DRUGS, SOCIETY AND BEHAVIOR 90/91

Fifth Edition

Editor

Charles Ladley
California State University, Sacramento

Charles Ladley is a professor of criminal justice at California State University, Sacramento. His B.A. was earned at Fresno State University, his M.A. from Western State College, Gunnison, Colorado, and his Ph.D. from Michigan State University. In addition to being an educator, he has a background of several years in law enforcement and has practiced as a police psychologist for twenty years. He has also specialized in drug counseling and education in the university and in private practice.

Annual Editions
A Library of Information from the Public Press

Cover illustration by Mike Eagle

The Dushkin Publishing Group, Inc.
Sluice Dock, Guilford, Connecticut 06437

The Annual Editions Series

Annual Editions is a series of over fifty volumes designed to provide the reader with convenient, low-cost access to a wide range of current, carefully selected articles from some of the most important magazines, newspapers, and journals published today. Annual Editions are updated on an annual basis through a continuous monitoring of over 200 periodical sources. All Annual Editions have a number of features designed to make them particularly useful, including topic guides, annotated tables of contents, unit overviews, and indexes. For the teacher using Annual Editions in the classroom, an Instructor's Resource Guide with test questions is available for each volume.

VOLUMES AVAILABLE

Africa
Aging
American Government
American History, Pre-Civil War
American History, Post-Civil War
Anthropology
Biology
Business and Management
Business Ethics
Canadian Politics
China
Comparative Politics
Computers in Education
Computers in Business
Computers in Society
Criminal Justice
Drugs, Society, and Behavior
Early Childhood Education
Economics
Educating Exceptional Children
Education
Educational Psychology
Environment
Geography
Global Issues
Health
Human Development

Human Resources
Human Sexuality
Latin America
Macroeconomics
Marketing
Marriage and Family
Middle East and the Islamic World
Money and Banking
Nutrition
Personal Growth and Behavior
Psychology
Public Administration
Social Problems
Sociology
Soviet Union and Eastern Europe
State and Local Government
Third World
Urban Society
Violence and Terrorism
Western Civilization,
    Pre-Reformation
Western Civilization,
    Post-Reformation
Western Europe
World History, Pre-Modern
World History, Modern
World Politics

Library of Congress Cataloging in Publication Data
Main entry under title: Annual Editions: Drugs, Society, and Behavior. 1990/91.
        1. Drugs—Addresses, essays, lectures—Periodicals. 2. Drug abuse—United States—
Addresses, essays, lectures—Periodicals. 3. Alcohol—Addresses, essays, lectures—Periodicals.
4. Drunk driving—Addresses, essays, lectures—Periodicals. I. Ladley, Charles A., *comp.* II. Title:
Drugs, Society, and Behavior.
ISBN 0–87967–838–0   362.2'92'0973'05

Fifth Edition

Manufactured by The Banta Company, Harrisonburg, Virginia 22801

Editors/ Advisory Board

To the Reader

In publishing ANNUAL EDITIONS we recognize the enormous role played by the magazines, newspapers, and journals of the *public press* in providing current, first-rate educational information in a broad spectrum of interest areas. Within the articles, the best scientists, practitioners, researchers, and commentators draw issues into new perspective as accepted theories and viewpoints are called into account by new events, recent discoveries change old facts, and fresh debate breaks out over important controversies.

Many of the articles resulting from this enormous editorial effort are appropriate for students, researchers, and professionals seeking accurate, current material to help bridge the gap between principles and theories and the real world. These articles, however, become more useful for study when those of lasting value are carefully *collected, organized, indexed,* and *reproduced* in a *low-cost format,* which provides easy and permanent access when the material is needed. That is the role played by *Annual Editions.* Under the direction of each volume's *Editor,* who is an expert in the subject area, and with the guidance of an *Advisory Board,* we seek each year to provide in each *ANNUAL EDITION* a current, well-balanced, carefully selected collection of the best of the public press for your study and enjoyment. We think you'll find this volume useful, and we hope you'll take a moment to let us know what you think.

The decision regarding which articles to publish now and which to save for future consideration is a never-ending task. The decision of which articles should be recommended for publication was based upon one primary criterion—their educational value. It is the opinion of this editor that the world outside the classroom generates the information for more formal schooling, and that we all should never cease to be students. Whether scientist, researcher, practitioner, social commentator, parent, or child, the decisions made about drugs today will significantly impact each of us tomorrow. The stated purpose of this anthology is to educate, inform, and assist in the creation of a basis for rational thought and reasonable action respective to the use or misuse of drugs.

Drugs are such a pervasive part of our daily experience that they now dominate the contents of many magazines, newspapers, television specials, radio talk shows, and school curricula. Drugs have been a part of society ever since humankind banded together in caves. Over 70 percent of today's pharmaceuticals originated from herbs, plants, trees, and bushes common to nature. The discussions of the use and abuse of drugs contained in *Annual Editions: Drugs, Society and Behavior 90/91* are a sampling of the current thought and investigations of the researchers and writers of our generation. As a reader, keep in mind that the opinions of today will necessarily change with the information of tomorrow. Drugs and their use may stem from antiquity, but the consequences of their use remain fresh and critical today.

The initial unit of this anthology considers American culture and its history of drug use. Drugs are by no means a present-day phenomenon. Their consequences, however, have led to a "war on drugs" which many consider to be America's second Vietnam. Unit 2 explores the factors of use, abuse, and addiction, wherein the answers gained spawn even more critical questions. Unit 3 deals with the "legal" drugs and how they affect personal behavior. The "who" of drugs and their use and abuse is found in Unit 4. The many and varied models of dependency are discussed in Unit 5, while the final unit deals with the issues of prevention and treatment.

Evaluation of each article requires careful reading and an open mind. The experience and opinions stated by the author may be in direct opposition to those of the reader. This possibility requires the reader to examine his or her own opinions for personal bias engendered by a lack of experience or understanding.

In using this collection of articles, I feel it is particularly beneficial to employ them as methods to promote serious group discussion, carefully dissecting the points made by the authors. Keep in mind regional similarities and differences, and that although the particular drug or problem may not yet be in your area, it soon may be. Readers can have input into the next edition by completing and returning the article rating form in the back of the book.

Charles Ladley
Editor

Contents

Unit 1

Drugs in Perspective

Sixteen articles discuss the history of drug usage, current illegal drugs, and the progress and setbacks in the war against drugs.

To the Reader   iv
Topic Guide   2
Overview   4

A. OUR CULTURE AND THE HISTORY OF DRUG USE

1. **What It Was Like to Be Sick in 1884,** Charles E. Rosen-   6
   berg, *American Heritage,* October/November 1984.
   Health care 100 years ago was, in some respects, very different
   from health care today. According to Rosenberg, *narcotics* could
   be purchased *over-the-counter* and the *standard of care* involved more personal contact.

2. **The War Against Demon Rum,** Robert Maddox, *American*   15
   History Illustrated, May 1979.
   The *temperance* movement, begun by Dr. Benjamin Rush in
   1784, climaxed in the Prohibition era. Maddox suggests that
   cartoons, lively songs, religious tracts, and poems inspired the
   historical battleground and set the stage for the *disease model*
   of alcohol abuse.

3. **America's First Cocaine Epidemic,** David F. Musto, *The*   20
   Wilson Quarterly, Summer 1989.
   Cocaine has been a part of the recreational drug scene for more
   than a century. The words of the past have either been ignored or
   forgotten. Chronicled cases of cocaine abuse are legion, yet it
   appears that little has been learned from the pages of history.

B. CURRENT ILLEGAL DRUGS

4. **The Joys of Victimhood,** Joseph Epstein, *The New York*   26
   Times Magazine, July 2, 1989.
   Epstein delivers a stinging slap in the face to those who seek
   sympathy by publicly marketing themselves as *"victims" of the*
   drug wars. The author decries the shift from self-reliance to a
   system of pathetic acceptance.

5. **Madison Avenue Medicine,** Elisabeth Rosenthal, *Discover,* 29
   October 1988.
   Are the *ethics of the medical community* being contraverted by
   "drug company reps"? Rosenthal describes the tactics used by
   pharmaceutical salespeople to acquaint the medical community
   with their latest product line. Is this more than just "business"?

6. **The Fire of "Ice,"** Michael A. Lerner, *Newsweek,* November 32
   27, 1989.
   A devastating drug from Asia has begun to enter the West Coast
   of the United States. It's a type of *methamphetamine,* or speed,
   that purportedly gives a prolonged high and goes under the name
   of *"ice."* This article looks at the possible impact of this drug on
   our society.

7. **Crank Capital, U.S.A.,** Tom Johnson, *Sacramento News*   34
   and Review, August 31, 1989.
   The "homebrewing" of crank (methamphetamine) is the newest
   cottage industry in "River City," Sacramento, California. The
   manufacture and distribution of crank is the purview of ex-felons
   and outlaw biker gangs.

8. **Crack's Destructive Sprint Across America,** Michael   39
   Massing, *The New York Times Magazine,* October 1, 1989.
   Washington Heights has become known as *the nation's crack*
   capital. As this article points out, crack seems to have been
   developed there, and even more importantly, the area's Dominicans are credited with having developed it for a mass market.

9. **Cocaine Kids: The Underground American Dream,**   45
   Terry Williams, *New Perspectives Quarterly,* Summer 1989.
   Who other than a rock star can earn $20,000 a week at the age of
   sixteen? The lure of *drug profits* corrupts even the best.

The concepts in bold italics are developed in the article. For further expansion please refer to the Topic Guide, the Index, and the Glossary.

C. THE WAR AGAINST DRUGS

10. **Why Peru Won't Stop the Cocaine,** Sharon Stevenson, *The Sacramento Bee,* September 10, 1989. — 50

    The upper Huallaga valley of Peru is the major growing area on earth for cocaine. The political left has united with the growers of the area to resist governmental efforts to halt **cocaine production**.

11. **Caught in the Crossfire,** Candy J. Cooper, *Image,* August 13, 1989. — 52

    The shrapnel and fallout of our "**war on drugs**" creates more than unanswerable questions. What about the kids who live in the war zone who choose not to sell or use? What is to be the lot of those "caught in the crossfire between the crooks and the authorities?"

12. **Drug Frenzy: Why the War on Drugs Misses the Real Target,** Barbara Ehrenreich, *Utne Reader,* March/April 1989. — 56

    A drug is a drug is a drug. Regarding addictions, reality has little to do with legality. Ehrenreich has chosen an excellent vista for the viewing of our society's fascination with **recreational chemicals**.

13. **Drugs and the Dream Deferred,** John D. Kasarda and Terry Williams, *New Perspectives Quarterly,* Summer 1989. — 60

    Kasarda and Williams focus on the inability of the **underclass** to share in the "dream of America." Solutions offered include physical relocation and cultural regeneration.

14. **The Drug-Money Hunt,** Peter Ross Range and Gordon Witkin, *U.S. News & World Report,* August 21, 1989. — 65

    The amount of **money in the drug trade** is enormous and hard to hide. Government agents are after cash and assets. **Money laundering** has become a business in itself.

15. **Weed It and Reap,** Tim Wise, *Dollars & Sense,* March 1989. — 68

    The war on pot has created an effect exactly opposite of what was desired or expected. The **suppression of marijuana** has significantly increased domestic production of the drug, to the point where marijuana is considered America's leading cash crop.

16. **The War on Drugs: Let's Surrender,** Joseph Sobran, and **Is This Any Way to Fight a War?** Edward Grimsley, *Conservative Chronicle,* 1989. — 72

    Conservative thinkers and journalists are ready to throw in the towel. Those generally thought to favor means of combat other than capitulation are rethinking their positions. Sobran and Grimsley consider "the war" to be lost, with "**the surrender model" (or legalization**) as the only reasonable alternative.

Overview — 74

A. USERS, ABUSERS, AND ADDICTIONS

17. **Everybody Must Get Stoned?** Bob Sipchen, *San Francisco Chronicle,* August 18, 1989. — 76

    Getting stoned is a natural drive, relates psychopharmacologist Ronald Siegal. From catnip to alcohol, the urge to intoxicate is common to the animal kingdom. "Life in pursuit of artificial paradise" has been the preoccupation of birds, elephants, and presidents.

18. **Cycles of Craving,** Dan Hurley, *Psychology Today,* July/August 1989. — 78

    Drugs, like fads, are cyclic. The **sixties** brought psychedelics while the eighties embraced stimulants. The mood of the times dictates the drug of choice of an era. Knowing this helps predict drug abuse patterns of the future.

19. **Passing a Legacy of Drug Addiction,** Karen Diegmueller, *Insight,* September 4, 1989. — 82

    There is no defense for the defenseless. **Crack babies** fed a mixture of drugs while still in the fetal stage suffer the possibility of mental retardation and physical malformation. Better detection and prevention must be instituted to stem the tide of addicted infants.

Unit 2

Drug Action on the Nervous System

Eleven selections in this section examine the impact of drugs on the nervous system with regard to transmitters and receptors. The ramifications of "designer" drugs are also considered.

The concepts in bold italics are developed in the article. For further expansion please refer to the Topic Guide, the Index, and the Glossary.

20. New Ways to Crack a Cocaine Addiction, Dina Van Pelt, *Insight,* July 31, 1989.   84
Drugs used in the **treatment of depression and psychosis** are being used therapeutically to eliminate the frantic craving for crack cocaine. Researchers understand how cocaine manipulates the brain, but treatment for the intense craving it produces still escapes the medical world.

21. The Return of a Deadly Drug Called Horse, Gordon Witkin, *U.S. News & World Report,* August 14, 1989.   86
Heroin is back with a rush. "Horse" is more potent and plentiful than ever, and at a lower cost. The new purity of heroin has made smoking it a popular pastime. It lasts longer than crack and eliminates the stigma and complications of needles, thereby adding to its dangerous allure.

22. The Invisible Line, Maia Szalavitz, *High Times,* September 1989.   88
The border that divides those who can use **mood or mind-altering drugs** and those who cannot forms "the invisible line." The treatment involved in **cocaine, heroin, and alcohol addiction** fails to consider addiction as a disease rather than the specific reaction to a specific chemical.

23. Cocaine: Litany of Fetal Risks Grows, Jane E. Brody, *The New York Times,* September 6, 1988.   89
Cocaine usage by pregnant women causes lasting damage to the fetus. Recent studies of **babies exposed to cocaine** before birth suggest that the drug is responsible for numerous harmful effects that may stay with these individuals for the rest of their lives.

24. Marijuana, Winifred Gallagher, *American Health,* March 1988.   92
Marijuana use peaked in 1978, but the drug still remains enormously popular. The pot on the street today is stronger than ever before, and can command prices of more than $100 an ounce in big cities.

B.   DESIGNER DRUGS

25. From Crack to Ecstasy, Hal Straus, *American Health,* June 1987.   97
Until 1986 new drugs could be designed to skirt federal drug laws. Many of these "analogs," or **chemical cousins to illegal drugs**, proved even more dangerous than the drugs they were designed to imitate.

26. We've Already Said Yes, Bruce Sterling, *This World,* September 24, 1989.   100
The best and worst is yet to come. Sterling reports that "society gets the drug problem it deserves," and gives us a taste of the drugs of the future. Technology cannot be halted any more than one can unring a bell. The **drugs of tomorrow** offer both great promise and terror.

27. "Drug of Infamy" Makes a Comeback, Sally Squires, *This World,* July 9, 1989.   101
Thalidomide caused severe birth defects in over 12,000 newborns over a decade ago. Today this "drug of infamy" has been recycled as an effective treatment for bone marrow transplants, Hansen's disease (leprosy), and rheumatoid arthritis.

Overview   104

A.   ALCOHOL, CAFFEINE, AND TOBACCO

28. Alcoholism: The Mythical Disease, Herbert Fingarette, *Utne Reader,* November/December 1988.   106
Alcoholism was first considered a disease in the early nineteenth century. The author, calling on recent studies, contends that heavy drinkers must take responsibility for their own lives.

29. Caffeine, Gary Legwold, *Bicycle Guide,* August 1989.   110
Caffeine, or "Christian crank" as it has been dubbed by athletes, is used as a performance enhancer in big-time bicycle racing and other sports. Caffeine in cup, bottle, or pill form is allowed within limits by the International Olympic Committee.

Unit 3

Drugs and Behavior

Nine selections in this section look at drug-induced behavior. The drugs considered include alcohol, caffeine, tobacco, and prescription drugs.

The concepts in bold italics are developed in the article. For further expansion please refer to the Topic Guide, the Index, and the Glossary.

30. Smokeless Tobacco: The Fatal Pinch, Rachel Wolfe, *Multinational Monitor,* July/August 1987.   **112**

In 1971 the federal government made a move to reduce tobacco usage in the United States by banning cigarette ads from the airwaves; in response to this, the *smokeless tobacco* industry launched a highly successful campaign to encourage cigarette smokers to switch to snuff and chewing tobacco.

31. Nicotine Becomes Addictive, Robert Kanigel, *Science Illustrated,* October/November 1988.   **114**

"Smoking tobacco is a means of administering nicotine just as smoking opium is a means of administering morphine," stated Glasgow physician Lennox Johnston in 1942. Terms such as *"tobacco addict "* and "cigarette fiend" were popularized over a century ago, yet Americans refuse the "addict" designation.

32. Kick Me: I Smoke, Patrick Cooke, *Hippocrates,* July/August 1989.   **120**

In 1989, all the world hates a smoker. This has not always been the case. Although *nicotine is considered to be as addictive as heroin* and the medical world has proved a link between nicotine and cancer, stiff resistance remains against restricting the availability of the drug.

33. Achieving a Smoke-Free Society, K. H. Ginzel, *Priorities,* Summer 1989.   **125**

Ninety percent of all smokers take up their habit as children, yet there is no organized effort dedicated to educating the youth of the country about the *disastrous consequences of tobacco use*.

34. Warning: Sports Stars May Be Hazardous to Your Health, Jason DeParle, *The Washington Monthly,* September 1989.   **128**

What responsibility does the advertising industry bear to avoid promoting disease and disability? The use of sports stars and sports events as product models sends the wrong message to a society in love with sports and athletes. The *tobacco industry uses sports to sell tobacco* and sees no conflict in doing so.

B.   THERAPEUTIC AND OVER-THE-COUNTER DRUGS

35. Ordinary Medicines Can Have Extraordinary Side Effects, Christopher Hallowell, *Redbook,* May 1987.   **139**

Many *over-the-counter (OTC) medications*, as well as several common prescription medications, can change our moods and impair our ability to think and function normally, often without our even noticing.

36. Sneak Addictions to Over-the-Counter Drugs, Robin Reif, *Self,* August 1986.   **143**

Several *over-the-counter drugs* cause rebound effects which are similar to, though milder than, the *side effects* of withdrawal from drugs that are addictive. This article has some suggestions for *self-help*.

Overview   **146**

A.   PERSONALITY AND DRUGS OF CHOICE

37. Intoxicating Habits, Bruce Bower, *Science News,* August 6, 1988.   **148**

Why do *alcholics* have an irresistible urge to drink? Researchers cannot agree on why *the power of alcohol* is so great, nor on how to prevent an addict from returning to the drug. Some researchers feel that at least 15 to 20 percent of those considered "alcoholic" can engage in moderate social drinking.

38. How to Stay in Right Relationship With Everything From Chocolate to Cocaine, Jed Diamond, *Whole Earth Review,* Spring 1987.   **150**

Can a person have a "right relationship" with drugs other than abstinence? With so much confusion and conflict regarding drugs, how is an individual to choose? *More than 95 percent of us use some form of mind-altering substance*, and at least half have a problem with their *drugs of choice*.

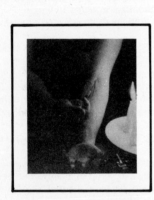

Unit 4

Who Uses Psychotropic Drugs?

Nine articles in this section examine the interrelationship between personality and the choice of drugs. The lasting changes wrought by drug usage are also considered.

39. **Wine and Winos: The Misery Market,** Alix M. Freedman, *The Saturday Evening Post,* July/August 1988. 152
Street alcoholics prefer the dollar-a-pint wines made with cheap ingredients and fortified with alcohol. The biggest bang for a buck has an alcohol content of up to 21 percent. The high sugar content in "big bang" wines obviates the need to eat, thereby creating associated health problems.

40. **A Male Problem?** Wendy Olson, *Los Angeles Times,* August 28, 1987. 155
Drug abuse among **women professional athletes** is less widespread than among men—and alcohol is almost always the substance abused. The author asks whether this is due to sex, or to the disparity in income between most male and female professional athletes.

B. *DELETERIOUS CHANGES FROM DRUG USE*

41. **Alcohol and the Family,** *Newsweek,* January 18, 1988. 158
What is the **impact on the family** when the life of an alcoholic becomes unmanageable? How do we educate the abuser that the consequences of alcohol are greater than a hangover? The adult children of **alcoholics** bear the scars of family drinking throughout their lives.

42. **Healing Scars of Parental Drinking,** Charles Wheeler, *Insight,* February 23, 1987. 164
Adult **children** of **alcoholics** have found that they have common problems. Banding together in **self-help** groups helps them to define the damage they have borne and to recover from it.

43. **Alcohol-Breast Cancer Link,** D. D. Edwards; **Nicotine: Addictive and Spreads Cancer?** D. D. Edwards; and **Cocaine Cardiology: Problems, Mysteries,** J. Silberner, *Science News,* April 4, May 9, January 31, 1987. 165
New evidence concerning the **side effects** of several commonly used drugs was brought forth in 1987. **Alcohol** has been linked with breast cancer in **women**. Not only tar, but **nicotine,** may cause cancer—bringing nicotine gum therapy for smoking into question. More research has also been done concerning the relationship of **cocaine** to heart attacks and other cardiac diseases.

44. **Shortcut to the Rambo Look,** *Time,* January 30, 1989. 167
With the current availability of **steroids,** many young males, in athletics or not, are overusing these potentially dangerous drugs. As this article points out, steroids cause moodiness, depression, and irritability, as well as damage to the heart and kidneys.

45. **Steroids: The Power Drugs,** Paul Pfotenhauer, *USA Today Magazine (Society for the Advancement of Education),* March 1989. 168
"If the National Football League's ban on **steroids** were enforced there would be a lot of offensive linemen playing indoor soccer next year," are the words of Bob Golic, the Cleveland Browns' nose tackle. The synthetic versions of testosterone present a **health risk to young athletes** that may not be reversible. Steroids are such risky drugs that the medical community is not sure of the results of non-therapeutic use.

Overview 170

A. *BIOLOGICAL AND BIOCHEMICAL MODELS: THE DISEASE MODEL*

46. **Control Yourself,** Stanton Peele, *Reason,* February 1990. 172
What is addiction? Today many addictions are being treated as diseases, which, as the author illustrates, misses the point. Peele notes that addiction is part of a much larger class of human behavior that is best counteracted by a sense of responsibility and respect for others.

47. **Breaking the Cycle of Addiction,** Deborah M. Barnes, *Science,* August 26, 1988. 176
The emerging **treatment strategies for combatting cocaine addiction** represent a radical departure from the conventional wisdom that the addiction was purely psychological in nature. The estimate that half of cocaine abusers have severe mood disorders requires rethinking of old ideas, and bold action in treatment.

Unit 5

Models of Dependency

Eight selections in this section discuss biological, biochemical, psychological, and social models of drug dependence.

48. **Ain't Misbehavin'**, Stanton Peele, *The Sciences*, July/   **178**
August 1989.

The word "***addiction***," while associated with a number of ***compulsive behaviors***, is most commonly associated with drugs. "Addictive personalities" has become the popular phrase for explaining the actions of those afflicted with such misbehavior.

49. **A Slip Doesn't Have to Lead to a Fall**, Daniel Goleman,   **183**
The Sacramento Bee, January 2, 1989.

The ***prevention of relapse*** is the greatest hurdle faced by therapist and client. A focus on changing self-defeating habits becomes a guidepost in therapy early in treatment. The application of "forewarned is forearmed" prepares people to prevent relapses and take advantage of slips, rather than being demoralized by mistakes.

50. **Drugs Don't Take People; People Take Drugs**, Mona   **185**
Charen, *Conservative Chronicle*, 1989.

Charen believes the ***precise nature of addiction is poorly understood*** by scientists, and varies from individual to individual. Much of the problem has been worsened by the loss of traditional societal supports such as family, church, and community. Americans have come to believe that drugs are an unstoppable outside force that overwhelms a person's pathetic attempts to resist.

B. *PSYCHOLOGICAL AND SOCIAL MODELS*

51. **Nasty Habits,** John Pekkanen, *The Washingtonian,* August   **186**
1984.

Nicotine is often overlooked as a drug. It can be compared to other, more familiar drugs, however, in the difficulty many users have in kicking the habit. The author introduces the notion that the ***reinforcement*** value of a drug determines its addiction potential—a key concept in many ***psychosocial models*** of dependence.

52. **Out of the Habit Trap,** Stanton Peele, *American Health,*   **189**
September/October 1983.

Self-help is proclaimed by this author as the only treatment which really works for addictions of any sort, regardless of their biological or ***psychosocial*** roots. He also discusses the role of ***genetics*** in addiction, and offers a short quiz to help readers ***diagnose*** their own habits.

53. **Addiction and IQ,** Linda Marsa, *Omni,* October 1989.   **194**

Addiction to cocaine is so powerful that individual cells in the brain learn to anticipate a drug reward, much as Pavlov's dog did. The fact that cells respond to a reward shows just how deeply imbedded in the design of the brain this reinforcement mechanism is.

Overview   **196**

A. *CONTINUUM OF CARE—PREVENTION*

54. **Epidemiology of Drug Abuse: An Overview,** Nicholas J.   **198**
Kozel and Edgar H. Adams, *Science,* November 21, 1986.

Is there a drug epidemic? National data indicate a decline in ***marijuana*** use among youth, and suggest that the number of novitiates to marijuana and to ***narcotics*** such as heroin is declining. Only ***cocaine*** use is rising.

55. **Taking Drugs Seriously,** John Kaplan, *The Public Interest,*   **205**
Summer 1988.

None of the ***drug policy options*** are attractive; all involve great costs either in expenditures on law enforcement or in damage to public health. The author reviews the various ways to loosen the grip that drug abuse has on our society.

56. **Cutting Costs of Drug Abuse,** Sabin Russell, *San Francisco Chronicle,* September 18, 1989.   **212**

The ***costs of drug abuse*** go far beyond the bloody excesses of the news. Industry has its back to the wall in the unwinnable war. Most employees feel that the $17 billion annual cost of alcohol and other drug abuse treatment programs is wasted.

Unit 6

Drug Abuse: Prevention and Treatment Issues

Twelve selections in this section discuss drug dependence and treatment. Topics covered include prevention, continuum of care, and alternatives to drugs.

57. **Megavitamin Therapy,** Stephen Barrett, *Priorities,* Spring 1989.   **214**

Polish scientist Casimir Funk is credited with the invention of the "vitamin" over a century ago. The truth about the effectiveness of vitamins and *"megavitamin therapy"* is as slippery as the proverbial eel. Vitamins have been proven to offer help in a significant number of instances.

58. **Advertising Addiction: The Alcohol Industry's Hard Sell,** Jean Kilbourne, *Multinational Monitor,* June 1989.   **216**

Alcohol is the most widely used and *advertised drug* in the United States. The alcohol advertising budget is in excess of one billion dollars per year, yet the industry claims that there is no conclusive proof that advertising increases consumption. The industry further claims that researchers who maintain the opposite are in error.

59. **A Drug History Revealed on a Strand of Hair,** William F. Buckley, *The Sacramento Bee,* October 12, 1989.   **219**

Drug testing using current methodology can be inaccurate and misleading. Only very recent drug usage can be detected. By testing hair samples, however, a record of daily usage with unquestionable accuracy for up to six months is possible.

B. CONTINUUM OF CARE—BEYOND PREVENTION

60. **The Dutch Model,** Eddy Engelsman, *New Perspectives Quarterly,* Summer 1989.   **220**

Under the title of "normalization" the *Dutch allow the use of even cocaine and heroin.* Use is not controlled, but possession is. Drugs are divided into the categories of "unacceptable risk" and "traditional cannabis products," with each category having a different level of punishment—a pragmatic prosecution policy.

61. **Why Not Decriminalize?** Arnold Trebach, *New Perspectives Quarterly,* Summer 1989.   **222**

Drugs may offer a societal benefit simply because they make the user "feel better." *The line that divides legal and illegal drugs* is an historical accident based primarily upon emotion rather than science. Between 50 and 60 million Americans use illegal drugs.

62. **A Long Time Coming,** Lily Collett, *This World,* August 6, 1989.   **226**

Twelve Step programs are the backbone of a *self-help recovery process.* The child of an alcoholic father tests their wisdom and traces the progress of the Al-Anon and Adult Children of Alcoholics programs in her life.

C. NATURAL HIGHS AND ALTERNATIVES TO DRUGS

63. **Drugs: The Power of the Placebo,** David Kline, *Hippocrates,* May/June 1988.   **229**

A *placebo* is an inert drug or substance that can affect the person taking it simply through the power of suggestion. The author looks at the extent to which placebos can affect the human body.

64. **Trances That Heal: Rites, Rituals, and Brain Chemicals,** Carol C. Laderman, *Science Digest,* July 1983.   **231**

Laderman reveals how, in Malaysia, shamans use trances when Western *therapy* fails. She argues that so-called primitive cultures may have tapped into *endorphin-produced highs* and *placebo* effects that scientists have only begun to study.

65. **Chasing Answers to Miracle Cures,** David Holzman, *Insight,* February 20, 1989.   **234**

Spontaneous remission recovery from a normally incurable disease causes the medical establishment discomfort and confusion. What part does the human mind play in "miracle cures"? Why and how does cancer yield to Zen meditation, laetrile, or placebos?

Glossary   **236**
Index   **242**
Article Rating Form   **245**

The concepts in bold italics are developed in the article. For further expansion please refer to the Topic Guide, the Index, and the Glossary.

Topic Guide

This topic guide suggests how the selections in this book relate to topics of traditional concern to students and professionals involved with the study of drugs, society, and behavior. It can be very useful in locating articles which relate to each other for reading and research. The guide is arranged alphabetically according to topic. Articles may, of course, treat topics that do not appear in the topic guide. In turn, entries in the topic guide do not necessarily constitute a comprehensive listing of all the contents of each selection.

TOPIC AREA	TREATED AS AN ISSUE IN:	TOPIC AREA	TREATED AS AN ISSUE IN:
Addiction	18. Cycles of Craving 20. New Ways To Crack a Cocaine Addiction 28. Alcoholism: The Mythical Disease 31. Nicotine Becomes Addictive 33. Achieving a Smoke-Free Society 37. Intoxicating Habits 38. How to Stay in Right Relationship 47. Breaking the Cycle of Addiction 48. Ain't Misbehavin' 53. Addiction and IQ	Children (con'd)	33. Achieving a Smoke-Free Society 41. Alcohol and the Family 62. A Long Time Coming
		Cocaine	3. America's First Cocaine Epidemic 19. Legacy of Drug Addiction 22. The Invisible Line 23. Litany of Fetal Risks Grows 26. We've Already Said Yes 43. Alcohol-Breast Cancer Link 47. Breaking the Cycle of Addiction 53. Addiction and IQ 54. Epidemiology of Drug Abuse 60. The Dutch Model
Advertising	10. Why Peru Won't Stop the Cocaine 34. Sports Stars May Be Hazardous 39. Wine and Winos 58. Advertising Addiction		
		Crank	7. Crank Capitol U.S.A.
Alcohol	2. The War Against Demon Rum 39. Wine and Winos 40. A Male Problem? 41. Alcohol and the Family 42. Healing Scars of Parental Drinking 43. Alcohol-Breast Cancer Link 54. Epidemiology of Drug Abuse 56. Cutting Costs of Drug Abuse 58. Advertising Addiction 62. A Long Time Coming	Decriminalization	60. The Dutch Model 61. Why Not Decriminalize?
		Designer Drugs/ Synthetic Drugs	26. We've Already Said Yes 27. "Drug of Infamy"
		Diagnosis	52. Out of the Habit Trap
		Disease Model	2. The War Against Demon Rum 22. The Invisible Line 28. Alcoholism: The Mythical Disease 41. Alcohol and the Family
Alcoholics Anonymous	49. A Slip Doesn't Have to Lead to a Fall 62. A Long Time Coming		
Alcoholism	1. What It Was Like to Be Sick in 1884 17. Everybody Must Get Stoned? 37. Intoxicating Habits 39. Wine and Winos 41. Alcohol and the Family 49. A Slip Doesn't Have to Lead to a Fall 62. A Long Time Coming	Drug Detection	59. A Drug History Revealed
		Drug Money	9. Cocaine Kids 14. The Drug-Money Hunt 15. Weed It and Reap
		Drug Trade	9. Cocaine Kids 10. Why Peru Won't Stop the Cocaine 14. The Drug-Money Hunt 15. Weed It and Reap
Athletes	26. We've Already Said Yes 29. Caffeine 34. Sports Stars May Be Hazardous 40. A Male Problem? 44. Shortcut to the Rambo Look 45. Steroids: The Power Drug	Education	3. America's First Cocaine Epidemic 12. Drug Frenzy 18. Cycles of Craving 33. Achieving a Smoke-Free Society 41. Alcohol and the Family
Brain	17. Everybody Must Get Stoned? 37. Intoxicating Habits 48. Ain't Misbehavin' 53. Addiction and IQ 63. Drugs: The Power of the Placebo 64. Trances That Heal 65. Chasing Answers to Miracle Cures	Endorphins	64. Trances That Heal
		Ethics	5. Madison Avenue Medicine 26. We've Already Said Yes 34. Sports Stars May Be Hazardous
Caffeine	29. Caffeine	Heroin	21. Deadly Drug Called Horse 60. The Dutch Model
Children	9. Cocaine Kids 11. Caught in the Crossfire 19. Legacy of Drug Addiction 23. Litany of Fetal Risks Grows		

TOPIC AREA	TREATED AS AN ISSUE IN:	TOPIC AREA	TREATED AS AN ISSUE IN:
History	1. What It Was Like to Be Sick in 1884 2. The War on Demon Rum 18. Cycles of Craving 25. From Crack to Ecstasy 31. Nicotine Becomes Addictive	Self-Help	36. Sneak Addictions 38. How to Stay in Right Relationship 42. Healing Scars of Parental Drinking 49. A Slip Doesn't Have to Lead to a Fall 52. Out of the Habit Trap
Law Enforcement	7. Crank Capitol U.S.A. 11. Caught in the Crossfire 14. The Drug-Money Hunt 15. Weed It and Reap 55. Taking Drugs Seriously	Side Effects	23. Litany of Fetal Risks Grows 24. Marijuana 26. We've Already Said Yes 27. "Drug of Infamy" 29. Caffeine 30. The Fatal Pinch 35. Ordinary Medicines 36. Sneak Addictions 43. Alcohol-Breast Cancer Link 44. Shortcut to the Rambo Look 45. Steroids: The Power Drugs
Legalization	12. Drug Frenzy 16. The War On Drugs		
Marijuana	15. Weed It and Reap 18. Cycles of Craving 24. Marijuana 54. Epidemiology of Drug Abuse 60. The Dutch Model 61. Why Not Decriminalize?	Smokeless Tobacco	30. The Fatal Pinch 34. Sports Stars May Be Hazardous
		Socioeconomic Issues	9. Cocaine Kids 13. Drugs and the Dream Deferred 61. Why Not Decriminalize?
Medical Model	20. New Ways to Crack a Cocaine Addiction 48. Ain't Misbehavin' 53. Addiction and IQ 56. Cutting Costs of Drug Abuse 57. Megavitamin Therapy	Steroids	44. Shortcut to the Rambo Look 45. Steroids: The Power Drugs
		Technology	7. Crank Capitol U.S.A. 26. We've Already Said Yes 25. From Crack to Ecstasy 27. "Drug of Infamy"
Nicotine	30. The Fatal Pinch 31. Nicotine Becomes Addictive 32. Kick Me: I Smoke 33. Achieving a Smoke-Free Society 34. Sports Stars May Be Hazardous 43. Alcohol-Breast Cancer Link 51. Nasty Habits	Thalidomide	27. "Drug of Infamy"
		Therapy/Treatment	20. New Ways to Crack a Cocaine Addiction 47. Breaking the Cycle of Addiction 48. Ain't Misbehavin' 49. A Slip Doesn't Have to Lead to a Fall 57. Megavitamin Therapy 64. Trances That Heal
Over-the-Counter Drugs	1. What It Was Like to Be Sick in 1884 29. Caffeine 35. Ordinary Medicines 36. Sneak Addictions 57. Megavitamin Therapy		
		Tobacco	*See* Nicotine
Personality	17. Everybody Must Get Stoned? 39. Wine and Winos 47. Breaking the Cycle of Addiction 48. Ain't Misbehavin'	Victims	4. The Joys of Victimhood 11. Caught in the Crossfire 19. Legacy of Drug Addiction 41. Alcohol and the Family 62. A Long Time Coming
Placebos	57. Megavitamin Therapy 63. Drugs: The Power of the Placebo		
Prevention	3. America's First Cocaine Epidemic 12. Drug Frenzy 37. Intoxicating Habits 38. How to Stay in Right Relationship 49. A Slip Doesn't Have to Lead to a Fall 50. Drugs Don't Take People 52. Out of the Habit Trap 58. Advertising Addiction 59. A Drug History Revealed 58. The Dutch Model	Women	23. Litany of Fetal Risks Grows 27. "Drug of Infamy" 40. A Male Problem? 43. Alcohol-Breast Cancer Link
		Workplace	56. Cutting Costs of Drug Abuse
		Youth	11. Caught in the Crossfire 30. The Fatal Pinch 33. Achieving a Smoke-Free Society 34. Sports Stars May Be Hazardous 44. Shortcut to the Rambo Look 45. Steroids: The Power Drugs
Psychosocial Model	32. Kick Me: I Smoke 36. Sneak Addictions 51. Nasty Habits 52. Out of the Habit Trap		

Drugs in Perspective

- Our Culture and the History of Drug Use (Articles 1-3)
- Current Illegal Drugs (Articles 4-9)
- The War Against Drugs (Articles 10-16)

I am trained as a criminal justice professional. Almost forty years of experience in the field have convinced me that we do not have a drug problem, we have a condition. By definition, a problem must have a solution in order for it to qualify as a problem. The thing we call the "drug problem" has stood thus far in defiance of every solution we have thrown at it. Therefore, in my world, it earns the title of "condition." What do you do with conditions? You live with them.

On occasion, we translate hopes into solutions only to find that they are limited, cumbersome, unworkable, or transitory at best. Has history taught us anything? Did we learn our lessons well with the war that was waged on "demon rum" over a half-century ago? Read "The War Against Demon Rum" carefully and see if there are any parallels today as our modern day reformers take on every problem with the fervor of the possessed. Think of your relationship with your doctor as you read "What It Was Like to Be Sick in 1884." Modern technology has exploded the clouds of ignorance that covered the medical world a century ago. We live in an era of "miracle medicine," yet we have more people with serious drug difficulties than we can possibly explain. Is this the price of progress?

Many modern thinkers, conservative and liberal alike, consider the war on drugs to have been lost a generation ago. Yet the soldiers remain in the trenches and the casualties mount. Many point to the inability to legislate morals as the prime lesson to be learned from the American experience with Prohibition. These advocates of the so-called "surrender model" are a significant and vocal minority. Articles such as "America's First Cocaine Epidemic," "Weed It and Reap," and "The War on Drugs: Let's Surrender" center on hindsight blindness, and beg our leadership to direct at least an occasional peek at the rearview mirror. "The Joys of Victimhood" looks at the field of "victimology." The author feels that the tendency to look at drug abuse in a manner that absolves the user from any personal responsibility or culpability for his or her actions has done little more than breed a vast horde of "victims." This attitude spawns a permanent underclass of people who are easily manipulated and misled.

"Madison Avenue Medicine" sheds light on an over-looked but important area of medicine: pharmacology. In our haste to consider drugs as being only a problem of the streets, we have ignored the realities of the legal drug business. The author explores her experiences as a physician with the pharmaceutical houses' "drug reps" and their sales tactics. Although it is difficult for the majority of us to accept medicine as a business, a business it is. "Why Peru Won't Stop the Cocaine," and "The Drug-Money Hunt" speak to the futility of the war on drugs. The massive profits generated by drugs attract the crooks, and there will always be more crooks than cops. Peru has a special problem within its borders, in that a civil war is in progress with the leftist insurgents holding power in the areas of cocaine cultivation and processing. Eradication of drugs is not easy in a land where all the odds are against the eradicators.

"Drug Frenzy: Why the War on Drugs Misses the Real Target" raises the question of the irrelevance of legality, while "Caught in the Crossfire," "Cocaine Kids," and "Crank Capitol U.S.A." help to explain the "hows" and "whys" of the underground stimulant industry. Few realize the magnitude of the temptations faced by inner-city youth, where a 10-year-old can pocket over $200 per day by merely acting as a lookout. What, then, of the youngsters who want to stay straight in a neighborhood held by the enemy? The news of the war does not look good.

Looking Ahead: Challenge Questions

Is present-day stress greater or less than that faced by the early pioneers who faced uncertainty at every turn of the trail?

Have the lessons of yesterday lasted only a short time?

What are we prepared to do with the victims of drug abuse of the next generation?

How do we separate the real victims from those lacking in self-control?

Will the United States continue to support governments responsible for the production of drugs while it condemns its own citizens for their use?

What can a society do to reclaim an underclass that feels that it has been abandoned?

WHAT IT WAS LIKE TO BE SICK IN 1884

*American medicine in a crucial era was at once
surprisingly similar and shockingly different from what
we know today. You could get aspirin at the drugstore, and anesthesia
during surgery. But you could also buy opium over the counter,
and the surgery would be more likely to be performed
in your kitchen than in a hospital.*

Charles E. Rosenberg

*Charles E. Rosenberg is Professor of History of Science
at the University of Pennsylvania.*

IN 1884 ALMOST three-quarters of America's fifty million people lived on farms or in rural hamlets. When they fell ill, they ordinarily were treated in their own homes by someone they knew, someone who might not be a trained physician but a family member, neighbor, or midwife. Only a handful of smaller communities boasted hospitals, for they were still a big-city phenomenon. And in those cities, only the workingman and his family, the aged and dependent, the single mother, or the itinerant laborer would normally have received institutional care. For the middle class, a bed among strangers in a hospital ward was a last resort. Even within the working class of America's rapidly growing cities, the great majority of patients too poor to pay a private physician never entered a hospital but instead received free outpatient care from dispensaries, from paid municipal physicians, and from hospital outpatient departments. The hospital was a place to be avoided—often a place in which to die—and not the fundamental element in medical care that it has become in the twentieth century.

Some of the ills Americans fell victim to a century ago were the same as those we still suffer from—bronchitis,

rheumatism, kidney and circulatory ailments; others have become either uncommon, like malaria, less common, like syphilis, or entirely banished, like smallpox. Tuberculosis was by far the greatest single killer of adults; gastrointestinal ills were the greatest scourge among children. Both tuberculosis and the "summer diarrheas" reflect and document the grim realities of a society in which food was sparse for many, work exhausting, living conditions filthy, and sanitation and water supplies well suited to the spread of infectious disease.

Americans still lived in the shadow of the great epidemics. Yellow fever had scourged the lower Mississippi valley only a few years before, and the threat of cholera that had scarred Europe in the early 1880s was just lifting; there was little reason to anticipate that Americans would be spared the devastation of any nationwide epidemic until the onslaught of influenza in 1918. But every year, of course, they had to contend with the usual exactions of typhoid fever, syphilis, malaria, measles, smallpox, and diphtheria.

Life expectancy at birth was a little over forty for the population generally—a bit more than half of what it is

From *American Heritage*, October/November 1984, pp. 23-31. Reprinted with permission of the author.

today. For those born in large cities it could be much lower. In Philadelphia, for example, life expectancy at birth was 40.2 for white males and 44.8 for white females —and 25.2 and 32.1, respectively, for black males and females. But for those fit enough to survive the hazards of infancy and childhood, life expectancies were not radically different from those prevalent in the United States today. A forty-year-old Philadelphian could expect to live to 65 if a man and to almost 69 if a woman; for blacks the figures were 58.6 and 64. Younger people died of ailments such as measles, diphtheria, diarrheas, croup, and pneumonia. Although a smaller proportion of Americans survived to die of cancer and the degenerative diseases now so important, their experience with them (excepting apparently a much lower incidence of most kinds of cancer) was similar to ours of the 1980s. Older people suffered and died from roughly the same sorts of things they still do.

MOST AILMENTS were, in the terminology of the day, "self-limited." In the great majority of cases a patient could expect to recover—with or without the physician's ministrations. This was understood and acted upon; even the wealthy did not ordinarily call a physician immediately except in the case of severe injury or an illness with an abrupt and alarming onset. The decision to seek medical help would be made gradually; first a family member might be consulted, then a neighbor, finally perhaps a storekeeper who stocked drugs and patent medicines—all before turning to a doctor. Many housewives kept "recipe books" that included everything from recipes for apple pie and soap to remedies for rheumatism and croup. Guides to "domestic practice" were a staple for publishers and peddlers. It is no wonder that doctors a century ago were so critical of the care provided by what they dismissed as uneducated and irresponsible laymen.

Perhaps most annoying to physicians was the competition provided by druggists. Pharmacists in cities and small towns often served as primary-care physicians. (In rural areas, on the other hand, doctors often served as pharmacists, buying drugs in wholesale lots and selling them at retail.) Aside from simply recommending patent medicine, druggists might well use prescriptions written by local physicians for the same patient in a previous illness or those issued to another patient suffering from what seemed to be the same ailment. As an indignant doctor put it, this amounted to "surreptitiously appropriating the doctor's brain and recipe to guillotine the doctor's income." No statutes regulated the use of prescriptions, and most laymen felt that, once paid for, a prescription was their property. Logically enough they had the prescription filled whenever "it" struck again. Similarly, no laws controlled access to drugs; no distinction was made between prescription and over-the-counter remedies. Only their pocketbooks limited laymen's drug purchases. Patients could and did dose themselves with anything from opium

to extremely toxic mercury, arsenic, and antimony compounds. It is no accident that some physicians were beginning to discern a growing narcotic-addiction problem and urged control over the sale of drugs. Their critics dismissed such demands as self-serving attempts to monopolize the practice of medicine.

Just as there were no rigid controls over the sale of drugs, so there were almost no legal constraints over medical education and access to medical practice—and it was also a period without health insurance and with an enormous number of working people and small farmers too poor to employ a private physician. America in 1884, then, was a highly competitive medical marketplace—one in which the number of paying patients was small in comparison with the total number of men (and a few women) calling themselves physicians and seeking to earn a living through practice. A handful of prominent urban consultants might earn as much as ten thousand dollars a year; but this relatively small group monopolized practice among the wealthy. Their far more numerous professional brethren had to scuffle day and night to make a modest living from the fees paid by artisans, small shopkeepers, and farmers. Codes of ethics adopted by medical societies at the time (though enforced only sporadically) were in good measure aimed at avoiding the most brutal aspects of competition: speaking behind another practitioner's back, for example, or selling and endorsing secret remedies, or guaranteeing cures. A more subtle tactic involved planting newspaper stories detailing a spectacularly successful operation or unexpected cure.

It was not until the end of the 1880s that the first effective state licensing laws were enforced. Before that almost anyone could hang out a shingle and offer to treat others. From the perspective of the 1980s, even the best-educated physicians had invested comparatively little time or money in their education, while many successful practitioners had trained as apprentices with local doctors and had never graduated from a medical school or seen the inside of a hospital ward. Even graduates of the most demanding medical schools had followed curriculums based on formal lectures with little or no bedside or laboratory training to supplement textbooks and lectures. In 1884 reformers had just succeeded in extending the length of medical school training at the best institutions to three years of classes. But each year's session lasted only six months and still failed to include much in the way of clinical training. Furthermore, not even the leading medical schools demanded more than a grammar school education and prompt payment of fees as an admission requirement. A minority in the profession had always found ways to supplement their limited formal education by hiring tutors, traveling to Europe for clinical training, and competing for scarce hospital staff positions. But even such efforts and the financial resources they implied did not guarantee economic success once in practice: patients often chose doctors on the basis of their personalities, not their skills.

Just as there were no rigid controls over the sale of drugs, so there were almost no legal constraints over medical education and access to medical practice—and it was a period without health insurance.

Medicine was a family affair. A successful practice was, by definition, what contemporaries termed a family practice. The physician treated not individuals but households: husband and wife, children and servants, and—in rural areas—farm animals as well. Minor surgery, childbirth, the scrapes, scars, and infectious diseases of childhood, as well as the chronic ills of invalid aunts or uncles and failing grandparents—all were the family doctor's responsibility. To call in a consultant was, in some measure at least, to confess inadequacy. Of course, in rural areas, and in most small towns, the option of consulting a specialist did not exist, while calling in another local practitioner was to risk the chance that the new doctor might "steal" the first practitioner's family. A few oblique words could undermine the confidence that a physician had spent years cultivating.

Not surprisingly, business relationships between doctor and patient were casual. A well-organized physician presented bills every few months, but this was regarded as optimistic; surviving financial records indicate that accounts could run on for years with small payments being made from time to time. In some cases only death would bring a final settlement (usually at a substantial discount). Practitioners in rural areas often were paid in kind when paid at all. A young Minneapolis physician in the early 1880s, for example, received oats, hay, cords of wood, a watch, and a dissecting case in lieu of cash, as well as services ranging from haircutting and mowing to buggy repair and housecleaning. The same physician also supplied his neighbors with a variety of drugs and patent medicines and served as house practitioner to a local bordello (at least this account paid cash!).

NATIONAL MUSEUM OF AMERICAN HISTORY, SMITHSONIAN INSTITUTION

Belladonna was used to treat asthma, whooping cough, and—when made into a plaster and placed on the patient's chest—cardiac disease.

DOCTORS SOUGHT TO IMPROVE their shaky circumstances in various ways. Some offered discounts for prompt payment—and threatened to add interest charges to bills remaining unpaid after ninety days. But most physicians were too insecure economically to take the chance of badgering patients and simply assumed that a substantial proportion of their accounts would never be paid. A rule of thumb was that bad debts should be limited to a third of the total billings.

Physicians also sought to bring some regularity to their economic relationships by adopting fee tables in their local medical societies—schedules specifying minimum charges for everything from ordinary home and office visits to obstetrics and assorted surgical procedures. In Scott County, Iowa, physicians agreed, for example, to charge one to five dollars for "office advice," a dollar for vaccination,

ten to twenty-five dollars for obstetrics—and ten to one hundred dollars (strictly in advance) for treating syphilis. Fee schedules always included rates for night attendance and mileage, which was particularly important in rural areas where the bulk of a doctor's time could be spent in travel. (Bicycles were already being suggested as a way of speeding the progress of an up-to-date physician's rounds.) In some counties physicians adopted an even more tough-minded stratagem: they blacklisted deadbeats—patients able but unwilling to pay. But none of these measures could alter the fundamentally bleak economic realities most practitioners faced.

One consequence, however, was a doctor-patient relationship very different from the often impersonal transactions to which we have become accustomed. Economic dependence was only one factor. Most physicians prac-

An alcohol burner heated the liquid in this vaporizer —eucalyptus, perhaps, for a chest cold—and the patient inhaled the fumes through the mouthpiece.

ticed in small communities where they knew their patients not simply as cases but as neighbors, as fellow church members, as people in families.

Physicians arrived at the patient's home with an assortment of ideas and practices very different from those available to their successors in 1984. Particularly striking was the dependence upon the evidence of the doctor's own senses in making a diagnosis. The physician could call upon no X rays to probe beneath the body's surface, no radioisotopes to trace metabolic pathways, no electrocardiograph to reveal the heart's physiological status. Most diagnoses depended on sight and touch. Did the patient appear flushed? Was the tongue coated? Eyes cloudy? Pulse fast or slow, full or shallow? What was the regularity and appearance of urine and feces? Was there a family history that might indicate the tendency toward a particular illness or an idiosyncratic pattern of response to drugs? Even more important than the doctor's observations, of course, was the patient's own account of his or her symptoms. (An infant's inability to provide such information was always cited as a problem in pediatric practice.) The physician's therapeutic limitations only emphasized the importance of diagnostic and prognostic skills. As had been the case since ancient times, a physician's credibility and reputation were judged inevitably in terms of the ability to predict the course of an illness.

T HIS IS NOT TO SUGGEST that medicine's diagnostic tools had remained unchanged since the days of Galen. The stethoscope had been in use since the

first quarter of the nineteenth century and had been improved steadily; available evidence indicates, however, that many practitioners were not proficient in its use, while some failed to employ it at all. Doctors who had never been taught to use the stethoscope found it easy to dismiss as an impractical frill.

The thermometer also was available to practitioners in 1884, and it was becoming more than an academic curiosity to the average doctor. Its hospital use was growing routine, although the first temperature charts in American hospitals actually date back to the 1860s. The thermometer was adopted slowly because mid-nineteenth-century versions were hard to use, expensive, and seemed to add little to what most physicians could easily ascertain by looking at a patient, feeling the pulse, and touching the forehead; any grandmother could tell when someone had a fever.

For the doctor, the challenge lay in predicting an ailment's course and suggesting appropriate treatment. The ophthalmoscope and laryngoscope could be of great value in diagnosing ills of the eye and throat; but although they had been known since the 1850s, their use was limited largely to a minority of big-city practitioners. They were still the specialist's tools, and the regular medical curriculum offered no training in their use. More ambitious physicians also had at their disposal a whole battery of urine tests. (A urinalysis manual of over five hundred pages had, in fact, been translated from the German a few years earlier.) Blood-cell counting was still an academic exercise, but many physicians tested routinely for albumin and sugar in the urine of patients suspected of having kidney ailments or diabetes. In the latter case, availability of a simple chemical test for sugar marked an aesthetic if not intellectual advance over the earlier practice of tasting the urine in question. But the availability of this handful of instruments and laboratory tests had not fundamentally altered traditional medical practice. The era of high-technology diagnosis still lay far in the future.

The physician brought three basic resources to the sickroom. First, of course, was the doctor's individual presence. In an era when patients with severe, and possibly fatal, infectious diseases were treated under the evaluating eyes of family, friends, and servants, nothing was more important than a physician's ability to inspire confidence. And contemporary medical doctrine specifically recognized that patient confidence was a key ingredient in the physician's ability to cure—even in surgery. The second resource available to the practitioner was the contents of the medical bag, the drugs and instruments of the physician's trade. The final resource lay in the doctor's mind: the assumptions about disease that explained and justified its treatment.

The doctor's bag was filled largely with drugs: pills, salves, and powders. Medical therapy revolved around their judicious use; in fact, physicians used the term *prescribe for* synonymously with *treat*. Doctors often complained that patients demanded prescriptions as proof that the physician had indeed done something tangible for them. And in most cases patients and their families could see and feel the effects: most drugs produced a tangible physiological effect. Some induced copious urination, while others caused sweating, vomiting, or—most commonly—purging. In addition, the majority of physicians carried sugar pills, placebos to reassure the anxious or demanding patient that something was being done.

PHYSICIANS WERE WELL AWARE that, in part at least, the efficacy of any drug lay in the realm of psychology and not of physiology. The danger, as one warned, was that practitioners might become so conscious of such effects that they would lose sight of the utility of genuinely active drugs. Another practitioner noted that he did not use sugar pills in treating patients in whom he had "confidence"—presumably those better educated and more congenial to him.

In the half-century before 1884, physicians had become increasingly skeptical of the staggering dosage level of drugs routinely employed in the first quarter of the century. Few drugs had actually become obsolete, but mild doses and a parallel emphasis on tonics, wines, and a nourishing diet had come to be considered good practice. Bleeding, too, had dropped out of fashion, though it was still regularly employed in a number of conditions—the beginning of a fever, for example, or with unconscious victims of severe head injuries.

None of this was meant to give the impression that remedies used in 1884 exerted only psychological effects. Even from the perspective of 1984, medicine a century ago had a number of effective tools at its command. Opium soothed pain and allayed diarrhea, digitalis was useful in certain heart conditions, quinine exerted a specific effect on malaria, and fresh fruits relieved scurvy. Vaccination had made major inroads against smallpox (even though technical problems and lax enforcement had made it less than 100 percent effective). Aspirin (although not under that name) had just come into widespread use in the treatment of fevers and rheumatism; it was, in fact, so fashionable that cautious physicians began to warn of its possibly toxic effects. Mercury did have some effect on syphilis, even if it could be dangerous and debilitating. (Some doctors still believed that mercury compounds were not exerting a curative effect until the patient was "salivated" — that is, beginning to show symptoms of what we would now regard as mercury poisoning.)

But the effectiveness of these drugs did not undermine the traditional home and family orientation of medical practice: in contrast to 1984, every weapon in the physician's armory was easily portable. Contemporaries sometimes complained of difficulties in finding competent nurses and continuous medical help in critical ailments, but neither problem was serious enough to convince middle-class patients that they might best be treated away from their families.

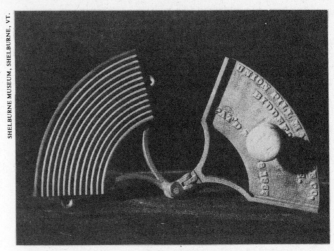

Once the pharmacist had prepared a medicinal paste and laid it across the grooves, this oddly sculptural pill maker would carve it into pellets.

Even surgery was most frequently undertaken in the patient's home—despite the fact that revolutionary changes already had begun to reshape surgical practice. One source of this change was the rapid dissemination of anesthesia, which by 1884 was employed routinely. The question was not whether to administer an anesthetic in a serious operation but which one it should be; ether, chloroform, and nitrous oxide all had their advocates.

Despite the availability of anesthesia, however, major operations remained comparatively uncommon. Many of the technical problems of blood loss, shock, and infection had not been solved. But the style of surgery certainly had changed, as had the surgical patient's experience. "Formerly," as one surgeon explained the change, the "great aim of the surgeon was to accomplish his awful but necessary duty to his agonized patient as rapidly as possible." Surgeons even timed their procedures to the second and vied with each other in the speed with which they completed particular operations. Now, the same surgeon explained, "we operate like the sculptor, upon an insensible mass." The best surgeon was no longer necessarily the fastest.

But doing away with surgical pain had not removed the more intractable dilemma of infection; by increasing the amount of surgery and length of time occupied by particular procedures, it may actually have worsened the problem of surgical infection. In the mid-1860s the Glasgow surgeon Joseph Lister had suggested that such infection might be caused by microorganisms—ordinarily airborne—and proposed a set of antiseptic procedures to keep these organisms from growing in exposed tissue. Immediate reactions were mixed. At first Lister's ideas were seen as extreme and wedded arbitrarily to a particular antiseptic, carbolic acid—"Lister's hobbyhorse" as skeptics termed it. But Lister gradually modified his technique, and by 1884 his point of view had come to be accepted by most American surgeons. This was also the year when surgeons learned that Queen Victoria had awarded

...BUT IT WAS WORSE IN 1784

J. Worth Estes, M.D.

TWO CENTURIES AGO drugs were thought to counteract illness by correcting certain dynamic imbalances in the body. The principal pathological imbalances were in the four liquid "humors"—blood, phlegm, yellow bile, and black bile —and in the tone, the strength, the irritability of the solid organs, especially the blood vessels and nerves.

These imbalances were most often attributed to the weather or to contagions transmitted in the air from sewage, stagnant water, or other patients; the microbes that actually were responsible would not be understood for another century. Other illnesses were blamed on factors ranging from alcohol to volcanic eruptions.

Whatever the supposed causes, treatments were designed to counteract the associated symptoms. Diarrhea, coughing, pain, weakness, convulsions, flushed skin, and skin rashes were common clues that both patients and doctors understood. The doctors also interpreted fast pulse rates as signs of fever: the short clinical thermometer had not been invented.

Treatments were usually unpleasant, but eighteenth-century patients accepted their violent effects as evidence that the medicines were doing *something*: the normal equilibriums of the strong laxatives and enemas may have kept patients on their chamber pots for hours each day, but the cathartic effect guaranteed that unbalanced humors were being flushed from the body. Neither patient nor doctor knew that catharsis itself does not contribute much toward restoring health. Nevertheless, if the patient recovered, it was easy to conclude that the drug had helped.

Drugs that cause vomiting—emetics—were thought to eliminate foul humors via the stomach and to strengthen the weakened patient by stimulating the stomach fibers so that their strength could be transmitted, via the nerves, to the rest of the body. Thus, emetics were important in the treatment of fevers, as were diaphoretics or febrifuges, drugs that made the patient "sweat out" a disease.

Two treatments were reserved for the sickest patients. One was a solution of a powdered Mediterranean beetle; applied to the skin, it raised a large, painful blister into which disturbed humors could escape. More important, the artificial irritation was presumed to neutralize the natural inflammation associated with most fevers and injuries. The other drastic treatment was to induce bleeding from an arm vein, about twelve ounces at a time, to remove chemically unbalanced blood and relax the tensions in the fibers of fevered blood vessels.

The application of cathartics, emetics, diaphoretics, blisters, and bleeding continued until the mainstay of fever treatment, the tonics, did their work. These bitter drugs were thought to increase the tone of weakened bodies. Similarly, red meat was added to weak patients' diets as a stimulant, while a bland, watery diet was prescribed to calm feverish bodies— hence, "Feed a cold, starve a fever."

One drug had several distinct effects. This was opium, usually given as the alcoholic solutions called laudanum and paregoric. Because the morphine and codeine in opium do produce sedation and relieve pain, coughing, and diarrhea, it was thought to decrease the tone and irritability of all organs, especially of the nervous system, lungs, and intestines.

Although the therapy of 1784 might be repellent to our own senses, it was entirely logical to the men and women who endured it. After all, it seemed to work: no matter how they were treated, nineteen out of twenty adult patients recovered, thanks to the body's remarkable ability to heal itself even when assaulted by both disease and eighteenth-century drugs.

J. Worth Estes is a professor of pharmacology at the Boston University School of Medicine.

Lister a knighthood; he already had become a historical figure.

But the problem of surgical infection was still far from solved in practice. Most surgeons and hospitals paid due homage to Lister but had no consistent set of procedures for keeping microorganisms away from wounds and incisions. Medical memoirs of this period are filled with stories of surgeons operating in their street clothes, of their using dressings again and again without intervening sterilization. Natural sponges were washed and reused. The day of aseptic surgery, in which every aspect of the operating room was calculated to keep contaminating objects as well as the atmosphere away from wounds, was still a decade away.

PART OF THE DIFFICULTY surgeons experienced in understanding Lister's theories paralleled the more general problem of relating microorganisms to infectious disease: physicians had difficulty envisaging how such tiny living things could bring about catastrophic change in individuals so much bigger. And why did one person exposed to a disease fall victim while another continued in good health?

Tuberculosis was a particularly good example. The sin-

Most diagnoses depended on sight and touch. Did the patient appear flushed? Was the tongue coated? Eyes cloudy? Even more important was the patient's account of his or her symptoms.

gle most important disease of the century, in terms of mortality, tuberculosis always had been seen as caused by a combination of constitutional and environmental factors such as diet, work, and cleanliness. The simple announcement that a particular bacterium was associated with the disease could not change these age-old views. One needed both seed and soil to grow a crop, as a frequently used analogy ran: in their enthusiasm for the germ theory, physicians should not lose sight of the fundamental role played by the soil—that is, the individual's life history and constitutional endowment—in preparing the way for infection. These views would not be changed easily, for they incorporated centuries of acute clinical observation as well as the authority of tradition.

Nevertheless, these ideas were in the process of rapid change at precisely this moment. The previous year the German bacteriologist Robert Koch had announced his discovery of the organism responsible for cholera and the year before that, in 1882, of the tuberculosis bacillus. Thus, within the space of two years, one scientist had unearthed the cause of the century's greatest killer and its most feared epidemic disease. (Cholera killed far fewer than tuberculosis, but its abrupt and unpredictable nature made it particularly terrifying.) Both discoveries had made front-page news, but it was not yet clear what they meant in practical terms. Like many physicians, most well-informed laymen were still a trifle skeptical. "Now the microbe may be a very decent fellow, after all, when we get acquainted with him," as one whimsical observer put it, "but at present I only know him by reputation, and that reputation has been sicklied o'er with the pale cast of thought of medical men . . . who have charged him with things that we, unprofessionals, look to them to prove." Not only did many Americans share such sentiments, but the technical means to turn this new knowledge into public health practice and effective therapeutics still lay in the future.

Bacteriological techniques, for example, had not yet become so routine that suspected cases of typhoid or tuberculosis could be diagnosed—and thus made the basis for a program of isolating sufferers. Public health departments, in any case, were unaccustomed to exercising such power or supporting laboratory work. And there were other problems as well. Physicians were still unaware that certain ills might be spread by individuals displaying no apparent symptoms—so-called healthy carriers—or by insects. (Though careful readers of the medical journals in 1884 might have taken notice of the report from a Cuban pub-

lication that a Dr. Juan Carlos Finlay had suggested that yellow fever might be spread by mosquitoes—a conjecture proven correct by a team of American investigators at the end of the century.) Perhaps most frustrating to doctors sympathetic to the germ theory was the difficulty of turning this insight into usable therapeutic tools. Knowing what caused a disease, after all, was not the same thing as treating it.

W E CAN HARDLY EXPECT age-old medical ideas to have changed overnight—especially in the absence of new ways of treating patients. Physicians still found it difficult to think of diseases as con-

Depending on what your physician believed, the camphor in this pharmacist's jar was a stimulant or a sedative. Bolstered with laudanum, it treated gout.

NATIONAL MUSEUM OF AMERICAN HISTORY, SMITHSONIAN INSTITUTION

Physicians had difficulty envisaging how microorganisms could bring about catastrophic change in individuals so much bigger. But these views were in the process of rapid change.

crete and specific entities. Fevers, for example, still tended to melt into each other in the perceptions of many doctors; diphtheria and croup, even syphilis and gonorrhea, were regularly confused. It was not simply that such ills were hard to distinguish clinically but that many physicians believed that they could shift subtly from one form to another. Perhaps most interesting from a twentieth-century perspective, physicians still were very much committed to the idea that environmental factors could bring about disease. Every aspect of one's living conditions could help create resistance or susceptibility to disease; and some factors, such as poor ventilation or escaping sewer gas, seemed particularly dangerous. Stress or anxiety also could produce any number of physical ills. Thus, a leading medical school teacher could explain to his class in 1884 that diabetes often originated in the mind.

Medicine always had found a place for stress and the "passions" in causing disease, and by the early 1880s physicians had begun to show an increasing interest in what we would call the neuroses: complaints whose chief symptoms manifested themselves almost entirely in altered behavior and emotions. Such ills were becoming a legitimate—in fact, fashionable—subject for clinical study. Depression, chronic anxiety, sexual impotence or deviation, hysteria, morbid fears, recurring headaches all seemed to be increasing. One particularly energetic neurologist from New York, George M. Beard, had just coined the term *neurasthenia* to describe a condition growing out of environmental stress and manifesting itself in an assortment of fears, anxieties, and psychosomatic symptoms. Beard himself believed that America was peculiarly the home of such ills because of the constant choice and uncertainty associated with the country's relentless growth.

This interest in emotional ills is not important only in and of itself; it is also evidence of the significance of a new kind of specialist, the neurologist. Even if such big-city practitioners represented only a small minority of the total body of physicians, and even if they treated a similarly insignificant number of patients, these specialists were forerunners of a new and increasingly important style of medical practice. By 1884 urban medicine was in fact already dominated by specialists—by ophthalmologists, orthopedic surgeons, dermatologists, otologists and laryngologists, obstetricians and gynecologists, even a handful of pediatricians—as well as the neurologists. Many such practitioners were not exclusive specialists; they saw patients in general practice, but their reputa-

tions—as well as the bulk of their consulting and hospital practice—were based on their specialized competence. They were the teachers of a new generation of medical students, and it was their articles that filled the most prestigious medical journals.

The availability of such new tools as the ophthalmoscope plus an avalanche of clinical information meant that no individual could hope to master the whole of clinical medicine as might have been done a half-century earlier. Coupled with the realities of an extremely competitive marketplace, this explosion of knowledge guaranteed that the movement toward specialization would be irresistible. Significantly, however, ordinary physicians remained suspicious of specialists, whom they saw as illegitimate competitors using claims to superior competence to elbow aside family physicians. In 1884 the handful of specialist societies already in existence were well aware of such hostility, and most adopted rules forbidding members from advertising their expertise in any way.

THERE WERE OTHER STRAWS in the wind indicating the directions in which medicine was to evolve. One was the gradually expanding role of the hospital. Though still limited almost entirely to larger communities, hospitals were playing an ever larger role in the provision of medical care to the urban poor. In 1873, when America's first hospital survey was undertaken, it found that only 178 hospitals of all kinds (including psychiatric) existed in the United States; by 1889 the number had risen to over 700. Even in small towns, local boosters and energetic physicians were beginning to think of the hospital as a necessary civic amenity; by 1910 thousands of county seats and prosperous towns boasted their own thriving community hospitals.

America's first few nursing schools provided another, if less conspicuous, straw in the wind. The movement for nurse training was only a decade old in the United States in 1884 and the supply of trained nurses and number of training schools pitifully small; the 1880 census located only fifteen schools, with a total of 323 students. But the first products of these schools (reinforced by a handful of English-trained administrators) were already teaching and supervising the wards in many of our leading hospitals. They were also beginning to provide a supply of nurses for private duty in the homes of the middle and upper classes.

Before the 1870s, both male and female nurses ordinarily had been trained on the job in hospitals or, even more

Physicians still found it difficult to think of diseases as concrete, specific entities. Fevers tended to melt into each other; diphtheria and croup, even syphilis and gonorrhea, were often confused.

informally, alongside physicians in the course of their private practice. But no matter how long they practiced or how skilled their ministrations, such individuals were inevitably regarded as a kind of well-trained servant. By the time of the First World War, the hospital and the nurses who staffed, taught, and trained in them had become a fundamental aspect of medical care for almost all Americans, not just for the urban poor.

Some aspects of medicine have not changed during the past century. One is a tension between the bedside and the laboratory. At least some clinicians in 1884 were already becoming alarmed at the growing influence of an impersonal medical technology. Even the thermometer could be a means of avoiding the doctor's traditional need to master the use of his eyes, ears, and fingertips—and thus disrupt the physician's personal relationship with the patient. Such worries have become a clichéd criticism of medicine a century later; the growth of technology seems to have created an assortment of new problems as it solved a host of old ones.

But whatever the physician's armory of tools, drugs, and ideas, some aspects of medicine seem unlikely to change. One is death. Euthanasia was already a tangible dilemma in 1884—when the physician's technical means for averting death were primitive. "To surrender to superior forces," as one put it, was not the same as to hasten or induce the inevitable. "May there not come a time when it is a duty in the interests of the survivors to stop a fight which is only prolonging a useless or hopeless struggle?"

Some of our medical problems have not been solved so much as redefined; and some have changed only in detail. A century ago an essay contest was announced in Boston; its subject was the probability of a cure for cancer. No prizes were awarded.

The War Against Demon Rum

With alcohol consumption on the rise in 19th-century America, the temperance cause took root.

Robert Maddox

Robert Maddox, of Pennsylvania State University, is a distinguished historian whose article "War In Korea: The Desperate Times" appeared in the July 1978 issue of AHI. For those interested in reading further on the subject of temperance he suggests The Origins of Prohibition *(1925), by John Allen Krout and* Ardent Spirits *(1973), by John Kobler.*

"Good-bye, John Barleycorn," cried the Reverend Billy Sunday to an approving crowd, "You were God's worst enemy. You were Hell's best friend. I hate you with a perfect hatred. I love to hate you." The date was January 16, 1920, the day when the Eighteenth Amendment to the Constitution went into effect. Drys across the nation celebrated happily, while drinkers cursed and contemplated a future without alcohol. Both were premature. John Barleycorn was by no means dead, though he did go underground for more than a decade. But on that first day, those who had worked on behalf of prohibition could congratulate themselves on a victory over what at times had seemed insurmountable odds.

From the first settlements at Jamestown and Plymouth Rock, Americans have brewed, fermented, and distilled everything they could. Though their drinking customs were from Europe, the colonists displayed remarkable ingenuity in devising additional reasons for having a cup of this or a mug of that. Writers of early travel accounts express surprise as to the amount of alcohol the colonists consumed. Everything from the crudest beers and ciders to the most elegant wines ran down American throats in amazing quantities.

During the colonial period there were few attempts to restrict the availability of alcohol, much less to prohibit it entirely. Public houses and taverns abounded. Even in Puritan New England, contrary to popular legend, the people had virtually unrestricted access to spirits of all kinds. Indeed, alcohol was seen as one of God's blessings, to be enjoyed as He intended. When taken in moderation, it was believed to be beneficial for both the mind and the body.

Drunkenness was another matter. Defined in one colony as "drinking with excess to the notable perturbation of any organ of sense or motion," public inebriation was dealt with harshly. The penalties varied from place to place but ranged from fines for first offenders to hard labor or whippings for chronic indulgers. Still, drunkenness was seen as a personal weakness or sin, and the guilty party had no one save himself to blame. Alcohol bore the repsonsibility scarcely more than did the fire which burned down a careless person's home.

A number of people, principally clergymen, spoke out or wrote locally distributed tracts denouncing the intemperate use of intoxicants. This was particularly true after the middle of the 17th century when rum and whiskey replaced the milder ciders and wines. To some it appeared their communities were in danger of drowning in alcohol. It was not until 1784 that any single temperance tract received wide attention. In that year the eminent Philadelphia physician, Dr. Benjamin Rush, published his "An Inquiry into the Effects of Spiritous Liquors on the Human Body and Mind." This pamphlet went through many editions and portions of the work were widely reprinted in newspapers and almanacs across the entire country.

The reception accorded Rush's tract undoubtedly reflected a growing concern about the problems concerning alcoholic consumption. Aside from its popularity, the pamphlet differed from earlier ones in several ways. First of all, as a physician-general in the Continental Army during the Revolution, Rush had had ample opportunity to observe the effects of drinking on soldiers. Thus his words had the backing of what appeared to be scientific examination, rather than mere moral exhortation. Rush denied the popular notions that drinking helped prevent fatigue, protected one against cold, and many other popular myths of the day. Quite the contrary, he argued, in general the consumption of alcohol helped *bring on* diseases of both the mind and of the body. Second, his pamphlet differed from previous ones in that he not only warned against excessive amounts of drink, but claimed that even moderate use over an extended period of time would have harmful effects. It is interesting to note, however, that Rush's

From *American History Illustrated*, May 1979. Reproduced through the courtesy of Cowles Magazines, publishers of *American History Illustrated*.

broadside was directed against distilled spirits only. Beers and light wines, he thought, *were* beneficial if taken in moderation.

How much effect, if any, Rush's pamphlet had on the consumption of alcohol at the time is uncertain. But it did inspire a number of reformers who took up the temperance cause in the years following. Perhaps the most important, and colorful, of these was the Reverend Lyman Beecher of East Hampton, Long Island. Father of thirteen children (including the famous Henry Ward Beecher and the even more famous Harriet Beecher Stowe), Beecher had been appalled by the drinking habits of his fellow students while at Yale and little he saw thereafter reassured him. Indeed, he came to believe, alcohol posed the greatest threat to the society's physical and spiritual well-being. Though males were the worst offenders, even women consumed impressive amounts. Nor were the clergy immune.

Beecher spoke of attending one convocation where, after a time, the room came to look and smell "like a very active grog shop." Worse yet were the amounts of alcohol given to children of all ages. Fairfax Downey, in a recent article about Beecher, tells the story of a 7-year-old girl who visited her grandmother in Boston. When she learned she would be given no spirits, she angrily notified her parents. "Missy," the grandmother learned, "had been brought up as a lady and must have wine and beer with every meal." Beecher was so concerned about the situation that he claimed he never gave a child even the smallest amount of money without adding the warning "not to drink ardent spirits or any inebriating liquor."

Beecher frequently lectured his congregation on the dangers of drink, and became even more active in the cause after taking the pastorate at Litchfield, Connecticut, in 1811. He was instrumental in forming one of the first temperance groups, the Connecticut Society for the Reformation of Morals. Among other things, the Society printed and distributed large numbers of Dr. Rush's pamphlet. In 1825 Beecher delivered six sermons on the temperance issue which later were published in pamphlet form. Widely reprinted in the years following, the "Six Sermons" according to one scholar, "were as widely read and exerted as great an influence as any other contribution to the literature of the reform."

The Reverend Beecher went beyond earlier temperance leaders in several respects. Like Dr. Rush, he believed that the sustained use of liquor was harmful even if one never actually got drunk. "Let it therefore be engraven upon the heart of every man," he wrote, "that the daily use of ardent spirits, in any form, or in any degree, is intemperance." Beecher's prescription was radical; he called for nothing less than total abstinence from distilled beverages. He differed from Rush on the question of drinking wine as well. Rush had recommended it; Beecher thought it a treacherous way station on the road to stronger potions. Under the influence of Beecher, and others like him, the temperance movement had come a long way from mere denunciations of drunkenness.

The 1830's witnessed a remarkable growth of temperance societies. The United States Temperance Union (later renamed the American Temperance Union) was founded in 1833, though four years passed before it held its first national convention. Despite its increasing popularity, the cause suffered grievously from internal disunity. For some, temperance meant what the word itself meant: moderation. For others, such as Beecher, it had come to mean abstinence. And what was to be included in the list of harmful beverages: distilled spirits only, or wines and beers too? Finally, should temperance (however defined) be promoted exclusively by moral suasion, or should the societies enter the realm of politics? Members of the various groups wrangled over these questions in seemingly endless debates which did little to achieve effectiveness.

A new development took place after 1840. Until this time, the most visible leaders of the cause were opinion leaders such as clergymen, newspaper publishers, and college presidents. Beginning with a group which called itself the Washington Temperance Society, however, a new element came to the fore: reformed drinkers. These were men who, some way or another, had seen the light and who wanted to help save others. Who knew better the evils of drink than those who once had been in its clutches themselves? This "Washington revival," as it became known, spread throughout the country and produced a number of eloquent spokesmen for the temperance cause.

One of the most popular of the reformed drunkards was John H.W. Hawkins. Hawkins began drinking as a young lad while serving as an apprentice to a hatmaker. For more than twenty years he alternated between periods of excessive drinking and relative sobriety. Finally, as his bouts with alcohol became longer and more debilitating he was no longer able to provide for his family and became a public ward. According to his own account, Hawkins was redeemed when members of the Washington Temperance Society in Baltimore convinced him to sign a pledge of total abstinence. Possessing impressive oratorical talents, Hawkins went on to become one of the cause's most sought-after speakers. He later estimated that during his first ten years as a reformer he traveled more than 100,000 miles and delivered some 2,500 lectures.

John Bartholomew Gough was equally in demand. Gough too had begun drinking as a youngster, and his habit cost him job after job and several physical breakdowns. During one, when his seriously ill wife tried to nurse him through, the strain proved too much for her and she died. For some time after her death he rarely drew a sober breath. When finally converted by a friend, Gough pitched himself wholeheartedly into the cause. By several accounts he was a masterful speaker, able to manipulate the emotions of his audience as he wished. He boasted in his autobiography that singlehandedly he accounted for more than 15,000 converts to abstinence.

Things did not always go smoothly for Gough. Early in his career as a reformer he "fell off the wagon" and did so again at the height of his popularity in 1845. The latter occasion touched off quite a furor. While visiting New York City Gough disappeared for almost a week. After a desperate search, friends located him in a bawdy house in one of the seedier sections of the city. He was, it was obvious, recovering from a monumental drinking spree. The incident received wide publicity as the anti-temperance press had a field day at Gough's expense. He claimed innocence. An acquaintance, whose name he could not remember, had treated him to a glass supposedly containing only a soft drink. Having consumed the beverage, Gough claimed, he blanked out and did not know how he ended up where he did. How many people believed Gough's explanation—implying as it did that the liquor interests had conspired to do him in—is unknown, but he remained a popular speaker on the temperance circuit for another five years.

The temperance movement evolved one step more during the pre-Civil War years. It was becoming painfully evident to some that, despite the thousands of pamphlets issued, meetings held, and speeches delivered, the drinking habits of most Americans had not changed. Taverns and saloons prospered, men and women reeled about in the streets, and the gallons of drink consumed rose with each passing year. But what of all the converts? The usual evidence of success consisted of the number of signed pledges individuals or societies collected from "redeemed" individuals, who promised either moderation or total abstinence. There were two problems with this approach. First, even in the most rewarding years no more than a tiny percentage of the adult population signed such promises. Second, how valid were they? To be sure, an effective speaker such as Hawkins or Gough could cause people to struggle in the aisles to sign up. But when emotions cooled, it was obvious, many resumed their old habits. Indeed, as one anti-temperance joke had it, some individuals became so elated by taking the pledge that they could scarcely wait to celebrate by having a few drinks. Increasingly, therefore, temperance advocates sought to strengthen moral persuasion with legal enforcement.

Some reformers had advocated legal controls in the 1830's and 1840's, but they were always in the minority. True conversion could only come through education, the majority had argued, and there was great fear that the purity of the cause would become sullied by entangling it in partisan politics. But this position became increasingly untenable as time wore on; unaided moral suasion simply had not achieved the desired effects. Nor was local-option legislation sufficient. This tactic had been tried in many communities, but serious drinkers could always lay in a supply from nearby towns or cities. Some reformers, therefore, came to believe that nothing less than statewide prohibition could get the job done. A formidable undertaking to be sure, but the prospects were dazzling.

Neal Dow was a successful businessman who looked the part. He wore expensive clothes, a lace-trimmed vest, and kept the time by a fat gold watch reportedly costing more than $200. He was dynamic, aggressive, and exuded vitality. Although slight of stature, Dow feared no man and used his fists effectively when the occasion demanded it. He was also a devout reformer. Dow devoted his life to the temperance cause and, as early as the 1830's, had become convinced that state prohibition was the only answer.

Born and raised in Portland, Maine, Dow practiced the teachings of his temperance-minded parents with a vengeance. At the age of 18 he joined the volunteer fire department of Portland and before very long somehow convinced the group to stop serving alcohol at its social get-togethers. Later, as captain, he enraged many drinkers by allowing a liquor store to burn to the ground without turning a hose on it. Called before the city's board of alderman to account for his behavior, Dow claimed he had acted as he did to "save" adjacent buildings. On another occasion, when the casks of a wholesale dealer were erupting into fireballs, Dow remarked to an aide that it was a "magnificent sight." Small wonder that the liquor interests in Portland would have preferred another fire chief.

But Dow was after bigger game. Throughout the 1840's he worked tirelessly to bring the temperance issue into the political arena. At first he concentrated on turning Portland dry, but statewide legislation was his real goal. He was careful not to allow prohibition to become a partisan issue; he and his allies (he often used his own employees to do temperance work) supported all those who were "right" on the good cause. At last, in 1851, Dow won what had seemed an impossible victory. With many members of both houses indebted to him politically, he shepherded through the Maine legislature the first general prohibition law in American history. Dow, who was by this time mayor of Portland, prosecuted the new law to the best of his considerable abilities.

The Maine Law of 1851 served as rallying point for prohibitionists in other states. Dubbed "The Napoleon of Temperance," Dow became a hero to drys everywhere as the following song attests:

Come all ye friends of temperance, and listen to my strain,
I'll tell you how Old Alchy fares down in the State of Maine.
There's one Neal Dow, a Portland man, with great and noble soul,
He framed a law, without a flaw, to banish alcohol.

Unfortunately, as Dow himself admitted privately, alcohol was not "banished" from Maine, but flowed rather freely through illegal channels. Still, it was a step forward, and in the next four years two territories and eleven states enacted similar laws. Many people deserved the credit, if such it be, but no one more than Dow who advised and counseled his fellow reformers across the nation.

The hope that prohibition would become an irresistible tide proved illusory after the mid-1850's. The most important reason was the growing sectional struggle which culminated in the Civil War. As compared to the great issues of slavery and secession, prohibition seemed almost trivial except to the faithful. More than twenty-five years were to pass before another state would adopt prohibition. Equally ominous, though less obvious, was a simple statistic. During those years of temperance victories the per capita consumption of wine, whiskey, and beer *rose* from slightly over four gallons to almost six and one-half. Later prohibitionists ignored or downplayed the grim truth that laws in the books were ineffective so long as a sufficient number of people were willing to disobey them.

By the early 1870's, the temperance movement began stirring again. One of the most significant developments of this era was the role women played. Women always had constituted the backbone of the movement in terms of numbers, but men invariably held the positions of leadership. The first sign of change occurred in what became known as the "Women's Crusade." In communities across the nation groups of women assembled in front of saloons and taverns, vowing to remain until owners agreed to close. For hours, days, and even longer the women sang and prayed, and tried to discourage men from entering. Some places indeed did close, but usually only temporarily and the Crusade dwindled after a few years. Veterans of the Crusade were not about to quit, however, and in 1874 formed the Woman's Christian Temperance Union. This organization would play an important part in the drive for national prohibition.

The dominant force of the WCTU until her death in 1898 was Frances Willard. Born into a family dedicated to reform (her father was a member of the Washington Society), Willard was a zealous temperance advocate from youth. Endowed with a formidable intelligence and incredible energy, she received a good education and was a college faculty member at age 23. In 1871 Willard was named president of Northwestern Female College and, when that institution merged with Northwestern University, became dean of women. She subsequently resigned from this post, however, and thereafter dedicated herself to the temperance movement.

Under Willard the WCTU became the largest, best organized, and most powerful temperance organization in the country. It published tons of pamphlets, provided speakers, lobbied legislators. There were few aspects of society the organization failed to penetrate. Willard herself was a dynamo who, when not giving a speech or chairing a meeting, wrote letters and articles in behalf of the cause. Described by one individual as "organized mother

love," the WCTU under Willard reached into every community.

Less important than Willard, though far more colorful, was Carry A. Nation ("carry a nation for temperance," she liked to say). A member of the WCTU, Nation circled in her own orbit and in fact was an embarrassment to some of the members. Having grown up in a family where eccentricity was the norm, Carry at age 19 married a man who drank himself to death very quickly. When the daughter of that union developed chronic illnesses of the cruelest sort, Carry concluded they were the results of her husband's addiction to alcohol and tobacco. These two substances became her lifelong enemies. Though she became involved in temperance work earlier, Carry made the full commitment after claiming to have received a direct communication from God during the summer of 1900.

Nation's methods were similar to the Women Crusaders—with a difference. She too prayed and sang that saloon keepers and their customers would repent. But in addition to her words she hurled bricks and bottles. Her favorite weapon came to be a hatchet which she wielded with remarkable verve for a middle-aged woman. "Smash! Smash! For Jesus' sake, Smash!" was her battle cry as she broke up saloons from Kansas to New York. Though she garnered a great deal of publicity, and caused some other women to take up their own hatchets, Carry's impact was not lasting. Indeed, in later years she became a curiosity, touring county fairs and carnivals. At age 64 she collapsed after a lecture and died a few months later in the summer of 1911.

The temperance movement took on new life with the founding of the Anti-Saloon League of America in 1895.

This temperance cartoon was captioned "Commit him for manslaughter in the greatest degree." ("Harper's Weekly," March 21, 1874)

As was the WCTU, it was misnamed. Just as "temperance" really meant abstinence, the Anti-Saloon League was dedicated to banning all alcohol rather than just that dispensed by saloons. It was an effective ploy because the term "saloon" conjured up all sorts of negative images: drunken fistfights, scarlet women, and husbands drinking away their wages. The word "League" was accurate, however, because the organization was nonsectarian and accepted any individuals or groups dedicated to prohibition.

The League's dedication to a single goal made it more effective than its predecessors. It took on no other reforms, rarely got bogged down in internal disputes, and appealed to everyone interested in the cause. The organization was pragmatic to say the least, and subordinated everything to its goal. "Ethics be hanged," as one of the leaders put it, and they very often were. The League regularly supported politicians who were known drinkers, for instance, provided they could be depended upon to vote dry. In the South, League speakers and pamphlets often played upon racial prejudices by describing in lurid terms how alcohol heightened the lust black males had for white women. Dedicated, unscrupulous as to means, the League was able to bring great pressure to bear upon politicians across the country.

During the first decade of the 20th century, the League, the WCTU, and other organizations, succeeded in getting a number of state legislatures to pass prohibitory laws of various kinds. By 1913 the League went on record as favoring a constitutional amendment to make prohibition nationwide. Bills were introduced in Congress and the issue aroused considerable debate, which spurred the drys on to greater efforts. When the 1914 elections were over, men committed to voting dry had gained in both houses of Congress. During the next session a prohibition bill introduced in the House won by a 197-190 majority. This was a good deal short of the two-thirds necessary to start the amendment process (three-fourths of the states

have to concur), but still constituted a victory of which earlier temperance advocates could not have dreamed.

Would the prohibitionists ultimately have prevailed because of their own efforts? Or would the movement have peaked short of its goal, and then perhaps waned as had earlier temperance crusades? The answer is speculative. For it was the onset of World War I—and more particularly, American entry into the conflict—which assured a prohibitionist victory.

American participation in the war gave the drys two additional weapons which they employed with deadly effect. The first stemmed from the simple fact that various grains and sugar are the main ingredients of beer and liquor. At a time when Americans were being called upon to conserve food for the war effort, how could one defend the diversion of these materials into alcohol? Few politicians were prepared to defend themselves against charges that they were willing to see drunks get their liquor while boys in the trenches went hungry. That most breweries and many distilleries bore Germanic names provided a second boon to the drys. They were able to concoct all sorts of horror stories about German plots to undermine the war effort by encouraging soldiers and civilians to drink their vile products. Such allegations may seem absurd today, but they carried weight during a period when sauerkraut was renamed "victory cabbage."

Under these circumstances the prohibition movement was unstoppable. What was to become the Eighteenth Amendment was adopted by the Senate in August 1917 and by the House in December. The wets thought they had outmaneuvered their opponents when they worked in a seven-year time limit on the ratification process, but they were badly mistaken. The required number of states ratified within thirteen months of submission and the Eighteenth Amendment became law on January 16, 1919, (though it was not to take effect until one year from that date). The "Noble Experiment" would soon begin.

AMERICA'S FIRST COCAINE EPIDEMIC

Only a decade ago, many prominent Americans tolerated and even touted the use of cocaine. From Capitol Hill to Wall Street, the young and moneyed set made the drug its favorite "leisure pharmaceutical." Some talked of decriminalizing the "harmless" white powder. But that changed after cocaine overdoses killed several celebrities—including Hollywood's John Belushi in 1982 and college basketball star Len Bias in 1986. Last year, the drug claimed 1,582 lives in the United States and was a factor in countless crimes. Crack, a cheap form of cocaine, is now considered a scourge of the nation's ghettos; teenage dealers wage murderous turf battles within blocks of the Capitol dome. Lawmakers clamor for a war on drugs but despair of finding a way to win it. All this has a familiar ring to it, says Yale's David Musto. Here, he recalls what happened a century ago, when America entered its first cocaine craze.

David F. Musto

David F. Musto is professor of psychiatry and the history of medicine at the Yale School of Medicine. Born in Tacoma, Washington, he received a B.A. from the University of Washington (1956), an M.A. in history from Yale (1961), and an M.D. from the University of Washington (1963). He is the author of The American Disease *(1987).*

I have tested [the] effect of coca," wrote a youthful Sigmund Freud in his famed essay "On Coca" (1884), "which wards off hunger, sleep, and fatigue and steels one to intellectual effort, some dozen times on myself." Like other doctors who had tested the drug, he found that the euphoria it induced was not followed by depression or any other unpleasant aftereffects. Furthermore, wrote Freud, "a first dose or even repeated doses of coca produce no compulsive desire to use the stimulant further."

With obvious wonder, Freud described the remarkable experiments of 78-year-old Sir Robert Christison, a world-famous toxi-cologist at the University of Edinburgh: "During the third experiment he chewed two drams of coca leaves and was able to complete [a 15-mile] walk without the exhaustion experienced on the earlier occasions; when he arrived home, despite the fact that he had been nine hours without food or drink, he experienced no hunger or thirst, and woke the next morning without feeling at all tired."

Freud's "song of praise to this magical substance," as he described it, was only one of many that were sung by various medical authorities before the turn of the century. Indeed, Freud had become interested in coca because American physicians, the drug's earliest and heartiest enthusiasts, had "discovered" that it could reduce the cravings of opiate addicts and alcoholics. Freud's interest was not academic. He was seeking a cure for the addiction of his colleague, Ernst von Fleischl-Marxow. "At present," Freud observed in 1884, "there seems to be some promise of widespread recognition and use of coca preparations in North America, while in Europe doctors scarcely know them by name."

In America, where the cocaine fad would reach greater heights than in Europe, the ability to cure opiate addictions was regarded as only one of cocaine's marvelous powers. While morphine and other torpor-inducing opiates were beginning to seem positively un-American, cocaine seemed to increase alertness and efficiency, much-prized qualities in the industrializing nation. In 1880, Dr. W.H. Bentley, writing in Detroit's *Therapeutic Gazette*, hailed coca as "the desideratum . . . in health and disease." The *Gazette*'s editors, quoting another medical journal, cheerily endorsed this view: "'One feels like trying coca, with or without the opium-habit. A harmless remedy for the blues is imperial.' And so say we."

Encouraged by the nation's leading medical authorities, and with no laws restricting the sale, consumption, or advertising of cocaine (or any other drugs), entrepreneurs quickly made cocaine an elixir for the masses. Lasting from around 1885 to the 1920s, America's first great cocaine epidemic went through three phases: the introduction during the 1880s, as cocaine rapidly gained acceptance; a middle period, when its use spread and its ill effects came to light; and a final, repressive stage after the turn of the century, when cocaine became the most feared of all illicit drugs.

North Americans, to be sure, were not the first inhabitants of this hemisphere to discover or extol the powers of the "magical leaf." For centuries before (and after) the arrival of the Europeans, the Indians of the Andes had chewed coca leaves to gain relief from hunger and fatigue. The drug spread beyond South America only after 1860, when an Austrian chemist named Albert Niemann learned how to isolate the active ingredient, cocaine. When Freud published his first praise of the elixir, pure cocaine, along with the milder coca, was already available to Americans in drug and grocery stores, saloons, and from mail-order patent-medicine vendors. By 1885, the major U.S. manufacturer, Parke, Davis & Co., of Detroit and New York, was selling cocaine and coca in 15 forms, including coca-leaf cigarettes and cheroots, cocaine inhalant, a Coca Cordial, cocaine crystals, and cocaine in solution for hypodermic injection.

Parke, Davis reported that it had repeatedly stepped up production during 1885 in order to satisfy the public's growing appetite. A Parke, Davis advertisement informed doctors of the drug's uses:

Advertisements idealized coca's past. During the 16th century, conquistadores learned of coca from the Incas. The drug's use by Spaniards was promptly outlawed, its effects condemned by Church and king as a demoniacal illusion.

An enumeration of the diseases in which coca and cocaine have been found of service would include a category of almost all the maladies that flesh is heir to . . . . Allowing for the exaggeration of enthusiasm, it remains the fact that already cocaine claims a place in medicine and surgery equal to that of opium and quinine, and coca has been held to be better adapted for use as a popular restorative and stimulant than either tea or coffee.

The American craving for cocaine was not satisfied by domestic producers alone. From Paris came a variety of popular cocaine concoctions manufactured by Angelo Mariani. "Vin Mariani," a mixture of wine and coca, arrived on the drugstore shelf with a raft of celebrity endorsements, including those of Pope Leo XIII, Thomas Edison, Sarah Bernhardt, Emile Zola, Henrik Ibsen, and the Prince of Wales. "Since a single bottle of Mariani's extraordinary coca wine guarantees a lifetime of a hundred years," exclaimed novelist Jules Verne, "I shall be obliged to live until the year 2700." Mariani boasted that Ulysses S. Grant took another of his products, "Thé Mariani," once a day during his last illness in 1885, allowing the ex-president to complete his famous *Memoirs*.

For consumers on a budget, the new wonder drug was available in less exalted forms. Coca-Cola, for example, contained a minute amount* of cocaine—enough to

---

*Coca Cola's cocaine content was .0025 percent in 1900, and may have been greater during the 1880s.

provide a noticeable lift, if not a "high." The "real thing" began life as a coca wine in 1885. In deference, ironically, to the widespread temperance sentiment of the day, the company replaced the alcohol content of the drink with soda water and flavorings, which allowed it to market Coke as a healthful "soft drink"—a "brain tonic" to relieve headaches and cure "all nervous affections." With the successful marketing of Coca-Cola and similar refreshers, the neighborhood drugstore soda fountain of late-19th-century America came to serve as the poor man's Saratoga Springs. There, the weary citizen could choose from among dozens of soda pop pick-me-ups, including Cola Coke, Rocco Cola, Koca Nola, Nerv Ola, Wise Ola, and one with the simple and direct name, Dope.

Cocaine also was offered as an asthma remedy and an antidote for toothache pain. (Other patent medicines contained opiates, such as morphine and heroin.) Dr. Nathan Tucker's Asthma Specific, a popular catarrh powder, or snuff, considered to be an excellent cure for hay fever and asthma, contained as much as half a gram of pure cocaine per package. Thanks to its remarkable ability to shrink the nasal mucous membranes and drain the sinuses, cocaine became the official remedy of the American Hay Fever Association.

In the six states and innumerable counties that were "dry" during the mid 1890s, workingmen found snuffs, soft drinks, and

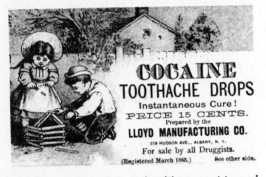

As much a part of everyday life as aspirin and decongestants are today, cocaine remedies were widely advertised during the 1880s and '90s.

other cocaine products a cheap substitute for hard liquor. In states where teetotalers had not prevailed, bartenders often put a pinch of cocaine in a shot of whiskey to add punch to the drink. Peddlers sold it door to door. And some employers in the construction and mining industries found practical uses for the drug, reportedly distributing it to their workers to keep them going at a high pitch.

How much cocaine did Americans consume? Judging from its wide legal availability, and given its seductive appeal,

it is safe to assume that they were using substantial amounts by the turn of the century. The limited import statistics for the leaf and manufactured cocaine suggest that use peaked shortly after 1900, just as co-

---

CONDEMNED TO REPETITION

By the 1970s, America's early experience with cocaine was largely forgotten, and some medical authorities praised the drug. One advocate was Dr. Peter Bourne, who was President Jimmy Carter's drug policy adviser until forced to resign by charges that he had written illegal prescriptions and used cocaine. In 1974, he wrote:

Cocaine . . . is probably the most benign of illicit drugs currently in widespread use. At least as strong a case could be made for legalizing it as for legalizing marijuana. Short acting—about 15 minutes—not physically addicting, and acutely pleasurable, cocaine has found increasing favor at all socioeconomic levels in the last year . . . .

One must ask what possible justification there can be for the obsession which [U.S.] Drug Enforcement Administration officials have with it, and what criteria they use to determine the priority they give the interdiction of a drug if it is not the degree of harm which it causes the user?

---

caine was being transformed in the public mind from a tonic into a terror.* Legal imports of coca leaves during that period averaged about 1.5 million pounds annually and the amount of cocaine averaged 200,000 ounces. (Today, the United States has roughly three times the population it did in 1900 but consumes more than 10 times as much cocaine—perhaps 2.5 million ounces annually.)

At first, there were few reports of chronic cocaine abuse. Confronted with one example in 1887, Dr. William A. Hammond, former Surgeon General of the Army, and one of the most prominent cocaine advocates of the era, dismissed it as a "case of preference, and not a case of irresistible habit." However, by 1890 the *Medical Record* cited some 400 cases of habit mostly among people being treated, as Freud and others had recommended, for addiction to morphine and other opiates.

---

*It is also difficult to determine how many Americans were addicted to cocaine. Because they can live with their addictions for 20 or 30 years, opium addicts (of whom there were perhaps 250,000 around the turn of the century) are a relatively stable population, and thus easier to count. Cocaine addicts, on the other hand, do not live long if they do not quit, so their ranks are constantly changing.

In fact, Freud himself watched his friend Ernst von Fleischl-Marxow disintegrate into a state of "cocainist" delirium before he died in 1891. Freud claimed that he had not intended for von Fleischl-Marxow to inject the drug, and he withdrew his support for its use as a treatment for morphine addiction. But he never publicly renounced other uses of the drug.

By the turn of the century, cocaine was becoming more and more suspect. A thorough investigation by a committee of the Connecticut State Medical Society in 1896 concluded that cocaine cures for hay fever and other ailments had been a major cause of drug dependency, and "the danger of addiction outweighs the little efficacy attributed to the remedy." It recommended that cocaine be made available only to physicians, for use as a local anesthetic. Scattered newspaper reports—"ANOTHER PHYSICIAN A VICTIM TO THE BANEFUL DRUG"—books such as Annie Meyers' *Eight Years in Cocaine Hell* (1902), word of mouth, and articles in *Ladies' Home Journal*, *Collier's*, and other popular magazines brought more bad news. The debilitating effects of Sherlock Holmes's cocaine habit were familiar enough to earn a place in an 1899 Broadway play bearing the name of the brilliant British detective.

Once the miracle drug of upper-class professionals, cocaine came to be considered a curse of both the American demimonde and pathetic middle-class victims of patent medicines. The "Report of Committee on the Acquirement of Drug Habits" in the *American Journal of Pharmacy* (1903) declared that most users were "bohemians, gamblers, high- and low-class prostitutes, night porters, bell boys, burglars, racketeers, pimps, and casual laborers." That year, reflecting the public's growing suspicion of cocaine, the Coca-Cola company replaced the stimulant with a milder, more acceptable one, caffeine—the first, one might say, of the "new formula" Cokes.

A 1909 *New York Times* report on "The Growing Menace of the Use of Cocaine"—published even as use was declining—noted that the drug was used at lower-class "sniff parties," destroying "its victims more swiftly and surely than opium." In the *Century Magazine*, Charles B. Towns, a national anti-drug activist, issued a grave warning: "The most harmful of all habit forming drugs is cocaine. Nothing so quickly deteriorates [sic] its victim or provides so short a cut to the insane asylum."

As early as 1887, the states had begun enacting their own (largely ineffective) laws against cocaine and other drugs. In 1913, New York passed the toughest statute to date, completely outlawing cocaine, except for certain medical uses. By the beginning of World War I, all 48 states had anti-cocaine laws on the books. Fourteen states also inaugurated "drug education" programs in the public schools.

And what role did the federal government play? A small one, at first. According to the Constitutional doctrines of the day, Washington had virtually no power to police the drug trade directly. The federal Pure Food and Drug Act of 1906 merely required labelling of any cocaine content in over-the-counter remedies. But official Washington was jolted by the effects of the cocaine "epidemic" in its own backyard, much as it has become alarmed today by hundreds of crack cocaine-related killings in the Federal District. For years, the District of Columbia's chief of police, Major Sylvester, had been warning Congress (which then governed the city directly) of cocaine's horrifying effects. "The cocaine habit is by far the greatest menace to society, because the victims are generally vicious. The use of this drug superinduces jealousy and prodisposes [sic] to commit criminal acts," he declared. In 1909, President Theodore Roosevelt's Homes Commission presented the testimony of Sylvester and other officials to an alarmed Congress, which promptly restricted legal drug sales in the nation's capital.

At the same time, the drug problem took on an international dimension. Roosevelt's State Department, under Elihu Root, had assumed the lead in attempting to regulate the free-wheeling international opium trade. Root's motives were mixed. By siding with the Chinese against Britain and other European powers that were reaping large profits in the Chinese opium market, Root hoped to gain trade concessions from the Chinese. Moreover, Root hoped, like some officials in Washington today, that he could solve America's drug problem by stamping out the cultivation of opium poppies and coca bushes abroad. But a nation that led such an international moral crusade, Root realized, would have to have exemplary anti-drug laws of its own.

In 1910, President William Howard Taft presented a State Department report on drugs to Congress. Cocaine officially became Public Enemy No. 1:

> The illicit sale of [cocaine] . . . and the habitual use of it temporarily raises the power of a criminal to a point where in resisting arrest there is no hesitation to murder. It is more appalling in its effects than any other habit-forming drug used in the United States.

The report also stirred racist fears, adding that "it has been authoritatively stated

A NEW COCAINE UNDERCLASS?

After the anti-cocaine reaction of the early 20th century, only a few Americans continued to use the drug. Today, as journalist Michael Massing recently warned in the New York Review of Books *(March 30, 1989), a different "two-tier" system may be emerging, with a large, permanent "underclass" of crack cocaine users.*

Contrary to the popular notion that narcotics are used throughout American society, drug use seems to be developing along well-defined class lines. On the one hand, the consumption of cocaine by the middle class has been steadily falling. Once considered glamorous and safe, cocaine is now widely viewed as a menace. The newsweeklies, movies, TV commercials, [and] books . . . all send the same message: Cocaine can kill. Educated Americans are responding. Recently, for instance, the Gordon B. Black Corporation of Rochester, New York, in a survey of 1,461 college students, found only 6 percent acknowledged "occasional" use of cocaine in 1988—down from 11 percent in 1987. Those who said they had friends who used cocaine socially dropped from 36 percent to 31 percent. Citing such surveys, the *Washington Post* concluded that "use of cocaine and marijuana among many segments of the population, particularly middle-class professionals and college students, has declined sharply."

In the inner cities, the story is very different. There the use of drugs—especially crack—is soaring. Three years ago, crack was sold only in large cities like Los Angeles and New York; today, it's available in places like Kansas City, Denver, and Dallas—everywhere, in fact, with a large minority population. Cocaine, once popular in Hollywood and on Wall Street, is fast becoming the narcotic of the ghetto. Mark Gold, founder of the nation's first cocaine "Hotline" six years ago, told the *Washington Post* that, when the service was introduced, most callers were whites with college degrees and high salaries; now, more than half are unemployed and only 16 percent college educated. . . . As drug use comes to be associated more and more with minorities, public support for treatment could dry up, giving way to renewed demands for more police, more jails, and harsher sentences—none of which . . . has much promise of reducing the demand for drugs.

that cocaine is often the direct incentive to the crime of rape by negroes of the South, and other sections of the country." (Likewise, opium was considered to be a special vice of the nation's Chinatowns.) Terrifying rumors told of criminals who gained superhuman strength, cunning, and efficiency under the influence of cocaine. Convinced that black "cocaine fiends" could withstand normal .32 caliber bullets, some police departments in the South reportedly switched to .38 caliber revolvers.

By December 1914, when Congress passed the Harrison Act, tightly regulating the distribution and sale of drugs, the use of cocaine and other drugs was considered so completely beyond the pale that the law itself seemed routine. The *New York Times* did not even note the passage of the Harrison Act until two weeks after the fact. The vote was overshadowed by a popular crusade against a more controversial target, Demon Rum, a crusade which brought thousands of temperance demonstrators to Washington that December. From the gallery of the House of Representatives, temperance advocates hung a Prohibition petition bearing six million signatures.

But the public's adamant anti-cocaine sentiment, which had reduced the drug's appeal after the turn of the century and resulted in legal restrictions, now facilitated operation of the laws. Unlike Prohibition, which was not backed by a public consensus, the Harrison Act—which Congress made more restrictive over the years—was largely successful.

What happened to cocaine? Of course, some Americans continued to acquire and use it, but their numbers eventually shrank. Peer pressure and the threat of punishment combined to drive cocaine underground. Only occasional—and often negative—references to it appeared in movies and popular songs during the 1920s and 1930s. Cole Porter announced, "I get no kick from cocaine" in his 1934 musical, *Anything Goes*, and an impish Charlie Chaplin, in the movie *Modern Times* (1936), gained such superhuman strength from sniffing "nose powder" that he was able to break out of jail.

By the time I was in medical school, during the late 1950s, cocaine was de-scribed to medical students as a drug that used to be a problem in the United States. It was news to us.

The people who had lived through the nation's first cocaine epidemic and knew that the euphoria induced by the drug was a dangerous delusion had grown old and passed from the scene. Cocaine's notorious reputation died with them. By the 1960s, America was ready for another fling with this most seductive and dangerous drug.

THE JOYS OF VICTIMHOOD

Joseph Epstein

Joseph Epstein's most recent book is "Partial Payments."

 SHAME THERE ISN'T A MA-chine, the sociological equivalent of a seismograph, that registers fundamental shifts in social attitudes and concerns. In the absence of such a machine, we all have to operate with our own often rather primitive social radar, taking our signals where we find them. When one's dentist, for example, begins to say "pasta" instead of spaghetti or noodles, one knows that the interest in cookery has fully swept the middle classes. When one sees Mafia men jogging and worrying about their cholesterol, one knows that anxiety about health really is endemic. What began as a fad becomes a trend, which becomes a shift, which finally becomes a serious change in the way we live and think about ourselves.

My own fairly low-voltage radar has been pinging away for some while on another such shift, and last summer, while I was watching the Democratic National Convention on television, it began to bleep furiously in my mind. The noise could no longer be avoided when, at the moment that Ann Richards, the Texas State Treasurer, completed her strong keynote speech, the commentator on the television network I was watching remarked (as near as I can recall), "Ann Richards is a divorced mother of four who has undergone rehabilitation for an alcohol problem." Earlier in the campaign, Kitty Dukakis had announced that she had undergone treatment for an addiction she had to diet pills. During his speech at the convention, Jesse Jackson, in speaking of his own origins, declared that he was an illegitimate child, and then he wove a speech around the metaphor of the Democratic Party being a quilt both made by and supplying warmth to all those elements in American life — minority groups, homosexuals, American Indians (or Native Americans, as they're now known), welfare families, and many others — who, in Mr. Jackson's reading, were America's victims. Eight and even four years earlier, the Democratic Party had advertised itself as the party of concern. Last summer, though, the Democratic Party seemed to have cut out the middleman and gone from "caring persons" straight to victims. The logic of the convention seemed to call for Michael Dukakis, on the night of his nomination, to arrive in an iron lung and announce that he was a lesbian mother.

Victims have never been in short supply in the world, but the rush to identify oneself as a victim is rather a new feature of modern life. Why this should be so isn't very complicated: to position oneself as a victim is to position oneself for sympathy, special treatment, even victory. It's not only individuals who benefit. In international politics, one sees the deliberate strategy of positioning for victimhood played out in the Middle East. Although Israel is a country of fewer than four million Jewish people surrounded by Arab nations numbering some 200 million people, very few of whom mean the Israelis well, the Arabs have somehow been able to make themselves — or at least the Palestinians as their representatives — seem the great victims in the Middle East. Every time a woman or a small child is injured in the organized riots known as the *intifada* — one might ask why small children are allowed anywhere near such danger — the victimhood of the Palestinians is reinforced and their cause, as victims, made all the stronger.

Gandhi was the great teacher of the art of victimhood, of setting one's victimization on full public display. Part of the genius of the Rev. Dr. Martin Luther King Jr. was to recognize the value of Gandhi's lessons for the American civil rights movement, and most especially the lesson of nonviolent resistance, which not only highlights victimhood but gives it, in a good cause, a genuinely moral aura. Their moral and physical courage lent civil rights workers in the South an appeal that was irresistible to all but the most hard-hearted of segregationists. Americans, all of whose families began in this country as immigrants, have a built-in tradition of having known victimhood, at least historically, and hence a strong tendency toward sympathy for victims.

Yet it was the civil rights movement, by my reckoning, that changed the tenor, the quality, the very nature of victimhood in the United States. I happened to be living in the South in the early 1960's, working as a director of the antipoverty program in Little Rock, Ark., while the civil rights movement was under way in full earnest. What I saw was a number of bad laws called into question and ultimately removed by acts of courage and wise restraint on the part of the victims of those laws. One really had to have nailed shut the shutters to one's heart not to have been moved by the spectacle of men and women risking everything to gain only what in fairness was coming to them. It was immensely impressive, on every level. Why? Because the early civil rights movement's appeal was unmistakably not to the guilt but to the conscience of the nation.

An appeal to conscience is an appeal to one's ethical nature, to one's sense of fair play; it is fundamentally an appeal to act upon the best that is in one. An appeal to guilt is almost entirely negative; rather than awaken the best in one, it reminds one what a dog one is. Conscience seeks its outlet in action, or right conduct; guilt seeks assuagement, or to find a way to be let off the hook.

The civil rights movement, like a spiritual oil spill, left a vast residue of guilt in its wake. Suddenly, if you were white you couldn't possibly be in the right. Such civil rights figures as Stokely Carmichael and H. Rap Brown — and not they alone — were endlessly reminding everyone that their forebears were brought to this country against their will in chains by our forebears. (That my forebears themselves fled a 25-year conscription in the czar's army and your forebears fled the peril of another potato famine was judged beside the point.)

This abundant stirring up of guilt may have produced little in the way of direct social change, but it did without doubt strike its target — so profoundly that social scientists began to write about a "culture of guilt." The guilt that was loosed, moreover, was of a kind that had no outlet. What are you supposed to do, after all, if someone blames you for slavery, a hideous institution, to be sure, but one defunct for more than a century? Say you are sorry it ever happened? Should you clear your throat and announce that there are historical reasons for some of these things?

And yet if you couldn't fight 'em, you could, spiritually at any rate, attempt to join 'em. The most efficient way to do so was not to deny the claims of militant blacks but instead set out claims of your own to victimhood alongside theirs. One saw this happen straightaway with the student protest movement of the late 1960's and early 1970's. Many students of those days not only claimed victimhood but claimed it precisely on the black model. Students were powerless, they said, they were exploited. Powerless, exploited, thoroughly alienated. Those were the claims of one group after another — 60's students, feminists, homosexuals, Vietnam veterans, the handicapped, even artists. Yea, verily, they would all overcome, except over whom? Who was left to be overcome? It soon began to seem as if there wasn't anyone in American life who couldn't find grounds for claiming to be a victim.

Small wonder, too, for victimhood has not only its privileges but its pleasures. To begin with, it allows one to save one's greatest sympathy for that most sympathetic of characters — oneself. Of the various kinds and degrees of pity, easily the most vigilant is self-pity. To stake out one's own territory as a victim, or member of a victim group, also allows one to cut the moral ground out from under others who make an appeal on the basis of their victimhood — to go off singing, as it were, "You've got your troubles, I've got mine."

HE PLEASURES OF VICTIM-hood include imbuing one's life with a sense of drama. The drama of daily life is greatly heightened if one feels that society is organized against one. To feel oneself excluded and set apart is no longer obviously or even necessarily a bad thing. A victim cannot properly be thought bourgeois or middle-class in any significant way, which in some circles is itself meritorious. Excluded, set apart, alienated, the victim begins to sound like no one so much as the modern artist.

Artists have for some while now liked to think of themselves as victims. Whole books — usually overwrought, rather boring books — have been written about the alienation of the artist in modern society. The bill of complaint states that the artist is undervalued, underappreciated — like the soft drink Dr Pepper in an old television commercial, so misunderstood. Best-selling novelists are driven in limousines to give lectures whose main message is that the artist in America has no place

to rest his head. Painters with serious real estate holdings rant against a vile and philistine country. Artists meanwhile maintain permanent victim status, which, it is understood, no public recognition or financial success can ever hope to diminish.

Like other victim groups, artists can be exceedingly touchy. I once sat in a room where grants in the arts were being discussed, and I had the temerity to wonder aloud about the usefulness of a series of grants to support places where writers might meet to discuss their own and one another's work. Did writers truly need such institutions, I asked, being in the trade some years myself and never having felt the need of them. In response, a rather famous novelist replied with a lengthy exegesis on the loneliness of the writer who spends months, often years on the same project, filled with doubt, encouraged by no one, stirred only by the passion to create something that no one may eventually want. . . . Did she, I wondered (this time to myself), show slides with that talk? It reminded me of H. L. Mencken's remark that whenever he heard writers complain about the loneliness of their work he recommended that they spend a few days on the assembly line, where they would have plenty of opportunities for camaraderie with their mates.

Sometimes it must be difficult for the spokesmen for victims to keep up the anger—Jesse Jackson in an expensive suit, Gloria Steinem at a socialite party at the New York Public Library—but, whether simulated or real, the note of outrage always seems to be there when they need it. A victim, especially a professional victim, must at all times be angry, suspicious, above all progress-denying. He or she is ever on the lookout for that touch of racism, sexism, or homophobia that might show up in a stray opinion, an odd locution, an uninformed misnomer. With victims everywhere, life becomes a minefield in a cow pasture— no matter where you step, you are in trouble.

As if all this isn't nervous-making enough, there has come into being a large number of people, many of them in universities, who, if not victims themselves, wish to speak for victims or rouse other people to a sense of their injury as victims. They are the intellectual equivalent of ambulance chasers.

Perhaps the best place to see the traffic of victims and ambulance chasers in full flow is in the contemporary university. I don't think it's stretching things to say that nowadays if you cannot declare victim status, or find some way to align yourself with putative victims, in the contemporary university you don't figure to have much standing. *Victimisme,* to Frenchify the condition, is very much where the action is in universities. Women's centers, African-American studies programs, student gay and lesbian programs, and those ultimate intellectual ambulance chasers, academic Marxists, all hammer cheerfully away at revealing what a perfect hell life has been, and continues to be, for almost everyone in the world. And yet they all seem so happy in their work: the young man wearing a smile and a black T-shirt with the pink triangle that Hitler forced homosexuals under the Nazis to wear; the young female professor and her graduate student sharing an intimate scornful laugh at the hopeless sexist assumptions of an older male professor; the recently tenured Marxist theorist in the black leather jacket and Bertolt Brecht haircut. Happy victims all.

One might conceivably be a victim if one works in a coal mine or a steel mill or in the fields as a sharecropper, but no one who works as a teacher in a university, or for that matter is a student there, is a victim. To have a teaching job in a university is to work roughly seven months a year in a generally Edenic setting at intellectual tasks largely of one's own choosing. Relativity of relativities, a victim among university teachers is someone who isn't permitted to teach the Shakespeare course, or who feels he has stupid students, or whose office is drafty, or who doesn't get tenure (which is lifetime security in the job) and therefore must find another job within (usually) the next 16 months. These are not exactly the kinds of problem faced by, say, boat people fleeing Cambodia.

Yet an increasing number of university teachers nowadays teach one or another branch of victimology—what might not unfairly be called Victim Lit. The most prestige-laden the school, the more victimological studies are likely to be a strong component in its curriculum. "Unfortunately," writes a black Harvard graduate named Christopher H. Foreman, Jr., in a letter to The New Republic about ethnic sensitivity training at Harvard, "the psychological comfort of being simultaneously privileged and oppressed seems too enticing for many people to forgo." Harvard, Yale, Princeton, Stanford and other only scarcely less august institutions compete among themselves lest they be caught without a goodly supply of angry teachers of victimological subjects. Irony of ironies, nuttiness of nuttinesses, the scene thus presented is that of the fortunate teaching the privileged that the world is by and large divided between the oppressed and the oppressors, victims and executioners, and that the former are inevitably morally superior. As a tuition-paying parent, I used sometimes to think, writing out those heavy checks to universities, that the only true victims in this entire arrangement were those of us who helped to pay for it all.

Such a situation could never have come about without certain fundamental confusions having been firmly established, and these begin with language itself. Victims have traditionally been minority groups, but in fact women, who in the United States are a slight majority, have been deemed victims, whereas the Jews and the Chinese in America, though clearly minorities (and vastly less numerous than blacks or Hispanic people), are not usually counted as victims and thus rarely get included in affirmative action or other quota favoritism programs. A victim, then, is someone who insistently declares himself a victim.

VICTIMS HAVE TO FIND ENEMIES, THE AUTHOR SAYS. SOCIETY IS AGAINST THEM. BUT THE DRAMA OF LIFE IS HEIGHTENED IF YOU FEEL THAT SOCIETY IS AGAINST YOU.

People who count and call themselves victims never blame themselves for their condition. They therefore have to find enemies. Forces high and low block their progress: society is organized against them; history is not on their side; the malevolent, who are always in ample supply, conspire to keep them down. Asked by an interviewer in Time magazine about violence in schools that are all-black—that is, violence by blacks against blacks—the novelist Toni Morrison replies, "None of those things can take place, you know, without the complicity of the people who run the schools and the city."

For victimhood to be taken seriously, there has to be a core of substance to the victim's complaints. Blacks were discriminated against, de facto and de jure, in this country for a very long while. Women were paid lower wages for doing the same work as men and they were indubitably excluded from jobs they were perfectly capable of performing. Mexican-Americans often worked under deplorable conditions. A case for victimhood cannot simply be invented, though some people try. I recall some time ago watching a television program that stressed the problems of the unwed teen-age father. Greatly gripping though they doubtless were, I remember muttering to myself: the unwed father, another victim group—who'd've thunk it?

Even when there is a core of substance to the victims' complaints, they tend to push it. A subtle shift takes place, and suddenly the victim is no longer making appeals but demands. The terms *lady* and *homosexual* are out; it's only *woman* and *gay* that are acceptable. Public pronouncements from victims take on a slightly menacing quality, in which, somehow, the line between victim and bully seems to blur. At some point, one gets the sense that the victims actively enjoy their victimhood—enjoy the moral vantage point it gives them to tell off the rest of the country, to overstate their case, to absolve themselves from all responsibility for their condition, to ask the impossible and then demonstrate outrage when it isn't delivered.

Apparently, the victims of our day rather like this state of affairs. I say "apparently" because it has been many years since any of the victim groups have shown anything approaching a genuine interest in organization. Instead, they seem to function chiefly as loose repositories for the expression of resentment. A strong sign of this is the striking absence of leadership in any of the major victim movements of the time: black, women, gay. The Rainbow Coalition—it might more accurately be called the Victim Coalition—isn't cutting it. Like the wild rookie pitcher in the movie "Bull Durham," the various victim groups are "all over the place"; blaming racism for black teen-age crime, male psychology for capitalism, the Government for AIDS. There is something fundamentally unserious about all of this. Whereas once the idea was to shake off victimhood through courage and organization, nowadays the idea seems to be to enjoy it for its emotional effects.

Not many other people seem to be enjoying it, though. The reserves of guilt that victims once felt they could draw on now appear all but depleted. White ethnics and others have begun to feel themselves the victims of affirmative action and other favoritism programs, so that we have the phenomenon of victims created by victims. Those whom the victims have been attacking all these years are themselves beginning to feel like victims. It's a real growth industry. When I recently read, in The Times Literary Supplement of London, at the close of a review of two books on adultery, that "Adultery is built upon, even aimed at, female unhappiness," I wondered if the T.L.S. would one day soon carry an angry answering letter from a man representing a society of cuckolds.

Just the other day I heard a fresh euphemism for what used to be known as "the handicapped." Take a moment to breathe in deeply before I set it out on the page, for I think it might take your breath away. The handicapped, in this new euphemism, are "the physically challenged." Somebody, obviously, has been working overtime.

Yet I cannot help think of the contempt in which that euphemism is likely to be held by the people I know who are seriously handicapped. These people do not in the least think themselves physically challenged; instead, they know that they have to undergo endless small and infuriating difficulties that the rest of us have been spared. They have been kicked, very hard, in the stomach by fate. Without denying or attempting to disguise the effects of this devastating kick, they neither whine about it nor protest it.

As it happens, these people are all intensely political (they are liberals and conservatives), but the last thing I can imagine any of them doing is using his handicap for political advantage or for that matter in any public way either to define or advance himself. Because they neither act as nor think of themselves as victims, in the end they seem, far from victimized, immensely dignified and quietly heroic. Although it was never their intention to do so, they make the contemporary joys of victimhood—the assumption of moral superiority, the spread of guilt and bad feeling, the shifting of responsibility for one's own destiny onto others or the "system" or society at large—seem rather dreary, if not pathetic. They also remind the rest of us that the most efficient way to become truly a victim is to think and act like a victim.

MADISON AVENUE MEDICINE

Elisabeth Rosenthal

Elisabeth Rosenthal is a resident in internal medicine.

Drug-company reps drown me with gifts and don't even ask me to remember their name. They don't need to.

I am about to bite the hand that feeds me. Really. Today it fed me and my fellow residents a very pleasant barbecue dinner of chicken and hamburgers, on a roof overlooking a river. The party marked the end of our second year of residency, two years of hard work and exhaustion. Most of the people knew one another extraordinarily well. There was only one stranger at the party, a pretty young woman dressed in blue high heels and a miniskirt.

Ostensibly, she fitted in perfectly, alternately flirting with the men and gossiping with the women. She danced to the reggae that issued from a tape deck, and she pitched in to turn the burgers. Yet I regarded her with suspicion. This young woman was in fact a "detail man" for Wyeth, the pharmaceutical company that was bankrolling our burgers. While we were celebrating, her purpose at our party was to promote an antianxiety drug called Ativan.

The party had been organized by several of my colleagues. As is fairly common practice for hospital department functions, they had approached the drug company for "sponsorship" of the event. The clues that Wyeth had anything to do with our party were few: the popcorn tins were all labeled Orudis, another Wyeth medication, and at one point the young woman balanced herself on a lawn chair and delivered a 30-second speech about Ativan's superiority to its competitors. But the plugs for the drug were easy enough to ignore, or at least not too difficult to rationalize: Ativan, after all, is a good

medication. So why did this woman's presence make me squirm?

The seduction of doctors by drug companies begins early. Immediately upon arriving at medical school, I remember, I received a box of reference books courtesy of Upjohn. A year later, just before the start of clinical rotations, a $50 stethoscope appeared from a company whose name I have long since forgotten—every second-year medical student in the country receives one. As a fourth-year student I somewhat guiltily picked up a drug-company pen at a company-sponsored lunch; it would be almost a year before I could return the favor by writing a prescription.

The arrival of the stethoscopes prompted the first and last official ethical discussion during my medical training regarding the wisdom of accepting drug-company gifts. The entire second-year class was invited to a debate that echoed my internal musings. The devil on my left shoulder urged me to take up the tempting offer; although I had already purchased my own stethoscope, it would be nice to have this perfectly adequate instrument as a backup. The angel on my right shoulder warned me that accepting the stethoscope would set a bad precedent. I'm afraid, after endless discussions, the devil won out: I, and everyone else I knew, kept the tainted instrument. The class ahead of mine at least had had the ingenuity to send their free stethoscopes to a clinic in Central America.

After I received my medical degree, and with it the license to write prescriptions, the gifts became more frequent and the sales pitches more shameless. Each morning thousands of drug-

company detail men arrive at hospitals around the country to promote their wares. Where I now work there is a detail man I'll call Jerry; he is known as the Zantac man. He's the high priest of a popular antiulcer drug manufactured by Glaxo Pharmaceuticals. As far as I know, this gentleman's one and only job is to patrol the halls where I work and make sure that Zantac is never far from anyone's mind. He is good at it.

I am sitting in the library with another doctor, discussing the management of a particular patient, and in comes the Zantac man with his briefcase overflowing with samples. Zantac is actually a wonderful drug, but nonetheless he reminds me of a snake-oil salesman.

"Do you have just a few minutes," he implores, "to discuss once-a-day Zantac dosing? Studies have shown that . . ." My mind starts to wander. He drones on about new studies demonstrating still more ways in which Zantac is infinitely superior to its primary competitor, a drug called Tagamet from Smith Kline & French. Jerry knows a lot about Zantac, and there is probably some useful information in his speeches, but I have long since ceased to hear it. He is like a piano player in a seedy bar where the din of conversation is drowning out the music. "Thanks for your time," he says when he's finished. He begins to pack up, leaving behind Zantac datebooks and Zantac pens and offering free samples of Zantac to each of us.

Every doctor has to make a separate peace with these drug reps. Personally, I find they make me nervous with their affable manners and their attempts to

To those outside medicine a sandwich may not seem like much of an incentive.

become my pal, and I prefer to keep my distance—but that is a gut reaction rather than a reasoned decision or a moral stance. I am cordial and will listen to them if time permits, but I would never dream of returning their friendly overtures or requesting free Zantac for my Uncle Jack in Cleveland.

Not everyone I know is so aloof. Some of my colleagues, fine doctors whom I generally respect, meet drug reps for lunch. They call the reps up every so often to chat—just to keep the conduits open between the drug-company coffers and the department social fund. When I tease my colleagues about their antics, they shrug their shoulders as if to say it's just good business. They remind me, rightly, that I am not above eating Wyeth hamburgers on the right occasion.

Why do the Jerrys of this world even exist? After all, the medical journals I read are replete with pharmaceutical advertising. The answer is simple: Within most classes of drug there are many brands marketed, all of which are essentially the same from the clinician's standpoint. They may vary a bit in chemical structure, and a little in cost, side effects, and dosing frequency, but they will all do the job.

In the antiulcer department Zantac and Tagamet are the current leaders. To treat minor muscle and joint pain there are dozens of nonsteroidal anti-inflammatory medications: Feldene, Motrin, Naprosyn, Anaprox, Clinoril, Orudis. They will all treat a strained tendon. It is the detail man's job to convince me somehow that Feldene or Motrin or Clinoril is far superior to the competition. Barring that, it is his task to turn my fancy toward the drug, the same way Kellogg's advertising seeks to ensure loyalty to its brand of cornflakes. And barring *that*, it is his job to keep my world so full of, say, Naprosyn—Naprosyn pens, Naprosyn pads, Naprosyn meals—that the letters *N-A-P-R-O-S-Y-N* flow reflexively from my pen.

To be fair, the detail men can at times be valuable sources of information. They can tell me about the resistance patterns of microbes to their antibiotics. They can find out if my patient's rash might be due to a rare side effect of their drug. But the hype always seems to outweigh the content.

Any number of tactics are used by drug-company reps to ingratiate themselves with the people who prescribe their wares. Judging from the number of meals we're offered, they must feel that the way to a doctor's heart is through his stomach. During the first years of training these are generally free lunches on the hospital premises—we'll bring you sandwiches if you'll listen to a five-minute spiel about Naprosyn. There are two or three of these lunches a week.

To those outside medicine a sandwich may not seem like much of an incentive, but the drug companies know their audience. Internship is memorable for its long hours of sometimes degrading work, few thanks, and even fewer concrete rewards. So when a detail man comes in, treats you with respect, values your opinion (okay, so it's only about antacids), and offers you lunch, you're grateful.

As training progresses, meals become more sumptuous, and the settings more exotic. A dinner for 20 at an elegant Spanish restaurant sets the scene for a presentation on balloon angioplasty (a procedure to clear blocked blood vessels) and a plug for Cardizem, a cardiac drug made by Marion Laboratories, which picks up the tab for the occasion. In time, pharmaceutical firms actually offer to pay you to eat with them. One company recently invited several of my co-workers out to a very expensive ($100 a head) Italian restaurant and paid them each a $150 consultancy fee to discuss what they thought about the firm's new antibiotic. With very little resourcefulness, young doctors can line up two or three dinners a week and make a handsome second income from offering their opinions over pasta primavera.

Tickets to sports events are also frequent enticements. So I imagine if you play the game really well, you could enjoy dinner at Le Cirque sponsored by one drug company, followed by a Knicks game at Madison Square Garden courtesy of its competitor. To the average resident, who earns somewhere around $25,000 a year and is shouldering twice that much in medical

school loans, such luxuries are tempting, and you tend to dismiss the favors they imply. Who bought these seats anyway? Was it Feldene? Or Motrin?

Most doctors I know feel they are above being influenced by drug-company propaganda and laugh at the notion that the care of their patients might in any way be affected. If anyone is swayed, it's always the other guy.

But I'm willing to bet that Syntex and Glaxo wouldn't be paying a huge sales force millions of dollars a year unless their strategies were working. And I suppose that their success is staring us in the face. Thanks to Glaxo's efforts, the hospital where I work is clearly Zantac turf: Zantac is the only antiulcer medication in the pharmacy, and I can recite the dosing of Zantac—by mouth or intravenously—in my sleep. Should I for some reason switch to prescribing Tagamet, I would have to fetch the hefty *Physicians Desk Reference* from the shelf to figure out the proper dose.

Some of the more intellectually pure hospitals in the country have sought to stunt the influence of drug companies by banning detail men from the buildings. But these are persistent suitors, and in my experience this sort of decree generally moves the seduction to restaurants several blocks from the hospital's front door. The struggle for markets is a form of guerrilla warfare, and all tactics are fair.

Drug-company knickknacks are scattered liberally about the hospital and hawked shamelessly at medical conventions. Some of the medical paraphernalia is quite useful: calipers for reading cardiograms, from Squibb (makers of Capoten, a heart medication); reflex hammers courtesy of Syntex; penlights and tourniquets from two antibiotics manufacturers. At conventions, where doctors in a festive mood are gathered in high concentrations, the connection between the gift and the advertisement is often more elusive: umbrellas for an antibiotic called Imipenum, wall clocks from a maker of transdermal nitroglycerin, hard hats advertising Cardizem.

Some people, I'm sure, will react to my tales of detail men with a big "So what?" Brokers take out their

The luxuries are tempting, and you tend to dismiss the favors they imply.

bankers for dinner; lawyers treat prospective clients to basketball games. So what? Maybe I am overreacting to the appearance of Madison Avenue sales techniques in what I've always considered a helping profession. But the hard sell of the drug companies makes me nervous. Does using that tainted stethoscope from medical school make me somehow more closely allied to the pharmaceutical industry? Does eating Wyeth barbecued chicken make me more likely to prescribe Ativan?

I must admit, I like my nifty pen from Nitro-Dur, the nitroglycerin-patch medication. And I am quite fond of my Amikin antibiotic mug with its inscrutable inscription, TOO MANY VARIABLES, TOO LITTLE TIME. Perhaps these gifts might influence someone—not me, of course, but maybe the other guy.

The Fire of 'Ice'

A devastating drug from Asia has triggered a crisis in Hawaii and now threatens the mainland

M I C H A E L A. L E R N E R

Twenty years old and fresh out of college, Tad Yamaguchi saw a good future for himself at an air-freight company in Honolulu. So when one of his superiors offered him a puff from the small glass pipe—a little something to help him get through the grueling 20-hour .shift—Yamaguchi felt he couldn't refuse. He says he was instantly hooked. "I felt alert, in control. It didn't seem to have a downside," recalls Yamaguchi. No wonder so many people in his office were using it. Four months later Yamaguchi, who had never done drugs before, was smoking every day. "I'd smoke as much as I could. I started buying large quantities to sell so I could support my habit," he says. Soon Yamaguchi, who kicked the habit a year ago, had lost 35 pounds and was smoking four days at a time, then "crashing" in a comatose sleep that lasted up to 36 hours. Next, paranoia and hallucinations set in.

The Japanese call it *shabu*, to Koreans it's *hiroppon*. To American addicts just discovering its intense highs and hellish lows, the drug is simply "ice," after the clear crystal form it takes in the manufacturing process. As addictive as crack cocaine but far more pernicious, ice—a type of methamphetamine, or speed—is a drug that seems culled from the pages of science fiction. In contrast to the fleeting 20-minute high of crack, an ice buzz lasts anywhere from eight to 24 hours. Unlike cocaine, which comes from a plant indigenous to the Andes, ice can be cooked up in a laboratory using easily obtained chemicals—a drug for the scientific age.

Methamphetamine's side effects are devastating. Prolonged use can cause fatal lung and kidney disorders as well as long-lasting psychological damage. "We're seeing people with dysfunctions two and a half years after they've stopped using. That's scary," says Earlene Piko, director of substance abuse at the Wai'anae Community Mental Health Center in Hawaii,

Highs and Lows: Counting Costs in the Drug Market

Ice
Cost: $50 per "paper" (less than 1 gram)
Duration: 8 to 24 hours
Effects: Immediate, intense euphoria; increased alertness
Side effects: Aggressive behavior, hallucinations, paranoia, fatal kidney failure

Crank
Cost: $50 to $120 a gram
Duration: 2 to 4 hours
Effects: Wakefulness, excitability, mood elevation
Side effects: Irritability, insomnia, palpitations, severe anxiety

Crack
Cost:: $3 to $20 a vial (less than 1 gram)
Duration: 20 to 30 minutes
Effects: Immediate, intense exhilaration, sense of well-being
Side effects: Anxiety, depression, stroke, heart attack, seizure

Heroin
Cost: $10 for a "dime bag"; $70 to $200 a "bundle" (less than 1 gram)
Duration: 4 hours per dose
Effects: Relaxation
Side effects: Drowsiness, nausea, heart and skin infections

the first American state to be afflicted by ice. The drug also tends to make users violent. The Honolulu Police Department estimates that ice was a factor in 70 percent of spouse-abuse cases the force handled last month.

Ice is not a new drug, but a more powerful form of a substance that has been popular in Western states for several years. Purer and more crystalline than the "meth" or "crank" manufactured in cities like San Diego, ice comes from Asia. So far, the spread to the United States has been largely confined to the Hawaiian Islands. But the quickness with which it has overtaken that state is startling. In just over four years, ice has surpassed marijuana and cocaine as Hawaii's No. 1 drug problem.

Korean connection: Now law-enforcement officials fear Hawaii may be a beachhead for the drug's spread to the rest of the United States. Congresswoman Patricia Saiki of Honolulu has started lobbying drug czar William Bennett to declare her city a "high-intensity drug-trafficking area" so it would qualify for more federal anti-drug money. "[Bennett needs to act now] to quell this plague before it gets to the mainland," she says. It may already be too late. In recent months, federal drug and customs agents have made several ice busts in the continental United States.

Hawaii's ice trail goes back to South Korea, which—along with Taiwan—leads the world in the manufacture and export of the drug. The Koreans learned about methamphetamine from the Japanese, who invented the stimulant in 1893. During World War II, Japan's military leaders supplied it in liquid form to weary soldiers and munitions-plant workers, leading to the addiction of hundreds of thousands of Japanese to the then legal drug. Japan banned shabu in the '50s, but many labs that produced it simply relocated to South Korea and smuggled the drug back across the Sea of Japan. In recent years use has leveled off—though Japan remains the drug's largest market. At the same time, Korea's once negligible domestic consumption has boomed, spreading from prostitutes and entertainers to students, housewives and businessmen; 130,000 Koreans are addicted to ice, medical experts believe. A common factor among some users: jobs with high stress and long hours. "It's a very suitable drug for workaholics," says journalist Cho Gab Je, author of "Korean Connection," a book about the hiroppon trade.

The link between Korea and Hawaii was forged in the early 1980s through Paciano (Sonny) Guerrero, a Hawaiian of Filipino origins who last month was sentenced in Hawaii's federal court to 25 years in prison without parole for the sale and distribution of ice. Known as the King of Batu (the word for rock in the Filipino language of Ilocano), Guerrero established the first ice-distribution network on Hawaii, using mostly local Filipino gangs to distribute it. Authorities estimate that Guerrero sold $7.3 million worth of the drug in 1987 and 1988 alone. "Sonny was selling mainly to Filipinos and Koreans, but it quickly spread. And it's spreading still—right into middle-class high schools," says a Drug Enforcement Administration agent in Honolulu.

Gang members: Korean drug organizations are trying to expand the ice market to mainland America. NEWSWEEK has learned that federal authorities are currently pursuing a Korean drug ring that is distributing ice in the United States. Last August U.S. Customs agents in Portland, Ore., seized about five ounces of ice sent by mail from Korea. Last month Honolulu police arrested five suspected members of a violent New York-based Korean gang called K.P. (Korea Power) that allegedly arrived in Honolulu with 17 other gang members to set up an ice pipeline to the East Coast. Police seized $72,000 in cash along with guns and ammunition.

At first puff, ice seems irresistible. Cheap and long lasting, the drug provides users with a sense of well-being. A penny-size plastic bag called a paper costs $50 and, when smoked, can keep a novice high for up to a week. Addicts call the sensation from smoking ice "amping" for the amplified euphoria it gives them. Odorless and hard to detect, ice is used as much for recreation as for staying alert on the job. "On the front end, it doesn't seem so bad. You stay awake, focused on what you're doing. And you feel good about yourself," says Dr. Joseph Giannasio, director of Castle Medical Center Alcoholism and Addictions program in Oahu. "Where it gets scary is at the tail end."

If Hawaii is any indication, a surge in ice use in America could be as destructive as the current crack crisis. Last month Honolulu Police Chief Douglas Gibb told Congress that the number of drug-exposed newborns reported to welfare officials has jumped from two a week to six a week in the past year. Ice largely accounts for the dramatic increase, say health experts, and the fallout is straining Hawaii's social services. "It's totally overwhelming. We're in a crisis," says Dr. Jane Stump, a psychiatry professor at the University of Hawaii and a member of the Child Protective Services medical team. "This ice, it's like a great tidal wave."

No bonding: The little that is known about ice's effects on newborns is alarming. "If you thought cocaine dependency was bad, that's in the minor leagues compared to this drug," says Earlene Piko. As with cocaine babies, ice babies tend to be asocial and incapable of bonding. Some have tremors and cry for 24 hours without stopping. They have to be swaddled to be held. "We know children who didn't bond are likely to be sociopaths," says Daniel Bent, U.S. attorney in Hawaii. "We're now producing 200,000 cocaine babies a year, and nurses tell us ice babies are worse in that area."

Rehabilitation clinics in Hawaii report there are now as many ice addicts as cocaine addicts seeking treatment. Doctors believe it's just the beginning. "You have to build up a large base of users before you start seeing people come in for help," says Giannasio. Most clinics are treating ice addiction as they would cocaine addiction. But ice is proving more difficult to kick. "Some people get hospitalized, start on psychotropic drugs to stop the hallucinations and after a month they're OK. But we have others who after two years haven't improved," says Piko. Honolulu police are preparing a number of public-service announcements to warn the population about the hazards of the drug. "We were ready for crack. We had commercials on TV, we learned how to bust the dealers and prosecute them," says Major David Benson of the Honolulu police. "But in its place, whammo, we got nailed with crystal meth." Federal authorities hope the continental United States won't face the same fate.

with DAVID BANK *and* PETER LEYDEN *in Seoul and* BRADLEY MARTIN *in Tokyo*

CRANK

Capital, U.S.A.

Sacramento's Homemade Methamphetamine Industry

Tom Johnson

A CRANK Lexicon

The methamphetamine subculture has its own lingo. Here are some common expressions and words used.

Crank. Methamphetamine.

Crankster, Crankster Gangster. Someone who uses or manufactures methamphetamine.

Cooker. A person who actually mixes the chemicals to make methamphetamine. Because part of the process involves heating, the cooking metaphor developed.

Eight Ball. An eighth-ounce package of crank. Most transactions are in grams.

Ephedrine. An ingredient in many antihistamine and asthma medications, it is now used as a key ingredient in the manufacture of crank. In California its purchase requires special reporting by chemical warehouses, but it can be bought without restrictions in nearby states.

Glass. High-quality methamphetamine.

Go-Fast. Another name for crank, as "Have you got any go-fast?"

Mule. A person who moves or carries drugs. Evolved from the time when Mexican nationals would carry heroin across the border from Mexico.

Point. A needle.

Red. Red phosphorous used in the manufacture of methamphetamine.

Rig. Syringe, needle and other paraphernalia used in injecting crank.

Speed. Another name for crank.

Spun. To overdose on one shot of meth and induce a kind of psychotic confusion. "Man, she's spun."

Thing. Another name for a needle apparatus. "I got some crank. You got a thing?"

Tweaked. The anxious, paranoid state a user gets into at the end of a multi-day session of shooting crank.

A drug more popular than rock cocaine lurks—no, swaggers—through Sacramento. You might call it the all-American drug. No foreigners export it to the United States. It's mostly manufactured and used by ex-felons and blue-collar whites. It's methamphetamine, known popularly as crank. And Sacramento is its national capital.

"Sacramento is to crank like Bogota is to cocaine," says Detective Gary Horat, an undercover narcotics agent and a member of the Sacramento Clandestine Lab Task Force.

"Crank is by far the drug of choice for Northern Californians," echoes Gilbert Bruce, special agent in charge of the Drug Enforcement Administration here.

Horat and his team of officers last week were called to an abandoned apartment building a block from McClellan Air Force Base. The inside of one of the units was awash in trash—gallon cans of acetone, rubber tubes, flasks, cat litter (to cut the smell) and a vacuum pump littered the floor. A strange glass-and-hose apparatus was stuck in the toilet, to vent the toxic wastes.

The abandoned crank lab was the 129th lab case the officers have investigated in northeast California this year. Just four years ago, when it first formed, the lab task force busted only 35 labs in a whole year, mostly in Sacramento, Butte and San Joaquin counties. "The extent of this thing still boggles me," says DEA agent Bruce. Horat estimates that at any given moment some 60 clandestine methamphetamine labs are operating in Sacramento.

Someone with no chemistry skills, working at a homemade setup in a kitchen and using legally available equipment and chemicals can turn out pound after pound of methamphetamine. "Most of these guys look like they couldn't make a peanut butter sandwich," says Deputy District Attorney Dale Kitchings, who has prosecuted meth cookers in both local and federal court. "It's difficult to convince juries" of the extent of their manufacturing. But big money at low overhead awaits the savvy cooker. The market price of crank now is $10,000 a pound, about the same or a little more than cocaine.

Horat has busted labs in rental trucks, in storage units, in motel rooms, in underground culverts. His office gets 200 tips a week from people who suspect the house next door—full of parked cars and tough-looking guys, with people coming and going at all hours of the night—is selling crank. The manpower required to bust one suspected dope house is so awesome and stretches Horat's eight-person unit so far that he seldom goes after small-time peddlers.

It's the source—the manufacturers—local drug agents want to squelch. And both police and drug chemists are getting more sophisticated. As police learn more about the drug chemistry and expand their field of informants, the crank cookers are constructing increasingly convoluted paper trails to distance themselves from the purchase of supplies and distribution of product. Narcotics agents are virtually ignoring individual users.

Methamphetamine is an analog of amphetamine developed by chemists after amphetmamine became increasingly difficult to obtain. Like cocaine, it stimulates the central nervous system. The drug itself is not the source of stimulation, but by chemically interacting with the central nervous system it releases stored energy from body reserves.

People who regularly use crank often inject it with a needle. It can be snorted, but the powder is abrasive to the nostrils and, with repeated use, injures the inside of the nose.

Like cocaine, the first injection sends a rush to the brain that some users equate with an intense orgasm. Crank makes you stay awake, elevates your mood and suppresses your appetite. But it can also make you irritable and nervous. Toward the end of a multi-day run, cranksters become paranoid, aggressive and confused, called tweaking in street parlance. Horat tells the example of a Sacramento paper boy who tried to collect from a "tweaking" crankster. When he rang the doorbell, he was answered with 20

rounds from an Uzi through the door.

Crank has been hailed by users as an enhancement to sex. In a study by the National Institute on Drug Abuse of 56 admitted addicts a third of the females and males said it increased sexual pleasure, a third of females and 14 percent of males said it had no effect either way on sex and a third of females and 54 percent of males had no opinion on the relationship between crank and sex.

Crank can take a physical toll: cardiac arrhythmia, headaches, hypertension, and constriction of blood vessels in the kidneys. True cranksters, even after leaving the drug, can suffer psychosis and severe anxiety for several months.

Crank abuse also leads to societal problems. Cranksters tend to ignore other parts of their lives, like children, rent and bill-paying. Staying awake for a week then crashing in a stupor for several days is not conducive to holding a job or operating even minimally in society.

Aquarian House, the one free residential treatment program in Sacramento County, now numbers crank abusers as half its 75 clients. (The other half is equally divided between heroin and crack cocaine users.) Just three years ago, says Brian Weiss, the senior counselor at Aquarian House, three-fourths of the residents were heroin addicts. Weiss, who has talked to hundreds of cranksters, says, "The nature of the drug is it makes you more violent and leads to erratic behavior. It's a real powerful drug, and without it users feel inadequate."

Almost anyone with the desire can make crank. The recipe is routinely passed around prison; and narcotics officers often find it scrawled on scraps of paper on people they arrest.

To call the makers of meth "chemists," police say, is a misnomer. Within the trade they are known as "cooks." Some cooks get a reputation and are hired solely to make crank; but more frequently, anyone with access to a recipe gives it a go.

A decade ago the crank trade was controlled by the Hell's Angels. Horat says the Angels still play a significant part in its manufacture, but far more independent manufacturers and labs have sprung up. Also, the Hell's Angels have become less visi-

ble publicly and more sophisticated in their illegal dealings.

Nowadays, says Horat, a Hell's Angel is likely to drive a shiny car, sport a short haircut and live in a snazzy house. He'll ride his Harley on weekends. He will own a semi-legitimate business through which to launder his money and pan out all the hands-on dirty work of crank manufacturing to people without prison records or who cannot be traced to him.

But no matter if you're an amateur or veteran crank manufacturer, your first stop is at one of two chemical-supply companies in the area: Grau-Hall Scientific Company on Elvas Avenue or Sierra Chemical in West Sacramento.

When drug agents are gathering evidence against a suspected manufacturer, they sit outside these establishments and watch the comings and goings of the suspects. The most popular method of manufacturing crank is the reduction of the chemical ephedrine (see sidebar). Except for ephedrine, a restricted substance, virtually all the equipment and chemicals needed can be legally purchased at Grau-Hall: red phosphorus, hydrogen-chloride gas, methyl alcohol, hydriodic acid, sodium thisosulfate, condensers, triple-neck flasks, thermometers, scales, a substance called Vita-Blend (to cut the finished product), and other paraphernalia.

Cranksters generally pay for these materials in cash and don't ask for a receipt. Because the process of making crank gives off distinctive odors—like rotting fish, fingernail-polish remover or ether—the labs are usually set up in rural or secluded spots. Buyers often rent vehicles to make their pick-ups at Grau-Hall, thereby frustrating the tracing process by drug agents.

By documenting the purchases at Grau-Hall and proving that all the materials were exactly needed to cook crank, drug agents have obtained search warrants for big labs. Also based on that information, prosecuting attorneys have been able to make convictions for conspiracy to manufacture stick.

Nowadays, the one problematic area for meth manufacturers (besides the cops) is ephedrine. This synthesized chemical derived from a desert plant called ephedra is restricted. That means if you want to buy it in

1. DRUGS IN PERSPECTIVE: Current Illegal Drugs

California, you must tell wnat you'll use it for, show identification and wait a certain period. If you have prior convictions, you'll probably be rejected.

But ephedrine is still legal in Oregon, Utah and many other states. Thus, cranksters simply travel out of state or send a "mule" off for the ephedrine. Horat recalls how a car from Oregon was stopped recently in Sacramento carrying 10 pounds of ephedrine and two shady-looking people. Police knew what their intention was; but the time, manpower and money required to build a case weren't worth it, and the transporters were released.

Crank exacts another toll, an environmental one. Whenever a lab is seized, narcotics agents call in a company called American Environmental to remove the toxic chemicals and clean up the site. Cleanup can be as minimal as stripping the wallboard and replacing it or as extensive as replacing all the tainted soil in the yard. The cost, borne by taxpayers, is a minimum $2,000 for each lab and often runs 10 times that much.

American Environmental General Manager Doug Lockwood says meth labs are increasing sources of groundwater pollution as cookers release waste products directly into septic systems or nearby water supplies.

Horat has been a narcotics agent long enough to have developed a certain cynicism about humankind's problems. "I used to laugh at Nancy Reagan's 'just say no' business," he says. "But now we have to do something, and we have to teach the young to say no."

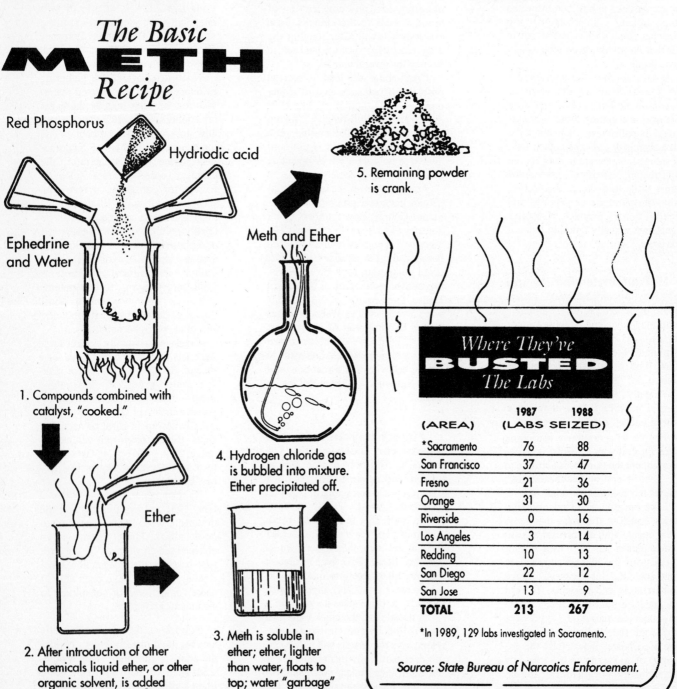

The Basic METH Recipe

Red Phosphorus

Hydriodic acid

Ephedrine and Water

5. Remaining powder is crank.

Meth and Ether

1. Compounds combined with catalyst, "cooked."

Ether

4. Hydrogen chloride gas is bubbled into mixture. Ether precipitated off.

2. After introduction of other chemicals liquid ether, or other organic solvent, is added to mixture, called "meth oil."

3. Meth is soluble in ether; ether, lighter than water, floats to top; water "garbage" compounds discarded.

Where They've BUSTED The Labs

(AREA)	1987 (LABS SEIZED)	1988 (LABS SEIZED)
*Sacramento	76	88
San Francisco	37	47
Fresno	21	36
Orange	31	30
Riverside	0	16
Los Angeles	3	14
Redding	10	13
San Diego	22	12
San Jose	13	9
TOTAL	213	267

*In 1989, 129 labs investigated in Sacramento.

Source: State Bureau of Narcotics Enforcement.

CRANK
60 Years Old And Still Popular

The use and abuse of manufactured crank extends back at least 60 years. But ephedra, the plant from which one of its prime modern-day ingredients, ephedrine, is synthesized, has been used by humans for thousands of years.

Some 40 species of ephedra—a woody, flowering shrub—grow worldwide. In the United States, ephedra is found mostly in semi-arid parts of the West and in the Rocky Mountains.

The Coahuilla Indians called ephedra *tu-tut;* Mexican and Spanish settlers referred to it as *tepopote* or *popotillo.* Anglo mountainmen and cowboys boiled and drank the crushed branches of ephedra, often preferring it over coffee. They called ephedra Mexican tea, teamsters' tea, Mormon tea, desert tea or Brigham Young's weed.

In addition to drinking it as a stimulant, these old-timers used ephedra potions to cure venereal disease, "purify" the blood and combat pneumonia.

Amphetamine was discovered in 1927, and two years later its derivative, methamphetamine, was synthesized. From the 1930s to the 1950s,

amphetamine was used as a substitute for ephedrine in nose inhalers. It was prescribed by doctors to treat asthma, sleeping disorders, chronic depression, overeating and low blood pressure.

Amphetamine and methamphetamine work on a body chemical called norepinephrine. Norepinephrine is a chemical messenger used to communicate electrical impulses from nerve to nerve.

When an amphetamine compound enters the body, there are more releases of this chemical, which triggers more nerve firings. When those firings take place in the brain and spinal cord, methamphetamine users feel the well-known effects—alertness, arousal and euphoria.

During World War II, amphetamine was distributed to some soldiers to keep them alert during combat. Methamphetamine was also doled out to Japanese civilians to help them meet production quotas. Large stockpiles of crank were discovered and used by American GIs in postwar Japan.

Nose inhalers containing amphetamine were so abused during the 1940s and 1950s that the chemical was banned. Manufacturers soon sub-

stituted methamphetamine, and by the mid-1960s both amphetamine and methamphetamine were added to the federal drug schedule, severely curtailing their legal distribution.

Chemists continued to manufacture the drug in Mexico, however, using legal ingredients from Europe and smuggling the finished product into the United States. Crank use declined a bit in the early 1970s when the Controlled Substances Act was passed, increasing penalties for manufacture and possession of certain crank ingredients.

Underground chemists continue to search for analogs of methamphetamine, that is, rearrangements of the molecules that provide the same effect. These analogs, sometimes called "designer drugs," would ostensibly be legal until a law was passed prohibiting their manufacture. For example, the chemists have tried stringing more carbon atoms onto the methamphetamine molecule, producing methylmethamphetamine. But that compound has proven 10 times weaker than regular meth.

Since many designer drugs are dependent on the same precursor chemicals, such as ephedrine or methylephedrine, law enforcement people are concentrating their efforts on squelching and restricting their possession.

CRANKSTERS

THE DANCER

Candy is ready to leave crank behind and regain her family's trust.

Candy was working as a topless dancer in Florida making $200-$300 a day when she sold the undercover cop the cocaine. A year later, she gave birth to her son while serving a year and a day in the county jail.

The little guy was born with an array of respiratory problems— unrelated to Candy's drug use—and spent his first month of life in an intensive-care unit.

Candy no longer sees her son. She gave him up for adoption last year. "I knew I was going nowhere," says the 27-year-old woman.

Today Candy lives at the Aquarian House residential treatment center

on a side street off Del Paso Boulevard. Aquarian House provides year-long drug counseling and residency programs to people with no money. It treats 75 people each year and has a six-month waiting list.

This is Candy's second stay at Aquarian House, and she's made it 90 days without going back on the street. This time, she says, she has the strength to clean herself up.

Born in Fresno, the daughter of a jockey, Candy spent her youth moving from race track to race track all over the United States with her parents and four of her nine siblings. By 1974, the whole crew settled in a trailer behind Cal Expo. Then tragedy struck. Her

father was blinded when a nervous horse charged through a stall and slammed a gate against his temple.

By age 15, she was on her own, living in Florida, out of school, smoking pot and dropping Quaaludes.

Drugs entered her life and she embraced them. Even jail and a sick child didn't quell her desire. After she was released, she bundled up her son and headed back to Sacramento. The first things she obtained were an apartment and some crank.

"I rented an apartment and spent five days wired to the gills." She managed to find a job in a topless and bottomless bar. "I was working six days, giving my son medicine every three hours and shooting crank." She also gave birth to her second child, a daughter.

She'd stay up two or three days at a time and then pass out. Her life started falling apart. She stayed in the house, paranoid and skinny.

Meanwhile her son's condition had worsened. He entered the hospital for an operation. While he was being cut open, Candy was at home crashing down from a crank run. She fell into such a stupor she neglected to visit her son, and the hospital accused her of abandonment.

After the boy was released, Child Protective Services suggested he stay two weeks in a foster home. Candy agreed. She also decided her life was such a mess and the boy needed so much care that she would seek counseling and give him up for adoption.

Tears well up in her eyes as she sits on the worn couch at Aquarian House and relates her tale. She gets letters from her son at Christmas and will be able to see him when he's 21.

She never mentions the whereabouts or responsibility of the father.

But after she gave up her son, Candy's life slid farther into the abyss. Her behavior didn't moderate even with the threat of AIDS. "I did so much crank, I didn't care where I got a needle," she says. At the same time, she switched her $60-$80 a day habit from crank to rock cocaine. "It's a lot more intense high."

Candy's daughter deplored her habit and would beg her not to shoot up. "I knew I was burning all my bridges, that I was going nowhere," says Candy. "I was always dumping her at places while I went to get loaded." Candy's mother eventually took over care of the girl, who will turn 7 in November.

Candy finally turned herself in to Aquarian House, made it 89 days and split.

With no roof over her head she

slept under bridges. She ate at soup kitchens. She weighed 90 pounds.

"I was too embarrassed and ashamed to go around my daughter."

She was eventually arrested in a park in Woodland for possession of a syringe and a little crank. Candy did six months in jail and entered Aquarian House after she was released. She has gained weight and looks healthy and content.

"I know I want recovery this time," she says. "I need to stick it out and have faith in myself." If for no other reason than to regain the trust of her daughter. "When I shut the bathroom door, no matter what I'm doing, she thinks I'm getting loaded. She wants me here. She told my mom she wants me off drugs. I love her very much."

As for her mother? "My mother isn't mad, she's hurt. She still doesn't trust me." □

THE DEALER

Bryant Wilson pulled a stick-up with a toy gun and ended up serving 23 months. He's been clean for over a year.

Bryant Wilson was so stoned one night, the policeman had to tap his flashlight on Wilson's noggin to wake him up. The youngster had doused his marijuana joint with lidocaine and "froze up." He was arrested but escaped conviction when his lawyer proved the police conducted an illegal search and seizure.

That was half a lifetime ago. His mother had died and Wilson was a 17-year-old high school dropout living in East Sacramento with his alcoholic father. He had great dope—pharmaceutical dexedrine straight from the loading dock—and runaway girls were living at his house. They exchanged sex for rent.

It's been a long road since then, and Wilson, now 34, is living at Aquarian House. He hasn't shot dope in more than a year and says he's found a new source of support—his comrades in Narcotics Anonymous.

The first doper Wilson met was his dad, who sent the boy mixed messages about his pot and dexedrine. "My dad found my stash box and said, 'That shit's illegal. Bury it in the backyard.' It was hard for him to lecture me because he was drunk all his life."

After his father died, Wilson at age 20 went to work in a gas station and snorted crank several times a week. He was also engaged in petty dealing but decided that level of

drug business was not for him. "Dealing is hard work," he says. "You're pestered all night by people begging, stealing from you, offering you their asses."

Wilson married, stayed at the gas station, but eventually blossomed into a full-on crankster. He started shooting methamphetamine daily and staying up for 11-12 day runs.

Unlike many cranksters, Wilson's life was not dominated by paranoia. But it was marked by a sense of power. He would spend his nights walking around Sacramento daring the police to catch him, or he would swagger down alleys waiting for someone to confront him. "I wasn't bold or brassy, and I've talked to a lot of cops with my mouth full of dope."

He kept no weapons, but sported a set of stainless-steel rings that could play the role of brass knuckles.

Wilson also had established a no-hassle system of crank dealing. He would take phone orders at his house each morning, make his connection, and then dole the crank out to the dealers' runners. At one point he even bought disposable needles and included them with the sale. "I was spending $100-$200 a day on my habit and selling two or three times that to support it."

He hung out with prostitutes, whom he would pick up and bring to

his house, simply for mutual friendship. He'd also share dope with them.

"You learn to manipulate people with drugs," he says. "Now I'm learning I can attract people on my own merits rather than for what I have."

But the crankster life soured. "A guy bigger and badder than me took my last $300." Plus, his dope was getting cut to nothing.

He ended up pulling two "armed" robberies—he used a fake gun—at convenience stores.

Because he didn't actually use a weapon, Wilson got six months. He ended up serving 23 months county time because of probation violations.

Wilson knows the criminal-justice system has run out of patience with him. Next time he does his time in the joint.

He last shot dope just more than a year ago, but now is sure he can stay away from the people and situations that lead to a crankster life.

But he's paying a lifetime price, the specter of AIDS. Every six months he must take an HIV test. Bryant remembers all the times neither he nor his shooting cohorts were concerned about the virus. "When you got a room full of tense people and one rig, no one stops to clean it," he says. "I've used a needle behind people in a porta-potty, shooting out of a eye-dropper cap. When it comes to getting loaded, it doesn't matter."

CRACK'S DESTRUCTIVE SPRINT ACROSS AMERICA

Michael Massing

Michael Massing, a New York writer, is a 1989 Alicia Patterson Fellow.

AS BROADWAY CUTS UP through the Upper West Side of Manhattan and into Washington Heights, it gradually turns into a giant Caribbean bazaar. The avenue abounds with *bodegas*, *farmacias*, unisex beauty salons, bargain clothing outlets, restaurants serving *pollo* and *plátanos*, and travel agencies offering bargains to the Dominican Republic. Women squeeze mangoes, children lick flavored ices, men play hard at dominoes, all to the accompaniment of a hundred different radios blaring salsa music. Long a magnet for immigrants, Washington Heights today is home to large colonies of Irish, Jews and, most numerous of all, Dominicans. As the ever-present crowds make their way up and down the street, the Heights seems a living embodiment of the American Dream — a vibrant, energetic urban melting pot.

Wander off Broadway, though, and the neighborhood quickly seems like an American nightmare. On side streets in the 150's and 160's, clusters of tough teen-agers wearing beepers, four-finger gold rings and $95 Nikes offer $3 vials of crack, the high-octane, smokable derivative of cocaine. On every block there are four or five different "crews," or gangs, each touting its own brand of the drug, known to aficionados as "Scotty" (as in "Beam me up"). Some blocks are "hotter" than others, depending on the availability of the crack. On the hottest blocks Scotty is available "24/7" — 24 hours a day, seven days a week. So much business is transacted on these streets that Washington Heights has gained a reputation as the crack capital of America.

The experience of the Heights has been repeated in large cities throughout the country. And now, in smaller communities, too, crack is striking with swift fury, From rural woodlands to shady suburbs, prairie townships to Southern hamlets, no community seems immune. The roster of the infected reads like a roll-call of Middle America itself: Roanoke, Va.; Seaford, Del.; Sioux Falls, S.D.; Cheyenne, Wyo.; Sacramento, Calif.; Portland, Ore. Fort Wayne, Ind., once known as the City of Churches, is now home to an estimated 70 crack houses, causing law-enforcement personnel to christen it "the crack capital of Indiana."

How did it happen? How did a drug once confined to a handful of large-city neighborhoods make its way to Main Street in just a few short years? Much of the answer can be found in data generated by the Federal Government's unprecedented intelligence-gathering operation against crack. In 13 cities across the country, crack teams created over the last three years by the Justice Department are methodically tracking the importation, distribution and consumption of the drug. In New York, the United States Drug Enforcement Administration (D.E.A.) operates a special Unified Intelligence Division staffed by experts from a dozen agencies, including the F.B.I., the I.R.S., Customs, Immigration and the local police department. Twenty-four hours a day, the information pours in — from wiretaps and surveillance teams, witnesses and informants, police raids and drug busts. By combining this data with testimony from D.E.A. agents, police captains, sociologists, undercover agents, community leaders, criminologists, prosecutors, addicts and treatment experts, it is possible to trace crack's destructive sprint across America.

WASHINGTON HEIGHTS HAS COME NATU-rally by its status as the nation's crack capital. It would be difficult to design a better location for marketing a new drug. First, the area is highly accessible. To the west, the George Washington Bridge brings in potential customers from New Jersey; to the north the Henry Hudson Parkway pulls them in from Westchester County. For residents of Passaic or Peekskill who want a quick high, the Heights offers easy-in, easy-out convenience. By all accounts, Washington Heights transacts more out-of-town drug deals than any other neighborhood in New York City.

The manufacturing and marketing of crack can be traced to the upper west side of New York City

The neighborhood itself provides a substantial pool of users. For every newcomer who has made it as a shopkeeper on Broadway, there are others who have dropped out of school, had a child out of marriage, become permanently unemployed — likely candidates for drug use. Here, as throughout the country, crack does best where Americans — especially minorities — do worst.

Finally, Washington Heights is home to New York's most enterprising drug dealers. No, they are not Colombians. Although most people associate Colombians with cocaine and crack — especially now that open warfare has broken out between the drug lords and the Government in Bogotá — Colombians are not generally involved in the retailing of crack in the United States. They just produce cocaine in South America and smuggle it into the United States. The Colombians living in New York are too few in number and too insular to have the array of contacts necessary to move drugs on the street.

The Dominicans, New York's fastest-growing immigrant group, do have such contacts. They also have the marketing talent. Crack dealing, like more legitimate lines of work, requires the ability to exercise quality control, hire a dependable workforce and develop a steady clientele. At all of this, the Dominicans (only a small percentage of whom are involved in the drug trade) have had a lot of experience. In the Caribbean, they are known as merchants and tradesmen. In New York, they have applied their savvy to become highly successful shopkeepers — and the city's top crack traffickers.

ALTHOUGH CRACK'S ORIGINS REmain obscure — no one really knows who invented it — the Dominicans are generally credited with having first developed it for a mass market. The breakthrough seems to have come about by accident, an improvised response to shifting consumer tastes. Until 1983, cocaine was used almost exclusively in powder form (known as cocaine hydrochloride). Extremely expensive, the drug was often consumed at parties and discos, where it was sprinkled on mirrors and snorted — usually through a high-denomination bill.

Gradually, though, many snorters, seeking a more intense high, turned to freebasing. This involved treating cocaine powder with ether and reducing it to a crystalline base, which, when smoked, produced a sharp, pleasurable rush. Unfortunately, freebasing was complicated and messy, the subject of instruction booklets running on for many pages. It was dangerous, too, risking explosions like the one that hospitalized the comedian Richard Pryor. To avoid the hassle, customers began demanding that their dealers convert the powder to freebase in advance.

This presented dealers with a dilemma. For, when cocaine is converted to freebase, it loses much of its weight. If they wanted to sell ready-made freebase at popular prices, dealers would have to absorb the loss — unless they could find an undetectable filler.

The search was on. One researcher who observed it was Terry Williams, a sociologist at the City University of New York who in 1982 began hanging out with a teen-age cocaine gang in Washington Heights. Williams, who recounts his experiences in a recently published book, "The Cocaine Kids," recalls that the local Dominican gangs "came up with something called 'comeback,'" a chemical adulterant akin to lidocaine, a prescription anesthetic. "When comeback is blended with cocaine powder and cooked, all of it remains in the mix," Williams explains. "This became the first chemical that you could cut freebase with." The result was the prototype for crack.

Eventually dealers found other, less expensive substances that worked in conjunction with comeback. The cheapest and most effective was common baking soda. Formulas varied, but the typical instructions were as simple as a recipe out of "The 60-Minute Gourmet":

Take two ounces cocaine hydrochloride. Mix with two ounces comeback and one ounce Arm & Hammer. Add water. Bring to a boil. Let cool into a solid mass. Break into small pieces. Smoke. Intense rush should follow instantly. Serves 2,000.

Before long, Dominican dealers were out on the streets of Washington Heights peddling the new substance in pellet form at a few dollars a pop. (The name came from the crackling sound the drug made when smoked.) The "champagne" of drugs, once limited to the elite, was now available — somewhat diluted — to drifters and dropouts, welfare mothers and unemployed youths. Dealers set up shop across the street from schools, enticing teen-agers with free samples. They also offered two-for-one deals and "Mother's Day" specials timed to coincide with the arrival of welfare checks. Soon, customers were seeking out dealers rather than the other way around, helping establish Washington Heights as America's first major crack market.

The Dominicans then began fanning southward into Harlem and eastward into the South Bronx. They also began supplying cocaine to other ethnic groups. In Harlem, in South Jamaica, Queens, in the Brooklyn neighborhoods of Bushwick and Brownsville, poor young blacks — jobless, uneducated and desperate — hungered for a piece of the "crazy money" crack offered. To get started, it took as little as an ounce of cocaine, an investment of perhaps $1,000.

Obtaining it was not much of a problem. By the mid-1980's, cocaine was arriving in New York by the *ton*. Importation was controlled by the Cali Cartel, Colombia's second-largest syndicate, after the Medellín Cartel. Desperate to unload their supplies, the Colombians found dependable customers in the Dominicans of Washington Heights. The two groups got along well, joined not only by a common language but also by similar entrepreneurial values. The Dominicans became New York's chief middlemen. As sales boomed to aspiring young dealers outside Washington Heights, the city was eventually carved up along ethnic lines, with Dominican-supplied blacks controlling Harlem, Queens and Brooklyn, and the Dominicans dominant in upper Manhattan and the South Bronx.

FROM THE START, CRACK'S DISTRIbution system distinguished it from all other drugs. Heroin, for instance, was highly centralized. From poppy cultivation to street sales, the trade was dominated by a single organization — the Mafia, which, though ruthless, imposed a certain order on the trade. Gang wars were rare, and police officers were never fired upon. Because distribution was so tightly controlled, it was possible, with diligent police work, to put an entire network out of business, as occurred in the French Connection case.

With crack, there could be no French Connection. In effect, it took the "organized" out of organized crime. "The unique thing about crack is that for a relatively small investment you can buy some cocaine, convert it to crack in the kitchen, and begin distributing almost immediately," says John Featherly, staff coordinator of the D.E.A.'s cocaine section in Washington. "This makes for a lot of entrepreneurs."

If heroin was the Fortune 500, crack was Mom and Pop. A typical crack organization would have no more than seven or eight people—a street seller or two, a steerer to direct customers, a guard to protect the merchandise, a police lookout, a weigher (known as a "scale boy"), a manager and a "Mr. Big" to count the profits. Competition was intense. In busy areas like Washington Heights, one block might host four or five crews, all contending for the same consumer dollar.

With no overall hierarchy or command structure to impose order, turf wars broke out over the most lucrative spots. Dealers regularly ripped off customers and stole from one another, leading to frequent shootouts, stabbings and executions. Crack created a new breed of urban guerrilla, members of a fierce, proliferating army that left the police badly outnumbered and outgunned.

By late 1985, when crack first came to the attention of the national press, it was deeply entrenched in New York's poor neighborhoods. In the rest of the country, only two cities—Los Angeles and Miami—had comparable crack problems. All three cities were major distribution points for cocaine, so it was natural that crack would engulf them first. Soon, however, the drug began to move out from these gateway cities and into the heartland. It would travel via a fearsome new set of traffickers—illegal immigrants from Jamaica—who would quickly and radically transform the way crack was distributed around the country.

Delroy Edwards grew up poor in the tough, stifling shantytowns of Kingston, Jamaica. In 1980, at the age of 20, he went to work as a street enforcer for the Jamaica Labor Party of Edward Seaga. Seaga was locked in bitter election duel with the People's National Party, headed by Michael Manley, and each side was forming armed gangs to intimidate the other. The gangs did their job only too well, killing 800 people by election day. After his victory, Seaga launched a crackdown, and many gang members, feeling the heat, headed for the United States. Among them was Delroy Edwards. Slipping into Brooklyn on a tourist visa, he eventually made his way into the marijuana business, selling nickel bags out of a neighborhood storefront.

At the beginning of 1985, Edwards learned to make crack. Soon he was selling little else. He worked out of two "flagship" spots in Brooklyn—one, a two-story house, the other, an abandoned brownstone near a housing project. Enough poor blacks coughed up enough $5 bills to enable Edwards to buy a $150,000 home on Long Island—and to pay for it in cash.

That wasn't enough for Edwards, who began looking to expand his business. Unfortunately, New York was already crowded with crack dealers; outside the city, however, lay plenty of virgin territory. In Washington, Baltimore and Philadelphia, for instance, crack was just beginning to catch on. Enterprising local dealers would travel to New York, buy a few ounces of cocaine, return home, convert it into crack, and sell the product for three or four times the New York street price. In the fall of 1986, Edwards traveled to Washington and set up shop; by the following spring his lieutenants had established thriving businesses in Philadelphia and Baltimore as well. At its peak, Edwards's organization, known as the Rankers, employed 50 workers and made up to $100,000 a day.

The glory days did not last. Edwards—nicknamed "Uzi" for his taste in weapons—was pathologically violent. People who crossed him were pistol-whipped, beaten with baseball bats, shot in the legs. One 16-year-worker, suspected of cheating, was beaten unconscious with bats, scalded with boiling water, and suspended by a chain from the ceiling until he died. Eventually, the police caught up with Edwards, and in July a Brooklyn jury convicted him on 42 counts of murder, assault, kidnapping and drug dealing. Edwards is now awaiting sentencing. The Rankers have disintegrated.

But there are 40 other groups just like the Rankers, running crack out of New York and Miami to points across the country. Posses, they're called, after their members' affection for American westerns (and for the guns used in them). Most, like the Rankers, took shape as gangs during the 1980 Jamaican election, then fled to the United States and regrouped. Here, their 10,000 to 20,000 members, organized in posses with as few as 25 members and as many as several hundred, keep incessantly on the move, slipping in and out of the many Jamaican communities scattered across the country. To maintain loyalty, each posse generally restricts membership to the residents of a particular neighborhood in Kingston. Posse members travel with fake IDs, making it tough for policemen to identify them. Sometimes, as a cover, they attach themselves to reggae groups touring the country. Today, Jamaicans are believed to control 35 percent to 40 percent of the nation's crack network.

Today, 35 to 40 percent of the nation's crack network is controlled by Jamaicans

"They're very good businessmen," says John A. O'Brien, an agent with the Bureau of Alcohol, Tobacco and Firearms (B.A.T.F.), the Federal agency that most closely monitors the posses. "They follow the law of supply and demand. When they see that a vial of crack selling for $5 in New York will get $15 in Kansas City, they'll move in." New York is their "training school," O'Brien says, "like going to Wharton. They'll take a guy doing a good job in Harlem and send him to open an office in the Midwest." On his arrival in the new area, the posse sales rep will rent a motel room and conduct a market survey of sorts to determine the most lucrative spot in town. Then he'll rent an apartment or, better yet, get a single female to lend him one in return for crack.

When asked how the posses move the drug from city to city, Bill McMullan, the assistant special agent in charge of the D.E.A.'s Washington office, jokingly cites the title of a recent movie: "Planes, Trains and Automobiles." Amtrak, Greyhound, commercial airlines, Federal Express, U.P.S.—the posses use them all, regularly.

To carry cocaine on commercial flights, the Jamaicans tend to recruit overweight women able to conceal one- or two-pound packages on their person. Also popular are rental cars, preferably Volvos, sent over the nation's highways, preferably Interstates. "When I see some of the places the posses are operating, I can't find any other explanation than the presence of a nearby Interstate," says Stephen Higgins, the B.T.A.F.'s Director in Washington.

In deciding where to strike, the Jamaicans generally follow the path of least resistance. Cities with well-organized criminal groups, such as Newark, St. Louis and Chicago, tend to get bypassed. At first glance, Chicago would seem to be an ideal posse target. It is a major transportation hub, has a vast inner-city population and offers block upon block of public housing projects, a favorite crack target. But Chicago also has plenty of established home-grown gangs doing a brisk business in cocaine and heroin. Intent on protecting their trade, they have worked determinedly to keep outside traffickers from entering. "When crack first appeared, some groups did try to come here and stake out some territory, but they quickly left," says Vincent Lang, chairman of the Chicago Housing Authority. "They wanted to remain alive." Today Chicago is awash in powder cocaine, but crack is very hard to find. Perhaps wary of the anarchic market forces crack has unleashed elsewhere, local dealers have opted out of selling it themselves.

In other cities, dealers tend to be too weak and disorganized to stand up to the posses and their tactics. The Jamaicans are fanatics for weapons. Taking advantage of lax gun laws in Texas, Florida and Virginia, they have stockpiled Uzis and AR-13 assault rifles. When breaking into a new area, the Jamaicans come in with all barrels blazing. "One cause of the violence we're seeing in many cities is Jamaican traffickers pushing out American blacks," says Jonny Frank, a prosecutor in the Delroy Edwards case.

According to the B.T.A.F., the posses have been responsible for approximately 1,000 murders since 1985. Washington, Philadelphia, Dallas, Houston, Kansas City, Denver—all have suffered Jamaican invasions. In New York, the posses have succeeded in taking over much of Brooklyn and Harlem, establishing themselves as the city's second largest traffickers, after the Dominicans.

Many smaller cities have been hit, too. New York-based posses have set up a thriving operation in Hartford, shipping their merchandise there via bus and train. In New York State, the Jamaicans are moving crack up Interstate 87, hitting such tiny Hudson Valley towns as Newburgh, Kingston and Saratoga Springs. In West Virginia, the posses have established crack houses in Martinsburg (population 13,000) and Charles Town (3,000). From there they have moved out along Interstate 81, shipping crack as far north as Chambersburg, Pa., and as far south as Roanoke, Va.

Roanoke! It would be hard to imagine a more unlikely setting for crack. A town of only 90,000, Roanoke is nestled in the heart of Virginia's dairy and orchard country, several hours' drive from the nearest city. Yet members of the Shower posse, the largest in the country, have managed to find their way there from New York.

On closer examination, though, the presence of crack in Roanoke is really not so surprising. Even towns with Norman Rockwell-like reputations have pockets of alienation and despair, open sores in which crack can take hold and fester. Roanoke has its own modest ghetto, beset by the same social ills afflicting larger cities. "We have a sizable minority community, and that's where the Jamaicans set up," observes Tom Bondurant, an assistant United States attorney in Roanoke. Demand was obviously high: crack was selling for $25 to $30 a vial—more than enough to catch the attention of big-city traffickers.

Roanoke's case is typical. Across the country, crack has displayed remarkable consistency, taking root in those sectors of society least able to resist it. In places like Charles Town, Newburgh, and even Fort Wayne, Ind., crack has found a foothold among poor blacks and—to a far lesser degree—Hispanics.

Will it stay that way? Or will crack break out like some contagion into the middle-class population, white and black? In some places, it already has. In Washington—the city with the nation's highest rate of drug-related violence—crack has leaped across the city lines into the middle-class suburbs of Maryland and Virginia. Until June 1988, for instance, crack was virtually unknown in Howard County, a tranquil, middle-class area midway between Washington and Baltimore; today the drug is being distributed in 20 locations, including some attractive town houses.

Dr. Mark F. Gold, the director of research at Fair Oaks Hospital in New Jersey and the founder of the national "800-COCAINE Helpline," detects a subtle shift in the profile of America's crack users. Until recently, he says, virtually all of those calling in to seek help with crack were young inner-city residents, poor and unemployed. Today, they remain the most common users, but, Gold says, "crack appears to be making some inroads into suburban and rural America. I now get many calls from the Sunbelt, whereas before I didn't." Gold, a member of William Bennett's kitchen cabinet, says that the nation has reached a "turning point. Whether crack expands and changes the typical crack user or not, only time will tell."

Today's reality, meanwhile, is most visible in Kansas City, Mo. A year ago, the city was declaring victory in the war on crack. A Federal organized-crime task force had succeeded in dismantling a thriving crack operation run by the Waterhouse posse. Working out of a fortresslike house in the heart of the inner city, the Jamaicans had employed an estimated 1,000 people at one point. Demand was so great that the posse had had to import Jamaicans from New York and Miami. This proved to be its undoing. The new workers felt little loyalty to the group, and when arrested, tended to talk, providing the task force with invaluable information. In late 1986, the Feds struck, raiding ghetto crack houses and rounding up dealers. Eventually, 178 traffickers were prosecuted and 25 more deported. By the start of 1987, no more than 75 posse members remained in town. Across the nation, Kansas City was hailed as a stunning success story.

The sense of triumph was short-lived, however. "A year ago, we were really feeling good about the successes we had had," says the first assistant United States attorney Rob Larsen, who directed the task force from 1983 to 1987. "Then the L.A. gangs began arriving."

Los Angeles's black street gangs are the fastest-growing set of crack traffickers in the country. Already they have established a national network second only to that of the posses. They are grouped into confederations known as the Bloods and the Crips, each with its own color (blue for Crips, red for Bloods), slang and hand signals. Fiercely territorial, the gangs have traditionally concentrated on fighting one another over impoverished patches of south-central Los Angeles.

Crack has changed that. Sensing the enormous profit potential in the drug, the Bloods and the Crips are now paying less attention to one another and more to transporting crack. Today, more than 10,000 gang members are at work in some 50 cities from Seattle to Baltimore. Generally, they emulate the tactics of the posses, infiltrating black communities by working through local contacts. So far, the gangs and the posses have avoided fighting one another. In fact, they seem to be dividing up the country between them—the gangs working eastward from California, the posses westward from New York. The two national networks are gradually crisscrossing—with devastating consequences for towns caught in the middle.

Thus, in Kansas City, when the crackdown on the posses created a vacuum, the Bloods and Crips quickly filled it. Today, crack is just as plentiful in the city as it had been before the Waterhouse roundup. Meanwhile, the Waterhouse posse, routed from Kansas City, is beginning to resurface in Des Moines and Omaha—even across the river in Kansas City, Kan. "It was a startling experience" says Larsen. "Nobody feels like we're making any substantial progress at all." Crack, he adds ruefully, "is a

very difficult thing for law enforcement to deal with."

Indeed, even if the posses and L.A. gangs were somehow tamed—an extremely unlikely prospect—there are plenty of other groups ready to take their place. Both Cubans and Guyanese have established fledgling interstate operations, while Haitian traffickers based in Fort Pierce, Fla., are transporting crack along the East Coast, via migrant farm workers. In Miami, Detroit and countless smaller cities across the country, local black rings are at work, looking intently for opportunities to expand.

Not everyone has lost hope. Robert M. Stutman, special agent in charge of the D.E.A.'s field office in New York, points to a natural selection process taking place in the crack trade, with smaller organizations gradually being absorbed by larger ones. "The crack business is becoming more highly organized, more like heroin," says Stutman. In New York, he observes, "crack is now controlled by a finite number of groups. That was not true two years ago." The effect, he says, is to provide law-enforcement officials with a "more discernible target."

Stutman cites a Dominican organization in Washington Heights that, in three short years, went from being streetcorner peddlers to becoming a multitier conglomerate selling more than 10,000 vials of crack a day. The group was so well organized that it marketed its crack under a brand name ("Based Balls"). Such practices eventually attracted the attention of the D.E.A., which, after an intensive investigation, put the group out of business.

No matter how determined the effort to root it out, crack continues to thrive

Unfortunately, the D.E.A.'s efforts had little effect on the supply of crack in New York—the usual outcome of law-enforcement action aimed at the drug. No matter how determined the effort to root it out, crack seems always to thrive. That has been the experience in Kansas City. In Brooklyn, crack continues to sell for $3 a vial despite the prosecution of Delroy Edwards. In Washington, the police recently seized Rayful Edmond 3d, allegedly the city's largest dealer, but crack remains available in 120 locations throughout town. "Right after we locked up Edmond, the homicide rate slowed down for a while," says Collin Younger, commander of the narcotics branch of the D.C. police. "Now it's beginning to pick up again as other dealers fight over his territory." Crack is getting so plentiful in the District of Columbia that Younger expects the price to drop any day now.

As if crack weren't enough to contend with, a new drug has recently appeared on the horizon. Called ice, it is a smokable version of methamphetamine, or speed. It creates a high that lasts for up to 24 hours, compared with crack's 20-minute high, followed by a "crash" so severe that it can resemble paranoid schizophrenia.

President Bush's anti-drug strategy, unveiled on Sept. 5, calls for a heavy reliance on police and prosecutors. Fully 70 percent of its projected $7.9 billion spending will go for law enforcement, including $1.6 billion for new prisons and $3.1 billion for state and local police. The remaining 30 percent will go toward treatment, prevention and education.

1. DRUGS IN PERSPECTIVE: Current Illegal Drugs

Judging from the record of the police to date, though, the Bush plan seems unlikely to make any real dent in the amount of crack on the streets. A sense of resignation is settling over America's drug agents. More and more of them are beginning to sound like Francis Hall. For four years, until his retirement in March, Hall served as commanding officer of the New York Police Department's Narcotics division, making him, in effect, New York's top narc. Hall helped design the Tactical Narcotics Teams (T.N.T.)—the special police units that carry out sweeps through drug-infested neighborhoods—that today are the city's principal weapon in the fight against drugs.

Looking back over his four years on the front lines, Hall compares the war on crack to another conflict. "Drug enforcement," he says, "is like the Vietnam War. In Vietnam, we underestimated the number of Vietcong and their will to fight. We appear to be doing the same thing with street-level drug traffickers." Noting that the staff of the narcotics division has increased from 525 in 1985 to 2,000 today, Hall observes, "It's like Westmoreland asking Washington for two more divisions. We lost the Vietnam War with a half-million men. We're doing the same thing with drugs."

The Vietnam analogy might be taken a step further. The Vietcong grew largely because of the social, political and economic breakdown engulfing Vietnam. No matter how much firepower the United States expended, the guerrillas always managed to regroup, nurtured by the poverty and injustice around them. Much the same is true of crack in America. No matter how many sweeps, raids and busts our police departments mount against crack traffickers, they always manage to resurface. Only when we address the conditions that have given rise to crack— the desperation of our inner cities—will we begin to see the light at the end of the tunnel.

Cocaine Kids: The Underground American Dream

Terry Williams

Terry Williams, an ethnographer at City University of New York, spent thousands of hours in the last four years documenting, from the inside, the lives and culture of teenage drug dealers in New York City's Washington Heights.

We spoke with Williams about his new book, Cocaine Kids, *based on his research. Following our adapted conversation are excerpts from* Cocaine Kids, *published by Addison-Wesley.*

Being poor sucks. That's what this teenage drug scene in the inner city is all about. "Fuck being poor! Why should I be poor?" they say. Like everyone else, these kids want what America projects: the big payoff, the Lotto. They want what adults want: power, respect, prestige, wealth. And they want it now.

Every teen aspires to make good. They have the desire to show family and friends they can succeed at something; that they can move up the career ladder and make money. Shut out from disappearing entry-level jobs in the mainstream economy, the cocaine kids find illegal employment opportunities in the highly profitable, rapidly growing, multinational drug trade.

In the cocaine hustle, making good means to "get behind the scale" – to be in command of significant quantities of drugs. It is like landing a top sales job in a major corporation, or being named partner after a long apprenticeship in a brokerage firm that has a seat on the stock exchange. The kids who get that far have control over prices and selling techniques, they direct the work of subordinate employees, and, above all else, they make large amounts of money.

In large measure, the cocaine kids are the offspring of a marriage between poverty and the American Dream. Their story is the story of the American Way.

So, young drug dealers – including Max, who headed the distribution "crew" near Washington Heights for the Colombians and made $20,000 a week at 16 – have rejected the cultural myth of the American Way. Max's choice was rational. He could have pursued the American myth of upward mobility by slinging burgers in the secondary labor market, or he could, and did, buy into the mystique of the street, drive a baby Benz, wear gold chains and have lots of money.

In large measure, the cocaine kids are the offspring of a marriage between poverty and the American Dream. Their story is the story of the American Way.

The Culture of Refusal | The alternative economic life of these kids is embedded in an alternative culture: the culture of refusal. They refuse to be part of a system that has rejected them. They are refusing to learn because teachers have told them they can't; social workers have told them they can't change; journalists and police officers have called them animals; their parents have refused, or are perhaps unable, to parent.

These kids are far from blame themselves for not taking personal responsibility. To be sure, their problems are not all society's fault. But the dimensions of the culture of refusal suggest that something is seriously, and structurally wrong with America's window of opportunity. In New York City alone, the school drop-out rate is more than 40 percent and a new, lost generation has emerged: 500,000 people are not even looking for jobs or applying for work. These numbers indicate mass refusal: Remember what it looked like when 500,000 people crowded into Beijing's Tiananmen Square to protest? The American culture of refusal is not even connected to the

By Terry Williams. From *New Perspectives Quarterly*, Summer 1989, pp. 21-25. Adapted conversation are excerpts from *Cocaine Kids* by Terry Williams. Copyright © 1989 by Terry Williams. Reprinted by permission from Addison-Wesley Publishing Co.

legitimate economy, and the drug culture is only a part of this great refusal.

Young people in poor, black urban areas start out with a belief that they can make decisions about what happens to their lives. They believe that they can be President of the United States. Then they walk out into the street, put their hand up for a cab and it passes them by. The guy at the grocery store says he can't hire them. The landlord won't rent them the apartment they want. As these young people begin putting all the pieces together, the feeling that they are part of society begins to erode.

The strong sense of possibility slowly turns into a kind of rage. Through this rage, the youth says, "No, I am not going to learn and I am not going to participate in this society. I am going to do what I need to do to get what I need and I don't need any help. I'm going to hustle for myself." The fury and violence of the individualist survivor's rage is usually turned back on the poor blacks in the community. The violence is aimed at the black neighbor. As a black male living in Harlem, for example, my chances of dying violently are 1 in 25.

While otherwise unnoticed, the rage of this lost generation is ominously broadcast to the society at large during degradation ceremonies in the "halls of shame," called courts, where, in the flash of camera lights, these kids are led away to jail, heads down, arms shackled. These kids are only visible through that imagery.

The Individualist Survivor | Every ethnic group that came through New York trod an illegitimate path to establishing a stake in the mainstream. The Italians, the Irish and other communities were all involved in some manner of organized crime. But, in a generation or so, they became legitimate and their kids attended Harvard and Princeton and became district attorneys. They came to America, found their niche – legal or illegal – and moved on.

That is what the Dominicans and the blacks I worked with are trying to do in the illegitimate drug economy. They are trying to get a stake in the system. Drugs are the nexus between the culture of refusal and economic opportunity. The illegitimate economy is the only economy where the refused can employ their entrepreneurial talents.

The difference between the immigrants and

> Drugs are the nexus between the culture of refusal and economic opportunity. The illegitimate economy is the only economy where the refused can employ their entrepreneurial talents.

these young kids in the culture of refusal is their penultimate American belief – which the immigrant groups never shared – that they can make it as individuals. This is one of the most significant causes of black immobility. The lack of collective will is picked up by the teenagers. Their troubles stem from absorbing the ideology that the American Dream is an individual one.

None of the cultural nationalism and solidarity responsible for the Koreans' collective upward mobility is evident in the black community. The Koreans are out there working 24 hours a day, and they are taking each other up the ladder, with their Korean-owned businesses, banks, and savings and loans.

The black kids also work 24 hours a day selling drugs. Their work is known as a "24/7" job: 24 hours a day, 7 days a week. They are out there day and night trying to make a dollar. But they are doing it alone, for themselves.

As far as I can see, only the infusion of a sense of collective self-awareness in the black community can help this lost generation turn pursuit of the American Dream from collective self-defeat to upward social mobility.

Market, Price and Violence | In 1983, a market glut in the cocaine producing countries of Peru, Bolivia and Colombia forced foreign suppliers to cut their prices. This had an immediate, beneficial effect for dealers, who continued to charge their retail customers the old price and realized extraordinary profits for a time. Word eventually got out, but even at lower prices sales could not keep up with production and total dollar receipts were down.

At that point, as classically happens in cases of market saturation, a new product was introduced which offered the chance to expand the market in ways never before possible. Crack, packaged in small quantities and sold for $5 and sometimes even less – a fraction of the usual minimum sale for powder – allowed dealers to attract an entirely new class of consumers. Once crack took hold, the market change was very swift and very sweeping.

The value of the commodity itself is very volatile. In New York, for example, a kilo (2.2 pounds) of cocaine worth $50,000 in 1980 brought only $20,000 in 1983. Now, due to the glut resulting from overproduction, a kilo brings only $12,000. The price differentials between "copping zones," which now encompass entire cities, often cause market rivalries that result in violence. One of the reasons there is so much violence in Washington, DC today is that a gram of cocaine there costs $100, while it only costs $25 a gram in New York becuase of the glut. So, distribution "crews" are going down from New York to battle for the higher profits in the Washington, DC territory.

Paradoxically, heightened law-enforcement efforts also lead to more violence. In New York, for example, when the Tactical Narcotics Team (TNT) closes down trading on a particular block, the dealers look for new territory. That inevitably produces competitive violence between competing "crews."

Cocaine Kids

From Cocaine Kids by Terry Williams. Copyright © 1989 by Terry Williams. Reprinted by permission of Addison-Wesley Publishing Company.

Those who recruit teenagers are following a tradition that dates back almost twenty years, and was the direct effect of the harsh "Rockefeller laws," mandating a prison term for anyone over eighteen in possession of an illegal drug. This led heroin dealers to use kids as runners, and cocaine importers have followed this pattern: young people not only avoid the law but are, for the most part, quite trustworthy; they are also relatively easy to frighten and control.

The Crew | The apartment is crowded with teenagers, all wearing half-laced sneakers and necklace ropes of gold. Doorbells ring every few minutes; white powder dusts the table tops; jagged-edge matchbook covers and dollar bills seem to flow from hand to hand. The talk is frenetic, filled with masterful plans and false promises. Everybody has a girl. Everybody has cocaine. Everybody has a gun.

The crew sits around as Max prepares the crack. Max is a master at mixing. He uses his own recipe and is familiar with the effects of the drug in various combinations.

Jake snorts from a large bag of cocaine resting on the glass table, telling Chillie about a woman he met at Jump-Offs, an after-hours club. *"La jeva no era muy grande, pero tenia lo de atras* [The girl was not too big, but she had a big behind]." He kisses his fingers. *"Hombre, 'mano."*

Max's recipe calls for an "eighth" of cocaine

Crack, packaged in small quantities and sold for $5 and sometimes even less – a fraction of the usual minimum sale for powder – allowed dealers to attract an entirely new class of consumers. Once crack took hold, the market change was very swift and very sweeping.

He will only admit he made a mistake when he is high and "the cocaine is talking."

(1/8 kilo, or 125 grams), 60 grams of bicarbonate of soda (ordinary baking soda) and 40 grams of "comeback," an adulterant that has allowed Max to double his profits from crack: this chemical can be cooked with base and, when the base is dried, it smells, tastes, and looks very much like cocaine. At $200 an ounce in 1984, it costs far less than the real thing.

He fills the Pyrex pot with tap water, and sets it on the stove. After 20 minutes, he places the material in cold water to coagulate into crack, and members of the crew come forward to cut the hardened chunks with razor blades and pack the chips into red-topped capsules.

Hector | Hector is skinny and freckle-faced. He is only three years older than Max, but he moves with the gait of an old man. His hands are rough, his bloodshot eyes dart from object to object with a twitchy nervousness. Though he was once a major dealer, and in many ways Max's mentor, he now looks to his little brother for support during hard times. He will only admit he made a mistake when he is high and "the cocaine is talking."

["Hector fell from grace after he began free-basing cocaine, lost his discipline and Max was asked to replace him 'behind the scale.' In the drug business, free-basing is a no-no. Snorting cocaine is permissible because the user/dealer can still take care of business." — from *NPQ* interview with Terry Williams.]

"I know I fucked up and made some vicious mistakes when I was behind the scale, but it's not gonna stay that way. I'll be back. Everybody is entitled to one mistake. I used to handle the weight [pounds, half pounds, kilograms] and I still can. It ain't no problem."

But Hector is not a kid anymore, and he knows it. As he talks, nobody looks up. When he asks, *"Mira, loco, si tu quieres, yo te puedo ayudar con eso* [Hey man, if you want me to, I can help you with that]," Max does not answer. Hector's eyes focus on Jake's hands counting crack chips into the capsules.

Jake | Jake is rotund, and always wearing faded jeans, dirty unlaced sneakers, a soiled T-shirt and a bummy-looking leather jacket. He is the odd man in. He looks older than his seventeen years and is sometimes shy. Jake has been sniffing until it's time to pick and pack the white

The Drug-Violence Nexus

Crack-related violence appears to be on the rise in many urban areas of the US. While general drug-related violence remained at a fairly constant level in New York City throughout the early 1980's, it increased significantly in 1988.

In an eight-month period in 1988, we focused our research on one-fourth of the police precincts in New York City and found that of the 414 homicide events reported there, 221, or 53.4 percent, were drug-related. Of those, a total of 61 percent were crack-related.

There has been a significant increase in crack-related homicides, with a corresponding decrease in certain other drug-related homicides. For example, only one percent of the drug-related homicides in our study were heroin related, 10 percent were alcohol related, and 20 percent were cocaine powder related.

The question of whether crack has significantly increased violence generally in our society is difficult to answer. Research in Washington, DC, for example, shows a significant numerical increase in crack-related homicides. Because Washington, DC is the center of government, this fact seems to be leading to a perception that drug-related homicides all over the country have increased dramatically. This is simply not the case. While the proportion of crack-related homicides has risen
in certain areas – New York, Los Angeles, Washington, DC – the proportion of other drug-related homicides has gone down, and the proportion of non-drug-related homicides nationwide has remained fairly constant.

Demographically, nearly half of the drug-related homicide victims in New York City in 1984 were in their twenties and the vast majority of them were male. In terms of race, the victims were overwhelmingly black or Hispanic.

The perpetrators of drug-related homicides in New York City were not strikingly different from their victims. They, too, were mostly young, male, and black or Hispanic.

In 1988, in terms of both ethnicity and age, the profile of the perpetrator and the victim of homicide in New York City was not significantly different from 1984. Even with the increase in the crack trade and the influx of younger dealers, runners, etc., both victim and perpetrator remained in the 20-30 age bracket.

Paul Goldstein is deputy director for criminal justice research at Narcotics and Drug Research, Inc. in New York City.

Henry Brownstein is principal specialist for the New York State Division of Criminal Justice Services in Albany.

This research was supported by the National Institute of Justice.

chips. He says cocaine gives him courage to face the unpredictable street.

"Did you hear about Max's uncle?" he asks so quietly one can barely hear him. Max interrupts, tells him to get some foil to wrap some powder. Jake straightens up, gets the foil, and places it on the table in front of Max. Again, he mentions Max's uncle, but nobody pays much attention. Jake seems as if he is about to explode – it turns out he badly wants to know if Max's uncle was killed because he owed a dealer for crack. Max does not answer.

A tireless worker, honest and loyal, Jake would never hurt Max. "I never lived in New York until my mother brought me here," he says, in a tone that is almost apologetic. He met Max by accident in the street. "He told me to go to this spot with him. He said he needed some back [backup or help] and he didn't have anybody. I went with him and made the move OK. After that we go back to see Chillie – Chillie used to have this spot in the Bronx then.

"After this happened we come to Max's house and he asked me to go to work for him. I knew
him because my sister knew his wife. Then we find out we're kin because of my aunt. I like working for him because it's easy money"

Chillie | Chillie is the boss at *la oficina*, which means that he supervises the work of Masterrap and Charlie. He and Max are the same age, and have worked together three years. He has dark, wavy hair and a sneaky smile that rarely surfaces; when it does it gives him a handsome, but sinister look. He lets everybody know that he, not Max, should be controlling the cocaine business because he takes in more money than anyone in the crew except Max. "I made over a million dollars selling this stuff. If the connect [connection; the importer] knew what I was doing, he would want to see me. Max knows I do the best business out here. I don't want except a little money and a little respect." But Max won't introduce him to the Colombian supplier.

Masterrap | Masterrap is slick, articulate and cool. He is quick to inform you that he is a ladies' man. "Rap is my name, females my game." When Chillie is busy or out of the office, he takes over. While he does not appear ambitious, he is the first in the crew to see the bigger picture and is well aware that time is against everyone in the cocaine trade. He does not overindulge like the others do.

Masterrap has his heart set on a musical career and has written many "rap" songs that he hopes one day to record. "Coke is just a way for me to make some money and do some of the things I would otherwise not have the chance of doing in the real world. Coke ain't real. All this stuff and the things we do ain't real."

Charlie | Charlie is the only African-American on the crew. He is a body guard at the office; he and Chillie were high school friends, and now they are partners. He has taken three martial arts courses and learned how to shoot a gun after his uncle – a New York City corrections officer – took him to a rifle range.

Charlie is eighteen and looking to be the next man behind the scale.

Splib | Splib is the only person present who deals as an independent, though he sometimes functions as a member of Max's crew. At nineteen, he is the oldest here. He is wise, handsome and, above all else, a survivor. He also takes great pleasure in his ability to con and manipulate people.

For an example, Splib proudly tells about his birthday, when he took two ounces of cocaine and two women to a hotel in New Jersey. They stayed three days and three nights. Afterward, broke and depressed, he called his supplier and told him he had a buyer who wanted four and a

> **While Masterrap does not appear ambitious, he is the first in the crew to see the bigger picture and is well aware that time is against everyone in the cocaine trade. He does not overindulge like the others do.**

half ounces – then worth $5,000 – right away, explaining that the two ounces were "on the street" (being distributed), but were not yet paid for. His supplier agreed to meet him with the cocaine, and Splib was able to sell enough to pay for the two birthday ounces as well as the new consignment.

"I never worry about money," he snaps. "I can always make money." Excited by his own story, he takes a folded dollar bill from his shirt pocket, and opens it to reveal what he announces to be the "purest cocaine in the world." Bending the edge of a matchbook cover into a vee, he takes two quick snorts. Refolding the bill with one hand, he is now ready to go into the street.

Splib, like most of the crew, is Dominican, but his ability to speak both Spanish and African-American slang with facility, and to mingle in both worlds is a valuable asset to the operation. He is aware of this, and high-handed about it: "The Indians [Colombians] have so much coke they can't off [sell] it without finding new markets. Blacks have proved they can organize and sell the shit, but the Indians don't know how to deal with Black cats. They don't understand their world or the way they do business. I do. And they know it."

The crack is packed in vials, the powder allotted. Max tells Jake when to return for more. The money is to be dropped off at another location, Chillie and Kitty get their consignments; Charlie and Masterrap take one last snort before they depart. Everybody is ready to deal.

Why Peru won't stop the cocaine

Maoist rebels protect the growers

Sharon Stevenson
Special to The Bee

Sharon Stevenson, a former editor for NBC News, has lived in Latin America for the past five years. She has been visiting the Upper Huallaga valley, Peru's major growing region for coca, the source of cocaine.

UCHIZA, Upper Huallaga, Peru — Invariably, they want to make you understand *la realidad,* the reality. The plain folk of the Upper Huallaga River Valley — probably the major growing region on Earth for the coca plant, the source of cocaine — try to impress on newcomers a crucial point that seems to elude U.S. policy makers: Sendero Luminoso, Peru's nine-year-old Maoist insurgency, and thousands of coca farmers are inextricably welded together in large part out of a shared animosity toward the Peruvian government.

Residents maintain that as long as Sendero is strong, going after coca production in a big way will only drive the farmers more deeply into guerrilla ranks.

After key command changes in January, the Peruvian military finally weighed in with a new strategy of divide and re-conquer. Accepting "reality," their object is first to sever Sendero from its base population, the coca farmer. They are trying to offer a pittance of government presence through civic works, put the military heat on the armed Sendero columns roaming the valley and use small commando units to root out political operatives. While they're

warning the *cocaleros* that cocaine is only a "fad" and they better begin switching crops, the armed forces say they have resources to fight only one battle at a time. They'll worry about narcotraffickers later.

But this strategy flies in the political face of U.S. desires for an all-out fight against drugs. Many U.S. government representatives persist in the illusion that the drug war in Peru can be fought without dealing directly with subversion, in effect, denying the depth of Sendero's penetration into the population.

Politicians acknowledge Peru's democracy is in trouble. In a July confidential memo labeled "Strategic Situation," President Alan Garcia concedes that Sendero "is capable of operating in almost the entire country, demonstrating an efficient organizational force," adding that they have the capacity to arm platoons. It's well accepted that Sendero is financing its activities nationwide from its "taxes" on farmers and narcos in their "liberated territory" in the Upper Huallaga.

Most worrisome, Sendero has vowed to sabotage upcoming municipal and presidential elections. And the rebels flexed their muscles Tuesday by blowing up a high-tension power pylon, causing a widespread blackout that prevented Peru's major radio network from broadcasting President Bush's anti-drug speech. The area is so guerrilla-ridden that Reuters news service has forbidden its cor-

respondents to enter the valley.

The Peruvian military and the U.S. Drug Enforcement Administration — like two animals — maintain their territorial imperatives. The military says it will combat narcotraffickers only when encountered with Sendero; the DEA will fight Sendero only when found with narcos. Yet for the DEA and the anti-drug police they advise, the line between fighting narcos and fighting subversion is virtually invisible.

The official story that the DEA is not involved in counterterrorism sounds good, but it was Sendero's combat against DEA-advised operations in 1988 in the Upper Huallaga — and its announcement of a $50,000 bounty for any dead DEA agent — that halted the eradication campaign and DEA participation in interdiction efforts in the valley. The emphasis on the need for a "secure" base of anti-drug operations, now being constructed near the Upper Huallaga town of Uchiza, and the specialized courses in jungle warfare being given by 12 Southern Command Green Berets to the anti-drug and anti-subversion police give the lie to the logic of stated U.S. policy.

The Peruvian government has declared the Upper Huallaga an emergency zone, making the army in its principal fight against subversion the commander of all forces. Gen. Juan Zarate, head of the anti-drug police, says, "The police continue to act normally against narcotrafficking and also do anti-subversive operations alone or jointly with the army."

THE ARMED forces' task of re-conquering the people from Sendero is daunting. Imagine the beauty of the tropical rainforest, mornings of lazy clouds in a slow-motion tumble down the green, dense hillside vegetation. And hear the farmers talk of the rich possibilities of agriculture in these high jungle valleys. Then, perhaps, you can appreciate their despair and finally their rejection of a government that has for years not only abandoned them, but actively made life more miserable.

Sendero is government here. It's *raison d'etre* is its mediation be-

 Reprinted from *The Sacramento Bee,* September 19, 1989, pp. 1, 6.

tween the narcos and the coca farmers, who have planted an estimated 250,000 acres in the Upper Huallaga alone. Sendero by all accounts brought order and justice out of chaos over the last two years, demanding that the narco-traffickers give fair prices and treatment to the cocaleros. Then digging in, it threatened or killed what few government agents were around (six mayors in six years in one tiny district alone) and began to offer protection from the police as well.

Sitting in his little stationery store in Tingo Maria, the owner, who asked not to be identified, said bitterly, "The police have done more to drive people to Sendero than anything else." At the airport in another town, the police — in front of two journalists — openly ripped off bills from a stack belonging to a local farmer. But a police spokesman in Lima showed no concern for such corrupt behavior. "What can you do?" asked the spokesman. It is the police, however, that are in direct charge of the drug fight. The army refused, saying it was not its job.

The new political-military commander in the emergency zone, army Gen. Alberto Arciniegas, vows he will keep police under wraps, that he'll act on reports of corruption. But a recent visitor to the region says the police outside the town of Tocache, the second largest town in the valley, still openly steal. Traditionally, the army has been welcomed in this zone (although not in others) because they have not indulged in the petty hassling habitual from the police.

In July the army went on a major offensive against Sendero, counting 100 rebels dead in just one weekend. Human rights abuses from artillery soldiers and disappearances have been reported, although Gen. Arciniegas maintains a dirty war would only run counter to his campaign to win back the people.

THE ARMY is trying to woo those very civilians who have to live under Sendero's justice system (the death penalty for adultery, stealing and informing) and who have to put up with *charlas* — late-night compulsory indoctrination talks and classes. Sendero's power is such that in one town it has told a school that it must hire only "approved" non-government teachers and teach only math, "revolutionary history," language and natural sciences.

Most sources who know the cocaleros well say they are tired of Sendero's rule but until recently have had no choice. An army intelligence officer, Capt. Jose Lariviere, says the army's intelligence is getting better as it uses more officers in civilian clothes to give people a chance to inform without being seen by Sendero.

The military's rationale is that you cannot win these hearts and minds and at the same time cut out from under them the first decent livelihood many of these people have had for generations. Although some diplomats close to the drug fight say most of the residents are in reality transients who will simply go back to the mountainous Sierra from whence they came, a recent internal AID study estimated that, of the 52,000 potential agricultural workers in the Upper Huallaga, only 30 percent are migrants. Except for the very few farmers without coca acreage, the entire population of some 183,000 in the valley profit from or depend in one way or another on coca.

But the military and non-military battle is uphill with scarce money or political will from the government in Lima to combat Sendero. An army captain with 13 years' experience complains about his $60 monthly salary in a valley awash in coca dollars, and

the military has put badly needed helicopters first on its wish list to Washington.

The Peruvian economy is one big crisis. While inflation has evened off at 25 percent a month, the government, according to recent leaks, is risking expulsion from the IMF for non-payment on a foreign debt of $2 billion. Basic economic structures don't work. In the latest of a series of government fiascos, tons of guano (bird-dung fertilizer) desperately needed for the next agricultural season have been sitting unsold on the docks at Callao for six months. Medical personnel have scandalized Lima in a three-month strike for better pay and more equipment, a shortage of kerosene has hundreds of desperate people lining up for the only fuel within their reach.

The military command, 350 miles away from Lima, is telling residents there's no extra money for development in the jungle. Gen. Arciniegas tells them, "If you want better roads, you have to pay taxes to your local government. If you want non-Sendero teachers, then you have to pay *and* protect them." With little or no resources available, one source familiar with the area says the customary protection money — ranging up to $15,000 a pop and normally paid by Colombian drug-smuggling pilots for landing privileges to the powers-that-be, be they police, army or Sendero — is now going to the local government in the army's show-case town of Uchiza to help pay for civic projects and for fresh foods for the army.

Pointing to the Upper Huallaga on a map of Peru, a high army officer said, "This area was another country. We're getting it back now. Whatever little they give me, I'll use. We have no choice."

Caught in the Crossfire

Whether you live in the wrong neighborhood, your skin's the wrong color or you wear the wrong clothes, you're an automatic suspect in the crack war.

Candy J. Cooper

Candy J. Cooper is an Examiner *staff writer.*

The grass grew wildly, the rose bushes jutted out around the modest Berkeley house a prostitute hoping to shake a charge had said was full of crack. But the two new women homeowners plotted not drug sales but petunia beds. A short surveillance *before* the cops broke in might have revealed the truth.

But no, there was just the informant. So the search went forward. Eight heavily armed Berkeley police officers surrounded the house in late July of 1987, smashed out all five back windows and broke out the front door, lock, jam and sill. They overturned mattresses, rifled drawers and scoured personal mementoes, including a carefully wrapped lock of an old friend's hair. They read personal letters and clientele lists and left with a mortgage payment book.

As the officers replaced their artillery, Sally Barrett drove up. She approached a front door held shut by a nail, pushed it open and stepped inside. She looked around at the glass on the floor and the rest of the upheaval. "You might as well have raped me," she said.

The truth was this: She and Lynn Robertson hate drugs; this was their first fixer-upper in a "transitional" neighborhood in South Berkeley; Robertson buys and sells not crack but houses for a living; and Barrett, a contractor, builds them. The truth was that the Berkeley police had made a terrible error in their war against crack, and the city paid the women $19,500.

Barrett and Robinson were mistaken for crack dealers, just like a young mother in Oakland and an accountant in Sacramento. Armed policemen broke into the Oakland house last October, chased a 29-year-old woman into the street, threw her to the ground and handcuf-

fed her with a gun pressed to her head while she pleaded "Don't kill me" and her 8-year-old son cried.

"It's an unfortunate mistake, and we apologize," an Oakland police captain said last October. In Sacramento, police apologized after busting into the wrong home in April and, in search of crack, pouring out a bag of cremated remains.

The wrong house, the wrong dealer, the wrong buyer and user. The odds of police stopping, searching, even stripping the wrong people in the intensified war against crack cocaine multiply with the disastrous epidemic. Police know it: "I think we need to make a greater effort to distinguish between the people who are involved in drugs and those who are not," said San Francisco police Capt. Jim Arnold. The people who live in drug neighborhoods, from the hills of Hunter's Point to the flatlands of the East Bay, know it.

Young black men know it best. Young black men comprise 82 percent of youth drug arrests in San Francisco, so it is young black men who are stopped for nothing. Take LaMerle Johnson. Seventeen, a summer intern at Channel 7, college-bound, Johnson was stopped by police in the Lakeview district on the way to the barber shop. They searched his jacket and pockets and tore out the soles of his shoes. The elderly neighbors watched this and shook their heads.

"I was really embarrassed," said Johnson, who once dealt crack but now organizes anti-crack rallies as a youth leader in the Omega Boys Club, an anti-drug, academic organization for urban youths. "The old people just looked at me and said, 'What a shame.'"

"I was really embarrassed. The old people just looked at me and said, 'What a shame.' " —LaMerle Johnson.

What is shameful, young black men say, is that if you have money in your pocket and dress in the clothing that is the trademark of drug dealers but also just the fashion — the sweatsuit, the pendant, the dark glasses, the earring — then you are a suspect.

You stand at a bus stop and a police officer aims a gun at your chest and searches your pockets, one young man says. In the past year, the year before he goes on to college, Jermaine King has felt like a suspect a dozen times, the number of times he estimates he's been stopped by police. One day on Potrero Hill they slapped 15-year-old DeWayne Williams across the mouth, threw his gold nugget earring in the grass and tripped him onto the ground, the boy said. His father and leaders of the Omega Boys Club went to the police to file a complaint.

"You can't even stand on the street here," said Phillip Brown, a 30-year-old cook who said he was never involved with police until he was stopped, handcuffed and made to sit on a sidewalk by Oakland police in January. "It's just like South Africa. If you don't have I.D., they take you to jail."

How many houses have been mistakenly entered with guns drawn, how many young men who are avowedly against drugs stopped, or searched, or arrested for crack? The Office of Citizen Complaints began in April to keep track of crack-related complaints after it seemed that their numbers had increased.

Though OCC police complaints dropped from last year, across the Bay, attorneys in John Burris' Oakland law office have interviewed some two dozen people who say police mistook them for crack dealers. Many are family members, friends or neighbors of people involved in drugs. They want the drug plague to end, but not at their expense.

"I have a strong sense that martial law has been declared," said Burris, "and my concern goes to those innocent people who are being victimized just because they're in the neighborhood."

Not all are young men. Ida Mae Hollins is a career postal worker and grandmother of 10 whose only brush with the law came when she once turned herself in for parking tickets. In April, Hollins set out on an errand of mercy in the Sunnydale housing project — to take her estranged husband to a nurse. When she stepped out of the car to ask a man if he had seen her son, he yelled "Narcs" and ran off.

A man in street clothes approached the 110-pound woman, searched her, cursed at her, hurled her to the ground and handcuffed her tiny wrists tightly behind her back, she said. Hollins was so startled she lost control of her bowels. "It's degrading, degrading, it's really degrading," said Hollins, who filed a complaint with the OCC.

Some of those who complain carry badges themselves. Oakland officer Derrick Norfleet made an undercover buy last July, only to have his white colleagues hit him with their car, according to his lawsuit filed in U. S. District Court. He flew over the hood and landed face down. The officers got out and punched and kicked Norfleet with their fists, feet and flashlight until he rolled over and they recognized him, the complaint said. City attorneys cannot comment on the case.

Two other black Oakland police officers may also have been assaulted by colleagues in the line of work. They fear that if they come forward, they might lose their jobs, their attorney says.

The injustice of the streets has become apparent to some in the courthouse. Deputy public defender Patricia Lee has collected 10 police reports at the Youth Guidance Center that she plans to turn over to the OCC because she believes they show a pattern of police arresting youths for crack they never possessed.

"I feel that what's happening is that when the police presence is known, kids are dropping the crack and running all over the place. Whoever's closest to the crack gets nailed," she said. It is easier for police to make an arrest stick when the word of a young black against that of a trained police officer is heard by a judge rather than a jury, a number of public defenders and defense attorneys said. Unlike adults, juveniles are not afforded the right of trial by jury.

But numbers show that while kids are being arrested more frequently for crack sales or possession, police are not necessarily winning in court. Youth arrests for crack-related crimes have multiplied by five between 1986 and last year. But nearly 40 percent of last year's arrests were not sustained, according to the Youth Guidance Center.

Civil rights abuses in the war on crack have surfaced around the country, most recently in southwest Los Angeles, where 38 police officers were disciplined in June for their involvement in an anti-gang raid last August. Residents of Dalton Avenue alleged that they were hit and kicked by officers and their apartment walls spray-painted with anti-gang slogans. Officers smashed out walls and TV sets with hammers, slashed furniture with knives, sledge-hammered toilets and sinks and destroyed a shed in what one attorney described as an "orgy of violence."

Some residents complained that on the way to the police station they were ordered to whistle the theme from the old "Andy Griffith" television show. Those who did not comply were allegedly punched and had steel flashlights dropped on their heads.

"The police department just suspended the Constitution in that area of town," said Los Angeles attorney Thomas E. Beck.

"If nothing's done, sooner or later those kids, they've got weapons, are going to start shooting at those officers."

Another four law enforcers at L.A. County's Central Jail faced discipline in June for taking part in burning two crosses outside the cells of gang members.

City officials have also stepped on civil liberties in their desperation to end crack's violence. In Washington, D.C., a U.S. district judge struck down a city council-ordered curfew in May, ruling that the right to walk the streets and meet with one's friends is integral to life in a free society. A curfew, he added, "casts these rights aside like so much straw."

Such overzealous solutions to the terrible drug plague were shot down at a national conference on crack and the black community held in April in San Francisco. Baltimore circuit court Judge David Mitchell asked a crowd of 1,200 people: "How do you separate me from a gang member? I'd like to know that I'm a free man. We can become so hysterical about what's going on, we can begin indicting whole races of people because we are concerned about an immediate problem."

There is another side to the story played out in the drab office buildings, the black and white patrol cars and the tinted, unmarked police vans where officers sit with binoculars surveilling drug buys. Sgt. Kit Crenshaw tells part of the story. The soundtrack to his job as an undercover San Francisco police officer is a song by Niggers with Attitudes, or NWA, called "F--- the Police." As he makes arrests of suspects in public housing, the muscular black officer hears that same song over and over, blasted at him at full volume.

Crenshaw grew up in Hunter's Point. When he was a kid, he parked his bike outside his house and found it there in the morning. Then he became a cop, and watched baseball bats and fist fights turn into assault rifles, drive-by shootings and gang wars. Crack changed everything. Now dealers have placed contracts on the lives of Crenshaw, his colleagues and his family. And his work, like all police work, has gotten tougher. The narcotics task force has doubled. The numbers of search warrants, drug buys and surveillances have all jumped. There is less time for service, almost no time to solve lesser crimes like car burglaries, and all work sharpens and points to crack. "We can't afford anymore to have the cop walking the street, patting kids on the head," said a veteran captain.

Police, on the contrary, are instructed to be "pro-active," meaning that they "create the action," instead of waiting for the crime to occur, said Crenshaw.

So police work grows more complicated. Surveillance is trickier because there are so many look-outs, and crack makes everything more unpredictable. "You set up in an empty unit in the projects (to watch an apartment across the street) and the next thing you know you've got a basehead wanting to cook up next door," said Lt. Billye Morrow.

Department supplies are dwindling. Unmarked cars fall apart or become intentionally "marked" by dealers. There are no more cars, so suddenly four narcotics officers are riding in one car, half as effective. Buy money evaporates, as dopers literally chew up the limited cash officers have available for buys. Morrow saw a man eat $1,000 once. "If they eat it," he said, "the evidence is gone."

Court cases don't stick, so police bust the same dealer four times before he goes to prison. They blame the district attorney's office when their work unravels in the courthouse, and much of it does. San Francisco leads the state in so-called "bad" arrests, where arrested persons are never prosecuted for lack of evidence.

And then there is the violence. Crenshaw is alone making an undercover buy and his foes have combat weapons. Some people want him dead. Neighborhoods are powderkegs. A patrol officer answers a call on a marital dispute and a crowd of 100 gathers. The streetlights are shot out, so they form squads to disperse the crowd in the dark. "You've got people at 4 a.m. with resting pulses of 160," said one Berkeley lieutenant. "They're literally on fire inside. They're so jacked, so prone to violence, so uninclined to be rational."

The pressure mounts. It comes from concerned parents. Just this year, the City's drug task force has received 900 complaints and calls for help from residents citywide. They want dealers off their front yards, out of their school yards. They want to protect the value of their homes.

The pressure comes from the rising national hysteria about the crack epidemic — likened in dimension to the Vietnam War. President Bush and Mayor Agnos contemplate bringing in the National Guard.

Is it surprising that if five officers conduct 110 searches in the course of one year they should one day raid the wrong house on a South Berkeley street on the word of an unreliable informant? "Nobody does a search warrant in the wrong place because they want to," said the Berkeley lieutenant.

In San Francisco, narcotics officers swoop into an area and people scatter — the guilty and the innocent. Maybe the innocent should have been at a playground, and parents should note who the crooks are and on which doorsteps they do business, officers say. If they allow their kids on those doorsteps, they should take what comes when there are arrests in response to complaints. If young black men dress in a certain manner, they too must be prepared to take what comes.

"I'm 42, make $60,000 a year and have $14 in my pocket," said Sgt. Rene LaPrevotte. "I see some kid playing hookie from school who has $600 in cash telling me it's for his auntie's phone bill? The public defender takes umbrage. 'Why should they have to justify where they get their money?' But if they're dressed like a

"If they're dressed like a drug dealer, if there are hand-to-hand exchanges, a reasonable and prudent person would assume they're a drug dealer." —Sgt. Rene LaPrevotte

prototype drug dealer, if there are hand-to-hand exchanges, a reasonable and prudent person would assume that they're a drug dealer."

On a Tuesday in May at the Sunnydale housing project, young men and women wander in to a weekly neighborhood meeting that is interrupted by shotgun fire and the sounds of a car skidding away. The frightened people at the meeting take their positions along the front wall, away from the windows.

A police community relations officer arrives and wants to know who the shooters are. But the young men in attendance, angry that no patrol car is in sight, refuse to help because they say police do not protect but harass them. The meeting breaks up early.

At other San Francisco meetings, a Hunter's Point anti-crime group has asked the police department to instruct them on how to file complaints against officers, and a Sunnydale group of concerned parents has suggested that youths keep track of badge numbers and patrol cars. The Rev. Aurelius Walker, of the True Hope Church of God In Christ in Hunter's Point, worries aloud at community meetings that "If nothing's done, sooner or later those kids, they've got weapons, they're going to start shooting at those police officers."

So police have begun a measured response. Police Chief Frank Jordan, in an effort to improve relations, has made some 70 undercover police officers get back in uniform and walk a beat. "That's the old-fashioned way of policing," said Gayle Orr-Smith, deputy mayor for public safety. "That way an officer can better determine who the bad guys and the good guys are."

Jordan said that so far citizens like the switch, because they feel safer walking to the playground, store or laundry. Some have begun to help officers solve crimes, he said.

Still, for many, the damage is irrevocable. People like Ida Hollins, stopped in Sunnydale in April, have decided simply to stay off the street, even in broad daylight.

"I feel hurt," said Hollins, who shows bruises on her hips, elbow and wrist. "There's no such thing as a good citizen anymore. I don't break any laws, I don't rob, I don't steal, but I feel as if my rights have been violated. I feel I don't have any rights. If I can't walk down the street and talk to anybody, what rights do I have?"

Drug frenzy: Why the war on drugs misses the real target

BARBARA EHRENREICH
MS.

Americans can't kick their addiction to reading about drugs. And publications of all sorts keep us supplied with a steady dose of details on the subject. So why another article? Because Ms. *columnist Barbara Ehrenreich talks about drugs with a wry wisdom. She not only pokes fun at the excesses of our current drug frenzy, she also probes for the deeper reasons so many people are attracted to addictive substances—not only cocaine, but booze and cigarettes and credit cards. And Kalamu ya Salaam, writing in a magazine published for New Orleans' black community, reminds us that America underwent a similar drug frenzy at the turn of the century.*

If there is anything more mind-altering—more destructive to reason and common sense—than drugs, it must be drug frenzy. Early signs include memory loss, an inability to process simple facts, and a belligerent narrowing of the eyes. Almost everyone is susceptible: liberals and conservatives, presidential candidates and PTA moms, the up-and-coming and the down-and-out. In fact, even *drug users*—a category that, scientifically speaking, embraces wine-sippers and chocolate addicts—are not immune.

Drug frenzy is not, as many people like to think, just a quick and harmless high. It is an obsession, overshadowing all other concerns, and capable of leaving a society drained, impotent, and brain-damaged. It easily overwhelms poverty, homelessness, and the federal debt as an issue.

There seems to be no stopping drug frenzy once it takes hold of a nation. What starts with an innocuous "Hugs, Not Drugs" bumper sticker soon leads to wild talk of shooting dealers and making urine tests a condition of employment—anywhere. There's talk of issuing "drug-war bonds," and worse talk about incarcerating drug offenders in "prison tents" to be set up in the Nevada desert. In drug frenzy, as in drug addiction, the threshold necessary for satisfaction just keeps rising.

Now I have as much reason to worry about drugs as anyone. I am the mother of teenagers. I am also, it pains me to admit in print, the daughter of drug abusers. Drugs disrupted my childhood home, eventually rendering it, as the social workers like to say, "dysfunctional." But the drugs that worry me most, the drugs that menaced my own childhood, are not those that our current drug warriors are going after. Because the most dangerous drugs in America are *legal* drugs.

Consider the facts: Tobacco, which the Surgeon General recently categorized as an addictive drug, kills over 300,000 people a year. Alcohol, which is advertised on television and sold in supermarkets, is responsible for nearly 100,000 deaths annually, including those caused by drunk drivers. But the use of all illegal drugs combined—cocaine, heroin, marijuana, angel dust, LSD, etc.—accounted for only 3,403 deaths in 1987. That's 3,403 deaths too many, but it's less than 1 percent of the death toll from the perfectly legal, socially respectable drugs that Americans—including drug warriors—indulge in every day.

Alcohol is the drug that undid my parents. When my own children reached the age of exploration, I said all the usual things—like "no." I further told them that reality, if carefully attended to, is more exotic than its chemically induced variations. But I also said that, if they still felt that they had to get involved with a drug, I'd rather it was pot than Bud.

If that sounds like strange advice, consider this: Unlike alcohol, cocaine, and heroin, marijuana is not addictive. Twenty million Americans—from hard hats to hippies—use it regularly. In considering whether to legalize it for medicinal purposes, a federal appeals court judge found that "marijuana, in its natural form, is one of the safest therapeutically active substances known to man." And unlike alcohol, a frequent factor in crimes such as child abuse, marijuana does not predispose its users to violence.

Not that marijuana is harmless. Although marijuana is not chemically addictive, some people do become sufficiently dependent on it to seek help. According to the National Institute of Drug Abuse,

From *Utne Reader*, March/April 1988, pp. 76-81. Excerpted from *Ms*, November 1988. Reprinted by permission.

however, there are no deaths that can be unequivocally attributed to marijuana use. Nor is there any

The biggest pusher of all is consumer culture.

clear evidence that marijuana "leads to" harder drugs, unless you count alcohol and the occasional truly dire drugs, such as PCP, that have been known to contaminate marijuana bought from street dealers. Taken alone and in moderation, it is still the safest high on the market.

But one of the first symptoms of drug frenzy is an inability to make useful distinctions of any kind. The drug that set off the "war," the drug that is enslaving ghetto youth and enlisting them into gun-slinging gangs, is cocaine, specifically crack. But who remembers crack? We're after "drugs"! In an alarming example of drug-frenzied thinking, a recent *Time* magazine drug cover story lumped cocaine, heroin, and marijuana together as the evil drugs in question.

Nineteen years ago, before drug-frenzy-induced brain damage set in, *Time* was still able to make distinctions, as this quote from the January 5, 1970, issue shows: ". . . the widespread use of marijuana, sometimes by their own children, is leading many Middle Americans toward a bit more sophistication, an ability to distinguish between the use of pot and harder drugs."

So what turned all these sober Middle Americans into drug-frenzied hawks? Historians point out that Americans have long been prone to episodes of "moral panic." One year it's communism; the next it's missing children—or terrorism, or AIDS, or cyanide-laced cold pills.

Usually, the targeted issue conceals a deeper anxiety. For example, as historian Barbara Epstein has argued, the late 19th and early 20th century temperance crusade—which was every bit as maniacal as today's war on drugs—was only incidentally about alcohol. The real issue was women's extreme vulnerability within the "traditional marriage." Husbands leave, husbands get violent, husbands drink. But you couldn't very well run a mass crusade to abolish *husbands* or—in the 19th century—to renegotiate the entire institution of marriage. The demon rum

Drug frenzy is nothing new in the U.S.

In any discussion of drugs (both legal and illegal) in America, two points must be kept in mind. One, there is a racial or ethnic factor in the drug problem. Two, America is a drug culture.

Morphine was the first major narcotic widely used in the United States. Its popularity escalated after the Civil War. Some analysts attributed the increase to the widespread use of morphine as a medication for the wounded in the war, but as David Musto, author of *The American Disease: Origins of Narcotic Control,* points out, "This line of reasoning does not explain the relatively few addicts proportionally or absolutely in such nations as France, Germany, Great Britain, Russia, and Italy, which also fought wars during the latter half of the 19th century and also used morphine as an analgesic. By the turn of the century, America had an estimated 250,000 addicts.

"In the United States, the exhilarating properties of cocaine made it a favorite ingredient of medicine, soda pop, wines, and so on," Musto adds.

"The Parke Davis Company, an exceptionally enthusiastic producer of cocaine, even sold coca-leaf cigarettes and coca cheroots to accompany their other products, which provided cocaine in a variety of media and routes such as a liqueur-like alcohol mixture called Coca Cordial, tablets, hypodermic injections, ointments, and sprays."

Need we point out that today Parke Davis is one of the most respected pharmaceutical companies? But while the entire American nation was con-

suming narcotics, the thrust of the anti-narcotic legislation at that time was built around the "opium smoking Chinese" immigrant population and "cocaine-crazed Negroes."

"Projection of blame on foreign nations for domestic evils harmonized with the ascription of drug use to ethnic minorities," Musto notes. "Both the external cause and the internal focus could be dismissed as un-American. This kind of analysis avoids the painful and awkward realization that the use of dangerous drugs may be an integral part of American society."

The first major campaign of narcotic suppression in America began at the turn of the century. Whipped into a purification frenzy by demagogic politicians, within the space of two decades America tried to go from a wide-open libertine nation to a dry, drug-free land.

It didn't work. Although drug use was curtailed, it was not eliminated and prohibition was eventually overturned. The by-product of this period of purity was the development of organized crime and its enrichment via the illegal trade in narcotics and alcohol.

—Kalamu ya Salaam
The New Orleans Tribune

Excerpted with permission from The New Orleans Tribune *(Sept. 1988). Subscriptions: $6/yr. (12 issues) from The New Orleans Tribune, 2335 Esplanade Av., New Orleans, LA 70119. Back issues: $1 from same address.*

Should drugs be legalized?

NO

A growing number of political and cultural figures in this country, conservatives as well as liberals, seriously advocate legalization of drugs. They claim that enormous criminal excesses of various kinds will thereby be eliminated. I recently heard one law professor say, "Overnight [with legalization] we'll be rid of drug wars, and the crime rate will drop significantly, because people won't have to steal to maintain their habit."

Meanwhile, in the ghetto where I work, not to mention in every other kind of neighborhood across the nation, parents struggle on behalf of their children. Matters debated publicly by big-shot experts or politicians are also considered by ordinary parents. In a Boston ghetto these words were recently uttered by a 35-year-old mother of four children:

"The other day on the news a man who's a professor said they should make drugs legal. He kept talking about 'the drug epidemic' and the 'teenage pregnancy epidemic,' and he had the answers—make the drugs legal, and give the kids contraception and abortions. I sat and wished he was right here in my living room, so I could talk with him. I'd ask him if he had any kids. I'd ask him if he'd want us to make the drugs legal for *his* kids. He's writing all of us off—

we're below him. He doesn't give a damn about us—so long as we stay out of his way. Give them drugs and condoms and abortions and some welfare money! Just stay out of my way!"

She had much more to say, but her remarks amounted to a pointed analysis of the way class and race affect our judgment as we contemplate certain important social and moral problems. For our own sons and daughters we want a decent, sturdy, solid life of no drug abuse. For others "below" us, quite another point of view applies: Stop their stealing or violence by making drugs legally available.

What children of *all* classes and races need is a social order that responds to and clearly evokes a firm moral tradition. Children need to know what is right, decent, and responsible—and also what is wrong, harmful to themselves and others, and not to be encouraged or allowed. Serious problems are not solved by repeated acts of moral surrender. The mother quoted above is crying for a world that helps her struggle against a range of troubles.

—Robert Coles
New Oxford Review

Excerpted with permission from New Oxford Review *(Sept. 1988). Copyright © 1988 New Oxford Review. Subscriptions: $19/yr. (10 issues) from New Oxford Review, 1069 Kains Av., Berkeley, CA 94706. Back issues: $3.50 from same address.*

YES

When we reinstated alcohol after prohibition, we knew that it was a dangerous drug, but realized that the dangers of legal use were outweighed by the penalties of prohibition: crime and violence, corruption, poisoning from bathtub gin, the immoderation that goes with surreptitious indulgence. But at that time we failed to attach a suitable program of education and warnings about alcohol's dangers. We are now catching up and sending the right messages about alcohol and tobacco—with impressive results.

We can make a better start with any other drugs we allow into the legal market, through a conscientious system of consumer information and warning labels. We could ban *all* advertising of recreational drugs, including alcohol and tobacco. We could also institute severe laws against the sale to kids of all recreational drugs, including tobacco. In these ways, legalization can be coupled with serious efforts to cut down usage, paradoxical as that may seem on the surface.

In addition, by eliminating the illicit market,

legalization would silence a terribly destructive and seductive message that's now getting through to inner-city kids: that drugs spell wealth and power. In the ghetto, they're now seen as the most (and sometimes the only) visible means of upward mobility.

Opponents of legalization say such a measure is elitist and racist; it would consign the underclass to a perpetual hell of addiction in order to be free of the threat of crime. But the inner cities are already awash in crack and other drugs, and all the violence and waste that goes along with high prices for drugs. Inexpensive crack is not the solution in itself. But by freeing our attention and resources from futile enforcement, we can begin to attack the immense and complex problems of education, unemployment, family structure, and internalized racism that nurture a growing and entrenched underclass.

—Eric Scigliano
Seattle Weekly

Excerpted with permission from Seattle Weekly *(Oct. 26, 1988). Subscriptions: $33/yr. (52 issues) from Seattle Weekly, 1931 2nd Av., Seattle, WA 98101.*

> No street-corner crack dealer ever had a better line than the one Madison Avenue delivers at every commercial break: Buy now! Quick thrills!

became what the psychohistorians call a "condensed symbol" of male irresponsibility and female vulnerability—focusing the sense of outrage that might otherwise have gone into the search for feminist alternatives.

Drugs also play a powerful symbolic role in our culture. Generically speaking, we imagine drugs as a kind of pact with the devil: What you get is ecstasy or something pretty similar. But the price you pay is eternal thralldom, dependency, loss of self. Only a few drugs—"hard" ones—actually fit these imaginings. But in mundane, drugless, ordinary life, we're offered a deal like this every other minute: buy this—sports car, condo, cologne, or whatever—and you'll be happy, suave, sexy . . . forever!

We are talking about the biggest pusher of all—the thoroughly legal and entirely capitalist consumer culture. No street-corner crack dealer ever had a better line than the one Madison Avenue delivers at every commercial break: Buy now! Quick thrills! You deserve it! And, of course, we love it—all those *things,* all those *promises!* If we could only have a little *more!* But, deep down, we also mortally resent it, this incessant, hard-sell seduction. The sports car does not bring fulfillment; the cologne does not bring love. And still the payments are due.

Drug frenzy, we might as well acknowledge, is displaced rage at the consumer culture to which we are all so eagerly addicted. Consider this recent statement in *Time* magazine by Harvard psychiatrist Robert Coles, who is otherwise a pretty thoughtful guy. We can't legalize drugs, he said (including, presumably, marijuana), because to do so would constitute a "moral surrender," sending what *Time* called "a message of unrestricted hedonism." What a quaint concern! We are already getting "a message of unrestricted hedonism" every time we turn on the TV, glance at a billboard, or cruise a mall. But we can't

very well challenge *that* message or *its* sender, even as mounting personal and social debt lends the message a mean and mocking undertone.

So we feed our legal addictions and vent our helplessness in a fury at drugs. We buy our next chance at "ecstasy" on credit and despise those poor depraved fools who steal for heroin or kill for crack.

> If my teenagers had to get involved with a drug, I'd rather it was pot than Bud.

The word for this is "projection," and it's the oldest, most comforting form of self-delusion going.

The only hopeful sign I can see is the emerging debate on drug legalization. The advocates of legalization, who include such straitlaced types as the New York County Lawyers' Association's Committee on Law Reform, argue that drug *prohibition* has become far more dangerous than drug abuse. Prohibition causes about 7,000 deaths a year (through drug-related crime, AIDS, and poisoned drugs) and an $80 billion-a-year economic loss. And prohibition drives up the price of drugs, making dealing an attractive career for the unemployed as well as the criminally inclined.

There are problems with wholesale legalization. Crack, for example, is so highly addictive and debilitating that it probably shouldn't be available. But I agree with the *New York Times* that we consider legalizing marijuana. We could then tax the estimated $50 billion spent annually on it and use the revenue to treat people who want to get off the hard drugs, including alcohol and tobacco.

But we're not even going to be able to have a sane debate about legalization until we come down off the drug frenzy. The only cure is a sturdy dose of truth, honesty, and self-knowledge—and those things do not, ancient countercultural lore to the contrary, come from drugs. Since there's no drug for drug frenzy, we're all just going to have to sit down, cold sober, to face the hard questions: Who's hurting, what's hurting them, and what, in all kindness and decency, can we do about it?

Drugs and the Dream Deferred

John D. Kasarda, Terry Williams

Director of the Center for Competitiveness and Employment Growth at the University of North Carolina, John Kasarda has perhaps the best grasp of any analyst in the country on the profound changes taken place in urban America.

His last article for NPQ, entitled "A Tale of Dual Cities" appeared in the winter 1987 issue.

Opportunity Foreclosure Zones

Drug-related violence in the American inner city – violence that has sparked the call for a drug war from Washington – is inextricably linked to the increasing isolation of the underclass, or "new immobiles," from the dynamism of the service and information sectors that dominate today's urban employment opportunities. With no prospect of upward mobility in the mainstream economy, unskilled and uneducated black youth have sought access to a surrogate economy in which there is mobility – the illicit and exploding underground drug economy. The rise of drug use, violence and crime clearly coincides with the growing disassociation of these communities from the mainstream.

The "underclass" is not synonymous with the persistently poor population of America, which in 1985 numbered approximately eight million. The "underclass" resides in segregated, deprived neighborhoods where social problems such as joblessness, out-of-wedlock births, welfare dependency, school dropout and illicit activities – especially drug use and trafficking – are so highly concentrated that there is a mutually reinforcing "contagion effect" of behavioral characteristics that conflict with mainstream values.

By waging the opening battle of the drug war in Washington, DC, Drug Czar William Bennett has placed the focus on the poor and the so-called "underclass."

Is the poor inner city the zone where the drug problem becomes a drug disaster? We turned to two of the most original thinkers about urban life in America today – sociologist John Kasarda and ethnographer Terry Williams – to address this question.

The best estimate of the size of this underclass was provided in a 1988 study by Erol Ricketts and Isabel Sawhill. Looking at 1980 Census tracts of neighborhoods where people simultaneously exhibited disproportionately high rates of school dropout, joblessness, female-headed families and welfare dependency, they concluded that about 2.5 million people could be defined as "underclass," disproportionately located in the major industrial cities of the Northeast and Midwest. In breaking down the data, the researchers delineated the makeup, on average, of the underclass neighborhood: 63 percent of the adults had less than a high school education; 60 percent of the households were headed by women; 56 percent of the adult men were not regularly employed; and 34 percent of the households were receiving public assistance. Further, their research revealed that although the total poverty population grew only eight percent between 1970 and 1980, the number of people falling within the poverty population but also living in the underclass areas grew by 230 percent, from 752,000 to 2,484,000.

It is clear from this data that urban poverty and underclass populations grew dramatically in large northern cities, despite targeted infusions of public assistance, affirmative action, and civil rights legislation. These populations have also persisted in the face of national and urban economic recovery.

Neither liberal nor conservative prescriptives have worked, I propose, because both were overwhelmed by fundamental changes in the structure of the economies of these cities – changes that affected the employment prospects of the

By John D. Kasarda and Terry Williams. From *New Perspectives Quarterly*, Summer 1989, pp. 16-21. Reprinted by permission.

urban, disadvantaged black population.

Modern advances in transportation, communications and industrial technologies, interacting with the changing structure of national and global economic organization, have transformed major northern cities from centers of goods production and distribution to centers of information exchange and higher-order service provision. In the process, many blue-collar industries that once constituted the urban economic backbone and provided entry-level employment opportunities for lesser educated residents either vanished or relocated elsewhere. These blue-collar industries have been replaced, in part, by knowledge-intensive, white-collar industries. Because employment in the white-collar industries often requires some education beyond high school, they are inaccessible to most disadvantaged blacks, even though expanding white-collar jobs are relatively close to the core ghettos.

Aggravating blue-collar employment declines in the cities' traditional goods-producing industries has been the urban exodus of white, middle-income residents and the neighborhood businesses that once served them. This exodus further diminished blue-collar service positions such as domestic workers, gas station attendants, and local delivery personnel. Concurrently, many secondary commercial areas of these cities withered because lower income levels of the minority residential groups that replaced the suburbanizing whites were unable to economically sustain them.

Black Flight | Economic distress created by urban industrial transformation and white-flight tells only part of the story, however. With important civil rights gains during the 1960s and '70s, selective "black flight" from the ghettos accelerated, resulting in a socioeconomic and spatial bifurcation of urban black communities.

According to 1980 Census data, Chicago's North Lawndale community, for example, lost half its black population during the decade between 1970 and 1980; the South Bronx lost 37 percent; nearly 100,000 black Chicagoans moved to the suburbs; and more than 50,000 blacks in Washington, DC moved from the city to the suburbs. Most of those who moved were among the economically stable who could afford to do so.

Prior to the 1960s, black communities in the

With important civil rights gains during the 1960s and '70s, selective "black flight" from the ghettos accelerated, resulting in a socioeconomic and spatial bifurcation of urban black communities.

inner city were far more heterogeneous in socioeconomic mix and family structure because *de facto* and *de jure* segregation bound together blacks of all income levels. The presence of working and middle-income blacks within or nearby the ghettos sustained essential local institutions such as neighborhood clubs, churches, schools, and organized recreational activities for youth. Working-class and middle-income black residents also provided mainstream role models for youth, greater familial stability and sanctions against deviant behavior.

Yet, as William Julius Wilson has argued, it was precisely these more economically stable blacks who disproportionately benefited from civil rights gains like affirmative action and open housing: Since artificial barriers to job access were removed, their exodus from ghetto neighborhoods was expedited. Left behind in increasingly isolated concentrations were the most disadvantaged with the least to offer in terms of marketable skills, role models, and economic and familial stability. Under such conditions, ghetto problems became magnified.

Capital Flight | With the flight of working- and middle-class blacks from the ghettos, not only were mainstream role models and neighborhood leadership resources lost, but it also became extremely difficult for most small, black-owned stores and shops that served ghetto residents to survive. It was often these smaller, neighborhood establishments that provided ghetto youth with their initial job experience and, in so doing, also offered locally visible models of employed teenagers. When these establishments closed, both important functions were lost.

Additionally, prior to the 1960s, racial segregation in business and shopping patterns resulted in black earnings being expended primarily in black-owned establishments. Money earned by blacks who worked in white-owned businesses was much more likely to be funnelled to a black-owned neighborhood establishment or local black professional than was the case in the 1970s and '80s. In effect, what occurred was both a decline in aggregate black community income and a decline in the number of blacks who could be employed in the neighborhood.

Finally, affirmative action programs were far more effective in the public sector than the private sector. Between 1970 and 1980, upper-echelon white-collar employment gains by blacks were highly concentrated in the public sector, whereas such gains by non-Hispanic whites were almost exclusively in the private sector. By the mid-seventies, administrative growth in the public sector had already begun to slow, especially in the major cities, and it further slowed during the Reagan years.

At the same time, a burst of entrepreneurship and private-sector self-employment commenced that bypassed blacks. In fact, black self-employment, in contrast to most other racial and ethnic groups, actually declined. It seems plausible that the differential success in affirmative action in the public sector disproportionately attracted better-educated, more talented blacks from private sector pursuits where most upper-income growth opportunities emerged in the past 15 years. Entering the more secure public sector, I propose, also reduces the prospects of these persons starting their own businesses and thus economically bolstering the black community.

The Economic Importance of Kinship | If spatial confinement and poor education are such handicaps to gainful employment in industrially transforming cities, why is it that America's new urban immigrant groups, especially Asians, have had high rates of success in carving out employment niches and climbing the socioeconomic ladder? Like blacks, many Asian immigrants arrived with limited education and financial resources and are spatially concentrated in the inner city. Research into this question reveals the critical importance of *ethnic solidarity* and *kinship networks* in fostering social mobility in segregated enclaves through self-employment.

Unlike most urban blacks, many Asian immigrants and certain Hispanic groups have been able to utilize ethnic-based methods to assemble capital, establish internal markets, circumvent discrimination and generate employment in their enclaves that are relatively insulated from both swings in the national economy and urban industrial transformation. Ethnic businesses are typically family-owned and operated, often drawing upon unpaid family labor to staff functions during start-up periods of scarce resources. They are also dependent upon ethnic contacts to obtain credit, advice and patronage. These businesses are characterized by thriftiness and long

Unlike most urban blacks, many Asian immigrants and certain Hispanic groups have been able to utilize ethnic-based methods to assemble capital, establish internal markets, circumvent discrimination and generate employment in their communities.

hours of intense, hard work with continuous reinvestment of profits.

As they expand, ethnic-enclave enterprises display strong hiring preferences for their own members, many of whom would likely face employment discrimination by outside firms. They also do business with "their own." In San Francisco, for example, a dollar turns over five or six times in the Chinese business community, while in most black communities dollars leave before they turn over even once.

Kinship and household structures of ethnic immigrants have significantly facilitated their entrepreneurial successes. Among recently arrived Asian immigrants, for instance, "other relatives" – those beyond the immediate family – constitute a substantial portion of households: 55 percent among Filipinos and Vietnamese, 49 percent among Koreans, 46 percent among the Chinese, and 41 percent among Asian Indians. In addition to serving as a valuable source of family business labor, these extended-kin members enable immigrant households to function more efficiently as economic units by sharing fixed household costs such as rents or mortgages, furnishing child-care services, and providing economic security against loss of employment by other household members. In short, by capitalizing on ethnic and family solidarity, many new immigrant businesses – ranging from laundries to restaurants to green groceries – have started and flourished in once downtrodden urban neighborhoods, providing employment and mobility options to group members in an otherwise unfavorable economic environment.

In contrast, non-immigrant urban blacks have been burdened by conditions that have impeded their entry and success in enclave employment, including lack of self-help business associations, limited economic solidarity, and family fragmentation. A 1986 survey by *Black Enterprise* magazine, for example, reported that 70 percent of self-employed blacks consider lack of community support as one of their most formidable problems. This, together with the documented flight of black-earned income to non-black establishments, led the black TV journalist Tony Brown to comment: "The Chinese are helping the Chinese, the Koreans help the Koreans, Cubans help Cubans, but blacks are helping everyone else. We have been conducting the most successful business boycott in American history – against ourselves." Apparently, racial political unity that has led to significant black electoral successes in major northern cities during the past two decades has not carried over to the economic sphere.

Given the importance of family cohesiveness and kinship networks in pooling resources to start businesses, providing day-care assistance, and contributing labor to family businesses, the black underclass is at a distinct disadvantage. As William Julius Wilson has noted, approximately two-thirds of black families living in Chicago's ghettos are mother-only households. These households are the poorest segment of our society, with female householders earning only one-third as much as married male householders.

Self-Employed Depression | All the factors previously mentioned have converged to depress black self-employment rates during the past two decades, especially in the inner city. According to 1980 Census data on the percent of the self-employed among all employed males in major cities with less than high school educations, blacks are consistently under-represented in self-employment, particularly when compared to less-educated Asians. In Washington, DC, for example, 16 percent of non-Hispanic whites are self-employed and 18 percent of Asians are self-employed, compared to 3.2 percent of blacks. In St. Louis, non-Hispanic white self-employment is also approximately 16 percent, Asian self-employment approximately 25 percent and black self-employment approximately two percent.

Among more recent Asian immigrants, self-employment rates are even higher. Korean immigrant self-employment rates range from a low of 19 percent in Chicago to a high of 35 percent in New York.

Just as striking are Asian-black contrasts from the most recent Census survey of minority-owned businesses. Between 1977 and 1982, the number of Asian-American-owned firms with paid employment expanded by 160 percent. During the same period, the number of black-owned firms with employees actually declined by 3 percent. With small business formation becoming the backbone of job creation in America's new economy, blacks are falling further behind in this critical arena.

No Exit | Financial weakness and family frag-

> The racial political unity that has led to significant black electoral successes in major northern cities during the past two decades has not carried over to the economic sphere.

mentation among the black underclass not only preclude capital mobilization for self-employment, but also creates barriers to their children's social mobility. Living in a mother-only household increases the risk of a black youth dropping out of school by 70 percent. The link between female headship and welfare dependency in the urban underclass is also well established, leading to legitimate concerns about the inter-generational transfer of poverty.

At the root of this concern is the paucity of employment among welfare mothers and the question of how this unemployment affects the attitude of their children toward work. Of those receiving welfare benefits, 85 percent have no reported source of income other than public assistance. Furthermore, 65 percent of the recipients of Aid to Families with Dependent Children at any one point in time are in an interval of dependency that has lasted for at least eight years.

One doesn't require a deep sociological imagination to sense the attitudinal and behavioral consequences of growing up in an impoverished household where there is no activity associated with the world of work, and a household that, in turn, is located in a commercially abandoned community where pimps, drug pushers, and unemployed street people have replaced working fathers as the predominant socializing agents.

Rekindling Underclass Mobility | It is clear that strengthening the black family and reducing the exceptionally high percentage of impoverished mother-only households must be key foci of policies to rekindle social mobility among today's urban underclass. These policies should be complemented with programs that allow ghetto youths to be reared in household and neighborhood environments where adult work is the norm, and to attend public schools that will provide them with necessary skills and social networks for employment in a rapidly transforming economy. For example, low-income black youths who moved from inner-city Chicago to predominantly white suburbs as part of a subsidized housing experiment performed remarkably well, both academically and socially.

As cities have functionally changed from centers of goods processing to centers of information processing, there has also been a significant rise in the education level required for urban employment. If greater proportions of disadvantaged black youth do not acquire the formal education necessary for employment in the white-collar service industries beginning to dominate urban employment bases, their jobless rates will remain high. For this reason, and because demographic forces portend potential shortages of educationally qualified resident labor for the white-collar industries expanding in the cities, there have been appropriate calls from both the public and private sectors to upgrade city schools, reduce black youth drop-out rates, and increase the proportion who continue on for higher education.

Such policies, however, are unlikely to alleviate the unemployment problems currently facing large numbers of economically displaced older blacks and yet-to-be-placed younger ones with serious educational deficiencies – those caught in the web of urban change. Their unemployment will persist because the educational qualifications demanded by most of today's urban growth industries are difficult to impart through short-term, nontraditional programs. In the major northeastern cities, only 22 percent of black males between 16 and 64 had more than one year of education beyond high school and 43 percent had not completed high school. Yet, since 1970, for example, New York City alone lost more than a half million jobs where the jobholders typically had not completed high-school, while it added 322,000 jobs where the average jobholder education exceeded one year of college. At the same time, lower skilled jobs mushroomed in the suburbs.

Out and Up | Rebuilding urban blue-collar job bases, or providing sufficient education to large numbers of displaced black laborers so that they may be re-employed in expanding white-collar industries, seems implausible. Instead, I think we need to look at the traditional means by which Americans have adapted to economic displacement – that is, moving out in order to move up. Despite the mass loss of lower-skilled jobs in many cities during the past decade, there have been substantial increases in these jobs nationwide. For example, between 1975 and 1985, more than 2.1 million nonadministrative jobs were added in eating and drinking establishments, which is more than the total number of production jobs that existed in 1985 in

> In the major north-eastern cities, only 22 percent of black males between 16 and 64 had more than one year of education beyond high school and 43 percent had not completed high school.

America's automobile, primary metals, and textile industries combined. Unfortunately, essentially all of the net national growth in jobs with low educational requisites has occurred in the suburbs and nonmetropolitan areas, which are far removed from large urban concentrations of poorly educated minorities. Tragically, this economy has surpluses of unemployed lower-skilled labor in the inner cities at the same time that suburban businesses are facing serious shortages in lower-skilled labor.

The inability of disadvantaged urban blacks to follow decentralized, lower-skilled jobs has increasingly isolated them from the shifting loci of employment opportunity and has contributed to their high rates of joblessness and associated social problems.

Relocation and Cultural Regeneration | It is clear to me, after years of studying the seemingly intractable problems of the underclass, that only two types of solutions will be truly effective: relocation and cultural regeneration.

Relocation means helping people move out of the isolated enclaves of the underclass into areas where the mainstream economy functions. Cultural regeneration of the underclass areas calls for something beyond government and policy. Government can't weave integrity back into the community and restore the family and discipline to poor and socially deprived people. The moral authority for that task must come from within the community, from voluntary and religious organizations like the Protestant church or the Nation of Islam, with its very effective family training and anti-drug, anti-crime programs.

In the end, restoring cultural and familial solidarity to the black underclass is the primary transformation that will enable it to once again join the social mainstream. Migrating and relocating, in the tradition of past acts that linked social mobility to spatial mobility, are the primary avenues that will bring the underclass into the economic mainstream. With cultural regeneration and relocation advancing together, the root problems of the ghetto underclass will be ameliorated. Symptomatic problems such as teenage pregnancy, school drop-out, and crime will be substantially reduced in the process.

The drug-money hunt

Narcotics warriors target dealers' cash as well as their stash

The war on drugs is undergoing a subtle but far-reaching shift. America's many-faceted drug-enforcement attack is gradually broadening its focus from the traditional targets of narcotics shipments, traffickers and users to the increasingly critical element that keeps the whole illicit system moving: Money. Federal authorities now believe that damming the flow of drug money that passes through myriad laundering schemes can cripple a trafficking network just as effectively as arresting dealers and seizing narcotics. "The old school was bodies and kilos," says Drug Enforcement Administration agent Albert Latson. "But when you seize money, you're seizing the trafficker's end product, his profits."

Drug money is the invisible scourge of narcotics-ridden America. Tainted dollars course through the nation's banking arteries like a polluted stream, commingling bad cash with good and infecting many who touch it along the way. The physical connection between money and drugs is so pervasive that random lab tests show virtually every U.S. bill in circulation bears microscopic traces of cocaine. That amounts to 12 billion bills worth about $230 billion.

Stanching the flow of dirty dollars

The fight against laundering has just now risen to the top of the international agenda. At last month's summit in Paris, President Bush and other leaders of the Group of Seven industrial nations announced plans for multilateral efforts to stanch the flow of drug dollars through the global financial vascular system. A joint financial-action task force will convene next month in France to follow up the new United Nations Convention Against Illicit Traffic in Narcotic Drugs and Psychotropic Substances. The trea-

ty, now signed by 67 nations, calls for all countries to make money laundering a crime and adopt measures allowing for confiscation of drug-related assets. The need to ferret out dirty traces in the $615 billion daily exchange of wire transfers in and out of the U.S. is made especially urgent by Europe's race toward financial integration in 1992, which will allow both clean and tainted money to flow even more freely across all Common Market borders.

Gripped by the notion that money is the drug dealers' lifeblood, the Bush administration this month launched a series of antilaundering initiatives. Treasury Secretary Nicholas Brady urged drug czar William Bennett to form a "national money-laundering control center" as part of his new national drug strategy due to be unveiled September 5. The NMLCC would coordinate the complex, often arcane laundering investigations that now fall into the jurisdictions of dozens of federal, state and local agencies. Atty. Gen. Dick Thornburgh called for the formation of a Justice Department office of international affairs to handle the rising tide of overseas laundering cases, among other things. In Mexico, Secretary of State James Baker urged the Carlos Salinas government to make money laundering an extraditable offense.

Yet America's drug warriors know they are only beginning to nudge at the edges of the problem. Some law-enforcement experts estimate that all laundering prosecutions, though on the upswing, touch no more than 2 percent of the money being washed. For all the new international cooperation, the millennium is not quite at hand. Luxembourg, Liechtenstein, the Netherlands Antilles, the Cayman Islands, Panama and Uruguay remain relatively safe places for dirty money, federal officials argue. "It

only takes one or two countries agreeing to be renegades, and you have an opportunity to pollute the entire system," says a knowledgeable U.S. Senate staffer.

Still, some new crackdowns on laundering are already paying off. The 1986 Money Laundering Control Act for the first time made money laundering itself a crime, and last fall's omnibus drug law expanded the federal government's ability to go after laundering schemes. Assistant U.S. Attorney Wilmer Parker III reached a plea-bargain agreement in a precedent-setting case in Atlanta federal court, which calls for a foreign-owned bank to plead guilty this week to laundering drug money. With a $5 million penalty, it is the largest laundering conviction ever obtained by prosecutors against any bank and the first time that any foreign bank without any operations in the U.S. has been convicted. At the Panama branch of Colombia's Banco de Occidente, two officers were caught washing more than $10 million. Not only were the bank officers indicted, so was the bank.

The Crockett and Tubbs takedown

The scope and subtlety of the probe is a good example of how hard it is to make money-laundering cases and how complex laundering schemes can be. The players in this undercover game were John Featherly, a pudgy New York Irish DEA agent in the middle years, and his sidekick, César Díaz, a dapper young Cuban-born DEA agent who was raised in Miami. Posing respectively as Jimmy Brown, a sometime Mafia money mover, and Alex Carrera, a Hispanic hustler on the way up, the unlikely pair were the equivalent of "Miami Vice's" Crockett and Tubbs as they penetrated the cash trail of Colombia's notorious Medellín cartel. Díaz met with a top cartel launderer, Eduardo Martínez, in the very heart of the Banco de Occidente, where "they treated him like the president of the bank," reported Díaz. The undercover duo then lured Martínez to another meeting at a posh hotel on the Caribbean island of Aruba. They became friends over drinks and dinner in a $500-a-night suite while discussing laundering techniques. Martínez never knew he was being secretly videotaped.

Once the evidence became overwhelming, prosecutor Parker moved aggressively to secure a new level of cooperation by the governments of Canada, Switzerland and Germany and that led to the freezing of $82 million in Banco de Occidente's deposits—half the bank's total. Even though charges against the parent bank in Colombia were dropped, the freezing of funds had the salutary effect of forcing the bank into a plea bargain. Under a never-before-used portion of the 1986 law, the U.S. government hopes to share the $5 million penalty money with the cooperating foreign governments. This is a breakthough that is bound to get the attention of countries that until now have been ambivalent about helping zealous U.S. prosecutors.

The Banco de Occidente plea agreement also sends a dramatic new signal to banks at home and abroad that even the actions of a few corrupt employes can be a costly oversight. "The word is out that if you launder, the U.S. can prosecute. It has absolutely terrified every bank in South America. They're shook," says Jerome Froelich, Banco de Occidente's attorney.

The largest laundry ever

In size, the Atlanta case pales by comparison to the largest laundering ring ever uncovered in the U.S. The ring, called La Mina, which means "the mine" in Spanish, was smashed in February by a four-agency federal investigation called Operation Polar Cap that led to 127 indictments. La Mina is alleged to be a multicontinent scheme that authorities say sluiced $1 billion in dirty dollars in three years through a floodgate of U.S. and foreign banks, jewelry fronts, gold brokerages and international wire transfers (see graphic). The cash was finally wrung dry in the coffers of Colombia's notorious Medellín cartel, which narcotics experts estimate supplies 80 percent of the cocaine consumed in the U.S.

La Mina was based in Montevideo, Uruguay. But it employed a cosmopolitan bazaar of Armenians, Turks, Arabs, Syrians, Vietnamese and Latin Americans working mainly in the U.S. Two jewelry firms operated by Armenian immigrants in the Los Angeles diamond district were cornerstones of the scam, secretly counting and depositing hun-

La Mina: The $1 billion laundering "mine"

THE SCHEME. *La Mina was the largest laundering operation ever uncovered, washing more than $1 billion in three years through a ring of Los Angeles-based Armenian jewelers. This is the federal government's account of how all the money landed in the coffers of Colombia's notorious Medellín cartel.*

1. THE COURIERS. *The money trail began with cash deliveries by Colombian couriers to bogus jewelry fronts in Manhattan's diamond district. A federal agent watched from a stairwell.*

2. THE PACKAGER. *A launderer packed the hundreds of thousands of dollars in small cartons, swathed in duct tape and labeled as jewelry. Then, he telephoned an Armenian jewelry front in Los Angeles and announced his shipment in code ("kilos" meant $100,000 and "grams" meant $10,000). He did not bother with amounts less than $10,000.*

3. THE CARRIERS. *Armored-car couriers picked up the cash, thinking it was jewelry. They transferred it to a plane for overnight delivery to Los Angeles. One day, a box broke open in the back of an armored car, revealing thousands of dollars "packed like bricks." The armored-car company notified federal agents.*

4. THE COUNTERS. *In a secluded room in the Los Angeles diamond district, the cash was sorted and counted on a high-speed machine. It was then rebundled for delivery to several banks. Members of the laundering network frequently argued over money counts and late shipments. Counting such huge volumes of cash was so tedious that one launderer often laid his head down on layers of cash to take a nap. Federal investigators set up a video camera in the ceiling and made extensive tapes of the scene.*

5. THE MONEY. *The Armenian jeweler and his accomplices delivered satchels of money to several Los Angeles banks—the first stage of laundering. One bank became suspicious when one jeweler's account took in $25 million in cash in three months. Apparently, the jewelers thought their paper trail would be covered by trading gold with one another.*

6. THE TRANSFERS. *The day after each deposit, the launderers ordered the banks to wire-transfer hundreds of thousands of dollars by computer to gold brokerages and to banks in New York. This laundered the money again, because it changed banks and accounts. Some of the money was then transferred to a London commodities broker for gold purchases—another wash cycle. Finally, the funds were wire-transferred to drug-cartel bank accounts in Panama and Uruguay controlled by agents of the Colombian drug cartels.*

7. THE GLOBAL TRADES. *La Mina's grand plan called for ill-gotten cash to jump countries and continents in a series of computer flashes. Money transfers designed to get drug proceeds from the streets of America back to the drug-producing cartel were masked by shipments of bullion in a circular gold-trading scheme. At first, gold was shipped from a Uruguayan exchange house to a Florida gold refiner. It was then traded to the Los Angeles jewelers, who sold it back to the original Uruguayan company that had started the transaction. In effect, it was a closed system. The Uruguayan exchange house "lost money" on the trades because it bought back the gold at a price higher than it had sold the gold. But that did not matter, because the exchange house was raking in hundreds of millions in drug profits. After federal investigators tracked the scheme for some time, they noticed that the traders often made their transactions entirely on paper and did not even bother shipping the gold. But by then, agents had hundreds of hours of video and audio tapes.*

dreds of thousands of dollars in local banks every day for a 3 to 7 percent commission. La Mina's unique method, according to prosecutors, was to move huge sums of money through the legitimate banking system. That generated a detailed paper trail of federal currency transaction reports, which are required when more than $10,000 in cash is deposited. But the launderers attempted to legitimize this banking record by creating among themselves a corresponding set of intramural gold trades, sometimes real, sometimes bogus.

The image of "laundering" is apt for the process that turns drug money into something indistinguishable from other legitimate assets. Those who launder money pass illegally obtained funds through some mechanism so that it comes out looking clean, or legal. The money can be transformed into some other kind of asset, such as property, foreign currency, cashier's checks or even cash that has been mixed with untainted money and cannot be traced back to the scene of the crime. Washing cash is crucial to the drug kingpins because of the enormous sums generated by sales of narcotics, often estimated at more than $100 billion annually, almost as much as the revenues of General Motors, the world's largest corporation (1988 sales: $123 billion).

Laundering schemes function as an alternative underground banking system for the narcotics industry, moving money around the world the way regular banks do it for legitimate businesses. Colombian drug bosses need large and steady remittances to maintain production and distribution, just the way a foreign car manufacturer must repatriate its U.S. profits to keep building cars for the U.S. market. One accused trafficker, Juan Francisco Pérez-Piedrahita, told an informant that $400 million in drug cash once rotted in a California basement because Medellín-cartel boss Pablo Escobar could not export it quickly enough through a laundering operation. The tale is probably apocryphal, but authorities treated it as a vivid illustration of the dimensions of the traffickers' laundering needs—and their vulnerabilities.

Laundering has bred a new kind of white-collar criminal. The quick-bucks, clean-hands allure of the trade sometimes leads otherwise upstanding citizens to the shady side of the law. "The people we're focusing on now are respectable-type people who live in the suburbs, talented people with business savvy," says DEA financial specialist Doug Ross. Then Georgia Representative Pat Swindall was in 1988 secretly taped by undercover agents discussing a laundering scheme designed to finance an $850,000 cash mortgage on his $1.4 million home. He was convicted this summer of perjury. Former California state budget director Richard Silberman, now a San Diego businessman, was arrested in April while negotiating to launder $1.1 million in purported drug cash.

Wherever there is a drug problem, there is money laundering. In Washington, D.C., with one of the most violent drug cultures in America, three brothers operating a luxury-car dealership were charged last month with laundering drug funds through the old-fashioned technique of "smurfing"—breaking large cash deposits into chunks of less than $10,000 each to avoid filing a currency transaction report. Even without drugs, small-town America feels the effects of drug cash. In depressed Atoka, Okla. (pop. 3,409), free-spending Mexicans suddenly began showing up in the economically depressed area. Authorities then discovered that almost $10 million in Mexican drug money was being laundered through a score of banks and used for purchases of 5,000 acres of ranch land. In Roma, Tex., drug-enforcement officials contend that an influx of drug cash into the dust-blown border town has distorted its tiny economy and driven land prices way up.

The bank connection

Banks are the most frequently used vehicles for money laundering. The international financial system is a computer-driven labyrinth of instantaneous electronic transfers ideally suited for launderers. In 1988, the Clearing House Interbank Payments System (CHIPS), the unique U.S.-based wholesale-electronic-transfer network in and out of the U.S., processed 33.9 million international transfers with an aggregate value of $165 trillion—plenty of cover for an average laundering ring. Because their volume is so great, wire transfers are virtually impossible to saddle with the same federal reporting requirements that are applied to cash transactions.

Since a sensational 1985 case against the prestigious Bank of Boston for not filing currency transaction reports, most banks seem to be diligently complying with the law, say federal investigators. But some officials argue that banks should take more-aggressive steps to identify and report potential launderers, as the Wells Fargo Bank of Los Angeles did in the La Mina case when a clerk reported suspiciously high deposits. Banking experts argue that this is an improper role for a financial institution. "It puts an impossible burden on the banks, which don't have the expertise to make that judgment," says John Villa, a Washington attorney who is an expert on banking crime.

American drug warriors note that every time they uncover a new laundering method, their foes seem already to have mastered another, harder-to-penetrate way to exploit the global banking system. "Every day, they find a new technique," says David Binney, chief of the FBI's drug section. "They're limitless in the ways they can expatriate that money. Trying to stay abreast of that—not ahead, just abreast—is a difficult task for law enforcement." Yet authorities insist they will press into this new area with more vigor because it lets them squeeze drug traffickers from the profit side, the place where it hurts them the most.

by Peter Ross Range with Gordon Witkin

WEED IT AND REAP

Domestic marijuana production soars with drug war

Tim Wise

TIM WISE is a staff editor at *Dollars & Sense.*

Last August, the daily pollen count in Tucson, Arizona contained a surprise for city officials: leading the list of allergens was marijuana pollen.

Tucson is not alone. Air samples taken the previous November in West Los Angeles by the Asthma and Allergy Foundation revealed as much as 40% of the airborne pollen coming from flowering marijuana plants. Given the urban setting and the time of year, the pollens were undoubtedly from indoor gardens in the area.

With all due apologies to allergy sufferers, the domestic marijuana crop is nothing to sneeze at. Marijuana may well be the country's largest cash crop, with annual harvests valued at anywhere from $10 billion to $33 billion. Even using conservative estimates, the United States now ranks just behind Mexico and Colombia among leading world pot producers. What's more, thanks to the importation of the world's best seeds and the wonders of hybridization, the best grass on the planet is now produced at home. And home is not just on the Western range: six of the top 10 marijuana-producing states are in the South and Midwest.

The reason is simple: with an investment of $200 to $400, one plant can earn the grower as much as $4,000 a year. We're not talking depressed farm prices here, which explains why Dick Kerth, a prominent Montana rancher and former Republican state committeeman, turned to weed farming. Left $2 million in debt by drought and low farm prices and facing foreclosure, the Kerths turned their barns into hothouses for some 2,000 plants. Kerth told CBS's "West 57th Street" program that if they hadn't gotten caught they would have been out of debt in just two years.

THE WAR COMES HOME

This is not the first time in the history of the United States that marijuana has been one of the country's principal crops. Prior to the introduction of the cotton gin in the early 1800s, cannabis hemp — farmed for its non-psychotropic stalks — was the country's main source of fiber for everything from ropes and paper to fabric (see box).

The recent marijuana boom, of course, is based not on the plant's stalks but on its leaves and buds, which are rich in the psychoactive chemical tetrahydrocannabinol (THC). Outlawed in 1937, marijuana use blossomed in the 1960s with the counterculture. By the early 1970s, a relatively small number of hippies had withdrawn into the hills of Northern California to commune with nature and grow their own dope. At the time, the price on the street was only $10 to $20 an ounce, hardly incentive for profiteers. What's more, domestic pot was relatively poor quality, harsh and with low THC content. The best stuff still came from Colombia, Mexico, and Southeast Asia, and the big drug importers controlled the distribution networks.

At the time, U.S. producers supplied a negligible percentage of the domestic market. But then the U.S. government's war on drugs brought the evil weed home. In 1978, the U.S. government sponsored an intensive campaign to eradicate foreign marijuana plantations. With the cooperation of the Colombian and Mexican governments, the herbicide paraquat was sprayed on large quantities of the weed, poisoning the product. The paraquat was like an amphetamine for domestic growers. As U.S. consumers grew mistrustful of foreign supplies, producers on the West Coast and in Hawaii, encouraged by a price jump of over 75%, expanded production to fill the void.

While the supply was fluctuating wildly, demand remained stable. The federal National Institute on Drug Abuse (NIDA) Household Survey for 1985 revealed an estimated 18 million people who admitted having smoked marijuana in the last month, with another 10 million who admitted using it in the last year. According to the federal government's National Narcotics Intelligence Consumers Committee (NNICC), that translates into demand for roughly 22 million pounds a year.

The National Organization for the Reform of Marijuana Laws (NORML) says such surveys are biased by the respondents' fear of prosecution. NORML estimates there are up to 50 million users consuming up to 38 million pounds a year. Government and grower sources may disagree about the size of the U.S. market, but they agree that demand has changed little since the mid-1970s.

The paraquat-induced boom gave Northern California a modern-day gold rush. Growers expanded their plots and began to import high-potency seeds instead of the finished product. If the best Colombian grass was poisoned, they would grow clean Colombian themselves. Marijuana being the hardy weed it is, they had little trouble. Soon high-quality, made-in-the-USA marijuana was readily available in many parts of the country. Also available was indoor pot, grown under artificial lights with the latest in hydroponic technology mostly in the Northwest, where the climate is more hostile to the cannabis plant.

The second stimulant for the domestic marijuana industry was cocaine. In the early 1980s, cocaine became the drug of choice for those who could afford it. More important, it became the drug of choice for importers. Although marijuana's price had risen to $40 an ounce on the street, coke was the real thing when it

Ad for indoor growing supplies from the trade magazine, Sinsemilla Tips.

came to profitability. With a street value of $600 a gram (more than $16,000 an ounce), cocaine was hundreds of times more valuable than marijuana. Cocaine was also far easier to smuggle into the country than the relatively bulky marijuana. With the penalties for marijuana and cocaine smuggling nearly identical, coke was it.

Between 1976 and 1984, cocaine shipments to the United States more than tripled. As importers concentrated on cocaine, marijuana became relatively scarce on the U.S. market. The price again jumped, 45% this time, and domestic growers were not long in responding. According to government estimates, by 1985 19% of the U.S. market was being supplied by domestic growers.

In less than a decade, U.S. producers had grown from a relatively obscure counterculture fringe into a multi-billion-dollar industry. In 1975, U.S. producers weren't even considered significant enough to measure; by 1987, 25% to 50% of the grass consumed in this country was grown at home. What's more, like U.S. winemakers, domestic growers were increasingly going upscale, producing so-called "lawyer bud": a more potent form of cannabis called sinsemilla. In 1987, between one- and two-thirds of domestic marijuana was sinsemilla, with THC content well beyond that of even the best foreign grass in the 1960s.

THE LOW AND THE HIGH

Not surprisingly, accurate data on an outlaw industry are hard to come by. The Justice Department's Drug Enforcement Agency (DEA) is the principal source of government data. For 1987, DEA estimates the harvested crop at 6.6 million pounds, up nearly 50% over the previous year. Since 1981, domestic cultivation has increased 150%, according to government figures. DEA estimates the number of commercial growers at between 90,000 and 150,000, with another million people growing for their personal use.

The DEA figures must be taken with more than a grain of white stuff. The only sure figure they have is the amount law enforcement officials seized or eradicated. In a highly subjective measure, they calculate the size of the domestic crop by estimating the effectiveness of their own work, which gives them an estimate of the amount they missed. For 1987, the DEA gave themselves a self-congratulatory 66% effectiveness rating. This is the same agency that in its 1982 report explained that "38% more domestic marihuana was *eradicated* than was previously *believed to exist*." (Emphasis in original.) (In a repeat performance in Mexico in 1984, Mexican police raided five farms, seizing eight times more marijuana than U.S. and Mexican authorities previously thought was grown in the whole country.)

For these reasons, government figures for domestic marijuana cultivation are generally taken as the low end of a wide range of estimates. At the upper end is NORML, which produces an annual crop report relying on a broader range of data—from consumption surveys to grower reports. NORML estimates the DEA and other law enforcement agencies seized or eradicated only 16% of the crop, meaning an estimated 22 million pounds made it to market, more than three times the government estimate. If the NORML figures are accurate, marijuana is by far the largest cash crop in the country, worth $33 billion, at least twice the value of the corn crop. It also means U.S. growers are supplying more than half the marijuana for the domestic market.

NORML estimates there are closer to 250,000 commercial growers and nearly two million "personal-use" growers. And the farmers are in every state in the country. According to NORML, 10 states each harvested more than $1 billion worth of weed in 1987. Thanks to successful government eradication efforts in Hawaii and California, the number-one pot-producing state in 1987 was Oregon.

According to Tom Alexander, a former grower who now publishes the trade magazine "Sinsemilla Tips" (circulation 15,000), Oregon's predominantly indoor cultivation represents the wave of the future. While increasingly sophisticated aerial surveillance makes outdoor growing risky, "the indoor growers are untouched. So many people have moved indoors that overall there is as much marijuana as ever," according to Alexander. He estimates as much as half of the U.S. crop may now be grown indoors.

And why not? For as little as $2,000, a suburban basement can be turned into a hydroponic cash machine. Powerful grow lights supply near-sunlight conditions and offer greater control over the environment. Seed varieties of the most potent sinsemilla have been bred for indoor growing. And a rotational hydroponic system provides year-round harvests. According to Alexander, the typical basement grower can make $20,000 a year producing some of the finest sinsemilla in the world.

AN INDUSTRY IN TRANSITION

But the question remains: if domestic cultivation has increased so rapidly and demand has remained stable, why is the price so high? Government officials cite high prices as proof of their successful eradication efforts. Indeed, the largest price hikes came in response to supply interruptions, first with paraquat, then with the importers' shift to cocaine. But current high prices seem to reflect not continuing short supplies but a temporary disruption, as the industry makes the transition from foreign to domestic supply.

Despite the predominance of domestic grass, it still lacks an efficient distribution structure. As the U.S. market has shifted from foreign to domestic supply, distribution networks have been disrupted. Local shortages of foreign marijuana are still common, and this keeps prices high. The foreign distributors won't handle domestic stuff because it competes with their own merchandise, and besides, they are pushing coke and crack rather than marijuana.

In a sense, domestic marijuana is a protected industry. The U.S. government's "supply-management" policies have been fairly effective at curtailing foreign marijuana and disrupting distribution networks. In the meantime, U.S. growers are responding to the artificially high prices by expanding production. But government harassment of domestic growers has prevented the industry from consolidating and developing an efficient distribution system.

"Marijuana is the only illegal drug that's not controlled by the cartels and the CIA," claims Tom Alexander. "That's because it's moved into our country in such a way that independent growers control it."

While there is no easy way to pinpoint the role of organized crime in distributing domestic marijuana, the federal government doesn't entirely disagree with NORML on this point. According to NNICC, "local trafficking organizations usually controlled the intrastate and interstate distribution of their marijuana."

One of the effects of the heavy eradication efforts in California and Hawaii has been to accelerate the decentralization of growing operations. The largest outdoor farms were the first to be spotted and raided, while many small growers escaped detection.

But decentralized growing doesn't necessarily mean decentralized ownership. As the industry moves indoors, "franchise" operations are becoming more common. One owner will set up indoor operations in houses all over the country and pay an operator to tend the crop. This lowers the risk to the owner and gives him or her easy distribution on the market where the crop is grown.

GREENER PASTURES AHEAD?

While there may be differences of opinion about the industry's future, marijuana is clearly a weed that won't go away. But as the industry makes its transition and law enforcement officials exploit drug-war hysteria to gain approval for more invasive surveillance techniques, the status quo is anything but secure.

With profit margins as high as they are, organized crime is certain to move in sooner or later. "I've been warning for the last couple years that the Mafia and organized crime will take it over," explains Tom Alexander. "They didn't want a piece of it when it was up in the hills: it was too much work." Now that it's moved indoors and into an urban setting, the industry is there for the taking. According to Alexander, they

---

Marijuana was outlawed in 1937 under the Marijuana Tax Act. So what was the federal government doing in 1942 exhorting U.S. farmers to plant cannabis?

It was part of the war effort. The plant that produces the psychotropic buds and leaves we know as marijuana is also the source of one of the strongest natural fibers known to humankind. The stalks from cannabis hemp contain no THC, the active ingredient in marijuana, but can be processed into a wide variety of essential products. Most ropes and cords used to be made from cannabis hemp, as did most paper. And cannabis hemp produces one of the strongest fabrics in the world: in fact, the word "canvas" derives from the word "cannabis."

The invention of the cotton gin and the mechanization of the weaving process in the early 1800s put much of the cannabis hemp industry out of business. No one had yet discovered a way to mechanize the harvesting and processing of hemp fibers. Still, into the 1930s cannabis hemp remained a common source of hand-woven fabric and was used for ropes, cords, and rigging, particularly on U.S. Navy ships.

Some claim that marijuana was outlawed in 1937 not because it was a narcotic but because a new mechanized harvester and processor made cannabis hemp a viable competitor for everything from paper products to clothing. According to this conspiracy theory, the co-conspirators included: William Randolph Hearst, who controlled vast pulp interests; the Dupont family, which produced the chemicals for pulp processing and was preparing to market the first synthetic clothing; and the oil companies (what conspiracy theory is complete without them?), which recognized the high methane content in the stalks as a threat to their oil-powered vision of the future.

After cannabis hemp was outlawed in 1937, the U.S. government began relying on Manila hemp, a strong but less versatile fiber, to supply the Armed Forces with everything from parachute cords to ship rigging and rope. When, in 1942, the Japanese took the Philippines, U.S. hemp supplies were cut off. The outlawing of marijuana had caused a national security emergency.

The government was quick to act. The U.S. Department of Agriculture produced a 15-minute film called "Hemp for Victory." Under the stirring cover of a "Yankee Doodle Dandy" soundtrack, the film instructed farmers in the wonders of cannabis hemp and how to grow it. Suddenly, growing dope was the patriotic thing to do. As soon as the Philippines was "ours" again, the cannabis ban was once more enforced and the plant's non-psychotropic applications were quickly hushed. "Hemp for Victory" was reportedly removed from the national archives at the government's request.

SOURCES: U.S. Department of Agriculture, *Hemp for Victory*, 1942; Jack Herer, "The Emperor Wears No Clothes: Everything you should have learned about marijuana but weren't taught in school," 1986.

---

probably already control distribution in major cities like Los Angeles.

Alexander sees a parallel with Prohibition. The first illegal stills "started up in the hills operated by independents," he explains. "When the stills moved closer to the urban centers, organized crime moved in, took the stills, and put them in their warehouses and speakeasies."

The alternative scenario is legalization or, at least, decriminalization. Ironically, deficit reduction may be the ultimate rationale for legalizing marijuana. Why spend millions each year on eradication efforts when you can reap a harvest of sin taxes on legal weed? Given that marijuana could probably be grown as cheaply as tobacco, there is every reason to believe taxes on the product could bring in as much revenue as current sales taxes on alcohol — over $9 billion on the federal and state levels.

Not surprisingly, some growers are opposed to legalization. The only thing keeping prices high is the illegal nature of the business. With legalization, prices to the grower would drop precipitously, governments would capture the bulk of the current windfall, and the gold rush would be over. But for most small growers, legalization would be more than welcome. According to Alexander, some would band together in grower cooperatives to counter the entry of corporations into the market. "Eventually the conglomerates will take over," admits Alexander, but as long as personal-use growing isn't outlawed, most growers would support legalization.

For now, though, such a reasonable resolution of the "marijuana problem" seems a pipe dream. If anything, Congress and state legislatures are mandating harsher penalties for possession and cultivation and are increasingly willing to abridge constitutional privacy rights to nab offenders. Harvest season in Northern California is now an annual military training exercise, with spy helicopters overhead and armed units on the ground carrying out their holy war against the evil weed.

Such eradication efforts, of course, only drive the price up to new heights, making marijuana cultivation even more attractive. Meanwhile, farmers like the Kerths, who can't make a living growing food in a hungry world, will continue to turn to grass to save their farms. As with the prohibition of alcohol, the government seems to be fighting a losing battle in a war long on self-righteousness but short on sense. The only lasting legacy of that war may well be the infringement on the privacy rights of all U.S. residents.

SOURCES: The National Narcotics Intelligence Consumers Committee, "The Supply of Illicit Drugs to the United States from Foreign and Domestic Sources in 1985 and 1986"; National Organization for the Reform of Marijuana Laws, *Common Sense for America*, various issues; *Sinsemilla Tips*, various issues; Ray Raphael, *Cash Crop*, 1985.

The War on Drugs:
Let's Surrender

Joseph Sobran

WASHINGTON, August 17 — A few days before our "drug czar," William Bennett, announced his new strategy to fight the drug trade, police in Lebanon, Pa., found two children, ages 7 and 9, playing drug dealer. They were selling little packets of sugar as cocaine and of grass (the lawn kind) as grass (the other kind). One officer moaned, "We just lost the war on drugs."

I agree. And it's high time we surrendered. We can surrender on reasonable terms now, or we can wait until many more people have died and surrender unconditionally.

WHEN OUR LEADERS talk of "war," they mean to inspire us with declarations of resolve. A real war is fought against a specific enemy whose defeat is the object. But war on impersonal things, forces and abstractions — such as poverty, terrorism and drugs — veers close to meaninglessness. How do you know when you've won?

Even in a real war, success may be hard to measure. Generals don't like to admit they're losing. They call for more troops, more money, more authority to widen the conflict.

If this is the case against flesh-and-blood foes, how much truer it's likely to be against more elusive realities. The "war on poverty" was supposed to end poverty. It didn't. It may have worsened it. All we really know is that this "war" has given us expensive and sometimes corrupt bureaucracies, like HUD. The staggering amounts of illegal drug money sloshing around would make bribery an even greater temptation to the anti-drug troops than is already the case in other government agencies.

Two items have clinched the argument for me. One is the estimate of Llewellyn Rockwell of the Ludwig von Mises Institute that decriminalizing drugs would cut street crime 75 percent. If that figure is anywhere near accurate, it's hard to imagine any consideration on the other side that could contravene it.

The other decisive fact is that drugs are out of control even in our prisons. If that's the case, turning the entire nation into a prison would not solve the problem.

THE WORD "PROBLEM" reminds me again of James Burnham's dictum: "when there's no solution, there's no problem." In that sense a certain range of drug use and abuse is not so much a problem that can be banished as a condition that has to be coped with.

We have reached the point where what we mean by the drug "problem" is less the consumption of drugs than the violence associated with their distribution. The gang warfare of the prohibition era never constituted a daily menace to ordinary citizens remotely approaching the nationwide terror that prevails in our cities now.

Prohibition was not a total failure; few things are. But it was a net failure. We still have alcohol abuse, but distributing whiskey doesn't get people killed anymore. Decriminalizing drugs would probably bring a marginal increase in drug consumption (though commercial drugs could be made safer than the uncontrolled substances in the streets, such as crack) But the main thing is that a criminal industry would be destroyed, and the sales of drugs would become non-violent.

Notice I say "decriminalizing," not anything-goes, laissez-faire legalizing. Drugs would still be banned from minors. The restricted adult market would be less profitable, and the risk of penalties for giving drugs to kids would hardly be worth the little money to be gained by it. Decriminalizing drugs for adults might actually reduce consumption by minors.

Americans are a moralistic people, and they tend to think that whatever is immoral should be illegal. By the same token, they tend to assume that whatever is legal must be a "right." But permitting drugs need not imply social approval. Legal liability (as for driving under the influence) would impose other constraints. Partial legalization would make drug abuse more legally reachable.

I HAVE COME to this position slowly and reluctantly, knowing how serious an irreversible mistake can be. But we are already making the mistake, and it's reversible. In an act of impressive political courage, Baltimore's Mayor Kurt Schmoke has made a similar proposal.

Like so many things in life, decriminalizing drugs would be a sad compromise, an admission of defeat. But defeat is what you court when you attempt the impossible.

For decades we've been decapitating Hydra, as Mr. Bennett has suggested decapitating drug dealers. That may work in Iran, but in America the heads grow back, and the beast has more heads now than when we started. We can't kill it. Let's domesticate it.

Is this any way to fight a war?

Edward Grimsley

MARCH 31 — Each day brings fresh evidence that the nation needs to reverse one of its main tactics in the war on drugs. Instead of trying to protect law-abiding citizens by building maximum-security facilities for offenders, society ought to erect maximum-security facilities for law-abiding citizens and concede the streets to the criminals.

They are controlling more and more of the neighborhoods anyway, the headlines show, no matter how many prisons governments build. Because of lenient judges and prison officials, abetted by such organizations as the American Civil Liberties Union (ACLU), offenders often go in one prison door and right out the other. Police who arrest a drug-crazed criminal one day may shoot him the next at the scene of another crime — or get shot by him.

SOMETHING LIKE THIS happened recently in Alexandria, Va., which is just across the Potomac River from the nation's crime-infested capital. A man who had walked away from a District of Columbia Corrections Department halfway house seized a hostage and killed a policeman in the ensuing confrontation, during which he also died.

This ambulant convict, who had gone to an Alexandria public housing apartment in search of crack, had been sentenced to two consecutive six-month sentences for carrying a pistol without a license and for at-tempting to possess cocaine. In other words, he was not your typical white-collar sniffer. Yet, a judge ordered him transferred from a regular prison to the halfway house for the final 90 days of his sentence. An official at the house subsequently gave him a weekend pass, and he never returned.

Obviously, then, building walls to keep criminals inside, where they can do society no harm, is not working. So why not try establishing secure areas for decent people and building walls to keep criminals out?

USING RIVER OR coastal barges as prisons for drug offenders, as federal drug czar William J. Bennett reportedly is contemplating, probably wouldn't improve the situation noticeably. Putting prisoners on floating Alcatrazes wouldn't prevent judges from ordering them transferred to halfway houses. And while it should be more difficult for prisoners to escape from such water-bound jails, the ACLU probably would ruin their effectiveness by persuading the courts to order authorities to include swimming on the prisoners' recreational programs.

Prisons for criminals might work, making maximum security facilities for law-abiding citizens unnecessary, if judges and prison officials could be induced to become more realistic about crime and punishment. Treating the officials as accessories to any crime resulting directly from their leni-ency, and subjecting them to a jail term or the loss of their pensions might do more than anything else to bring revolving prison doors to a screeching halt.

As for the ACLU, which often prods judges and prison officials into leniency, it needs to acquire new concepts of constitutional rights. While vigilance against oppression is essential, it is important to remember that the Constitution protects law-abiding citizens as well as criminals. If forcing inner-city residents to huddle behind bolted and chained doors, afraid even to stroll around the block, is not a violation of their constitutional rights, it ought to be.

MAYBE THERE SHOULD be another law providing that no one could seek to invalidate anti-drug laws and programs without first living a month — unprotected — in a ghetto house or an apartment in the middle of a drug zone. Any ACLU official who survived such a harrowing experience probably would desert that organization and become an ardent member of the National Rifle Association.

Surely constitutional purity does not require greater respect for a criminal's "right" to enjoy weekend furloughs than it requires for a police officer's right to live. But Alexandria Police Cpl. Charles W. Hill is dead because certain authorities were more sensitive to a criminal's comfort and happiness than they were to the interests of society. That's no way to fight a drug war.

Drug Action on the Nervous System

• **Users, Abusers, and Addictions (Articles 17-24)**
• **Designer Drugs (Articles 25-27)**

People use drugs because they produce a desired result. This unit will help the reader to understand the "how" and "why" of drugs. A drug acts upon the central nervous system and we behave in a different, but internally consistent, manner. For example, with few exceptions, when we drink, we can get drunk, and when we drink plenty, we can get plenty drunk. Seldom does this analogy break down. Without this consistency, drug treatment would be dangerous or impossible. *Why* we make the conscious decision to drink or get drunk is quite another matter.

To understand the workings of the brain is one thing, to understand behavior is quite another. There is no way of knowing how long humans have been tinkering with the brain or when drug use became ritual in an attempt to bridge the spiritual unknowns. The field of investigation called neuroscience has given medicine significant new information about brain function and control mechanisms, many of which involve drugs. "Better living through chemistry," an advertising slogan of the past, gained new meaning in the sixties and ever greater meaning today.

"Everybody Must Get Stoned?" is the thesis of psychopharmacologist Ronald Siegal. The subject of this article contends that getting "stoned" is a natural drive in birds, elephants, and presidents alike, and the urge to get intoxicated is not only a drive, but is a common preoccupation within the animal kingdom. In "Cycles of Craving," we discover the cyclical nature of the use of drugs. The mood of the times seems interlocked with the drugs of choice, according to the author. Drugs' side effects are the topic of discussion in "Passing a Legacy of Drug Addiction" and "Cocaine: Litany of Fetal Risks Grows." The truly innocent in our midst are the most vulnerable to drug use. Infants exposed to drugs when in the womb often suffer mental retardation, physical malformation, and early death. As children, they can expect a poor quality of life while their support system faces bankruptcy. "The Invisible Line," and "New Ways to Crack a Cocaine Addiction" discuss the craving that marks addiction. Cocaine was thought to be nonaddictive until a few years ago. These articles detail the severity of cocaine craving and offer specific treatments. "The Return of a Deadly Drug Called Horse" tells of the new popularity of smoking heroin. Its purity is up and the price is down, the answer to a drug user's prayer. And while heroin is back, "Marijuana" never went away. The drug continues to be more in demand than ever before. The strength is up, and so is the price, and so are the dangers to health.

The second subsection investigates "designer drugs." Designer drugs, the "magic bullets" from the lab, are described in "From Crack to Ecstasy," and "We've Already Said Yes." "Drug of Infamy Makes a Comeback" tells how thalidomide, the scourge of over twenty years ago, has been recycled as an effective treatment for a number of medical conditions once thought incurable.

Looking Ahead: Challenge Questions

Are hallucinations real?

Does the brain function by design or accident?

What makes my brain similar to or different from yours?

Why do I forget? Why do I remember? Why do I remember some things and not others? Are there drugs that will enhance or cancel my memory?

Do all drugs have side effects?

Can the urge to use recreational drugs be totally and permanently suppressed? Should it? Who will make those decisions?

Will the advancement of science significantly limit our freedom of choice? If it does, will we be given drugs to make us unaware of our loss?

Unit 2

EVERYBODY MUST GET STONED?

Bob Sipchen

Los Angeles Times

Stoned, smashed, bombed, tight, tipsy, tanked, stewed, plastered, looped, blotto, swacked, schnockered, fried, ripped, besotted, blasted, shikker, reeling, soused, soaked, canned, potted, bent, crocked, shellacked, squiffy, jug-bitten, oiled, polluted, raddled, high, lit, loaded, stinko, pie-eyed.

There are reportedly more synonyms for intoxication than any other word in the English language. For good reason. Catnip-sniffing kittens and alcoholic American presidents alike know that the urge to get high is a strong one.

The $6.1 billion the White House Office of Drug Control Policy is likely to spend fighting drugs next year isn't going to change that. Ollie North's anti-drug community service work won't change that. Nor will Nancy Reagan's urging kids to "Just Say No."

At least that's the view of University of California at Los Angeles psychopharmacologist Ronald Siegel, whose new book, "Intoxication—Life in Pursuit of Artificial Paradise," argues that the motivation to achieve an altered state of mood or consciousness is "a fourth drive," as much a part of the human condition—and as important to most other species—as sex, thirst and hunger.

"I find it helpful to picture America in a tug-of-war between the laws of the land and the drives of the people," he writes. Siegel doesn't advocate legalizing the drugs that society is now battling. But 20 years of research have convinced him that until America comes to grips with the reality of the powerful intoxication drive, the tug-of-war will be a stalemate at best.

Siegel speculates that his curiosity abut altered states of consciousness may have been triggered in boyhood,

when a dentist gave him nitrous oxide. "William James, one of my heroes in psychology, had some very interesting experiences and thoughts about psychology as a result of his intoxication on nitrous oxide."

Siegel said that his own use of controlled substances since then has been minimal and limited to research.

"I've been really lucky," he said. "I've been able to hire people to take it for me. I've had some very brave volunteers, and there's no lack of drug users out there to study."

Until a recent injury knocked him out of the running, Siegel was a marathoner and something of a health nut. "I've always been extremely conservative about my own body. I could probably count on one hand the number of times I've had alcohol in a year," he said.

If anything, Siegel appears intoxicated with curiosity; his addiction is to research.

Siegel did his undergraduate work in sociology at Brandeis University, and received a Ph.D. in psychology from Dalhousie University in Halifax, Nova Scotia, where he experimented with the effects of LSD, marijuana and other drugs on pigeons and mice. He then went on to postdoctoral work at Albert Einstein College of Medicine in New York.

At Albert Einstein, "a professor made the statement that man is the only animal that intoxicates himself deliberately. I thought, 'Gee, that has to be wrong,'" Siegel said.

Stoned Grasshoppers

In 1970, Siegel went to Czechoslovakia to study insects that were eating marijuana plants. Contrary to local folklore, he did not find that stoned grasshoppers were able to make enormous leaps.

But later he did find evidence that some insects seemed attracted to some plants, such as the opium poppy, as an intoxicant as well as a food source. For two decades, Siegel and research associates have been working their way way up and down the phylogentic spectrum and around the world, watching California robins get smashed on Pyracantha berries and divebomb cats; observing jimsonweed-addled cattle in Hawaii; hearing tales of tigers in Sumatra that attack children to eat the fermented durian fruit they've gathered, and stories of elephants on the African savannahs that get as drunk as Dumbo in the Disney cartoon.

"During the Vietnam conflict, our observers found that water buffalo were nibbling opium poppies more often than they naturally do. This was very similar to what our soldiers were doing with heroin," Siegel said. "You can understand that in terms of both animals reacting to stress."

Sometimes the detective work took odd spins. Armed with a strand of John Keats' hair he acquired from a private 19th century collection of literary celebrities' locks, Siegel used a process called radioimmunoassay to determine that the poet was an opium user.

In fact, lots of important people—maybe most—used some kind of drug, he said. For example, his files contain prescription records, historical accounts and correspondence on the drug habits of most of this country's presidents. According to Siegel's book, presidential drug preferences ran from cigars to whiskey and beyond.

As the book points out, "President Andrew Johnson was said to be rarely sober"; Abraham Lincoln used chloroform, "a popular recreational drug of the day"; and Ulysses S. Grant was an alcoholic and after retirement wrote his memoirs "sustained by cocaine."

In all his research, he said, he has yet to find a contemporary or historical culture that hasn't pursued some form of intoxication or consciousness altering. "There may have been pockets but they probably utilized other nondrug methods of intoxicating themselves: Religious ecstasy . . . ritual dancing, drumming, jumping up and down.

Traffickers to the World

"What I'm saying is, we have always done this. The tobacco industry financed the American Revolution. We were the drug traffickers to the world," he said.

Which is not to say that Siegel discounts the tragic consequences of this or any of America's more modern drug habits. Nor does he endorse legalization of outlawed drugs.

"My position is that none of these drugs are good," he said. "I'm not advocating the use of any of the drugs we have today. I don't think any of them are healthy or safe. I wish to God we could reevaluate and reconsider alcohol and let that go through an FDA trial. I don't think it would ever make it." People use drugs, from caffeine to heroin, for one purpose, Siegel believes. "They're medicating themselves. They're changing their mood. They're changing the way they feel. These are legitimate medical uses.

"Our choices of drugs may not always be legal or prudent or safe, but that's what we're doing." The way to clean up our drug problem "is to clean up the drugs themselves," he said.

"The problem is we're messing around with Mother Nature. We're taking relatively safe medicines, benign intoxicants, and turning them into poisons by concentrating the dose and changing the pattern of use. All the problems that I've seen on this planet . . . are really problems of misusing the dosage and the pattern of use," he said.

If society would invest as much money as it does on the drug war in finding a safe natural drug, or in creating safe synthetic drugs, the war might become unnecessary, Siegel said.

"It is natural that being chemical organisms, we're going to react with the chemistry around us," Siegel said. "It's too late to take a step back. To 'just say no' is to deny everything that we are and all the things we could be."

77

Cycles of Craving

Society's drugs of choice appear to come in waves: LSD and marijuana, cocaine, now crack. But cutting across the gradual shifts in drug-use patterns and the severe crisis in many of our cities is a growing disenchantment with it all.

Dan Hurley

Dan Hurley is a contributing editor of Psychology Today. *For reprints of this article, see the classified section.*

Lenard Hebert is an expert of sorts on America's patterns of drug abuse over the past 25 years. He hasn't studied them; he's lived them.

"I did each drug of the decade," says Hebert, a 40-year-old man now glad to be recovering in New York City's Phoenix House, one of the largest residential drug treatment centers in the world. Sitting in a lounge at the center, dressed neatly in white shirt and tie, he recalls his time as a Marine in Vietnam in 1967: "We'd wear peace signs on our helmets and love beads around our necks. Drugs were another way to get in touch with home. And LSD was definitely the most popular drug at the time."

When he returned home in the early '70s, Hebert became a black militant, bought a beret and, as he says, "did strictly reefer. A good militant did natural, herbal things. Then I went disco. I snorted cocaine for 10 years. It was chic because it was so expensive."

Along came crack, the smokable, highly addictive form of cocaine with its five-minute high. Hebert stopped dealing cocaine and turned his middle-class high-rise apartment into a crack den. Before he made it to Phoenix House, he was sleeping in abandoned cars and shelters for the homeless.

Spotting National Trends

The cycles of drug abuse that nearly ruined Hebert's life represent fairly well the way that different drugs sweep across our country in waves. "It's as if we've been conducting a huge social experiment since the early 1960s," said the late Norman E. Zinberg, a psychiatrist at Harvard who, since 1963, had been studying national drug abuse patterns. (He died in April.) In his view, the nation has gone through four major waves of drug use, beginning with LSD in the early 1960s, marijuana in the mid- to late-'60s, heroin from 1969 to 1971 (Hebert escaped this heroin wave somehow) and cocaine in the late '70s and '80s.

Zinberg believed shifting patterns in drug abuse are signs of the times, reflections of the country's shifting zeitgeist. "Cocaine became the drug of the '80s because it's a stimulant," he said. "People were looking for action. It fit the mood, just like psychedelics fit the mood of the early '60s."

For years, experts have been trying to spot large trends in drug abuse with the hope that they might better prepare and adapt treatment, prevention and law enforcement efforts, according to David E. Smith, a specialist in addiction medicine who opened the Haight Ashbury Free Clinic in 1967 and has been monitoring drug-use patterns ever since. Although we have become increasingly sophisticated in identifying patterns, several factors muddy tidy calendars of drug usage such as Zinberg's. Most notably, researchers have found that: 1. Drug use varies tremendously from region to region, even city to city; 2. Drugs of choice move with some predictability through the social class structure; and 3. Rather than a simple succession of drugs in use, one drug often will piggyback on another, complicating efforts at prevention.

The East-West Transfer

In 1976 the National Institute on Drug Abuse (NIDA) took the first step toward monitoring regional trends when it formed the Community Epidemiology Work Group, an assembly of drug-abuse experts from 20 cities around the country who meet biannually to exchange data. "Drug-abuse problems sometimes develop very quickly at the local level," says Nicholas J. Kozel, chief of NIDA's statistical and epidemiologic analysis branch and chairman of the group.

"Up until about a year and a half ago, there wasn't much of a crack problem in Washington, DC," Kozel explains. "Then all of a sudden we had more violence and murder than we'd ever seen, most of it associated with drugs, especially crack. Drug abuse is different from Boston to Buffalo to Washington. It pops up this month and recedes the next. That's why we need local surveillance. It keeps you on the edge of your seat, trying to stay alert to these changes and their impact on the health of our nation."

Class Distinctions

Compounding these regional variations is the movement of particular drugs through social classes. In a fairly predictable pattern, drug epidemics seem to begin among a

The middle class, experts have shown, is losing interest in drugs.

small, elite group, then filter down into the broad middle class and finally permeate the ghetto. In 1983, half of the callers to 1-800-COCAINE, the national cocaine-abuse hot line, were college-educated, 52% had family incomes of at least $25,000 and only 16% were unemployed. By 1987, only 16% of the callers were college-educated, a mere 20% had incomes of $25,000 and fully 54% were among the unemployed.

"Cocaine use is going down among the people who work and can't afford not to show up for their jobs," says psychiatrist David F. Musto, a Yale medical historian and author of *The American Disease: Origins of Narcotic Control*. "The first people to go on a drug are the avant-garde and the wealthy, and they're the first to go off it, too. But in the inner city, drugs become a source of status and money, at least for the dealers."

Demand for illegal drugs has been dropping in the middle class for 10 years, according to two national surveys sponsored by NIDA. The most recent National Household Survey on Drug Abuse showed that drug use among 18- to 25-year-olds leveled off between 1979 and 1985. The first substantial decline in cocaine consumption among American high-school seniors, college students and young adults showed up in a 1987 survey conducted by the University of Michigan's Institute for Social Research. The most recent available poll shows that the decline continued in 1988.

Drugs that Travel Together

Despite regional variations, there do appear to be predictable patterns of abuse once a drug arrives on the scene. For instance, heavy abusers of cocaine or speed often use heroin simultaneously, usually at the end of a binge to ease themselves down. It shouldn't be surprising, then, that in 27 cities across the country the number of deaths associated with both heroin and cocaine leapt between 1984 and 1988. From 1987 to 1988 alone, domestic heroin seizures by the Drug Enforcement Agency more than doubled, jumping from 382.4 kilograms to 793.9 kilograms.

"It's predictable that we've had an increase in heroin abuse," says Smith. "Anytime you see a stimulant upswing, you see an opiate upswing. The stimulant epidemic was the door for the opiate epidemic."

And Smith is now worried by a disturbing new trend—a simultaneous increase in the use of *both* speed and cocaine. "Normally the trends go in different directions," he says. "The speed curve went up and the cocaine curve went down. But since the advent of crack, it's the first time I've ever seen both the speed curve and the cocaine curve go up. The current stimulant epidemic is without a doubt the worst I've seen since 1967—and in fact it's worse than 1967."

What Shapes the Patterns?

Experts have found the patterns of drug abuse are formed not only by vague national moods and fashions but also by the ordinary stuff of any business: packaging, marketing, distribution, research and development. "Crack has grown because of new marketing techniques," says Jim Hall, executive director of Up Front, a national drug-information center based in Miami. "When the yuppies were buying cocaine, they bought it in somebody's apartment, usually at prices of at least $50. The crack user buys it on the street or at a crack den in a vial that costs $10. This less-expensive alternative is what has brought cocaine to a whole new user group in the poverty pockets." It's not unlike the single-serving marketing strategy that has been successfully adopted by the food industry.

Arguably the strongest regulator of drug use is the public's perception of a drug's safety. America's first epidemic of cocaine abuse a century ago began when doctors had only good things to say about it. In 1884, Sigmund Freud wrote in *Uber Coca* that "The psychic effect of cocaine consists of exhilaration and lasting euphoria which does not differ from normal euphoria of a healthy person . . . . Absolutely no craving for further use of cocaine appears after the first or repeated taking of the drug." Thirty years later, the U.S. Congress passed the Harrison Act, designed to restrict severely traffic in opiates and cocaine, which by then had come to be considered serious public health hazards.

Cocaine's perceived risks have followed much the same trajectory in its second epidemic. As recently as 1985, psychiatrist Lester Grinspoon and lawyer James B. Bakalar wrote in a chapter of *The Comprehensive Textbook of Psychiatry* that "High price still restricts consumption for all but the very rich, and those involved in trafficking. . . . If used moderately and occasionally, cocaine creates no serious problems." In that same year, the University of Michigan's annual survey of high-school students and young adults found that only 34% believed that trying cocaine once or twice was a "great risk." By 1987 amidst thundering anti-drug news in the national media, that proportion had jumped to 47.9%, and by 1988 more than half of those polled thought that even experimenting with cocaine was very risky. "The perceived risks have shifted enough that they could fully account for the shifts in use," says Jerald G. Bachman, one of the survey researchers.

Drugs for the '90s

Even now, as the uproar of negative publicity about

New marketing trends are helping to shape drug-abuse patterns.

crack's debilitating effects has checked its spread among middle-class users, another stimulant — a smokable, fast-acting form of methamphetamine — has entered the drug scene in the West and, according to some experts, has begun moving eastward. Police officers in various areas have been seizing unprecedented numbers of clandestine methamphetamine laboratories, and there has been a sharp rise in both hospital emergency-room reports and deaths related to use of the stimulant.

In contrast to crack, which gained its foothold in the East and then began moving westward, methamphetamine seems to be a West Coast phenomenon. It also differs from crack in that "methamphetamine use tends to be highest among white, blue-collar types," says Smith. "The clandestine labs tend to be controlled by the white biker gangs, while crack tends to be controlled more by inner-city blacks."

The growth of methamphetamine seems to stem from the ease with which it is manufactured in secret labs. A drug that can be made here at home avoids the problem of smuggling across our increasingly patrolled borders. In addition, its effects are advertised as similar to those of cocaine, without the reputation for deadliness. Hall, of Up Front, says that the spread of methamphetamine "looms as a potential national drug crisis of the 1990s."

The Empathy Drug

A case study in the progression of a new drug trend can be seen in the recent emergence of MDMA, better known as Ecstasy. First produced in 1914 but forgotten for years, the drug attracted the attention of psychotherapists in the '70s because, besides its stimulant and mildly psychedelic qualities, it could also increase patients' insight and empathy. "There's very little question in my mind that it can facilitate insight-oriented psychotherapy," says psychiatrist Lester Grinspoon.

By 1985, however, Ecstasy had become a recreational drug associated with a distinct type of music and dancing called "acid house" that originated on the Spanish island of Ibiza where wealthy people vacation. It served as a sort of new, improved brand of cocaine: It was exclusive, it provided the energy for dancing until dawn, it was allegedly "harmless," and—perhaps most attractive—it made people not only want to talk— as most stimulants do—but also to listen.

Researchers quickly found, however, that Ecstasy can damage brain cells in animals, even in low doses that correspond to the dosages people use for recreation, and the DEA outlawed it for most purposes in 1985. Recently made illegal in most of Europe, it drew the kind of sensational headlines there last summer that crack had garnered in America. Yet that publicity

failed to cross the Atlantic, and Ecstasy continues to enjoy a safe and exclusive image here.

"It's a very white, very middle-class drug," says Bill Brusca, general manager of The Tunnel, a popular Manhattan nightclub. "It's not the kind of drug you're going to hear a lot about, because it's not habit-forming."

But positive accounts such as these, says Nicholas Kozel of NIDA, "are similar to what was said about cocaine in the early '80s. They're looking for the safe drug, and we're realizing that there isn't any." Even so, Kozel isn't prepared to predict that Ecstasy abuse will reach epidemic proportions. "Forecasting is difficult," he says, "and MDMA is an especially difficult drug to track."

What Does the Future Hold?

Despite the advances in trend analysis for drug abuse, nobody seems prepared to forecast the future. Some — including, most notably, psychiatrist Jerome Jaffe, the country's first "drug czar" under President Richard Nixon and the current head of federal addiction research efforts — are skeptical about our ability to make accurate predictions at all. Although he concedes that, without question, drug abuse follows a "trendy, fashionable popularity cycle," he doesn't believe we know enough about those cycles to predict what will happen next.

Historian Musto thinks that the most important trend is the decreased use of illegal drugs by the middle class that has cut through all of the various cycles since 1979. "We're 10 years into a phase of growing intolerance toward drugs," says Musto. "If history is a guide, it will take 20 to 30 more years for drug use to hit the nadir." History is indeed a guide to Musto, who investigated long-forgotten documents on America's first drug epidemic at the turn of the century for *The American Disease*. To him, the year-to-year shifts in drug use are all-but-imperceptible "blips" in our declining interest in illicit drugs.

According to Musto, "Crack seemed to be the ultimate drug problem, one so frightening that it crystallized our intolerance toward all drugs. It has created a consensus in society against drugs and ended the ambivalence that had been prevalent for decades."

Musto fears that America's turn against drugs could have serious social repercussions. "My concern is that as demand goes down in the middle class, instead of channelling efforts into long-term plans to help, people will get angrier and angrier at those in the inner city who still use drugs," he explains. "If we triple the amount of money we spend to battle the drug problem and if we pass a death-penalty measure expecting to solve the problem in a year, we'll only become frustrated by the results. The decline in drug use will be a long, gradual process. We're going

Will ignoring history make a third drug epidemic inevitable?

down a road, and we've still got a long way to go."

A drug epidemic takes on a different character when it reaches the ghetto: There are more deaths—including the killing of innocent standers-by—and other tragedies such as addiction in newborns. Failure to recognize these people as victims, Musto says, and consequent failure to pursue aggressive public education and jobs programs, will only exacerbate an already difficult social problem.

Breaking the Cycle

Once this, America's second drug epidemic, bottoms out, will we begin cycling inexorably into a third? Musto is willing to make one prediction: A society that forgets its history of abuse is doomed to repeat it. Unfortunately, says Musto, when America's first cocaine epidemic began fading in the '20s, "it became policy in the federal government to mention drugs as little as possible, and if they did mention them, to give descriptions so exaggerated and disgusting that no one would try them even once." Many adults are familiar with the 1936 propaganda film *Reefer Madness* that was circulated in the late 1950s and became

a cult favorite in the '60s and '70s. When the young people who experimented with drugs in the '60s discovered that the exaggerations couldn't be trusted, they discarded all cautions to explore the reality of drugs in earnest.

Tragically, America's ahistorical attitude toward drug abuse continues to this day. "The Department of Education in California recently came up with a new syllabus of American history," Musto says. "There's no mention of the history of drug abuse. And in one place it lists drug abuse among the unacceptable topics for history electives. The largest education system in America gives no space on its syllabus for the important history of drug abuse in the United States."

In Musto's opinion, "The history of drugs and alcohol should be integrated into American history. If people had had a vivid knowledge of the first cocaine epidemic, the second epidemic might have taken a different route."

As we live with the fallout of America's second great drug-abuse epidemic in decline, a national commitment to remember the toll it has taken may be the only way to avoid a third.

Passing a Legacy of Drug Addiction

SUMMARY: Crack has infiltrated the human life cycle. Fetuses exposed to the drug in the womb of drug-abusing mothers face a number of medical complications, including mental retardation and physical malformations. Pregnant addicts have taken to smoking the drug to induce an easier, earlier labor. But it is not so easy on the babies, who suffer withdrawal and other symptoms of their mothers' drug addiction.

Tales of motherhood in America are not what they once were. When the crew of an ambulance in Oakland, Calif., arrived at the home of a pregnant woman who had gone into labor, the attendants "had to pry [drugs] out of her hand," says Donald Sutton, a member of the Oakland Crack Task Force.

Since researchers began documenting the potentially harmful effects that certain chemical substances have on the fetus, many pregnant women have refrained from consuming or have reduced their intake of caffeine, alcohol, nicotine and even seemingly harmless analgesics.

As conscientious as some women are, however, a growing number of them abuse drugs while carrying children, a practice that has alarming consequences for the mother and child as well as the community that must bear the financial and social costs.

Drug use by mothers is frequently difficult to detect. Few hospitals routinely test for drugs among their maternal and newborn patients. As a result, researchers suspect that the incidence of pregnant women using drugs is higher than what has been documented. The National Association for Perinatal Addiction Research and Education estimates that as many as 375,000 infants born annually may be affected by their mothers' drug use. Half the babies born at Boston City Hospital, which treats a large majority of impoverished patients, show traces of some form of drug.

Crack, the cheap, highly addictive derivative of cocaine, has become the preferred drug. A hospital in Houston reported to the House Select Committee on Children, Youth, and Families that the percentage of pregnant drug abusers using cocaine, most of it thought to be in the smokable form of crack, jumped from 2 percent in 1980 to more than 80 percent this year. And health care workers are seeing an increase in accidental pregnancies — and affected infants — as more women turn to prostitution to support drug habits.

Infants who were exposed to cocaine in the womb often are born prematurely with low birth weights. They face a multitude of risks, such as mental retardation and congenital malformations. They can experience drug withdrawal and its symptoms of depression and irritability.

Researchers at the federal Centers for Disease Control in Atlanta recently discovered a strong association between maternal cocaine use and abnormalities of the urinary tract. Among infants whose mothers reported using cocaine during the first trimester of pregnancy, there was a fivefold increase in kidney obstructions. These children are in jeopardy of eventually losing their kidney function, depending on the severity of the obstruction, unless the problem is discovered and treated. The study looked at some 500,000 births in the five-county metropolitan Atlanta region from 1968 to 1980. "At the time when these babies were born, the use of cocaine was very low," says Dr. Jose F. Cordero, acting chief of the birth defects and genetic diseases branch of the CDC. If the study were conducted today, he says, "we would be even more likely to find an association."

Fetuses exposed to cocaine have also been known to die. One study found a higher rate of spontaneous abortion among pregnant cocaine users than among pregnant heroin users.

Even if the fetus survives birth, the baby may not make it beyond the first year. One preemie at D.C. General Hospital weighed 1 pound, 11 ounces at birth. A hospital worker laments, "She's about to die."

Drugs are killing more than teenagers and adults in the District of Columbia. After several years in which the District's infant mortality rate tapered off, it rose last year to 23.2 deaths per 1,000 births, the highest rate since the beginning of the decade and among the highest in the nation. City officials blame a large portion of it on mothers' use of crack.

What is making an already disastrous situation deadlier is the intentional use of crack in the later stages of pregnancy. "It's the word on the street — if you take crack, you can get the baby delivered easier. Clearly that is a fallacy. It's a highly dangerous practice and it doesn't accomplish what they hope it will," says Dr. David B. Schwartz, chairman of maternal and fetal medicine at Sinai Hospital in Detroit.

"With crack cocaine, you don't have the ability to think straight. You would tend to believe anything that anybody will tell you," says the Oakland Task Force's Sutton, who is also program coordinator for the Richard Allen Institute, an Oakland drug prevention center. "Any drug that would take away the maternal instinct — we know [is] a horrendous and horrible drug."

It is not as though drug-free women smoke crack to speed up their deliveries. For the most part, these are drug users who believe the myth that smoking crack will induce an easy, early labor. As taxing as the late stages of pregnancy are for healthy women, the substance abuser's tolerance level is lowered by the physical and psychological toll of the drugs. More than the healthy expectant mother, the drug user may be so anxious to deliver her baby that she will smoke crack. If women sell sex for drugs, they need to deliver their babies to get back on the street to earn more money to buy more drugs.

Women may very well go into labor earlier if they use cocaine, but it will not be an easier labor. Researchers at Northwestern University Medical School found that women who use cocaine throughout their pregnancies are much more likely to deliver premature babies that are more prone to physical ailments than are babies carried to full term. "Actually, the contractions are harder," says Dr. Ira J. Chasnoff, director of the Perinatal Center for Chemical Dependence at Northwestern Memorial Hospital.

By taking cocaine to induce labor, "the mother can have a stroke and die. It can cut off the oxygen supply to the baby and the baby can die," says Schwartz, who attributes the practice to ignorance and addiction.

Addicted, strung-out mothers are taking other hazardous cues from the streets, too. They are dusting nipples with cocaine to subdue fussy infants who may be particularly irritable due to the effects of the drug on their nervous systems.

"It's almost a moot point whether women are [using crack to induce labor] deliberately or not," says a social worker at a hospital in Washington, because the outcome is the same.

Alerting the female drug abuser to the additional risks to both her and her unborn child is a monumental task. Such women are reluctant to seek health care in general, and the majority turn up at hospitals to deliver their babies without having sought any prenatal care. "You're trying to reach the hardest-to-reach people," says Alonzo Plough, deputy commissioner of health and hospitals and director of public health in Boston.

Even if addicts can be enticed into seeking help, treatment programs are frequently filled to capacity. Boston squeezes 380 people into a methadone program with a capacity for 280. Furthermore, because of the high cost of malpractice insurance associated with their specialties, fewer obstetricians and midwives are willing to work in urban clinics, says Plough.

Unlike heroin addicts who are given methadone as an aid to combating their addiction, cocaine addicts have no such alternatives. Researchers at Lincoln Hospital in New York have had some success, in

a short span of time, with the use of acupuncture in treating cocaine addiction. Boston City Hospital has adopted a similar program, particularly for pregnant addicts. This fall the acupuncture treatment will be part of an outpatient program that combines counseling and, when called for, antidepressants. Participants also will be able to come to a drop-in center. "We don't have the capacity to do treatment on demand for all addicts," says Plough. At the very least, "we want to provide treatment on demand for pregnant addicts."

While education and treatment are the preferred strategies for many health care workers to deal with pregnant addicts, others are recommending prosecution. Two women have been arrested in Florida after delivering babies who tested positive for cocaine. A grand jury in Illinois this spring refused to indict a woman on charges of manslaughter after her infant died from what authorities described as prenatal cocaine use. In recent weeks, authorities in Minnesota and Connecticut have also pondered charges against pregnant addicts.

Although more cases are being referred to prosecutors, "there is no epidemic of

criminal prosecutions," says Patricia Toth, director of the National Center for the Prosecution of Child Abuse. "My gut feeling is it's going to be a combination of strategies. People often do not have the wherewithal to control their drug addiction," says Toth. But, "there are children who are born whose lives are either physically or otherwise very negatively affected. We can't ignore that."

If, by some miracle, pregnant women stopped using drugs, the chain would not disappear. Many of the exposed children, even if they grow up in a healthy environment (an unlikely event if their mothers continue abusing drugs), will be plagued with developmental and emotional afflictions. "These children are certainly at risk for long-term problems," says Chasnoff.

Sutton knows a woman who has been raising her nephew since her sister, a cocaine addict, abandoned him at birth. Five years later, the woman is having trouble getting him into kindergarten. The boy has severe behavioral problems, a suspected legacy of his cocaine-complicated birth.

— Karen Diegmueller

New Ways to Crack a Cocaine Addiction

SUMMARY: Many experts view cocaine as the most habit-forming of drugs and its addictive lure as the most difficult one to control. Several new treatments are being tested that have shown promising results so far. But researchers still do not know whether the therapeutic drugs will help users maintain permanent abstention.

In years past when a cocaine craving set in, Richard A.'s only priority was to get a fix. When he had some ready cash, it was no problem to drive into the city and buy an ounce. But on the few occasions when he was short, the overpowering urge for the drug led him to commit robberies. On some occasions, he robbed someone at gunpoint or went after a convenience store, where he was assured of a full cash register.

Those episodes ended after he was arrested and convicted of armed robbery, but he still craved the cocaine high and knew he could not control it. Richard had tried Cocaine Anonymous counseling and a few other specialized treatment programs during his 20-year on-again, off-again relationship with the drug, but he repeatedly fell back into the binge routine, which became progressively more frequent in the years following his discovery of the ecstatic high he could achieve by injecting the drug directly into his veins.

Richard is in a new program now and finally feels he is not destined to repeat those dark, long years of addiction. He is a member of a group of test subjects being treated for cocaine addiction with carbamazepine, an anticonvulsant drug routinely prescribed to epileptics to control seizures. He has been clean for five months and is impressed by the fact that the drug eliminates his frantic craving for cocaine. Taking carbamazepine, in addition to undergoing weekly counseling sessions, has made him confident, for the first time, that he can keep the drug out of his life.

"When you do cocaine for a long time, you don't have fun doing anything else," he says. "Carbamazepine isn't the only thing working for me, but it was the first thing to break my cycle of going out for cocaine, and it gave me time to get my life back together."

The progress he and others are making is triggering new optimism among researchers who are treating cocaine and crack addicts with various medications that have been around for years to treat depression and psychosis. Several drugs are undergoing clinical trials to test their effectiveness in subduing the craving for cocaine that some medical experts consider the most intensely powerful sensation known to man. Using these pharmacological agents as an adjunct to counseling and behavior therapy, researchers hope that by lessening the craving, patients may benefit more from other forms of therapy and counseling.

Researchers understand how cocaine manipulates the brain to constantly want more, but how to treat addiction successfully has proved a Herculean task. While it may be considered the most habituating drug, its withdrawal symptoms are much less obvious than those of an alcoholic, for example. In the early phases of treatment, minimizing craving is extremely important; the highest risk of relapse occurs within the first 10 weeks of treatment. Statistics show that as many as half of all patients resume drug use within a year after leaving the sheltered environment of a treatment facility, often due to psychological cues linked to their drug past.

Unlike antidepressants, the effectiveness of carbamazepine is not wholly attributed to its influence on dopamine receptors, the pleasure centers in the brain that become flooded under the influence of cocaine. It addresses craving specifically, zeroing in on the supersensitivity of brain cells, says James Halikas, professor of psychiatry at the University of Minnesota, who reported impressive results in his initial clinical trials with the drug and is about to complete a more comprehensive trial.

The similarity between what occurs in the brain to produce certain kinds of epileptic seizures and what takes place during cocaine use accounts for the apparent effectiveness of carbamazepine. The anticonvulsant appears to reverse "kindling," a rapid firing of neurons by brain cells triggered by cocaine use, he says. Kindling produces a sensitivity in the cells, which in the cocaine user translates into craving. Based on preliminary animal research conducted by Robert Post and Susan Weiss of the National Institute of Mental Health, Halikas theorized that by reducing this sensitivity with carbamazepine, craving would be minimized.

In a sample of 13 cocaine users, approximately half abstained from cocaine for several months on average when taking daily doses of carbamazepine. The remaining patients tended not to be as faithful about taking the doses but were able to abstain from cocaine for varying periods when they took the treatment. All 13, however, agreed that when they were taking carbamazepine, their craving for cocaine was significantly reduced, according to Halikas and his colleagues.

Carbamazepine also appears to possess an added deterrent. Several patients who used cocaine while also taking the treatment admitted that the intensity of the high was diminished significantly and that it took at least twice as much cocaine as usual to achieve their customary high. Halikas predicts that if further studies bear out what the researchers have observed so far, carbamazepine could be distributed from clinics and treatment facilities in much the same way that methadone is made available to heroin addicts.

"We are at the forefront of the consumer

By Dina Van Pelt. From *Insight*, July 31, 1989, pp. 54-55. Reprinted by permission. All rights reserved.

"The concern I have about the use of these drugs is the false message that they can simply come in, give a urine sample, get some more and then be OK."

end of drug abuse," says Halikas. "From the treatment view, this approach is a major breakthrough because it gets at the biochemical heart of how these abusive drugs work. If this discovery looks as good a year from now as it does at this point, I think everyone will be using it."

Another treatment that shows promise is an antidepressant and antipsychotic drug called flupenthixol decanoate, which has shown abstinence-promoting properties in two preliminary studies on smokers of crack, the highly potent rock form of cocaine. Crack smokers often have a harder time staying off the drug because crack is more concentrated, a greater amount is absorbed into the brain sooner and the high is immediate.

Just as the quick hit is a blockbuster, so are the craving and the crash of depression that follow if more crack is not smoked. Addiction often occurs within weeks or even days after crack is first tried, while a casual snorter of cocaine may take years to become addicted. And because crack smokers tend to have such a difficult time staying off the drug with just counseling therapy, some pharmacological agent is also used early on in treatment.

In one study of 10 crack smokers at an outpatient treatment program in the Bahamas, intramuscular injections of flupenthixol not only appeared to decrease the users' craving and facilitate abstinence but also increased the average amount of time that users remained in treatment. The drug also produced positive clinical effects in one to three days, which is sooner than the seven to 14 days characteristic of other medications.

The researchers, led by Frank H. Gawin of Yale University School of Medicine, say they are particularly impressed because flupenthixol appears to eliminate craving without exacerbating the crash depression that often intensifies the need. As with carbamazepine, those treated reported a diminished euphoria when they resumed smoking crack. Flupenthixol is not marketed in the United States but is available clinically in the Far East, Europe and the Caribbean.

Gawin also has conducted trials to determine the effectiveness of desipramine, an antidepressant drug, on stimulating initial abstinence from cocaine. He and his colleagues report that out of 72 addicts treated with the drug, almost 60 percent stayed off cocaine during a short-term trial of three to four weeks. The subjects also reported reduced craving.

The double-blind study compared desipramine with lithium carbonate and a placebo. In Gawin's view, desipramine may represent a new class of substance abuse treatment that does not work as a cocaine antagonist but instead speeds up the return to normal of a central nervous system that has been damaged by years of abuse.

Bromocriptine, a drug used to treat victims of Parkinson's disease, is also given to some cocaine addicts to stunt craving when they begin treatment. Bromocriptine increases the uptake of dopamine in the brain and offsets the jerky physical movements characteristic of patients with Parkinson's, often evidenced in heavy cocaine users.

None of these new treatments is habit-forming or has any overwhelming side effects and, unlike methadone, using any of them is not considered to be a replacement of one addiction with another, doctors say.

And in most cases, patients cannot build a tolerance to them. The main question that the experts cannot answer is if and when craving ever diminishes, even if a user gets treatment with drugs and behaviorial therapy.

Tests on animals indicate the craving is indefinite, but it is not known whether this is the case in humans. Researchers know, however, that even after several years of abstinence and extensive counseling, a relapse can occur spontaneously, most often triggered by a cue from the past. This is where medications given to alleviate craving early on in treatment leave off, argue those who are more in favor of psychosocial counseling.

"The concern I have about the use of these drugs is the false message that we may be giving clients that they can simply come in once a week, give a urine sample, get some more desipramine, carbamazepine or whatever and then be OK," says James Cocores, medical director of the outpatient recovery center of the Fair Oaks Hospital in Summit, N.J. Cocores urges a structured outpatient counseling program in conjunction with these medications.

Although the early research is promising, researchers cannot predict at this stage whether treatment with drugs such as carbamazepine involves a lifelong commitment or is simply an initial stepping-stone to getting straight. It could take years to determine whether this approach has any effect on reducing the staggering relapse rate of those addicted to cocaine. But it is a new direction in treating a very specific and mystifying aspect of cocaine addiction that has not been responsive to much else.

— *Dina Van Pelt*

The return of a deadly drug called horse

Heroin is back on the streets, more potent and more plentiful than ever

At first, Etonia would drink beer to feel more mellow during the crashing aftereffects of coming down from a crack-cocaine high. Then, the 30-year-old New York City woman found something better: Heroin. "I'd buy heroin and crack and cook them all up together. It was like I was on a ride at Coney Island," she says. "I'd reach my euphoria and then come down, and hit the corners and slow down, and my body was gone."

There are thousands of Etonias in urban America today, and their number is rising. While cocaine remains America's worst drug problem, a fact confirmed by last week's National Household Survey on Drug Abuse, authorities say heroin is showing ominous signs of a resurgence, and this time it is piggybacking onto the crack-addiction crisis and perhaps spreading far beyond its previous boundaries. "We are on the verge of another heroin epidemic . . . that may be the worst in United States history," says Senate Judiciary Committee Chairman Joseph Biden (D-Del.). And that could produce a large new generation of ad-

dicts, while overloading an already strained treatment system and creating a potent new drug cartel.

Reports from the streets are chilling. Purity levels have jumped from 4 percent to 7 percent two years ago to about 40 percent today, a leap termed "unbelievable" by Robert Stutman, the Drug Enforcement Administration's chief in New York. "The more potent the heroin that's available, the more overdoses we're going to see, and the easier it is to become addicted," says Dr. Stanley Yancovitz, a chemical-dependency expert at Manhattan's Beth Israel Medical Center. Heroin-related hospital emergencies climbed 9.5 percent from 1987 to 1988.

On "deck." As heroin has gotten more plentiful, wholesale prices have dropped from $190,000 to $200,000 per kilogram four years ago to $160,000 to $170,000 today and are expected to drop further, which officials fear could fuel an expanding market. A "dime bag" of "horse"—about 0.05 grams—typically costs $10 and is often sold as part of a 10-pack, known as a "deck," which

might sell for $100. Heroin seizures by the DEA rose 288 percent between 1981 and 1988. Officials fear the addict population is growing. Assistant FBI Director Tony Daniels believes the last official government estimate of 490,000 heroin addicts is grossly underestimated. A new estimate is being prepared, and a Justice Department report said last week the total could be as high as 750,000.

What alarms drug experts most is the increasing popularity of smoking heroin, as opposed to injecting it. The greater purity of heroin has enhanced the "kick" available from smoking it, and the heroin high lasts longer than that of crack. More important, smoking heroin eliminates the stigma and complication of using needles and thus removes the fear of AIDS as well, which dangerously broadens heroin's allure. And after years of believing heroin devotees to be an aging group in their 30s and 40s, authorities now report seeing younger users. "Smoking opens up the specter of heroin addiction to a whole new population," says Stutman.

Authorities report that growing numbers of crack addicts are smoking heroin

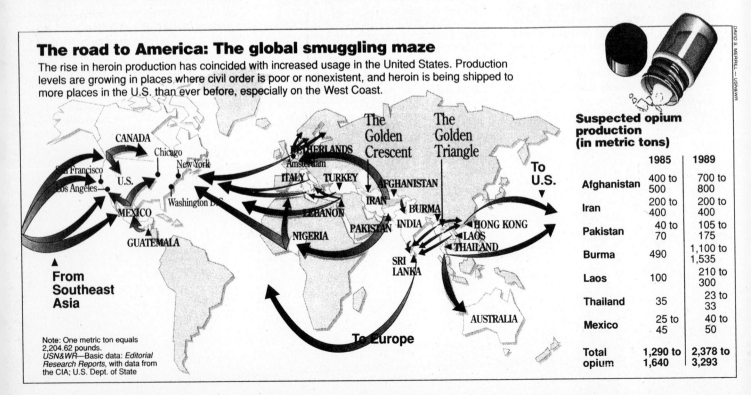

The road to America: The global smuggling maze

The rise in heroin production has coincided with increased usage in the United States. Production levels are growing in places where civil order is poor or nonexistent, and heroin is being shipped to more places in the U.S. than ever before, especially on the West Coast.

Note: One metric ton equals 2,204.62 pounds.
USN&WR—Basic data: *Editorial Research Reports*, with data from the CIA; U.S. Dept. of State

Suspected opium production (in metric tons)

	1985	1989
Afghanistan	400 to 500	700 to 800
Iran	200 to 400	200 to 400
Pakistan	40 to 70	105 to 175
Burma	490	1,100 to 1,535
Laos	100	210 to 300
Thailand	35	23 to 33
Mexico	25 to 45	40 to 50
Total opium	1,290 to 1,640	2,378 to 3,293

with crack, a phenomenon known as "chasing the dragon." The appeal of the combination is that it prolongs the high, while slowing down the racing feeling of crack and reducing the anxiety, depression and paranoia that would otherwise occur when the crack wears off. "Doing the dragon gave you that little drowsiness so you could kick back and be a little more aware, instead of just having that full-tilt feeling from crack," says David, 23, a recovering New York addict. "Heroin cut some of the intensity off of it." Officials at New York's Phoenix House, a drug-rehabilitation program, were shocked to find that 37 percent of recently admitted crack users reported mixing it with heroin. Not surprisingly, the newest problem in treatment programs is coping with a growing population of those addicted to two separate drugs. "A polydrug addiction is harder to treat than a single drug addiction," says Yancovitz of Beth Israel.

Heroin has come back because production and distribution systems have been re-established. Recent seizures suggest demand may be magnitudes beyond previous estimates. The DEA's 1987 estimate of heroin consumption in New York was about 3,000 pounds annually. But in February, 1988, some 2,400 pounds destined for New York was seized in Bangkok, and this past February, federal agents snatched 800 pounds of heroin hidden in golf-cart tires in Queens, N.Y. Yet no one believes the police are finding more than 15 percent of the supply.

Distribution of the product has grown deadly efficient. Successful law-enforcement strikes against the Mafia earlier in the 1980s left a void in heroin marketing that has been aggressively filled the past three years by ethnic-Chinese gangs peddling a high-quality product from Southeast Asia. The Chinese groups are secretive, intimidating, tightly knit and speak a dizzying array of dialects, while operating in the crazy-quilt atmosphere of Chinatowns in New York and San Francisco. All that makes them devilishly tough for law enforcement to penetrate. Fewer than 2 percent of DEA and FBI agents are Asian. The DEA's New York office formed a Southeast Asian task force in 1986. They have scored some successes, like the recent New York guilty plea of kingpin Johnny Kon, who faces up to life imprisonment for a heroin-smuggling conspiracy. But, a knowledgeable Senate staffer says, "federal agencies just don't have the expertise to go after these rings like they have after more-traditional organized crime."

Flourishing in lawless lands. The driving force behind heroin's renaissance can be found in the poppy fields of lawless, mysterious lands with names like the Golden Triangle (in Southeast Asia) and the Golden Crescent (in Southwest Asia). Worldwide opium output is skyrocketing, thanks in part to prime growing conditions and political turmoil that makes government control virtually hopeless. American officials say there is little they can do about that, because 90 percent of the world's opium production takes place in areas over which the U.S. has little control—places like Burma, Laos, Iran, Lebanon and Afghanistan. Afghanistan has seen opium production rise significantly in the recent years of civil war. American authorities fear that if the situation there ever calms down, returning refugees will seize on opium as a quick cash crop instead of the more traditional wheat farming or fruit harvesting, thus increasing opium production even more. In Burma, where ruthless warlord armies produce the world's largest crop of illicit opium, a U.S.-funded eradication program was scrapped when aid was cut off following last fall's military takeover and political violence there. American officials say the Burmese are now too focused on repressing opposition to care much about narcotics control. They predict Burmese opium production will probably jump another 25 percent or more. In addition, recent discovery of opium-poppy fields and a makeshift heroin lab in Colombia have authorities concerned that the South American drug cartels may seriously be contemplating entry into the heroin business.

In coming months, the nation's attention will be focused on the war on cocaine. Drug czar William Bennett says his upcoming drug strategy will concentrate on the ravages of crack, and few would argue with that tack. The federal household survey of drug use showed that, while casual drug use is declining, cocaine addiction continues to rise. But some policymakers like Senator Biden believe the time to attack heroin is now, before it mushrooms into a full-blown crisis that forces beleaguered American drug agents into a hopeless two-front war.

Gordon Witkin

THE INVISIBLE LINE

Maia Szalavitz

His eyes are vacant, his posture twisted. His greyish-green skin color identifies him as "sick." He sits on the stoop of a graffitied brownstone amid broken glass, scattered crack vials and syringes. He's an addict. A loud street noise startles him. His eyes make contact with a passerby. They're like black holes, sending out disturbing, conflicted messages of fear, anger and despair. The passerby looks away and moves quickly down the block.

What drug did this to him? Those who have had success in treating addicts say it doesn't matter. He has crossed what people in the business of treating addiction call "the invisible line"--the border which divides those who can use mind and mood altering drugs safely and those who cannot.

Take another look at the addict on the stoop. His dilated pupils indicate the beginnings of heroin withdrawal or the actual high of crack. Both are dangerous states during which addicts commit acts of violence. When people are high on opiates (and not in withdrawal), they tend to "nod out" into a dreamy, quiet state that lasts 4-6 hours; as long as they have their drug, they're harmless.

On the other hand, cocaine addicts are dangerous whether they are high--which lasts, at most, 20 minutes per dose--or craving the drug. The coke crash is more extreme than the heroin crash. Junkies usually sleep and are unaware of the crash, while coke addicts can't sleep, often becoming depressed and experiencing manic paranoia These effects are even more pronounced when the extremely impure freebase, crack, is the form of coke being abused.

"Crack's the worst," says Joe L., a former coke dealer. "The cocaine used to make it is the lowest quality, and the chemicals used to produce it often remain in the crack. Smoking those chemicals alone is bound to make you crazy, but in combination with freebase cocaine, it's sick. Guaranteed psychosis."

This explains why so much violence is associated with crack. One addict, Roger J., described the high and the ensuing comedown: "I felt invincible, really fast. It made me wild. I just had to keep that high going. I was definitely insane. Coming down was a new experience in pain. I tried to sleep, but couldn't. My body was shaking, weak, drained of energy and rational thought. I was completely null and void--zero. It was like I was on top of the Empire State Building going down in an elevator without brakes."

What can be done to treat this fearsome addiction? First, we have to examine what's been done to treat other addictions. For much of the history of substance-abuse treatment, addiction has been viewed as the inability to control the use of a specific substance--heroin, coke or alcohol. Whole methodologies of treatment have long been based on this mistaken assumption. Methadone, for example, is substituted for heroin with the idea that heroin addicts have a problem solely with that substance, not with their way of dealing with life in general. This narrow approach has prevented many addicts from getting the kind of help they really need.

While cocaine brings you "up" and heroin brings you "down," both take you "out," to the psychological escape routes all addicts seek. So, of course, does alcohol. Researchers have found a chemical produced in the brains of alcoholics, and not normal drinkers, which is also produced in heroin addicts. This chemical, THIQ, never metabolizes and stays in the brain forever. THIQ is an extremely addictive painkiller that causes rats, which normally would rather starve than drink alcohol, to prefer booze to water. (For more information, see *THIQ Is Alcoholism: Clinical & Experimental Research,* Grove & Stratton, NY, 1983.) One can begin to see here an actual physiological basis for the disease of addiction.

Addiction treatment in this country has overlooked these facts for years. Methadone maintenance is the classic example, and is especially important to examine in light of recent calls by public officials to produce a methadone "clone" as a treatment for crack addiction.

Supposedly, methadone blocks the physical craving for opiates without producing the high. But, in reality, as a synthetic opiate, it generates classic opiate activity--painkilling, mild euphoria--in the brain. Methadone blocks heroin the way vodka blocks gin. If you're too drunk to get any more drunk, it doesn't matter how much more you drink--you just won't feel it. Methadone proponents may say otherwise, but this is how methadone really works.

Other drugs, such as naltrexone and nalozone, do block opiates. However, no junkie would willingly line up at a clinic at 6 a.m. to take them, nor would anyone resell them on the street--as is commonly done with methadone--for one simple reason: they don't get you high. Even worse for the junkie, they produce withdrawal symptoms.

Withdrawal from methadone is also more severe than from heroin. Treatment centers are rife with stories about people who were kept awake a month kicking methadone. (Insomnia usually lasts a week when kicking heroin.) Says one counselor, Mary C., herself a former addict: "It would be better to maintain them on heroin."

New York Newsday recently ran a four-part series on methadone treatment in New York. It reported that more than 60 percent of patients on methadone take illegal drugs--usually crack or intravenous cocaine. Joe L. told HIGH TIMES about his experience at a methadone clinic. "All methadone did for me was increase my cocaine use," he said. "I never had a clean urine the whole time I was on the stuff--and those who did were usually faking it. I saw people use their children's urine, even sell their children's urine. And the counseling was a joke. I can't think of one person there who wasn't using something else--alcohol, drugs or whatever."

Despite these claims, methadone maintenance continues to be funded. Why? Why else? Money. Methadone makes millions of dollars for those who run the clinics, which are little more than drug dealerships. According to *Newsday,* even though some New York clinics have not been inspected in years, hire the barest minimum of personnel and are almost always severely neglected, they're still allowed to stay in business. *Newsday*'s investigation also revealed that a flourishing black market for methadone exists outside the clinics.

Nevertheless, New York recently expanded methadone treatment as an attempt to halt the spread of AIDS. But since most people who shoot heroin also shoot coke, this idea is ludicrous. Now, even more methadone will be sold, at the expense of cutting what's left of the clinic's bare-bones counseling staffs. As it is, "there's no instruction in living sober," says Mary C. "No career counseling. Nothing."

At the clinics, addicts are told that they must resign themselves to lives of waiting in line for their cups of methadone. In fact, they are discouraged from trying to get off drugs, told that escaping the claws of methadone will only lead them back to the iron grasp of street drugs. Methadone has become an end--make that, a dead end--in itelf.

From *High Times,* September 1989, p. 21. Reprinted by permission.

Cocaine: Litany of Fetal Risks Grows

Researchers find that a majority of exposed newborns suffer damage.

JANE E. BRODY

The first detailed studies of babies exposed to cocaine before birth suggest that this widely used drug is causing an epidemic of damaged infants, some of whom may be impaired for life because their mothers used cocaine even briefly during pregnancy.

The new evidence of fetal hazards is the latest addition to the growing medical indictment of cocaine, which until this decade was thought by many to be a relatively innocent drug. In recent years, cocaine has been shown to be addictive and dangerous, even potentially fatal for adult users.

The new research has found a wide spectrum of ill effects that can result from fetal exposure to cocaine. These include retarded growth in the womb and subtle neurological abnormalities, which may afflict a majority of exposed newborns. In more extreme cases, cocaine can cause loss of the small intestine and brain-damaging strokes.

The researchers offer one hopeful note: Doctors and therapists who work with babies of cocaine users have discovered that a variety of parenting techniques can help minimize the behavioral and movement difficulties that afflict many of the babies. These experts hope that with such techniques, the effects of cocaine on many infants can be largely or entirely countered.

The litany of threats to newborns is long and growing. Cocaine-exposed babies are more likely to die before birth or to be born prematurely. They tend to be abnormally small for their age at birth and have smaller-than-normal heads and brains. They face an increased risk of deformities of the genital and urinary organs, including kidney malformations that can lead to life-threatening infections.

Cocaine-exposed babies also face a tenfold increase in the risk of crib death. These sudden, unexplained deaths usually follow several episodes in which the babies stop breathing for abnormally long periods. More serious cocaine-induced handicaps such as strokes are believed to be relatively rare. But researchers said that other problems, like inhibited prenatal growth and subtle neurological abnormalities, may affect the majority of babies exposed to cocaine.

The emerging medical findings are especially ominous in view of new indications of widespread use of cocaine, either snorted or smoked in its potent form of crack, by pregnant women. A survey released last week of women having babies at 36 hospitals around the country found that, on average, 11 percent were exposing their unborn babies to illegal drugs, with cocaine the most common. The rates varied among hospitals from less than 1 percent to 27 percent; the hospitals included some in urban and some in rural areas, some serving the poor and some serving higher income groups.

Studies conducted among 115 pregnant women at Northwestern Memorial Hospital in Chicago have shown that some of the worst effects on unborn children occur when cocaine is used during the first three months of pregnancy, when a baby's organs are forming, and often before the woman realizes she is pregnant.

Even if a woman stops the drug once pregnancy is diagnosed or uses it only intermittently, her baby can suffer physical or behavioral problems, the studies revealed.

Single 'Hit' Is Dangerous

In fact, the research suggests that a single cocaine "hit" during pregnancy can cause lasting fetal damage. While a single dose of cocaine and its metabolites clear out of an adult body within 48 hours, an unborn baby is exposed for four or five days, according to Dr. Ira J. Chasnoff, who directed the survey of 36 hospitals.

Cocaine, which is soluble in fat, readily crosses the placenta, where the baby's body converts a significant portion of it to norcocaine, a water-soluble substance that does not leave the womb and that is even more potent than cocaine. Norcocaine is excreted into the amniotic fluid, which the fetus swallows, re-exposing itself to the drug. As a result, the researchers believe, almost no cocaine-exposed baby fully escapes its damaging effects.

The new findings on cocaine hazards to infants, as well as the survey on drug abuse by pregnant women, were discussed last week at a meeting in New York sponsored by the National Association for Perinatal Addiction Research and Education. Dr. Chasnoff is director of the group, which is based in Chicago.

At the meeting, Dr. Chasnoff described the tragic results of "recreational" cocaine use by a suburban couple. Although the couple had snorted cocaine from time to time for years, the woman stopped using it in the second month of pregnancy and she remained drug-free until she was nearly ready to give birth. Then her husband gave her 5 grams of cocaine as an anniversary gift, prompting her to break her abstinence.

The drug-precipitated labor and the baby, a boy, was born with limited use of his right arm and leg. He had suffered a cocaine-induced stroke that damaged a large segment of his brain just before he was born.

Dr. Chasnoff, director of the Perinatal Center for Chemical Dependence at Northwestern Memorial Hospital and founder of the national as-

Babies exposed to cocaine often suffer subtle neurological abnormalities.

sociation, explained that strokes occur because cocaine causes a sudden increase in fetal blood pressure. The baby's heart rate rises dramatically and remains elevated for hours. A stroke that cuts off circulation to the small intestine can cause the gut to atrophy, making it impossible for the baby to digest food after birth.

"It takes only one hit of cocaine to cause a stroke in the baby before or just after birth," Dr. Chasnoff said in an interview. The physician will also present his findings later this week at a meeting on prenatal drug abuse. The meeting will be at the Hyatt Regency in Bethesda, Md., under the sponsorship of the New York Academy of Sciences.

Among the more worrisome effects of fetal exposure to cocaine are often-subtle impairments in the development of the nervous system. These can interfere with a child's ability to learn and interact normally with people and the environment. Such problems can result in a poor relationship with parents and lead ultimately to failure in school and society.

But these are also the problems that may diminish with time and that the researchers said could be minimized if parents were shown how best to handle their drug-damaged child.

Dr. Dan R. Griffith, developmental psychologist at Northwestern University, said parents could be taught to recognize when their babies are becoming unduly agitated and to take simple steps to calm them, such as swaddling them in a blanket.

'Easily Overloaded'

He explained that cocaine-exposed babies are often born with "a very fragile, easily overloaded nervous system." They tend to be hypersensitive and irritable, screaming inconsolably at the slighest provocation. A sudden noise or change in position, even talking to and looking at the baby, can trigger prolonged crying.

Other cocaine-exposed babies escape into a deep sleep for 90 percent of the time to shut themselves off from outside stimulation. They will not wake up even if undressed, talked to, rocked or physically manipulated, Dr. Griffith said.

The neurological problems can persist for months, interfering with a wholesome attachment between mother and baby, Dr. Griffith said. In

some cases, he said, frustrated mothers have abused their children.

"The baby tends to shut the mother out and become very irritable when she tries to attend to his needs," he said. "The mother becomes withdrawn from the infant and resents

him for not returning her attentions."

Learning Disabilities Possible

Moreover, Dr. Griffith's preliminary findings on older cocaine-exposed children suggest that the neurological problems may later

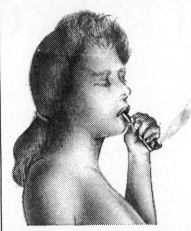

A Vicious Assault On the Unborn Child

New research shows that a pregnant woman who uses cocaine exposes the fetus to stresses that continue long after the drug is used. The risks of miscarriage, premature birth and stillbirth are increased, and because of cocaine's chemical properties, a byproduct lingers in the system, repeatedly battering the developing child.

Cocaine is fat-soluble, letting it easily penetrate the placenta, which nourishes the fetus. A byproduct, norcocaine, is water-soluble and remains trapped there.

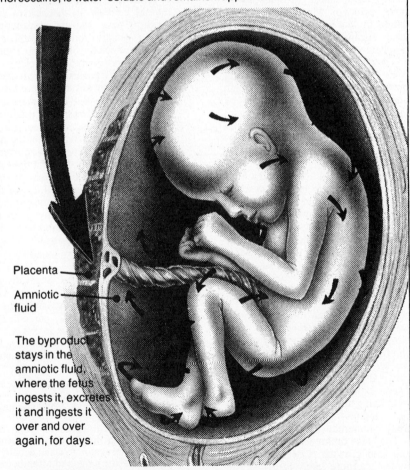

Placenta

Amniotic fluid

The byproduct stays in the amniotic fluid, where the fetus ingests it, excretes it and ingests it over and over again, for days.

LASTING DAMAGE. Effects can include retarded growth, stiff limbs, hyper-irritability, tendency to stop breathing with higher risk of crib death, and, in extreme cases, malformed genital and urinary organs, a missing small intestine and strokes and seizures.

Illustration by Judith Glick

show up as learning disabilities, hyperactivity and difficulty focusing.

Jane Schneider, a physical therapist at Children's Memorial Hospital in Chicago, said that cocaine-exposed babies also often have motor difficulties that can prevent them from exploring their bodies and nearby objects and that may interfere with their ability to crawl and walk. Her studies indicate that cocaine babies are 40 times as likely to suffer delays in motor development as infants not exposed to drugs before birth.

Dr. Griffith, who is studying the development of 400 cocaine-exposed babies, has found that parents can be taught to "read" their babies' signals of distress and to help keep the baby calm and responsive. Ms. Schneider, the therapist, said parents can also learn how to hold and move their babies to counter the motor abnormalities caused by cocaine.

"We teach the mothers how to stimulate their babies without overstimulating them," Dr. Griffith said. "Many mothers hold the baby too close. If the baby tries to ignore the mother, the mother becomes more intrusive and the baby becomes more agitated or rejecting. They both end up frustrated and unhappy."

Early signs that the baby's nervous system is being overloaded include hiccoughs, yawns, sneezes, grimaces, jerky movements, flushed skin, averted or closed eyes and crying. A baby showing such signs of distress will often lose control if pushed further. When this happens, removing all

Doctors say that even one 'hit' of the drug can inflict damage on a fetus.

stimuli and swaddling the baby in a blanket can help calm the infant.

Simple Stimulus Recommended

Dr. Griffith has shown that cocaine-exposed infants do better when presented with one simple stimulus at a time. The mother, for example, might talk to the baby without moving, or move without talking. The human face is often too complicated a stimulus for these babies to handle and thus they remain calmer if held close but facing away from the mother. Looking at a ball and trying to follow its movements is easier for these babies than watching a face, he said.

Sucking on a pacifier, the psychologist has found, is often critical to the baby's ability to remain calm. If the baby starts to get agitated, he will usually calm down if held vertically with support under the thighs and rocked gently up and down.

"These babies need a lot of help from caretakers to maintain control of their hyperexcitable nervous systems," Dr. Griffith said, adding that it is also important not to let the baby cry. "Mothers should not worry about spoiling the babies by picking them

up when they cry. They should not let the babies scream but rather do what they can to calm the babies down."

Ms. Schneider's studies have shown that by four months of age, cocaine-exposed babies tend to be very stiff, even rigid. They have difficulty rounding their hips and raising their legs to explore their feet.

Babies Remain Standing

They also have problems bringing their hands together and relaxing their fists. They seem to enjoy standing up and will remain standing on their toes for very long periods, apparently unable to relax their bodies enough to sit back down.

Parents can help, she said, by holding the babies in a relaxed posture, upright against the parent's hip with a hand under the thighs to keep the legs flexed and the baby's shoulders rounded to permit the hands to come together.

"These babies should be discouraged from standing until they are ready to lift themselves up to a standing position," Ms. Schneider said. "And they should not be left lying on their backs for long periods; they're too stiff in that position."

"Infant walkers and jumpers are also very bad — for all babies, but especially for stiff babies," she added. "Rather than training the baby to walk, the walker may impede progress by keeping the infant from crawling around. It is far better to put the baby in a playpen or on a blanket on the floor."

MARIJUANA

Is there new reason to worry?

Winifred Gallagher *is a Senior Editor of* American Health.

America just can't decide what to do about marijuana. Some people equate smoking pot with sipping wine, others with abusing hard drugs. Most rank it somewhere in between. The confusion is awkward but understandable: Marijuana is the nation's most popular but perhaps least understood illegal psychoactive substance.

So far, studies of pot's health effects suggest what many who've smoked it would predict: For most people, occasional use probably isn't particularly harmful. Heavy use over long periods is likelier to be dangerous, although the kind of expensive, long-term studies that proved the destructive effects of tobacco and alcohol remain to be done. At present, those who seem most at risk include young people, pregnant and nursing women, heart patients and the emotionally unstable. Harvard psychiatrist and drug researcher Norman Zinberg summarizes the inadequate and conflicting data this way: "Nothing's been proved, but there's reason to worry."

There's a pressing reason to learn more about marijuana's effects: The pot on the street has increased in strength and potential harmfulness. Thousands of professional growers, many of them in Northern California,

have transformed American homegrown from a cottage industry into a multibillion-dollar-a-year agribusiness. These knowledgeable farmers use sophisticated technologies like hydroponics to cultivate pot powerful enough to command astronomical prices—more than $100 an ounce in big cities.

Recent studies show there are plenty of customers, though not quite as many as there used to be. Pot smoking peaked in 1978, and has declined since, especially among teenagers. The number of high-school seniors who smoke it daily fell by over half from 1978 to 1986. However, the drug remains enormously popular: Some 62 million Americans have tried it, and 18 million smoke it regularly. Many of today's smokers are the babyboomers who first lit up in the '60s and '70s. But some have found that the drug that mellowed them as hippies can make them uptight as yuppies.

One reason that pot smoking makes many graying members of the Woodstock generation anxious these days is that even occasional use can jeopardize their livelihoods; Many face tests to detect traces of the drug in their urine as a condition of employment. Even long-ago indulgence

can damage reputations, as Judge Douglas Ginsburg learned when he was forced to withdraw himself from consideration for the U.S. Supreme Court.

The uncertainty over almost every aspect of marijuana has created confusing, contradictory policies. At the same time that the practice of urine testing spreads, laws in many states increasingly treat users with leniency. Although smokers can still be jailed in some states, they are now merely fined in others where the drug has been "decriminalized." In Alaska they can even legally grow their own. Smoking marijuana continues to become more socially acceptable, but the question remains: Is it safe?

What Pot Is, How It Works

Marijuana is not a simple—or even a single—drug. Its wide range of effects on body and mind is caused by the more than 400 chemicals of the Cannabis sativa plant especially the 60 or so that are unique to it—the cannabinoids (see "Medical Benefits?"). Some of these may contribute only minimally to the "high," but THC (delta-9-tetrahydrocannabinol) produces most of the psychoactive effects. While the potency of street

Pot mellowed the hippies, but can make yuppies uptight.

Signs of Trouble

"There are no simple signs that a person has a serious problem with marijuana, but there are some common patterns," says Dr. Robert Millman, of the New York Hospital-Payne Whitney Clinic. "An interaction of the drug, the person and the environment is usually involved." According to the American Psychiatric Association, 4% of adults in this country suffer from "cannabis dependence" at some time in their lives.

Doctors stress that it can be very difficult to distinguish whether a pot problem is a symptom or a cause. The problem is that users in trouble often have pre-existing personality or mood disorders, which are aggravated by the drug. However, indications of a dependence on marijuana include:

■ A pattern of daily or almost daily use, usually developed over a long period. Chronic heavy users generally increase the frequency of smoking over time, rather than the dose. But they also find, with long-term use, that they eventually get less pleasure from smoking.

■ Impaired ability to function socially or on the job.

■ Use of other drugs together with marijuana.

■ Lethargy.

■ Anhedonia—the inability to feel pleasure.

■ Attention and memory problems.

drugs varies greatly, the average concentration of THC by weight has increased from about 1% or less in the '60s and '70s to anywhere from 4% to 10% in the '80s.

When marijuana is smoked, THC enters the lungs, passes into the blood stream and is carried to the brain in minutes. Both THC and its chemical by-products dissolve in fatty tissue—such as the brain, the adrenals, the gonads and the placenta—and remain there for three or more days. (These chemicals can be detected in the urine of frequent smokers for four weeks or more.) It's worrisome that these compounds linger in the body and accumulate with repeated smoking, but there's no evidence yet that they cause harm.

In the brain itself, according to Dr. Billy Martin, a professor of pharmacology at the Medical College of Virginia in Richmond, THC seems to turn on a number of biochemical systems. In low concentrations it may cause two or three changes; in stronger doses, 10 or 12. Says Martin: "The high is probably a combination of effects—sedation, euphoria and perceptual alterations—each caused by a separate mechanism." He thinks that molecules of THC produce their effects by fitting into special receptor cells in the brain, like keys in locks. If Martin and his colleagues could prove the existence of the receptors, their discovery would suggest that a THC-like biochemical occurs naturally—the body's own version of marijuana. "Such a substance could serve in the maintenance of mental health," Martin says, "perhaps by helping the individual to calm down or protect himself against stress."

High Anxiety

During the marijuana high, which lasts for two to four hours after smoking, users often experience relaxation and altered perception of sights, sounds and tastes. One of pot's commonest side effects is the "munchies"—a craving for snacks, especially sugary ones. Participants in a study at Johns Hopkins ate more snacks—and consumed more calories per day—while they had access to marijuana in a social situation.

The high can be subtle and somewhat controllable, and intoxicated users can seem sober to themselves and others. But this *feeling* of sobriety is one of pot's greatest risks to well-being. Hours after the sensation of being stoned is over, the drug can still impair psychomotor performance.

The user's coordination, visual perceptions, reaction time and vigilance are reduced, which can make it dangerous to drive, fly or operate machinery. In a study done at Stanford University, simulated tests of pilots' skills showed they were affected for up to 24 hours after smoking, although they felt sober and competent. Another California study showed that a third of the drivers in fatal car crashes had been smoking marijuana. Driving under the influence of pot may be especially dangerous, because the driver may not know when his ability to function is askew.

Short-term memory and learning ability are also curtailed for hours after smoking. This delayed effect could be a serious problem for students, especially frequent smokers. Because the duration and extent of marijuana's psychomotor effects are not known for sure, the practice of testing urine to determine workers' competence is very controversial. "For the first two to four hours, say, on a Saturday night, the drug decreases one's ability to think, drive and work," says Dr. Reese Jones, a drug researcher and professor of psychiatry at the University of California, San Francisco. "But it's yet to be determined if those effects are still present on Monday morning."

Dr. Robert Millman, director of the alcohol and drug abuse service of the New York Hospital-Payne Whitney Clinic, agrees. "Most of the urine screenings that test positive for drugs

Medical Benefits?

Marijuana can be a useful medicine, but it's no wonder drug. People have used it for 5,000 years to assuage a variety of complaints, most recently in the effort to help treat glaucoma, asthma, spasticity, seizures and certain other nervous system irregularities, as well as the nausea that accompanies chemotherapy. In fact, doctors can now legally prescribe THC, pot's most active ingredient—usually in a capsule marketed as Marinol—for chemo patients.

However, marijuana has not proved itself to be superior to other drugs for most patients. So far, it's just an alternative that may work better for certain people. Many scientists doubt it will ever be a truly significant addition to the pharmacopeia. Its action is neither potent nor focused enough to produce the predictable, clear, isolated effects of first-class drugs. Moreover, the intoxication it causes often makes THC medication undesirable.

On the other hand, marijuana does have limited but documented medical potential. With further research, its components could be teased apart. Those that produce the desired effects—say, the suppression of vomiting or relaxation of muscles—could be isolated, and the rest, causing euphoria and sedation, could be eliminated. Its remedial action is sometimes different from that of standard drugs, which could point pharmacologists to new research directions—one reason scientists are dismayed over the reduction of research funds.

Marijuana may have some medical uses, but it's no wonder drug.

man Zinberg, author of *Drug, Set, and Setting* (Yale University Press, $10.95), studied a group of marijuana smokers, he concluded that "essentially, marijuana doesn't cause psychological problems for the occasional user." Many of his colleagues agree. Most of Zinberg's subjects described the drug as not particularly deleterious to normal functioning, and difficult (though not impossible) to abuse; they tended to restrict smoking to leisure time and special occasions, often planned around food.

Deadheads & Other Potheads

The researchers' consensus on long-term heavy marijuana smokers is bleaker, although hard data are more elusive than those on the drug's acute effects. For the vast majority of users, pot isn't physically addictive. It ranks far below drugs such as cocaine and heroin—or alcohol and tobacco—in inviting compulsive use. Nonetheless, a significant number of smokers use the drug frequently, often daily. Such regular use is one of the most obvious signs of a serious marijuana problem; heavy daily smokers are usually at least a bit out of it (see "Signs of Trouble").

Being out of it is less noticeable in the countries where the three large field studies of chronic users were conducted than in the fast-paced United States. Marijuana is widely accepted in Jamaica and Costa Rica, and within certain subcultures in Greece. These studies found that pot smokers were by and large as healthy and functioned as well—as nonsmokers. However, although these surveys didn't prove any major, permanent health consequences of long-term pot use, that doesn't mean there aren't any. Researchers caution that the subjects of these studies were mostly poorly educated, working-class adults who have lower standards for produc-

pick up signs of pot—a very widely used drug," he says. "Companies are confused about what to do—should they fire everybody?"

Evaluating marijuana's impact on mental ability is difficult, but gauging its effects on emotional health is even more so. Responses are subjective and unpredictable. Marijuana is often associated with a feeling of mellowness, but it causes anxiety as well. It might make one user drowsy, and another—or the same user on a different occasion—hyperactive. One smoker becomes chatty, another withdrawn.

The strength of the drug, frequency of use, and physiological differences among users—for example, in body size and neural sensitivity to the drug—help account for the wide range of reactions. "About a third of people who smoke it feel no effects, a third feel ill and a third feel high," says Dr. Renaud Trouvé, a drug researcher and assistant professor of anesthesiology at Columbia-Presbyterian Medical School in New York.

What Timothy Leary and others called "set and setting"—the mental state of the user and the environment in which the drug is taken—also plays a part in emotional reactions to marijuana. According to Millman, many

people now in middle age found smoking pot relaxing as youths within the laid-back '60s counterculture. As they've increased in age, power and responsibility, they've tuned out, turned off and dropped in.

"There's a natural history to marijuana use," he says. "The baby boomers have acquired a sense of their vulnerability and of the finiteness of time—'This is my life we're talking about!'" he says. "Feeling lethargic and giving up control make them anxious now."

That fear of losing control, or even one's mind, can induce paranoia and anxiety—pot's commonest unpleasant side effects—in people who would not have had these problems if they hadn't taken the drug, according to Millman. Moreover, he says, "marijuana can open a door to psychosis in predisposed persons similar to the action of many hallucinogens like LSD." Many doctors suspect that in these rare instances of users losing touch with reality, the drug has simply activated a latent psychiatric problem. Because of marijuana's potential for stirring up the psyche, psychiatrists say those with pre-existing disorders should stay away from it.

However, after Harvard's Dr. Nor-

tivity and health than middle-class Americans. And it took decades, not years, to determine the serious risks now known to be associated with alcohol and tobacco.

For those who look on pot as a buffer against stress, so-called "self-medication" can be dangerous: The person who smokes in an effort to "treat" his depression, anxiety or personality quirks may only add to his trouble. The psychological problem most often associated with chronic marijuana smoking is the "amotivational syndrome." Those thought to have it—many of them teens and young adults—show diminished goal-orientation, passivity and an inability to master new problems. However, the syndrome poses a chicken-or-egg question: Does heavy pot use cause poor motivation, or vice versa?

New York Hospital's Millman prefers the term "aberrant motivation" to describe the inert attitude of some heavy smokers. "When parents arrive at my office with a son in a ponytail and a tie-dyed shirt, they don't have to say a word. The kid is abusing drugs and doing badly in school and at home—but somehow he can get himself to a Grateful Dead concert in Ohio with $7 in his pocket. He doesn't lack motivation, he's just focusing it in the wrong direction."

Millman, who thinks such flawed motivation is caused by the combination of pot and pre-existing psychological problems, has found that some adolescents smoke grass not only to escape from their troubles, but to explain them. Such self-handicapping protects their egos against feelings of failure. "Many of the kids I see have made pot smoking the rationalization for psychopathology—they and their peers can say they act weird because of dope, rather than because they have an untreated learning disability or an emotional disorder," he says.

Some teens smoke to give themselves an excuse for failure.

Children and teenagers are endangered by any drug, because their bodies and minds—especially their judgment—are immature. A study of middle-class adolescents dependent on marijuana, reported in the May 1987 issue of the journal *Clinical Pediatrics*, helped identify those who may be at highest risk from the drug. Many were learning-disabled, had family histories of alcoholism, and personal and academic problems. Their parents and in some cases therapists hadn't suspected their pot smoking for a year after they started, perhaps because other problems may have disguised the drug use.

The connection between pot, poor motivation and learning disabilities is particularly troubling in an era when 28% of students drop out of high school. The sedation, skewed psycho-motor functioning and involvement with other drugs and drug-abusing peers associated with marijuana make any use by teens unwise. A kid who tries pot also has an estimated 10% risk of becoming a daily smoker—and frequent use, at this age, can become truly disastrous.

Revving Up the Heart

Proof of the physical risks of marijuana is as elusive as proof of its dangers to the mind. The lack of comprehensive long-term human studies and the limits of animal research frustrate scientists like Renaud Trouvé. He's convinced that marijuana stresses the heart, lungs and immune and endocrine systems, particularly when it's used frequently. "As for the short-term physiological effects of marijuana, one can believe what is written," he says. "As for the long-term effects, we just don't know."

For example, it seems reasonable that pot smoking would be bad for the lungs. Marijuana contains more tar and carcinogens than tobacco and is inhaled longer and harder. But while heavy users do show a measurable airway obstruction and seem more prone to bronchitis and sinusitis, no links to serious lung diseases like cancer or emphysema have been established. In

Marijuana has more carcinogens than tobacco does.

fact, perhaps the worst threat to the lungs of pot smokers is the herbicide paraquat, which was sprayed widely on marijuana fields, especially in Mexico. The use of the chemical, which can cause severe lung damage, has been discontinued, although it's being considered as a way to deter growers in California and Hawaii.

The effects of marijuana on the reproductive system also seem ominous, but remain unproved. The drug temporarily lowers the level of the sex hormone testosterone in men, and decreases the number, quality and motility of sperm, but the impact on fertility is unknown. However, testosterone also helps govern puberty's changes in boys. Some researchers think that low levels of the hormone could impair adolescent development.

Women who smoke heavily may experience menstrual irregularities, including a failure to ovulate. When pregnant monkeys, rats or mice are exposed to heavy doses of pot, their offspring are more likely to have a low birth weight or to be stillborn. There's no clear proof that marijuana causes birth defects, but doctors urge pregnant and nursing women to treat pot with the same caution they give to alcohol and tobacco.

Similarly grim but inconclusive observations suggest that marijuana use can adversely affect other organs and systems in the body. Some researchers have found that marijuana can cause microscopic brain-cell damage in monkeys—but human brain damage hasn't been shown. Some studies suggest that marijuana can suppress immune function to some extent, but scientists don't yet know whether that degree of dysfunction affects health. What's more, marijuana increases the heart rate by as much as 90 beats per minute. This added workload could be very dangerous for those with cardiovascular disorders such as angina, but

Pot can change sex hormone levels, for men and for women both.

there's no evidence that it causes any permanent harm to healthy hearts.

Toward a Sound Pot Policy

What state-of-the-art marijuana research tells experts is that we need to know more. In 1982, the Institute of Medicine published "Marijuana and Health," a 188-page report based on solid research and compiled by a committee of 21 scientists. Its conclusion, echoed by many marijuana researchers today: "Marijuana has a broad range of psychological and biological effects, some of which, at least under certain conditions, are harmful to human health. Unfortunately, the available information does not tell us how serious this risk may be."

The uncertainty that surrounds marijuana use is compounded when it's compared to the nation's other drugs—both legal and illegal. Despite increasing decriminalization and public tolerance of pot, half of all drug arrests made by local police in 1985—almost 500,000—involved marijuana, according to *The New York Times*. Many citizens consider this police enforcement an inappropriate use of resources that could be used to fight the greater menace of deadly drugs like heroin and cocaine—or, for that matter, tobacco and alcohol, which cause hundreds of thousands of deaths each year.

It's unlikely that either of these two legal, lethal drugs would be lawful if they were discovered today. "The light use of marijuana is certainly not as bad for you physically as alcohol or tobacco," says Harvard's Zinberg. "Our drug policy is based on morals, not on health considerations. The person with a drink in his hand says to himself, 'I'm bad enough, but that guy smoking pot over there is worse.'"

Zinberg says the best approach toward a sound policy on marijuana would be continued decriminalization accompanied by 15 years of serious long-term research. By then, the public would have enough information to make personal choices and public policy decisions. Reese Jones believes

We need more money for basic research, not for drug testing.

that, regardless of policy changes, marijuana's popularity may gradually die out as the group of heavy users ages.

The one point on which all those concerned with marijuana agree is that having so little knowledge of the drug is a dangerous thing. Despite its prevalence and the unanswered questions about its use, federal support for marijuana research, still in its infancy, has decreased— diverted to less-used but "hotter" drugs like cocaine. "I'm a researcher with conservative views on drug use who hasn't found the hard data on the health effects of marijuana," says Jones. "There's a lot of uncertainty about it—you can't say it's unsafe, but there's no proof it's benign, either. We should be studying it to find out, but all the research money is going to help figure out how to detect it in people's urine instead."

FROM CRACK TO ECSTASY

Basement chemists can duplicate almost any over-the-border drug.

Hal Straus

Hal Straus *is a freelance writer specializing in medicine and science.*

In an age that can produce designer cigarettes and designer toilet paper, someone was bound to come up with designer drugs. But you won't find a fashionable name on the label. Designer drugs are concocted by underground chemists who tend to move frequently, a jump ahead of the law. One thing they don't need is fame.

The drugs are designed to skirt federal drug laws, which (until recently) permitted the manufacture and use of any drug not *precisely* defined and scheduled as a controlled substance. By altering the molecular structure of an illegal drug like heroin or PCP (Angel Dust) just slightly, a basement chemist could make a substance as legal as, well, designer chocolate.

This may no longer be the case. A tough new federal drug bill passed in October 1986 bans these chemical cousins or "analogs" outright, *en masse*, even before they are invented. Such a sweeping law, however, must be vague scientifically, and thus far it remains unused and untested in the courts.

Besides slight modification of chemical structure, designer variations differ in one other important respect from the "originals": Some have proved even more dangerous than the drugs they were designed to imitate.

First was Lethal and Legal

Designer drugs first hit the street in 1979 in Southern California, where a batch of "China White"—the street name for the finest Asian heroin—was actually found to be an analog of fentanyl, a narcotic painkiller.

The appearance and euphoric effects of heroin and designer-fentanyl were almost identical but there was a difference: Fentanyl packed from 20 to 2,000 times the wallop of heroin. Novice or low-grade users who unknowingly shot their normal doses soon discovered that the designer-fentanyl was completely lethal. It was also completely legal.

In 1982 another synthetic heroin appeared in Northern California. This one didn't kill; it crippled. Users arrived at a San Jose hospital paralyzed, twisted, unable to speak—victims of brain damage similar to advanced-stage Parkinson's disease. After exhaustive laboratory investigation, neurologists analyzed the culprit as MPTP, an analog of meperidine, another narcotic painkiller commonly known under the trade name Demerol. Though a clandestine chemist could not legally produce Demerol, no laws at the time prevented the synthesizing of a meperidine-like drug, which had turned seven people into living mannequins.

Law enforcement clearly had a problem. Though underground labs had been illegally producing LSD, PCP, speed and methaqualone (Quaaludes) since the 1960s, these designer-heroin episodes marked the first time they had made and sold *legal* heroin substitutes on a large scale. Up to its ears trying to control *imported* heroin, the Drug Enforcement Administration (DEA) now had to contend with domestic chemical entrepreneurship—without a strong legal arsenal for the job. As DEA scurried to outlaw one fentanyl analog, another fentanyl "weed" would sprout almost overnight.

100 Californians Died

In 1984, Congress handed the DEA emergency scheduling (restricting) powers as a new weapon to combat the imposing threat of designer drugs. "Before then, it took us one to three years to schedule one of these drugs because of all the red tape involved," recalls Gene Haislip, DEA deputy as-

New drugs sprout up overnight.

sistant administrator. "We just couldn't afford all the time. After the 1984 law, we could schedule a drug in three to four months."

But the "schedule lag" was still too long. Using $500 worth of easily obtainable chemicals and lab equipment, an underground chemist could cook up and ship $1 million worth of designer heroin in a matter of days or even hours. Says Haislip: "Millions of doses could be placed in the general drug traffic, people would die—and no crime would have been committed! So we went back to Congress for more powers."

The result is Section 1201 of the Anti-Drug Abuse Act of 1986. It bans analogs with chemical structures "substantially similar" to presently controlled substances. In other words, designer drugs are now illegal even before they are designed—at least that's the intent. Many experts believe that the law has weaknesses.

"The wording of the law is vague," says Gary Henderson, professor of pharmacology at University of California at Davis. He has studied the fentanyl drugs for a dozen years. "What is an analog? How much can you change a chemical before it becomes an entirely new entity?"

DEA's Haislip concedes that the 1986 law might run into problems, but sees no better solution. "Yes, the question (of substantial similarity) can and probably will come up. But it's an issue that can be attested to by experts in a trial, which would be the case even if the law weren't passed."

According to Haislip, "all is now quiet on the fentanyl front," but not before close to 100 Californians died from fentanyl-analog overdoses. What's more, lab tests from state methadone clinics suggest that thousands more drug-tolerant users—perhaps 20,000 addicts—may be regular, unsuspecting users of the fentanyls. And finally, fentanyl analogs have been found as far east as New York and Georgia, mixed in with heroin and cocaine.

Likewise, MPTP has not re-emerged, but 300 probable users of the contaminated 1982 batch are being closely monitored for Parkinson's symptoms. Preliminary signs of the disease have been detected in half of the subjects tested.

Too Expensive for Drug Barons

The reason that designer-heroin has not been even more prevalent has as much to do with the structure of organized crime as the structure of molecules. Drug syndicates have shown no predilection for abandoning old-world drug sources, nor allowing upstart domestic chemists to get in on the action.

In addition, fentanyl production is an intricate chemical process. Most likely, Dr. Henderson speculates, the fentanyl analogs were brewed by one smart "independent," who anticipated the analog game and made a dozen or more designer variations simultaneously, releasing them one at a time as each became illegal.

Though the mafia is not likely to go into wholesale synthetic production overnight, the looming menace of designer-heroin should not be underestimated. Federal drug policy has long been predicated on intercepting foreign organic heroin and persuading foreign governments to control their own agricultural output. The flood of cheap heroin on the streets suggests that the policy has not been entirely effective. However, the more successful the policy becomes, the more the stage will be set for designer analogs and the kind of poor quality control exhibited by the California designer-heroin debacles. With advances in American synthetic chemistry, foreign organic heroin may become obsolete.

There is, unfortunately, more bad news: The potential for designer or otherwise menacing drugs is not limited to heroin. Analog possibilities for other illegal drugs are virtually limit-

less. The same natural laws that provide the molecular backdrop for medicine create the context for thousands of drugs of medical use and for thousands of drugs of recreational abuse.

■ "Designer" Coke. Street chemistry has recently come up with a purified, highly potent, cocaine distillate known as "crack." It brought an epidemic of addiction and several deaths. Crack preparation is within the grasp of any cook who has a kitchen, a box of baking soda, and a kitchen stove.

But though cocaine purification is fairly simple, *imitation* is not. The underground chemist's usual method— mixing a mild stimulant like caffeine with a topical dental anesthetic such as benzocaine or lidocaine—numbs the sinuses, but falls far short of the coke "rush." While naive users (or those accustomed to lousy cocaine) may be fooled, habitual snorters can typically detect the deception in a short time.

Producing synthetic cocaine in the lab is even more problematic, requiring thousands of dollars in lab apparatus.

The potential for producing designer-cocaine, however, may mean that this drug problem won't be solved just by tightening our borders. A crackdown on imported cocaine could make the synthetic version cost-effective. As Henderson says, "If the government were able to cut off the foreign supply . . . we would have synthetic designer-coke in this country in 30 days."

■ Black Beauties. In the late 1970s, a rash of legal amphetamine "lookalikes" were marketed by speed pill minifactories to cash in on the drug and diet craze. Ads for some were even carried in mail-order sections of mainstream consumer magazines. Made to look just like "black beauties," "purple hearts," or other popular pill forms, they actually contained caffeine, ephedrine (a vascular constrictor), and phenylpropanolamine (PPA), an amphetamine analog that is an active ingredient in many over-the-

Many drugs can be cooked in kitchens.

counter diet pills and cold remedies such as Contac.

Real amphetamine production is as widespread as ever, of course.

■ **Female Marijuana.** "Designer botanists" have been able to grow especially potent strains of pot known as "sensimilla." Removing the male part of a marijuana plant before sexual maturity stimulates the female buds to exude several times the amount of cannabis resins.

The case of synthetic marijuana, however, is similar to synthetic heroin and cocaine: Underground chemists have found it difficult to match the ultimate Underground Chemist—nature.

THC, the active ingredient in marijuana, was first synthesized in the early 1970s through a complex, costly procedure far beyond the skills of most clandestine labs.

■ **Ecstasy.** It was probably inevitable that the DEA's sweeping pounce on designer drugs would trap at least one small animal along with the dangerous big game. Consider MDMA, better known by its exotic street name, Ecstasy.

A mild psychedelic, similar in effect to mescaline and LSD yet reportedly without visual hallucinations, MDMA

was first synthesized in 1914 by Merck but was never marketed. It was all but forgotten until the mid-1970s when several psychiatrists—impressed with the drug's insight-enhancing benefits—began to use it as a catalyst in therapy.

In July 1985, DEA classified MDMA in Schedule I, alongside heroin, LSD, and the designer-fentanyls as a drug with "high potential for abuse and no medical usefulness." The action roused a storm of protest from psychiatrists and researchers who believe that MDMA has enormous therapeutic potential.

"It enhances trust, empathy, positive feelings, and makes people less defensive, allowing them to explore internal areas that are ordinarily unavailable to them," says Lester Grinspoon, Harvard professor of psychiatry.

Even the drug's most ardent advocates do not support de-scheduling but re-scheduling, into Schedule III, where research on MDMA would not be so severely restricted. Though DEA insists that special registration procedures will expedite legitimate MDMA research, the drug's proponents are skeptical. "Anyone who has attempted to do research on a Sched-

ule I drug knows that one year of his professional life will be devoted to hopping over bureaucratic jump ropes," states Dr. Grinspoon. "On MDMA, we need data from the laboratory and the clinical setting, not the streets."

Safety Vs. Progress

Not all consequences of designer drugs have been bad. Besides MDMA's apparent psychotherapeutic value, other drugs like THC are used in cancer chemotherapy and glaucoma treatment, and the tragic MPTP episode has ironically led to a better understanding of Parkinson's Disease, a complex neurological disease that afflicts 350,000 Americans.

Many experts believe that some of the money now spent on enforcement would be much better applied to research on the psychological and social causes of addiction, research on the drugs themselves, and public education. The MDMA controversy is a case in point. Classifying the drug in Schedule I has effectively halted all clinical use and research but has done little to curb underground production or street abuse.

We've Already Said Yes

Drugs are part of our culture, inherent in the way we live and think. In the future, we won't use drugs to escape reality, but to lash ourselves into superhuman effort. We'll use drugs to enhance memory, enhance intelligence and enhance sexuality.

Bruce Sterling

Bruce Sterling is a science fiction writer whose latest book is "Islands in the Net."

Every society gets the drug problem it deserves. Drug-hunger is essential to our modern way of life; it's a constant, like electricity, or air pollution. We lie to ourselves about drugs and the nature of their attraction for us. Because of that, we risk being blindsided in the 21st century—when the hidden cultural logic of drug use will reach a bizarre crescendo.

Not long ago, President Bush told an audience of astonished Amish that Wall Street yuppies use cocaine. That uncomfortable truth discredits the silly myth that drugs are the exclusive province of derelicts, teenagers, bohemians and the *lumpenproletariat*. Those well-heeled professionals do cocaine, not because it's fun (although it is), but because it gives them a vital short-term edge that helps them prosper in the crazed environment of a futures pit.

The coming thing in drugs is not intoxicants but performance enhancers. In the future, we won't use drugs to "escape reality," but to lash ourselves to superhuman effort.

You can see this trend coming already. The cozy, dreamy days of marijuana and LSD are history; what people want now is crack, amphetamine and anabolic steroids—headlong speed and muscle by order. Steroids provide no pleasurable "high"—in fact, they ruin your sleep, your temper and your complexion—but it's estimated that 1 million Americans abuse them. The market is vast and growing, and the steroids scandal of the last Olympics perversely gave this market a tremendous popular boost.

The reasons are obvious. Ben Johnson is, in fact, the fastest man in the world. He may have been deprived of his gold medal, but of his frankly superhuman abilities there is no doubt. Athletes are caught in a bind that will eventually spread into many other corners of society.

Put yourself in Ben Johnson's place. It will happen soon enough, so you might as well get used to it. Steroids enhance strength, but soon we are going to discover substances that will enhance memory, enhance intelligence, enhance mood, enhance sexuality. The drugs we have today already do this, in halting ways—amphetamine, for instance, has been found to raise the IQ by about 10 points, though for short periods, and at great cost to health.

As we come to understand the nature of our own neurochemistry, we are going to discover a galaxy of extremely potent substances with greater specificity and fewer side effects. The drugs we use today are mostly vegetable extracts that crudely mimic human biochemistry. But beta-endorphin, for instance, is a natural human brain chemical, an analgesic 10,000 times more potent than morphine. The high-tech development of drugs will eventually lead us to abuse our own body chemistry.

With the advent of monoclonal antibodies and genetic engineering, we are learning to produce pure biochemicals cheaply, artificially, by the ton. Imagine the vast coca fields of South America reduced to a few stainless steel vats neatly hidden in a basement in Medellin or San Francisco. Cheaper drugs, better quality, less risk, more profit—the logic of industrial commerce is very powerful. We have found no way to date to defeat the black-market drug industry, and the social, financial and technological factors are all very strongly on its side.

Now imagine yourself as a 21st century student, taking entrance exams for the law, or for medicine perhaps, while your competing fellow students enjoy the secret luxury of photographic memory, enhanced IQ and perfect concentration. Could you resist that temptation when "everyone else is doing it"—and the cost of failure means the humiliating sacrifice of your ambitions?

Or imagine yourself as a failing TV journalist, when the stringers on the other networks can instantly remember every campaign promise the president ever made. Imagine yourself a 21st century president, and facing some Panamanian drug-monarch who never sleeps and whose eyes blaze with preternatural cunning.

The irresistible logic of drugs confounds all attempts at repression, creating a maelstrom of money, guns and violence that has turned our inner cities into unprecedented war zones. The problem isn't stopping there, and it's not going to stop anywhere else in our society, either, because it is part of us, and inherent in the way we live and think.

Drugs are a technology like others. Like nuclear power, for instance, the tremendous potency of high-tech pharmacology has fearsome side effects. We are not masters of the destiny of our technologies. The changes they bring to our society may force us into dilemmas we never would have chosen.

That is the milieu in which we were born and raised—the culture that invented cosmetic surgery, genetic engineering, antibiotics, telephones, jet travel and a thousand other glittering short-cuts to the Artificial Paradise. Our unstoppable cultural hunger for drugs is overwhelming evidence for this simple fact.

Already, today, we are busily investing billions in the basic medical research that will open a Pandora's box. The alternative is Luddism, to virtuously ignore this medical knowledge and plod on with the burdens of schizophrenia, cancer, AIDS, Alzheimer's disease and the simple God-given limits of what we used to call "the human condition." We are not going to accept those limits, under any circumstances. We may give them pious lip service, but when it comes to the crunch, we will vote otherwise with our bloodstreams.

Sooner or later, we will stop trying to bail back the sea with a fork, and come to terms with this horrifically powerful transformation in our lives. The war against drugs is a lost cause. The only question is how many will die in the service of empty rhetoric.

'Drug of Infamy' Makes a Comeback

Thalidomide, notorious a generation ago as a cause of birth defects, is staging a resurgence as an experimental medication for patients with bone-marrow transplants, Hansen's disease (leprosy) and rheumatoid arthritis.

Sally Squires

For the 30-year-old District of Columbia man with chronic myelogenous leukemia, time was running out. The bone-marrow transplant he had to fight the leukemia was going bad for the second time and he was beset with liver problems, cataracts, nerve inflammation and arthritis. Heavy scars appeared on his legs and feet, making it almost impossible for him to walk. Despite strong doses of steroids and other treatment, nothing seemed to work.

"How would you like to try a drug of infamy?" asked his doctor, Georgia Vogelsang, an assistant professor of oncology at the Johns Hopkins Medical Institutions in Baltimore.

In November 1986, the patient began taking eight tiny pills a day of thalidomide. Although never approved for use in this country, thalidomide was widely prescribed nearly three decades ago as a sedative and ended up causing severe birth defects and missing limbs in some 12,000 children worldwide.

But for the leukemia patient, the thalidomide story has a different ending. Within two months, the patient showed marked improvement. Most of his acute symptoms—liver damage, arthritis and nerve inflammation—had disappeared. Seventeen months later, his skin was almost back to normal. Now, almost three years since treatment began, he is back at work full time and his illness remains in remission, although he continued taking thalidomide daily until last summer.

Thalidomide, notorious a generation ago as a cause of birth defects, is staging a quiet resurgence as an experimental medication for patients with bone-marrow transplants and other conditions, including Hansen's disease (leprosy) and rheumatoid arthritis, which sometimes do not respond to traditional treatments.

In studies at Hopkins, 65 percent of bone-marrow transplant patients with a chronic severe complication known as graft vs. host disease responded to treatment with thalidomide. The drug proved effective enough for the Food and Drug Administration to approve within the last several weeks an expanded seven-center study of 120 more patients.

Graft vs. host disease develops when transplanted cells mount an attack against the patient's body. It afflicts an estimated 50 percent of patients who receive bone-marrow transplants. "Between one-third and one-half of patients die as a result," Vogelsang said. If thalidomide proves safe and effective in a larger number of patients, it could significantly improve the survival odds for bone-marrow-transplant patients, she said.

Since those who undergo bone-marrow transplants are rendered sterile by whole body radiation used to destroy their own bone-marrow cells, there is no danger that thalidomide will cause birth defects in patients' offspring.

Thalidomide seems to help bone-marrow-transplant patients by shutting down the immune system, similar to the way the drug cyclosporin works. The benefit of thalidomide, however, is that it is much more selective. Instead of uniformly shutting down the immune system and leaving patients vulnerable to infection, thalidomide appears to affect only the white blood cells known as T-cells that trigger graft vs. host disease.

To date, thalidomide has only been used in bone-marrow-transplant patients for whom all other means of conventional treatment have failed. Whether the drug will also be useful—and safe—in less-severe forms of transplant rejection is not yet known. Researchers also don't know if thalidomide might be effective as well for other types of transplant patients. Graft vs. host disease can plague those who have had transplants of a kidney, heart, liver or other organ. Preliminary results from animal studies of heart trans-

Use remains limited because of the potential for lawsuits. Drug companies' legal departments 'absolutely nix it,' said Dr. Georgia Vogelsang.

plants "look like thalidomide works there, too, although we haven't used it extensively yet," said Vogelsang.

Thalidomide is also being used to treat Hansen's disease. An estimated 15 million people worldwide suffer from Hansen's (or leprosy). Thalidomide has helped thousands of patients with leprosy avoid the severe complications of the illness, which when left untreated cause permanent damage to limbs. "It works like magic," said Robert C. Hastings, the physician who heads the National Hansen's Disease Center's laboratory research branch in Carville, Louisiana.

Beyond Hansen's disease and transplant problems, researchers are treating a number of other conditions with thalidomide on an experimental basis. Among the other conditions:

• **Rheumatoid arthritis.** In 1984, researcher O. Gutierrez-Rodriguez added thalidomide to the medication given to seven women patients who had suffered from rheumatoid arthritis from eight months to 13 years. Joint inflammation and pain disappeared within several weeks after the women began taking thalidomide. Blood tests showed other improvement, including a marked reduction in red blood sedimentation rate and a significant drop in blood levels of rheumatoid factor. In four of the women, the improvements lasted long after thalidomide was stopped. In a 1988 study of 17 patients with rheumatoid arthritis, 12 showed complete remission.

• *Lupus.* Discoid lupus erythematosus (DLE), an inflammatory skin disease, showed significant improvement in 19 out of 20 patients who took thalidomide for two weeks, according to a study published in the Mexican scientific journal Dermatologia Revista Mexicana.

Despite its promise, the major concern about thalidomide remains its potential for birth defects—one reason that the FDA, Johns Hopkins and others are searching for new analogs of the drug.

Newer forms of thalidomide might also help overcome another problem sometimes associated with thalidomide use. Nerve damage known as peripheral neuropathy has been associated in a small percentage of patients.

In the late 1950s, reports of nerve damage caused by the drug first prompted then-FDA director Frances Kelsey to hold up thalidomide's approval in the United States. In the intervening months, the reports of the devastating birth defects began to surface at medical meetings. By 1961, the drug had been withdrawn from the market.

Thalidomide emerged in a heyday of drug development after World War II, when there was less concern about the potential risks of new wonder drugs coming out of the laboratory. The thalidomide tragedy greatly changed this attitude.

The drug company CIBA first described thalidomide in 1953, but dropped research on it when it appeared to have no pharmacological effects. The following year, the West German drug company Chemi Gruenenthal synthesized thalidomide, and three years later marketed it as a sedative hypnotic.

Soon afterward, thalidomide, which was cheap and available without a prescription, became the most popular sleeping pill in West Germany. Fourteen other drug companies began producing it and sold it in 46 countries, including Canada, Britain and New Zealand. American women who traveled or lived abroad also were able to obtain the drug.

In 1961, letters began appearing in the journal *Lancet* reporting severely deformed babies born to women who had taken thalidomide during pregnancy. Nearly 12,000 children were ultimately affected. Most were born without limbs and with other congenital abnormalities ranging from cleft palate to phocomelia—a condition known as "seal limbs."

Exactly how those birth defects were caused is still not completely understood. Studies do show, however, that thalidomide appears to be dangerous during a small window of pregnancy from day 35 to 55 when limbs are forming, said Trent Stephens, associate professor of anatomy and embryology at Idaho State University in Pocatello.

The drug might have faded into medical history had it not been for the observations of Israeli dermatologist J. Sheskin. In 1965, Sheskin reported that the drug was effective in treating six leprosy patients suffering from a complication called ENL—or erythema nodosum leprosum. Severe cases of ENL cause fever, nerve inflammation, swelling of lymph nodes, weight loss and mania, in addition to the more common red tender skin nodules.

Sheskin, who had been prescribing thalidomide as a sedative in patients with severe ENL, noticed that patients who received the drug showed remarkable improvement in just 12 hours. Within two days, nodules were gone and fevers had broken. Other studies, including one conducted in four countries by the World Health Organization, confirmed those results.

In the United States today, the FDA classifies thalidomide as an orphan drug, meaning that it can be used only on an experimental basis in clinical trials.

The drug is available in this country from just two sources—the National Hansen's Disease Center in Carville, Louisianna, and from Pediatric Pharmaceuticals, a firm in Edison, New Jersey.

Use remains limited because of the potential for lawsuits. "It's a very predictable scenario," said Vogelsang. "When we talk to the drug companies, the scientific groups are wildly enthusiastic, but when it get to the legal department they absolutely nix it."

Because the drug can produce such severe birth defects, many experts believe thalidomide will never be widely distributed. "Nonetheless, it would be unfortunate if patients who respond favorably to thalidomide after failing to respond to conventional therapy are denied access to it," Kaitin wrote in the journal *Pharmaceutical Medicine* last fall. "The time has come for the medical establishment, national drug agencies and (the) public to reconsider the unjustified blanket stigmatization of this drug."

Drugs and Behavior

- Alcohol, Caffeine, and Tobacco (Articles 28-34)
- Therapeutic and Over-the-Counter Drugs (Articles 35-36)

All the drugs mentioned in this unit are "legal" drugs, having been given special consideration by the government. This is not to say they present no danger to our health and well-being. Alcohol is considered America's number one drug problem. Cigarettes are directly responsible for almost 1,500 deaths per day in the United States, yet, like alcohol, they are the stuff that billboards, television commercials, and government subsidies are made of. Tobacco's power of addiction has been compared as being equal to or greater than that of heroin. Nicotine is a powerful drug. Caffeine is addictive too, and the side effects can be severe. The rationale for the distinction between "legal drugs," and "controlled substances" is, at best, vague.

According to "Alcoholism, The Mythical Disease," the legality of a drug has nothing to do with its "hardness." In terms of money and lives lost, alcohol and tobacco are near the top of the list. Most scientists are in agreement on the tobacco-cancer link. This is explained in "Smokeless Tobacco: The Fatal Pinch," and "Kick Me: I Smoke." Education about the effects of smoking is the theme of "Achieving a Smoke-Free Society." In "Caffeine," we discover the use of caffeine as a performance enhancer in athletic competition. This drug is allowed in limited quantities by the International Olympic Committee. "Sports Stars May Be Hazardous to Your Health" challenges the responsibility of the advertising industry as a "drug pusher." The high visibility use of sports figures and entertainers in the sale of injurious products creates still another social quandry.

The final subsection of this unit deals with drugs obtainable without prescription. Over-the-counter preparations are also subject to abuse, and have the capability of serious consequences. The articles "Ordinary Medicines Can Have Extraordinary Side Effects" and "Sneak Addictions" speak to the unsuspecting about the traps of self-medication with products that include aspirin, nasal spray, and other headache and allergy preparations not generally considered to be drugs. Serious dependency or addiction can occur from use of seemingly innoculous medicines.

Looking Ahead: Challenge Questions

How does a government decide which drugs to control? Who makes these decisions? What part does politics play in making these decisions?

Why are the drugs demonstrated as being the deadliest both sanctioned and subsidized?

Why do drugs become so popular once they have been banned? When is a drug safe? How much protection does a society need from itself?

If drugs were not available, would humankind find other ways to promote self-abuse? What is the duty of the advertising industry respective to "legal" and "illegal" drugs? How different would matters be if all drugs were legal?

Unit 3

Alcoholism: The mythical disease

HERBERT FINGARETTE/*THE PUBLIC INTEREST*

Herbert Fingarette is a professor of philosophy at the University of California, Santa Barbara. He has served as a consultant on alcoholism and addiction to the World Health Organization.

The idea that alcoholism is a disease is a myth, and a harmful myth at that. This assertion obviously conflicts with the barrage of pronouncements in support of alcoholism's classification as a disease by health professionals and organizations such as the American Medical Association, by the explosively proliferating treatment programs, and by innumerable public-service organizations.

But the public has been profoundly misled, and is still being actively misled. Credulous media articles have featured so many dramatic human-interest anecdotes by "recovering alcoholics," so many "scientific" pronouncements about medical opinion and new discoveries, that it is no wonder the lay public responds with trusting belief. Yet this much is unambiguous and incontrovertible: The public has been kept unaware of a mass of scientific evidence accumulated over the past couple of decades, evidence familiar to researchers in the field, which radically challenges each major belief generally associated with the phrase "alcoholism is a disease."

Why is it important whether alcoholism is a disease? To begin with, "disease" is the word that triggers provision of health-insurance payments, employment benefits such as paid leave and worker's compensation, and other government benefits. The direct cost of treating alcoholism is rapidly rising, already exceeding a billion dollars annually. Add in all related health costs and other kinds of benefits, and the dollar figure is well into the tens of billions annually.

Alcoholism is, of course, profoundly harmful, both to the drinkers themselves and to others. But if it ceased to be characterized as a disease, all the disease-oriented methods of treatment and resulting expenditures would be threatened; this in turn would threaten the material interests of hundreds of thousands of alcoholics and treatment staffers who receive these billions in funds. The other side of the coin would be many billions in savings for taxpayers and those who pay insurance premiums.

It is not surprising that the disease concept of alcoholism is now vigorously promoted by a vast network of lobbies, national and local, professional and volunteer, ranging from the most prestigious medical associations to the most crassly commercial private providers of treatment. This is big politics and big business.

Use of the word "disease" also shapes the values and attitudes of society. The selling of the disease concept of alcoholism has led courts, legislatures, and the populace generally to view damage caused by heavy drinkers as a product of "the disease and not the drinker." The public remains ambivalent about this, and criminal law continues to resist excusing alcoholics for criminal acts. But the pressure is there, and civil law has largely given in. In regard to alcoholics, civil law now often mandates leniency or complete absolution from the rules, regulations, and moral norms

The public has been profoundly misled about alcoholism.

to which non-diseased persons are held accountable. Such was the thrust of a recently denied appeal to the U.S. Supreme Court by two veterans, who claimed certain benefits in spite of their having failed to apply for them during the legally specified 10-year period after discharge from the Army. Their excuse: alcoholism, and the claim that their persistent heavy drinking was a disease entitling them to exemption from the regulations.

When the facts are confronted, what seems to be compassion done in the name of "disease" turns out to subvert the drinker's autonomy and will to change, and to exacerbate a serious social problem. This is because the excuses and benefits offered heavy drinkers work psychologically as incentives to continue drinking. The doctrine that the alcoholic is "helpless" delivers the message that he might as well drink, since he lacks the ability to refrain. As for the expensive treatments, they do no real good. Certainly our current disease-oriented policies have not reduced the scale of the problem; in fact, the number of chronic heavy drinkers reported keeps rising. (It is currently somewhere in the range of 10 to 20 million, depending on the definitions one uses.)

The disease concept of alcoholism not only has no basis in current science; it has *never* had a scientific justification.

The understanding of alcoholism as a disease first surfaced in the early 19th century. The growing popularity of materialistic and mechanistic views bolstered the doctrine that drinking problems stemmed from a simple malfunctioning of the bodily machinery. The new idea was popularized by Benjamin Rush, one of the leading medical theorists of the day.

Rush's claim was ideological, not scientific, since neither Rush nor anyone else at that time had the experimental facilities or the biological knowledge to justify it. It seemed plausible because of its compatibility with the crude biological theories of the time, assumptions that we now know to be erroneous. Nevertheless, the idea seized the public imagination, in part because it appealed to the growing mercantile and manufacturing classes, whose demand for a disciplining "work ethic" (especially among the working class) was supported by this new "scientific" indictment of drinking. We should realize that the 19th-century version of the doctrine, as advanced by the politically powerful temperance movement, indicted *all* drinking. Alcohol (like heroin today) was viewed as inherently addictive. The drinker's personal character and situation were considered irrelevant.

The 19th-century temperance movement crested in 1919 with the enactment of the Prohibition Amendment; but by 1933 the idea of a total prohibi-

The disease model of alcoholism is big business.

tion had lost credibility, and the amendment was repealed. For one thing, the public no longer accepted the idea that no one at all could drink alcohol safely. In addition, the costs of prohibition—such as gangsterism and public cynicism about the law—had become too high. Most people wanted to do openly and legally, in a civilized way, what large numbers of people had been doing surreptitiously.

For the temperance impulse to survive, it had to be updated in a way that did not stigmatize all drinking on moral or medical grounds. Any new anti-alcohol movement had to be more selective in its target, by taking into account the desires of drinkers generally, as well as the interests of the now legal (and growing) alcoholic beverage industry.

A new sect arose with just the right formula. Alcoholics Anonymous (AA), founded in 1935, taught that alcohol was not the villain in and of itself, and that most people could drink safely. (In this way the great majority of drinkers and the beverage industry were mollified.) A minority of potential drinkers, however, were said to have a peculiar biological vulnerability; these unfortunates, it was held, are "allergic" to alcohol, so that their drinking activates the disease, which then proceeds insidiously toward addiction.

This contemporary version of the disease theory of alcoholism, along with the subsequent minor variants of the theory, is often referred to now as the "classic" disease concept of alcoholism. Like the temperance doctrine, the new doctrine was not based on any scientific research or discovery. It was created by the two ex-alcoholics who founded AA: William Wilson, a New York stockbroker, and Robert Holbrook Smith, a physician from Akron, Ohio. Their ideas in turn were inspired by the Oxford religious movement, and by the ideas of another physician, William Silkworth. They attracted a small following, and a few sympathetic magazine articles helped the movement grow.

The "alcoholism movement," as it has come to be called among those familiar with the facts, has grown at an accelerating rate. Its growth results from the cumulative effect of the great number of drinkers indoctrinated by AA, people who passionately identify themselves with the AA portrait of "the alcoholic." AA has vigorously supported the idea of "treatment" for alcoholics; in turn, the rapidly proliferating treatment centers for the "disease of alcoholism" have generally supported AA. All this has generated a kind of snowballing effect.

By the 1970s there were powerful alcohol-related lobbying organizations in place at all levels of government. The National Council on Alcoholism (NCA), for example, which has propagated the disease concept of alcoholism, has been a major national umbrella group from the early days of the movement. Until 1982 the NCA was subsidized by the liquor industry, which had several representatives on its board. The alliance was a natural one: At the cost of conceding that a small segment of the population is allergic to alcohol and ought not to drink, the liquor industry gained a freer hand with which to appeal to the majority of people, who are ostensibly not allergic.

Large and powerful health-professional organizations (such as the American Medical Association) now have internal constituencies whose professional power and wealth derive from their role as the authorities responsible for dealing with the "disease" of alcoholism. As usual, these interest groups lobby internally, and the larger organization is persuaded to take an official stand in favor of the disease model of alcoholism.

Judges, legislators, and bureaucrats all have a stake in the doctrine. They can now with clear consciences get the intractable social problems posed by heavy drinkers off their agenda by compelling or persuading these unmanageable people to go elsewhere—that is, to get "treatment." Why should these public officials mistrust—or want to mistrust—this safe-as-motherhood way of getting troublesome problems off their backs while winning popular approval? The ample evidence that treatment programs are ineffective, and waste considerable amounts of money and resources, is ignored.

There is a consensus among scientists that no single cause of alcoholism, biological or otherwise, has ever been scientifically established. There are many causal factors, and they vary from drinking pattern to drinking pattern, from drinker to drinker. We already know many of the predominant influences that evoke or shape patterns of drinking. We know that family environment plays a role, as does age. Ethnic and cultural values are also important. The belief in a unique disease of alcoholism leads many to wonder whether these sorts of influences can make much of a difference when it comes to the supposedly "overwhelming craving" of alcoholics. Once one realizes that there is no distinct group of "diseased" drinkers, however, one is less surprised to learn that no group of drinkers is immune to such influences or is vulnerable only to other influences.

Even if the disease concept of alcoholism lacks a scientific foundation, mightn't it nevertheless be a useful social white lie, since it encourages alcoholics to enter treatment? This common—and plausible—argument is flawed because medical treatment for alcoholism is ineffective. Medical authority has been abused for the purpose of enlisting public faith in a useless treatment for which Americans have paid more than a billion dollars. To understand why the treatment does no good, we should recall that many different kinds of studies of alcoholics have shown substantial rates of so-called "natural" improvement. As a 1986 report concludes, "the vast majority of [addicted] persons who change do so on their own." This natural rate of improvement, which varies according to class, age, socioeconomic status, and certain other psychological and social variables, lends credibility to the claims of success made by programs that "treat" the "disease" of alcoholism.

Many of the clients—and, in the expensive programs, almost all of the clients—are middle-class, middle-aged people who are intensely motivated to change, and whose families and social relationships are still intact. Many, often most, are much improved by the time they complete the program. They are, of course, delighted with the change; they paid money and went through an emotional ordeal, and now receive renewed affection and respect from their family, friends, and co-workers. They had been continually told during treatment that they were helpless, and that only treatment could save them. Many of them fervently believe that they could never have been cured without the treatment.

One of the most fiercely debated issues is whether "controlled drinking" is a legitimate goal.

The sound and the fury signify nothing, however, for the rates of improvement in these disease-oriented treatment programs (which cost between $5,000 and $20,000) do not significantly differ from the natural rates of improvement for comparable but untreated demographic groups.

There is some disagreement about the effectiveness of more modest forms of treatment. Some reports—for example, a major study done for the Congressional Office of Technology Assessment—conclude that no single method of treatment is superior to any other (a judgment made by all the major studies). But according to the study, the data appear to show that "treatment seems better than no treatment." That is, some help-oriented intervention—it doesn't matter what kind—may contribute modestly to improvement.

The more pessimistic reading of the data is that elaborate treatments for alcoholism as a disease have no measurable impact at all. In a review of a number of different long-term studies of treatment programs, George Vaillant states that "there is compelling evidence that the results of our treatment were no better than the natural history of the disease." Reviewing other major treatment programs with long-term follow-ups, he remarks that the best that can be said is that these programs do no harm.

In recent years, early evaluation studies have been re-examined from a non-disease perspective, which has produced interesting results.

The new perspective suggests a different conception of the road to improvement. Instead of hoping for a medical magic bullet that will cure the disease, the goal here is to change the way drinkers live. One should learn from one's mistakes, rather than viewing any one mistake as a proof of failure or a sign of doom.

Also consistent with the newer pluralistic, non-disease approach is the selection of specific strategies and tactics for helping different sorts of drinkers; methods and goals are tailored to the individual in ways that leave the one-disease, one-treatment approach far behind.

Much controversy remains about pluralistic goals. One of the most fiercely debated issues is whether so-called "controlled drinking" is a legitimate therapeutic goal. Some contend that controlled drinking by an alcoholic inevitably leads to uncontrolled drinking. Disease-concept lobbyists, such as the National Council on Alcoholism, have tried to suppress scientific publications reporting success with controlled drinking, and have excoriated them upon publication. Some have argued that publishing such data can "literally kill alcoholics." Even so, hundreds of similar reports presenting favorable results have appeared. One recent study concludes that most formerly heavy drinkers who are now socially adjusted become social drinkers rather than abstainers.

In any case, the goal of total abstinence insisted upon by advocates of the disease concept is not a proven successful alternative, since only a small minority achieves it. If doubt remains as to whether the controversy over controlled drinking is fueled by non-scientific factors, that doubt can be dispelled by realizing that opposition to controlled drinking (like support for the disease concept of alcoholism) is largely confined to the U.S. and to countries dominated by American intellectual influence. Most physicians in Britain, for example, do not adhere to the disease con-cept of alcoholism. And the goal of controlled drinking—used selectively but extensively—is widely favored in Canada and the United Kingdom. British physicians have little professional or financial incentive to bring problem drinkers into their consulting rooms or hospitals. American physicians, in contrast, defend an enormous growth in institutional power and fee-for-service income. The selling of the term "disease" has been the key to this vast expansion of medical power and wealth in the United States.

What should our attitude be, then, to the long-term heavy drinker? Alcoholics do not knowingly make the wicked choice to be drunkards. Righteous condemnation and punitive moralism are therefore inappropriate. Compassion, not abuse, should be shown toward any human being launched upon a destructive way of life. But compassion must be realistic. It is not compassionate to encourage drinkers to deny their power to change, to excuse them legally and give them special government benefits that foster a refusal to confront the need to change. Alcoholics are not helpless; they can take control of their lives. In the last analysis, alcoholics must *want* to change and *choose* to change. To do so they must make many difficult daily choices. We can help them by offering moral support and good advice, and by assisting them in dealing with their genuine physical ailments and social needs. But we must also make it clear that heavy drinkers must take responsibility for their own lives. Alcoholism is not a disease; the assumption of personal responsibility, however, is a sign of health, while needless submission to spurious medical authority is a pathology.

CAFFEINE

Using caffeine to enhance your performance may backfire in ways that you might not expect.

Gary Legwold

Gary Legwold is a contributing editor to BICYCLE GUIDE.

John Brady, a member of the 7-Eleven pro racing team, doesn't use caffeine as an aid to his performance in cycling anymore. Not only that, he believes this doesn't put him at a disadvantage. "I think I'm at an advantage because I don't feel I need to use it," says Brady. "I know where my strength comes from; it's not from caffeine."

Brady is in something of a minority. A good portion of competitive cyclists believe caffeine will give them a boost, an edge, a way of backing off the bonk. Experts estimate that as many as one-third to one-half of competitive cyclists drink tea, coffee, espresso, colas, and cola syrups. Other variations on the theme are stay-awake pills, citrated caffeine, and time-released caffeine suppositories that supposedly get into the system faster and with less stomach distress.

What they're doing is legal within limits. The International Olympic Committee has restricted the amount of caffeine a cyclist can use to the equivalent of six to eight cups of strong coffee consumed in two or three hours. If one exceeds the limit, punishment is comparable to that of using other drugs. For example, in the 1988 U.S. Olympic Trials, track rider Steve Hegg was disqualified for having exceeded the IOC limit for caffeine in urine following an event.

The most widely known sources of caffeine are coffee beans, cola nuts, tea, and cocoa beans, although the substance is found in a total of 60 different plants and trees. It is absorbed by the body quickly, peaking at 15 to 60 minutes after consumption, and stays in the body for variable amounts of time.

Caffeine increases heart rate, digestive secretions, respiration rate, and alertness, while delaying fatigue and shortening reaction time. On the negative side, it can cause headaches, irritability, insomnia, diarrhea, hyperactivity, depression, heartbeat irregularities, and dehydration related to its diuretic qualities, which cause increased urine output—something to consider on hot days when keeping properly hydrated is a major challenge anyway. Excessive use of caffeine, which is not unheard of among cyclists, has been linked, though inconclusively, to heart disease, various cancers, and birth defects.

Caffeine was once touted as a way to burn fat instead of glycogen. But that view has now been discredited.

Cyclists who swear they get a lift and improved performance from caffeine got an additional lift in the late 1970s and early 1980s, when respected researchers found that in endurance activities, caffeine caused the body to use more fat as fuel, thus sparing the reserves of glycogen, the muscles' primary source of energy.

In a study done at Ball State University, researchers gave one small group of competitive cyclists two cups of regular coffee containing a total of 330 milligrams of caffeine. A second identical group was given two cups of decaffeinated coffee. It took the caffeine group 19.5 percent longer to exercise to exhaustion than the decaf group. Also, there were signs that free fatty acids in the caffeine group's blood were elevated, and that there was a shift from the use of glycogen to fat as fuel for the exercise.

Another study, headed by John Ivy, PhD, associate professor in the Department of Kinesiology and Director of Exercise Science Laboratories at the University of Texas at Austin, found that 500 mg of caffeine increased work production in trained cyclists by 7.4 percent, with no increase in perceived exertion.

This kind of information filtered out to the cycling community, which welcomed the news. Now they had a simple explanation of how caffeine supposedly worked: it caused glycogen sparing. But while cyclists were hearing what they wanted to hear, researchers were a bit more skeptical. For them, there remained too many variables—caffeine dosages and varying individual sensitivities to caffeine, for example—to draw ironclad conclusions from the published research.

Skepticism grew as follow-up research often failed to confirm that caffeine did indeed lead to glycogen sparing. Sometimes researchers found an increase in free fatty acids (FFAs) with caffeine; sometimes they didn't. When they did show a caffeine-induced increase in FFAs, sometimes the anticipated glycogen sparing failed to show. And no one could offer a cogent explanation as to why sparing seemed to work with cyclists and not runners, as studies showed. And carbohydrate loaders saw no increase in FFAs, and thus, no glycogen sparing, according to work done by Jane Weir, PhD, at the University of Cape Town Medical School, South Africa.

Recently, William Winder, PhD, published research that came down hard on caffeine. In a series of experiments on endurance-trained, non-trained, and fasted rats, Winder's group in the Division of Physiology and Anatomy, Department of Zoology at Brigham Young University, concluded that, based on biopsies of muscle and the liver where glycogen is stored, caffeine produced no glycogen sparing even though there was an increase in free fatty acids. Winder says that human studies have also found no sparing. Based on these experiments he says, "caffeine should not be used as an ergogenic aid. I don't believe that it is effective in sparing carbohydrates during long-term exercise."

Nonetheless, many pro-caffeine cyclists are not likely to be swayed by the methodological soul-searching, or even the opinions of experts. Researchers such as Ivy say that maybe everyone is hung up on sparing, but the more relevant point is that some athletes believe caffeine works for them, and that's enough.

The fact is, the athletes are right in their intuition that caffeine is doing something. Studies agree that caffeine stimulates the nervous system enough to lower perceived exertion scores and generally make athletes feel more alert. Those alertness and fatigue reduction factors, however slight, are not to be ignored in endurance events, say many experienced cyclists.

"I believe cyclists are taking caffeine much more for central nervous system stimulation and to lower perceived exertion than they are for glycogen sparing," says Ed Burke, PhD, former USCF technical director who is currently director of new products and research at White Rock Products Corp.

Ivy agrees. "The effect of caffeine may not be this increased sparing of carbohydrate," says Ivy. "It may be part of it, and I think it is part of it later in the exercise [session]." But, he adds, the mental aspects of caffeine use "may be actually more important than the metabolic changes."

However, that increased central nervous system stimulation isn't always a benefit. Dale Stetina, a two-time Coors Classic winner and a member of two U.S. Olympic cycling teams, stays off caffeine most of the year. He has drunk coffee for a couple of important races, but he sees danger in being "wired" and caffeine-confident versus just plain confident. Being too juiced up can lead to tactical errors.

"If you don't normally have caffeine in your diet and take some strong coffee, you feel especially alert," he says. "It's good that you believe in yourself that day; because you feel alert, you feel quick. But it can almost make you antsy and hyper. If you're like that you can get carried away attacking when you shouldn't. And if you don't conserve energy, you just blow up sooner."

And you'll very likely blow up if you try to use caffeine as bonk prevention. The sugar and caffeine of a cola may momentarily pick you up, but only diet and training can help you avoid bonking. "Anybody who's bonked has depleted glycogen, and I think that's more a function of not knowing when to eat or what to eat rather than metabolizing fat in-

Caffeine makes you think you're not working as hard as you are. That's risky, because you could end up bonking even earlier.

stead of glycogen [from taking caffeine]," says Len Pettyjohn, director of the Coors Light cycling team.

John Brady has seen this first-hand. "During the Tour of Texas I did have a Coke because I was working really hard one day, and it didn't do anything for me. I blew up anyway," says Brady. "If you get yourself in situations where you bonked, you definitely did something wrong in your diet and training as a whole," he says.

The bottom line is that most experts, and many elite cyclists, think the ergogenic use of caffeine should not apply to recreational riding. The potential negative effects don't outweigh the positives. Asks Burke, "Why are you out there? To enjoy your ride, or to knock 30 seconds off your time?"

"Quite frankly, the stance that I take is that caffeine is a drug," says Peter Van Handel, PhD, who is a sports physiologist with the U.S. Olympic Committee and has written a review article on caffeine. "You can't prescribe it for someone and say that it's going to enhance their performance." However, Van Handel has no problem with the pleasurable cup of coffee before a race and the cola near the end when you're fading. The amount of caffeine in these drinks (40 to 150 mgs) is not going to do much. The problem comes about when cyclists lose their perspective about caffeine and rely on it too much.

So recreational riders should put the caffeine away, or at least put it in perpective. "If I were you," says Burke, "I'd be more concerned about training and diet and fluid replacement than I would be worrying about caffeine in a recreational situation. You know, we all look for shortcuts sometimes."

Smokeless Tobacco

The Fatal Pinch

Rachel Wolfe

Long after the Marlboro Man quit hawking cigarettes on television, baseball players were still chewing Red Man, "dipping" Skoal, and encouraging millions of young television viewers to develop another, more dangerous habit – using smokeless tobacco.

When cigarette ads were forced off the airwaves in 1971, the smokeless tobacco industry launched a massive promotional campaign to take up the slack. Smokeless tobacco producers pumped millions of dollars into television ads featuring sports stars and country-western singers. Their mission: to change the stigma of chewing tobacco and snuff. What was once considered low-brow, socially unacceptable and dirty had to become desirable.

They were amazingly successful. The use of chewing tobacco and moist snuff skyrocketed at a time when smoking in the United States and other industrialized countries was on the decline. Between 1970 and 1979, production and sales of the fine cut tobacco used in moist snuff increased 188 percent, according to the National Cancer Institute. Sales of snuff are now increasing at the rate of seven to 11 percent every year. The World Health Organization (WHO) describes it as a "new threat to society," estimating that there are now 12 million users of snuff and loose-leaf chewing tobacco in the United States.

Relatively few companies control the smokeless tobacco industry in the United States. U.S. Tobacco, which produces the two best-selling brands on the market, leads the pack in sales. Its Skoal, Skoal Bandits and Copenhagen brands alone account for approximately 27 percent of the smokeless tobacco market. Liggett & Myers, Lorillard, Brown & Williamson, and Culbro, Incorporated share the rest of the market.

Smokeless tobacco was left out of the initial debate that raged over smoking and health, and its producers attempted to capitalize on the windfall. In 1985 the industry spent over $22 million on advertising. Skoal Bandits ads told the public to "take a pouch instead of a puff." Print ads referred to it as "good clean chewing tobacco," or "clean enjoyment."

"Advertisements for smokeless tobacco imply that the habit is less harmful than smoking," noted Dr. Christopher Squier in an American Cancer Society report. "Unfortunately, this impression is common among the public and even among health professionals."

By 1981 several major studies had surfaced linking chew and snuff to oral cancer. Each year, the studies linking smokeless tobacco to various diseases grew more damning. Finally in August, 1986, amidst pressure from public interest and health groups, smokeless tobacco ads were banned from electronic media in the United States, and mandatory labels warning of oral cancer, tooth decay and gum disease were required on all packages.

Now advertisers have switched to new tactics. Instead of claiming that smokeless tobacco is a safe alternative to cigarettes, ads are increasingly aimed at young people. Smokeless tobacco ads feature swarthy outdoorsmen and athletes, despite the 1985 Smokeless Tobacco Council voluntary code which prohibits the use of "active athletes" in advertisements.

And according to the Federal Trade Commission, advertisers are increasingly using sports events and rock concerts as forums to distribute free samples of the tobacco as well as t-shirts and tote-bags bearing the logo of tobacco brands. Only two states—Minnesota and Utah—have banned free distribution of smokeless tobacco products. Free samples are also available through special mail-in offers in magazines such as *Field and Stream*, *Outdoor Life*, and *Sporting News*, despite state laws prohibiting minors from using smokeless tobacco. "Spitting contests" held at fairs and festivals have different age categories, including pre-schoolers. Youth groups around the country have started "chewing clubs," and some public schools set aside special areas where students can chew tobacco.

Industry innovation seems to have offset the decline in consumption health professionals hoped would result from the 1986 ad ban and warning label requirements. In fact, sales of snuff and chewing tobacco have continued to rise dramatically among young people. Twelve surveys from the past seven years have found that 8 to 36 percent of male high school and college students in the United States are regular users of smokeless tobacco, especially snuff. The National Institutes of Health estimated that at least three million of all U.S. users are under age 21. Surveys in Massachusetts, Texas, Oregon and Oklahoma indicate that approximately 30 percent of teenage males are "chewing" or "dipping."

One shocking study conducted by the U.S. Centers of Disease Control found that 17 percent of five-year-old girls and 10 percent of five-year-old boys in Alaska used smokeless tobacco and had been using it for an average of about a year. More than 30 percent of 11-year-olds were regular users. A survey of kindergarten children in Arkansas found that 21 percent had used smokeless tobacco. Fourteen U.S. states still allow sales of smokeless tobacco to minors.

Like cigarette producers, the smokeless tobacco industry is also looking outside the U.S. for new markets. "We're investing our good, hard-earned dollars in what we call 'mining,' laying a good foundation, in certain areas of the U.K., France, Italy," said U.S. Tobacco president Nicholas Buonicanti (a former Miami Dolphins linebacker) in 1985. Other targets included Sweden, Latin America, Taiwan, China, and Japan. Smokeless tobacco is "now being promoted cynically and aggressively around the world," says a WHO study group.

With the increased use comes increased dangers. "The problem is," says Allen Greenberg, an attorney formerly with the Public Citizen Health Research Group, "smokeless tobacco is not only addictive but also deadly." Snuff and chew are linked to many serious health problems: cancers of the cheek and gum; oral leukoplakia (precancerous lesions); cancers of the esophagus, larynx and pancreas; and tooth decay and gum disease.

In India, where more than 40 percent of cancers are in the oral cavity, there is an extremely high rate of tobacco use. J.J. Pindborg, who conducted long-term epidemiological studies in India in the 1960s, found that oral cancer and leukoplakia occurred almost exclusively in Indians who had a tobacco habit. Another study found that Indian women who chewed tobacco had a higher percentage of stillborn babies than those who didn't use tobacco.

In the United States, the American Cancer Society estimates that oral cancer accounts for 27,000 deaths each year. Of these, a large percentage are thought to be caused from tobacco use. Risks of developing cancers increase with the duration of smokeless tobacco use.

In addition, surveys have shown that young people who use smokeless tobacco often "graduate" to cigarettes. "Many smokeless tobacco users are young people who may experience deleterious health effects from long-term snuff use or may try other forms of tobacco," says the National Cancer Institute.

But despite the number of studies indicting smokeless tobacco, it was the widely publicized case of Sean Marsee, a high school athlete and regular user of Copenhagen snuff, that first awakened America to its dangers. Marsee began using snuff at the age of 12. At age 18 he was diagnosed as having tongue cancer in the spot where the "quid" touched his tongue. In 1984, after a series of disfiguring operations including partial removal of his tongue, Marsee died. He was 19 years old. In one of the few lawsuits against smokeless tobacco producers, Marsee's mother sued U.S. Tobacco. Although the suit was ultimately unsuccessful, it sparked widespread debate on the safety of smokeless tobacco and spurred Congress into taking action.

Today, the World Health Organization, the Surgeon General, the American Medical Association, the American Cancer Society, the American Dental Association and the American Heart and Lung Association have joined ranks to battle smokeless tobacco. In June of this year a WHO study group called for a "pre-emptive ban" on the production, importation, and sale of smokeless tobacco all over the world, in order to "prevent a new public health epidemic from a new form of tobacco use." For areas already afflicted, WHO is urging litigation against the industry, prohibition of sales to minors, total advertising bans, and involvement of health personnel and teachers in the fight.

Progress is visible, if slow. Smokeless tobacco has been completely banned in Ireland, Hong Kong, New Zealand and Israel. The U.K. has prohibited electronic advertising, and is now debating whether to ban smokeless tobacco sales altogether. The battle is uphill, but there is strong determination to convince youth throughout the world that a pinch between the cheek and gum could be all it takes to end up dead.

NICOTINE BECOMES ADDICTIVE

It has taken more than half a century to prove finally and indisputably that the colorless, oily liquid in tobacco hooks smokers just as surely as heroin does junkies.

ROBERT KANIGEL

Robert Kanigel, author of Apprentice to Genius, *is working on a biography of the Indian math prodigy Ramanujan.*

1942. British tanks battled Rommel's Panzers in North Africa. The pages of *The Lancet*, Britain's leading medical journal, told of physicians killed in battle and tuberculosis patients denied extra rations at home. Meanwhile, Glasgow physician Lennox Johnston was shooting up with nicotine.

Three or four times a day he'd inject himself with a hypodermic syringe of nicotine, the colorless oily liquid that, on exposure to air, gives tobacco its pungent smell and brownish color. After eighty shots, he found that he liked them better than cigarettes and felt deprived without them. He observed a similar pattern among 35 volunteers to whom he also gave nicotine shots. "Smoking tobacco," he'd assumed from the start, "is essentially a means of administering nicotine, just as smoking opium is a means of administering morphine." And nothing in the course of his study led him to change his mind.

Later, critics objected to Johnston's lack of scientific controls. "And they were right," says Jack Henningfield, a smoking researcher at the Addiction Research Center in Baltimore. "But Johnston was right, too": nicotine was why people smoked—a judgment embodied in the very title of the Surgeon General's latest report on smoking, *Nicotine Addiction*, issued last spring.

The 618-page report drew sneers from the tobacco industry, but no full-dress rebuttal. "We haven't had to," insists Tobacco Institute spokesman Gary Miller, pointing to newspaper editorials that damned the report as the work of zealots and painted its conclusions as ill-founded. "Smokers and non-smokers are just not buying it." But if anything, Surgeon General Everett Koop's report—which summarized the work of hundreds of scientists in thousands of studies, and was itself reviewed by dozens of outside experts—granted scientific legitimacy to folk wisdom and anecdotal evidence of centuries' standing.

The phrase, *tobacco addict*, goes back at least to the eighteenth century, when Samuel Johnson used the expression. *Dope fiend*'s entry into the language during the 1870s was followed by *cigarette fiend* just a few years later; today *nicotine fit* is in common usage. More than half a century before the Surgeon General's report, John L. Dorsey, a Baltimore physician writing in *The Practitioner*, took as a given "that the use of tobacco in its various preparations is a form of drug addiction. . . . The real addict, the smoker of 20 to 50 cigarettes a day, cannot lay aside the habits of years with an easy nonchalance. He has ahead of him wretched days of withdrawal symptoms which will usually end with surrender to the habit." In the devastated cities of Europe after World War II, people cheated, stole, and prostituted themselves for a smoke, and German prisoners of war on diets of 900 calories a day would sometimes swap food for cigarettes.

Indeed, midst today's climate of inhospitability to smoking, and confronted with a thick, citation-studded government report fairly bursting with proof that smoking is addictive and nicotine is its agent, it can be hard to recall that anyone ever thought otherwise. Yet for all those, like Dr. Dorsey, who deemed tobacco addictive,

> *"The cloud of white smoke*
> *rising before the smoker*
> *is soothing and companionable.*
> *The gradual ascent of the completed rings,*
> *their changing forms*
> *and their picturesque movements*
> *disappearing into thin air*
> *all tend to rouse the imagination."*

others had insisted its hold on the smoker was weak. "Smoking," pharmacologist W.E. Dixon had written in the same journal just a few years before, "does not lead to addiction comparable with that of morphine or cocaine. . . . The loss of one's smokes is an annoyance, but not a tragedy."

Why, then, *did* smokers reach for their cigarettes 20 or 30 or 40 times a day—or as was more common in Dixon's day, their pipes and cigars? "The cloud of white smoke rising before the smoker is soothing and companionable," noted British pharmacologist Sir Robert Armstrong-Jones in the 1920s. "The circular shape of the completed rings are attractive. Their gradual ascent unaided and without apparent effort from the 'gurgling briar,' their changing forms and their picturesque movements disappearing into thin air, all tend to rouse the imagination." Smoking, then, granted pleasure—even, as Armstrong-Jones would have it, aesthetic pleasure. Indulging in it hardly made you a drug addict. Oral gratification, "pulmonary eroticism," and all manner of other psychological explanations were trotted out over the years, too. Was it not these that held the smoker in thrall, and not anything so insidious as an addictive drug?

Until recently, of course, the issue wasn't really thrashed about much. After all, smoking, in the view of most scientists, physicians, and smokers, was harmless. So whether or not it was addictive didn't *matter*.

And then, almost all of a sudden, it did.

First came the early studies, in the 1950s, linking smoking to lung cancer and other health problems. Then, the Surgeon General's landmark 1964 report saying as much. Then, over the next 15 years, the steady drumbeat of data buttressing that conclusion: Smoking *was* dangerous to your health. It gave you lung cancer. It contributed to heart disease. It was responsible, yearly, for 300,000 people dying before their time . . .

Mort Levin, a retired Johns Hopkins School of Medicine epidemiologist who established some of the earliest

ties between smoking and lung cancer, still remembers the press conference, at the Hotel de la Paix in Paris in the early 1950s, at which he first presented his findings to the world. Afterwards, some in the audience came up and told him they planned to sell their cigarette company stock. When Levin's evidence became known, they said, people would simply give up smoking and the tobacco companies would go under.

Well, people *didn't* stop smoking. The tobacco companies *didn't* go under. All during the 1950s, the prevalence of smoking among adult males barely budged from its long-steady figure of just over fifty percent. The 1964 report brought it down to the mid-40s, but meanwhile more women were smoking—from less than 20 percent of them in the 1930s to about 30 percent in the 1960s. All told, cigarette sales rose.

Nor was it that people hadn't gotten the message. A 1969 poll found that 81 percent of Americans in their twenties, and 71 percent of all Americans, thought smoking caused cancer. Every magazine ad, every billboard, every cigarette packet carried the word. People apparently wanted to give it up; one recent Gallup Poll, for example, found that 77 percent did. But they didn't, or wouldn't, or couldn't. Why? A question previously accorded scant attention now beginning in the 1960s and then more insistently during the 1970s became one of consuming interest: Was smoking, in some meaningful sense of the word, "addictive"? And if so, was nicotine responsible?

* * *

Of the 4,000 chemical constituents of tobacco, nicotine, which takes its name from Jean Nicot, the sixteenth century French ambassador to Portugal who introduced tobacco to the French court, constitutes 1.5 percent of it by weight and has long been known to have powerful pharmacological effects. Indeed, its use to study transmission of nerve impulses even before 1900 left a whole branch of the cholinergic nervous system forever dubbed "nicotinic."

In his 1931 study, *Phantastica: Narcotic and Stimulating Drugs*, L. Lewin asserted that "the decisive factor in the effects of tobacco, desired or undesired, is nicotine and it matters little whether it passes directly into the organism or is smoked." In 1961, F. S. Larson and two other Medical College of Virginia pharmacologists came out with their classic, encyclopedic survey of the tobacco literature. That nicotine played a role in maintaining tobacco use was to them abundantly clear; but as to how central a role, or whether smoking was a habit, or an addiction, or something else altogether, they reached no consensus. Meanwhile, when it came to hard data, Lennox Johnston's war-time experiment remained largely alone.

And that's how matters stood for a quarter century, until 1967. In that year, B. R. Lucchesi and his colleagues at the University of Michigan Medical School, took another swipe at the question. It was Johnston's work all over again, but this time *with* the controls.

Experimental subjects would arrive at the lab in the morning, having gone without food, drink, or cigarettes since midnight. After blood pressure and heart rate tests, they would enter sound-proofed air-conditioned isolation booths, get hooked up to instruments, and have 23-gauge hypodermic needles inserted in their forearms. To each needle was attached a Y-shaped extension, one arm of which dispensed salt solution, the other nicotine. During some six-hour sessions they got nicotine equivalent to one or two cigarettes an hour. During others they'd get only saline solution. They never knew which. Throughout each session, while kept busy with tests of reaction time, hand steadiness and the like, the volunteers could smoke whenever they wished.

Would they smoke less when they were getting nicotine fed into their veins?

They did. Subject No. 4 consistently smoked about 11 cigarettes per session when he wasn't getting IV nicotine, eight when he did. For Subject No. 2, it was seven and four. Moreover, subjects tended to smoke less of the cigarettes they did consume. "Small but significant," the authors labeled nicotine's effect. There were plainly other factors in their smoking. But just as plainly, the nicotine they got through the needle was nicotine they didn't have to get from their smokes.

During the 1970s the evidence mounted.
And yet none of it
made smoking an addiction.
Because for many people, even today,
addiction meant only one thing.
It meant morphine or heroin. It meant **bad.**

In 1971 came evidence of quite a different sort. Sponsored by the American Cancer Society, William A. Hunt and two colleagues at Loyola University of Chicago compared relapse rates of smokers trying to give up smoking, as reported in dozens of earlier studies, with those of alcoholics trying to give up alcohol and heroin addicts trying to give up heroin. The studies had been performed under vastly different circumstances and so the results of the comparison, the authors apologized, were merely "illustrative."

But *illustrate* they did, in the form of a memorable graph. The horizontal axis represented time since going off heroin, alcohol, or tobacco. Plotted on the vertical axis was the percentage of those still off—100 percent at first, then a fall-off over subsequent weeks and months. And the thing you could never get out of your mind once you'd seen it was that laying the curves for any of the three atop the others, you could scarcely distinguish one from the other: Smokers, the graph said, had as much trouble staying off cigarettes as alcoholics did in staying off drink—and as heroin addicts did in staying off junk.

During the early and mid-1970s, a series of seemingly small, methodological improvements helped give re-

searchers a clearer sense of how nicotine exerted its addictive spell. Puff on a cigarette and nicotine reaches its primary site of action, the brain, within seven seconds, being taken up by the circulatory system through capillaries in the lungs. Nicotine levels in the blood, then, give a measure of how much has reached the brain. And now, more reliable methods for measuring blood levels began to be reported in the literature.

When they were applied, the same figure would crop up with uncanny regularity in experiment after experiment. For some smokers it was 20, for others 50, but on average 35 nanograms per milliliter was how much nicotine, in billionths of a gram per milliliter of blood, smokers seemed to "want." When his blood level fell substantially below it, the smoker lit up—whereupon the figure would shoot up to perhaps fifty. Then, over the next half hour or hour, it would decline, to perhaps 20 or 25. Which meant it was time for another cigarette. And so on during the smoker's waking hours. Plot blood concentration over the course of a day and you'd wind up with a saw tooth marching across the paper.

The "titration hypothesis," researchers called it, using lab terminology for the precise adjustment of a chemical's concentration to some particular value. And while the data never made for so tidy a picture as the model implied, a wide variety of evidence supported its general outlines: smokers manipulated their smoking pattern to get the desired blood levels of nicotine, inhaling more or less deeply, or more or less often. When smoking a low-nicotine cigarette, they might cover up the air vents designed to dilute the smoke—and wind up with blood levels far higher than otherwise. It was as if smokers could "read" their own blood. Thirty-five nanograms per milliliter? They were happy. Twenty? They'd want a cigarette, but could manage without one. Five? They were climbing the walls.

During the early and mid-1970s, the evidence mounted. And yet to most lay people, most physicians, and even most smoking researchers, none of it made smoking an addiction, and none of it made nicotine an addictive drug. Because then—and for many people even today—"addiction" meant one thing. It meant addiction to the opium poppy. It mean morphine or heroin. It meant *bad.*

* * *

B efore World War I, the line separating "good" drugs from "bad" was hazier than it is today. Anyone could go out and buy McMunn's Elixir of Opium or any of at least 600 such "soothing syrups," "pain killers" and "cough medicines," all containing opiates. According to E. M. Brecher in *Licit and Illicit Drugs*, it wasn't unknown for a prominent physician to take morphine every day for 30 or 40 years and never lose a day of work because of it. Sigmund Freud used cocaine for years.

"An opium den at the beginning of the century was a social club. When you say 'opium den,' think 'bar,'" says Neal Grunberg, a psychologist at the Uniformed Services University of the

Health Sciences in Bethesda, Maryland who helped write some of *Nicotine Addiction's* key sections. Being addicted carried few of the connotations—evil, crazed, criminal—it does now. Etymologically, to be addicted means to be *bound over* against one's will like a prisoner or a slave—whether to a drug or anything else. That older, broader, more innocent sense of the word lingers today in such expressions as being addicted to chocolates, or addicted to love.

By the 1980s, it had become clear that while abstaining from tobacco did not induce a withdrawal syndrome like that seen among heroin users, the symptoms were just as distinct, just as specific, and just as measurable.

Then, in 1914, came the Harrison Narcotics Act which, aimed at regulating the drug trade, came to be interpreted as a ban on narcotics use for all but the most narrowly medical purposes. For the first time, morphine and its opiate cousins were illegal. The nation's estimated 200,000 addicts turned to illicit drug dealers—and became criminals.

During the 1940s, classic studies with narcotics addicts imprisoned at the federal facility in Lexington, Kentucky, began to lay the groundwork for an understanding of addiction. But in the process, addiction began to lose its earlier, broader meaning and to ever more intimately fuse with heroin abusers in the public mind. Between about 1940 and 1965, as Jack Henningfield reckons it, addiction came to *mean* opiate addiction, with all its intimations of back alley drug deals and junk-crazed muggers.

So that when, in 1957, the World Health Organization established its definition of addiction, the opiates model was about the only model around. To be addictive, WHO said, a drug had to cause physical dependence, pronounced changes in behavior, and withdrawal symptoms. Cocaine and amphetamines, both today universally regarded as addictive, were excluded, being classed as merely "habituating."

In 1964, WHO discarded the distinction between habituating and addictive. "It was refuted, disowned, by the very committee that put the old definition together," says Jerome Jaffe, director of the Addiction Research Center. But the change came too late to influence the Surgeon General's landmark study appearing that same year. Applying the old definition, the Surgeon General

ruled that nicotine was not addictive. Because, says Jaffe, evidence for withdrawal symptoms and behavioral changes among tobacco users was, at the time, still scanty. Yes, nicotine was so potent that barely one smoker in ten could keep to fewer than five cigarettes a day. Yes, it might be "habituating," to use the discarded WHO definition. Yes, it might be "dependence-producing," to use jargon that came into use later.

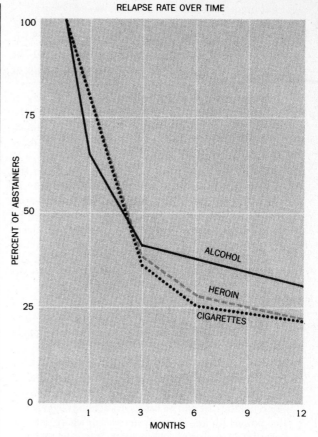

RELAPSE RATE OVER TIME

Smokers trying to give up the weed backslide about as frequently as alcoholics and heroin addicts trying to give up their favorite drugs.

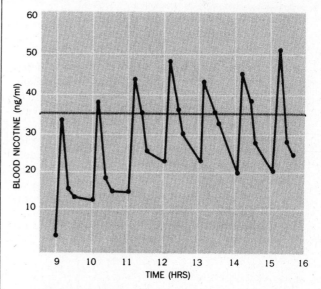

This subject who smoked one cigarette an hour illustrates the titration hypothesis—how smokers manipulate their smoking pattern, inhaling more or less deeply or more or less often, to get the desired blood levels of nicotine—on average 35 nanograms per milliliter.

But no, it wasn't addictive. *Heroin* was addictive.

"We tend not to believe that the things we do routinely and normally are bad," observes Neil Grunberg. So it was with smoking. All through the 1930s, 40s, and 50s cigarette smoking had been advertised as a symbol of success, of healthy sexuality, of the American way of life. It was socially acceptable. It didn't make you crazy. It wasn't heroin. And so, as evidence mounted through the early 1970s that smokers were—to again invoke addiction's etymological roots—*bound over* to the drug, resistance to the idea lingered.

You could see it at a conference, "Smoking As a Dependence Process," held by the National Institute of Drug Abuse in 1978. At it, many of the presentations given were fairly riddled with ambivalence. On the one hand, *of course* smoking was addictive, and *of course* nicotine was responsible. On the other hand, there was reluctance, reaching even beyond normal scientific caution, to say so as long as any gaps remained in the scientific record.

M.A.H. Russell of Maudsley Hospital in England, for example, reviewed the evidence for nicotine's role—how it affected behavior and performance in ways that might be reinforcing, how it induced tolerance in animals, and so on—only to add a cautionary note: "If we could prove that nicotine is what smokers seek, we could be confident that the puzzle was virtually completed. Unfortunately this is not the case and we cannot escape the nagging fact that powerful addictive syndromes occur where pharmacological factors clearly play no part." How did we know, in other words, that smoking, with its comforting little rituals, wasn't more like such persistent habits as gambling, say, or nail biting?

Jerome Jaffe, then at Columbia University's College of Physicians and Surgeons, also expressed doubt. In a paper with Maureen Kanzler, he noted that, while nicotine *seemed* responsible for smoking's hold on the smoker, "reliable laboratory evidence that nicotine is a reinforcer of drug-taking behavior has been more difficult to develop than comparable evidence for drugs like morphine, amphetamine or cocaine." It was hard to get animals to give it to themselves. And when they did, they did so less compulsively than they did other drugs.

"We believe that most drinkers of gin and tonic want the gin more than the fizz or the quinine, that people who drink paregoric want the morphine and not the camphor," wrote he and Kanzler. But their personal convictions aside, they weren't *quite* ready to say it was nicotine that smokers craved more than the flare of the match, the lung-filling pull of the inhalation, or the leisurely rise of smoke rings into the air.

* * *

How did we know that smoking, with its comforting little rituals, wasn't more like such persistent habits as gambling, say, or nail biting?

The doubts, though, were soon to be dismissed once and for all. Just as a generation earlier hundreds of millions of dollars had poured out of the National Cancer Institute to pin down smoking's effects on health, now NIDA sank resources into the study of tobacco addiction. "This is a psychoactive drug with effects that fit the most stringent definitions of addiction," Jack Henningfield remembers NIDA director William Polling pronouncing with certainty; now it was time to make the case airtight. "All of a sudden," recalls Henningfield, "this behavior-controlling drug was being studied by people trained to study behavior controlling drugs." And within a few years beginning in the late 1970s, the remaining doors through which nicotine might escape the label of addictive were slammed shut.

One measure of addictive potential can be gained by simply asking human subjects how much they like whatever they're being fed through an intravenous needle, comparing the drug at various dosages to a placebo. Give a small dose of morphine and people like it significantly more, on a standard five-point scale, than a placebo. Up the dose and they prefer it still more. Do the same for a drug like chlorpromazine, known not to encourage compulsive use, and subjects like it no more than a placebo; a higher dose changes matters not at all. Give them nicotine, as Jack Henningfield reported in a key experiment, and the scores climb with higher dosages just the way they do for morphine.

Around this time came a series of studies by the Addiction Research Center's Steven Goldberg and colleagues at Harvard. One anomaly long nagging at the composure of smoking researchers had been nicotine's apparent failure to satisfy the self-administration test. If a drug is addictive, you'd expect people and animals to fairly lap it up—or, the way such experiments are done, to eagerly press a lever that metered it out to them. At the 1978 conference, there'd been reports of self-administration in rats, but at unimpressively low levels. And other researchers had been unable to demonstrate it at all.

What Goldberg and his colleagues did was to mimic human smoking behavior in monkeys. When people smoke, any effects of the nicotine become intimately linked to—and amplified by—environmental cues: *Dinner's over. Time for a smoke.* So with the nicotine they delivered intravenously, the experimenters periodically flashed an amber light. Sure enough, the monkeys would press away, usually about once or twice a second, self-administering the drug. When the nicotine, unbeknownst to the animals, was replaced by saline, lever pressing fell off dramatically. When the monkeys were given mecamylamine, a drug known to block nicotine's pharmacological actions, pressing likewise fell. The results were clear. "In one fell swoop," says Henningfield, "all the equivocal studies were out."

During the same period came key work on nicotine's withdrawal effects. Three hundred years before, following tobacco's introduction to England, King James I observed that smokers "are not able to forebear the same, no more than an old drunkard can abide to be long sober, without falling into an uncurable weakness and evil constitution." But difficulty in giving up smoking is one thing, withdrawal effects quite another. "You feed a vending machine that doesn't deliver, and you start beating on the machine," offers Jerome Jaffe, playing attorney for the defense. His point? "*Any* time you interrupt a habit, you can get irritable. Now if I give up smoking, do I vomit? Do I have seizures? Do I fall down on the floor, have hallucinations?" Junkies and alkies do. Smokers don't. Q.E.D., tobacco was not addictive, Jaffe portrays the skeptics insisting.

But by the early 1980s it had become clear that while abstaining from tobacco did not induce a withdrawal syndrome like that seen among heroin users, the symptoms were just as distinct, just as specific and just as measurable. Retrospective studies consistently showed signs of irritability, restlessness, difficulty concentrating, and weight gain. Now, the same symptoms showed up in more reliable prospective studies. Why, you could give smokers a battery of psychological and cognitive tests, watch their performance deteriorate within eight hours after their last smoke, then watch it return to normal once they started smoking again—or even, for that matter, when you fed them nicotine-laced chewing gum.

There had been other arguments long raised against calling nicotine addictive. Smoking, some said, doesn't exhibit tolerance; you don't require ever-increasing doses to achieve the desired effect. Sure it does, Henningfield points out. You don't *start out* smoking two packs a day. "And there are *no* drugs that people escalate their use of forever."

But wasn't it so, insisted critics like Gary Miller of the Tobacco Institute, that most ex-smokers gave it up on their own without outside help, or drugs, or treatment programs? What kind of an addiction is that? An addiction like any other, says Henningfield. Of alcohol users, for example, only 15 per cent are alcoholics. And nine in ten servicemen addicted to heroin in Vietnam got off once they got home. Because a drug exerts a powerful hold, doesn't mean it exerts an absolute hold.

Proponents of nicotine's central role in keeping smokers smoking don't say, and never said, that nicotine was the whole story. Give nicotine intravenously and smoking drops—but does not stop. Give nicotine chewing gum to would-be quitters and, without counseling and support, their relapse rate is almost as high as if you just let them go cold turkey. As Jerome Jaffe points out, "there's a lot of conditioning that goes with the inhalation of cigarette smoke. You have thousands of couplings" between the pleasure you get from smoking and the rituals surrounding it. To give up smoking means giving up nicotine—but also much more.

Later in the 1980s would come studies holding up whole new areas of nicotine's workings to the scientist's searchlight. Kenneth Kellar and his colleagues at Georgetown Medical Center, for example, discovered binding sites in the brain at which nicotine presumably acts. Other researchers experimented with nicotine gum, introduced in 1984 as a means of supplying smokers with a more benign source of nicotine while weaning them off cigarettes. Still others explored nicotine's role as a mood regulator and its ability to improve scores on cognitive tests through subtle nervous system effects.

But in essence, by the early 1980s, the case was already made; smoking was addictive—not just by the new, 1964 WHO definition but by the earlier, more rigid 1957 one—and nicotine was what made it so. So it was just a matter of time before the full force of the federal government lined up behind that determination.

In 1982, NIDA director William Pollin formally testified before Congress that nicotine was an addictive drug.

Later that year, summarizing Pollin's testimony and bearing the imprint of the U.S. Department of Health and Human Services, appeared a Public Health Service pamphlet, *Why People Smoke*. Placing tobacco right beside heroin, alcohol, and marijuana among drugs of abuse, the pamphlet reckoned it "the most widespread example of drug dependence in our country," one that drew its power and compulsion from nicotine.

In 1987, the American Psychiatric Association, which seven years before had included tobacco dependence within its Diagnostic and Statistical Manual of Mental Disorders, established "nicotine withdrawal" as an organic mental disorder.

Then, finally, on May 16, 1988, Surgeon General Koop stood before the cameras and microphones. . . .

* * *

About ten years earlier, in a hospital in Jaipur, India, a three-year-old Hindu child from a rural family was admitted to the pediatrics ward for malnutrition, anemia, and acute bronchitis. Two days later, the child was given a transfusion. During it, despite two shots of tranquilizer, he could not be stilled. Later, "the child was unable to sleep," the doctors who wrote up the case in *Clinical Pediatrics* reported, "crying and fretting through much of the night, begging for bidis."

A bidi is a crude, indigenous form of cigar popular in India, typically a three inch-long wad of sun-cured tobacco wrapped in Tendu leaf. It turned out that the boy's grandmother had surreptitiously supplied them to him for the past six months, and that he now smoked, inhaling deeply, eight to ten of them daily. When denied the bidis at the time of the transfusion, he became cranky and irritable and could neither eat nor sleep comfortably.

The three Indian physicians had little doubt about what they were seeing. They entitled their case study, "Probable Tobacco Addiction in a Three-Year-Old Child."

Kick Me: I Smoke

Patrick Cooke

Contributing editor Patrick Cooke's last story for HIPPOCRATES *was about "imported nurses."*

I was sitting at a corner table in a Washington, D.C., restaurant not long ago, enjoying good conversation and good coffee, and was about to enjoy the cigarette I have come to associate with both, when a woman across the room stood up and shouted at me, "Put that thing out!" Evidently it made no difference to her that I was far away in the restaurant's smoking section—or that I was still patting my pockets for a match.

It's 1989, and all the world hates a smoker. A little more than a decade remains until the surgeon general's deadline for the dawn of the smoke-free society—the year 2000—and already you can tell what a mean little world *that's* going to be.

If you don't believe it, listen closely to the cheerful threat now included in your flight attendant's pre-takeoff instructions: " . . . and we remind you that federal law prohibits tampering with the smoke detector in the lavatory." Or belly up to a certain roulette table in Caesar's Tahoe Casino, where it's okay to dwizzle away the family farm but no longer acceptable to smoke while you're doing it. Come on down to friendly Del Mar in Southern California, where a local initiative, citing the danger of second-hand tobacco smoke *outdoors*, called for banning smoking on local beaches and sidewalks; the proposal suggested roping off two town smoking corrals.

From sea to shining sea the American smoker is being shown his place. And that place, you might have noticed, is the far end of the company parking lot, or outside a city highrise in the rain.

I smoked my first serious cigarette 17 years ago and have, more or less, smoked a pack a day ever since. I knew it was a stupid thing to do, people around me were concerned for my health, but back in the early seventies, smoking was considered a personal decision. Folks pretty much left you alone to wallow in your own idiocy. The surgeon general had made his point eight years earlier: If you smoke, expect to die early and horribly. Millions had already heard the message and quit. They did

so because organizations like the American Cancer Society nudged them along with assurances of a better, longer life.

My, but we've come a long way. The anti-smoking bandwagon has since changed course and gathered momentum like few social movements of the past decades. Along the way it has pushed aside the good-hearted quit-smoking programs whose work was steady but apparently too slow. Instead, crusaders now advocate smoker bashing.

Groups like the American Cancer Society are still doing their best to encourage quitting, but concern for the smoker's health has been pretty much shouted down—when was the last time you heard anyone mention it? No, the road to the smoke-free society now promises to be littered with ugly billboards of the depraved smoker filling public spaces with poison gas, compromising the morals of children, ripping out the airplane smoke detector. In nonsmoking America, every week is hate week.

I recently saw a woman leap from line at the motor vehicle department and assail an elderly Asian man who was smoking nearby. The man spoke no English. "No smoke!" the woman screamed, and pointed to a sign. The man apparently read no English either because he smiled and bowed and went on happily puffing. "NO SMOKE!" she bellowed. Suddenly, it dawned on the little fellow that he might be attacked, and probably more out of fear than understanding he dropped his cigarette. *She* stomped it out. "This is a public space! You may not smoke here!"

What produces this kind of aggressive and pompous behavior in many anti-smoking advocates? Maybe the frustration is more than they can bear after decades of misery caused by cigarettes. What enrages them is the impossibility of simply outlawing the cause of all that suffering. And now they've turned that rage on the smoker.

But this is not the first group to show its contempt for smokers. That distinction belongs to the tobacco companies. And you must begin in their dark lair to understand how far we have come, and where we are going.

L IKE ANYONE ELSE, smoker or nonsmoker, I cannot hear the words "Tobacco Institute" without getting the creeps. So to sit in their plush suite in downtown Washington, D.C., is to invite the serious willies. One aspect of the place I find comforting, however: You can smoke anywhere you like. It may be the only office left in America where smokers are not frog-marched to the exits for lighting up.

In the 1950s, the six major tobacco companies formed the institute to lobby for their interests and to respond to the uncomfortable questions beginning to arise about smoking and health. As scientific evidence piled up that cigarettes were killing people, the companies wheeled out their own scientists, who declared that a link between smoking and lung cancer did not exist. Today, one of the institute's chief functions is still to wheeze out that mantra any time someone mentions the more than 300,000 Americans who die each year of smoking-related illnesses. "Studies showing smokers have a higher risk for disease are merely statistical," the chant goes. "And statistics don't prove cause and effect."

The statement would go well above the display case adorning the institute's reception area. Inside the lighted case are dozens of packs of cigarettes, antique and contemporary, representing all the tobacco companies who pay the institute's bills: "Bright," "Now," "Oasis," "St. Moritz". . .

The mood has not been as carefree around the institute as those happy packs would suggest, however, since Rose Cipollone died of lung cancer in Little Ferry, New Jersey. It's not that anyone here is in mourning because Mrs. Cipollone died from consuming an estimated 370,000 cigarettes over a period of 40 years—"statistics don't prove cause and effect." It's that her case may soon put an end to the long-standing industry boast of never having lost a dime in a liability case involving a smoker's death.

Mrs. Cipollone began smoking in 1942. She continued on through the decades as radio personality Arthur Godfrey, sponsored by Chesterfield, urged fellow smokers to ignore critics who imagined poisons lurking in cigarettes—and advertisements featured even doctors enjoying every smooth puff. Mrs. Cipollone smoked while in labor with her first child. She smoked after an operation to remove part of her lung. She continued to buy cigarettes almost all the way up to the end of her 58 years, which seems to be the only thing that mattered to the cigarette companies.

When her husband sued the manufacturers of the brands she had smoked, claiming that they had misled his wife about the risks, nearly everyone expected it to end as all 100 previous liability actions had since the first, in 1954—either in a mistrial or dismissal.

But it didn't. The jury heard evidence never before presented in court, like the 1972 Tobacco Institute memorandum bragging about the policy that worked best for the cigarette industry: a "brilliantly conceived and executed strategy" of "creating doubt about the health charge without actually denying it."

A legion of attorneys for the tobacco companies huffed and puffed the mantra, but in the end one of the manufacturers, Liggett, was ordered to pay Mr. Cipollone $400,000.

Today the chief spokesman for the Tobacco Institute is Walker Merryman. He is a 23-year smoker who says he feels "just fine," though as I sit across from him in his large, well-ventilated office, he looks older than his 41 years.

Not surprisingly, he won't discuss the Cipollone

In the old days, folks pretty much left you alone to wallow in your own idiocy. My, but we've come a long way.

verdict, which is, also not surprisingly, under appeal. He will, however, talk about the industry's efforts to counter the bad publicity cigarettes have gotten since the trial.

This year, for example, the institute launched the "Enough is Enough" campaign, prompted by its own national survey that reported, contrary to all other evidence, that Americans do not support tougher anti-smoking measures. Last year, the Philip Morris Company, the institute's biggest member, began a newspaper and magazine blitz, entitled "The American Smoker: An Economic Force." At a reported cost of $5 million, the ads remind boorish nonsmokers that smokers have a $1 trillion impact on the economy—so watch how you treat them.

"One of the points Philip Morris wants to drive home," says Merryman cheerfully, "is that you have the right to make a choice about smoking and we want to help you defend that right."

That may well be the kind of help some smokers are looking for. But it makes me nervous to think of the tobacco industry as my pal, guarding me from the anti-smoking loonies. It makes me nervous because the industry was Rose Cipollone's pal, too, and in their eyes I'm as disposable as she was.

Apparently the industry believes that if I am dumb enough to smoke, I am dumb enough to think they are looking out for my best interests. And what's more, that I will offer them my loyalty. But their motives are black-hearted, and exploitation, a form of smoker bashing, doesn't come any more cruel or cynical.

I think there was a time when the anti-cigarette forces understood this, when they saw smokers as manipulated by an evil empire, and that what they offered was better health through escape from the cigarette companies' grasp. They saw no reason to bash smokers any worse than the $35 billion industry already was. At some point they decided instead

If You Must Quit, Please Try...

EARLY THIS YEAR, William Bennett vowed that before taking office as the nation's drug policy czar, he would break his own addiction: a two-pack-a-day habit. With a little more than a week to go, he checked into a six-day live-in program at a resort in West Virginia. Thanks to a regimen that included yoga classes and a breaking-free-from-cigarettes balloon-releasing ceremony, Bennett stubbed out his last cigarette. It wasn't his first "last cigarette"—most smokers quit several times before they finally stop—but, with the nation's eyes upon him, Bennett may well stay clean this time.

Quitting isn't easy. Surveys show that 70 percent of the nation's 55 million smokers have tried at least once. One of the biggest hurdles, especially for women, is a fear of fat. About two-thirds of those who quit gain five to ten pounds—but that's a small price for dramatically reducing your risks of both heart disease and lung cancer.

Although 90 percent of quitters do it on their own, there's plenty of help for those who need it.

BEHAVIOR MODIFICATION: Learning to take a short walk after dinner or to doodle while talking on the phone are just two new habits that can replace smoking. Counselors teach such coping tips at clinics sponsored by the American Lung Association, the American Cancer Society, and private groups such as Smokenders. Other tactics include pairing up with a buddy to talk to when temptation strikes, avoiding or changing situations that trigger smoking, or switching to brands successively lower in nicotine. The group quits together usually midway through a six- or seven-week program. On average, 40 percent of graduates are still free from cigarettes a year later. Costs range from $50 to $300.

RESIDENTIAL TREATMENT: There are about ten live-in programs nationwide. One of the oldest, run by the Seventh-Day Adventists, has been helping smokers for 20 years. The week-long course costs $1,750 and includes coping strategies, a health improvement plan—exercise, massages, vegetarian meals—and the support of other participants. After one year, 35 percent of the graduates remain ex-smokers.

ACUPUNCTURE: It remains unclear how—or even whether—getting poked with tiny needles eases quitting. Enthusiasts say this fairly painless technique lessens the physical symptoms of withdrawal, but there's no solid evidence. A course of treatments—usually half-hour sessions at a clinic—lasts from two days to three months. Each session costs from $35 to $65. Acupuncture helps 27 percent of aspiring quitters stay off cigarettes for at least a year.

HYPNOSIS: Suggestions that breathing deeply will quiet a craving or that quitting makes food taste better help 20 percent of those wanting to stop. But motivation is the key, researchers say: The more you want to quit, the better hypnosis works.

NICOTINE GUM: By chewing gum, smokers can work on breaking the psychological habit without suffering nicotine withdrawals. Serious addicts—people who smoke soon after waking and who go on to light up more than 40 times a day—benefit most from the gum. To get a full nicotine hit, you have to chew slowly and intermittently for almost 30 minutes—a bitter experience, many say. If you don't chew correctly, be prepared for hiccups, upset stomach, and a sore mouth. By itself, the gum helps 11 percent of smokers to quit for at least a year. Combined with counseling it unhooks 29 percent. Doctors suggest people try gradually weaning themselves from the gum after smoking urges fade, usually in three to six months. Five to 10 percent of gum chewers become gum addicts, but better that than a cigarette addict, doctors say. A box of 96 pieces costs about $28.

DRUGS: A handful of drugs now being investigated may ease the psychological urge to smoke. Clonidine, used to treat alcohol and opiate addiction, helped twice as many heavy smokers stop in a recent trial as did a placebo. An early report suggests the anti-anxiety drug buspirone may help reduce irritability while smokers try cutting back. Would-be quitters can ask their doctors to write a prescription for either drug.   —*Mary James*

that we were the enemy, and that the thing to do was grab a club and get in on the action.

GREGORY CONNOLLY, director of the Massachusetts Office for Nonsmoking and Health, was quoted in the *Journal of the American Medical Association* rightly taking store owners to task for selling cigarettes to minors, but this is what he said: "We have to make merchants feel like the person who lights up in a restaurant. Embarrass them."

This belligerent tone would have been unthinkable a decade ago. Now it is fairly commonplace. Northwest Airlines, in fact, commercialized the mood last year when it introduced a no-smoking program. The television ad shows a lone smoker banished to the back of a plane taking his last puffs on the airline. All around him, fed-up passengers applaud the announcement that soon every domestic flight on Northwest will be completely nonsmoking. *That's* the way you handle a smoker.

What brought about this new attitude can in part be laid to the most recently publicized of cigarettes' evils, second-hand smoke, or, the new phrase in fashion, "environmental tobacco smoke"—the ambient smoke from cigarettes that reaches nearby nonsmokers.

Perhaps the most vocal and influential organization warning of this new threat is the Group Against Smoking Pollution (GASP). At the Boston chapter I called on, for example, they talked proudly of having established no-smoking ordinances in 58 communities in Massachusetts, and of pushing the airline ban that now prohibits smoking on 80 percent of all domestic flights. It's an impressive record for what began in 1972 as only a loosely knit collection of people who, honest, used to sit around evenings talking about how much they hated cigarette smoke.

"Early on we didn't have the medical documentation we have now, just a strong suspicion, knowing what's in cigarette smoke, that it was having an effect on people," says GASP's legal counsel, Ed Sweda, who every year goes to the Virginia Slims Tennis Tournament dressed up as the Grim Reaper. "Now we stress the health hazards over and above the annoyance factor, which everybody recognizes anyway."

Obviously GASP never did think much of smokers, but when the "passive smoking" debate came along it justified all of their ill feelings: Like drunk drivers, smokers were endangering the innocent with their deadly vice. Add to that the surgeon general's later assertion that cigarette smokers are addicts, one of the most loaded words of the decade, and a social mandate was sealed. Nicotine is as addictive as heroin—the surgeon general said so—and there's no telling what a smoker might do alone in an airplane lavatory. Why, we could *all* be killed!

"Five thousand nonsmokers a year die from being exposed to tobacco smoke," says GASP's exuberant executive director, Jerry Maldavir, who, along with Sweda, works in a small musty office in the Red Cross building opposite Boston's Fenway Park. "I don't give a damn what the smoker does by himself. But the minute that smoke interferes with the health of others, it's another problem."

That toll, 5,000 deaths, is at the heart of GASP's effort to sling smokers out of the room. It is also at the root of Connolly's recent comment that it's okay, possibly even one's duty, to embarrass smokers in restaurants.

I certainly would not minimize the tragedy of 5,000 deaths. But is environmental tobacco smoke the "epidemic" that Sweda insists it is? In 1986, the surgeon general gathered the results of 13 studies on the link between environmental smoke and lung cancer. That is not an overabundance of literature, considering that concern about second-hand smoke was first raised 25 years ago. Only six of those 13 studies arrived at results that researchers regard as statistically significant.

Moreover, most of those studies—and nearly all of the other literature I have seen on death due to passive smoking—centers on spouses who lived a long time with smokers and who developed a higher incidence of disease than spouses who lived with nonsmokers. Estimates of the national body count range inexplicably from 500 to 46,000 individuals per year. I don't doubt that cigarette smoke has some effect on the mates of smokers, but this seems to me to have been rather a personal matter for those people. And if they did decide to endure that suffocating atmosphere, what was their propensity for disease? Was the window ever opened? Was radon creeping up from the basement? The studies don't answer these questions.

The government report acknowledges a number of difficulties with the studies. Yet Surgeon General Koop has apocalyptically concluded, "The two-thirds of this country who do not smoke are assaulted by the one-third who do smoke, and that assault can be lethal."

People are *not* keeling over in restaurants or in line at the motor vehicle department, although it's easy to get that impression from anti-smoking dogmatists. Cigarette smoke is extremely unpleasant if you don't smoke and I can certainly see a case for clearing many public places of it. But the evidence scarcely constitutes an epidemic or lethal assault, and it does not justify a bigoted social movement that encourages the bullying of little old men minding their own business.

GASP, heady with success, doesn't seem inclined to wait for further returns before pressing on, however—even though the number of deaths, Sweda admits, "is still a matter of some debate."

"You can argue about whether it's five thousand or one thousand or somewhere in between, but the essential fact is that environmental tobacco smoke is harmful," Sweda says. "Our position is to be overly protective rather than underprotective of the public health."

Nicotine's as addictive as heroin, the argument goes, and there's no telling what a smoker might do in an airplane lavatory.

Good enough. But the problem with this sort of half-cocked high-mindedness is that it has a way of becoming infectious. Swayed by claims that smokers cost companies more than nonsmokers, an increasing number of employers nationwide are simply not considering smokers for new positions. GASP of New Jersey gleefully publishes a list of employers who hire only nonsmokers. In Massachusetts, newly hired firefighters and police are being told that they can be fired if caught smoking on or *off* the job.

In Indiana, a "sin" tax on cigarettes subsidizes child care—a noble cause, but why should smokers foot the bill? They already pay $10 billion more a year in taxes nationwide than nonsmokers. In California, voters last year approved a proposition that called for raising the cigarette tax by 250 percent, or 25 cents a pack. Approximately a fifth of the estimated $600 million raised yearly goes toward educating children about smoking. No one, including most smokers, would argue with that—Rose Cipollone's story should be required reading. But a portion goes as well to funding state parks and recreational facilities, and the rest, the largest allocation, to offsetting medical care for people who can't afford health insurance and aren't covered by federal programs. Again, these are terrific objectives. They are also society-wide problems in which smokers share responsibility but that their smoking did little to create.

From town halls all across the country to Capitol Hill, lawmakers have discovered the anti-smoking issue to be popular, safe, ethically defensible, and therefore politically irresistible. In 1989, the smoker is the lunatic junkie waving a handgun around in a crowded room—imperiling innocent lives, making trouble. So tax them, embarrass them, corral them, it's the new public entitlement. Go ahead, take a whack, no one is going to stop you.

AT HOLIDAY SEASON around the Cooke ménage, my five-year-old niece, Kathleen Meara, makes a game of stealing my cigarettes and hiding them somewhere deep in the house. She informs me that smoking is disgusting—the little darling—and refuses to tell me where she's put them. In 12 years she will be a member of the smoke-free society's high school class of 2001, and I hope that once this game ends, cigarettes will never again be a part of her life.

I take it as a good omen that kids are

now at least more knowledgeable about the dangers of cigarettes than ever before. But what about the rest of us, the militant grown-ups whose minds appear to be made up about smoking? Will we spend the next decade woffing at one another, or can we, fellow Americans, reason together?

The truth is that despite being universally despised, many of America's 55 million smokers have readily conformed to all the new rules. A *New York Times*/WCBS poll of smokers in New York City found that 43 percent of them agreed with the new ban on smoking in most public places—New York City, mind you. I, too, have found the new regulations easy enough to live with. Nonsmokers generally find smoke annoying, so smokers do not mind sitting in the restaurant's smoking section; the nonsmoking domestic flights of two hours or less are no real burden.

My own theory is that smokers go along with the bans because they do not really want to smoke. Last year, a Gallup poll asked 300 of them if they would like to quit. More than 200 said yes. If that ratio held true nationally, the total would be something like 36 million smokers.

I believe it, because after 17 years I know something about the way the smoker thinks. You are a voluntary toxic dump for 43 cancer-causing chemicals. The butts pile up, the room stinks, life starts its crawl down the actuarial charts, farther away from friends and family who dance merrily along the life expectancy line that reads "Never smoked." You begin to believe that you will not be around long, or at least long enough to see the end of certain things. Quitting cigarettes is the single most important change you can make to turn all that around. But you don't. And added to the hatreds already heaped on the smoker by the reprehensible companies who encourage you to light up, and the nincompoops who glare when you do, comes a certain self-disappointment that is hardest of all to hide from.

What good does it do to ostracize, ridicule, and isolate smokers? They can't be threatened with anything worse than knowing their end may be no different from Rose Cipollone's. Getting them to quit—that dusty old crusade of years ago—is the *only* way to the smoke-free society. If all the antismoking energy of the last decade had worked toward that end, instead of setting moronic goals like making the beaches of California a safer place

Getting smokers to quit—that dusty old crusade of years ago—is the *only* way to a smoke-free society.

to breathe, the current cycle of animosities might already have been broken.

Ask yourself what would happen if those 36 million targets of opportunity really were ready to quit. At an average of a pack and a half a day, and averaging $1.22 (including tax) per pack—or $667.95 per smoker a year—that's a $24 billion-a-year loss to the tobacco companies. Wouldn't that make everyone feel pretty good? Now ask yourself if that's likely to be accomplished by barking "Put that out!" across a crowded restaurant.

I don't know how you win over that many hearts and minds, but it is encouraging to see companies like General Electric, Prudential Bache, and Texas Instruments subsidizing cessation programs for their employees instead of simply banning smoking and self-righteously walking away.

That's a start anyway. It's a little old-fashioned since there are no embarrassments involved. But if the idea doesn't catch on soon, you'd better keep a few ashtrays around for the year 2000.

ACHIEVING A

SMOKE-FREE SOCIETY

Dr. K. H. Ginzel

K. H. Ginzel, M.D., is Professor of Pharmacology and Toxicology at the University of Arkansas. His work is concentrated in the area of nicotine and its effects.

The health of a new generation could go up in smoke if the institutions dedicated to protecting our country's youth continue to turn their backs on the long-term hazards of tobacco.

Johnny turns 18 this spring. It is a magic time, a coming of age that will mark his graduation from high school and the first time he will be eligible to vote. In New York State, Johnny will also be old enough to buy and smoke cigarettes. Like a lot of other young people, Johnny already smokes. After all, what is the harm? It is not an illicit drug; it is not even alcohol. It is only a cigarette.

ONLY A CIGARETTE?

Our greatest health threat, according to the world's leading medical authorities, is tobacco. In the United States alone, every year an estimated 350,000 to 485,000 smokers fall victim to heart attacks, strokes, lung cancer, chronic bronchitis, and emphysema. By comparison, alcohol kills close to 100,000 people, while

all other dependence-producing drugs combined are responsible for some 35,000 deaths annually. These grim statistics point to only one logical goal: To place tobacco at the top of the list in our war against drugs. But, how likely are we to succeed?

NINETY PERCENT OF ALL SMOKERS BEGIN THEIR HABIT AS CHILDREN. THAT'S WHY IT IS CRUCIAL TO EDUCATE YOUNGSTERS AT HOME AND AT SCHOOL ABOUT THE DANGERS OF SMOKING AS EARLY AS POSSIBLE.

Confronted with the ever-growing menace of bad news from the health front and the daily attrition of 1,000 deaths and 4,000 quitters, the tobacco firms have launched advertising and promotional campaigns unparalleled in modern history in volume and moti-

From the American Council on Science and Health's *Priorities*, Summer 1989, pp. 5-7. Reprinted by permission.

vational wizardry. Specifically, they have aimed at allaying the fears of smokers to keep them smoking, and at enticing youth to secure a new generation of reliable customers. To these ends, the industry has persistently denied that tobacco causes disease, and has adopted a marketing strategy that artfully exploits the perceived needs, wants, and vulnerabilities of the adolescent. Although their ads are allegedly geared to adults, there can be little doubt that they appeal to children. A case in point is Parliament Lights' advertising campaign. Its headline reads: "The Perfect Recess." At first glance, the headline seems to refer to Parliament's special filter. But the implied message to school children, and to the child in all of us, is plainly obvious.

From the "recess" that can be "perfect" to candy cigarettes, toys, and T-shirts, all embellished with logos of cigarette brands, to the industry-sponsored athletic events and rock concerts, the young are virtually inundated with the seductive imagery of tobacco use to make sure that they will either become active consumers themselves, or at least accept smoking and dipping tobacco as a perfectly natural, normal, even desirable behavior of their peers and elders.

GOVERNMENT APPROVED?

Ninety percent of all smokers begin their habit as children. That's why it is crucial to educate youngsters at home and at school about the dangers of smoking as early as possible. Yet there is no organized nationwide effort dedicated to educating children about the disastrous consequences of tobacco use.

The much publicized "Just Say No" program, which teaches children to stay away from addictive drugs, focuses on drugs and alcohol, with tobacco hardly ever being mentioned. Indeed, "drugs and alcohol" is the ever-present label one encounters when programs, projects, task forces, legislative bodies, treatment centers, or schools deal with substance abuse. It is almost like telling society, "Say NO to drugs and alcohol, but say YES to tobacco."

Even the U.S. Department of Education gets failing grades when it comes to informing students about smoking. In the department's booklet "School Without Drugs," of which 1.5 million copies were distributed to schools nationwide, the former Secretary of Education, William Bennett, states: "The foremost responsibility of any society is to nurture and protect its children." He goes on to say, "Alcohol is an illegal drug for minors and

FRIENDS IN HIGH PLACES

A close mutual relationship between tobacco interests and government has existed for a long time. The clout of the tobacco industry is so strong that the very institutions created by government to protect its citizens from preventable disease and premature death have had their credibility severely compromised.

The ties between the federal government and the tobacco industry became closer last April when Bonnie St. Claire Parker, staff director and administrator of the Senate Select Committee on Ethics, joined the Tobacco Institute as Senate Liaison of Federal Government Relations. The Tobacco Institute, an association of cigarette manufacturers, is dedicated to the increased use of tobacco for the financial gain of its members. They openly state that the health risks of tobacco are "alleged", not proven!

The tight bonds between government and tobacco interests surfaced once again when former President Reagan appointed Tobacco Institute Vice President Judy Wiedemeier to serve on the President's Child Safety Partnership, a study group to help choose better ways to protect children.

The "long arm" of the Tobacco Institute also embraces the nation's educational system. In a

canny move, the Institute helped publish two parent guides that are used by the "Just Say No" program. The Tobacco Institute introduces itself in the brochures as a trade association that doesn't want young people to smoke because it believes that "smoking is an adult custom." This is a clever way of telling kids that lighting a cigarette is a rite of passage into adulthood. The "errand boy" distributing the brochures with the institute's message is none other than the National Association of State Boards of Education.

Taxes levied by local, state and federal governments on tobacco manufacturers' products have also united these unlikely partners in a common cause—the creation of revenue. Government has blinded itself to the fact that cigarettes are a lethal commodity that is injurious to the health of the public it is pledged to protect.

It's quite obvious that politics and health don't mix. Former President Reagan acknowledged this last spring when he formed a nonpartisan coalition of Republicans and Democrats to conduct the "War on Drugs."

"If we cannot remove politics from drugs, how can we hope to remove drugs from our...schools?" asked the former President. How, indeed?

should be treated as such." Tobacco is also an illegal substance for minors, yet the Secretary of Education avoids this and all other issues concerning tobacco. Adding insult to injury, the entire 78-page booklet contains only four brief and innocent references to smoking.

Mr. Bennett's and the Department of Education's non-position on smoking is puzzling. It ignores a top authority, the U.S. Surgeon General, who reports that tobacco is one of the most addictive substances known to man. Just consider this single fact: a pack-a-day smoker inhales 70,000 puffs a year. Mr. Bennett's head-in-the-sand attitude also failed to consider that tobacco use is recognized by prominent scientific investigators as a "gateway" drug that often opens the doors to the use of illicit substances. The exclusion of tobacco from drug and health educational programs may still have other adverse consequences for both students and teachers. Any message that does not implicate tobacco as a serious health hazard will, in fact, be most persuasive to the younger child whose naive sense of fairness cannot comprehend that the government would permit the sale and promotion of a product "if it were really that bad." This simplistic logic will render children easy prey to the industry's recruiting tactics and usher them more readily into the drug world. As for teachers, tobacco's low profile in drug prevention programs may prevent them from seeking adequate knowledge that should be transmitted to their students.

CONSPIRACY OF SILENCE
An unfortunate reason why tobacco is so low on the nation's list of concern is that, quite simply, it brings in too much tax revenue at every level to expect government to ban or control tobacco marketing, or even to enforce existing restrictions. The profits made by cigarette makers and promoters, and the tax revenues levied by local, state, and federal agencies have united these beneficiaries in a common cause that has given

tobacco a clout that is totally unique for a commodity that maims, kills, and, unlike alcohol, is virtually devoid of any socially redeeming value. Regrettably, there is only slim hope that Congress will place the welfare of the people ahead of the financial gain of the tobacco industry. A recent court opinion even cites Congress' "carefully drawn balance between the purposes of warning the public of the hazards of cigarette smoking and protecting the interests of the national economy." This so-called "balance," however, translates into a national death toll of almost a half-million people per year at a monetary loss of $65 billion for health care and lost productivity.

The smoking gun also points at newspapers and magazines that accept cigarette advertisements and suppress information about the dangers of smoking in order to protect their publications' advertising revenue. Harvard epidemiologist John Baylar aptly called "the sharp and continuing rise in deaths from lung cancer, nearly all from cigarette smoking ... a medical, social and political scandal."

HOPE FOR TOMORROW
In spite of an increasingly powerful tobacco industry, we can help our children achieve a smoke-free society. To start, we must expose the duplicity of the tobacco industry, the government, and the media. All of them ignore or deny the hazards of tobacco while they harvest substantial financial gain. The real cost is not measured in dollars; it is measured in lost lives.

Ideally, a new initiative against tobacco should begin on a national level with full support from the top—the White House. This initiative should deal with tobacco, along with alcohol and drugs of abuse, in an even-handed fashion that is in correct proportion to the damage they inflict. Only then can we hope to achieve a smoke-free—and drug-free—America.

Warning: Sports Stars May be Hazardous to Your Health

Sports celebrate health. Cigarettes cause death. So what's that Marlboro sign doing at Shea Stadium?

Jason DeParle

Jason DeParle is an editor of The Washington Monthly. *Daniel Mirvish, John Larew, John Heilemann, Michael Carolan, and Anita Bose provided research assistance.*

In case you missed it, this year's press guide to the Women's International Tennis Association is an impressive volume. Its 456 glossy pages bear tribute to what the guide immodestly calls "one of the greatest success stories of the modern sports world"—how women's tennis stepped from obscurity into the limelight of the Virginia Slims circuit, where this year players will compete for more than $17 million in prize money. Just twenty years ago, the nation's best women tennis players languished before small crowds on high school courts. Now, the guide says, with their own massage therapists and "state-of-the-art forecasting system," they've become "synonymous with style."

They're synonymous with wealth, too: Chris Evert's $8.6 million in lifetime earnings places her a distant second to Martina Navratilova's $14 million. But most of all, they're synonymous with fine physical form. Sprinkled throughout the media guide are photos of athletes in peak physical condition: Manuela Maleeva bends "low for a forehand volley," "Hana Mandlikova intently awaits a return," "Gabriela Sabatini puts to use her 'smashing' backhand."

Those of us less physically gifted than Hana Mandlikova can't help but envy the strength in her legs, power in her arms, and stamina in her lungs as she pauses, racket poised, before exploding into her backhand. It's precisely the rareness of these qualities that brings us to admire her so, and to pause a moment when looking at her picture. Because as Hana Mandlikova intently awaits a return, she does so in front of a big sign that says "Virginia Slims"—a product not known for promoting the powers of heart and lung that lie at the center of her trade. In fact, throughout the guide—not to mention the nation's

sports pages and television broadcasts—we find these stars showcasing their enviable talents in front of cigarette ads. The bold corporate logo of the Virginia Slims series emphasizes the bond: a woman, sassy and sleek, holds a racket in one hand and a cigarette in the other.

This is odd. Tennis champions, after all, are models of health, particularly the health of heart and lungs, where endurance is essential. And cigarette smoking, as the Surgeon General recently reminded, "is the chief avoidable cause of death in our society"—death, more precisely, from heart and lung disease.

Struck by this seeming contradiction, I called Renee Bloch Shallouf, whom the guide lists as Media Services Manager for the players union, and asked if she, too, was impressed with the incongruity. "I think I'll defer this one over to Virginia Slims," she said. "They're the sponsor. We're just the players union. All I can do is give you a personal opinion."

"What is your personal opinion?"

"Noo—hoooo," she said, keeping the answer to herself.

Shallouf ended the conversation by saying, "If I find somebody opinionated—someone willing to give their opinion—around here, I'll call you."

Turning back to the media guide, I flipped to the section marked "Virginia Slims Personnel," and, to my surprise, found a familiar face on the page. There, bearing the impressive title of "Director, Worldwide Operations," was Anne Person, a college classmate of mine. Perhaps she would have some thoughts on the compatibility of tennis and tobacco. But, though she answers a phone at Philip Morris headquarters, she said she was only a "consultant" and that she worked "only on the tennis end." As for her thoughts about tobacco, she said, "I just can't do it. I don't choose to do it. . . . Regarding the tobacco issue, I don't choose to share my opinions." She suggested I call Steve Weiss, the manager of media relations for Philip Morris, U.S.A.

When I did, Weiss sounded astonished. He said he found the question—is there a contradiction between the vigor of athletics and the disease caused by cigarettes?—a breach of journalistic ethics. "Are you editorializing?" he said. "I disagree with your premises. . . You're saying that cigarette smoking causes a disease? Can I ask you something? Is that your opinion? That's a very opinionated statement. I'd appreciate a little more openmindedness. . . . I disagree with a journalist who calls and issues a very opinionated statement, when the credo of journalism is balance, fairness, and accuracy." He referred me to the code of reportorial probity, as articulated by the professional society, Sigma Delta Chi.

We backed up and started again.

Q: Does smoking lead to disease?

A: "I'm not a doctor. I would leave that to more informed individuals."

Q: Is the Surgeon General an informed individual?

A: "I think the Surgeon General is but one voice among many in the continuing debate about cigarette smoking."

On it went for about an hour, a stock recitation of the Philip Morris line. Or almost—there was a momentary point of diversion. Insisting that Philip Morris was not trying to make cigarettes seem glamorous, Weiss said, "We don't ask any of our players to smoke. *I doubt many, if any, do.*"

Hmmm. . . . and why is that?

Pause.

Then, growing agitated, Weiss said, "That's their choice. You have to ask them. I'm not qualified to answer that. I am absolutely not qualified to say what anybody does or does not do. *I'm retracting that, Jason. . . .*"

At that point, Weiss's voice took on the tin echo of a speaker phone. "*I want you to know that I'm recording this conversation,*" he said.

Smokes Illustrated

The fit athletes of the Virginia Slims circuit who swat balls in front of cigarette ads, in a tournament named for a cigarette brand, pocketing large sums from a cigarette company's largesse, are but a small subset of the great marriage of sports and tobacco. A large and growing number of sports now lend their athletes' credibility as fine physical specimens to the tobacco companies, whose products, by the Surgeon General's estimate, kill about 1,000 people a day. Cigarette manufacturers exploit sporting events in a variety of ways, ranging from such old-fashioned strategies as stadium advertising to the virtual invention of eponymous sports, like Winston Series Drag Racing or Marlboro Cup horseracing. When the pitchmen of Philip Morris say, "You've come a long way baby," they could very well be congratulating themselves; their success in co-opting the nation's health elite to promote a product that leads to an array of fatal diseases is extraordinary.

But they couldn't have done it alone. For starters, they needed the cooperation of the athletes, and, with a few praiseworthy exceptions, they've gotten it. When Billie Jean King set out 20 years ago to find a sponsor for women's tennis, she may have needed Philip Morris as much as it needed her. But these days, she and the other stars of women's tennis have actually had to fight off other corporate sponsors who would welcome the chance to take over. The tobacco companies have also needed the help of sports journalists, and, again, they've gotten it. The daily papers have been silent. The big magazines, like *Sports Illustrated*, are thick with tobacco ads and thin on tobacco critics. And the networks have been perfectly happy to show an infield decked with Marlboro banners, race cars painted with Marlboro signs, officials wearing Marlboro logos—while pretending that cigarette ads are still banned from the air.

The marriage of cigarettes and sports has at least three insidious consequences. The first, and perhaps most troubling, is that it obscures the connection of cigarettes and disease, subliminally and perhaps even consciously. Quick: speak the words "Virginia Slims"

> "I'm sure that's why Virginia Slims put up that money—so they could get the recognition, the association with sports and health. . . ," said one ABC executive. "I think it's clever. They found a loophole."

and what do you see? A) Chris Evert, or B) the cancer ward? If you answered A)—and most people do—then Philip Morris has you right where it wants you. (The recognition of this power is why the soccer star Pele won't pose near cigarette signs.) The second troubling fact about cigarettes' tryst with sport is that it allows them to penetrate the youth market. Cigarette spokesmen self-righteously insist they have no such goal. But tobacco companies desperately need teen smokers for the simple reason that few people start smoking once they are adults; and there's scarcely anyone more glamorous to a teenager than a star athlete. The third reason why cigarettes' infiltration of athletics is bad is that it circumvents the ban on television ads. Previously, cigarette companies had to hire actors to play athletes in their commercials, but now they've got the real thing.

Emphysema Slims

For those keeping moral score, cigarettes' involvement with aerobic sports, like tennis and soccer, is probably the most indefensible, since the respiratory fitness those sports require and represent is precisely what cigarettes deprive people of. That is, race car drivers can smoke and drive, but soccer stars certainly can't smoke and sprint. That doesn't mean race car drivers are welcome to promote cigarettes, of course. Their ties to tobacco endanger the public health by continuing to make cigarettes seem glamorous to kids, and by keeping the cigarette signs on T.V.

For leads on many of the following items, I am indebted to Dr. Alan Blum, a Baylor physician whose anti-smoking research and protests (like the staging of an "Emphysema Slims") makes him the Don King of the anti-smoking world:

◆ **Soccer:** Besides the world's most enviable lungs, soccer offers cigarettes two other advantages: wild overseas popularity at a time when American tobacco companies are stepping up their Third World trade, and a growing popularity among American youth.

Camel cigarettes, manufactured by R.J. Reynolds, was one of four major sponsors of the 1986 World Cup in Mexico City. Among the privileges it received in return was the chance to post four seven-meter Camel signs next to the field, where the world-wide television audience of 650 million for the final game alone could see them.

A brochure by ISL Marketing, a firm that handles World Cup marketing, explains: "The launch of their Camel Filters in Mexico was arranged to coincide with World Cup 86. . . .The team of Camel girls was stationed at each stadium distributing free samples . . . . Sponsorship of World Cup 86 provided Camel with a golden profile that reflected its product image of independence, masculinity, and adventure."

Earlier in the decade, RJR even tried to field its own World Cup club. In sponsoring the 1983 "Winston Team America Series," it compiled an all-star team and held a 30-game series against the pros in major stadiums across the country. During half-time, fans joined a contest to kick a ball through the "o" in a Winston sign.

◆ **Baseball:** Cigarette companies have ads in 22 of the 24 Major League ballparks in the United States, typically in spots that enhance broadcast coverage. The camera near the visiting team dugout at Shea Stadium, for instance, which is used to capture men leading off first base, frames the player with the Marlboro sign in left-center. At Fenway Park in Boston, a sign for the Jimmy Fund for cancer research, a favorite Red Sox charity, hangs above the right field bleacher. So does a Marlboro sign.

◆ **Skiing:** For about eight years, until last season, Loew's sponsored the Newport Ski Weekend, which offered half-price lift tickets in exchange for cigarette boxes. Philip Morris invites skiers at a number of Western resorts to take the "Marlboro Challenge," a plunge down a timed race course festooned with Marlboro flags.

In the 1983-84 season, RJR's brand, Export A, became the official sponsor of the Canadian Ski Association, which oversees the country's major competitions. The company's original contract called for "the exclusive right. . . to identify itself or its products (including name, logo, and colours) on: flags, poles, course markers, scoreboards, award pre-

sentations, start banners. . . all buildings, podiums, backdrops. . . ." To be sure no one missed the point, the contract added: "The Association shall use its best efforts to have the events telecast on national network television."

But the Canadian skiers rebelled, with some refusing to accept league trophies. The contract was modified following the protest, and the controversy led finally to a ban on all tobacco advertising in Canada. Ken Read, who represented Canada twice in Olympic skiing and is now a broadcaster, was among the leaders of the protest. "I think it's inappropriate for a cigarette to sponsor any sporting event—period," he said. "It's incompatible with the objective of sport—to promote a healthy lifestyle."

I asked Read what he thought about the cigarette companies' argument that they're only promoting brand loyalty and, therefore, not encouraging kids to smoke. "That's absolute garbage," he said. "When you're using sports as a tool, you're influencing youth."

◆ **Horse racing:** Rather than take over an existing horse race, in 1973 Philip Morris simply went out and created one from scratch: the nationally-televised Marlboro Cup, which it sponsored until 1987.

In a interview with *The Daily Racing Form*, Ellen Merlo, director of marketing promotions at Philip Morris, explained the event's appeal: "First, it has created enormous visibility for Marlboro. There are newspaper stories leading up to and following the race that mention the Marlboro name frequently, and this is excellent exposure. Secondly the image of horse racing and the imagery of the Marlboro Man campaign seem to have reinforced each other. The man on the horse theme is central to both, and we feel it has worked well as a partnership."

◆ **Autoracing:** Since 1971, RJR has been the chief sponsor of NASCAR's premier circuit, the $18 million, 29-race Winston Cup Series. This is a sport that has other problems besides cigarette sponsorship, of course—such as encouraging 16-year-olds to play Richard Petty on the interstate. As they do, the word "Winston" may quickly come to mind: one of the races is called the Winston 500; another is simply known as The Winston. The driver who accumulates the most points during the season wins the $1 million Winston Cup. The driver who wins three of the top four races wins a bonus called, accurately, the Winston Million—you get the idea.

"We're in the cigarette business. We're *not* in the sports business. We *use* sports as an avenue for advertising our products. . . ." said Wayne Robertson, an RJR executive, in a trade journal. "We can go into an area where we're marketing an event, measure sales during the event and measure sales after the event, and see an increase in sales."

If this list seems lengthy, don't forget it omits the Vantage Golf Scoreboard, Salem Pro-Sail races, Lucky Strike bowling, the Winston Rodeo, Benson & Hedges on Ice, and any number of other cigarette-sponsored sports. It also omits Camille Duvall, champion water skier and the cover girl for the current issue of *Philip Morris Magazine,* where the company that insists its interest in athletes has nothing to do with glamour, describes her as "gorgeous—swimsuit issue, pack-it-in-Paulina, no-exaggeration, gorgeous."

Those who think that tobacco's conquest of sport is complete, however, can take heart—according to the *Chicago Sun-Times,* Philip Morris recently lost the $12,000 sponsorship of the U.S. boomerang team to an anti-smoking group called Doctors Ought to Care, which is run by Alan Blum. Philip Morris "promised us all kinds of publicity," the team captain, Eric Shouffer, told the newspaper. "If we'd wear big Philip Morris logos on our chest, they told us we'd be on 'Good Morning America' and so on."

It wasn't just conscience that governed the team's decision, Shouffer said, but practical considerations, too: One member is an asthmatic "who falls over dead when he gets near smokers."

The man with the cough

Lung cancer, which is almost always fatal, is a curiously polite disease. It glides through the body, making itself at home but careful not to cause a fuss. The chest may be its harbor but it can sail wherever the bloodstream goes, and it explores the body at leisure. It can list south toward the groin, or tack its way north to the brain; it can stretch out yawning on beaches of bone marrow. It is lazy and can afford to be. It is confident. It announces itself at the time of its choosing. One day, it knocks.

By then, the average man—or, increasingly, woman—hasn't been feeling his usual robust self for three months or so. He's 55 or 60 years old, and has been smoking most of his life, but never had any problems as a result. It was just a cough at first, with a bit of mucous, and sure to go away in another week. Then the mucous disappeared, but the cough kept hanging on. His appetite began to slow.

Let's have a look, the physician says. Though there's something oddly reassuring about the touch of his cold stethoscope on the patient's chest and back, it's less reassuring to be directed in front of the X-ray machine. There is something there, the doctor reports—pneumonia, maybe—but he's careful not to sound too alarmed. It might be nothing that 10 days of antibiotics can't cure. Ten days later, when the cough and the spot on the X-ray have endured, it's time for another look.

The word cancer *has been there all along, but no one's wanted to say it. And with good reason—from the time it first gets uttered, the average lung cancer patient will live less than three years. Perhaps the doctor will say it first: The purpose of the biopsy, he explains, is "to rule out cancer." A phrase like "let's not get worried until we know what we're dealing with" will almost certainly follow. We're just going to remove a small piece of tissue, the physician says; you can expect some discomfort.*

Draped in a soft blue gown, the man with the cough gets wheeled into a 65-degree room, where a surgeon

snakes an optic fiber down his throat and snatches a piece of lung. A pathologist slices the sample, using one portion to prepare a quick slide and saving the rest for future tests. In the waiting room, there is a human community—wife, children, friends from work, grandchildren perhaps—that is connected through nerves and fears, or, maybe, prayers. The initial indication may come as quickly as 15 minutes, but final confirmation can take three or four days—itself a sample of the waiting that will fill future months. Time seems to stop until the word arrives.

If the word is something like squamous cell carcinoma—*lung cancer—there will begin a difficult discussion indeed.*

Hacking hags

Whether or not the figure of 1,000 deaths a day presents tobacco companies with a moral challenge, it certainly presents them with an economic one: how to replace the thousands of people their products kill each week. To some extent, cigarette companies have been losing the war. In 1965, 40 percent of American adults smoked; by 1987, this figure had dropped off to 29 percent. But while cigarette consumption is declining, it's declining least among blacks, women, high school drop-outs, blue-collar workers, and other groups whose members tend to lead more difficult lives. The more marginal one's status in society, the more likely one is to smoke.

Since 1971, when the ban on televised cigarette ads took effect, the cigarette companies' efforts to reach their target audiences have grown more complicated. The story of the ad ban is an interesting one in itself, and perhaps its most salient moral is that, despite the immense wealth and power of the tobacco companies, there is, in fact, much that one person can do. In this case, the person was John Banzhaf, a 26-year-old law school graduate. Noting the saturation of TV with cigarette ads, he sent off a three-page letter to the Federal Communications Commission, arguing that the Fairness Doctrine required broadcasters to give anti-smoking groups their say. To nearly everyone's surprise, the FCC agreed, announcing in 1967 that henceforth broadcasters should air one anti-smoking spot for every three or four cigarette commercials.

Anti-smoking groups took to the air with an inordinate amount of creativity. Though television viewers were still being blitzed with ads that showed happy smokers in vigorous poses, now they received other visions too: a Marlboro-like man, bursting boldly through the saloon doors, only to collapse in a fit of coughs; a wrinkled hag on a respirator, cigarette in hand, asking, "Aren't I sexy?" Though still outnumbered, these hacking, wincing images of death began to register: cigarette consumption declined in each of the next four years. The cigarette companies weren't just losing the battle; through the Fairness Doctrine they were subsidizing the other side's artillery. In 1970, they went to Congress to say they wanted out.

The withdrawal wasn't as easy as it might seem, however. If one company withdrew its ads, it ceded an advantage to its competitors; if all withdrew at once, they were subject to antitrust reprisals for collusion. What they needed was an order: ban us, they asked. Perhaps the constituency least pleased by this prospect was the broadcasters, who were then banking about $250 million a year in tobacco ad revenues. Though Congress finally passed the ban over the broadcasters' objections, the TV executives, to whom the term "conscience-stricken" could not fairly be applied, did win a soothing concession: the ban didn't take effect until midnight on January 1, 1971—after the commercial-thick bowl games were aired.

Cigarette strategists now had to contend with a more complicated world. They still needed to saturate the culture with the idea that smoking leads to happiness, but television, their most powerful weapon, seemed off limits. *Seemed* is the operative word here. By channeling some of that $250 million ad budget into sports sponsorship, cigarette companies were right back on the air. Consider the timing: Virginia Slims, born 1971; Winston Cup racing, born 1971; Marlboro Cup horse racing, born 1973. Sports sponsorship has become such an spectacular success that by now all kinds of corporations want in—the John Hancock Bowl, the Mazda Gator Bowl. "We have a waiting list for inside billboards," says Jane Allen, who works in the marketing department of the Charlotte Motor Speedway. "Everybody in the business knows it's because of TV coverage."

A cardinal sins

But tobacco's problems extended beyond the TV ban, and sports was only part of the answer. Since 1964, the industry had been stuck with the Surgeon General's warnings and increasingly vocal criticisms of their products. What the tobacco industry needed was friends, and its strategy for finding them was sound: it decided to buy them. Donning the mask of philanthropy, the tobacco companies have courted not only athletes but ballerinas, modern dancers, jazz musicians, museum curators, unions, civil rights groups, feminists, religious leaders—almost anyone with a glimmer of uprightness and a use for cash. The Guggenheim Museum. The Joffrey Ballet. The Whitney.

The purpose of this fevered gift-giving has been to divert the public's attention from what tobacco companies really do: lure people, particularly young ones, into buying a highly addictive drug, which, if used as intended, courts death. In this, they are no different than crack peddlers. The Surgeon General has likened the addictive powers of nicotine to those of heroin and cocaine: all of them create psychological and *physical* cravings; each causes a chemical reaction that makes the body want more. As anyone understands who's watched someone they care for try to quit, the pack-a-day smoker "chooses" his habit as freely as the cocaine addict chooses his. Cocaine and

> "We're in the cigarette business. We're *not* in the sports business," said one RJR executive. "We *use* sports to sell cigarettes."

heroin inflict their damage more quickly; but cigarettes kill more widely. It is cigarettes, not cocaine, that cause about 390,000 deaths each year according to C. Everett Koop.

In respectable society today, cocaine peddlers are objects of scorn. But cigarette peddlers are jauntily strolling the halls of their latest museum exhibits. The tobacco companies need this false status as respectable corporations in order to survive. If the world saw them as the drug pushers they are, Congress would ban their ads, if not their product, and Drug Czars would join the fray. By accepting tobacco sponsorship, the country's singers, dancers, curators, and the like help ensure this doesn't happen. While accepting the Devil's money may be defensible if you give nothing in return, the recipients of tobacco largesse have given something very precious indeed, the one thing the cigarette sellers could never earn on their own: respect.

Thus comes Philip Morris beneficiary Alvin Ailey, writing the Surgeon General last year to call tobacco executives "enlightened. . . . generous patrons," and to argue that, "A nation has a cultural health as well as a physical health." Thus comes Terrence Cardinal Cooke to say a prayer at a cigarette-sponsored display of Vatican art, leading one Philip Morris vice president to boast, "We're probably the only cigarette company on this earth to be blessed by a cardinal."

While tobacco's been busy assembling this circle of courtiers, athletes aren't just any members of the court. Their unique evocation of health, access to television, and influence on teenagers makes them especially prized, and a report this year by the Surgeon General adds extra emphasis to the point about youth: "The uptake of smoking is now a phenomenon that occurs almost entirely during the teenage years. . . ."

Tobacco spokesmen have a way of sounding positively wounded when someone suggests they're scheming to entice the young—the Tobacco Institute even funds an anti-teenage smoking program. It's not advertising or athletes that cause teenagers to start smoking, but "peer pressure," says Steve Weiss, the

Philip Morris spokesman and ethics buff. As if peer pressure were something that filtered down through the ozone layer and had nothing to do with race cars and tennis stars.

Mets to RJR: Drop dead

Of course, cigarette companies couldn't co-opt athletics if athletics wasn't willing to be co-opted. For the most part, that willingness consists not of active promotion but of silence, which is just as necessary to the cigarette salesmen's success. Imagine how many baseball fans, teenage and adult, would get the message if Darryl Strawberry held a press conference to denounce the indecency the Marlboro sign lends to the Shea Stadium outfield. Or better yet, trotted out with a paint brush to cover it up. What could the Mets management do? Bench him?

While Strawberry's probably valuable enough to get away with it on his own, lots of lesser players aren't. Alone, that is. But imagine if the entire Mets roster signed a petition, refusing to play the 1990 season under the Marlboro banner—refusing to donate their authority as athletes, T.V. stars, and teen idols to the nation's number one health hazard. Look northward, New York Mets! The Canadian skiers told RJR to drop dead—you can, too!

What the athletes need is a little leadership, and one place where you might hope to find it is the office of Dr. Bobby Brown, the American League president, former New York Yankee, and *cardiologist*. In 1985, Alan Blum, the anti-smoking activist, wrote to Brown and suggested he do something to remove cigarette ads from stadiums. Brown wrote back a nothing-I-can-do letter ("legally permitted," "forced to recognize an individual's rights") promising serenely that, "This is an ongoing problem, however, that we will continue to address."

I called Brown recently to see how the progress was coming. Major League Baseball, after all, forbids athletes from smoking in uniform—why can't it forbid them from playing in front of cigarette billboards? Isn't the purpose of the uniform ban to keep baseball players from promoting cigarettes? Brown couldn't have been more disingenuous: he said he didn't know the reason athletes were forbidden to smoke in uniform, just that it was on the books and he didn't feel compelled to change it.

As for billboards, Brown agreed that "anytime you have advertising, the tobacco companies think you have a chance of increasing sales—that's why they're doing it." To remove them, however, would be "unrealistic," since tobacco companies could still advertise elsewhere, such as in subways. Maybe even Brown didn't want to hear himself offer this explanation, however, because he began to sound annoyed. "Who are you, sir?" he asked. "Who funds you?" When I suggested that subways might not pack the prestige of Major League Baseball, and, anyway, someone needed to take the first step, he got angrier. "It's *unrealistic* for tobacco ads to be removed from baseball parks," he said. Then he hung up.

Most athletes can probably claim to have given the issue little thought (some too convincingly). Brown at least can claim that he's not actively soliciting the billboards, just shrugging his shoulders while others do. But I'd like to know what people like Billie Jean King, Chris Evert, and Martina Navratilova—athletes who have thought it over, and pledged the cigarette companies their fidelity—can claim, but they aren't returning phone calls on the issue.

"I believe in free enterprise," King said in 1983, on one of the few times she's been publicly quizzed on her tobacco ties (significantly, it wasn't a journalist but an anti-smoking activist who asked the question). King went on to say that "Personally, I hate cigarette smoking. I hate cigarettes. Ninety-five percent of the girls do"—as though this excuses her prominent role in their promotion over the past two decades, as though this justifies her taking the court against Bobby Riggs in 1973 dressed in Virginia Slims colors, with Virginia Slims sequins on her chest. What she's saying is this: Let someone else get lung cancer; it won't be me; and I'll get rich and famous in the process.

In the two decades that King's been selling Philip Morris her image of vigor—she not only played Riggs, remember, she beat him—lung cancer has overtaken breast cancer as a leading cause of women's death. And what are King & Co. doing about it now? Continuing to coo about how "loyal" Philip Morris has been, while rebuffing a bid by Proctor & Gamble last year to take over the women's tour.

Pam Shriver's career earnings are $3.9 million. "I don't feel bad at all about looking somebody in the eye and saying, 'Virginia Slims is our sponsor,' cause they're a great sponsor," she said in 1986. "Too bad they're a cigarette."

The tissues' revenge

The average American smoker consumes about 7,000 cigarettes a year. If he inhales each one six times—a modest estimate—then 42,000 jet streams a year travel down his throat and into his lungs and out his mouth and nose, bathing the tissues of the respiratory tract in clouds of smoke and nicotine. Lung cancer is the tissues' revenge. Sometime, somehow, a cell rebels and begins to divide. One cell becomes two, the two become four, the four become eight, and the cancer is off and racing.

If lung cancer is caught in an early stage, that is, if it's anatomically confined, there's a chance it can be surgically removed. But the disease rarely gives itself away before spreading so far that surgery is no longer an option. Back from biopsy, then, the man with the cough will have two options. The type of lung cancer known as "small cell" may respond to chemotherapy, although the response, even when complete—driving the cancer from all medical detection—almost never stays that way.

Doctors know how to kill cancer cells. The problem is what they call the "therapeutic-to-toxic ratio"—*how to kill cancer cells without killing other cells too. During chemotherapy, the patient will almost surely succumb to wild fits of vomiting. His hair will fall out. His body will go limp. For days afterwards he may feel too exhausted to lift himself from bed. If the process works and the cancer goes into retreat, chemotherapy can earn the patient a modest extension of life.*

The second type of lung cancer, known, straightforwardly enough, as "non smallcell lung cancer," does not respond to chemotherapy. It may respond to radiation. When it's time for the bombardment to begin, the patient will stretch out beneath a linear accelerator—a hulking structure that, resembling a 10-foot microscope, hunches over his form. When technicians turn on the switch, a 12.5 ton medical marvel will send between 180 and 300 "rad" burning into the diseased cells. A tumor the size of a cubic centimeter—the size, say, of a bouillon cube—will contain about a billion cancerous cells. If treatment kills a billion minus one, the patient is still left with a fatal disease, for the one that survives will continue to divide.

Breast cancer, testicular cancer, prostate cancer, and others have all been known to succumb to the linear accelerator's might. But lung cancer rarely loses. Within five years of diagnosis, 87 percent of those afflicted can expect to be dead.

Lying on the table, the man with the cough feels nothing. Only the tension of waiting.

'A loophole'

Just as it takes a certain physiological culture for cancer to conquer a lung, it takes a certain journalistic one for tobacco to conquer sports. And sports journalists, for the most part, have provided it. The major components of this culture are indifference ("I just report the news; I don't make it") and rationalization ("It's a legal product; people can make their own choices")—with a generous sprinkling of publisher's greed, in the form of cigarette ads. Relish for a moment the thought of a Sam Donaldson of sport trailing Chris Evert and you get a sense of how vulnerable athletes would be to a determined inquiry: "Ms. Evert, lung cancer has just surpassed breast cancer as a killer of women; why do you display your athletic talents in front of that Virginia Slims banner? Don't you care about the welfare of women? Does money mean that much to you?"

And it's not as though sports journalists can't see what's going on. As Lydia Stephans, programming manager for ABC Sports, said, "I'm sure that's why Virginia Slims put up that money—so they could get that recognition, the association with sports and health. Otherwise why would they want to pump millions of dollars into sports? They can't do it by putting a commercial on the T.V. They used to show people sailing around smoking cigarettes. So now they do it through sports. . . On their half, I think it's clever. They've found a loophole."

As for the dailies, no one who has walked past the sports desk of an average American newspaper is likely to confuse it for a breeding ground of social reform. The idea that they have a moral obligation to speak out against tobacco's role in sport is likely to strike many sportswriters as about as compelling as their obligation to champion educational reform in Zambia. For lots of them, it's just not on the radar.

"We haven't done the piece you're doing. It's a legitimate story. I'm glad you're doing it," said Leonard Shapiro, sports editor at *The Washington Post,* who was more thoughtful about the topic than most of the journalists I spoke to. "Maybe it's become such an ingrained part of our culture, it's something we don't even notice."

What are the sports editors' options? One strategy might just be to rename the event. When Ellen Merlo of Philip Morris brags about "the newspaper stories leading up to and following the race that mention the Marlboro name frequently," sportswriters could decide that henceforth the "Marlboro Cup" will just become "The Cup." (Newspapers routinely make such judgments about proper editorial content, screening out, say, obscenity.) Failing that, how about a big "Surgeon General's Warning: Smoking Causes Lung Cancer, Heart Disease, Emphysema, and May Complicate Pregnancy" slapped on the photos of the tourney?

The sportswriter who, by chance, does develop a Donaldson complex on the issue isn't likely to find great encouragement from above. For one, a number of newspapers have actually allied themselves as co-sponsors of cigarette-backed sporting events. *The Houston Chronicle, The Houston Post, The Boston Herald,* and the *Los Angeles Times* have all joined Philip Morris as backers of Virginia Slims events, while the *Atlanta Journal* joins RJR in financing the Atlanta Journal 500.

Ad men

More to the point is a basic fact of American journalism: Publishers like the income from cigarette ads, and few are likely to regard an anti-tobacco crusade as a boon to business. Not many will respond as forthrightly as Mark Hoop, publisher of the *Twin Cities Reader,* who flatly fired the reporter whose preview of the Kool Jazz Festival pointed out that Duke Ellington had died of lung cancer. (When later asked by ABC News if he'd really said, "If we have to fly to Louisville, Kentucky and crawl on bended knees and beg the cigarette company not to take their ads out of our newspaper, we'll do that," Hoop said, "True.") But those with a subtler touch will still find a way to communicate that inordinate crusading on the issue does not enhance journalists' career advancement.

While actual cigarette advertising in many papers is modest, it's not so modest that publishers are anxious to lose it. (A recent 12-page advertising supplement for Marlboro Grand Prix racing in *The New York Times Magazine* cost close to $300,000, according to the *Times*'s advertising department.) And the conglomerate nature of cigarette ownership may mean that other ad revenues are also at stake: RJR's holdings include Nabisco, Del Monte, and Kentucky. Fried Chicken, while Philip Morris controls those of

> "It's *unrealistic* for tobacco ads to be removed from baseball parks," said Dr. Bobby Brown, the American League president. Then he hung up.

Seven-Up, the Miller Brewing Company, and General Foods, makers of Jello, Maxwell House, Tang, Oscar Mayer, and so forth. Let no one mistake the point—the cigarette companies haven't been shy about exercising this clout. After the advertising firm Saatchi & Saatchi produced a recent anti-smoking commercial for Northwest Airlines, RJR pulled its *$70 million* Nabisco account.

The media's own conglomerate status means it has more than one flank exposed. Denunciations of RJR in *The Washington Post* could mean fewer ads for Camels, Oreos, and Smirnoff in *Newsweek*, just as an attack on Virginia Slims in *The New York Times* could lead to the end of the $900,000 of tobacco ads that appeared last year in its wholly-owned *Tennis* magazine. Obviously, both the *Post* and *Times* have had unkind words for tobacco; but neither can claim to have provided the kind of unforgiving coverage that tobacco has earned with a product that *every two years* kills more Americans than have died in all the wars of this century.

And that's just the daily press. For a sense of how cigarette revenues have shaped the attitudes of the magazine world, consider the views of George Gross, executive vice president of the Magazine Publishers of America. He recently went before Congress to warn that restrictions on cigarette advertising could lead to a surge in smoking, since "the prominent health warnings now carried in all magazine tobacco advertising will not be seen by millions of readers." Now there's an original argument.

Meanwhile, a 1986 study by the University of Michigan School of Public Health found that no other category of magazines—fashion, politics, general-interest, and so forth—relies more heavily on tobacco ads than do sports magazines. On the average, tobacco provided 11.3 percent of the sports journals' income, down slightly from 14.0 in 1976—but

up impressively from pre-ad ban days of 1966, when it was only 2.1 percent. *Sports Illustrated*, the industry giant, weighed in at 11.3 percent—or $27 million.

The dangers of milk

What kinds of inhibitions might such revenues induce? It's certainly fair to say that *Sports Illustrated*, itself part of a larger Time, Inc. empire full of cigarette ads, hasn't brought an exceptionally skeptical view to the issue of tobacco and sports. "It's a fringe thing," says Peter Carry, the magazine's executive editor. In 1977, the magazine did find space for "Chaws," a nine-page celebration of chewing tobacco by an array of baseball stars. Sample? "I'll stick a chaw in my mouth and everything seems to get a little brighter," said pitcher Rick Reuschel.

Meanwhile, one could suggest that *Sports Illustrated* has been less than zealous in publishing alternative points of view. Ask Greg Connolly, a Massachusetts dentist hired by Major League baseball to help athletes quit chewing tobacco. In 1986, Connolly says he contacted the magazine and offered to write a piece about the program. He said that two different editors, including baseball editor Steve Wulf, warned him that higher-ups might find a possible "conflict of interest" with advertisers, but Wulf told him to try it nonetheless. Connolly turned it in, but the piece never ran.

So what—maybe Connolly can't write. But that wasn't the explanation that Wulf gave Howard Wolinsky, a *Chicago Sun-Times* medical writer, when Wolinsky asked what happened. Wolinsky says Wulf told him, "based on common sense, magazines do not like to upset their advertisers by publishing stories that are negative on an advertised product." When I called Wulf he confirmed that he had warned Connolly about possible conflicts of interest, and he acknowledged the conversation with Wolinsky. He said he was speaking to Wolinsky about magazines in general, not *Sports Illustrated*, which he said "does not let its advertisers dictate its editorial content." His fears about the possible conflict of interest, he said, "turned out not to be the case. The sole reason it didn't run was for editorial purposes."

Judging from another *Sports Illustrated* article, the magazine seems to think that tobacco isn't just a "fringe" issue in sports but also in health. In 1983, the magazine ran a 10-page article deploring the sad state of "fitness" in America, explaining how poor diet and a lack of exercise contribute to heart disease and general ill health. The article doesn't exactly ignore tobacco. Cigarettes show up twice. First the magazine argues, "The problem is not only too little exercise—the culprits in the case of children include TV and, recently, video games—but too many cigarettes, too many calories and a diet far too rich in salt and saturated fats. . . ." Next, it advises "'lifestyle' changes, such as cutting out cigarettes. . . . *Just as important* is the need to 'engineer' more activity into daily life. Use stairs instead of elevators. Leave your car at the far end of the parking lot. . . ." (Emphasis added.)

With the messy little business of cigarettes put behind, the magazine turned a tarter tongue toward a real social blight: sweetened water. The Los Angeles public pools were offering free admission to "to children producing wrappers from Kool-Aid packages," the authors said. "Of course, the appropriateness of such an association with Kool-Aid, a product not ordinarily thought of as promoting fitness, might be questioned." Imagine how heartless those Kool-Aid peddlers are! Of all the things to push on kids! The writers went on to document another crass exercise of corporate power, blasting the National Dairy Council for "disseminating educational material on nutrition that pointedly neglects to suggest that readers might want to restrict their intake of eggs, whole milk, butter." Why the dairy council even gave those milk pamphlets to kids! Rascals! Have they no shame?

The same issue that emphasized the dangers of elevators and eggs more than Marlboros, Camels, or Winstons, happened to have ten pages of cigarette advertising. Among the ads was a two-page spread from the Tobacco Institute, which asked "Is cigarette advertising a major reason why kids smoke?" and answered, "No." When I asked Jerry Kirshenbaum, the fitness article's co-author, how the ethics of that ad compared to the Dairy Council's plug for milk, he said, "I really don't think I want to discuss this any further."

Interestingly, *Sports Illustrated* did run a very hard-hitting article last year on beer's effect on sports, which shows the magazine hasn't just simply tuned out on moral issues. (See Monthly Journalism Award, November 1988.) Beer's involvement in sport, through sponsorship and advertising, led the magazine "to wonder just what kind of cultural hypocrisy is going on when Americans relentlessly insist on immersing sport—our most wholesome, most admired, even (sometimes) most heroic institution—in a sea of intoxicating drink." *SI* suggested that this was "cynical, ironic, immoral, hypocritical. . ." The magazine's beer-ad revenues in 1988 were $6.3 million—significant, but far short of tobacco's $35 million. And perhaps equally significant, beer companies don't feel as imperilled, and hence, as vindictive, as cigarette makers do.

Carry, the executive editor and a former smoker, said that quitting was one of the hardest things he'd ever done. But as far as tobacco's involvement with sports, "I would say on the level of the world's evils, I would say it ranks pretty low."

The 150 m.p.h. Marlboro

While it would certainly help if *Sports Illustrated* saved its righteous indignation for Kools instead of Kool Aid, the tobacco companies have friends in even higher places—television. It was the broadcasters, remember, who did their level best to keep cigarettes commercials on the air. These days, tele-

vised tennis and auto-racing doesn't sell cigarette ads but does sell equally lucrative car ads and truck ads and beer ads instead.

The small group of network executives who control the nation's sports programming have unique power where tobacco and athletics are concerned. If the heads of CBS, ABC, and NBC simply turned on the TV, saw the whirl of Marlboro cars, flags, and banners, and said, "Hey, that's a cigarette ad—don't show it," the game would be over. Without the magnifying effects of broadcast coverage, tobacco's 20-year outbreak of sports fever would meet its antibiotic. (To protect themselves from losing a competitive advantage to some less scrupulous, upstart station, the networks could seek a ruling from the FCC, pointing out tobacco's circumvention of the law. And, of course, the FCC needn't be shy; it could always instigate an investigation itself.) A few "sports" might go under, at least in their present forms. Then again, if the Winston Cup can't exist without Winston, then isn't it more cigarette ad than sport, after all?

The media employees who wait for the executives to move are likely to wait a long time. To push the process along, a little unity would help. Just as baseball players, acting together, could bring the necessary pressure to bear on ballparks, writers and producers can put pressures on the media corporations. Acting alone, the reporter who condemns cigarette ads may get branded an "activist" and sent to write obits. Joining together, the top 50 reporters at the *Times* or the *Post* or ABC could exercise real pressure—particularly if they said they were willing to take a cut in pay equal, on a percentage basis, to the loss in revenue, as long as the executives and shareholders did the same.

Judging from my recent discussions with sports broadcasters, however, the dangers of such an outbreak of moral zeal seem slight. It's certainly not expected at CBS, where CEO Larry Tisch happens to wear a second hat as chairman of the board of Loew's, owners of Lorillard Tobacco, makers of Kents, Newports, and Trues. The new anti-tobacco policy isn't on the horizon at ESPN either, where RJR/Nabisco owns 20 percent.

At ABC, Lydia Stephans, the programmer with a clear-eyed view of tobacco's clever loophole, argued that there's little the networks can do. If they didn't broadcast sporting events with cigarette ads, she said, there wouldn't be any left to broadcast—which is sort of the point. "I'm basically neutral," she said.

The fervor at NBC wasn't much greater. I asked Doug Kelly, an NBC spokesman, how the network deals with the tobacco ads that line scoreboards and racetrack infields. He called back a few days later to explain that "we only show the part that shows the scoreboard." Kelly did concede that it was hard to get a tight shot of the Indy 500, which NBC also broadcasts, at least one that would crop the Marlboro sign off the racecar's hood. When I asked if that all those 150 m.p.h. cigarette signs didn't violate at least the spirit of the ad ban, Kelly's tone became distinctly less friendly. "I'm not going to comment on that," he said.

"Is that K-e-l-l-y?" I asked in parting.

"No, it's s-p-o-k-e-s-m-a-n," he said. "I prefer to be known as an NBC spokesman. It's not our policy to identify our spokesmen here."

It's too bad that Pete Axthelm doesn't have a spokesman. It's not that he's been any more complicit in the promotion of cigarettes and sports than most other big-name sports writers. He hasn't. But the more loudly he defended the marriage of the two, the more embarrassing it became to listen, all the more so because he seemed like a terrifically nice guy.

This, remember, is a man who's been at the top of the profession that should be chasing cigarettes from sports:

"Obviously, I can be criticized since we all make our outrageous salaries as a result of tobacco and beer advertising, so I know I'm setting myself up," he began. "I have to keep coming back to the thing with our Constitution—free rights, free markets, whatever."

And if kids look to athletes as role models? Well, that's their fault, Axthelm said. "What we really should be striving for is not to have athletes conform

to more rules, but to have our kids realize that athletes are *not* role models," he said. (Philip Morris, no doubt, would be happy to sponsor another educational program, to help kids kick the hero-worship habit.)

Virginia Slims? "What I recall is the general slogan, 'You've come a long way, baby,' as being a good thing for women," he said. "I'm a feminist."

Q: "Isn't one of the areas in which women are achieving parity lung cancer?"

A: "I don't want to comment on that."

By the end of the conversation, Axthelm began to sound concerned. Perhaps, finally, he was as unconvinced by his own defense of the cigarette companies as I was. While Bobby Brown dealt with his lack of good answers by slamming down the phone, and Doug Kelly dealt with it by seeking anonymity, at least Axthelm stayed on the line. But the more he talked, the more his answers turned back against him: "I just don't want to be set up as an idiot," he said. "Don't set me up after a lung cancer paragraph and say, 'Virginia Slims has done a lot for women.'"

Sixty pack-years

There's an odd sign on the door to one of the cancer wards at the Bethesda Naval Hospital. It lets visitors know that the "smoking lounge is located on 6 center." Not long ago, Dr. Paul Sperduto, an oncologist at the National Cancer Institute, escorted me onto the NCI ward and pulled the medical chart of a patient, who, four years ago, coughing, had gone to see his doctor. "Metastatic small cell lung cancer to

the left neck, mediastinum, right hilum, and liver," Dr. Sperduto said. *"That's* definitely *not curable."*

But the mere fact of the patient's presence at such a sophisticated facility indicated he'd been luckier than most. If he hadn't been chosen for a government study, he probably wouldn't have been there. His chart tagged him as lucky, too. Under sophisticated "cancer management," his disease had disappeared twice, adding a few years to his life.

The first bout of management began in 1985 with the onset of chemotherapy, monthly for eight consecutive months—four or five days of chemicals followed by a week or so of vomiting and exhaustion; rest and repeat. It seemed to work. By July 1986, a CT scan could no longer find the lump in his chest. Cancer management then called for a round of brain radiation, since the disease is known to sojourn there.

By December 1987, it was back, and four more months of chemotherapy began, this time with different chemicals. Again the cancer fled. "That's great," Dr. Sperduto said. *"Relatively speaking." Six months later, in September, 1988, it returned. This time, the cancer managers tried the experimental therapy called* In Vitro *Best Regimen. They sent a piece of the patient's lung into the lab, grew his disease in petri dishes, and sprinkled them with competing chemicals, to see which seemed to work best. Cytoxan won. And into his veins it went, over the course of five monthly cycles. It was now January, 1989, and nothing was happening. The cancer held firm.*

Another experiment began—a monoclonal antibody, the discovery of which had earned a researcher a Nobel Prize. That didn't work either. The cancer now appeared throughout his chest and liver. In March, a tumor in the throat wouldn't let him swallow. The cancer managers radiated it down. In April, the pain medicine was locking his bowels. The physicians reduced his dosage—good for the bowels, bad for the pain. Next came an electolyte imbalance, which brings more vomiting and the possibility of seizures. The chemotherapy, meanwhile, had caused a "peripheral neuropathy," the sensation of burning in the patient's arms and legs. When I met him in July, the man with the lucky chart, a former auto mechanic now 58 years old, was back for more treatment.

Cancer doctors speak not in years but in packyears, and this man's number was 60: one-and-a-half packs of Lucky Strikes a day, times forty years, beginning at age 15. "My father smoked, both my brothers smoked," he said. "At that age, it makes you feel like you're a big man. . . .Of course, my daughters have always been after me to stop. They smoke now, too. Now I'm trying to get them to stop. The oldest one sent away for that Cigarrest, or whatever you call it. But her husband smokes too. She said it didn't work."

It was quiet in his room. He spoke in a monotone, with no peaks of anger or dips of despair. He wasn't mad, he said—not at Lucky Strikes, not at the disease, not at the clumps of hair that keep falling out

"all over the bed and all over the pillow." He'd had a full life, he said, and Dr. Sperduto nodded in support: his patient had been married for 33 years, with three daughters, and four grandchildren. By the time we said goodbye, all three of us knew he'd be dead by Christmas.

Driving out of the hospital, we passed an advertisement on the side of a city bus. It showed an athletic young woman, diving into a pool. "Salem," it said. "The Refreshest."

Ordinary medicines can have extraordinary side effects

CHRISTOPHER HALLOWELL

Elizabeth's cold was making her miserable—her throat was scratchy, her nose was so stuffed she could hardly breathe, and her head felt as if it were going to explode. After three days of suffering, she bought a popular over-the-counter decongestant and took the recommended dosage. "That night," she says, "though my congestion had let up, I felt as though my brain had been rewired. I was very jumpy and once I got to bed, I lay wide awake. I tossed and turned so much that my husband couldn't sleep either." The next morning she took another dose. "That day I felt even worse. I was so irritable I yelled at my kids over the littlest things."

It wasn't until her second sleepless night that Elizabeth began to suspect her medica-

tion as the cause. In the morning, she called her doctor, who explained that the preparation she'd been taking contained pseudo-ephedrine, a compound that can affect some people's nervous systems. The jumpiness, irritability and insomnia that Elizabeth experienced were direct reactions to the drug.

Elizabeth's story is not an unusual one, unfortunately. While we tend to hear about the physical side effects of certain drugs, we often are not informed that ordinary cold tablets, painkillers, allergy remedies and other common over-the-counter (OTC) and prescription medications can change our mood or affect our ability to think and function normally. Perhaps you, too, are being affected without even realizing it.

THE MENACE IN YOUR MEDICINE BOTTLE

It is still not known for sure exactly how medications cause mind- and mood-altering reactions—nor why some people experience them while others do not. But researchers do know that drugs are not always totally precise in performing their intended functions and that psychological side effects can result from a drug's unexpected interaction with the body's nerve circuitry. "Many drugs work by changing signals in the brain or the nerves, and problems can occur when they affect signals they weren't supposed to affect," says Bambi Batts Young, Ph.D., a scientist associated with the Center for Sci-

Drugs you take for a cold or headache, a cough or allergy, can cause surprising mind- and mood-altering reactions. Do you know what you're swallowing— and what it can do to you?

ence in the Public Interest, a Washington, D.C., consumer and research group. Dr. Young, who recently directed a Center-sponsored investigation into chemicals that affect the brain and nervous system, explains that adverse reactions also can result if, for some reason, the body is eliminating certain chemicals at a slower-than-normal rate.

Given the individuality of each person's chemical and neural makeup, it is all but impossible to predict who will be vulnerable to side effects from any given preparation. For the same reasons, it's hard to tell exactly what reactions may occur. Still, some medications do contain ingredients that have been known to cause problems. Fortunately, most of the side effects are temporary.

THE DANGERS OF DIET PILLS

Most over-the-counter diet pills contain a substance called phenylpropanolamine hydrochloride, or PPA for short, as the active ingredient. This compound is chemically related to amphetamine, a substance that is notorious for exciting the nervous system. Though the psychological reactions to OTC diet pills containing PPA are rarely severe enough to warrant medical intervention, they are sufficient to alter mood and behavior in some people. Typical is the case of former Congresswoman and Vice Presidential candidate Geraldine A. Ferraro. During a 1983 hearing on the safety and efficacy of OTC drugs before the House Subcommittee on Health and Long-Term Care, Congresswoman Ferraro reported that she began taking diet pills when she decided to lose weight. "I can recall . . . [that] my heart started beating very fast and I cleaned my house as if I was . . . the white tornado . . . ," she is quoted as saying in a transcript of the hearing. "I'd be up very early in the morning and I couldn't sleep at night. . . . I decided I didn't want to become a nervous wreck, so I stopped taking them . . . and immediately . . . the symptoms stopped."

PPA has been implicated in hundreds of similar reports, many of them emphasizing

the feelings of nervousness, anxiety and irritability that overcome some people who take pills containing the ingredient. But PPA can also cause more serious psychological problems. The *Journal of the American Medical Association* cited the cases of seven women who were brought to a hospital emergency room suffering from hallucinations, dizziness and anxiety after taking PPA-containing tablets. Within several hours, all the women had recovered except one, who suffered a psychotic episode.

While such extreme reactions from PPA use are rare, feelings of euphoria are more common. These are thought to be the result of PPA's causing the release of chemicals in the brain in much the same way that amphetamines do. "Medications containing PPA used to be sold on the street as substitutes for amphetamines or 'speed,'" says Sorell L. Schwartz, Ph.D., a professor of pharmacology at Georgetown University School of Medicine in Washington, D.C. "I don't feel that there is any sound reason for supporting their use as diet aids."

CULPRITS IN COLD REMEDIES

The use of PPA is not restricted to diet pills. More than 100 OTC medications—including cough syrups, cold remedies and decongestants—contain the substance. The same mood shifts can occur with these preparations as with diet pills, but the threat is often doubled. In addition to PPA, these medications may contain ephedrine or pseudoephedrine, substances that relax air passages and constrict blood vessels not only in swollen nasal passages but also in the brain, thus affecting the nervous system. Among the common reactions are the ones Elizabeth experienced: nervousness, irritability and insomnia. Other possible side effects include dizziness and general malaise.

Children, because of their size and age, can be more severely affected than adults— even when the recommended dosages are followed. A report in the *British Medical Journal* warns that a frequently used over-

the-counter cough medicine that contains pseudoephedrine and triprolidine (an antihistamine) can occasionally cause nightmares in children. Mood changes are also caused by the surprisingly high percentages of alcohol that many cold and cough medications contain. As one parent of a three-year-old girl recently said, "I gave my daughter the recommended child's dose of a cough medicine I usually take. She lay in bed wide-eyed until midnight, when she suddenly started giggling about something. It helped fight her cough, but the next day she was tired and cranky."

THE PROBLEMS WITH PAINKILLERS

Aspirin and acetaminophen are two common remedies for minor pain; both are relatively safe. In large doses, such as might be taken to quell arthritic pain, however, aspirin can cause a ringing in the ears that may lead to feelings of disorientation.

For greater pain, prescription drugs are the best bet, but with their increased effectiveness also comes increased risk. The most frequently used of these are the synthetic opiates such as codeine, propoxyphene and meperidine. Their mood- and mind-altering side effects include irritability, disorientation, dizziness and drowsiness. And added to these problems is the possibility of addiction. "A person can easily become addicted to one of these drugs after three or four months of continued use," explains Charles Dackis, M.D., an expert on drug addiction and medical director of Hampton Hospital in Mount Holly, New Jersey. "Once addiction begins, psychological side effects become much worse. Personality changes, such as impulsive, irresponsible and antisocial behavior, are common. The person becomes less and less concerned with the relationships in his life."

ALLERGY TREATMENTS CAN SPELL TROUBLE

The symptoms of hay fever and other allergic reactions—itchy eyes, runny nose, etc.— are caused by histamine, a compound that is released from cells when allergy-inducing substances are present. Allergic reactions are often treated with antihistamines, which interfere with the effects of histamine by blocking its receptor sites.

But many antihistamines, such as chlorpheniramine, brompheniramine and diphenhydramine—to name but a few found in typical OTC and prescription antiallergy medications—are infamous for the drowsiness they can cause. Cheryl, a 35-year-old self-employed publicist, learned this the hard way. Although drowsiness is so common a reaction that physicians and pharmacists often caution patients about this side effect, Cheryl was given no warning when she purchased an OTC antihistamine to relieve a

a sexual TURNOFF

Among the most disconcerting side effects of some over-the-counter and prescription medications are a decrease in sexual desire and a lack of physical or emotional responsiveness to sex. "When an individual or a couple comes to me for help with a sexual problem, the first thing I want to know is what medications are being used," says Shirley Zussman, Ed.D., a New York City sex therapist. "Many common drugs diminish libido far more than anyone might expect."

For example, antihistamines can cause drowsiness and lack of concentration, so many allergy sufferers using these drugs find themselves too sleepy or unfocused for sex. Barry J. Klyde, M.D., an endocrinologist associated with Cornell University Medical College in New York City and a member of the staff at the New York Hospital, adds, "Because antihistamines interfere with the chemicals that carry nerve impulses—including those necessary for normal sexual function—they may hinder erection or lubrication, as well as orgasm in both men and women."

Tranquilizers also affect nerve impulses and so can induce similar reactions. Another way they can inhibit normal sexual responses is through their muscle-relaxing effects. And, adds Dr. Klyde, "Some sedatives have a depressive effect, which makes it even more difficult to become aroused or to reach orgasm."

Painkillers also can be a culprit. Dr. Klyde points out that people taking frequent doses of painkillers often experience a decrease in *all* their basic biological drives. According to Dr. Charles Dackis, these drugs suppress sexual desire and sometimes cause impotence.

Likewise, birth-control pills can reduce a woman's sex drive, says Dr. Zussman. This is due to the low estrogen levels in most pills prescribed today. Dr. Klyde explains: "The Pill can have effects similar to but not as severe as those experienced at menopause—thinning of the vaginal lining, decreased lubrication, painful intercourse and lessened desire." Women who notice such symptoms should speak to their gynecologists about changing to a Pill with slightly higher levels of estrogen.

Women may not always be aware of subtle changes in their sexual responsiveness, while with men the effects can be much more obvious. This is especially true with medications that often cause impotence, such as some prescription drugs used to treat high blood pressure, ulcers, heart disease and depression. "I know of more than two hundred drugs that cause sexual dysfunction in men," says E. Douglas Whitehead, M.D., a New York City urologist and a director of the Association for Male Sexual Dysfunction in New York City.

Changing a patient's prescription can often alleviate impotence, however, so it is important that a man alert his doctor to any problems he may be having. In fact, Dr. Zussman advises that anyone taking medication on a continual basis discuss its possible effects on sexuality with his or her doctor.

some, adds Dr. Sly. And another fairly new drug, cromolyn sodium, is sometimes prescribed as an alternative to antihistamines because it has virtually no side effects. Used as a nasal spray in the treatment of allergies involving the nasal passages, the drug prevents the release of histamine from cells. "However, cromolyn sodium is not effective for everyone," cautions Dr. Sly.

The drugs used to treat asthma also cause a multitude of changes in mood and frame of mind. Among the most frequently prescribed are bronchodilators, which open constricted airways. Theophylline, the most common in this class of drugs, produces nervousness, insomnia, irritability, behavioral problems and difficulty in concentrating in many patients, according to Dr. Sly. Another group of bronchodilating drugs called beta-agonists—including albuterol, terbutaline and bitolterol mesylate—can cause some of the same side effects, although to a lesser degree than does theophylline, especially when they're inhaled through the mouth (via a nebulizer or metered-dose inhaler) rather than taken as tablets. (Albuterol is prescribed in tablet, liquid and inhaler form; terbutaline in tablet and inhaler form; bitolterol mesylate, only in inhaler form.) The reason inhaled drugs have fewer side effects than those taken in tablet, liquid or injected form: They're deposited directly at the site they're intended to treat (in this case, the airways) rather than absorbed through the bloodstream, which circulates the drug throughout the body. Also, less of the drug is needed when it doesn't have to take a roundabout route to reach its target. But unfortunately, inhaled drugs are not always effective in severe cases of asthma, because the airways may be too constricted for enough of the drug to penetrate.

Epinephrine (also know as adrenaline) is yet another beta-agonist drug. This one is associated with more side effects than the other drugs in this category—even when it is inhaled—according to François Haas, Ph.D., director of the Pulmonary Function Laboratory at New York University Medical Center in New York City and coauthor of *The Essential Asthma Book: A Manual for Asthmatics of All Ages* (Scribner, 1987). These include jitteriness, disorientation due to dizziness, and even anxiety, often resulting from the very rapid heartbeat the drug can bring on. "For this reason, epinephrine is usually limited to use in asthma emergencies, during which time it would most likely be injected," Dr. Haas says. Epinephrine *is* present in some OTC asthma medications, however, and he and other specialists warn against using these.

Finally, a class of drugs called steroids, prescribed both for asthma and persistent allergies involving severe inflammation, can cause feelings of euphoria and, in rare cases, psychotic behavior, according to Dr. Sly. Restlessness is another, although infrequent, reaction. But again, these side effects are

case of the sniffles. She took the drug in the morning, before going to the office. An hour later, during an important meeting with a potential new client, Cheryl felt so sleepy she could hardly concentrate on what she was saying. She cut the meeting short and lost the account as a result.

But drowsiness is not the only problem with antihistamines, says R. Michael Sly, M.D., chairman of allergy and immunology at the Children's Hospital National Medical Center and professor of child health and de-

velopment at the George Washington University School of Medicine in Washington, D.C. "In some individuals, especially young children, antihistamines can have the opposite effect, causing restlessness, irritability and insomnia—side effects your doctor is less likely to mention." Nightmares are another, though rarer, reaction, he says.

A new prescription antihistamine called terfenadine does not appear to cause the side effects typically associated with antihistamines, although drowsiness may occur in

usually associated with the tablet, not the inhaler form of the drug. Steroid sprays can be inhaled through the nose or, in the case of asthma, through the mouth.

UNEXPECTED EFFECTS OF TRANQUILIZERS

The usual preparations prescribed for anxiety include diazepam, lorazepam, oxazepam, prazepam, triazolam and chlordiazepoxide, all made from a class of compounds called benzodiazepines. These can cause drowsiness, depression or euphoria, dulled thinking and impaired motor coordination, according to Dr. Dackis. In addition, they can be addicting, he says. "Addiction can come on so quickly that many people are not even aware that they are addicted. And even after a few months of use, anxiety—the very problem these drugs are supposed to cure—can become much worse. Withdrawal causes additional problems: Irritability, increased nervousness and depression can result."

The use of diazepam also can have another effect, one that worries Dr. Young. She is concerned about how it may affect a newborn infant. When the drug is given to a woman in labor, it quickly crosses the placental barrier via the umbilical cord. But because an infant's kidneys and liver are not completely developed at birth, the drug may not clear out of the baby's body for days. Dr. Young cites studies finding that babies born of mothers who took diazepam during labor showed a lack of responsiveness for up to several weeks. "We're not sure yet whether this is anything but a short-term effect, but it needs to be looked into," she says.

A new antianxiety medication on the market only a few months—buspirone—avoids many of the side effects of the benzodiazepines, according to John Feighner, M.D., associate clinical professor of psychiatry at the University of California Medical School in San Diego, who has tested the drug for seven years in his research institute. "Buspirone is a totally new type of compound that alleviates anxiety but is nonsedating," he says. He emphasizes, however, that it is most effective for long-term rather than occasional anxiety. "What is exciting," Dr. Feighner adds, "is that here is a drug that will not interfere with daily living. It is not addictive, produces no withdrawal symptoms, shows no complications with alcohol use and does not impair motor coordination or mental functioning." He does warn of possible side effects including restlessness and dizziness, but these reactions have occurred in less than ten percent of his patients.

HOW TO PROTECT YOURSELF

Because there is no government policy stipulating that drugs must be tested for their effect on mood, the mind and behavior, it is the consumer who must protect herself, advises Dr. Young. "Mental side effects are often so transitory or their origin so difficult to pinpoint that regulation against the chemical compounds in some drugs is slow in coming or is nonexistent. The Food and Drug Administration (FDA), the Federal Government agency that approves the sale of drugs, is likely to take action only if someone has a dramatic reaction or dies after having taken a recommended dosage," she says.

The FDA's stance concerning PPA is a case in point. In 1972 the agency began investigating PPA along with all other OTC drugs; in 1979 an advisory panel concluded that PPA was an effective dietary aid. Since then, scores of researchers as well as the American Medical Association and the influential *Medical Letter*—an authoritative and well-respected newsletter that keeps doctors abreast of the latest developments in drugs—have criticized it, but without effect in the marketplace. "Consumer assume that because a drug's sold over the counter, it must be safe," says Dr. Young. "But this is just not true." Though the FDA is continuing to investigate claims against PPA, it has made no move to restrict its sale.

What, then, can you do to avoid unnecessary psychological side effects from your medications? "While no magic potions exist, there are a large number of therapeutic alternatives to turn to if the adverse effects of one medication are too severe," says William Barr, Pharm.D., Ph.D., chairman of the department of pharmacy at the Virginia Commonwealth University in Richmond. "Given professional advice, most people can generally find something suitable for them." So be sure to report to your doctor any side effects you may be experiencing from a drug—whether it's a prescription or OTC remedy. Ask him if there's another suitable medication you might take instead. More advice from pharmacology experts:

• **Read package labels.** Package labels and inserts include warnings of any known possible adverse reactions that can occur with use.

• **Never exceed the recommended dosages.** Information about how much medication you should take can be found on the package labels of OTC drugs; if you're taking a prescription drug, make sure you understand your doctor's directions on the correct dose.

• **Question your doctor and pharmacist.** Survey after survey has shown that doctors write prescriptions far more freely than they offer information about what a drug may do besides bring relief. If you have any doubts as to whether a medication is appropriate for you, ask. Your pharmacist, as well as your doctor, is qualified to answer questions.

• **Consider switching pharmacists if you're not getting the information you need.** "Pharmacists are trained professionals," says Dr. Barr. "If yours won't take the time to answer questions about a medication, you should find a new one."

Being a well-informed consumer is probably the best defense against the potential side effects of any drug. Used carefully and sensibly, over-the-counter and prescription drugs can help us feel better—rather than worse.

Sneak addictions to over-the-counter drugs

Such innocents as aspirin, laxatives and nose drops can hook you—how to taper off if they have

ROBIN REIF

Robin Reif is a New York-based freelance writer who frequently contributes medical articles to Self.

ver-the-counter (OTC) drugs are available over the counter only because they're deemed safe enough for use without a doctor's okay. But that doesn't mean they can't cause problems, and sometimes it's the way we use them that's at fault.

Overuse of over-the-counter drugs can result in some surprising dependencies. The body can "forget" how to perform a particular function without the drug to help it along, for example. Or a psychological reliance—continuing a drug because you think you need its real or perceived effect—can develop. While most people can taper off and "unhook" themselves from these drugs, one key is to first recognize that you're an overuser. Even more important is simply knowing which drugs are most likely to cause a problem so you can use them with an extra measure of care

Drugs that cut down on digestive efficiency

Some of the most problematic OTC drugs are laxatives. Taken as directed—never for more than a week at a time—these are safe and provide effective relief from constipation. But if they're relied on for longer periods, the colon may actually "forget" how to evacuate on its own. The reason varies with the type of laxative. With stimulant laxatives (those containing phenolphthalein, cascara or senna) the colon's nerves get so used to the drug's high chemical stimulation that the stool's lower stimulation no longer triggers the elimination reflex. Dulled reflexes can also result from overusing saline laxatives (products whose main ingredients are sodium, potassium or magnesium salts), which draw large amounts of water into the colon. Nerves continually sparked by this high volume eventually aren't stimulated by the lower volume of natural waste material, explains Robert Sause, Ph.D., associate professor of pharmacy at St. John's University College of Pharmacy and Allied Health Professions in New York City. These changes, called "lazy bowel syndrome," can start after as little as several weeks of repeated use. A dependency tip-off is needing more laxatives more frequently, says New York City gastroenterologist Ellen Scherl, M.D.

People who may run into these problems include those who think that "regularity" means a bowel movement every day, when in fact regularity can range from three times a day to once every three days, says Dr. Sause. Others who may be at risk are people with ''irritable bowel syndrome.'' This common, stress-linked syndrome (which some experts believe may have a familial basis) is characterized by alternating periods of constipation and diarrhea, explains gastroenterologist Arnold Levy, M.D., vice president of education for the American Digestive Disease Society. While it's best treated with diet and stress-management measures, some people with irritable bowel syndrome tend to start overusing laxatives at times when constipation hits, thereby aggravating the syndrome, says Dr. Levy. People whose constipation stems from fiber-poor diet and pregnant women, whose hormonal shifts can cause a sluggish bowel, may also be tempted to fall into frequent laxative use.

Most people with a laxative habit can retrain their bowel by temporarily substituting bulk-forming laxatives for stimulants and salines while adding more fiber and eight to ten glasses of nonalcoholic fluid per day to their diets, says Dr. Scherl. Then, over a period of a couple of weeks, they should slowly wean themselves from the bulk laxatives. Moderate exercise can also help ease the colon back into action. If, after trying these measures over the course of a couple of weeks, constipation persists, it's wise to consult a physician. While constipation itself is not dangerous, it may be the only noticeable symptom of a more serious underlying problem, such as an abnormal thyroid condition.

The best way to avoid problems is to use bulk-formers, if laxatives need to be used at all. These are made essentially from indigestible plant fibers like cellulose, bran and psyllium seed. In fact, some doctors don't regard these products as laxatives at all, but as just another way to up dietary fiber, says Dr. Levy.

Noses that stuff up long-term

A different kind of dependency problem can arise with OTC nasal decongestants (sprays or drops) because of a process known as ''rebound.'' When people use these drugs too often or for too long, as the medication wears off, nasal stuffiness bounces back—sometimes worse than it originally was, creating the need for even more medicine. If taken again, the new dose sparks more rebound stuffiness and a continuous cycle can start, explains Bruce Kimelblatt, Pharm.D., assistant director of the pharmacy at The Mount Sinai Medical Center in New York City.

Experts don't know for sure what sets the rebound cycle in motion. Some think that if swollen blood vessels remain shrunk by decongestants for too long a period of time, there's a buildup of cellular waste which could otherwise be carried out by normal blood flow. When the drug wears off, blood rushes back to clean out the waste, ballooning the vessels once again, says Dr. Kimelblatt.

Problems with nasal decongestants tend to start when the stuff-up source—usually a cold or allergy—outlives the

amount of time you can safely use the products (for most OTC sprays or drops, it's three days). With symptoms still there, it's tempting to keep treating them. To avoid this, anyone who's been using nasal decongestants for more than a few days and is relying on them to clear a constantly clogged nose should simply go cold-turkey, says Sol Katz, M.D., professor of medicine, Georgetown University School of Medicine. There may be rebound stuffiness for several days or even weeks, says Dr. Katz, but eventually nasal tissue almost always returns to normal, although in very rare instances it needs to be drained or surgically excised to open breathing passages. Meanwhile, use of humidifiers or vaporizers can ease the discomfort, as can saline nose drops.

To avoid problems in the first place, read the product label and use only as long and as frequently as the manufacturer recommends. Products containing naphazoline hydrochloride or preparations of 1-percent phenylephrine hydrochloride should be used with special care since they wear off more quickly, inviting overuse.

Getting hooked by headaches

Headaches are another annoyance which, due to overmedication, can bounce back worse than they began. Some experts think this occurs only with drugs containing caffeine (it's added to some aspirins and menstrual-cramp products). Caffeine keeps blood vessels in a constant state of constriction. After several weeks of high doses, stopping can produce caffeine-withdrawal headaches as vessels painfully expand, says Seymour Diamond, M.D., director of the Diamond Headache Clinic in Chicago. This causes people to reach for pills again to quell their pain, thereby continuing the cycle.

 ome researchers believe rebound headaches and possible psychological dependence can also occur with caffeine-free drugs like pure aspirin and pure acetaminophen (Tylenol, for example). Vulnerable to this problem are those who have an inherited tendency toward frequent headaches, in which pain hits more days than not, says Joel Saper, M.D., director of the Michigan Headache and Neurological Institute, Ann Arbor.

Doctors don't know for sure why this kind of rebound pain occurs, but some speculate that when headache-prone people self-medicate with a combination of OTC analgesics almost continuously, the constant presence of artificial painkillers may inhibit production of the body's natural painkillers, such as morphinelike endorphins.

To avoid both these headache problems, follow strictly dose recommendations on product labels and never use OTC painkillers for more than ten days straight, except under a doctor's direction. If headache problems hang on longer than that, see a family doctor, who may in turn refer you to a specialist. Since there are over 3,000 causes of headaches, self-treating with nonprescription painkillers for too long not only puts people at risk for dependency problems, but may also mask more serious conditions (hypoglycemia and aneurysm are two) that need medical attention. In many cases once the true cause is learned, lifestyle changes (diet and stress reduction, for example) or more-effective medications can provide relief.

People who may already have an overuse habit (more than 100 pills a month is one guideline, according to Dr. Saper) can usually stop cold-turkey. Those whose painkillers are laced with caffeine or use more than ten pills per day should cut their dose by two tablets daily until they're off. Quitting analgesics often produces strong rebound headaches. If these don't pass after several days or if they become very uncomfortable, seek help from your doctor, who may prescribe a painkiller with a different method of action to tide you over till the headaches subside.

The mind hook

Sometimes people start taking an OTC drug for a genuine problem, but because they like the medication's real or perceived effect, they may increase the dose or prolong use beyond what the label suggests. Appetite suppressants are sometimes misused this way.

While most people stop these drugs after 12 weeks (as product labels advise), others are reluctant to give up the pills, believing that they can't lose weight without them. Prolonged use, however, can easily lead to increased doses since the drug has only a modest effect on appetite, which people may become accustomed to as time goes on. Some people use higher doses from the start to get greater appetite suppression.

Excessive use of appetite suppressants ups the odds of side effects—the main one being high blood pressure, triggered by the active ingredient in these products—PPA (short for phenylpropanolamine). The chances of temporarily elevated blood pressure are greater when the drug is overused by overweight people—who are more prone to high blood pressure to begin with, says Nathan Rawls, Pharm.D., assistant professor of clinical pharmacy at the University of Tennessee's College of Pharmacy. And one study showed that even when taken at recommended doses by young, healthy adults, PPA can have this effect. At the extreme, diet pills have been controversially associated with complications of high blood pressure, such as irregular heartbeat and stroke.

PPA is further known to exacerbate other health problems that tend to occur more frequently in overweight people: diabetes, heart and thyroid troubles. While product labels do warn against use by those who have such problems, studies show that some people may not necessarily be aware that they have these conditions.

To avoid overuse of these diet aids, some experts recommend that they not be used at all. But anyone who does opt for them should realize from the start that these drugs are intended only as temporary aids to help reduce hunger during the first weeks of switching to a lower-calorie diet, says Dr. Rawls. If taking them, strictly adhere to limits stated on the label. Anyone currently over the limit should taper off by eliminating one dose per day.

Antidrowsiness drugs can also spark a psychological attraction, due to the boost in alertness and energy provided by the caffeine or other stimulants they contain. If used for several weeks, though, tolerance can develop and higher doses may be needed to get the original effect. With higher doses, however (over 500 mg per day or more), symptoms of "caffeinism" can occur, including nervousness, insomnia, irritability and irregular heartbeat, says Stephen J. Levy, Ph.D., author of *Managing the Drugs in Your Life*. The problem is that cutting out the pills can bring on withdrawal headaches, lethargy and low moods, which another dose can quell.

The discomfort of quitting these products can be minimized by tapering off rather than stopping suddenly, says Dr. Rawls. Switching to decaffeinated coffee and avoiding other caffeine-containing drugs can also help to ease the transition. Some diuretics have as much as 100-200 mg of caffeine per dose, and some cold remedies have about 30 mg, notes Dr. Levy.

Other OTC medicines can present psychological dependency problems because of the alcohol they contain. Alcohol-laced cough/cold remedies—some of which are as high as 50 proof—should be considered off limits to anyone who has alcohol problems, advises Dr. Kimelblatt.

While it's highly unlikely that others will get hooked on these products, some people may start using them for colds and enjoy the "floating" feeling caused by the alcohol and enhanced by the antihistamines in these medicines. They may then start using these products as sleep aids or even recreationally for a mild "high"—a practice which should be avoided. All over-the-counter label information pertaining to dose and duration is regulated by the Food and Drug Administration; and although the guidelines tend to be conservative, they draw boundaries which are designed to keep consumers from getting hooked on OTC drugs.

Who Uses
Psychotropic Drugs?

- Personality and Drugs of Choice (Articles 37-40)
- Deleterious Changes From Drug Use (Articles 41-45)

Who is likely to abuse drugs? "Intoxicating Habits" raises the question of whether or not alcoholics can handle "social drinking." The author cites research which infers that at least 20 percent of those considered "alcoholic" can engage in moderate social drinking. This opinion draws heavy criticism from Alcoholics Anonymous and other recovery groups which claim that "alcoholics who practice social drinking become drunks." "Wine and Winos" deals with street alcoholics and their drug of choice, sugar-fortified wines. These "big bang" dollar-a-pint vintages kill the appetite and suppress the desire to eat, which creates attendant health problems. "How to Stay in the Right Relationship With Everything From Chocolate to Cocaine" shows the difficulty of establishing a "right relationship" with drugs when abstinence is not chosen. "A Male Problem" indicates that drug abuse among female professional athletes is less widespread than among males, with alcohol being the most abused chemical among the women.

An examination of the deleterious effects of drug use shows that the damage goes far beyond the life of the individual user. The articles "Alcohol and the Family" and "Healing Scars of Parental Drinking" demonstrate the destruction done to close family members by the abuse of alcohol. "Alcohol-Breast Cancer Link" details several unexpected side effects of some commonly used drugs.

Examples of muscle-building drugs in use today are cited in "Shortcut to the Rambo Look," and "Steroids: The Power Drugs." These "builders of muscles and men" are now so common among high school and university students as to be deemed a genuine health threat. The fact that few of these athletes will go on to professional sports careers has not stopped them from using these performance-enhancers.

Looking Ahead: Challenge Questions

Why would an athlete choose the "Olympic gold" over longevity? Is there a "right relationship" with drugs? What is it?

Do children of alcoholic parents have a reasonable chance of a good life? Can an alcoholic safely practice controlled drinking?

Why do many drug users not become drug abusers? Define "drug abuse."

When should drug education begin? Must parents abstain from all drugs in order to prevent drug abuse in their children?

What part do cigarettes play in the war on drugs? Why do many smokers find moderation impossible?

Differentiate between "hard" and "soft" drugs.

Unit 4

Intoxicating Habits

Some alcoholism researchers say they are studying a learned behavior, not a disease

BRUCE BOWER

Most alcoholism treatment programs in the United States operate on the assumption that people seeking their help have a disease characterized by physical dependency and a strong genetic predisposition. The goal of treatment, therefore, is total abstinence.

Herbert Fingarette, a philosophy professor at the University of California, Santa Barbara, pored over alcoholism and addiction research and came up with a suggestion for the many proponents of this approach: Forget it.

In a controversial new book (*Heavy Drinking: The Myth of Alcoholism as a Disease*, University of California Press, 1988), Fingarette says alcoholism has no single cause and no medical cure, and is the result of a range of physical, personal and social characteristics that predispose a person to drink excessively.

"Let's view the persistent heavy drinking of the alcoholic not as a sin or disease but as a central activity of the individual's way of life," he contends. Seen in this context, alcoholism treatment must focus not just on the drinking problem, but on developing a satisfying way of life that does not revolve around heavy drinking. Total abstinence — the goal of medical treatment centers as well as Alcoholics Anonymous — is unrealistic for many heavy drinkers, holds Fingarette.

Disputes over the nature of alcoholism have a long and vitriolic history. But Fingarette's arguments reflect a growing field of research, populated mainly by psychologists, in which alcoholism and other addictions — including those that do not involve drugs, such as compulsive gambling — are viewed more as habits than as diseases. Addictive behavior, in this scheme, typically revolves around an immediate gratification followed by delayed, harmful effects. The habitual behavior nevertheless continues and is often experienced by the addict as uncontrollable.

"Addiction occurs in the environment, not in the liver, genes or synapses," says psychologist Timothy B. Baker of the University of Wisconsin in Madison. Biology may, in some cases, increase a person's risk of developing a dependency, but "an individual chooses to take drugs in the world. The likelihood of a person trying a drug or eventually becoming addicted is influenced by his or her friends, marital happiness, the variety and richness of alternatives to drug use and so on," Baker contends.

Expectations and beliefs about alcohol's power to make one feel better shape the choices leading to alcohol addiction, according to one line of investigation. The most notable of these beliefs, says psychologist G. Alan Marlatt of the University of Washington in Seattle, is that alcohol acts as a magical elixir that enhances social and physical pleasure, increases sexual responsiveness and assertiveness, and reduces tension (SN: 10/3/87, p.218).

The initial physical arousal stimulated by low doses of alcohol pumps up positive expectations, explains Marlatt. But higher alcohol doses dampen arousal, sap energy and result in hangovers that, in turn, lead to a craving for alcohol's stimulating effects. As tolerance to the drug develops, a person requires more and more alcohol to get a short-term "lift" and a vicious cycle of abuse picks up speed.

Despite falling into this addictive trap, Marlatt says, some people drastically cut back their drinking or stop imbibing altogether without the help of formal treatment. In these cases, he maintains, external events often conspire to change an individual's attitude toward alcohol. Examples include an alcohol-related injury, the departure of a spouse, financial and legal problems stemming from drinking or the alcohol-related death of another person.

When treatment is sought out, Marlatt advises, the focus should be on teaching ways to handle stress without drinking and developing realistic expectations about alcohol's effects. Marlatt and his co-workers are now developing an "alcohol skills-training program" for college students, described more fully in *Issues in Alcohol Use and Misuse by Young Adults* (G. Howard, editor, Notre Dame University Press, 1988). Preliminary results indicate many students who consume large amounts of alcohol every week cut down considerably after completing the eight-session course. In fact, says Marlatt, children of alcoholics show some of the best responses to the program and are highly motivated to learn how to drink in moderation.

Psychologists teach the students how to set drinking limits and cope with peer pressure at parties and social events. Realistic expectations about alcohol's mood-enhancing powers are developed, and participants learn alternative methods of stress reduction, such as meditation and aerobic exercise.

The program does not promote drinking, says Marlatt, and students showing signs of hard-core alcohol dependency are referred for treatment that stresses abstinence. "But it's inappropriate to insist that all students abusing alcohol are in the early stages of a progressive disease," he contends. "Our approach acknowledges that drinking occurs regularly and gives students more options and choices for safer drinking."

A similar approach to helping adult alcoholics has been developed by psychologists W. Miles Cox of the Veterans Administration Medical Center in Indianapolis and Eric Klinger of the University of Minnesota in Morris. Their model, described in the May JOURNAL OF ABNORMAL PSYCHOLOGY, holds that although a number of biological and social factors influence alcohol abuse, the final decision to drink is motivated by conscious or unconscious expectations that alcohol will brighten one's emotional state and wipe away stress. An alcoholic's expected pleasure or relief from a drinking binge, for example, may outweigh fears that it eventually will lead to getting fired or divorced.

Cox and Klinger's technique aims at providing alternative sources of emotional satisfaction. They have developed a questionnaire to assess an alcoholic's major life goals and concerns. A counselor then helps the alcoholic formulate weekly goals based on his or her responses. Counseling also attempts to reduce the tendency to use alcohol as a crutch when faced with frustration. "Alcoholics often have unrealistically high standards and lack the capacity to forgive themselves for not meeting these standards," Cox says.

The focus on an alcoholic's concerns and motivation is intended to complement other treatments, say the researchers. It is consistent, they note, with the efforts of Alcoholics Anonymous to drive home the negative side of drinking and the benefits of not drinking.

The context in which people consume alcohol is another part of the addictive process under study. Any combination of drinking and mildly pleasant activity, such as television viewing, conversation or card games, appears to provide the best protection against anxiety and stress, report psychologists Claude M. Steele and Robert A. Josephs of the University of Michigan's Institute of Social Research in Ann Arbor. Alcohol's ability to draw attention away from stressful thoughts and onto immediate activity may play a key role in its addictive power, they suggest.

Steele and Joseph tested this theory in their laboratory. They gave enough vodka and tonic to adult subjects to induce mild intoxication. Another group expected to receive vodka and tonic, but was given tonic in glasses rubbed with alcohol to create the odor of a real drink. Everyone was told that in 15 minutes they would have to give a speech on "What I dislike about my body and physical appearance." Researchers asked some from each group to sit quietly before making the speech, while others were asked to rate a series of art slides before speaking.

Those subjects who drank alcohol and rated slides reported significantly less anxiety over the speech than the other participants. Viewing the slides when sober had no anxiety-reducing effects.

According to the researchers, this supports the notion that alcohol's reduction of psychological stress has less to do with its direct pharmacological effects than with its knack for shifting attention with the aid of distractions.

On the other hand, being intoxicated and doing nothing before the speech significantly increased subjects' anxiety, note the investigators in the May JOURNAL OF ABNORMAL PSYCHOLOGY. Without any distraction, alcohol appears to narrow attention to the upcoming situation.

Recent investigations also suggest alcohol users are motivated by alcohol's ability to reduce psychological stress among people who are highly self-conscious and constantly evaluating themselves. Steele and Josephs did not, however, evaluate the "self-awareness" of their subjects.

A different approach to unraveling drinking behavior involves the search for cues that set off an alcoholic's craving or irresistible urge to drink. Just as Pavlov's dogs were conditioned to salivate after hearing a bell that previously had preceded the appearance of food, there are internal and external "bells" that provoke craving in many alcoholics, explains psychiatrist Arnold M. Ludwig of the University of Kentucky Medical Center in Lexington.

These cues are often quite specific, he says. For instance, recovered alcoholic and major league baseball pitcher Bob Welch has reported experiencing a craving to drink during airplane flights, after a game of golf and after pitching.

In a survey of 150 abstinent alcoholics reported in the fall 1986 ALCOHOL HEALTH & RESEARCH WORLD, Ludwig finds nearly all of them can identify one or more "bells" that trigger craving. With the exception of "internal tension," mentioned as a cue by more than half the subjects, there was considerable individual difference in reported drinking "bells." These included going to a dance, feeling lonely, having a barbecue, seeing a drink in an advertisement and driving past former drinking hangouts.

Alcoholics Anonymous, notes Ludwig, teaches that four general conditions — hunger, anger, loneliness and tiredness — make recovered alcoholics more vulnerable to drinking urges, an observation supported by research on craving.

Other evidence, Ludwig says, suggests that the more times uncomfortable withdrawal symptoms — shakiness, agitation, hallucinations or confusion — have been relieved by drinking in the past, the greater the likelihood that familiar drinking cues will elicit craving in alcoholics.

Many alcoholics feel helpless and bewildered when craving strikes, seemingly out of the blue. "But craving is not the elusive, mysterious force many believe it to be," says Ludwig. To successfully recover, he contends, alcoholics must become aware of the emotional and situational cues that trigger drinking urges.

The first drink in the right setting, he adds, often whets the appetite for more. Alcoholics should seek out "safe havens" where drinking is discouraged, he suggests, such as workplaces, Alcoholics Anonymous and outdoor activities.

Whereas Ludwig sees drinking cues as stoking the internal embers of craving, other researchers focus solely on external "reinforcers" that affect an alcoholic's drinking behavior. When important reinforcers outside the realm of drinking, such as a job or marriage, are lost, say psychologists Rudy E. Vuchinich and Jalie A. Tucker of Wayne State University in Detroit, a recovered alcoholic becomes more likely to resume drinking.

"The growing consensus from clinical studies [points to] the important role of environmental variables and changes in life circumstances in influencing the drinking behavior of alcoholics," they write in the May JOURNAL OF ABNORMAL PSYCHOLOGY. But the development of appropriate environmental measures to study drinking is still in the early stages, the investigators add.

While research into the psychology of alcohol addiction is beginning to mature, it remains largely ignored by the biologically oriented advocates of alcoholism-as-disease, says Marlatt. The research and clinical communities are especially polarized over suggestions from addiction studies that some alcoholics — about 15 to 20 percent, according to Marlatt — can safely engage in moderate or social drinking.

The characteristics of alcohol abusers who can handle controlled drinking are not clear, but Marlatt and other researchers see milder alcoholics as prime candidates for this treatment approach.

Given that most current alcoholism treatment is based on the disease model of total abstinence, which has been endorsed by the American Medical Association and the American Psychiatric Association for many years, reconciliation between opposing theoretical camps is not imminent.

"But biological and genetic approaches to alcoholism need to be integrated with psychological and social approaches," Marlatt says. "This really hasn't been done yet."

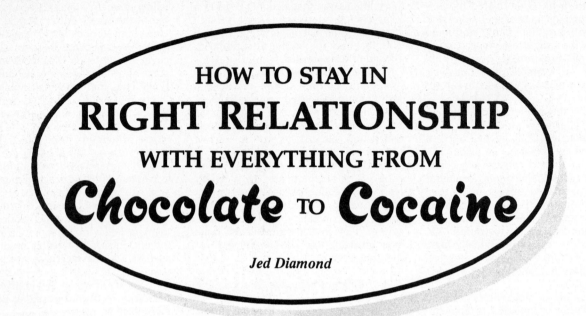

HOW TO STAY IN
RIGHT RELATIONSHIP
WITH EVERYTHING FROM
Chocolate TO *Cocaine*

Jed Diamond

PEOPLE IN THIS COUNTRY USE OR EXPERIMENT with a variety of drugs, including alcohol, cocaine, marijuana, and heroin. We use substances not always thought of as drugs, such as coffee, sugar, cigarettes, and chocolate. We get other drugs from physicians for use as medications, including Valium, codeine, and Seconal. All these substances are "mind-active drugs."

Nicotine, in the form of cigarettes, is probably the most addictive drug we know, yet it continues to be advertised widely and is still used by over a third of the population. Caffeine, in coffee, tea, chocolate, and soft drinks, is the most widely used stimulant and is often abused. But since it is not viewed as a drug, problems go unnoticed.

With so much confusion and misinformation about drugs, it is difficult for the individual to decide how to relate to them. More than 95 percent of us use some mind-active drug, and studies indicate that as many as half of us have some problem with the drugs we use.

For most of us, the issue isn't whether to use drugs, but which ones to use and how to remain in good relationship with the drugs we do use.

Most of us wait until we are having a crisis before exploring our relationships with drugs. The purpose of this questionnaire is to help you decide for yourself if you are in good relationship with the drugs in your life *before* you begin to have problems.

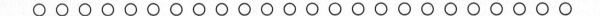

Before reading, pick up a pencil. If you are so inclined, you can assist the author by sending him your responses. A certified alcoholism and drug-abuse counselor, Jed Diamond is investigating the profile that drug relationships take within a given individual. He also solicits comments about the questionnaire. Send them to Jed Diamond, P. O. Box 9355, San Rafael, CA 94912.
—Kevin Kelly

First, ask yourself which of the following drugs you use:

1. Stimulants:
coffee, nicotine, refined sugar, cocaine, amphetamines

2. Depressants:
alcohol, barbiturates (i.e. sleeping pills), tranquilizers (i.e. Valium, Librium, Dalmane), narcotics (i.e. codeine, morphine, heroin)

3. Psychedelics
(LSD, mushrooms, MDA)

4. Marijuana

5. Prescription drugs
not commonly thought to be psychoactive (i.e. antihistamines, steroids, cough suppressants)

6. Over-the-counter preparations
not commonly thought to be psychoactive (cold remedies, decongestants, appetite suppressants)

Whether a given drug is legal or illegal, approved or disapproved, obtained from a physician or bought on the street, some people can use it with good results while others have problems.

For each drug you presently use or think you may use again, ask yourself the following questions:

1. Am I aware that _____ is a drug, and do I know what the effects are on my body, mind, and spirit?

☒ **YES**
☐ **NO**
People who remain in good relationship with a drug have a deep understanding of what the drug is and what it does. Those who begin to have problems lack such awareness. They think coffee is just a beverage, smoking just a bad habit, marijuana only a simple herb, and cocaine a safe drug if snorted.

2. Am I experiencing useful effects of _____ over time?

☒ **YES**
☐ **NO**
People who have the best relationship with a drug get continued positive effects over time with the same amount of the drug. People in the worst relationship with a drug often use it heavily but get the least out of it.

3. When I use _____, do I always use the amount I want and no more?

☒ **YES**
☐ **NO**
People in good relationship almost always use just the amount they want. If they decide to have two drinks and no more, they stick to the decision without problem. Those beginning to have bad relationships often go beyond their decided limit.

4. When I find I'm not getting the effects I want, do I take a break from using _____?

☒ **YES**
☐ **NO**
People in good relationship with a drug realize that too much of a good thing can be bad. If they aren't getting the effects they want, they stop for a while. Those who begin to have problems tend to use more of the drug, more frequently, in an attempt to regain the lost pleasure.

5. Do I find it easy to stop using _____ whenever I want?

☒ **YES**
☐ **NO**
People in good relationship with a drug can take it or leave it. They find that they frequently leave it, even when the drug is readily available. Those in bad relationship have trouble stopping when they want and have great difficulty turning down the drug when it is offered.

6. When I'm not using _____, do I feel comfortable?

☒ **YES**
☐ **NO**
When we're in good relationship, we naturally have periods when we don't use the drug and feel fine. People who begin to have bad relationships notice that they have to make a conscious effort to cut back and are often uncomfortable when they're not using.

7. Are my family and friends in good relationship with ____?

☒ **YES**
☐ **NO**
Those with one or more family members or friends who have had problems are much more likely to have problems themselves.

8. Do those who know me well think I am in good relationship with the _____ that I use?

☒ **YES**
☐ **NO**
Those who are in good relationship are never questioned about their drug use. People who are beginning to get into trouble may hear it first from others. "Maybe you ought to slow down," or similar comments, may indicate that others are beginning to see a problem developing.

9. Do I have rules about when and when not to use _____?

☒ **YES**
☐ **NO**
Those in good relationship rarely think consciously about when to use. They have a "body sense" of what's right for them. When they do think consciously about it, they easily follow their own rules. Those beginning to have bad relationships have lost their inner controls and find it difficult to consistently follow their own rules.

10. Am I open and comfortable with others about my use of ____?

☒ **YES**
☐ **NO**
People in good relationship with drugs are quite open and comfortable with others when they are using. Those beginning to have problems feel uncomfortable about letting others see how much or how often they use. They begin to hide the truth.

11. Do I often celebrate good times and deal with bad times without _____?

☐ **YES**
☒ **NO**
Although celebrations can be times for using a drug, people in good relationship often celebrate without it. When they're anxious, depressed, or lonely, they may talk it out, meditate, or run. Those beginning to get into bad relationship find that good times and bad times are most often associated with the use of the drug.

12. Am I free from adverse effects on my health and well-being?

☐ **YES**
☐ **NO**
People in good relationship with drugs rarely, if ever, experience damage to their physical, psychological, social, or spiritual health and well-being. Those in bad relationship begin to notice adverse effects, but find that they continue to use despite these effects.

IF you honestly answered "yes" to the 12 questions listed, you are probably in good relationship with drugs. If you answered "no" to one or more questions, you might want to talk with an expert about your relationship. Since relationships often change over time, you may want to answer the questions again in six months.

WINE AND WINOS: THE MISERY MARKET

Winos are a major embarrassment to big companies producing the cheap wines bought by down-and-out drunks.

Alix M. Freedman

In the dim light of a cold February morning, a grizzled wino shuffles into the Bowery Discount liquor store muttering, "Thunderchicken, it's good lickin'." Fumbling for some change, he says: "Gimme one bird." Raymond Caba, the store clerk, understands the argot and hands over a $1.40 pint of Thunderbird, the top seller in what he calls "the bum section."

The ritual is repeated a thousand times a day in dead-end neighborhoods across the country. Cheap wines with down-and-dirty names—and an extra measure of alcohol—are the beverage of choice among down-and-out drunks. But winos are an embarrassment to the big companies that manufacture these wines. With rare exceptions, they aren't eager to acknowledge their own products.

Thunderbird and Night Train Express are produced by the nation's largest wine company, E. & J. Gallo Winery, though you'll not learn that from reading the label on the bottle. MD 20/20 is made by Mogen David Wine Corporation, a subsidiary of Wine Group Limited, which refuses to talk about its product. Richards Wild Irish Rose Wine, the very best seller in the category, is produced by Canandaigua Wine Company. Canandaigua is volubly proud of the wine but quick to point out that it enjoys wide popularity with people who aren't alcoholics.

The Biggest Bang

People concerned about the plight of street alcoholics are critical of the purveyors of dollar-a-pint street wines made with cheap ingredients and fortified with alcohol to deliver the biggest bang for the buck. At 18 percent to 21 percent alcohol, these wines have about twice the kick of ordinary table wine, without any of the pretension.

The consumption of alcohol in the United States *is* declining in virtually every category, but the best-selling of the low-end brands keep growing, in large part because customers can't stop drinking. Says Paul Gillette, the publisher of the *Wine Investor* in Los Angeles: "Makers of skid-row wines are the dope pushers of the wine industry."

Vintners generally try hard to filter their wines through the imagery of luxury and moderation, stressing vintage, touting quality. So they are understandably reluctant to be associated in any way with what some call a $500 million misery market.

Suppliers deny that the most popular street wines sell as well as they do because they appeal to dirt-poor, hard-core drinkers. Companies contend that their clientele is not like that at all, and besides, any alcoholic beverage can be abused. The wine people say they face stiff competition from high-alcohol malt liquor and 200-milliliter bottles of cheap vodka. The future for the high-proof business, vintners say, isn't particularly rosy in any case. The wine category they call "dessert" or "fortified"—sweet wines with at least 14 percent alcohol—has lost favor with drinkers.

Markedly Profitable

Wino wines are inexpensive to produce. They come in no-frills, screwtop packaging and require little or no advertising. Although they generally aren't the major part of vintners' product lineups, they are especially profitable. All told, net profit margins are 10 percent higher than those of ordinary table wines, Canandaigua estimates. Gallo says that isn't true for its products, but it won't say what is true.

The wines are also a rock-solid business. Of all the wine brands in America, the trade newsletter *Impact* says, Wild Irish Rose holds the No. 6 spot, Thunderbird is 10th, and MD 20/20 is 16th. In contrast to the lackluster growth of most other wine brands, unit sales of the leading cheap labels, Wild Irish Rose and Thunderbird, are expected to be up 9.9 percent and 8.6 percent respectively this year, *Jobson's Wine Marketing Handbook* estimates.

So unsavory is this market that companies go to great lengths to distance themselves from their customers. If suppliers are willing to talk about the segment—and few are—they still don't acknowledge the winos' loyal patronage. Gallo and Canandaigua leave their good corporate names off the labels, thus obscuring the link between product and producer.

The "No-Name Market"

"This is the market with no name," says Clifford Adelson, a former executive director of sales at Manischewitz Wine Company, which once made low-end wines. It was recently acquired by Canandaigua. "It's lots and lots of money, but it doesn't add prestige."

Cheap wines typically aren't even sold in many liquor stores. For instance, Frank Gaudio, who owns the big Buy-Rite Twin Towers Wine & Spirits store in New York's World Trade Center, doesn't stock any of these brands, though many homeless alcoholics spend their days just outside his door. "We don't want that clientele in our store," he says. "We could sell [fortified wines] and probably make money, but we don't." The wines, however, are staples of the bullet-proof liquor stores of low-income neighborhoods. Although you can't say the whole market for items like Thunderbird and Night Train consists of derelicts, down-and-outers do seem to be its lifeblood. Fifty current and reformed drinkers interviewed for this article claim to have lived on a gallon a day or more of the stuff.

"The industry is manufacturing this for a select population: the poor, the homeless, the skid-row individual," says Neil Goldman, the chief of the alcoholism unit at St. Vincent's Hospital in Manhattan's Greenwich Village.

• • •

Dawn finds a small bottle gang near the Bowery, chasing away the morning shakes with a bottle of Thunderbird they pass from hand to hand. Mel Downing tugs up the pant leg of his filthy jeans to reveal an oozing infection on his knee. He is drinking, he says, to numb the pain of this "wine sore" and other ones on his back before he goes to the hospital later in the morning. "We're used to this stuff," the 39-year-old Mr. Downing quickly adds. "We like the effect. We like the price."

A cheap drunk is the main appeal

of the wines that winos call "grape" or "jug," but most often just "cheap." Winos say that these wines, even when consumed in quantity, don't make them pass out as readily as hard liquor would.

Walter Single, a recovering alcoholic, recalls that on a daily diet of nine pints of Wild Irish Rose, he was still able "to function well enough to panhandle the money he needed to drink all day and still have enough left for a wake-up in the morning."

Obviating the Need to Eat

Some drinkers say the high sugar content of the wines reduces their appetite for food, so they don't have to eat much. Others say they can still drink wine even after their livers are too far gone to handle spirits. Still others appreciate the portability of pint bottles.

"I feel more secure with a pint," explains Teddy Druzinski, a former carpenter. "It's next to me. It's in my pocket." Canandaigua estimates that low-end brands account for 13 million gallons of the dessert category's 55 million gallons and that 50 percent is purchased in pints.

Many people in the wine industry eschew producing skid-row wines. "I don't think Christian Brothers should be in a category where people are down on their luck—where some may be alcoholics," says Richard Maher, the president of Christian Brothers Winery in St. Helena, California. Mr. Maher, who once was with Gallo, says fortified wines lack "any socially redeeming values."

"The consumers are we alcoholics," agrees Patrick Gonzales, a 45-year-old wino who is undergoing a week of detoxification at a men's shelter on New York's Lower East Side. "You don't see no one sitting at home sipping Mad Dog [MD 20/20] in a wine glass over ice."

Major producers see their customers otherwise. Robert Huntington, the vice president of strategic planning at Canandaigua, says the Canandaigua, New York, company sells 60 percent to 75 percent of its "pure grape" Wild Irish Rose in primarily black, inner-city markets. He describes customers as "not super-sophisticated," lower middle-class and low-income blue-collar workers, mostly men.

Daniel Solomon, a Gallo spokes-

man, maintains that Thunderbird "has lost its former popularity in the black and skid-row areas" and is quaffed mainly by "retired and older folks who don't like the taste of hard products."

According to accounts that Gallo disputes, the company revolutionized the skid-row market in the 1950s after discovering that liquor stores in Oakland, California, were catering to the tastes of certain customers by attaching packages of lemon Kool-Aid to bottles of white wine. Customers did their own mixing at home. The story goes that Gallo, borrowing the idea, created citrus-flavored Thunderbird. Other flavored high-proof wines then surged into the marketplace. Among them: Twister, Bali Hai, Hombre, Silver Satin, and Gypsy Rose. Gallo says that the Kool-Aid story is "a nice myth" but that Thunderbird was "developed by our wine makers in our laboratories."

"Thunderbird Princess"

Vintners advertised heavily and sought to induce skid row's opinion leaders—nicknamed "bell cows"—to switch brands by plying them with free samples. According to Arthur Palombo, the chairman of Cannon Wines Limited and one of Gallo's marketing men in the 1950s and '60s, "These were clandestine promotions." He doesn't say which companies engaged in the practice.

Today, such practices and most brands have long since died out. Companies now resort to standard point-of-sale promotions and, in the case of Canandaigua, some radio and TV advertising. There is still an occasional bit of hoopla. In New Jersey, Gallo recently named a Thunderbird Princess, and Canandaigua is currently holding a Miss Wild Irish Rose contest. But to hear distributors tell it, word of mouth remains the main marketing tool.

The market is hard to reach through conventional media. Winos will drink anything if need be, but when they have the money to buy what they want they tend to hew to the familiar. (Sales resistance may help explain why the handful of low-end products that companies have tried to launch in the past 20 years have mostly bombed.) Besides, "it would be difficult to come up with an advertising campaign that says this will go down smoother, get you drunker, and help you panhandle better," says Robert Williams, a reformed alcoholic and a counselor at the Manhattan Bowery Corporation's Project Renewal, a halfway house for Bowery alcoholics.

Companies see no reason to spend a lot of money promoting brands they don't want to be identified with. "Gallo and ourselves have been trying to convey the image of a company that makes fine products," says Hal Riney, the president of Hal Riney & Partners, which created the TV characters Frank Bartles and Ed Jaymes for Gallo's wine cooler. "It would be counterproductive to advertise products like this."

Richards Wild Irish Rose purports to be made by Richards Wine Company. The label on a bottle of Gallo's Night Train reads, "Vinted & bottled by Night Train Limited, Modesto, Ca." Gallo's spokesman, Mr. Solomon, says, "The Gallo name is reserved for traditional [table] wines."

Industry people chime in that it isn't at all uncommon for companies to do business under a variety of monikers. But they also agree with Cannon's Mr. Palombo: "Major wine producers don't want to be associated with a segment of the industry that is determined to be low-end and alcoholic."

Winos have their own names for what they buy, Gallo's appellations notwithstanding. When they go to buy Night Train, they might say, "Gimme a ticket." They call Thunderbird "pluck," "T-Bird," or "chicken." In street lingo, Richards Wild Irish Rose is known as "Red Lady," and MD 20/20 is "Mad Dog."

Getting Through Sundays

If skid-row wines are cheap to market, they are even cheaper to make. They are generally concocted by adding flavors, sugar, and high-proof grape-based neutral spirits to a base wine. The wine part is produced from the cheapest grapes available. Needless to say, the stuff never sees the inside of an oak barrel.

"They dip a grape in it so they can say it's made of wine," says Dickie Gronan, a 67-year-old who describes himself as a bum. "But it's laced with something to make you thirstier." Sugar probably. In any event, customers keep on swigging. Some are so hooked that they immediately turn to an underground distribution system on Sundays and at other times when liquor stores are closed. "Bootleggers," often other alcoholics, buy cheap brands at retail and resell them at twice the price. The street shorthand for such round-the-clock consumption is "24–7."

At nightfall, Mel Downing, the member of the bottle gang with the leg infection, is panhandling off the Bowery "to make me another jug," as he puts it. As his shredded parka attests, he got into a fight earlier in the day with his buddy, Teddy Druzinski, who then disappeared. Mr. Downing also got too drunk to make it that day, as planned, to the hospital for treatment of his "wine sores."

A short while later, Mr. Druzinski emerges from the shadows. He has a bloodied face because he "took another header," which is to say he fell on his head. Nevertheless, in the freezing darkness, he joins his partner at begging once again.

"I'm feeling sick to my stomach, dizzy, and mokus," Mr. Downing says. "But I still want another pint." He scans the deserted street and adds: "Another bottle is the biggest worry on our minds."

A Male Problem?

Substance Abuse Among Women Is Less Than Among Men—and It's Almost Always Alcohol

Wendy Olson
Special to The Times

At the height of her career on the Ladies Professional Golf Assn. tour, between 1964 and 1975, Carol Mann won 38 tournaments. The 6-foot 3-inch blonde from Maryland was known for her powerful swing, strong irons and knack for winning.

What the LPGA and Women's Sports Foundation Hall of Famer was never known for was her problem with alcohol and amphetamines.

As a child of alcoholic parents, she was already a strong risk to have her own drinking problem. As a top golfer, she used alcohol in her celebrations, to relieve the loneliness of the women's tour and to escape her own failings.

"I used alcohol as a relaxer and an escape from my own performance," Mann said. "I celebrated victory with it. When I won my first tournament, I popped every cork on a few cases of champagne for the media. I used it for joy as well as pain. Usually, when I didn't do well, my habit was to have some beer."

Mann has been a recovering alcoholic since her mother was admitted to the Betty Ford Clinic in 1981, where Mann discovered her own problem with alcohol.

"They had family week there, and when I went to family week, I thought I was going to discuss my mother's problem," Mann said. "But the facts are, I went to learn about me and how I have responded to the illness . . . I have not used alcohol for about 10 years, nor do I intend to.

"When I was trying to become successful early in my career, the first seven years, there was a lot of pain of failure. While that pain was significant, I really used it as a motivator. I was willing to keep [working on my game] more so I wouldn't keep being in pain. When I started being more successful, I started taking pills, am-

> *"When I was trying to become successful early in my career, the first seven years, there was a lot of pain of failure. While that pain was significant, I really used it as a motivator. I was willing to keep [working on my game] more so I wouldn't keep being in pain. When I started being more successful, I started taking amphetamines, although that was only for a short period."*
>
> —Carol Mann

phetamines, although that was only for a short period."

The list of male athletes whose lives and playing careers have been marred by drug and alcohol abuse is long. Former Maryland basketball star Len Bias, former Houston Rockets guard Lewis Lloyd and New York Giants linebacker Lawrence Taylor stand out from the last 15 months, and drug violators detected in the recent Pan American Games were men. Mann stands virtually alone as a top woman athlete who has had drug or alcohol problems.

From all appearances, the use of chemical substances—recreational and performance-enhancing drugs and alcohol—by female athletes is neither as prevalent nor as widely known as the use of chemical substances by male athletes.

"Frankly, for me as a women's athletic director, the use of drugs in women's sports is not a major concern," said Judith Holland, women's athletic director at UCLA.

"There are too many other things I have to be concerned about that are more pressing problems."

Holland said that among the 17- to 23-year-old female athletes she deals with, eating disorders are a more pertinent problem.

"The woman in athletics is basically invisible," she said. "I suppose in some cases, particularly when you read about so many [male] athletes' drug problems, that's good."

Although there are no reliable statistics comparing drug use among female athletes to drug use among male athletes, many involved in drug testing and women's athletics hold that although drug use among women athletes exists, it is not nearly as extensive as among male athletes.

Of 273 women athletes surveyed in a study done by Hazelden-Cork, a chemical abuse clinic in Minneapolis, with the cooperation of the Women's Sports Foundation, almost all reported having used alcohol at some point, 76% used alcohol in the last 30 days, and more than 90% reported that they have never used cocaine or marijuana. Only 1% reported using cocaine more than once, and none reported using anabolic steroids.

Results from the study, which were released in July, included responses from professional and amateur, retired and active female athletes. The study is the first attempt to paint a broad picture of chemical abuse among female athletes.

Dr. Robert Murphy, the outgoing chairman of the National Collegiate Athletic Assn.'s drug education committee and a member of the drug-testing committee at Ohio State University, said that in the three years Ohio State has administered three-times yearly drug tests to its athletes, no female athlete has tested positive. Among male athletes, the positive test response has dropped from 8% in the first year to 5% in the second and 2% in the third.

"Although in our experience there appears to be less use among women than among men, we think that when we test more frequently, we will get a similar pattern of use among women [as among men], but about half the incidence," Murphy said. "I think that as time goes on, we'll find some [drug] use among women, but not as much as the men."

The relative absence of drug use among female athletes apparently hinges mainly on the status of women's athletics and the professional athletic opportunities open to women. Most female athletes do not have the economic wherewithal to be frequent drug users.

"There's simply not a lot of money involved with [women's athletics]," Holland said. "I think money, in a lot of ways, is the root of all evil. Although I'd like to see the [money] become more fair and more equitable, in this case maybe it's good for women athletes."

Cheryl Miller, the All-American women's basketball player and Olympic gold medalist from USC, said that in her playing years she didn't notice any chemical abuse among female athletes.

"I think anytime there is a lot of drug abuse, it probably affects women as well," Miller said. "But I don't think it's as much of a problem as in men's sports. I think [one of the reasons male athletes have more problems] is that it's more available to men. In the professional ranks, you can afford drugs. Not too many women can afford it.

"Most women feel like you aren't going to have a professional athletic career. We're looking out for what our other career will be."

Only in tennis and golf can women pursue lucrative professional careers. But tennis and golf have never been known for having players with chemical-abuse problems. Whereas professional football, basketball and baseball teams have drug testing and drug-counseling programs and hardly a day goes by without a report of an athlete in those sports being involved in a drug- or alcohol-related incident, professional golf and tennis are relatively clean.

"There's sort of an end to women's athletics at the college level," said Dr. John Lombardo, a sports medicine specialist at the Cleveland Clinic in Ohio who works with the Inner Circle, the drug-counseling program of the National Football League's Cleveland Browns. "There's not much for women professionally. The high-risk sports are football, basketball, baseball and hockey, where there's a great deal of money involved. Players in these sports seem to have more temptation, more access to drugs.

"As far as women athletes at the high school and college level, there is still a different drive for playing the sport. For men, there's the added carrot of the professional career. Women know that's not their life. The sport is a big part of their life, but they have a different attitude toward playing the game. They always play because they like it. There's not the extra lure of money."

The professional organizations in women's golf and tennis don't perceive any kind of drug problem among their athletes. The LPGA currently has no drug-counseling or drug-education program, but the Women's International Tennis Assn. is instituting a series of drug-education seminars.

Merrett R. Stierheim, WITA executive director, said the seminars will be mandatory and that drug testing is under review by the association's board of directors and medical committee, but no decision will be made immediately.

Trish Falkner, a player services representative for the WITA, said the drug education seminars are aimed at preventing a chemical abuse problem from surfacing on the women's professional tour.

"We really think, looking at our staff and our trainer and the contact they have with the players, we would know if any of our players are drug users," Falkner said. "We just know we don't have a problem. That's not to say that down the line at some point we won't, with all of the pressure society is putting on us. We're not ignoring the possibility of a problem in the future, we're just not in any great hurry."

In her 1986 autobiographical account of life on the women's tennis tour, Pam Shriver said that women tennis players were too "cheap" to buy drugs.

Although part tongue-in-cheek, Shriver's statement captures the difference between individual sports, such as golf and tennis, and team sports, such as football and baseball. In individual sports, an athlete's playing income depends on his or her performance at each event, but in team sports, an athlete's playing income is based on a contract, which may be supplemented by individual performance incentives.

Chris Evert, who is WITA president and active in Nancy Reagan's "Just Say No" anti-drug program, said she is supportive of the approach the WITA is taking.

"Our emphasis as an association is on education," she said. "We don't feel there is a problem."

The primary figures involved in the Hazelden study — Karla Hill-Donisch of Hazelden, Deborah Anderson, executive director of the WSF, and Mann, president of the WSF, also say they believe that education is the best route to take with women athletes.

"I think that the results didn't really surprise us at all," Hill-Donisch said. "There are not a lot of women [athletes] who are substance abusers. But I think that women are looking for more information on women and chemical abuse, that came out loud and clear."

Eighty-six percent of the respondents said they wanted more information on women and chemical abuse.

Although Anderson said she views the results as good news, she also said that there is no room for complacency in dealing with the chemical dependency of female athletes. Barbara Hedges, women's athletic director at USC, agrees.

"I think the problems that have occurred have focused on the male athletes, but I don't see a big difference in the orientation between men and women that would lead to drug use only among men," Hedges said.

"It would be presumptuous to say women don't have the problems men do. We should continue to be vigilant. The media is not out of line in being vigilant. I see our testing program, the other collegiate testing programs and NCAA testing as a positive step, but we can't sit back and rest on the fact we've been successful."

And as Mann points out, women in general and female athletes are more likely to have problems with legally obtained prescription drugs and alcohol than recreational drugs, such as cocaine and marijuana.

Mann said she is out of touch now with what chemical abuse programs might exist on the LPGA tour — the drug and alcohol problms of golfer Muffin Spencer-Devlin were linked to her mood swings triggered by sugar imbalance and were treated by a Santa Barbara nutritionist before she even qualified for the LPGA tour. But Mann said she hopes that more female athletes will look at their own alcohol and drug behavior problems as the Hazelden study receives more attention.

"I've had to broaden my scope," Mann said. "I feel I have a responsibility to the whole of women's sports. The main thing that [the WSF] wanted to do with co-sponsoring the event at Hazelden was to open up the topic so that more and more women athletes would take a look at their behaviors, and it has occurred and it will occur."

Alcohol and the Family

The children of problem drinkers are coming to grips with their feelings of fear, guilt and rage

Believe it or not, there are still people who think that the worst thing about drinking is a hangover.

Oh, yeah, on New Year's Day I had a hangover that...

No. Forget hangovers.

Huh? So what should we talk about? Cirrhosis?

If you wish, but the liver, with its amazing powers of regeneration, usually lasts longer than the spouse, who tends to fall apart relatively early in the drinker's decline.

You're making it hard for a man to drink in peace.

Sorry, but even if spouses do not abuse alcohol, they can come to resemble drunks, since their anger and fear are enormous: way beyond what you'd find in a truly sober person.

I know, I know, it's terrible what goes on behind closed doors.

You make it sound like there are no witnesses. You're forgetting the children. They grow up watching one out-of-control person trying to control another, and they don't know what "normal" is.

I suppose it's hard for the kids, until they move out.

They may move out, but they never leave their parents behind.

Hmm. Listen, can we talk?

We already are. A lot of people already are.

We are, just now, learning more about heavy drinking, and, simultaneously, putting behind us the notion that what alcoholism amounts to is just odd intervals of strange, and sometimes comic, behavior: W. C. Fields, Dean Martin, Foster Brooks. Since 1935 the members of

Alcoholics Anonymous have been telling us, with awesome simplicity, that drinking made their lives unmanageable; Al-Anon brought us the news that relatives and friends of drinkers can suffer in harmony; and then came Alateen and even Alatot, where one picture of a stick person holding a beer can is worth a thousand slurred words. The Children of Alcoholics (COAs)—loosely organized but rapidly growing throughout the United States—reaffirm all of the previous grass-roots movements and bring us new insight into alcoholism's effects on the more than 28 million Americans who have seen at least one parent in the throes of the affliction. The bad news from COAs: alcohol is even more insidious than previously thought.

The good news: with the right kind of help, the terrible damage it does to nonalcoholics need not be permanent.

Imagine a child who lives in a chaotic house, rides around with a drunk driver and has no one to talk to about the terror. Don't think it doesn't happen: more than 10 million people in the United States are addicted to alcohol, and most of them have children. "I grew up in a little Vietnam," says one child of an alcoholic. "I didn't know why I was there; I didn't know who the enemy was." Decades after their parents die, children of alcoholics can find it difficult to have intimate relationships ("You learn to trust no one") or experience joy ("I hid in the closet"). They are haunted—sometimes despite worldwide acclaim, as in the case of

There's a Problem in the House

In "Adult Children of Alcoholics," Janet Geringer Woititz discusses 13 traits that most children from alcoholic households experience to some degree. These symptoms, she says, can pose lifelong problems.

Adult children of alcoholics . . .

- guess what normal behavior is.
- have difficulty following a project from beginning to end.
- lie when it would be just as easy to tell the truth.
- judge themselves without mercy.
- have difficulty having fun.
- take themselves very seriously.
- have difficulty with intimate relationships.
- overreact to changes over which they have no control.

- constantly seek approval and affirmation.
- feel that they are different from other people.
- are super-responsible or super-irresponsible.
- are extremely loyal, even in the face of evidence that the loyalty is undeserved.
- tend to lock themselves into a course of action without giving consideration to consequences.

artist Eric Fischl—by a sense of failure for not having saved Mommy or Daddy from drink. And they are prone to marry alcoholics or other severely troubled people because, for one reason, they're willing to accept unacceptable behavior. Many, indeed, have become addicted to domestic turmoil.

'Hurting so bad': Children of alcoholics are people who've been robbed of their childhood—"I've seen five-year-olds running entire families," says Janet Geringer Woititz, one of the movement's founding mothers. Nevertheless, the children of alcoholics often display a kind of childish loyalty even when such loyalty is clearly undeserved. They have a nagging feeling that they are different from other people, Woititz points out, and that may be because, as some recent scientific studies show, they are. Brain scans done by Dr. Henri Begleiter of the State University of New York College of Medicine in Brooklyn reveal that COAs often have deficiencies in the areas of the brain associated with emotion and memory. In this sense and in several other ways—their often obsessive personalities, their tendency to have a poor self-image—the children of alcoholics closely resemble alcoholics. In fact, one in four becomes an alcoholic, as compared with one in 10 out of the general population.

The anger of a COA cannot be seen by brain scans. But at a therapy session at Caron Family Services in Wernersville, Pa., Ken Gill, a 49-year-old IBM salesman, recently took a padded bat and walloped a couch cushion hard enough to wake up sleeping demons. "I came because I was hurting so bad and I didn't know why," he says. "A lot of things were going wrong. I was a workaholic, and I neglected my family." It took Gill only a few hours of exposure to the idea that he might be an "adult child," he says, to realize that his failings as a parent may be if not excused, then at least explained. Like a lot of kids who grew up in an alcoholic household, Gill, who is also a recovering alcoholic, never got what even rats and monkeys get: exposure, at an impressionable age, to the sight and sound of functioning parents. Suzanne Somers, the actress and singer, spent years working out her anger in the form of a just published book called "Keeping Secrets." "I decided that this disease took the first half of my life, and goddam it," she says, "it wasn't going to take the second half of it."

'Control freak': Not every COA has all of the 13 traits (see chart) ascribed to them by Woititz in her landmark work, "Adult Children of Alcoholics" (*1983. Health Communications, Inc.*), and not all have been scarred. (President Reagan, who has written of sometimes finding his father passed out drunk on the front porch, does not appear, from his famous management style, to suffer from any tendency to be a "control freak," a

COURTESY CLAUDIA BLACK

■ A nine-year-old's nightmare: Living in denial

most common COA complaint.) Some children of alcoholics are grossly overweight from compulsive eating while others are as dressed for success as, well, Somers. A few COAs are immobilized by depression. Another runs TV's "Old Time Gospel Hour." What these people *do* have in common is a basic agreement with George Vaillant, a Dartmouth Medical School professor who says that it is important to think of alcoholism not as an illness that affects bodily organs but as "an illness that affects families. Perhaps the worst single feature of alcoholism," Vaillant adds, "is that it causes people to be unreasonably angry at the people that they most love."

The movement is only about six years old, but expanding so rapidly that figures, could they be gathered for such a basically unstructured and anonymous group, would be outdated as soon as they appeared. We do know, though, that five years ago there were 21 people in an organization called the National Association for Children of Alcoholics; today there are more than 7,000. The 14 Al-Anon-affiliated children-of-alcoholics groups meeting in the early '80s have increased to 1,100. With only word-of-mouth advertising, Woititz's book has sold about a million copies; indeed, "Adult Children of Alcoholics" reached the number-three spot on The New York Times paperback best-seller list long before it was available in any bookstore—at a time, in other words, when getting a copy meant

collaring a clerk to put in an order and *saying the title out loud.*

"We turned on the phones in 1982," says Migs Woodside, founder and president of the Children of Alcoholics Foundation in New York, "and the calls are still coming in 24 hours a day." The COAs Foundation sponsors a traveling art show that features the work of young and adult COAs; often, says Woodside, an attendee will stand mesmerized before a crude depiction of domestic violence or parental apathy ("Mom at noon," it says beneath the picture of someone huddling beneath the bedcovers)—and will then go directly to a pay phone to find help. "The newcomers all tend to say the same thing," says Woodside. '"Wait a minute—that's my story, that's *me!*'"

"It's private pain transformed into a public statement," says James Garbarino, president of the Erikson Institute for Advanced Study in Child Development, in Chicago, "a fascinating movement." But when you consider that denial is the primary symptom of alcoholism and that COAs tend by nature to take on more than their share of blame for whatever mess they happen to find themselves in, the rapid growth of the COAs movement seems just short of miraculous—something akin to a drunken stockbroker named Bill Wilson cofounding AA, now *the* model for a vast majority of self-help programs throughout the United States. After all, who would want to spill the family's darkest secret after years of telling teachers, employers and friends that everything was fine? ("A child of an alcoholic will always say 'Fine'," says Ro-kelle Lerner, a counselor who specializes in young COAs. "They get punished if they say otherwise.") Who would voluntarily identify themselves with a group whose female members, according to some reports, have an above-average number of gynecological problems, possibly due to stress—and whose men are prone to frequent surgery for problems, doctors say, that may be basically psychosomatic?

The answer is, only someone who had, in some sense, bottomed out, just the way a drinker does before he turns to AA.

The concept of codependency is at the center of the COAs movement. Eleanor Williams, who works with COAs at the Charter Peachford Hospital in Atlanta, defines codependency as "unconscious addiction to another person's dysfunctional behavior." Woititz, in a recent Changes magazine interview, referred to it more simply as a tendency to "put other people's needs before my own." A codependent family member may suspect that he has driven the alcoholic to drink (though that is impossible, according to virtually all experts in the field); he almost certainly thinks that he can cure or at least control the drinker's troublesome behavior. "I actually thought that I could make a difference by cooking my husband better meals and by taking the kids out for drives on weekends [so he could rest]," says Ella S., a Westchester, N.Y., woman. "For all I know, it's a deeply ingrained psychological, and possibly genetic, disease, and here I am going at it with a lamb chop."

Mental movies: Obsessed with her husband's increasingly self-destructive behavior, Ella's next step, in typical codependent fashion, was to hide Bob's six-packs, which made him, to put it mildly, angry. Soon they were fighting almost daily and Ella was running mental movies of their scenes from a marriage all night long. "I was wasting a lot of time and energy trying to change the past, while he kept getting worse," she says. "There was a kind of awkward violence between him and me all the time; our hearts weren't really in it, but it wasn't until he had an affair with an alcoholism counselor *that I got him to* that I left." If you're wondering about children, Ella has a seven-year-old daughter, Ann. Her omission is significant. If life were a horse race, then Ann has been, as they say on the past performance charts, "shuffled back" among the also-rans.

What COAs—all people affected by alcohol—need to learn is that the race is fixed: when there is no program of recovery—either through the support of a group or the self-imposed abstinence of an individual—the abused substance will always win, handily, no matter what the competition. The first step of AA begins, "We admitted we were powerless . . ." But what will become of Ann, who is codependent on *two*

COURTESY CHILDREN OF ALCOHOLICS FOUNDATION

■ The fighting never stops: Living with fear

people? Perhaps, sensing that she is not exactly the center of attention, she will reach adulthood with a need for constant approval, a common COA symptom. Or maybe she will, even as a child, react to the chaos by trying to keep everything in her life under control, and thus give the impression that she is, despite everything, quite a trouper, a golden child.

"[Some] don't fall apart until they're in their 20s or 30s," says Woititz, and in some cases, especially those marked by violence or incest and sexual abuse (three times more common in alcoholic households than in the general population), that's the wonder of it all. One eight-year-old patient at Woititz's Verona, N.J., counseling center

woke up in the middle of the night to see her alcoholic mother shoot herself in the head. "The child called the 911 emergency number, got her mother to the hospital and basically saved her mother's life," says Woititz. "When I saw her she was having nightmares—that she wouldn't wake up and witness this suicide attempt. This is not a normal nightmare. The child had become mother to her own mother."

Each unhappy family, as Tolstoy said, is unhappy in its own way. Artist Eric Fischl, 39, in a short videotape he made for the COAs Foundation called "Trying to Find Normal," speaks of stepping over his passed-out mother, in their comfortable-looking (from the outside) Port Washing-

COURTESY CHILDREN OF ALCOHOLICS FOUNDATION

■ Out of control: Remembering hurts

Heredity and Drinking: How Strong Is the Link?

Research on the genetics of alcoholism took a curious turn a few weeks ago when Lawrence Lumeng analyzed his DNA to demonstrate why he can't tolerate liquor. Lumeng, a biochemist at the Indiana University School of Medicine, is among the 30 to 45 percent of Asians whose response to spirited beverages is a reddened face, headaches or nausea. This "Oriental flush," past studies have shown, arises in those who have an inefficient version of a liver enzyme that is crucial to the body's breakdown of alcohol; this "lazy" enzyme allows the buildup of an alcohol product, acetaldehyde, which is sickening and leads many Asians to shun alcohol. Working with biochemist Ting-Kai Li, Lumeng says that he pinpointed the gene that instructs cells to make the odd enzyme. The experiment offers dramatic evidence that a bodily response to alcohol is genetically dictated—and is thus inherited as surely as eye color.

There is no evidence for the opposite proposition: that a specific gene makes a person *crave* alcohol. Considering the wide variety of reasons why people consume the stuff, it seems unlikely that a "drinking gene" exists. But researchers have firmly established that, compared with other children, an alcoholic's offspring are around four times more likely to develop the problem, even if they were raised by other, nonalcoholic parents. In families with a history of alcoholism, explains C. Robert Cloninger, a psychiatrist and geneticist at Washington University in St. Louis, "what is inherited is not the fact that you are destined to become an alcoholic but varying degrees of susceptibility" to the disorder. So real is the predisposition that many researchers advise adult children of alcoholics (COAs) to drink no alcohol whatsoever.

Even the brains of COAs show faint signs of unusual activity, according to controversial studies by psychiatrist Henri Begleiter of the State University of New York in Brooklyn. Begleiter has found that young boys who have never consumed alcohol produce the slightly distorted brainwave patterns typical of their alcoholic fathers. Such signature brain waves, he says, may mark the son of an alcoholic as likely to develop a drinking problem and perhaps alert him to the risk. However, it remains to be seen whether such brain scans are sufficiently reliable and informative to distinguish potential social drinkers from future alcoholics. The technique,

comments psychologist Robert Pandina, scientific director of the Center of Alcohol Studies at Rutgers University, is "at this time not any more valuable" as a predictor of future drinking behavior "than collecting a good family history on an individual."

Other studies show that many COAs respond uniquely to booze. Marc Schuckit, a psychiatrist at the Veterans Administration Hospital in San Diego, has found that college-age sons of alcoholics often react less to a few drinks than other college men; in his studies, the drinkers' sons were generally not as euphoric or tipsy after three to five cocktails. Schuckit believes that this lower sensitivity makes it harder for the alcoholics' sons to know when to stop drinking, starting them down the road to alcohol problems. Preliminary experiments by Barbara Lex of McLean Hospital in Belmont, Mass., confirm that daughters of alcoholics respond similarly. Women from families with a history of alcohol abuse tend to keep their balance better on a wobbly platform after having a drink. Apparently women, too, can inherit traits that might predispose them to addiction, although there are far fewer female than male alcoholics.

Half a beer: The key unre-

solved issue, of course, is why some individuals from alcohol-scarred families succumb to alcoholism while others don't. Genes play some role in the development, most notably in abstinence. "People say that whether you drink or not has to do only with willpower," explains Indiana's Lumeng, "but the reason I can drink only half a beer is biological."

Yet heredity alone obviously isn't to blame for alcoholism's appalling toll. In fact, about 60 percent of the nation's alcohol abusers are from families with *no* history of the disorder. How much people drink is influenced by factors as prosaic as cost; partly to curb consumption, the National Council on Alcoholism is lobbying to raise federal excise taxes on beer and wine, which haven't changed since 1951. Social influences like cost and peer pressure "are just as important as genes," says Dartmouth psychiatrist George Vaillant. "All the genes do is make it easier for you to become an alcoholic." For now, the value of genetic studies is to warn COAs that they may well have a real handicap in the struggle against the family trouble.

TERENCE MONMANEY *with* KAREN SPRINGEN *in New York and* MARY HAGER *in Washington*

---

ton, N.Y., home and seeing her "lying in her own piss." His work, which has been the subject of a one-man show at the Whitney Museum in New York, is not autobiographical, he says, and yet "the tone [of it] has everything to do with my childhood." His painting "Time for Bed" "relates to my memory of all hell breaking loose," he says. "I guess you could say the boy is me and his shame, embarrassment and sadness is mine as well. The little boy's Superman pajamas are on backwards, so it's like looking in a mirror. I painted the woman standing on a glass table with spiked heels on to give it a sense of fragility and danger. The man only has one arm because I wanted a sense of impotence."

Alcohol leaves every alcoholic and codependent who does not admit his powerlessness over the substance in a constant state of longing. Fischl didn't realize how sad he'd been until his mother died, in an alcohol-related car accident, in 1970. "The thing about having a sick parent is that you think it's your problem," he says. "You feel like a failure because you can't save her." Even when there is no incest, there is seduction. Fischl's mother kept "signaling," he says, "that if you could just come a little bit further with me in this, you can save me."

Some of the other things that alcohol ruins, before it gets to the liver: family

meals ("Alcohol fills you up. My father was never interested in eating with us"); gloriously run-of-the-mill evenings around the hearth ("Alcohol makes you tired. My father was in bed most nights at 8"). When enough C_2H_5HO is added to a home, vases may start to fly across the room and crash into walls. All kinds of paper—court-issued Orders of Protection, divorce decrees, bounced checks—come fluttering down. The lights go on and off. Does that mean Daddy's forgotten to pay the bill again, or that the second act is starting?

Every alcoholic household is, in fact, a pathetic little play in which each of the members takes on a role. This is not an idea that arrived with the COAs movement; a 17-page booklet called "Alcoholism: A Merry-Go-Round Named Denial" has been distributed free of charge by Al-Anon for almost 20 years. Written by the Rev. Joseph L. Kellerman, the former director of the Charlotte, N.C., Council of Alcoholism, "Merry-Go-Round" takes note of the uncanny consistency with which certain characters appear in alcoholic situations. These include the Enabler ("a 'helpful' Mr. Clean . . .[who] conditions [the drinker] to believe there will always be a protector who will come to his rescue"); the Victim ("the person who is responsible for getting the work done if the alcoholic is absent") and the Provoker (usually the spouse or parent of the alcoholic, this is "the key person . . . who is hurt and upset by repeated drinking episodes, but she holds the family together . . . In turn, she feeds back into the marriage her bitterness, resentment, fear and hurt . . . She controls, she tries to force the changes she wants; she sacrifices, adjusts, never gives up, never gives in, but never forgets").

Some of the earliest books in the COAs movement explored the drama metaphor more deeply and defined the roles that children play. Sharon Wegscheider-Cruse, in her 1981 book, "Another Chance" (Science and Behavior Books, Inc. Palo Alto, Calif.), wrote about the Family Hero, who is usually the firstborn. A high achiever in school, the Hero always does what's right, often discounting himself by putting others first. The Lost Child, meanwhile, is withdrawn, a loner on his way to a joyless adulthood, and thus, in some ways, very different from the Scapegoat, who appears hostile and defiant but inside feels hurt and angry. (It is the Scapegoat, says Wegscheider-Cruse, who gets attention through "negative behavior" and is likely to be involved in alcohol or other drugs later.) Last and least—in his own mind—is the Mascot, fragile and immature yet charming: the family clown.

'Good-looking' kids: Virtually no one was publishing those kinds of thoughts when Claudia Black, a Laguna Beach, Calif., therapist, began searching for literature on the subject of the alcohol-affected family in the late '70s. "Half of my adult [alcoholic] patients had kids my age and older," she remembers, "but all I found was stuff on fetal alcohol syndrome and kids prone to juvenile delinquency." One thing that fascinated her about young COAs, she says, was that despite their developmental problems "they were all 'good-looking' kids"—presentable and responsible albeit not terribly verbal. "They had friends but weren't honest with them. Everything was 'fine and dandy'."

The title of Black's important 1981 book, "It Will Never Happen to Me" (M.A.C.

"NOT NOW I'M BUSY"

COURTESY CHILDREN OF ALCOHOLICS FOUNDATION

■ Trauma: Parental neglect

Denver, Colo.), reflects the typical codependent's mix of denial and false bravado. In it, she makes the point that the children in an alcoholic household never have an environment that is consistent and structured, two of the things they need most—and she, too, talks of such stock juvenile "roles" as the Responsible One and the Adjuster. Her unique

warning was that children who survive a parent's alcoholism by displaying unusual coping behavior often experience "emotional and psychological deficits" later on. They are also likely to become alcoholics, says Black, because "alcohol helps these persons become less rigid, loosen up and relax. When they drink they aren't quite so serious." Though those things happen to almost everyone who imbibes, Black says that "for those who are stuck in unhealthy patterns, alcohol may be the *only* thing that can provide relief."

Well, she guessed wrong there: a movement, manifested by often joyous meetings, has come along in the interim. At hundreds of COAs gatherings around the country tonight, people will talk and listen to each other's stories, to cry, to laugh and generally, as Ken Gill says, "recharge their batteries." "This program kept me from being an alcoholic myself," said a woman named Heather at a gathering in an affluent section of San Francisco last week. "Because I was the oldest, everything was always my fault. It's like when you make your parents breakfast and you bring them one scrambled egg and one fried egg—in my house I always scrambled the wrong egg." Heads bobbed in agreement. Who else but COAs could identify with a story about what happens when kids cook for their own mother and father?

Discovering self-esteem: Talking and listening: this is the way we've learned to

It happened once to me; I was but A child happy and Free. Then one day my daddy came Behind me and pushed me Down the stairs. I Just layed there. When I awoke that day was Gone and and I've been sick Forever long. I was but 3 and daddy always beat on me; He smelt of Beer and wine and the next day he kissed me and said things were Fine.

COURTESY CHILDREN OF ALCOHOLICS FOUNDATION

■ Physical abuse: An adult remembers

deal with problem drinking. And though it sounds wimpy, don't knock it; it's the surest way to alleviate not just the imbibing but the whole range of symptoms we call alcoholism. A woman named Nina stood up at a meeting in Boston last week, practically glossed over the fact that both her parents were alcoholics—and proceeded to speak about how well she was feeling and doing. COAs meetings and literature, she said, had allowed her to discover self-esteem. At another meeting, Carolyn told a story of complaining to her doctor about depression—and hearing the doctor shoot back a question about whether one of her parents was an alcoholic. "I was shocked," she said, and well she might be. Doctors, as a group, have yet to play a major role in helping mitigate the effects of alcohol, perhaps because the average medical-school student spends a grand total of between zero and 10 hours studying the affliction that kills 100,000 people annually.

An avalanche of information is coming, nevertheless, from another kind of M.D.—call them the Masters of Disaster, the people who've lived with alcoholism or worked with alcoholics so closely that they might as well be their kin. Robert Ackerman, a professor of sociology at Indiana University of Pennsylvania, has been studying the children of alcoholics for an exceedingly long time by the standards of the movement—since the early '70s. In his recent book "Let Go and Grow" *(Health Communications, Inc.),* he reports on a survey he took to test the validity of Woititz's 13 generalizations about COAs, as well as seven more observations of his own. What he found was that "adult children of alcoholics identified about 20 percent more with these characteristics" than did the general population. Other professionals are reporting success with therapies involving hugging, acting out unresolved scenes from long ago and even playing one of several board games for children of alcoholics called Family Happenings and Sobriety. Cathleen Brooks, executive director of a program called Next Step in San Diego, reports that her clients often make life-changing strides after six to 18 months of primary treatment and make the decision never to drink or take drugs.

The 7 million COAs who are under the age of 18 are harder to help, if only because their parents' denial tends to keep them out of treatment. For these children who never know what to expect when they come home from school each day, life, says Woititz, "is a state of constant anxiety."

Some pediatricians think there is a link between such anxiety and childhood ulcers, chronic nausea, sleeping problems, eating disorders and dermatitis. Migs Woodside, from the COAs Foundation, says that the trained teacher can pick the child of an alcoholic out of a crowded classroom. "Sometimes you can tell by the way they are dressed or by the fact that they never have their lunch money," she says. "Sometimes you can tell by the way they suddenly pay attention when the teacher talks about drinking, and sometimes you can tell by their pictures."

Someday, 20 or 30 years from now, those children may feel a vague sense of failure or depression and be hard pressed to explain why. In the meantime, it's their Crayolas that are hard pressed. Beer cans—and not liquor or wine bottles—form a leitmotif in the work of young children of alcoholics. Occasionally, Woodside says, looking a little sad, the big stick figures can be seen tipping the cans into the mouths of the little stick figures.

CHARLES LEERHSEN *with* TESSA NAMUTH
and bureau reports

Healing Scars of Parental Drinking

SUMMARY: Long after they have left their drink-dominated childhood homes, many people find that the alcoholism of their parents still disrupts their lives. Banding together in self-help sessions enables such adults to confront the damage and recover.

Lillian began going to weekly Adult Children of Alcoholics meetings a year ago. For three months all she could do was listen and fight back tears.

Like most of the nation's 22 million men and women raised in homes where one or both parents abused alcohol, Lillian grew up believing she was somehow responsible for her family's problems. It was a heavy burden for a little girl.

When Dad passed out at dinner and fell into his fried chicken, Mom, desperate to cover up "the problem," kept eating and insisted that everything was OK. Lillian thus learned to distrust and ignore even what her eyes and ears told her.

She felt anger toward her parents. But knowing such feelings were "bad," she instead turned the anger inward, blaming herself. Her spontaneous, expressive impulses died, and she became like a small, serious grown-up, stifling her feelings. She came to have only one priority: survival.

Despite their shared background of frequent conflict and tension, adult children of alcoholics — ACOAs they are called by those who work closely with them — usually look healthy and often perform well. But the survival techniques they developed as children persist. They frequently have low self-esteem, guilt and depression. They are at high risk to marry alcoholics and are four times more likely than others to become alcoholics themselves.

In recent years, however, more and more such adults have banded together to confront the effects of parental alcoholism. There is even a telephone referral service for such meetings, at (213) 651-1710. In meetings modeled after Alcoholics Anonymous sessions, borrowing from AA's 12-step recovery program, the adults focus on a different topic each week. For most, the pain of their chaotic upbringing has been buried under years of shame.

Partly as a result of therapist Janet Woititz's best-selling book "Adult Children of Alcoholics" and Claudia Black's "It Will Never Happen to Me," attendance at these self-help meetings nationwide is exploding. "People have started to pay attention the past few years. It was a lot harder 10 years ago for people to identify themselves" as children of alcoholics, says Woititz, who also heads the Institute for Counseling and Training in Verona, N.J.

The therapist initially came into contact with children from alcoholic families as an elementary school teacher in the early 1970s. "I noticed that about 25 percent of my students were different from the rest and I was real concerned. They were different in that there were skills they didn't have. They knew how to be compliant, but not how to cooperate. They knew how to handle a crisis or do something at the last minute, but not how to do anything systematically. They were worried and concerned most of the time. They didn't know how to relate to their peers, even though their peers liked them. They didn't know how to be friends."

Her 2-year-old clinic, which handles about 300 patients per week and has a long waiting list, also has therapy groups to work on deeper issues, including past sexual and physical abuse. In up to 90 percent of child abuse cases, alcohol is a significant factor, according to the National Association for Children of Alcoholics.

"It used to be that ACOAs didn't start to seek help until their late 20s," she says. "They really functioned quite well up to that point and were able to deny the things that were getting in their way. But as people become more aware, we are seeing younger and younger people."

Before discovering the self-help meetings, Lillian, a university professor in Washington, went through years of psychotherapy for bouts of depression. "I have a history of repressing anger and turning it against myself. In the program, I am learning tools that I never learned because my family life was so unhealthy. One of the things I have to learn is how to recognize when I'm angry and then how to express it: how to say things to the people I'm angry at and not be waylaid into expressing it indirectly to somebody else."

According to the Children of Alcoholics Foundation in New York City, the children commonly adopt one of four roles that persist into adulthood. The responsible child is a high achiever who always does what's right, is successful and puts everyone else first. The problem child gets attention by being a troublemaker. He is strongly attracted to a peer group outside the home and is likely to be involved with alcohol and drugs. The silent child is a loner, quiet and withdrawn, who survives by retreating inward, not rocking the boat. The clown is a charmer who works hard to be the center of attention and uses humor to distract family members from a painful situation.

Woititz estimates that 70 percent of those seen at her clinic have a past or current drinking problem. "There is no way that an ACOA ever takes a drink without being conscious of it; it means something."

Recent research indicates that many recovering alcoholics who relapse into drinking after two to five years of sobriety often have not dealt with issues resulting from growing up in an alcoholic family, she says.

While her work concentrates on children of alcoholics, she emphasizes that many of their experiences and symptoms are also valid for others whose homes were "different": families where there was other compulsive behavior such as gambling or drug abuse, or even chronic illness or unbearably rigid religious attitudes.

One year after discovering the Adult Children of Alcoholics organization, Lillian is decidedly upbeat about the future. "At this stage, the most important thing in my life is this program of recovery. Recovery is learning new tools, learning how to live. I let nothing interfere with it. When people come around who are real unhealthy and I think that my program of recovery is threatened, I tell them good-bye. Right now, I'm just committed to getting better, to healing. And it's happening."

— Charles Wheeler

From *Insight*, February 23, 1987, p. 64. Originally from *The Washington Times*.

Alcohol-Breast Cancer Link

Drinking three or more alcohol-containing beverages a week may double a woman's chance of developing breast cancer later, and even lower amounts can increase risk to a lesser degree, says one of two reports this week on the relationship between alcohol and breast cancer. The other study, which found increased risk only at higher intake levels, also concludes that alcohol can significantly increase the risk of breast cancer. But scientists from both groups — while emphasizing the importance of alcohol as a risk factor because it can be eliminated — stopped short of recommending that women quit drinking.

Using previously collected data from the National Health and Nutrition Examination Survey, researchers from the National Institutes of Health (NIH) found that any amount of alcohol, even the equivalent of less than one drink weekly, raises the breast cancer risk by at least 40 percent. In the study's heaviest-use category (three or more drinks per week), the risk increase jumps to 100 percent, or double, report the researchers in the May 7 New England Journal of Medicine. Data were not available on the types of drinks consumed or the age at which subjects began drinking. An earlier NIH study suggested the risk is elevated if drinking begins before age 30.

In another study reported in the same issue, based on data from the Nurses' Health Study begun in 1976, scientists at Harvard Medical School and Harvard School of Public Health in Boston estimate that women who consume from about three to nine drinks per week have a 30 percent increased risk of developing breast cancer compared with nondrinkers. (One drink is defined as 12 ounces of beer, a glass of wine or a drink with 1 ounce of liquor.) Greater alcohol intake raises the risk to 60 percent, according to Walter C. Willett and his coauthors. The group did not, however, find increased risk in those who drank fewer than three drinks per week, partly contradicting the NIH data.

Philip R. Taylor, a coauthor of the NIH report and acting chief of the National Cancer Institute's Division of Cancer Prevention and Control, told SCIENCE NEWS that the differences between the NIH results and the Boston data may have resulted from possible underreporting by NIH subjects of the amount actually consumed. He adds, however, that the two studies and an earlier one similarly designed are consistent and "right on target" in reporting an average 50 to 60 percent increased risk with moderate drinking. Willett says data collected by the Boston group "are probably more likely to be real," because the amount of alcohol ingested was validated with follow-up questionnaires given women chosen randomly from the larger group. Alcohol consumption among the NIH subjects was measured only during the initial interview.

In any case, both Taylor and Willett agree that alcohol must be considered a possible factor in breast cancer. "It still is not totally clear whether this is a true cause-and-effect relationship," says Willett. Taylor also says NIH "is not in a position to make a firm recommendation [regarding alcohol use by women] at this point." He notes that other NIH reports suggest that small amounts of alcohol may lower the risk of heart disease.

"There are a large number of risk factors [such as heredity] for breast cancer," says Taylor. "Almost none are things that a woman can do anything about. Alcohol may be one of those things . . . but there's a lot of thinking that has to go on before people start chucking their wine bottles."

In an accompanying editorial, Saxon Graham, chairman of Social and Preventive Medicine at the State University of New York in Buffalo, points out that 14 of the 17 studies that have looked at alcohol and breast cancer have found increased risk. Graham writes that women with other known risk factors for breast cancer "should curtail their alcohol ingestion." Those risk factors include obesity, having had first pregnancies after 25, having few or no children, and having a mother with breast cancer. Graham told SCIENCE NEWS he thinks women at high risk should quit drinking alcohol entirely.

Those interviewed agreed that the two epidemiologic studies have their shortcomings. The NIH's conclusions are based on a total of 131 cases of breast cancer identified among a group of 7,188 women. "[The 131 cases] is small in absolute numbers," says Taylor. "But the statistical analysis tells you the results are not likely to be due to chance. One still should be cautious [about interpreting results]." Based on 89,538 women, 601 of whom developed breast cancer during the four years following the original interviews, the Boston study has larger numbers but also is flawed, says Graham. He criticizes the study for the homogeneity of its nurse population, a "medically knowledgeable and middle-class" group. Middle- and upper-class women have a higher incidence of breast cancer, and Graham questions whether such results can be extrapolated to the general public.

— *D.D. Edwards*

Nicotine: Addictive *and* Spreads Cancer?

Nicotine appears to be one of those things some people could die for — in more ways than one. One new study suggests it may promote the spread of cancer cells, while another indicates higher doses of nicotine replacements may be necessary to help smokers stop using tobacco.

At first, nicotine managed to keep clear of the fiery debate over whether tar and other tobacco constituents caused health problems. Then it was indicted in heart disease, and later found to cause a true physical addiction in many users (SN: 1/18/86, p.44). No longer the hidden ingredient, nicotine now is being studied in a broad range of research projects, including two reported last week in San Diego at the American Cancer Society's annual science writers' seminar.

At the University of South Alabama in Mobile, Gesina L. Longenecker and her co-workers are assessing the interaction of tumor cells, nicotine and blood platelets. Other studies had shown that platelets (cell fragments essential in blood clotting) can be activated by tumor cells. These activated platelets attach to the cells, protect them from the immune system and apparently help them work their way through the blood vessel walls during metastasis, or spread, of the cancer.

The Alabama group found that cultured cells from a human muscle cancer also produce significant amounts of prostacyclin, a substance released routinely from blood vessel walls that *inhibits* platelet activation and prevents unwanted clotting in the circulation. Thus these tumor cells, paradoxically, appear to release a negative signal that in effect slows the spread of cancer while at the same time promoting it.

But nicotine upsets this balancing act, says Longenecker, by inhibiting the production of prostacyclin by cancer cells, much as it inhibits prostacyclin produced by blood vessels. In addition, preliminary data suggest that nicotine increases the number of circulating tumor cells that stick to the sides of blood vessels. Longenecker explains that this would make nicotine not an initiator or promotor of cancer by itself, but perhaps a cofactor that aids metastasis.

Although the effect has been studied in only one type of cancer, Longenecker says it could be important to varying degrees in numerous types of cancer. Does this mean that smoking could enhance the spread of many, if not all, types of cancer? And should cancer patients be told to stop tobacco use, given the pleasure they may receive from smoking or chewing tobacco?

The answers are complicated by the fact that only 20 percent of smokers are able to quit the habit "cold turkey."

At last week's seminar, Jack E. Henningfield, from the National Institute of Drug Abuse (NIDA), said nicotine addiction "is a special sort of compulsive behavior," similar to heroin and cocaine addiction in its behavioral and physical effects. Because a tolerance to nicotine builds over time, Henningfield says many tobacco users may require nicotine replacements like nicotine gum for a longer time and in larger doses than currently recommended by physicians. (Only half of the nicotine from the prescription chewing gum actually reaches the bloodstream.)

"The most desirable situation is no nicotine," he says, "but it could be given much longer safely." That would make it more likely to help the more than 60 percent of smokers who fail to stop, even after seven attempts, he says.

Despite the dangers of nicotine use, Henningfield feels that it is often a "trade-off" necessary to eliminate exposure to carcinogens in tobacco. Despite research on nicotine substitutes at NIDA's Addiction Research Center in Baltimore, nothing has been found to take its place for the addict, says Henningfield. NIDA studies are being done on smokeless cigarettes, suppositories and skin patches containing nicotine.

— D.D. Edwards

Cocaine Cardiology: Problems, Mysteries

As more and more cases of cocaine-related heart problems and deaths are recognized, researchers are beginning to get an idea of what types of heart disease the drug causes. But how the damage occurs, who is prone to problems and why so few users are affected remain a mystery, says Jeffrey M. Isner of Tufts University in Boston.

Isner, one of the first to publish in the scientific literature on the connection between cocaine and heart disease, is studying the physiological correlation between the two. He discussed some of the cases and their possible causes at last week's American Heart Association Science Writers Forum in Monterey, Calif.

Of the U.S. cases reported so far, three-quarters have been heart attacks and the rest were due to inflammation or arrhythmia. The problems occurred immediately after cocaine use, and none of the users had discernible underlying conditions that might have predisposed them to heart disease.

Isner and his colleagues' description of seven cases in the Dec. 4, 1986, NEW ENGLAND JOURNAL OF MEDICINE followed previous reports of 26 other incidents. Since he published, Isner says, at least four more cases have appeared and details of 19 more have been submitted for publication. Most of the people had snorted "normal" levels of the drug.

While researchers don't know how cocaine causes heart attacks, they are beginning to rule things out. Spasms in the coronary arteries and subsequent formation of a blood clot at the spasm are believed capable of causing heart attacks in non-users, but users are evidently not especially prone to such spasms.

Using a diagnostic test routinely used to test for coronary artery spasms, Isner and his colleagues, as well as researchers at several other laboratories, checked nine cocaine users who had suffered heart attacks. In the test, a drug that can cause spasms in susceptible people is injected via catheter directly into the coronary arteries. If the test shows the person to be sensitive to the drug, naturally occurring spasms are presumed to be causing the heart problems.

Isner and his colleagues tried the same test with cocaine after obtaining consent in a user with heart problems. Again, no signs of spasms were seen.

Some researchers have also linked cocaine use to myocarditis, or inflammation of the heart muscle. Isner has checked a tissue biopsy from someone with cocaine-related myocarditis and found an unusually large number of a certain type of white blood cell. The cells are characteristic of cardiac hypersensitivity to some therapeutic drugs, suggesting that an allergic reaction may be to blame for cocaine-related myocarditis.

Researchers are at a loss to explain the epidemiology of the association. Although the number of reports linking cocaine to specific instances of heart disease has been rising over the past five years, it is still extremely small compared with the estimated 5 to 6 million cocaine users in the United States. The apparent increase in the rate firms up the relationship, Isner says, but why the drug's effect on the cardiovascular system of most users is limited to a boosting of the heart rate and blood pressure, while a small percentage get heart disease, is unknown. "This is something that's going to affect a distinct minority of users," says Isner. "But we don't have any way of predicting who is going to belong to that subset.

"The drug has an awfully long history. It's still used by millions of Indians in Peru and Colombia. And at least in that population, the potential for sudden, fatal cardiac disorders has not been described or recognized." One potential source of the difference — impurities in the U.S. street product — has not been checked because of the difficulty of obtaining samples of the drugs used by the patients, he says.

— J. Silberner

Shortcut to the Rambo Look

97-lb. weaklings no more, teens take steroids to bulk up

Adolescence can be a trying time—particularly for the teenage boy. He is exultantly proud of his newfound sense of masculinity, but his body, alas, remains an embarrassment. Where are those flauntable biceps and triceps? Earlier generations of frustrated youth sought salvation in Charles Atlas' body-building exercises or strenuous programs of pumping iron. Many of today's teens, however, are subscribing to an ominously simpler solution. Explains Dr. Robert Willix, Jr., of Fort Lauderdale: "Before, the 97-lb. weakling on the beach turned to weight lifting. Now he turns to steroids."

Until recently, the drugs were considered mainly the bane of competitive sports and body building. But the alarming fact is that steroids, which are synthetic male hormones, are increasingly being abused by teenage boys for cosmetic reasons. A report last month in the Journal of the American Medical Association revealed that 6.6% of male high school seniors—and perhaps as many as 500,000 adolescents nationwide—have used steroids. Nearly a third of the students surveyed took the drugs to acquire that brawny look. Declares "Ian," a 5-ft. 6-in., 115-lb. 17-year-old from Boston, who has been popping pills for three months: "I'm sick of being small. I want to be bigger."

From early childhood, boys learn that the ideal man looks something like Mr. Universe. "Watch Saturday-morning television, and you'll see all these huge, abnormally muscled beings on cartoons and kids' programming," notes Chicago osteopath Bob Goldman. "Conan and Rambo are the heroes." So are sports stars, some of whom—like Olympic sprinter Ben Johnson and Seattle Seahawk linebacker Brian Bosworth—are known to have taken the steroid shortcut. Scrawny youngsters, some only 13, eagerly pay between $50 and $400 to black-market dealers for a six-to-13-week cycle of pills and injectables that could turn them into Hulk Hogans. "It takes years to build up a body like that," brags "Rick," 17, pointing to drug-clean weight lifters at a gym outside Los Angeles. "Steroids are

quick." Used in conjunction with training, the drugs stimulate cellular processes that build muscle.

But the drug-enhanced physiques are a hazardous bargain. Steroids can cause temporary acne and balding, upset hormonal production and damage the heart and kidneys. Doctors suspect they may contribute to liver cancer and atherosclerosis. Teens, who are already undergoing physical and psychological stresses, may run some enhanced risks. The drugs can stunt growth by accelerating bone maturation. Physicians also speculate that the chemicals may compromise youngsters' still developing reproductive

Charles Atlas body-building ad from the '50s

systems. Steroid users have experienced a shrinking of the testicles and impotence. Dr. Richard Dominguez, a sports specialist in suburban Chicago, starts his lectures to youths with a surefire attention grabber: "You want to shrink your balls? Take steroids."

Just as worrisome is the threat to mental health. Drug users are prone to moodiness, depression, irritability and what are known as "roid rages" Ex-user Darren

Allen Chamberlain, 26, of Pasadena, Calif., describes himself as an "easygoing guy" before picking up steroids at age 16. Then he turned into a teen Terminator. "I was doing everything from being obnoxious to getting out of the car and provoking fights at intersections," he says. "I'd just blow. You can walk in my parents' house today and see the signs—holes in doors I stuck my fist through, indentations in walls I kicked." Chamberlain grew so despondent, he recalls, that he "held a gun to my head once or twice." Others have succeeded in committing suicide. Warns Aaron Henry, 22, a St. Charles, Mo., drug counselor whose adolescent dependence on steroids drove him close to physical and mental ruin: "When you put big egos and big dreams together with steroids, that's a nasty combination."

Despite such horror stories, teens deny that the dangers apply to *them*. Willix recalls that after one session in which he warned students to avoid the drugs, two 15-year-olds came up and said, "We hear what you're saying about steroids, but could you tell us which ones to use?" Rick of Los Angeles takes 40 mg of the chemicals daily, but insists, "I'm being careful. I'm taking what I think a doctor would prescribe." Has he seen one? "I will when I'm 18."

Once on the drugs, adolescents find it hard to get off. "People say, 'I'll just take them for three months until I get the look I want, and then I'll quit,'" explains Adam Frattasio, 26, of Weymouth, Mass., a former user. "It doesn't work that way." Bulging biceps and ham-hock thighs do a fast fade when the chemicals are halted. So do the feelings of being powerful and manly. Almost every user winds up back on the drugs. A self-image that relies on a steroid-soaked body may be difficult to change. Chamberlain has a friend, now 29, who has been taking steroids for more than a dozen years. Says Chamberlain: "His mind is so warped that he said he doesn't care if he dies, so long as he looks big in the coffin." —**By Anastasia Toufexis. Reported by Naushad S. Mehta/New York and James Willwerth/Los Angeles**

STEROIDS:
THE POWER DRUGS

"Understanding the deleterious effects of steroids doesn't necessarily stop athletes from using them."

Paul Pfotenhauer

Mr. Pfotenhauer is a writer with the University of California, Davis News Service.

ASK athletes about anabolic steroids. They will say that, if you want size, strength, and endurance, these are the drugs for you. Their usage has been increasing among football players, track and field athletes, wrestlers, and body-builders, but athletes are not the only users of steroids. There also are a growing number of non-athletes—people who just want to cut a Herculean pose on the beach.

Athletes generally don't admit steroid use, so estimates vary as to how many are on the "juice." It is said that 70-90% of all professional football players are using steroids. When the Cleveland Browns' nose tackle Bob Golic was asked what would happen if the National Football League's ban on steroids were enforced, he responded, "There would be a lot of offensive linemen playing indoor soccer next year."

In college athletics, steroid use is on the increase. The head of the National Collegiate Athletic Association Drug Testing Committee says more than half of the nation's major college football players use illegal steroids. The pressure is subtle. No one orders players to begin a program of steroid use, but coaches may say their offensive line must get bigger and stronger, quickly. Athletes know that weight training is a slow process that takes years of hard work to increase size and bulk, so many turn to steroids.

Anabolic steroids are synthetic versions of testosterone, the male hormone. In small doses, they have legitimate medical uses in cases of soft-tissue injuries, skeletal disorders, malnutrition, and some types of anemia.

However, the health risks to the male athlete using these agents include edema, hypertension, conversion of latent diabetes into chronic diabetes, testicular shrinkage, increased cholesterol, jaundice, infertility, decreased libido, and significantly depressed testosterone production that may not be reversible. Prostate cancer, if present, will be stimulated. Kidney disorders, hardening of the arteries, and liver malfunction are among the side-effects of taking the drugs.

So, why would any athlete use steroids in light of the known health risks? Rob Rathbun, a starting defensive tackle on the University of California, Davis (UCD) varsity football team, says the majority of users resort to them so as to be competitive. "There's no question athletes get stronger using steroids. In high-powered collegiate programs, players are pressured to make the club, and if taking the drug helps them to do that, they will."

It's hard to convince young, powerful athletes that anything is a health risk to them. "Some players start to think that if they don't use a steroid, they will be at a disadvantage," notes Rathbun. "The scary part is that once a player has begun to use steroids, they're hard to give up."

Rathbun says he knows of no UCD athlete using steroids, but he has had suspicions about some. "I have seen athletes in the weight room who were not that strong a couple of months ago make fast gains in the amount of weight lifted."

Anabolic steroids first came into use in the late 1940's, when they were administered to survivors of concentration camps to stimulate weight gain. Their use to enhance athletic prowess began in the 1950's. In the Munich Olympic games in 1968, it was estimated that more than 65% of athletes involved in mid- and short-distance running and field events had taken steroids in preparation for participation.

"In Europe, many athletes are given prescriptions for anabolic steroids by the team doctor for the specific purpose of enhancing athletic ability," says Jon Vochatzer, men's track and field coach at UCD. He recently returned from a two-year program in which he worked with the West

German National Track and Field Team.

"Athletes there are encouraged to use steroids and are not tested for their use in European events. The only time they have to submit to drug tests is in international competition. Generally, these athletes stop taking steroids weeks before tests so that no traces of the drugs appear," claims Vochatzer. "What strikes me odd is the fear associated with steroid use in this country, whereas in Europe it is promoted."

Pressure on athletes

Vochatzer thinks more athletes will begin using steroids in the U.S. because of the pressure to do so. If American athletes want to remain competitive with their European counterparts, they see steroids as necessary.

"The use of steroids alone does not improve strength," says Dr. Jeffrey Tanji, director of the sports medicine program at the UCD Medical Center in Sacramento. "The combination of progressive weight training, calorie and protein supplementation, and anabolic steroids has been shown to effectively increase body mass."

He says that steroids causes muscle hypertrophy (growth to large size). When individuals lift weights without using steroids, they increase the size of the muscle cells and sometimes the number of cells. Steroids won't increase the number of cells, but they will increase the fluid in each cell and each cell will grow bigger. As a result, a person using steroids will retain more fluid.

"Since steroids are such risky drugs, the medical community doesn't know everything about their pharmacologic effects when used for non-medical purposes," claims Tanji. "The reason is that each time a drug study is undertaken, it has to be approved by a human subjects committee at each hospital or institution. The committee reviews the study in terms of its dangers and hazards to the human subjects. Because steroids are so dangerous, medical committees will not accept these kind of studies."

Since steroids cause chemical changes, users actually feel differently when they take them. Athletes taking anabolic steroids experience a state of euphoria and diminished fatigue, which enhances training. They also report increased aggression—making steroids ideal for competitive athletes, according to one source. Users have admitted that they like the feeling of being big. Football players say they feel "pumped-up" (as if they had just lifted weights) all the time. It's a very seductive feeling.

Females who use anabolic steroids to enhance athletic performance are not exempt from adverse health reactions. The masculinizing side-effects in women include the growth of body and facial hair, acne, deepening of the voice, clitoral enlargement, and depression of the menstrual cycle. Medical doctors think that some of these side-effects may not be reversible. Vochatzer says many women in the Soviet bloc countries use this drug for the weight events in track and field competition, and their use is readily noticeable in their physical appearance.

Users take steroids on a "cycle" or schedule. Sometimes, users may double-up their dosages—what they call "stacking" —to get the added energy boost. "With double and triple dosages, the medical risks climb dramatically. We have enough case studies to know that deaths have occurred among athletes as a result of abusing steroids," Tanji explains.

Sports injuries have increased as a result of steroid use, he says. The reason is that steroids help build muscle fiber, but, at the same time, decrease the body's ability to form scar tissue around an injury. "Inflammation is what leads to the formation of scar tissue and eventually heals the wound. Anabolic steroids increase fluid in the body, but they also decrease the body's ability to cause inflammation after injury."

Understanding the deleterious effects of steroids doesn't necessarily stop athletes from using them. Tanji cites an opinion poll that asked athletes whether they would take an anabolic steroid if they could be assured of receiving a gold medal in the Olympics, even if it meant their death from the drug within a short period of time. Nearly half of the respondents said "yes." "This worries me because it is short-term thinking. One athlete told me that he would rather die big than die small."

Steroid testing may not be the answer. Oral doses can be detected for five to six weeks, whereas injections can remain in a person's system for 11 months or longer. However, if an athlete stops using oral steroids six weeks before a post-season game or sports competition, the drugs may not be detected. Additionally, the tests are very expensive, and only sophisticated laboratories are equipped to uncover the use of steroids in the body. Therefore, testing is not routine.

Dr. Ron Sockolov, a Sacramento sports medicine specialist, points out that there is both a psychological and physical dependency on the drug. Steroids are addictive, but not in the sense of hallucinatory drugs such as heroin and cocaine. "Athletes can have a very difficult time trying to quit because the user loses weight [muscle size and mass], loses the aggressive behavior, and loses the euphoric sense of feeling and looking good."

Tanji thinks steroid use is gaining popularity among high school students, who utilize it not only to increase their athletic enhancement, but to look great on the beach. Young athletes who take steroids before their growth is complete actually may stunt their growth by sealing off the ends of their bones.

Many athletes and coaches think it will be next to impossible to eliminate steroids, just like it's almost impossible to get rid of drugs in society. An information and credibility gap concerning anabolic steroids continues to exist between athletes and the medical and scientific communities that can be closed only if both groups are better-informed about the effects of this alluring drug.

The Size Enhancers: A Steroid Glossary

Steroids are easy to obtain, even though they are illegal to use without a medical prescription. In 1987, California passed some of the toughest steroid laws in the nation, making possession or sale a felony. Yet, despite stricter criminal penalties—and growing medical evidence of its dangers—steroid use is spreading. Most steroids come through a $100,000,000-a-year black market, say Federal authorities. As a result, the risk of contaminated supplies increases because of lack of quality control.

Anabolic steroids are available to the user in two forms: oral tablets and injections for intramuscular use. Both forms are risky. Jeffrey Tanji, director of UCD's sports medicine program, says the only difference between an oil-base injection and oral tablets is the slower release of the drug when it is injected. The chemical is assimilated through the internal organs in either form.

Black-market steroids are acquired easily at many gyms. A number of anabolic steroids are available to individuals. Among the more popular drugs used are:
- Oxymetholone (anadrol): Comes in tablet form and makes users both stronger and bigger.
- Oxandrolone (anavar): Comes in tablet form and greatly increases strength.
- Nandrolone (deca-durabolin): An injectable drug that makes users gain size through protein synthesis (as do all the others).
- Methandrostenolone (dianabol): Comes in injectable and tablet form. Many users think this is the most effective strength- and size-building anabolic steroid.
- Methyltestosterone (metandren): Comes in tablet form and works into the system quickly. Makes users very aggressive.
- Testosterone cypionate: Injectable testosterone that is used to maintain testosterone levels when the body begins to stop producing its own due to heavy steroid use.
- Testosterone propionate: An oil-base injectable form of testosterone that is very fast-acting.
- Stanozolol (winstrol): Comes in tablet and injectable form and reportedly acts slowly.

Models of Dependency

- **Biological and Biochemical Models: The Disease Model (Articles 46-50)**
- **Psychological and Social Models (Articles 51-53)**

Dr. Arnold Washton, founder of the first National Cocaine Hotline, reports that while "Americans represent only 2 percent of the world population, we consume 60 percent of the world's illicit drugs." In addition to the illegal substances, millions of people abuse prescription drugs from tranquilizers to sleeping pills. Are we, as Dr. Washton says, a "chemical people," a nation of compulsive drug users? Every person who has suffered as a result of drugs would like to see the eradication of the drugs that caused their personal pain. Their desire is understandable. But, according to Dr. Washton, "It is a form of collective insanity to believe that if all illicit drugs were somehow removed from this country, we would become a society of non-compulsive, life-embracing people."

How is an "addictive personality" triggered or disarmed? Are those people included in this category born with severe "mood disorders" that engender a compulsion for chemical escape, or have they been created by the adverse demands inherent in a modern industrial society? "Breaking the Cycle of Addiction" and "Ain't Misbehavin' " focus on the personality of the user. The article "A Slip Doesn't Have to Lead to a Fall" deals with the treatment and prevention of relapse, while "Drugs Don't Take People, People Take Drugs" considers the poor understanding of the precise nature of addiction. The problem has been worsened by the loss of traditional support systems such as the church, the family unit, and the community.

An examination of the psychological and social models presented in the second subsection of this unit considers drug use as a problem of reward and reinforcement. How else can science explain a drug like nicotine being so addicting that some so-called "hard drugs" are easier to quit? "Nasty Habits" and "Out of the Habit Trap" examine the development of addiction and the shifting of dependencies from one drug or activity to another when the original chemical is substituted or unavailable. "Addiction and IQ" puts forth the possibility that addiction should be considered something other than a failure of character, given the evidence for the reward/reinforcement theory.

Looking Ahead: Challenge Questions

Why do members of the same "gene pool" behave differently when it comes to drug use and abuse?

How should the effectiveness of a therapy or therapist be judged?

Why are some people able to handle alcohol and others cannot?

Who should determine the kind of treatment an addict is to receive?

Define the difference between use and abuse. Why do so many people overcome their addictions? Do you have to have "been there" or be a former addict to adequately counsel others with dependencies?

If drug behavior is hereditary, what about other behavior characteristics?

Is therapy necessary or desirable for everyone who uses or abuses drugs?

Unit 5

CONTROL YOURSELF

STANTON PEELE

Stanton Peele is a senior health researcher at Mathematica Policy Research in Princeton, New Jersey, and the author of Diseasing of America: Addiction Treatment Out of Control.

Recently, the *New York Times* assessed the value of the Helmsley real estate empire at about $50 billion. Why, then, did Leona Helmsley steal a piddling million dollars or so by casting personal expenditures as business expenses? The crime was certainly an act of irrationality on Leona's part, like a millionaire's shoplifting.

It should be obvious to any trained clinician that Leona Helmsley is suffering from addiction to the acquisition of money, a compulsion to extract financial advantage in the most trivial ways, even when the potential gain could have no impact on her well-being. This would probably have been the most successful defense her lawyers could have presented at her tax-evasion trial. Indeed, Leona's failure to claim she was addicted could have been used as proof that she was, since one of the primary traits of addictive diseases is "denial" that one has the disease.

America is clearly moving into the 21st century in addictionology—the identification and explication of new addictions, defined as diseases. In addition to the standard drug and alcohol habits, these addictions include shopping and debt, sex and love, gambling, smoking, overeating, and just about anything people can do to excess. There are now A.A.-type support groups organized around several hundred types of activities. The crucial first step of the 12-step program that Alcoholics Anonymous and its derivatives have made famous is the obligation for the alcoholic or addict to admit he or she is "powerless over alcohol," or whatever the person's habit happens to be. This symptom is central to the disease, and A.A. focuses on loss of control as the definition, the etiology, and the excuse for addiction and addictive misbehavior.

It is not science that is fueling the movement to label so many activities as addictions. The tendency to see all addictions as cut from the same cloth returns us to 19th-century (and earlier) usage, in which to be addicted meant to be given over to a vice or activity in some unwholesome and morally reprehensible or weak-willed way. The observation that alcoholism (called inebriation and drunkenness in the last century) and drug addiction are items in a much larger class of human behavior is a fundamental realization that has been accepted throughout most of human history, but which American addictionologists have recently been rediscovering.

What is new in the 20th century is the claim that these compulsive activities somehow represent codifiable diseases. In the case of alcoholism, the inability to control one's drinking is today described as an inherited trait. This is wrong. In fact, even biologically-oriented research has shown that loss of control is not an inheritable trait, as A.A. originally claimed.

Rather, to the extent that genetic transmission of drinking patterns is indicated (and the scientific underpinnings for even this minimal proposition are far weaker than most lay readers suspect), researchers see alcoholism as the cumulative result of a long history of drinking. Some genetic theorists claim people continue drinking heavily for long periods of time to resolve neuro-psychological deficiencies or because they lack the inherited mechanism to determine when they have drunk enough. These theories nonetheless leave room for any number of environmental and personal factors to influence the development of alcoholism.

Research has shown decisively that alcoholics, even while drinking, are crucially influenced by value choices and environmental considerations. Alcoholics who seem to be out of control on the street are actually pursuing deliberate drinking strategies designed to achieve specific levels of drunkenness. Street alcoholics allowed to earn credit for booze in a laboratory will work until they accumulate enough chits to attain the exact level of intoxication they seek. Or, allowed to drink freely in an isolation booth, they will voluntarily cut down their drinking to spend more time in a comfortable, abstinent environment with other alcoholics watching television. Such alcoholics do get drunk a lot, and they prefer drinking to most other options available to them in their natural environments. Nonetheless, alcoholic drinking is a largely purposive behavior, even if alcoholics' purposes are quite alien to most people and even though alcoholics frequently regret their choices after they become sober (at least, until they become drunk again).

Much of the work on alcoholics' intentions while drinking has been conducted at the Baltimore City

Hospital, part of the federally supported Addiction Research Center. But many of these same investigators are now giving their work with cocaine addicts a very different slant from the one they gave their alcohol research. This research group is often shown on television working with addicts attached to electrodes or giving responses recorded on a computer as they take or come down from their cocaine doses. A researcher then explains to the interviewer how cocaine provides a tremendous uplift, followed by an enervating down.

Actually, this process is a standard one observed in human beings engaged in activities ranging from eating carbohydrates to sexual intercourse (hence the readiness with which these activities are equated with drug addictions). Often, the researchers observe how the anticipation of the cocaine high or the need to reintroduce cocaine to alleviate the low will drive the addict to do anything. Sometimes reference is made to laboratory studies in which animals continue to inject cocaine through an implanted catheter until they kill themselves.

Just how addictive are cocaine and crack? Cocaine in any form is less addictive than cigarettes by the two key behavioral measures of addiction. Five times as many regular cigarette as crack smokers become addicted, according to Jack Henningfield, a researcher at the National Institute on Drug Abuse, and addicts indicate it is easier to give up crack than cigarettes. In fact, if we go by the NIDA survey to which George Bush alluded in his nationally televised speech last September, very few cocaine users become addicted. The survey found that 21 million Americans had used cocaine, 8 million had used it in the last year, and 3 million were current users, but only 300,000 used cocaine daily or nearly so. Government statistics thus show that 10 percent of current users and 1.5 percent of all users take the drug close to every day.

What are we to make, then, of the addict who explains that he needed to steal or kill to get more of his drug, or the woman who sells sex—one notorious addict prostituted her teenage daughter—to get money for crack? Aren't these behaviors drug effects? No, they are not, and it is a mark of naiveté—not science—to mistake the behavior of some drug users with the pharmacological effects of the drug, as though addictive loss of control and criminal behavior were somehow chemical properties of a substance.

Notwithstanding all the pseudoscience associated with it, addiction engages age-old questions about will power, self-control, personal responsibility, and values. How are some people able to turn down a fattening dessert or an after-dinner cigar which they might enjoy consuming, but which they have decided is bad for them? Do those who instead indulge themselves have a disease? Or do they have less self-control or think it is less important to be healthy?

In fact, science, like law, cannot accurately proceed without taking into account individual responsibility and values. For example, given that cigarettes are harder to quit than crack, what should we learn from the fact that William Bennett gave up smoking to take his post as drug czar? The only possible answer is that he was wise enough to recognize that he couldn't hold an antidrug post and be a cigarette addict, and

that he wanted the drug post more than he wanted to continue smoking.

Of course, self-control and sound values are not immutable, Platonic ideals either. After all, Bennett inappropriately maintained his cigarette addiction throughout his tenure as secretary of education. Smokers and fat people demonstrate similarly weak self-control for years, until they successfully stop smoking or lose weight, after which we all envy them for their superior will power. People do refocus their values as their lives progress and they have different opportunities and options and become better prepared or more willing to change long-term habits. This is the nature of the beast, and nothing we learn about the chemistry of one drug versus another can change it. *Try* to say something sensible about nicotine's addictive properties as a way of explaining Bennett's new-found ability to abstain from smoking.

Why do we think crack/cocaine is so much more addictive than cigarettes, or heroin, or alcohol (all of which addicts with multiple addictions say are harder to quit than cocaine, whether smoked, injected, or snorted)? The drug's current reputation seems strange when we consider that cocaine was an ingredient in Coca-Cola and other soft drinks into the 20th century, and that research on cocaine's effects was conducted for 50 years before cocaine was announced to be addictive in the mid-1980s, coinciding with the explosion of recreational cocaine use in this country. Cocaine came to be addictive among some inner-city users and among a very small percentage of middle-class users who tried the drug.

Why didn't most of these people become cocaine addicts? The answer is so simple that we are left wondering why scientists can't figure it out: Most people have better things to do than to become addicted to cocaine. This is an example of a scientific concept—addiction—developing a symbolic meaning which is contradicted by the data. Nothing about drug use or any other addiction rules out choices and individual values. Without taking these facts of life into account, we cannot understand who becomes addicted and who does not, and why.

A study of middle-class users of cocaine by the Addiction Research Foundation of Toronto found not only that most regular users do not become addicted, but also that most of those who develop a steady craving for cocaine eventually cut back or quit the drug on their own. In other words, cocaine use resembles just about every other compelling experience in its potential to upset people's equilibrium, but this is not a permanent or inexorable condition for most people.

Counterpoised with these data are reports by the few who despair of kicking their cocaine habits on their own and enter private treatment centers, or by the addict-criminals who testify on television that you would kill and prostitute your children—as they did—if only you took crack. These claims are preposterous, the scientists and clinicians who encourage them are misrepresenting the facts, and we have reached a strange impasse in our civilization when we rely for information and moral guidance about habits on the most debilitated

Addiction can be initiated through habit, peer pressure, or life-style; which in turn can lead to a physical dependence. Addiction, however, is not a disease and controlling it is ultimately the responsibility of the individual.

segments of our population—groups who attribute to addiction and drugs what are actually their personal problems. What, really, are we to learn from people who stand up and testify that they couldn't control their shopping sprees, that they spent all their money and went bankrupt to get material possessions we were smart enough to resist, and that they now want us to forgive them and their debts?

The message in all this is that one of the best antidotes to addiction is to teach children responsibility and respect for others and to insist on ethical standards for everyone— children, adults, addicts. Crosscultural data indicate, for instance, that when an experience is defined as uncontrollable, many people experience such loss of control and use it to justify their transgressions against society. For example, studies find that the "uncontrollable" consequences of alcohol consumption vary from one society to another, depending upon cultural expectations. In arctic Finland, drinking ses-

sions regularly lead to knife fights and killings; in Mediterranean countries such as Greece, on the other hand, such violence is virtually unheard of, and people do not perceive a link between alcohol and aggression.

The modern "scientific" view of alcoholism and addiction has actually caused addictive behaviors of all kinds to grow. It excuses uncontrolled behavior and predisposes people to interpret their lack of control as the expression of a disease which they can do nothing about. Treatment advocates attack those who don't accept the disease model of addiction as being "unscientific" and "moralistic," or as practicing "denial." On the contrary, the refusal to accept the loss-of-control myth seems to inoculate people against addiction.

One of the worst consequences of the idea that addiction and alcoholism are diseases is the notion that substance abuse can be treated away, a view continuously propagated by a large and growing addiction-treatment establishment and bought by well-meaning public officials and private citizens. In fact, these treatments are exorbitantly expensive ($7,500 to $35,000 a month in a private treatment center) while being demonstrably ineffective.

One of the most remarkable works of addictionology of the 1980s was a tome by psychiatrist George Vaillant entitled *The Natural History of Alcoholism*. Vaillant defended throughout his book the medical model of alcoholism, but then revealed that the alcoholics he treated at Cambridge Hospital in Massachusetts with detoxification, compulsory A.A. attendance, and counseling fared no better than comparably severe alcoholics who went completely without treatment. Several times in this strange book, Vaillant warns professional readers not to interfere with "the natural healing process"—this, in a work by a psychiatrist who insists that we need to get more alcoholics into treatment.

What works in fact for alcoholism and addiction is giving people the options and values that rule out addictive drug use. Investing more in futile but expensive treatment programs simply subtracts from the resources that are available to influence people's actual environments in ways that can reduce their vulnerability to addiction. Even Dr. Herbert Kleber, Bennett's deputy in charge of "demand reduction," has indicated that addicts can only be treated by being "given a place in the family and social structures" that they may never have had before. In other words, as Kleber puts it, they require "habilitation more than rehabilitation."

The head of the NIDA, Charles Schuster, indicates that in treating drug addicts, "the best predictor of success is whether the addict has a job." Of course, the best way to avoid addiction in the first place is to have in place social structures, jobs, and values that militate against habitual intoxication. But these are hardly treatment issues, and to approach them as such is to attack the problem in a belated, piecemeal, and ultimately self-defeating way.

Thus, to the extent that Bennett and Bush's "war on drugs" focuses on external agents and supplies, it not only misses the point of addiction, it actually deprives domestic programs of the resources they need to have any impact on the conditions in inner cities that fertilize drug abuse. As for Bennett's resolve to stamp out casual drug use as a part of his attack on addiction, there really is no relation between the two. As Bush himself indicated in his nationally televised speech in September, the NIDA found that 23 million Americans had used an illicit drug during the previous month when questioned in 1985, a number that declined to 14.5 million in 1988. Yet during this same period, daily drug use—and especially cocaine addiction—climbed.

Clearly, although we convinced those with the most personal resources and responsibility to stop experimenting with drugs, those who are unable or unwilling to control their drug use grew more numerous and found themselves in a deeper hole. At the same time, as we have seen, the NIDA survey to which Bush alluded found that miniscule numbers of those who experiment with cocaine become addicts. Here we see how the administration's own statistics disprove the link between recreational drug use and addiction that Bennett seeks to claim.

In the area of addiction, what is purveyed as fact is usually wrong and simply repackages popular myths as if they were the latest scientific deductions. To be ignorant of the received opinion about addiction is to have the best chance to say something sensible and to have an impact on the problem.

Breaking the Cycle of Addiction

A mix of drug therapy, behavioral therapy, and psychotherapy may prove to be most effective as researchers examine clinical data on how to treat cocaine addiction

A DOCTOR WHO TREATS PEOPLE for drug addiction tells this story. "A woman was doing very well in treatment. Then one day she was changing her baby's diaper. She used baby powder and the sight of the white powder induced a tremendous craving for cocaine."

Charles O'Brien of the University of Pennsylvania in Philadelphia and the Philadelphia Veterans Administration Medical Center is the doctor. "The greatest clinical problem [in treating patients for drug addiction] is relapse," he says. Common, sometimes unexpected reminders of drug use can lure a chronic user to take cocaine again.

Faced with this intractable cycle of drug-taking behavior, those who treat cocaine addicts have been handicapped because until recently no one knew whether one method of treatment was any more effective than another. Now, physicians who are testing various methods in clinical trials are coming to believe that a combination of drug therapy, behavioral therapy, and psychotherapy is most likely to be effective. As yet, however, they are still in the early stages of evaluating these and other components of a more comprehensive treatment program.

The emerging treatment strategies represent a radical departure from the conventional wisdom that a person's addiction to cocaine was purely a psychological problem. People have used cocaine since the late 1800s, but not until 7 or 8 years ago did researchers recognize that it is a powerfully addictive drug. The delay helps to explain why efforts to identify specific programs for treating cocaine addiction are still in their infancy.

Many of the responses a person has to cocaine stem from neurochemical actions of the drug itself. For instance, several researchers think that one reason why cocaine initially causes such intense euphoria and pleasure is that it directly stimulates a so-called reward system in the brain that uses dopamine as a neurotransmitter (*Science*, 22 July, p. 416). Over time, however, the brain system behaves as if it is depleted and chronic users take cocaine to feel any pleasure at all. Habitually snorting cocaine powder or smoking "crack," a free-base form of the powdered salt, produces these effects, although many physicians think that people who smoke crack are more likely to become addicted and that they do so more quickly.

At the recent American Psychiatric Association meeting,* Frank Gawin and Herbert Kleber of Yale University School of Medicine in New Haven, Connecticut, discussed results of a controlled clinical trial in which they tested desipramine, a widely used antidepressant, in a group of chronic cocaine abusers. Of the 72 people enrolled in their 3-year study, one-third received desipramine, another third got lithium, and the rest were given placebo, each for 6 weeks. Sixty percent of those receiving desipramine were able to stop taking cocaine for 3 weeks or more, in contrast to 23% on lithium and 17% on placebo.

The Yale researchers view desipramine therapy as only one part of a treatment program that will ultimately include other therapies. "Desipramine is not being used as a cure for cocaine addiction, but as an adjunct to initiate abstinence," says Gawin. "It is somewhat like ameliorating the early withdrawal symptoms associated with opiate and alcohol withdrawal." Unlike the alcohol-related DTs or the muscle spasms, sweating, and nausea of heroin withdrawal, few physical symptoms result from cocaine withdrawal. Instead, users who stop repeatedly bingeing on cocaine go through three distinct stages.

The first, immediate phase is a crash, says Gawin, characterized in its early stages by a rapid descent of mood and physical activity,

---

*The annual American Psychiatric Association meeting was held 7 to 12 May in Montreal, Quebec.

fatigue, and an intense craving for more drug. Although the person ultimately feels exhausted toward the end of this phase, sleep is often difficult and addicts may drink alcohol, take tranquilizers such as Valium, or inject heroin to relax, which can lead to dependence on other drugs.

The second phase of drug abstinence lasts for several weeks. It begins as sleep patterns become more normal, the person's mood improves, and craving for drug decreases. During the middle and late parts of this phase, however, the person becomes anxious, craves cocaine again, and is typically unable to experience normal pleasures from food or sex, for instance—a state called anhedonia. "The most common complaint of chronic cocaine users is boredom, since they don't know the word anhedonia" says Gawin. He sees anhedonia as a major force that drives habitual users to take cocaine again.

If the chronic user makes it to the third stage of withdrawal, the ability to experience pleasure can return along with a better mood. But the person may still feel episodic craving for cocaine. Treatment programs are geared to help addicts reach this stage and remain free from cocaine use.

The role of desipramine in a program to treat cocaine abusers is still being debated. No one is certain exactly how the drug relieves depression, and researchers are even further from understanding how it helps some addicts stop taking cocaine for a while. The drug apparently blocks the reuptake of norepinephrine and serotonin into brain neurons. A prevalent theory is that the levels of these neurotransmitters are too low in depressed patients and that desipramine normalizes the levels. Gawin and Kleber speculate that in cocaine addicts desipramine relieves craving because it binds to a population of receptors in the brain reward pathway that regulate dopamine function.

While desipramine may help an addict to

break away from cocaine use for short periods of time, many researchers think that additional kinds of therapy will be needed to maintain long-term abstinence.

"No matter how many times you can get a person to stop smoking, drinking, or using cocaine, they often relapse," says O'Brien. "And this is where conditioned behavior is so important." He, Anna Rose Childress, A. Thomas McLellan, and George Woody, also of Philadelphia, and their colleagues, are testing a specific form of behavioral conditioning that is designed to disrupt patterns of behavior associated with repetitive drug taking. Alone it appears to be of little value, but in combination with psychotherapy or counseling it seems to help.

The Philadelphia researchers find that addicts are often not aware that the sight of drug paraphernalia or driving by the place where they used to buy drugs induces a tremendous craving for cocaine. For the addict, chronic cocaine use induces a kind of learning and memory much like the classical conditioning of Pavlov's dog in which the dog learned to salivate when he heard a bell that was previously associated with food.

"We hook the patients up to a polygraph and show them videos of people using drugs or handling the paraphernalia," says O'Brien. "They get an increased heart rate, reduced skin temperature, and other dramatic indications of physiological arousal. They get upset and scared and say things like 'My God, I didn't know I still had this in me.'"

O'Brien and his co-workers use the videos and various cognitive methods to train their patients in a safe environment where no drugs are available. The overall process, which is called extinction of conditioned behavior, involves "repeatedly exposing a person to the stimuli that produce arousal," says O'Brien. With repetitive exposures, the arousal and craving for cocaine diminish. "We have tested extinction as a behavioral therapy and alone it is not effective," he says. "So then we ask if it adds to the benefit of other therapies." A clinical trial that is just ending indicates that it does.

"The best results seem to occur in the group of patients receiving psychotherapy from professionals plus extinction, and the second best combination is counseling—by experienced people who are not health pro-fessionals—plus extinction," says O'Brien. Less effective were counseling alone or psychotherapy alone.

"None of these people is cured," says O'Brien. "Obviously we'd like to get them to the point where they never relapse, but our best results are to have longer periods of remission. It is like having arthritis or diabetes; people learn to live in spite of their illness."

Kleber adds another dimension to the problem of relapse. "We [physicians] have a different goal than the patient," he says. "The patients want to go back to controlled use of cocaine, but I don't believe that once you have been addicted you can return to a controlled use pattern."

To date, no one's rules for treating chronic cocaine users are hard and fast. Kleber and Gawin are testing other drugs in addition to desipramine, including sertralene (which blocks serotonin reuptake), mazindol (an antiobesity drug), buspirone (an antianxiety drug not related to Valium), and chlorpromazine (an antipsychotic). They are also testing a combination of desipramine therapy with other forms of behavioral therapy. "We don't do formalized extinction training as O'Brien does," says Kleber. "Instead, we teach patients to avoid high risk situations and train them how to handle dangerous situations. We also try to reinforce how bad their addiction to cocaine was."

An issue that complicates any drug treatment program, including one for cocaine addiction, is that patients may have an underlying psychiatric problem in addition to their dependence on drugs. "There is no doubt that anecdotally, a significant percentage of people who go to mental health facilities have combined psychiatric disorders and substance abuse problems," says Lewis Judd of the National Institute of Mental Health in Rockville, Maryland. The problem is compounded because few treatment centers are equipped to handle these patients, he says.

No one is certain of the exact percentage, but several studies indicate that about half the people who take cocaine chronically have a history of affective (mood) disorder—about 30% have been depressed at some time in their lives and roughly 20% have had cyclothymia, a mild form of manic depressive disorder. A smaller percentage have a history of attentional deficit disorder and a few were at some time diagnosed with antisocial disorder.

Estimating the number of people with specific combinations of mental disorders and drug abuse problems is not easy, because of the lack of statistically valid surveys on large populations. As a result, most of the information about patients with a dual diagnoses of mental illness and substance abuse comes from interviews of people who enter treatment programs, who may not be a representative group.

Researchers also need to understand how a mental disorder may affect someone's ability to stop using drugs, says Jerome Jaffe of the Addiction Research Center in Baltimore, Maryland. "For instance, people who are depressed often find it more difficult to stop smoking, or stop taking opiates or cocaine," he says. "We are not sure if the depression precedes or follows the drug use, but how important is that? What is important is the person's state of mind at the time." Besides, he says, clinicians must deal with the drug abuse first before they can separate depression due to drug withdrawal from an underlying depression.

Physicians now have a drug and a mix of behavioral and psychotherapy that seem to help people stop using cocaine, at least initially. The next steps will be to test other forms of therapy alone and to combine them in various treatment programs to see which are most effective for different populations of patients. In the process researchers will continue to learn more about addiction and how to break its cycle.

Deborah M. Barnes

ADDITIONAL READING

C. P. O'Brien *et al.*, "Pharmacological and behavioral treatments of cocaine dependence: Controlled studies," *J. Clin. Psychiatry* **49**, 17 (1988).

F. H. Gawin and E. H. Ellinwood, "Cocaine and other stimulants: Actions, abuse, and treatment," *New Engl. J. Med.* **18**, 1173 (1988).

AIN'T MISBEHAVIN'

Addiction Has Become an All-Purpose Excuse

STANTON PEELE

STANTON PEELE, a senior survey researcher at Mathematica Policy Research, Inc., in Princeton, New Jersey, is the author of several books on addiction, most recently DISEASING OF AMERICA: ADDICTION TREATMENT OUT OF CONTROL, *which is being published by Lexington Books in August.*

SWEPT UP in the hurly-burly of an American presidential campaign, Kitty Dukakis looked to be in her element. Throughout the gaudy carnival of speechmaking and handshaking, she exuded warmth and a kind of kinetic energy that, to many observers, offered a refreshing contrast to the rather stolid manner of her husband, Massachusetts Governor Michael S. Dukakis, the Democratic aspirant. And, though candidate Dukakis was repudiated at the polls, his wife seemed to have emerged a winner—popular and admired, with a lucrative career as an author and lecturer looming before her. But scarcely three months after the election, it was a weary, wistful Kitty Dukakis who appeared on the cover of *Newsweek*, with the headlines "Addictive Personalities: Who gets hooked on drugs and alcohol—and why" and "Kitty Dukakis: Her private struggle."

Inside the magazine were more photographs showing her face haggard and tormented, accompanied by an account of why she had checked herself into Edgehill-Newport, a Rhode Island treatment center for alcohol and drug dependency. Mrs. Dukakis (who, in the past, had frankly discussed her apparently successful recovery from a twenty-six-year bout with amphetamines) had suddenly begun drinking to excess. As Governor Dukakis said at the time, "She clearly recognizes she has a sickness—and it is a sickness—and she had to deal with it."

Two weeks later, *New York Newsday* ran a front-page photograph of Grace Ann Machate, taken as she followed a flag-draped casket bearing the body of her husband, police officer Robert Machate, down the steps of a Brooklyn church. In the early-morning stillness several days before, Machate, twenty-five years old, had been slain with his own revolver on a deserted city street while attempting to arrest a suspected drug dealer. He was the seventh New York–area law officer killed in the line of duty within

a year whose death was tied to drug trafficking. That day's newspaper also carried an Associated Press Wirephoto of Kitty and Michael Dukakis, smiling and waving buoyantly upon arriving home after Mrs. Dukakis's completion of treatment at Edgehill-Newport.

These stories exemplify the range of news about alcohol and drug problems that, through various media, bombards the American public. At one end of the spectrum are tales of high-powered celebrities—entertainers, athletes, political figures—some of whom, like Kitty Dukakis, enter expensive rehabilitation clinics. In stark contrast are grim reports from city streets, where random violence associated with heroin, cocaine, and, recently, crack (a potent, inexpensive cocaine derivative) has infected many neighborhoods, threatening grandmothers, toddlers, and police officers alike. Between these extremes are constant reminders of how substance abuse threatens children of the middle class: one is hard put to find a town in New Jersey, for instance, without a street sign bearing the caution Drug-free School Zone. Similarly, organizations such as Mothers Against Drunk Driving have arisen from suburban, middle-class roots.

In the minds of most Americans, narcotics and alcohol are linked inextricably with addiction, an idea that conjures up images of the crazed user, oblivious to anything but obtaining more of his or her particular poison, who will stop at nothing to get it. To be sure, drugs and alcohol have chemical effects, and withdrawal from habitual use of those substances can elicit a raft of irritating physical sensations. But beyond that, science, and now the public, has embraced the notion that addicts suffer from a physiologically well-defined phenomenon—as Governor Dukakis put it, "a sickness"—even though repeated attempts to prove that addiction is a clear-cut medical condition have been, at best, inconclusive. The addiction-as-disease idea has spread wildly, to encompass not only chemical dependency but also a host of other compulsive behaviors, including gambling, overeating, undereating, shopping, and fornication. The "addiction" issue of *Newsweek*, for example, carried an unrelated story about the travails of Boston Red Sox third baseman Wade Boggs, who was being sued for twelve million dollars by a woman who had long provided him with companionship on road trips. In explaining the liaison, the married Boggs confessed that he was "addicted to sex"—to which his former mistress responded, "I guess what I thought was love was just a disease."

The pervasive and growing influence of the disease model of addiction has serious ramifications for American society. The more psychologists and attorneys dismiss forms of misbehavior as uncontrollable compulsions, the less people are held accountable for their actions—even when they have harmed others. Often, the only penalty for gross, even criminal misconduct is undergoing counseling in a treatment center. Creating a world of addictive diseases may mean creating a world in which anything is excusable, one that must inevitably slide into chaos.

WHILE THE WORD is attached to a growing crowd of compulsive behaviors, addiction still is most commonly associated with narcotics use—so much so that *drug* and *addiction* seem almost synonymous. The drugs most often thought of as addictive are the opiates (derivatives of opium, the dried milky discharge of the poppy plant), which are unsurpassed as pain-killers and sleep inducers and include heroin, morphine, and the milder formula, codeine.

Though opiates have been used commonly for most of recorded history, only since the eighteenth century have their addictive effects been explored in any detail. In one of the earliest descriptions of withdrawal symptoms, written in 1701, the English physician John Jones cited perspiration, frequent urination, loose bowels, depression, and chronic itching as likely results of sudden curtailment of habitual opium ingestion. Similar notes were sounded in scattered English medical journals over the next one hundred and fifty years, and in 1850, Jonathan Pereira, in *Elements of Materia Medica and Therapeutics*, one of the most respected medical manuals of the time, warned that excessive opium intake brings on moral, as well as physical, deterioration and that children of drug addicts were apt to be "weak, stunted, and decrepit."

Despite these caveats, the use of opiates in Europe and the United States spiraled upward. Physicians dispensed narcotics indiscriminately, and for the most part, neither the general public nor the medical profession had any notion that opiates were especially dangerous. While their consumption often was described as addictive, the opiates themselves were not considered any more habit-forming than other pharmacological agents. Indeed, prominent turn-of-the-century pharmacologists, such as Clifford Allbutt and Walter E. Dixon, of England, were just as concerned about withdrawal from caffeine, often resulting from curtailment of habitual coffee drinking:

The sufferer is tremulous and loses his self-command; he is subject to fits of agitation and depression. He has a haggard appearance.... As with other such agents, a renewed dose of the poison gives temporary relief, but at the cost of future misery.

At that time, according to the English research team of historian Virginia Berridge and psychiatrist Griffith Edwards (writing in 1981, in *Opium and the People*, an extensive review of English opiate use during the nineteenth century), addiction was viewed as any indulgence in an act that was mildly damaging to health and perhaps a little bit of a nuisance.

In the final quarter of the nineteenth century, a small number of German scientists began to conduct research into drug addiction. In 1878, one of them, the physician Eduard Levinstein, published *The Morbid Craving for Morphia*, in which he described morphia addiction as "the uncontrollable desire...to use morphine as a stimulant and a tonic, and the diseased state of the system caused by the injudicious use of the said remedy." And, presaging modern notions, he argued, albeit without experimental evidence, that the compulsion to take narcotics results "from the natural constitution"—that, in effect, drug addicts are victims of physiology. Still, Levinstein remained true to the established view of his time (and, increasingly, our own), making no distinction between addiction to drugs and other "passions," including smoking, gambling, greed, and sexual excess.

The reclassification of drug addiction as a medical condition rather than a passion, vice, or other behavioral phenomenon did not occur as a result of startling new studies of narcotics users or even of animal experiments. Instead, the idea slipped unseen into the realm of conventional wisdom on the coattails of other scientific developments. In finding bacterial and viral causes for infectious diseases, Louis Pasteur, Robert Koch, and other researchers of a century ago helped create a climate in which a medical cure for almost any ill seemed possible. And since drug addiction has physical manifestations, it seemed safe to assume that it, too, was a disease that could be cured, even in the absence of evidence that addiction displays specific symptoms, follows a particular course, or responds to treatment as infectious diseases do.

Coincidental with the medicalizing of addiction was a dramatic rise in the number of drug addicts. The reasons are unclear, but when alcoholism and compulsive drug use gained acceptance as forms of illness, during the 1890s, narcotics addiction had ebbed in England and America. Then, during the next ten years the trend reversed, and by 1910 the level of English opium consumption had returned to its nineteenth-century peaks.

The situation in the United States was in some ways more extreme. Like the English, Americans consumed massive quantities of opium at the turn of the century, especially in the form of patent medicines available at local dime stores and peddled by itinerant salesmen. Another important catalyst for American addiction had come in 1898, with the invention by the Bayer company of the morphine derivative heroin. Legal at the time, heroin was easily administered by syringe and was ten times more potent than its parent drug.

America went on to become the world leader in narcotics addiction. In many nations the opium poppy is cultivated openly, yet addiction is virtually nonexistent: native peoples consider the drug harmless and use it only for ceremonial purposes. European nations—including France, where much of America's heroin supply is processed—

also have had negligible addiction problems. Even England has had dramatically lower levels of heroin addiction than the United States. Indeed, drug use in America has come to be surrounded by a kind of mystique, which intensified when control of narcotics began to shift from physicians to government and law-enforcement officials. (In 1914, the Harrison Act, passed by the U.S. Congress, regulated the use of opiates and other drugs.) And as drugs became an object of social disapproval, there was a change in the groups that used them.

During the 1800s, much attention was focused on Chinese opium smoking, but the leading consumers of opium were, in fact, white, middle-class women, who apparently preferred the drug to their husbands' alternative, alcohol. By 1920, however, drugs had moved underground, to urban ghettos, where they were used predominantly by poor immigrant and minority males. Narcotics, especially heroin, had become an exotic source of horror and fascination for Americans. What once had been available at any local apothecary now was seen as the agent of an insidious compulsion that was an inevitable consequence of its use. Still, despite all the research into the pathology of cholera, malaria, influenza, and other diseases, the first quarter of this century passed before any attempt was made to find physiological evidence that narcotics use meant inescapable physical bondage.

THE PIONEERING EFFORT to demonstrate a biomedical basis for addiction in human drug users was begun in 1925, at Philadelphia General Hospital. A team of researchers—an internist, a pathologist, a psychiatrist, and a chemist—administered a series of heavy doses of morphine to a group of drug addicts. To check for signs of physiological addiction, they measured the subjects' body functions and observed their performance on several tasks during withdrawal. But they found little evidence that addiction was much more than a result of the subjects' imaginations. In one of a series of articles based on this research, published in 1929 in the *Archives of Internal Medicine*, two of the Philadelphia physicians, Arthur B. Light and Edward G. Torrance, described the amazing behavior of their most recalcitrant subject, a man who was the quickest to express his displeasure when there was even the slightest delay in the administration of a drug. He refused to continue the experiment thirty-six hours after withdrawal, demanding instead that he be given more morphine. Light and Torrance administered a placebo and were bemused when the man "promptly went to sleep for a period of eight hours," never aware that he had been given "nothing but sterile water."

The researchers noted that, in general, though "the incessant begging and annoying behavior of the addict" during withdrawal "becomes at times almost unbearable," there were no marked changes in their patients' metabolism, circulation, respiration, or blood composition. Light and Torrance did observe such withdrawal symptoms as vomiting, diarrhea, perspiration, and nervousness, but because these occurred inconsistently, they did not appear to indicate a medical syndrome. In fact, the researchers reported that similar symptoms can be found among members of a university football team just before the proverbial big game—symptoms that disappear "when the whistle starting the game is blown."

Over the years, this work has been all but dismissed by the scientific community. Light and Torrance have been accused of ignoring the biological realities of addiction by mistaking physiological withdrawal for malingering. But this criticism fails to account for some of the most striking aspects of their findings. The addicts in their studies had been given extremely high levels of morphine—certainly in comparison with standard doses of narcotics available to American street addicts today—yet, when eventually denied their fixes, they overcame the ensuing withdrawal symptoms and lost their cravings. Some did so under forced regimens of physical exertion (when withdrawal set in, they were made to climb steps, for instance); others, after placebo injections.

In contrast, today's heroin addicts typically manifest severe, unremitting withdrawal symptoms when deprived of the drug at treatment centers—even though, as opposed to the addicts in the 1925 study, they often enter rehabilitation with no detectable concentrations of narcotics in their systems. (Drugs sold on the street typically are mixed with liberal amounts of benign substances, so the user is not exposed to large doses of narcotics.) Nevertheless, physicians continue to maintain that withdrawal and readdiction are inevitable consequences of habitual narcotics use, inherent in the chemical properties of the drugs—and that people who take these drugs are bound to consume them more frequently, compulsively, and invariantly than do users of other, so-called nonaddictive pharmacological products.

One of the most damning refutations of this belief is research into narcotics use by American soldiers who served in Vietnam. A vast proportion of the men used opiates at one time or another during the war. This panicked American officials, who anticipated a wholesale influx of addicts stateside when the veterans returned home. The U.S. Department of Defense commissioned a research team, led by the epidemiologist Lee N. Robins, to study the military drug problem. Robins and her colleagues interviewed more than five hundred men who had used narcotics in Vietnam (identified by urine screening upon their departure) one year and then three years after their return home. Most had received a concentrated form of the drugs while in Southeast Asia, and of those who took narcotics five or more times, nearly three-quarters reported becoming addicted: they suffered significant withdrawal symptoms when they were forced to stop using heroin for various reasons (they could not get any while out on patrol, for example).

According to all widely accepted ideas about heroin abuse, recovery depends on total abstinence. So, most of the returning soldiers who had been addicts, had they sought the drug back in the United States, should have become readdicted in short order. But Robins discovered that, while fully half of those who had been addicted in Vietnam used narcotics again upon their return home, only one-eighth became readdicted after three years back in the United States. And only half of those who used heroin frequently—more than once a week for what Robins described as "a considerable period of time"—became readdicted.

Robins's research yielded other surprising results. The

returning veterans in her sample commonly consumed a variety of drugs besides heroin, including marijuana and amphetamines, though heroin addicts supposedly are possessed by a monomaniacal obsession for heroin. Moreover, their indulgence in heroin was no more compulsive or uncontrollable than their consumption of the other substances. All this evidence calls into question the long-held claim that opiates are special agents of addiction. Remarkably, however, such findings have had virtually no impact on addiction research and theory.

More influential has been a large body of experiments in which rats or monkeys continually self-administer drugs in the laboratory—studies often cited in support of the argument that narcotics are uniquely addictive. Yet, what many of these experiments have demonstrated is that it can be extremely difficult to addict animals. John L. Falk, a behavioral pharmacologist at Rutgers University, in New Jersey, found it necessary to alter the accustomed feeding regimen of rats to get them to drink significant amounts of alcohol. When a normal feeding regimen was resumed, the rats lost nearly all interest in alcohol. As Falk pointed out in a 1983 article entitled "Drug Dependence: Myth or Motive?" these results are consistent with other investigations showing that the motivational power of drugs over animals is "altered radically by seemingly small changes in the behavioral context." For example, many studies in which animals are required to press a bar to earn a narcotic injection have shown that increasing only slightly the number of requisite bar presses can halt the animal's drug consumption.

In one series of experiments, Bruce K. Alexander, a psychologist at Simon Fraser University, in British Columbia, found that rats housed together in a large cage would not choose an opiate solution over water but that rats isolated in small cages drank significantly more of the opiate. Moreover, even after a period of being allowed to drink only the drugged liquid, the animals that had been isolated also chose water over the opiate when they were placed in the roomier cage and could once again enjoy the companionship of other rats. These experiments strongly suggest that drug dependence is a consequence of behavior *and* environment, and that, although animals and some people will, under certain circumstances, consume drugs excessively and compulsively, it does not follow that narcotics are inherently addictive.

Certainly, the Vietnam experience also served as a kind of laboratory demonstration of how environmental factors can create a climate hospitable to addiction. In Southeast Asia, most American soldiers encountered a range of emotions and sensations unlike anything they had experienced at home: incessant fear, constant physical discomfort, intense loneliness for family and friends, the necessity for killing, a sense of complete helplessness— the inability to control their own destinies or even to know whether they would live to see the next dawn. In this alien world, the numbing, analgesic effects of narcotics were welcomed. But when returned to the secure familiarity of home, most of the men who were hooked in Vietnam—even if they felt moved to take a drug now and again—did not find narcotics addictively alluring.

As Harold Kalant, a pharmacologist at the Addiction Research Foundation, in Toronto, observed after decades

of work, given that the drug user or alcoholic often continues to seek the intoxicated state even after completing the period of withdrawal, there can be no pharmacological or biological explanations for this behavior. Clearly, any habit has an impact on a person's body and mind, but interpreting how a pharmacological experience feels, deciding that this feeling is desirable, concluding that it is impossible to live without it, and seeking more of it all are matters of individual perception and choice.

GIVEN THAT THERE IS NO EVIDENCE for a purely physiological explanation of addiction, the whole process of labeling a drug addictive is arbitrary at best. One of the more telling examples of this is the evolution of American public policy concerning cocaine. As difficult as it may be to fathom today, cocaine once was an active ingredient in soda pop: Coca-Cola contained a dose of the drug until 1903. Though narcotics researchers have explored the addictive potential of cocaine for the past fifty years in the laboratory, only upon a sudden rise in recreational cocaine consumption, as well as a proportional rise in compulsive use, during the early eighties, did government agencies ordain that the drug be regarded as addictive. In fact, that judgment directly contradicted the most comprehensive experimental findings available.

In a recent survey, investigators at the Toronto addiction-research center found that twenty percent of the recreational cocaine users they studied had frequently been seized by an urge to continue taking the drug, but, even among this minority, most did not become fully addicted. A review of the literature on cocaine use, by the Yale University psychiatrist David Musto, pointed out that less than ten percent of regular cocaine users descend into a pattern of compulsive, uncontrollable consumption. Nonetheless, we are warned repeatedly that to "say yes" to cocaine is to slide inexorably into chemical bondage and, ultimately, death.

As Berridge and Edwards point out, this publicity campaign echoes an earlier time: "The nineteenth-century discovery that the addict is a suitable case for treatment is today an entrenched and unquestionable premise, with society unaware of the arbitrariness of this come-lately assumption." The researchers add that any suggestion that addicts be "left to their own devices would be dismissed only as outrageous and bizarre." In the light of the failure of researchers to link narcotics addiction or, for that matter, alcoholism with physiology, it seems all the more absurd that so many sexually driven people, compulsive shoppers, and other obsessive types have joined substance abusers in the special programs and treatment centers that have proliferated across the country.

WHAT, EXACTLY, goes on inside these rehabilitation facilities? Certainly, Edwards's disillusionment with them is based, in part, on his own research experience in England (where he is considered the leading psychiatric authority on addiction). In a controlled study of hospital treatment for alcoholism, he and his colleagues found that problem drinkers given a single session of counseling improved just as much as a comparable group receiving the full complement of inpatient and outpatient hospital services, including detoxification programs and follow-up counseling. Similarly, a study by the psychiatrist George Vaillant, of Dartmouth College, checked the progress of hospital-treated alcoholics two and then eight years after their release. Though some had cut down on drinking or ceased altogether, they had done so only in roughly the same proportions as untreated alcoholics.

Still, many graduates of treatment centers passionately proclaim that their lives have been saved by the help they sought. In part, this may be because alcoholics and addicts who enter such treatment programs often are effectively brainwashed into believing they have an incurable disease. The sociologist David R. Rudy, of Morehead State University, in Kentucky, who observed several chapters of Alcoholics Anonymous, reported, in *Becoming Alcoholic*, that a number of those who entered these groups did so believing that they had some kind of drinking problem but not that they had succumbed to uncontrollable alcoholism. Once inside the group, however, they quickly were shown the error of their thinking; new members were pressured into acknowledging that, because of their disease, their drinking was out of control.

This brainwashing exerts a powerful influence on the addict's perception of his or her addiction. An experiment conducted by the psychologist G. Alan Marlatt, of the University of Washington, in Seattle, demonstrated the effects on active alcoholics of believing that one slip off the wagon leads to a binge. Alcoholics in the study were given highly flavored drinks either with or without alcohol. Some were told that they were drinking liquor, others that they were consuming a nonalcoholic beverage. Marlatt found that alcoholics who believed they were drinking alcohol—whether or not they were—drank significantly more than those who were actually given alcohol without their knowledge. Having learned that even a casual brush with liquor means an inevitable relapse, the alcoholics given the placebo lived out their expectations. But it had nothing to do with physiology.

T HE FUNDAMENTAL TENET of Alcoholics Anonymous—that alcoholism is never cured—has been imposed upon almost every bad habit imaginable, and as a result, a thriving addiction-treatment industry has developed in the United States. Comparing statistics from 1942 with those from 1976, Robin Room, of the Alcohol Research Group, in Berkeley, California, found that the number of people being treated for alcoholism in America, per capita, had increased twentyfold. And in the ten years since Room's survey, treatment has continued to grow at an alarming rate. Yet Americans over twenty-one drink less today than a decade ago. One explanation for this paradox is that the threshold for labeling a person chemically dependent has been lowered—as with Kitty Dukakis, who referred herself to Edgehill-Newport because she had gotten drunk a few times after years of moderate drinking. By attracting such alcoholics as Mrs. Dukakis, private hospital chains that specialize in treating substance abuse continue to expand.

Meanwhile, new addiction-treatment groups modeled on Alcoholics Anonymous have proliferated, as well. The National Council on Compulsive Gambling, which coalesced from numerous Gamblers Anonymous groups, has grown even more rapidly during the eighties than the AA-inspired National Council on Alcoholism. Sometimes, compulsive gamblers are treated in hospitals, frequently on the same inpatient wards as alcoholics. And there is a National Association on Sexual Addiction Problems, as well as a nationwide network of Sex Addicts Anonymous branches, both of which support hospital treatment for "victims" of compulsive copulation.

Perhaps the most dire consequence of the disease model of addiction is that it has encouraged the abdication of individual responsibility for outrageous conduct. The addict is a victim and, thus, unaccountable for his actions. The misadventures of Wade Boggs, confessed "sex addict," may have provided the public with a measure of titillation. But another recent news event—the object of even more intense public and media preoccupation—had a more chilling aspect: jurors declined to deliver a murder conviction against Joel Steinberg (the disbarred Manhattan lawyer convicted of manslaughter in the fatal beating of his illegally adopted six-year-old daughter, Lisa), partly because they felt Steinberg, a habitual drug user, was under the influence of cocaine at the time of his daughter's death and, so, was not fully responsible.

Certainly, Joel Steinberg may have been impaired by the effects of a drug when he murdered Lisa. But was he suffering from a disease? Is there something in cocaine that interacted with the cells in Joel Steinberg's body to enslave him to the drug? And if so, must we forgive him for killing a child? There is no justification within the realm of science for making that conceptual leap.

A slip doesn't have to lead to a fall

Studies show ways recovering addicts can learn from their lapses

Daniel Goleman

New York Times

In news that should hearten anyone whose New Year resolutions are already in jeopardy, researchers say lapses do not necessarily mean that the effort is doomed.

Rather, they say, learning to overcome lapses is emerging as one of the most important parts of such efforts, whether they are trying to eat less or to give up smoking and other addictions.

"For any habit you want to change, the key to success is not just stopping, but keeping from relapsing," said Howard J. Shaffer, a psychologist at the Center for Addiction Studies at Harvard Medical School. "You can learn from a slip how to keep it from happening again."

Overcoming a relapse is the focus of a new treatment approach being used by therapists for patients with a wide range of addictions.

In addition to obvious applications, like alcoholism, overeating and drug addiction, the new techniques are being used with cardiac patients who must adopt a healthier way of life and also with sex offenders.

Their approach differs in emphasis from that of groups like Alcoholics Anonymous, which stress the need to avoid lapses altogether. "In AA people feel that if they slip and have a drink they're lost entirely, back to day one," Shaffer said.

"That attitude in itself can sometimes be enough to turn a slip into a full relapse, since it can lead to the attitude that if you've had one drink, you're off the wagon, so you may as well keep drinking."

Despite the difference in outlook, relapse prevention is often used along with treatment programs that involve Alcoholics Anonymous-type groups, said G. Allan Marlatt, a psychologist at the University of Washington who is an expert on breaking habits.

The approach is receiving wide recognition as a useful addition to virtually any of the dozens of therapeutic approaches now used to change self-defeating habits.

Researchers have found that most treatment approaches for all kinds of addictions have comparable long-term success rates and that they are all made more effective when techniques of avoiding and overcoming relapses are added.

"The key is what happens after the formal treatment ends and the patient returns to regular life," Shaffer said.

The importance of focusing on how people cope with temptations after they have changed a habit is highlighted by a study at Stanford Medical School, to be published next year by Oxford University Press.

In that study, people who had gone through one of five different treatment programs for alcoholism were studied for two years after completing the program.

A careful analysis of what contributed to their success or failure in staying dry was done by the researchers, Rudolph Moos, John Finney and Ruth Cronkite, all psychologists at Stanford.

"The results suggest that how people cope with stress after their treatment has a great deal to do with how well they will succeed," Finney said. "Relapse prevention is one of the most promising approaches these days."

The focus on relapse prevention has come largely from the work of Marlatt and a fellow psychologist at the University of Washington, Judith R. Gordon.

Theirs is a common-sense approach drawing on such homely wisdom as "forearmed is forewarned." But it not only prepares people to prevent relapses but also helps them take advantage of any slips rather than becoming demoralized by them.

Marlatt sees relapse prevention as applying to any habit people want to change.

It was inspired by studies in the early 1970s that found relapses in about three-quarters of those treated for addictions as diverse as smoking, alcoholism and heroin. The studies showed that two-thirds of the relapses occurred within 90 days of the end of treatment.

"About 20 percent of people can kick a habit on the first try, but most people need several attempts, no matter what the habit," Marlatt said.

In research with Susan Curry, a psychologist at the University of Washington, Marlatt and Gordon studied 123 heavy smokers who were trying to quit.

The participants had smoked for an average of 19 years and most had already tried to quit three or more times. The study was reported in the October issue of The Journal of Consulting and Clinical Psychology.

The researchers found that those

who succeeded in quitting tended to attribute their relapses to something in the situation rather than to a personal failing.

"The successful quitters focused on what they might have done differently, rather than on thoughts like, 'This just proves I'm addicted to nicotine,' " said Marlatt. "Those who went back to smoking tended to treat their first lapse as decisive. They felt guilty, blamed themselves for the lapse instead of the situation and saw the lapse as due to something in themselves they could not change, like a lack of willpower."

Many of those who eventually succeeded in quitting often had episodes when they smoked some cigarettes. But they were able to return to abstinence.

"They saw themselves as having made a mistake they need not repeat," said Marlatt. "For example, one man smoked when he went to a bar with an old friend who had come to town. He said afterward, 'That taught me I have to be particularly vigilant about smoking when I drink.' "

Part of the training in relapse prevention programs encourages people to identify those situations in which they are most likely to encounter temptation.

Often the pressures are social: being with friends who gamble or getting into family arguments.

Often the triggers are emotional. The triggering emotions are most often anger or frustration for men and depression for women, according to Marlatt.

In the training programs, one focus is on anticipating such situations, and finding more positive ways to deal with them.

Advising people just to say no is not enough, Shaffer said. "You need to rehearse exactly how you'll handle the situations when temptation is greatest," he advised. "At holiday parties, where there will be people plying you with rich foods, or alcohol, or even drugs, how will it be to refuse, and just what will you say?"

With his patients, Shaffer often plays the role of the person offering the temptation. He asks some patients to anticipate how they will spend every part of the day, virtually minute by minute, to identify what risky moments they face. Then, they can plan how they will deal with them.

One of the more novel applications of relapse prevention is with sex offenders, especially child molesters who receive psychological treatment in prison and are then paroled. The programs are being tried in California and in Florida.

"They've had to redefine what they mean by lapse in working with child molesters," Marlatt said. "If they commit the offense, it's already too late. So they count a lapse as simply having a sexual fantasy of the offense."

One principle in the relapse prevention training is to treat any slip as an emergency that needs to be dealt with immediately.

People going through the program are often given a small card they can take out for guidance. The card is described in "Relapse Prevention," a book edited by Marlatt and Gordon and published by Guilford Press.

The card advises that as soon as a lapse occurs, the person should stop and look carefully at what has just happened, and realize the need to take specific steps to assure that the slip does not undermine the effort to change the habit.

Card holders are advised that feelings of guilt and self-blame are likely, and they should allow it to pass until they become calm. They are reminded that a slip is a chance for learning, not a total failure. Card holders are then asked to remind themselves of the reasons they were trying to change the habit.

Then they are urged to review the situation that led to the lapse, paying special attention to their mood, who they were with and what they were doing, and if there were any early warning signals that they might use in the future to prepare themselves to ward off temptation.

They are then instructed to make an immediate plan for recovery from the slip.

"Throw away the rest of the pack of cigarettes," the card reads. "Pour out the remaining booze from the bottle."

Then, the card says, leave the scene of the slip. It urges the card holder to call a friend or psychotherapist for help, and to think of ways to avoid slipping.

The antidotes often take the form of a "positive addiction," finding something like regular exercise or gardening that the person can turn to when they feel most vulnerable to the old habit.

Perhaps most important is to keep trying instead of giving up. "Most people have several slips and lapses before they finally kick a habit," said Marlatt. "It's like mountain climbing; you may need several attempts before you reach the top."

Drugs don't take people; people take drugs

MONA CHAREN

AUGUST 24 — No doubt the Bush Administration's proposals for dealing with the drug scourge, to be presented after Labor bay, will contain lots of useful and even creative ideas. Bill Bennett has made creative ideas his specialty. But if President Bush really wants to make a contribution to solving this problem, he will start by acknowledging that we don't have a drug problem. We have a culture problem.

> *Heroin was listed as the hardest habit to kick, with cigarettes a close second. Cocaine, in all its forms including crack, was at the bottom of the list, behind alcohol.*

Sure, drugs are addictive, but the precise nature of addiction is poorly understood by scientists and varies from individual to individual. And yes, drugs do give rise to crime — but mostly indirectly, by creating a market for an illegal substance. This is not to say that widespread drug use is not a problem. It is. But the problem inheres in the kind of society which has so loosened its traditional supports — family, church, community — that its individual members are flying off in all directions like rivets from an exploding steel drum. It is the disintegration of traditional values, not the drugs themselves, that causes people to smoke and snort their lives away.

AMERICANS HAVE BECOME accustomed to thinking of drugs as some unstoppable outside force, utterly overwhelming a mere human's pathetic attempts to resist. But the truth is that drugs don't take people; people take drugs.

When heroin first burst into national consciousness in the 1960s, it was believed that the drug had stunning and unusual addictive properties. Today, though still considered the most difficult addiction to shake, heroin has lost its mystique.

In his book *The Hardest Drug*, John Kaplan examined the lives of heroin addicts in several cities and found, to his surprise, that withdrawal from the drug, far from the hellish torments he had expected, was actually very much like a bout of flu — definitely not pleasant, but endurable. So endurable, in fact, that addicts would voluntarily undergo withdrawal on a regular basis to regulate their need for the drug as the price fluctuated.

Now, reports the *New York Times*, new studies are debunking the current myth that crack addiction is too potent to be treated.

THE FASHIONABLE VIEW of crack as irresistible was bolstered by troubling animal studies. Monkeys who were taught that they could receive an injection of cocaine (the equivalent of crack) by pressing a bar in their cages would press the bar ceaselessly, stopping neither for food nor sleep, until they died. They would not do the same for heroin.

Scary. But a grain of salt is helpful. My confidence in the reliability of animal studies was profoundly shaken when my cat developed a fever. "I'll give him aspirin," I volunteered to the vet. "That's the worst thing you could do," she responded. "Aspirin is toxic to cats."

And people turn out to be different from monkeys too. Former human addicts at the Addiction Research Center in Baltimore, Md., were asked to compare withdrawal from various drugs. Heroin was listed as the hardest habit to kick, with cigarettes a close second. Cocaine, in all its forms including crack, was at the bottom of the list, behind alcohol.

So it is not the pharmacological properties of crack which have made it so difficult to treat. Rather, the specialists are saying, it is the culture to which detoxified addicts are returned that holds the key to the problem.

Dr. Michael Scheehe, president of a drug treatment center in New Canaan, Conn., told the *New York Times*, "We have to remove (addicts) from their communities. You have got to get them out of that drug environment. That environment is a morgue."

WE CANNOT EXPECT crack addicts to straighten out their lives when the norms of behavior among their families and peers include drug use, chronic unemployment, and crime. Studies of heroin addicts have found that the best predictor of successful rehabilitation was whether or not the addict had a job.

President Bush and William Bennett may think they're facing a drug problem. But in fact, drug abuse is merely one symptom among many — including teenage child-bearing, crime, and violence — of what happens when "traditional values" are trashed.

The drug problem is not pharmacological; it is moral.

From *Conservative Chronicle*, 1989, p. 25. Reprinted by permission of Mona Charen and Creators Syndicate, Inc.

Nasty Habits

Why Are Some Drugs, Such as Nicotine, So Addicting, While Other So-Called Hard Drugs Are Easier to Stop?

John Pekkanen

People usually think of addiction in terms of illicit mood-altering drugs, such as heroin. Over-the-counter or prescription drugs that are also mood-altering—tranquilizers, sleeping pills, and even pain-killers—are not thought to pose as great a threat of addiction, nor is the everyday consumption of alcohol, cigarettes, and coffee generally considered to be that hard to stop.

However, researchers are finding that in many cases the legal drugs are the most addictive, and the illegal ones easier to quit. In the words of Dr. Robert DuPont, a Washington psychiatrist and former director of the National Institute on Drug Abuse, "The way we've looked at drugs and drug abuse for the past 40 years has been wrong." Many drugs considered to be "hard" may actually be less likely to produce a dependency than seemingly more benign ones.

"The whole idea of separating physical addiction and psychological addiction has been very misleading, too," he goes on, "as if physical addiction were the real problem. I've seen people quit really powerful physical dependencies, such as long-term, high-dose heroin use, and I've seen others almost die to get a drug for which they supposedly had 'only' a psychological addiction."

Sweating, heart palpitations, and nausea are some signs of withdrawal from physical dependencies; if withdrawal produces no physical symptoms but leaves a craving for the drug, such as with cocaine, the addiction is termed psychological.

Several years ago I had a conversation with Dr. Maurice Seever, one of the leading drug-addiction researchers in the country. He was then at the University of Michigan. At the time, heroin was widely considered to be the most addictive of all drugs, and in many circles it is still believed to be. Dr. Seever designed a study to find out if this was true, as well as to determine the "addiction potential" of other drugs. He permitted monkeys to self-administer different drugs—each monkey could strike a handle in its cage, which activated a syringe that gave the monkey an intravenous drug fix. The monkeys were allowed to get as much of the drug as they wanted, and they became addicted. Dr. Seever then calculated the drug's addictive power by taking away the syringe and counting the number of times the monkey hit the handle for a fix. A myth was quickly dispelled. For physically addicting heroin, the monkeys would hit the bar several hundred times before giving up. But for cocaine, which causes only a psychological addiction, some monkeys hit the bar more than 10,000 times, "until their paws were bloody," Dr. Seever told me.

Mood-altering drugs can be divided into three categories:

Stimulants: Cocaine belongs to this class of drugs, as do nicotine and caffeine. Amphetamines and amphetamine-type drugs, such as Ritalin and Preludin, are stimulants, too, and go by the street name of speed. The appeal of stimulants is the energizing lift and sense of power the user gets. But used regularly, cocaine and amphetamines can create paranoia.

The strongest "rush" comes from cocaine, which is popular among professional athletes, entertainers, and others in high-pressure, high-visibility occupations. One would think, therefore, that cocaine would be the most addictive stimulant. But according to Dr. Donald Jasinski, scientific director of the Addiction Research Center in Baltimore and a widely recognized addiction expert, nicotine has more potential to addict.

"When we've given nicotine intravenously to addicts, they have described it as 'cocaine-like,'" says Dr. Norman Zinberg, a Harvard psychiatrist and recognized drug authority. Besides, he goes on, the effect of cocaine may last one or two hours, but people who smoke a lot of cigarettes get little nicotine highs all day long. When the nicotine is abruptly withdrawn, a powerful craving sets in. "Ninety-five percent of people who use nicotine [in cigarettes] become addicted to it. That is by far the highest addiction rate of any drug."

Although caffeine does not appear to be as strongly addictive as nicotine, people who drink half a dozen or more cups of coffee a day can suffer withdrawal

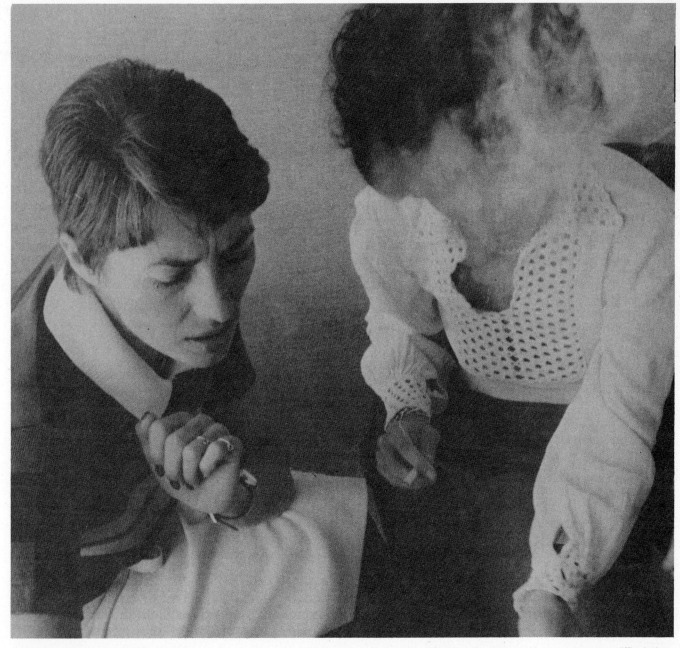

Cigarette smoking is a common habit, sanctioned by society, which often becomes an addiction. To stop smoking can be more difficult than breaking an addiction to hard drugs.

symptoms when they quit abruptly. Irritability, agitation, headaches, and nausea can occur.

Depressants: Included in this category are barbiturates, alcohol, opiates, and minor tranquilizers.

Barbiturates are probably the most physically dangerous of all drugs—far more so than cocaine or heroin. People have died from abruptly withdrawing from barbiturates. The short-acting ones, such as Nembutal and Seconal, are the most physically addictive drugs known. Although they are commonly used to help

induce sleep, they don't aid sleep after two weeks of use.

Other depressants have varying degrees of physical-addiction potential, with alcohol probably the strongest. It was once mistakenly thought that a single shot of heroin created addiction. However, perhaps half or even more of those who experiment with heroin don't become dependent on it.

Synthetic opiates, such as Percodan, are prescribed for pain and can be physically addictive. Although their euphoric effects appear to be minimal, they still

must be used cautiously because addiction is common for people with chronic pain. Codeine, an opiate used in cough syrups, is addictive but not at the levels usually prescribed.

Of the minor tranquilizers, Miltown is most like a barbiturate and is addictive. So are Valium and Librium, although they are less dangerous. However, they can create both physical and psychological dependencies because they are often taken to diminish stress. In this anxiety-ridden world, too many people rely on too many tranquilizers. Some people who grow used to high doses and then abruptly quit go into seizures.

Other depressants fall into the category called sopors, Quaaludes being the best known. Their physical-addiction potential lies somewhere between the minor tranquilizers and short-acting barbiturates. Originally devised by drug manufacturers as "safe" barbiturate substitutes, they can produce severe withdrawal symptoms.

The basic difference between stimulants and depressants, as far as addictive potential goes, is that depressants have a far greater tendency to produce a measurable physical addiction, while stimulants appear to create deeper psychological needs.

Hallucinogens: Included in this category are marijuana, peyote, LSD, STP, and others. Once thought not to create a dependency, some drugs in this group—particularly marijuana—are now believed to be addictive. Many long-term users of marijuana find it extremely difficult to quit. Says Dr. DuPont, "People who use marijuana for a long time can get addicted to it. It's not just a habit—I've seen it happen."

There are several reasons that some drugs are more addictive than others. One of the most important factors in drug dependency is enjoyment. Says Dr. DuPont, "The more a person likes a drug, the harder it is for him to quit." So it follows that the addictive potential of a drug depends partly on the person using it. For some, the stimulant effect of cocaine is unnerving and unpleasant; for others, it is pure euphoria.

Before Dr. Seever ever gave any of his monkeys a mood-altering drug, he always took it himself to test its effects. "The only one I'll never try a second time is cocaine," he says, "because it felt too good."

Dr. Zinberg adds that the more a drug alters your mood, the easier it is to quit. Because marijuana is a relatively mild hallucinogen, it may be the most addictive of this kind of drug.

Another consideration is genetic susceptibility. Some people, for instance, are biochemically more prone to alcoholism than others. The same is true for other drugs as well.

The circumstances under which a drug is taken can also make a difference in its potential to become addictive. Animal studies have revealed that rats kept alone in individual cages were much more likely to grow dependent on a drug than were rats with a "social life." Alcohol can be physically addicting, yet only 5 percent of those who try it become addicted to it. Dr. Zinberg believes that many people don't abuse alcohol because they drink in social settings where there are constraints against drunkenness, which is not the case with illicit drugs such as cocaine or heroin.

Out of the Habit Trap

Stanton Peele, Ph.D.

Stanton Peele, Ph.D., is a social psychologist who has been investigating the problem of addiction for over a decade. He wrote Love and Addiction *(with Archie Brodsky) and* A Unified Theory of Addiction: The Addictive Experience *(with Bruce Alexander).*

A man who had been drunk every night for many years arrived home late, bombed once again. The next morning his mother, with whom he was living, found him staring at himself in the mirror. He turned to her and announced: "I'm giving up drinking and, while I'm at it, smoking." Then he placed a pack of cigarettes and a bottle of beer on the mantelpiece. "What's that for?" his mother asked. He said: "That's so I'll know where to find a smoke or drink if I want one. Then I can just kill myself instead." He has touched neither cigarettes nor booze for nearly 10 years.

A union official, noting that the price of cigarettes had risen yet again, put the extra nickel in the vending machine. A coworker laughed at him: "You'll pay whatever they ask." The smoker thought: "God, he's right; the tobacco company has me where it wants me." Then and there, he quit his three-pack-a-day habit forever.

Talk-show host Merv Griffin watched a comedian imitating him—as a fat man. The comic had stuffed himself with padding and Griffin could not bear the caricature. He put himself on a diet and exercise program, and soon showed off his new, thin self to his audience.

Stories like these seldom make the newspapers; for that matter, people who quit their long-standing habits by themselves often go unrecognized by scientific studies. Instead, we hear dire stories about people who can't seem to quit, and gloomy statistics on relapse rates. Among people in therapy to lose weight, stop smoking, kick a drug or drink addiction, as few as 5% actually make it.

But here's the irony and the hope: Self-cure can work, and depending on someone else to cure you usually does not.

This is the case for addictions like cigarette smoking and alcoholism, as well as for some more-complex habits. Obesity, for example, may involve compulsive overeating—an addiction to food that some thin people also struggle with for years. But genetics and a lifetime of inactivity and bad eating habits also play a role. Whatever the cause, though, losing weight takes a major change in lifestyle—and the people who do it best are those who do it on their own.

Therapists tend to fail their clients by undermining self-reliance; they encourage people to rely upon others for cure, and to give up responsibility for their own behavior. But because therapy works so rarely, many researchers have come to view addictions as almost impossible to beat. And that mistake makes habits harder to break.

Many have begun to think of addiction as an exclusively biological process—one that cannot be overcome by psychological effort or will power. In this view, alcoholics have a "disease," a "genetic susceptibility" to liquor. Obese people have a preordained weight level. Smokers are hooked on nicotine, and their bodies cannot tolerate a depletion of the drug.

All of these theories stem from the grandfather addiction of them all, heroin. Everyone knows the image: the suffering heroin addict, inexorably bound to a physiological dependence. The penalty for withdrawal is intolerable agony, so the addict increases the doses until death. Remember *The Man with the Golden Arm*?

For more than 10 years, I have been conducting interviews with all sorts of addicts and reviewing the research on all kinds of addiction. Addiction, I've found, may be affected by biological factors, but they are not enough to explain it. True, addiction is caused partly by the pharmacological action of the drug (if it's a drug addiction), but also by the person's social situation, attitudes and expectations. Even people who are constitutionally sensitive to a substance can control their use of it, if they believe that they can.

There is now good evidence for these heretical assertions. The most compelling statistics come from the success of people who cure themselves without therapy:

☐ University of Kentucky sociologist John O'Donnell, analyzing a national survey of drug use among men in their twenties, found that only 31% of the men who had ever used heroin had touched the drug in the previous year.

☐ Similarly, when American soldiers who had used heroin in Vietnam returned home after the war, over 90% of them gave the drug up without difficulty. Addiction experts predicted an epidemic of heroin abuse by the vets, but it never materialized. Washington University psychologist Lee Robins found that even among men who had truly been addicted in Vietnam, only 14% became dependent on narcotics in the U.S.

☐ Harvard psychiatrist George Vaillant found that more than half of the one-time alcohol abusers in a group of several hundred men had ceased problem drinking (the men had been interviewed over a period of 40 years).

☐ Social psychologist Stanley Schachter at Columbia University, interviewing members of two different communities, discovered that about half of those who had once been obese or hooked on cigarettes had lost weight or quit smoking. The formerly overweight people said they had lost an average of 35 pounds and kept it off for an average of 11 years.

Some of these statistics, admittedly, are open to question. When you're asking people to talk about how they've changed over the past several years, they may paint an excessively rosy picture of their ability to improve themselves. But even if the percentages are inflated, the evidence is still good that people can change for the better, far more than they have been given credit for.

Often, people simply outgrow their bad habits. Sociologist Charles Winick of City College of New York has examined the lives of drug addicts. Many, in Winick's words, "mature out" as they get older. Long-term studies of alcoholics and smokers show the same pattern. Some people even outgrow their teenage cravings for Twinkies and sugar "fixes."

Why Biology Is Not Destiny

There's other intriguing evidence that hammers away at the theory of the "biological trap" of addiction. For example, most addicts, of all kinds, regularly overcome withdrawal pangs. As Harvard psychiatrist Norman Zinberg and his associates discovered, heroin addicts often cut down or quit their heroin use on their own. Alcoholics often don't need to "dry out" in a hospital, but frequently just go on the wagon with no particular anguish. Practically every cigarette smoker stops at some point—for anywhere from a few days to years. (Orthodox Jews quit weekly for the Sabbath.)

It is actually long *after* the phase of "withdrawal pangs" that most addicts slide back into their habits. When they do backslide, it is not because of a physiological craving as much as it's stress at work or home, or social pressures ("Come on Mort, join us . . . one for the road . . .").

It's also a myth that a single experience of a drug can catch you chemically (hence the "first fix is free" strategy of drug dealers). Most people have to learn to become addicted. As Zinberg found, hospital patients given strong doses of narcotics every day for 10 days or more—doses higher than those street addicts take—virtually always leave the hospital without even a twinge of craving for the drug.

For an addiction to develop, the pharmacological effects of a drug have to produce an experience that a person with certain needs, in a certain situation, will welcome. When the need is great enough, people can become "addicted" to almost anything. Addicts may switch not only from one chemical substance to another, but from a chemical to a social "high." Vaillant reports that former alcoholics often shift to new dependencies—candy, prayer, compulsive work, hobbies, gambling.

Addiction also depends largely on people's beliefs about what a substance will do to them. Psychologist Alan Marlatt at the University of Washington found that alcoholics will behave drunkenly when they only *think* they are drinking liquor—but when they're actually drinking tonic and lime juice. He also found the reverse: When alcoholics drink alcohol, but believe it's tonic and lime juice, they don't behave drunkenly.

Are You Addicted?

Addictions are not all-or-nothing. Even a casual habit can be mildly addictive. The more "yes" answers to the following questions, the more addictive the habit.

Addictions:

❶ Erase negative feelings—pain, anxiety and despair. Does your habit make you forget your problems? Do you indulge most when you feel worst?

❷ Detract from other involvements. Does your habit harm other aspects of your life? Does it prevent you from fulfilling other responsibilities, trying new experiences, dealing with people who don't share the habit?

❸ Artificially prop up self-esteem. Must you return to your habit regularly to feel okay about yourself and your world? And do you feel bad again when you stop?

❹ Routinize your life. Do you refuse to vary the routines surrounding your habit? Do you ignore all changes in your life circumstances while pursuing it?

❺ Are ultimately not pleasurable. Do you enjoy your habit less and less with time? Can you skip it when you don't even anticipate enjoying it? Do you continue mostly because the thought of *not* doing it horrifies you?

— S. P.

Despite such evidence, the search has continued, unsuccessfully, for a single physiological factor that might be the underlying cause of all addictions. The prime candidates have been endorphins, morphinelike substances found to occur naturally in the body. Some pharmacologists speculated that people are susceptible to drug addiction if their bodies don't produce a normal level of endorphins. Maybe all addictive involvements elevate your endorphin levels, the theory went.

When it turned out that people could even become addicted to serious jogging, biochemical studies of runners were also done. Sure enough, jogging was found to boost endorphin levels. But endorphins failed to explain the difference between those who stop running when they're injured or it's inconvenient and those who behave like true addicts.

One very lean man, who insisted on running hard every day regardless of inclement weather, family obligations or his own injuries, explained his addiction to me this way: "I feel great every day I run; but I'm afraid I'll balloon back up to 200 pounds the moment I quit." His desire to run was more than chemical; he saw running as a magical talisman against returning to his former self.

The best explanation of addiction takes both mind and body into account. The effects of a substance can't be isolated from the context of human experience. Thinking of addiction solely as a "disease" or a "chemical dependency" ignores the power of the mind in generating the need for the drug—and in breaking that need.

The cycle of addiction begins as a response to a stressful problem (getting drunk to avoid dealing with a bad job, running to get away from a bad marriage) or as an attempt to produce certain feelings (as Harvard psychologist David McClelland and his coworkers showed, many men feel a sense of power while drunk).

These feelings, in turn, lead into a cycle that makes the addiction harder to escape. For example, a man who abuses his family when he is drunk may feel disgusted with himself when

he sobers up—so he gets drunk again to boost his self-esteem. Soon the addictive experience feeds on itself. It becomes central to the person's life, and it becomes a trap.

The Steps to Self-Cure

How does anyone manage to kick a habit after years of living with it? To find out, San Francisco sociologists Dan Waldorf and Patrick Biernacki interviewed heroin addicts who quit on their own, and sociologist Barry Tuchfeld at Texas Christian University talked with some 50 alcoholics who recovered without therapy or AA. And in conducting our own field research with addicts of all types, my associate Archie Brodsky and I have outlined the critical steps in self-cure.

The key word is *self*: taking charge of your own problem. Some psychologists call this self-mastery; others, self-efficacy; others, the belief in free will. It translates into three components necessary for change: an urge to quit, the belief that you *can* quit and the realization that *you* must quit—no one can do it for you. Once you have quit, the rewards of living without the addiction must be great enough to keep you free of it.

The stages of successful self-cure are remarkably similar, regardless of the addiction:

1 Accumulated unhappiness about the addiction. Before a change can take place, unhappiness with the addiction has to build to a

point where it can't be denied or rationalized away. This phase of the process of self-cure, to use Vaillant's analogy, is like the incubation of a chick. Just because the chick hatches, rather abruptly at that, doesn't mean it happened spontaneously. A lot of changes go on first beneath the outer shell.

To break an addiction, you must believe the rewards you'll get (from not smoking, from exercising and losing weight, from cutting down on or giving up alcohol or drugs) will surpass what you got from the habit. Heroin addicts who "mature out" typically explain to interviewers that a life of hustling, prison and the underworld was no longer worth it.

2 A moment of truth. An alcoholic pregnant woman told Tuchfeld: "I was drinking beer one morning and felt the baby quiver. I poured the rest of the beer out and I said, 'God forgive me, I'll never drink another drop.'" Another woman who had quit (and resumed) smoking several times found herself sorting through the butts in an ashtray late one night, desperate for a smoke: "I saw a snapshot of myself in my mind's eye," she told us, "and I was disgusted." She has not been a smoker for 15 years now.

Most ex-addicts can pinpoint a moment at which they "hatched" from the addiction and left it behind. It is impossible to distinguish the real moment of truth from the addict's previous vows to quit, except in retrospect. But it is

---

Born-Again Behavior

People who cure themselves of bad habits go through stages of change that resemble those of religious conversion. So says University of Washington professor Rodney Stark, president of the Association for the Sociology of Religion.

1 Stage 1 in Stanton Peele's hierarchy of change—"accumulated unhappiness"—is known to evangelical Christians as "being burdened by sin."

2 What Peele calls a "moment of truth" sounds like St. Paul bathed in light on the road to Damascus, or a less-dramatic event that shocks the sinner into conversion.

3 and **4** Changing behavior, changing identity: In religious converts, the born-again identity comes first. But new lifestyles and friends soon follow.

5 The relapse problem, known to Methodists as "backsliding," is a constant concern for revivalists and other evangelists as they seek to help the "tender Christian" through the first stage of salvation. —*T.G.H.*

just as foolish to disregard these reports altogether. Because they are part of such a high percentage of successful cures, they seem to have an important meaning to the ex-addict.

Epiphanies that work can be brought on by dramatic, catastrophic events: an alcoholic becomes falling-down-drunk in front of someone he admires, or a cigarette smoker watches a friend die of lung cancer. But most moments of truth seem to be inspired by trivial remarks or chance occurrences. Either way, they work because they crystallize the discrepancy between the addict's self-image and the reality.

3 Changing patterns. People successful at self-cure usually make active changes in their environment—they may move away from a drug culture, become more involved in work, make new friends. But some people break a habit without changing their usual patterns. The man whose story began this article—the heavy drinker and smoker—was a musician who continued to spend nearly all his nights in bars. He wrapped himself in a new identity—"I'm a nondrinking, non-smoking musician"—that protected him from his familiar vices.

4 Changing the identity of addict. Once former addicts gain more from their new lives than from the old ways—feeling better, getting along with people better, working better, having more fun—the lure of the addiction pales. One long-time heroin addict quoted in the book *High on Life* quit the drug in his thirties, went to school and got a good job. Later, during a hospital stay, he was given an unlimited prescription for Percodan, a synthetic narcotic. He marveled at how he had no desire to continue the drugs when his pain stopped: "I had a different relationship with people, with work, with the things that had become important to me. I would have had to work at relapsing."

5 Dealing with relapses. One of the problems with biological theories of addiction is the image of imminent relapse it creates for the addict—the idea that one slip is a return to permanent addiction. Many of Schachter's

ex-smokers admit having a puff at a party. Half of those ex-addicts who had been in Vietnam did try heroin at home, Lee Robins found, but few returned to a full-fledged addiction. The addict who has successfully modified his or her life catches the slip, and controls it.

The steps out of addiction, therefore, are: to find a superior alternative to the habit you want to break; find people who can help you puncture your complacent defenses; change whatever you need to in your life to accommodate your new, healthier habits; celebrate your new, nonaddicted image whenever you can.

The common feature in all these steps is *your* action, *your* beliefs. Self-curers often use many of the same techniques for breaking out of an addiction that formal treatment programs do. But motivated people who have arrived at these techniques on their own are more successful than those in therapy.

Why should this be? One possibility, of course, is that the people who go for

Is Alcoholism Genetic ?

People with alcoholic relatives are three times more likely than their peers to have a drinking problem themselves. Does the high risk come from genetic factors, family environment, or a bit of both?

The fault is in the genes, said psychiatrist Donald Goodwin of the University of Kansas, who studied adopted children. He found that those whose biological parents were alcoholics—but whose adoptive parents were not—had a higher risk than kids who were born to nonalcoholics but raised by problem drinkers.

Other researchers, however, are still not sure. In *The Natural History of Alcoholism*, Harvard psychiatrist George Vaillant recently reviewed findings from over a 40-year study of some 600 men—136 of whom were alcohol abusers at some time—and eight years' work with 100 men and women in his alcoholism treatment clinic. "At the present time," he wrote, "a conservative view of the role of genetic factors in alcoholism seems appropriate."

Vaillant found cultural patterns to be stronger than genetic ones in determining alcoholism. People from Irish backgrounds, for example, were seven times more likely to be alcohol-dependent than those from Mediterranean backgrounds. Yet the Irish also breed many more teetotalers. This indicates the problem is not a gene that

commands "drink!" but a view of drinking as an all-or-nothing activity.

Recently, biochemists and neuroscientists have looked for clues to alcoholism in the body and brain. Some have proposed that the problem is abnormal metabolism of alcohol. Such inherited factors, however, may make only a small contribution to an alcohol problem. Asians, Eskimos and American Indians, for example, all show a metabolic reaction to alcohol called Oriental flush, a visible reddening due to acceleration of the cardiovascular system. But though both American Indians and Chinese Americans manifest this same syndrome, the former have the highest rate of alcoholism in the United States, and the latter have among the lowest.

Though biological theories of alcoholism are imperfect, they have been remarkably popular. And they have formed the basis for the disease theory of alcoholism, which presents total abstinence as the only solution to a life-long "illness." Yet life-history studies have shown that some alcoholics do teach themselves to drink in a controlled manner. In fact, alcohol abusers more often evolve into moderate drinkers than give up drinking completely, according to sociologist Don Cahalan at the University of California in Berkeley.

Vaillant also found that alcoholics recovered as well with the passage of time as they did with treatment in his clinic. The solution to addiction, he concludes, may be found more in the individual than in any therapy. —*S. P.*

those who have tried to change on their own and found it impossible. People may try to quit smoking a dozen times, or lose and regain a few hundred pounds, before deciding they need help. Therapy often represents only one attempt at cure, whereas people usually come to grips with a problem over a period of years.

But I also think that therapy itself may inadvertently impede cure, by lowering the addict's sense of self-mastery and self-control. In turning to therapy, addicts unwittingly acknowledge that they are powerless to break the addiction. Thus medical supervision of drug withdrawal, for example, can actually inflate the difficulty of doing something that drug addicts accomplish repeatedly on their own.

Therapy can be especially demoralizing when it's based on the notion that addiction stems from an unchangeable biological weakness. Such a philosophy can make quitting even more diffi-cult. Sociologist Charles Winick observed two decades ago that adolescents who failed to mature out of heroin addiction were those who "decide they are 'hooked,' make no effort to abandon addiction and give in to what they regard as inevitable."

We now see why that discovery applies to the general problem of breaking self-destructive habits. Only death and taxes, it now appears, are truly inevitable. Everything else is negotiable—and open for improvement.

ADDICTION AND IQ

Linda Marsa

ike crack addicts found dead with half-empty pipes clutched in their hands, rats in the lab have taken lethal doses of cocaine, pressing levers for the drug until they go into convulsion and die. Scientists are now beginning to understand why cocaine is so addictive and why this addiction rips away even the most ingrained instinct for survival. Two researchers at the University of California Irvine (UCI), have uncovered some clues to addiction's mystery. And in a bold conceptual leap they propose that addiction, learning, and intelligence may involve one and the same process at the cellular level.

In a series of experiments, Larry Stein, chairman of UCI's department of pharmacology, and psychopharmacologist James Belluzzi discovered that certain individual brain cells can be trained or "reinforced" to respond to a reward of cocaine. Like Skinner's rats, which pressed levers unremittingly in anticipation of being fed, these neurons literally burst with electrical activity for a coke fix. "We were actually surprised that a single cell can be reinforced, because it would seem you'd need a whole brain, or at least many of its subsystems, to reinforce behavior," says Stein. "The fact that *cells* respond to a reward shows just how deeply embedded in the design of the brain this reinforcement mechanism is."

Studying the neurochemistry of addiction, reward, and reinforcement has been Stein's lifework for 30 years, and he and Belluzzi are the only scientists in the world who have given over the control of the rewarding stimulus to the cell. Allowing a cell to "self-administer" a drug, as it were, "is an extremely difficult concept for my colleagues to accept," says Stein. Most investigators apply a drug to a cell, then wait to see what happens. But in Stein's test the cell first fires in a burst of electrical discharge,

then it gets the cocaine reward. Just as in animal operant conditioning, the pigeon, say, gets the piece of corn after it pecks the right button.

Stein and Belluzzi examine neurons from the hippocampus in the brain's limbic system because the electrical activity recorded when the tissue is thinly sliced is comparable to that in an intact brain. When the cells fire, microdroplets of cocaine are immediately applied to the cell body. The researchers give another group of cells cocaine randomly, whether or not they fire. When the scientists pair doses of cocaine with firing, the neurons "learn" to fire for more, while the neurons in the randomly dosed control group do not. Stein and Belluzzi then do the same test using the neurotransmitter dopamine as the reward. It works just as well as or better than cocaine. And when they perform the same experiment with the powerful natural opiate dynorphin A, other hippocampal neurons learn to fire for more of that reward, too.

"In a sense, the purpose of life is to activate our reward systems," declares Stein, who thinks dopamine and the opioid peptides function as the brain's own reinforcement transmitters and may be responsible for many forms of learning and conditioning, as well as addiction. "Dopamine and the opioid peptides are transmitters in very powerful control systems based on a certain chemistry, and along come poppy seeds and coca leaves that have chemicals very similar to, or can pharmacologically interact with, these central systems. They go right in, do not pass go. So if you're tapping into the natural, positive reinforcement systems, then to say that cocaine or amphetamines—or heroin or morphine—should be highly appealing is an understatement."

Why use cocaine as a reinforcer? In the whole animal, cocaine is probably the most addictive of the addictive drugs,

says Stein. "Of course, no one has found a good fast way to give dopamine centrally to see how addictive the transmitter is. Drug addiction should be treated as a biomedical brain disease rather than a failure of character. Until pharmacological approaches are developed to prevent the brain's reward system from being automatically switched on by these drugs, it will be difficult to break the cycle of addiction.

"But my primary interest is not addiction, although it's a fascinating perturbation of the system," he adds. "The big question is the neurobiology of reinforcement." Stein's tests demonstrate that consequences of an event can mold behavior: Cells fire; cocaine is applied as a reward; cells fire with renewed zeal. This pattern of selecting successful behavior by reinforcement has the same logical status as the natural selection of successful structures and functions in evolutionary biology. Both are examples of selection by consequence.

Stein constructs a thought experiment: "If we had a microelectrode in every cell in a rat's brain," he says, "and a giant Cray computer to keep track of all that, then we would get the rat to press a lever for food. We could see which neurons were active. If we allowed the rat to do that a hundred times, of all those cells there'd be a small subpopulation contributing directly to the lever-pressing behavior at the time of the lever press and just before food delivery. The food would, presumably, activate the reward system, giving the target cells a shower of dopamine or endorphin. Statistically," he adds, "only the cells involved in the correct behavior consistently would have been recently active. Only recently active cells are responsive to the reinforcing transmitter, so over many trials there would be selective reinforcement of correct response cells.

"I like to call these cells 'smart cells,'" he continues, "because they learn from the consequences of their action." The more smart cells, the more behavioral variations and flexibility. Intelligence—the ability to behave adaptively—may depend in part on the number of smart cells. Maybe, he says in what he admits is "rank and raw" speculation, "the general IQ factor can be quantified by counting up how many smart cells you have."

Stein's next step is to determine where these smart cells cluster. In addiction research everyone is looking for a place in the brain where the drugs exert a high. "The lore of the field is that the nucleus accumbens [a prominent area of the limbic system] is the main candidate. I don't have any problem with the nucleus accumbens; it is an important projection of

the dopamine system." But, Stein adds, the reward-seeking cells probably reside in the diverse areas of the brain where many different types of learning occur. Perhaps nature's way of endowing these centers with learning ability is by putting these smart cells in them.

Some scientists are reserved about smart cells. "It's a giant, albeit interesting, leap," comments Thomas H. Brown, a Yale psychologist studying the mechanisms of learning. "But there are a lot of *missing steps* between understanding the brain's systems of rewards and reinforcement, and the idea of global intelligence." Adds Andrew G. Barto, a computer scientist at the University of Massachusetts-Amherst, "Neurons are

probably more sophisticated machines than we currently believe. But how can you get these cells to interact as an aggregate unit to solve complex problems?" Artificial intelligence theorists like Barto would like to answer that question.

If Stein's assertion about smart cells and intelligence proves a key piece of that puzzle, will we arrive at a biotechnology to augment intelligence? Will we be able to improve our IQs by using drugs that enhance the activity or development of smart cells? "These gains have been hard won over the last thirty years," Stein says. "It'll be quite a while before we unravel the biological basis of intelligence. But this research may give us an interesting place to start."

Drug Abuse: Prevention and Treatment Issues

- Continuum of Care—Prevention (Articles 54-59)
- Continuum of Care—Beyond Prevention (Articles 60-62)
- Natural Highs and Alternatives to Drugs (Articles 63-65)

Matters of drug use or abstention are personal decisions. At what point should government interfere where it comes to the behavior of its citizens? How far should our leadership go to ensure a reasonable society without the abrogation of freedom of choice? Experience shows that successful drug treatment, like prevention, is dependent upon the capability and desire of the user to make correct decisions.

"Epidemiology of Drug Abuse" and "Taking Drugs Seriously" explain the patterns of drug abuse and consider America's national drug policies while "Cutting Costs of Drug Abuse" detail the costs to industry of drugs in the workplace. "Megavitamin Therapy" attacks the drug problem from the therapeutic viewpoint. "Advertising Addiction: The Alcohol Industry's Hard Sell" questions the responsibility of that industry in promoting alcohol consumption. The place of testing in prevention is shown in "A Drug History Revealed on a Strand of Hair." Although expensive, this form of examination offers incontrovertible evidence of drug use that spans a period of months, not just days. "The Dutch Model" and "Why Not Decriminalize?" points to facts, figures, and attitudes that run counter to the feelings of many who believe in a ban on all recreational drug use. "A Long Time Coming" describes the workings of the "Twelve Step" programs employed by some of the more successful treatment groups and examines the self-help movement in the lives of adult children of alcoholics.

The final subsection investigates some current nontraditional approaches to drug prevention and recovery. "The Power of the Placebo," "Trances That Heal," and "Chasing Answers to Miracle Cures" discomfit the scientific community with the positive results of therapies based on what many consider to be nonscientific principles. The occasional spontaneous remission from incurable diseases often baffles many trained professionals.

Looking Ahead: Challenge Questions

Who should be tested for drug use? How and by whom should testing be done? How often?

Does an employer have the right to dictate to an employee what may be done during off-hours? Who should determine the type of treatment program needed? Should an employer or insurer be expected to pay for three or four relapses requiring subsequent treatment?

Are recreational drugs necessary or desirable in our society? If yes, which ones and when?

How far should a government go in limiting freedom of choice in a society? Who should make the rules?

Comment on the fact that although illegal drugs are readily available, their use caused fewer than 5,000 fatalities in 1988, whereas alcohol and tobacco were responsible for nearly half a million deaths. What can be done to prevent this?

Nobody likes a quitter...
but we do!

American Cancer Society

Epidemiology of Drug Abuse: An Overview

Nicholas J. Kozel and Edgar H. Adams

The authors are with the Division of Epidemiology and Statistical Analysis, National Institute on Drug Abuse, Rockville, MD 20857.

Issues regarding the use of epidemiology in drug abuse research are discussed and systems for monitoring national trends and identifying risk factors are described. Data indicate a general decline in marijuana users, and increased prevalence and health consequences associated with cocaine use.

The application of epidemiology to the study of drug abuse is relatively recent. Despite the long history of drug abuse in society, the use of the epidemiologic approach to study this complex public health problem began in earnest less than two decades ago. It was during the outbreak of heroin abuse in the late 1960's that the use of the term "epidemic" to describe drug abuse came into vogue. Although most of the scientific community recognized both the validity and the benefit inherent in using the tools of the epidemiologist in understanding and addressing the problem of drug abuse during that era (1–8), the introduction of the technique was not without its critics (9, 10).

One focus of concern during that time was that the initial introduction of drugs into the body was voluntary. This was contrasted with diseases involuntarily contracted that were being investigated by the traditional medical epidemiology model. It was argued by some that since drug abuse was a self-imposed condition, it was automatically excluded from the jurisdiction of the epidemiologist, whose imperative was to study infectious disease. In response, Greene made a strong case that heroin addiction was a communicable disease in the classical sense, with the drug itself being the infectious agent, the host and reservoir being man, and the drug-using peer as the vector (11).

Another major concern of the day was the potential for indiscriminate use of quarantine (in this case also known as incarceration) as a preventative against the spread of drug abuse to the general population. This argument centered on the conclusion, held inevitable by some, that drug abusers once identified would be automatically imprisoned. Neither of these objections stimulated much action beyond debate and posed no serious impediment to the efficacious introduction of epidemiology to the study of drug abuse.

There was also much discussion about whether drug abuse more closely paralleled a chronic relapsing disease or an acute disease pattern. The popular view was that drug abuse was a unidimensional phenomenon, that is, no distinction was made between the type of drugs used, etiology, and populations at risk. There was an attempt to classify drug-using behavior into one of two apparently distinct categories. More recently, the recognition of the wide differences in classes of drugs abused and the diversity of abuser populations point up even further distinctions in the underlying motivations for initial use and resultant adverse health consequences. Over the years drug abuse has moved from the position of being challenged as an appropriate object for epidemiologic study to challenging the creativity of epidemiology itself.

Recent history shows that in contrast to the issues in which drug abuse differs from other types of epidemiologic investigation, the areas of similarity are immediately evident. Drug abusers demonstrate patterns of behavior that can be measured, incidence curves can be drawn, rates of prevalence can be computed, attack rates can be calculated, risk factors can be identified, etiologies and consequences can be determined, and prevention programs can be implemented.

As with most social behavior, the etiology of drug abuse is complex, varying through time, by geographic region, and by demographic characteristics. The underlying causes of drug abuse are as diverse as the populations that they affect. Peer pressure, curiosity, depression, hedonism, attempts to increase or improve performance, rebellion, alienation, and a wide variety of other reasons have been cited as responsible for abuse of substances ranging from solvents to stimulants to opiates. Changes have been observed in the types of drugs abused both in national waves as well as regional and localized ripples, from marijuana in the 1960's through heroin in the 1970's to cocaine in the 1980's.

Risk factors change and are subject to the same demographic and geographic variations that affect other aspects of drug abuse. The factors that placed populations at high risk for heroin abuse in the late 1960's and early 1970's have changed dramatically in the 1980's. In the earlier period, the profile of a heroin addict was a male in the middle to late teens who was initiated into heroin use during the previous several years, disproportionately from minority groups, and living in an inner city area. In the mid-1980's, the heroin addict population still is composed primarily of males, but in their early to mid-30's, the majority of whom have a history of heroin abuse that extends back to the late 1960's and early 1970's. They are, in fact, the earlier use cohort.

Not only are certain populations at risk for abuse of specific types of drugs, but drug abuse itself constitutes an antecedent condition for other adverse health consequences. Thus, intravenous drug abusers are at high risk for contracting acquired immune deficiency syndrome (AIDS) as well as a host of other diseases. The consequences of drug abuse vary just as widely and change just as substantially over time. Changes in patterns of abuse, such as engaging in more dangerous routes of administration, increasing dosage units, or using drugs in combination, increase vulnerability to toxic effect. For example, the recent domestic cultivation of sinsemilla marijuana has introduced much higher levels of tetrahydrocannabinol into the marijuana-abusing population, thus increasing the amount of psychoactive substance ingested and the probability of acute adverse health consequences. In addition, social and psychological problems resulting from chronic cocaine abuse have been identified that were totally unsuspected just a few years ago. In fact, the compulsive drug-seeking behavior associated with cocaine abuse has led to a redefinition of the term "addiction," which previously had been restricted to the physical withdrawal symptoms resulting from opiate and depressant dependence.

Measurement Issues

Measurement of the drug abuse problem is complicated by the fact that drug abuse is an illicit behavior and that populations of interest may not be studied by traditional research methodologies. In addition, drug abuse itself may be considered a deviant behavior or it may be considered a disease (that is, addiction), or, as mentioned above, it may be regarded as an antecedent to a disease, such as AIDS, subacute bacterial endocarditis, and others. In the first case, the population at risk

Table 1. Population using marijuana for the first time in the preceding year and incidence rates for marijuana use. Data from 1982.

Age group	First use (%)		Incidence	
	Males	Females	Males	Females
12 to 17	4.0	8.0	5.3	9.6
18 to 25	0.7	1.4	2.3	3.3
Sample size	1404	1460	845	938

is the general population of the United States. In the second case, the population at risk might be defined as those who had abused a certain drug more than a given number of times and, in the third case, the population at risk might be defined as intravenous (IV) drug abusers.

Analytical epidemiology has been used on many occasions to document specific risk factors associated with drug abuse (12–14), but findings in this paper are based on data from national drug abuse surveillance programs. One of the most effective measurement tools employed in the descriptive epidemiology program for drug abuse is surveys. Repeated cross-sectional surveys are used to monitor trends, changes in the attitude of the population, and the prevalence of drug use. Two such surveys, the National Household Survey on Drug Abuse and the High School Senior Survey, are sponsored by the National Institute on Drug Abuse (NIDA). These surveys use probability samples, thus allowing extrapolation to the general population.

The annual High School Senior Survey collects information from approximately 16,000 to 18,000 public and private high school seniors located in approximately 130 high schools in the contiguous United States. These survey data are used to monitor trends in drug abuse and, through a longitudinal study of a subsample of each class, to monitor maturational factors associated with drug abuse. The measures and procedures employed have been standardized and applied consistently in data collection since 1975.

Although the exclusion of dropouts and absentees from the study may result in somewhat conservative estimates of drug abuse in the high school senior class population, the stability of the survey provides an excellent measurement of drug abuse trends, including both prevalence and incidence data as well as changes in attitudes and beliefs about drugs. In addition, the follow-up design in the survey provides information on drug abuse subsequent to high school graduation, which is vital to determination of age-related risk factors. For example, these data indicate that while the extent of marijuana abuse does not change significantly after high school, the abuse of cocaine increases dramatically. This finding, in addition to findings from other studies, has been used to suggest that the age of risk for cocaine abuse may be different from that for other drugs (15).

6. DRUG ABUSE: Continuum of Care—Prevention

The National Household Survey on Drug Abuse, a general population survey of household members aged 12 and above, has been conducted every 2 to 3 years since 1971. This survey excludes populations in institutionalized settings (prisons, military bases, colleges) as well as transient and nonresidential populations. Therefore, estimates of drug abuse may be conservative. Still this household survey remains the single most important measure of drug abuse in our general population. In addition to monitoring trends by age, sex, and other demographic variables, the size of the database permits analysis of a variety of questions on drug abuse. For example, data from the 1982 survey suggested that current abuse of marijuana as well as annual prevalence (use in the past year) of marijuana abuse had decreased for both males and females between 1979 and 1982. These decreases were greater for males, pointing to the possibility that incidence rates during the period may have been higher for females (16). More detailed analysis of the 1982 survey data regarding first use of marijuana for the previous year indicated that the incidence of marijuana abuse was higher among females than males in the age group 12 to 25 (Table 1). The incidence rates in Table 1 represent new use of marijuana as a percentage of the population at risk and exclude those who have used marijuana previously.

In another study, the National Household Survey on Drug Abuse database was used in an attempt to define the population at risk for cocaine abuse. Analysis of the household data suggested that, not only were cocaine abusers likely to have abused marijuana prior to abuse of cocaine, but the probability of abusing cocaine increased with the frequency and recency of marijuana abuse (17). The inclusion of drug problem and dependency scales in the most recent survey will enable researchers to assess risks according to levels of abuse. For example, a recent study of high-risk cocaine abusers (defined as having abused cocaine at least 12 times in the previous year) indicated that the number of self-reported dependency symptoms increased with frequency of abuse (18).

There are two more data systems that are used by NIDA. The Drug Abuse Warning Network (DAWN) reports consequences of drug abuse as reflected by emergency room episodes for drug-related problems and medical examiner cases for drug-related fatalities. The Client Oriented Data Acquisition Process (CODAP) reports treatment data.

Both data systems have been used to monitor drug abuse trends and health consequences. For example, DAWN data have been used to measure recent changes in reported cocaine morbidity and mortality, increases in speedballing (the use of heroin and cocaine in combination), and increases in the median age of heroin abusers. In addition, DAWN data were used to monitor the spread of the combination of pentazocine and tripelennamine, known on the street as

"T's and blues." With the reformulation of pentazocine to include the narcotic antagonist naloxone, DAWN reflected a subsequent decline in the number of emergency cases and fatalities related to T's and blues (19).

An example of the use of CODAP data is a recent analysis of admissions for treatment in the Southwest which showed that the abuse of inhalants is particularly serious among the Hispanic population in that area. With a sample controlled for age it was found that 60% of Hispanics admitted to drug abuse treatment programs had less than a 12th-grade education. This figure rose to 85% when only inhalant abusers were examined (20). While each of the trend indicator or measurement systems cited has recognized methodological limitations, each provides a particular view of drug abuse behavior or consequences and together form a reasonably solid foundation for tracking epidemiologic trends.

Patterns and Trends of Selected Drugs of Abuse

Heroin. In many respects, heroin is one of the most difficult drugs to investigate. In spite of its visible presence during the past 20 years as a national social and health problem, its association with crime, and the recent relation established between IV drug abuse (predominantly IV heroin abuse) and AIDS, heroin abuse continues to be a relatively rare event and involves a population that seeks to remain hidden. These circumstances virtually preclude the use of traditional research methods, such as general surveys, in studying incidence, prevalence, and consequences of abuse.

Treatment data reported to CODAP, however, have been used to identify relative changes in incidence through calculation of year of first heroin use. Because

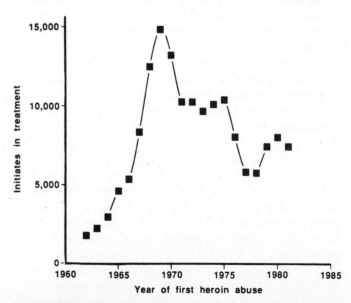

Fig. 1. Incidence of heroin abuse. Data are based on admissions to a panel of federally funded treatment programs.

of the difficulty in identifying denominator data, raw counts rather than rates have to suffice for incidence trend analysis. Figure 1 shows that epidemics of heroin abuse occurred in the United States during the mid-1960's, the mid-1970's, and the early 1980's.

The data show that the epidemics which occurred in the 1960's and 1970's were national in scope, whereas the epidemics of the 1980's were more localized in geographic location. In the latter case, the country in which heroin originated was identified as an important link to the area of the United States affected (21).

In comparison with incidence analysis, problems are even more complex in estimating the prevalence of heroin abuse. Over the years, various methods have been used, including snowball techniques and multiplier methods as well as mathematical and systems analysis models (22). In spite of the inherent difficulties of definition and measurement, various estimates of the heroin addict population have been surprisingly similar and consistent for the last decade, for the most part ranging between 400,000 and 600,000.

Although heroin prevalence appears to have remained relatively stable in recent years, changes have occurred in characteristics of abusers, most notably an aging effect, as evidenced in both treatment and DAWN emergency room data. For example, the percentage of all heroin-related nonfatal emergencies reported to DAWN, which involved persons 30 years of age or older, increased from 36% in 1979 to 58% in 1983, whereas a similar increase from 41 to 56% occurred during the same time period among heroin treatment admissions. These age data make a strong case when combined with declining incidence data, that the preponderance of current heroin abusers were initiated into heroin abuse between the mid-1960's and mid-1970's.

A variety of risk factors and health consequences have been related to heroin abuse over the years. Most recently, reports of the growing availability of "black tar" heroin, a type of heroin purported to be of high purity and low price, may be responsible for recent increases in heroin-related morbidity and mortality (23). Additional risk factors include abuse of heroin in combination with other substances. A particularly lethal combination in recent years has been the ingestion of heroin in temporal proximity to the consumption of alcohol (12). The most dramatic issue of the day, though, is the association between IV drug abuse and AIDS. Not only has the percentage of AIDS cases associated with IV drug abuse been increasing, but in some areas, such as New York and New Jersey, IV drug abusers are threatening to become the majority risk group, and this group is viewed as representing the potential bridge to the general population.

Marijuana. The most widely abused illegal drug in the country today is marijuana. The 1982 National Household Survey on Drug Abuse indicated that an estimated 56 million people in the United States had used marijuana at least once and slightly more than 20 million were estimated to have consumed it during the month before the survey (16, 24). By 1985, lifetime prevalence increased to 26 million, while use in the past month decreased to 18 million. These estimates represent a substantial percentage of the national population, but the lifetime (ever used), annual, and past month prevalence trends show a decline or leveling among all age groups during the most recent measurement points (Table 2).

The increase in the 26 and older age category was found to be the result of a cohort effect—that is, the entry of the 23- to 25-year-old age cohort into the 26 and older age group between 1979 and 1982. The net change in the older adult group was not statistically significant (17).

These national household trends are reflected in data from high school senior classes which reached their apex in marijuana use with the classes of 1978 and 1979 and have since declined through 1984 and leveled off in 1985 (Table 3). A clue to the reasons underlying the surge in marijuana abuse during the 1970's and its subsequent decline also may be garnered from the High School Senior Survey. The point at which marijuana abuse had reached its peak was the same point at which perceived harmfulness was at its nadir. For example, in 1978 monthly prevalence among high school seniors was at 37% and almost 11% used marijuana daily. At the same time, only 12% of seniors nationwide believed that there was great risk of harm associated with occasional use, and 35% perceived great risk with regular use. By 1985 monthly prevalence declined to 26% and daily use to below 5%, whereas perceived risk for occasional use rose to 25% and for regular use to 70%.

Thus, the belief that marijuana use, even once or twice, poses no great risk is highly correlated with an

Table 2. Trend in estimated prevalence of marijuana use among three age groups, 1971–1982.

Prevalence	Population using marijuana (%)						
	1972	1974	1976	1977	1979	1982	1985
12- to 17-year-olds							
Ever used	14.0	23.0	22.4	28.0	30.9	26.7	23.7
Used in past year		18.5	18.4	22.3	24.1	20.6	20.0
Used in past month	7.0	12.0	12.3	16.6	16.7	11.5	12.3
Sample size	880	952	986	1272	2165	1581	2287
18- to 25-year-olds							
Ever used	47.9	52.7	52.9	59.9	68.2	64.1	60.5
Used in past year		34.2	35.0	38.7	46.9	40.4	37.9
Used in past month	27.8	25.2	25.0	27.4	35.4	27.4	21.9
Sample size	772	849	882	1500	2044	1283	1804
26 years and older							
Ever used	7.4	9.9	12.9	15.3	19.6	23.0	27.2
Used in past year		3.8	5.4	6.4	9.0	10.6	9.5
Used in past month	2.5	2.0	3.5	3.3	6.0	6.6	6.2
Sample size	1613	2221	1708	1822	3015	2760	3947

Table 3. Trend in estimated prevalence of marijuana use among high school senior classes, 1975–1985.

Prevalence	High school seniors using marijuana (%)										
	1975	1976	1977	1978	1979	1980	1981	1982	1983	1984	1985
Ever used	47.3	52.8	56.4	59.2	60.4	60.3	59.5	58.7	57.0	54.9	54.2
Used in past year	40.0	44.5	47.6	50.2	50.8	48.8	46.1	44.3	42.3	40.0	40.6
Used in past month	27.1	32.2	35.4	37.1	36.5	33.7	31.6	28.5	27.0	25.2	25.7
Used daily in past month	6.0	8.2	9.1	10.7	10.3	9.1	7.0	6.3	5.5	5.0	4.9
Sample size	9,400	15,400	17,100	17,800	15,500	15,900	17,500	17,700	16,300	15,900	16,000

increase in prevalence trends and probably had its genesis in the social status afforded the drug during the 1960's and early 1970's and the lack at that time of conclusive findings regarding short- or long-term health consequences (25). Now it is clear that marijuana has a serious impact on social functioning as well as health. Behaviorally, use of marijuana, especially long-term heavy use, has been directly related to subsequent abuse of other illicit drugs (26). Marijuana has been called a "gateway" drug and, indeed, the single best predictor of cocaine use is frequent use of marijuana during adolescence (27).

Clinical effects of marijuana also have been documented, specifically the effect of marijuana on the nervous system as well as the cardiovascular, respiratory, and other major body systems (28). In addition, long-term marijuana abuse, just as long-term cigarette smoking, can produce serious chronic effects over time and recent evidence suggests that marijuana abuse adversely affects performance (29). With these considerations in mind, the Institute of Medicine has called for further epidemiologic study in the form of cohort and case-control studies to identify the long-term health consequences of marijuana abuse (28).

Cocaine. In 1973, the Strategy Council on Drug Abuse stated that morbidity associated with cocaine abuse did not appear to be great. It also stated that at the time there were virtually no confirmed cocaine overdose deaths and that a negligible number of people were seeking medical help or treatment for problems associated with cocaine abuse (30). In 1972, approximately 48% of young adults between 18 and 25 years of age had tried marijuana, but only 9% had ever tried cocaine. Between 1974 and 1985, lifetime prevalence of cocaine use increased from 5.4 million to 22.2 million. Estimates of current prevalence, use in the past 30 days, increased from 1.6 million in 1977 to 4.3 million in 1979, remained stable through 1982, and increased to 5.8 million in 1985. Data from the High School Senior Survey also show increases in current use of cocaine among high school seniors in the past 2 years. By 1985, 6.7% of high school seniors had used cocaine in the past 30 days. Additional data collected in five waves of the Gallup Poll in late 1984 and mid-1985 did not indicate dramatic increases in the use of cocaine overall, but did suggest increases in current use in males aged 26 to 34. Annual prevalence did not appear to increase.

Table 4. Trend in annual prevalence of cocaine use among follow-up populations, 1 to 4 years after high school, 1980–1985.

Sample	Used cocaine in past 12 months (%)					
	1980	1981	1982	1983	1984	1985
Total	18.0	18.1	19.2	17.5	17.5	17.2
Full-time college students	16.9	15.9	17.2	17.2	16.4	17.3
Sample size	2855	2862	2861	2821	2790	2690

As with marijuana, increase in lifetime prevalence of cocaine abuse were noted in the 1982 National Survey. Unlike marijuana, however, the increases in cocaine abuse in the 26 and older population were, in fact, due to new users in that population (17), suggesting that the age of risk for abuse of cocaine differs from other drugs. Further evidence of the different age risks for cocaine abuse is provided by an 8-year follow-up sample of students from the High School Senior Survey. In this study, all prevalence measures rose substantially with age. By 1985, lifetime cocaine prevalence was 40% for 27-year-olds who were seniors in 1976. Use in the past year was 20% compared with approximately 13% among graduating high school seniors in the class of 1985. Interestingly, both annual prevalence and current prevalence among college students and the total sample up to 4 years after high school has been relatively stable between 1980 and 1985 (Table 4).

Overall, the data suggest relative stability in the annual prevalence pool estimated at approximately 12 million, but an increase in use in the past month. As previously mentioned, data for the Gallup Poll suggest increases in use in the past 30 days in the 26- to 34-year-old population. This is consistent with previous follow-up data from the High School Senior Survey and from other studies that suggest a general progression of frequency of use of cocaine. The 26- to 34-year-old population ranged in age from 16 to 24 in 1976 when marijuana abuse had yet to peak, and the cocaine epidemic was just beginning. Of note, a recent sample of 100 cases of high-risk cocaine abusers, defined as having used cocaine at least 12 times in the previous year, indicates that 60% of this population had been smoking marijuana for more than 10 years.

Even with the current increase in abuse of cocaine in the older population, the rise does not match the epidemic increases noted in the late 1970's. However, sharp increases have been noted in treatment admissions, emergency room cases, and mortality associated with cocaine abuse. Between 1981 and 1985, the number of DAWN nonfatal emergencies associated with cocaine increased threefold from 3296 to 9946 and cocaine-related deaths showed a similar threefold increase from 195 to 580. Recent reports of heart attacks in relatively healthy individuals have been attributed to the abuse of cocaine and have heightened awareness of the severe consequences of a drug once thought to be benign (31–33).

The rise in treatment admissions parallels the trend noted for emergency room and medical examiner cases. In 1977, primary cocaine abuse accounted for 1.8% of all admissions to federally funded treatment facilities. By 1981, they accounted for 5.8%, and in 1984 the 15 states still submitting treatment data to NIDA reported that primary cocaine admissions accounted for almost 14% of total clients. If secondary cocaine problems were included, more than a fourth (28.7%) of treatment clients reported to NIDA had a problem with cocaine.

Route of administration is particularly important with cocaine. In the past, inhaling (or snorting) the drug has been the predominant mode of administration, whereas inhaling the vapors of cocaine, that is, freebasing, was virtually nonexistent. Although the reported incidence of heart attacks in cocaine snorters clearly demonstrates that intranasal abuse of cocaine is not safe, researches have suggested that more potent physiological and psychological consequences may occur from either the smoking or IV route.

On the basis of treatment data, it appears that freebasing cocaine has increased from less than 1% in 1977 to almost 5% in 1981 and 18% in 1984. Similarly, emergency room data show that in 1977 less than 1% of cases were associated with smoking cocaine compared with 6% in 1984 and 14% during the first quarter of 1986.

The increase in smoking cocaine in the first quarter of 1986 may reflect the introduction of a form of freebase cocaine known as "crack." An important aspect of "crack" is that it is sold on the street in the freebase form. In the past the user had to convert the cocaine from hydrochloride, the form that is snorted, to freebase. This new marketing tactic may bring about an increase in freebasing and subsequent casualties. In addition, the marketing of "crack" in 65- to 100-milligram doses for $10 rather than in gram lots for $100 initially removes the price barrier that has prohibited many, especially the young, from experimenting with cocaine. These are viewed as ominous signs with the potential to develop into a major public health problem.

Conclusion

Our knowledge of drug abuse has advanced substantially in a very short time. Much can be said about risk factors associated with other types of drug abuse. The variety and range of substances involved and the dynamic social nature of drug abuse sets it in a cycle of almost constant change. In addition, drug epidemics often are localized and involve specific subpopulations that make surveillance based on national data systems difficult. At the same time, the multifaceted nature of the problem has allowed us to apply investigative techniques from a variety of disciplines in public health, medicine, and the social sciences. Significantly, epidemiology has become a staple in the methodological armamentarium of drug abuse research.

REFERENCES

1. R.L. DuPont and M.H. Greene, *Science* **181**, 716 (1973).
2. L.G. Hunt and C.D. Chambers, *The Heroin Epidemics* (Spectrum, New York, 1976).
3. P.H. Hughes, E.C. Senay, R. Parker, *Arch. Gen. Psychiat.* **27**, 585 (1972).
4. M.H. Greene, J.L. Luke, R.L. DuPont, *Med. Ann. D.C.* **43**, 175 (1974).
5. D.X. Freedman and E.C. Senay, *J. Am. Med. Assoc.* **223**, 1155 (1973).
6. R.L. DuPont, *N. Engl. J. Med.*, **285**, 320 (1971).
7. P.H. Hughes and G.A. Crawford, *Arch. Gen. Psychiatr.* **27**, 149 (1972).
8. J.C. Ball and C.D. Chambers, Eds., *The Epidemiology of Opiate Addiction in the United States* (Thomas, Springfield, IL, 1970).
9. E.D. Drucker and V.W. Sidel, "The communicable disease model of heroin addiction—a critique," paper presented at the meeting of the American Public Health Association, San Francisco, 4 to 8 November 1973.
10. P. Jacobs, "Epidemiology abuse: Epidemiological and psychosocial models of drug abuse," paper presented at the National Drug Abuse Conference, New Orleans, 4 to 7 April 1975.
11. M.H. Greene, *Am. J. Public Health* (Suppl.), **64**, 1 (1974).
12. A.J. Ruttenber and J.L. Luke, *Science* **226**, 14 (1984).
13. Centers for Disease Control, *Morb. Mortal. Wkly. Rep.* **30**, 185 (1981).
14. C. Vandelli *et al.*, *Drug Alcohol Depend.* **14**, 129 (1984).
15. L.D. Johnston, P.M. O'Malley, J.G. Bachman, *Drug Use Among American High School Students, College Students, and Other Young Adults—National Trends Through 1985* (National Institute on Drug Abuse, Rockville, MD, 1986).
16. National Institute on Drug Abuse, *National Survey on Drug Abuse: Main Findings 1982* (National Institute on Drug Abuse, Rockville, MD, 1983).
17. E.H. Adams *et al.*, *Adv. Alcohol Drug Abuse*, in press.
18. E.H. Adams and B.A. Rouse, "Populations at risk for cocaine use and subsequent consequences," paper to be presented at the meeting of the American Psychiatric Association, Washington, DC, 18 to 22 November 1986.
19. C. Baum, J.P. Hsu, R.C. Nelson, *Public Health Rep.*, in press.
20. E.H. Adams, "An overview of drug use in the United States and along the U.S.-Mexico border," paper presented at the U.S.-Mexico Border Public Health Association meeting, Monterrey, Mexico, 28 to 30 April 1986
21. National Institute on Drug Abuse, *Epidemiology of Heroin: 1964–1984* (National Institute on Drug Abuse, Rockville, MD, 1985).

22. M.D. Brodsky, *Natl. Inst. Drug Abuse Res. Monogr. Ser. 57* (1985), p. 94

23. National Institute on Drug Abuse, *Community Epidemiology Work Group Proceedings* (National Institute on Drug Abuse, Rockville, MD, 1986).

24. National Institute on Drug Abuse, *Population Projections— Based on the National Survey on Drug Abuse, 1982* (National Institute on Drug Abuse, Rockville, Md., 1983).

25. National Commission on Marihuana and Drug Abuse, *Marihuana: A Signal of Misunderstanding* (Government Printing Office, Washington, DC, 1972).

26. R.R. Clayton and H.L. Voss, *Natl. Inst. Drug Abuse Res. Monogr. Ser. 39* (1981) p. 46.

27. D.B. Kandel, D. Murphy, D. Karus, *Natl. Inst. Drug Abuse Res. Monogr. Ser. 61* (1985), p. 76

28. Institute of Medicine, *Marijuana and Health* (National Academy Press, Washington, DC, 1982).

29. J.A. Yesavage, V.O. Leirer, M. Denari, L.E. Hollister, *Am. J. Psychiatr.* **142**, 1325 (1985).

30. Strategy Council on Drug Abuse, *Federal Strategy for Drug Abuse and Drug Traffic Prevention 1973* (Government Printing Office, Washington, DC, 1973).

31. J.S. Schachne, B.H. Roberts, P.D. Thompson, *N. Engl. J. Med.* **310**, 1666 (1984).

32. P.F. Pasternack, S.B. Calvin, F.G. Bauman, *Am. J. Cardiol.* **55**, 847 (1985).

33. L.L. Cregler and H. Mark, *ibid.* **57**, 1185 (1986).

Taking drugs seriously

JOHN KAPLAN

JOHN KAPLAN is associate professor of law at Stanford Law School. He is the author of *The Hardest Drug: Heroin and Public Policy*.

IT WOULD BE difficult to deny that the efforts and resources expended in our attempt to prevent the production of heroin and cocaine in other countries, and to keep out of the United States those drugs that are produced, have passed the point of diminishing returns. The outcry over drugs in the newspapers and on the political hustings, and a look at what is occurring in many public-housing projects and in the large lower-class black and Hispanic neighborhoods of our central cities, should be enough to convince sober observers that our present drug policies have simply not been successful enough.

Of course, there are politicians who still argue that our drug problems can be substantially improved by further attempts to push the Colombian, Mexican, Burmese, and other governments toward greater efforts. But with the military and internal strength they have at their disposal, they are doing about as well as one could expect.

Nor is the related demand to increase the use of our army or navy to stop drug smuggling a more likely source of improvement. The ingenuity of smugglers, the tremendous volume of legitimate trade, and the huge number of individuals crossing our borders make it impracticable to achieve the kind of increases in the interdiction rate that would make heroin and cocaine significantly less available or more expensive in the United States.

The problem, then, for those who realize that our present efforts have bogged down, is what to do. In this respect, drug policy must proceed by elimination. None of the policy options is attractive. All involve great costs—either in expenditures on law enforcement or in damage to public health. Since no option is without severe disadvantages, we can aim only to choose the policy that is least bad.

At one level, the simplest solution would be simply to get out of the way, legalize heroin and cocaine, and allow their sale as we do alcohol's. Until recently this was rarely advocated in print, though for years one would hear such recommendations in private conversation with intellectuals. Now, however, the legalization movement is becoming respectable, and even popular.

A repeal of drug prohibition?

Probably the central problem with the solution of legalization is that it ignores basic pharmacology. There is such a thing as a dangerous drug, and both heroin and cocaine undoubtedly fall into this category. It is here, of course, that the alcohol analogy is usually brought up. The analogy is indeed suggestive, because alcohol is by any standard a dangerous drug as well. And when we repealed Prohibition, we replaced a legal ban on alcohol similar to that now imposed on heroin and cocaine with a system of legal, controlled sale, presumably much like that contemplated for heroin and cocaine. There is no doubt that legalization has attractions. When Prohibition was repealed, the enormous inflow of profits to organized crime and the large-scale corruption of public officials caused by the illegal alcohol traffic dropped sharply. And the large number of civil-liberties violations by Prohibition agents ceased as well.

Several factors, however, made the repeal of Prohibition a much better social decision than would be the case with heroin or cocaine. Hard as it is to believe, the social cost of maintaining Prohibition was not only greater than that which heroin and cocaine currently impose upon us, it was even greater than that imposed by what is now our greatest drug problem—alcohol. Although the addict criminality caused by the high price of heroin and cocaine seems to have had no counterpart in the case of alcohol, the strain on our institutions was far greater. Corruption in the United States during Prohibition approximated that which we now associate with many Third World countries. It is true that the heroin and cocaine trades have corrupted many local police, some prosecutors, and a few local judges. During Prohibition, however, things were much worse. Federal judges, federal and state prosecutors, and countless politicians—

from congressmen and state governors to mayors, city councilmen, and chiefs of police—were in the pay of bootleggers.

Part of the difference is due to the passage of time. Wave upon wave of reform has made our government a far more honest one in the last fifty years. Perhaps more important is the fact that both before and during Prohibition, alcohol use was common among all social classes and in virtually every area of the nation, and had a much better "image" than heroin and cocaine do today. A society where many people in all walks of life considered themselves drinkers made this activity far more respectable than the use of "hard drugs" is today. And, of course, when an activity is more socially acceptable, it becomes easier for government agents to accept bribes and favors to allow it to continue.

The strain and social costs atrributed to Prohibition were not the only factors justifying the legalization of alcohol. The majority of drinkers enjoyed the use of alcohol without any harm to themselves or society. In a sense, the legalization of alcohol represented the willingness of these drinkers to shoulder their share of the social costs of legalized alcohol.

Nonetheless, the example of alcohol control illustrates a basic rule concerning all attempts to minimize the damage caused by habit-forming and destructive drugs. The principle also applies to a number of consensual (somewhat inaccurately called "victimless") crimes, such as gambling and prostitution. When one of these behaviors is made criminal, its enforcement is not particularly effective; it saddles the criminal-justice system with huge costs; it feeds organized criminal gangs; it causes official corruption; and it leads to large numbers of violations of civil liberties. Finally, the law does not really solve the problems of those engaging in the activity.

On the other hand, the legalization of the behavior produces an increase in the behavior, which can produce a public-health problem of enormous magnitude. Prohibition, for example, despite its faults—including the fact that it was not strictly enforced—did lower the amount of drinking in the United States. The comparative figures for cirrhosis of the liver demonstrate this clearly. With the repeal of Prohibition, both the number of drinkers and their per capita consumption of alcohol gradually but substantially increased, leading eventually to one of our major public-health problems—alcoholism. According to most estimates, alcoholism results in somewhere between 50,000 and 200,000 deaths per year. And regardless of whether the yearly social cost of alcoholism amounts to forty billion dollars or one hundred and ten billion dollars (two frequently cited figures), no one would deny that the social cost of alcohol use far exceeds that of all illegal drugs together. The issue then is not whether we were correct in legalizing alcohol or tobacco (I would strongly argue that we were), but what we should do about the drugs that are currently illegal.

A prescription system?

Of course, criminalization and legalization are not the only possibilities. We are probably correct in using a prescription system for valium, for example, which is quite a dangerous drug—but also a useful one. When heroin addicts in England consisted overwhelmingly of middle-aged, middle-class men and women who had become addicted during the course of medical treatment, a prescription system was successfully used to dispense the drug. (Sale without a prescription was a rather serious crime.) However, when an increasingly higher percentage of those addicted came to be more like American addicts—lower-class, criminal, and thrill-seeking—the "British system" was abandoned. England stopped using the pre-

scription system for more than a tiny and diminishing number of addicts, adopting instead a legal-control method much like that used in the United States.

In any event, no one seems to be arguing for a prescription system to control our major illegal drugs. If marijuana, cocaine, and heroin have legitimate medical uses (and the possibility that heroin is better than morphine at relieving intractable pain is the subject of heated debate, with most of the evidence apparently arguing against its superiority), then a prescription system seems most suitable. In fact, this is already being done: we allow prescriptions for medical use of cocaine and THC, the major active ingredient in marijuana.

Though we can regard heroin addiction itself as a disease, and hence a possible candidate for a prescription system, the problems in making such a system work seem insurmountable, as the British have discovered. The sizable pool of non-addicted heroin users forms a ready market for diverted prescribed heroin; the ranks of the addicted would thus swell. (It is impossible for a physician to determine how much heroin an addict really "needs," since this amount varies enormously over time.) Moreover, another drug—methadone—that is available by prescription (although only under certain conditions) is seen, both in the United States and in Britain, as much preferable to heroin for the medical treatment of heroin addiction.

The most important reason, however, why a prescription system for marijuana, cocaine, or heroin is just as inappropriate as it would be for alcohol and tobacco is that people generally use these drugs because they want to, and not to cure their ailments. We may be able to treat them and convince them not to use these drugs, but providing these drugs through prescription is not the way to do it.

If the choice for each of the "recreational" drugs is between criminalization and some kind of legalization, then it must be made on a drug-by-drug basis, as was the case with alcohol and tobacco (and coffee, for that matter), taking into account such variables as the pharmacological makeup of each drug and the cost of attempting to suppress it.

This is not an issue to be decided by John Stuart Mill's "simple principle"—that is, by letting each person decide for himself. No nation in the world follows his rule regarding self-harming conduct, and the rule is probably unworkable in a complex, industrial society—particularly one that is a welfare state. Mill's principle, moreover, seems singularly inappropriate when it is applied to a habit-forming, psychoactive drug that alters the user's perspective as to postponement of gratification and his desire for the drug itself.

No surrender?

On the other hand, certain arguments against legalization are even less impressive. Mill's principle, after all, is on the whole a rather sensible injunction to government, which tends—almost by reflex—to attempt to forbid any activity that it regards as harmful, immoral, or deviant. Far less sensible is the idea, advanced by Jesse Jackson and echoed by A. M. Rosenthal of the *New York Times*, that "you do not win a war by surrendering." Obviously, surrender is sometimes the better course. We did it with alcohol, and, if we go back further, we did it in many states with tobacco. (And in the international arena both we, in Vietnam, and the Soviet Union, in Afghanistan, seem to have improved our respective positions by abandoning a war.)

The non-pragmatic, no-surrender arguments are often coupled with warnings about the consequences of legalization. Such arguments, however, are insubstantial—particularly when compared with the serious arguments with which we should be grappling. Take Rosenthal's *Times* argument: "How can we continue to fight against alcoholism and tobacco addiction," asks Rosenthal, "if we suddenly say that other drugs—even more dangerous—should be made available?" This is not persuasive. First, virtually every scientist who has looked at the issue would acknowledge that one of the illegal drugs—marijuana—is certainly no more dangerous than alcohol. Second, the argument is a *non sequitur*. Legalizing drugs thought to be more dangerous than alcohol and tobacco might well make it even easier to convince alcohol and tobacco users that legalization does not guarantee that these drugs are safe. The educational message of treating what are patently dangerous drugs the same way we treat alcohol might be valuable for yet another reason. Many people still fail to understand that, by virtually any definition, alcohol is a drug. Treating alcohol the same way we treat cocaine and heroin might help drive this point home to many drinkers.

A similar fallacy lies behind a more common and somewhat more general argument—that legalization of a formerly illegal drug "sends the wrong message" to the public, implying that the drug is safe. The fact is that when Prohibition was enacted alcohol was regarded as dangerous, and Prohibition was not repealed because we changed our minds and decided that alcohol was safe. We all grew up believing that tobacco was habit-forming and stunted one's growth, at the very least. People who chose to drink and smoke did not do so because they believed that no one could be hurt by such behavior or that the government gave them its blessing. The simple increase in availability seems to account for all the increase in drug use when a drug is legalized. After all, those who use dangerous drugs that the public condemns tend not to be highly aware of the nuances of governmental messages.

As a result, the issue boils down to a careful weighing of the costs of criminalization of each drug against the public-health costs we could expect if that drug were to become legally available.

I will not consider the case of marijuana. It is the most used of the three major illegal drugs (although its use has decreased considerably in the last decade); but at present marijuana is also the least socially costly of the illegal drugs, in addition to being the drug that has been most effectively interdicted (because of its relatively large bulk). Finally, marijuana is the drug that promises the lowest public-health costs if legalized.

Various commentators have considered the social costs of marijuana's criminalization and the projected public-health costs of legalization. And though they have been shouted down by parent groups and those who seek their votes, these commentators, by and large, have leaned toward legalization. The report of the National Academy of Sciences Committee on Substance Abuse and Habitual Behavior made a rather conservative recommendation: it merely asserted that "the current policies directed at controlling the supply of marijuana should be seriously reconsidered."

Nor need we devote any attention to LSD, mescaline, PCP, or any number of other illegal drugs here; for the illegal status of these drugs has not created a significant social problem.

Needless to say, this is not the case with heroin and cocaine. The costs of restricting supply of these drugs are substantial. Since space does not permit discussions of both heroin and cocaine, I will discuss only the anticipated costs of legalizing cocaine. First, a reasonable calculation of the public-health costs of heroin legalization, based on our admittedly inadequate information, already exists.[1] Second, since cocaine is far more prevalent than heroin, it imposes

greater social costs upon us—from the amount of money flowing into criminal syndicates to the number of users arrested for predatory crimes. Third, there seems to be widespread public agreement—although it is probably mistaken—that cocaine is the more benign of the two drugs.

The case of cocaine

At a minimum, it is clear that anyone advocating the legalization of cocaine would have to make a serious estimate of how many more people would use the drug after it was legalized; how many of these users would become dependent on the drug; and how much harm this would cause them and society. Instead, there has been no serious discussion of all this. Moreover, no one has seriously considered the impact of a "new" drug upon a culture that has yet to develop patterns of self-control with respect to its use; by contrast, we should recall that over many generations our culture has developed a variety of informal controls over alcohol use, which allow most people to lessen the harm that alcohol does both to them in particular and society in general. Societies not accustomed to alcohol, however, such as England prior to the "gin epidemic" of the late seventeenth and early eighteenth centuries, and many Native American and Eskimo cultures, have experienced a public-health catastrophe of huge proportions as a result of the introduction of distilled spirits.

Nor have the advocates of the legalization of cocaine considered how we would be able to prevent teenagers from gaining access to the now legal drug. Many people assume that legalization of a drug would affect only adults, since, as with alcohol, we would make it illegal to sell the drug to minors. The problem, however, is that legal access for adults makes a drug *de facto* available to the young. This has been the experience with alcohol and tobacco. Cocaine is far less bulky and more concealable than alcohol, and its use does not leave the telltale aroma of smoke; thus it would be even more difficult to keep away from minors.

Yet another problem is the possibility of changes in public consciousness and values. Such changes can make use of a drug less dangerous, but they can also greatly augment its dangers. There are many examples of changes in public consciousness, entirely apart from governmental action, that have influenced drug use. The use of tobacco, alcohol, and marijuana seems to have dropped in the last several years, just as jogging and low-fat diets have increased, all as a consequence of the nation's greater fixation on health. Unfortunately, we cannot guarantee that such cultural trends will continue, or even that they will not be reversed, as has often happened in the past.

Youth culture, moreover, seems to be subject to dramatic fluctuations. The rapid changes in styles of dress, hair, music, and entertainment among the young have bewildered their elders for generations; and the appearance of a charismatic proselytizer for cocaine (as Timothy Leary was for LSD and marijuana) could change youth attitudes toward cocaine. Such a cultural change, even if only temporary, could present us with a permanent problem of large numbers of young people who became drug-dependent during the period of the drug's "window of acceptability."

Consider the case of heroin. Though most people have not noticed, the epidemic of heroin use stopped about ten years ago. Each year, the average age of heroin addicts goes up by about a year. Nevertheless, the last heroin epidemic has left us with an endemic problem of about 500,000 addicts who impose large social costs upon us.

---

[1] See my *The Hardest Drug: Heroin and Public Policy* (University of Chicago Press, 1983).

The dangers of cocaine

This is not to say that problems like these cannot be solved, or that more careful thought and research might not satisfy us. As far as we now know, however, there is no particular cause for comfort. The pharmacological nature of cocaine, in fact, is especially worrisome. We need not list all the serious negative effects cocaine may have on its users, since an impressive list of such effects can be drawn up for any of the psychoactive drugs. The problem is to determine just how prevalent these effects would be if the drug were legalized.

With cocaine, we do not have to consider the relatively rare stoppages of the heart muscle or the incidence of strokes; the common effects of cocaine are the most appropriate reasons for concern. The most important fact about cocaine is that it is an extremely attractive drug. In the 1950s a double-blind experiment on the "enjoyability" of a number of injected drugs was undertaken with twenty normal volunteers. Although fewer than half of the subjects found heroin or morphine euphoric, fully 90 percent liked an amphetamine (which is a pharmocological relative of cocaine), giving it by far the highest "pleasure score."

Probably related to its "pleasure score" is the fact that cocaine is the most "reinforcing" drug known to us. Animal studies corroborate the reports of many human users. Over the past four decades, self-administration equipment has been developed that permits animals to "work" for supplies of a drug and to administer all they want. It turns out that opiates such as heroin lie somewhere between alcohol and cocaine in their reinforcing power. Alcohol seems relatively unattractive; it is quite difficult to get most animals to drink alcohol, and unless they are already addicted, monkeys and many other animals will go to some length to avoid ingesting alcohol. Virtually all monkeys, however, will continue injecting themselves with opiates until they become addicted, and even nonaddicted animals will perform considerable amounts of work to "earn" their injections. But cocaine is the most impressive drug in this respect: animals will do enormous amounts of work to earn their cocaine shots. Indeed, if permitted, they will hit at their levers again and again to gain their reward of cocaine, neglecting food or rest until they die of debilitation.

This problem is exacerbated by several other properties of cocaine. Along with amphetamines, it is one of the few drugs that can improve one's mental and physical performance of a task. In fact, this improvement is limited to performance under conditions of fatigue, and the improvement is only temporary. Nonetheless, there will be many occasions during work, athletics, or studies when an individual will be willing to mortgage his future for a little more energy and mental clarity. Moreover—and in this respect unlike amphetamines—cocaine not only produces an alert high, but also subsequently causes a noticeable low, a kind of depression after its relatively short-term course has been run. This rather unusual effect results in the urge to use the drug again, both to re-create the past enjoyable high and to fight off the present dysphoric low.

The damage wrought by heavy cocaine use in terms of psychiatric symptoms and general debilitation is now widely known. What is less appreciated are the more subtle changes that regular cocaine use can cause. Unlike alcohol and heroin, cocaine use can easily be integrated with everyday activities. Its use can be quite inconspicuous, and, like cigarette smoking, can accompany a host of everyday activities. Cocaine use makes one feel good, then highly competent, then nearly omnipotent. It is easy to see why the use of such a drug would be damaging in a complex, mechanized, and interdependent society such as ours.

Nor should we take much comfort from the fact that most of those who use cocaine today have not become dependent upon the drug. As long as the drug is expensive and relatively difficult to procure, most of its users will be able to avoid dependence. When the drug is easily available, however, we can expect the temptations toward use to increase considerably.

We can see this by doing a quick calculation. Once the nonfinancial cost of cocaine (that is, incovenience and criminal danger to the user) is greatly reduced by legalization, the drug's financial cost looms as the dominating one. At present, a gram of cocaine sells for about $80-$100. Its cost of production is certainly less than three dollars. Presumably, legalized cocaine would be taxed as heavily as possible, though the cost including tax would have to be sufficiently low, so as to make bootlegging unprofitable. Profits in today's cocaine trade are so huge, though, that it is hard to believe that we could keep the retail price of a gram of cocaine above $20. (Keep in mind that the bootlegger, who tries only to cheat the government out of its tax receipts, is treated much more leniently by both the criminal-justice system and society than is the universally maligned drug pusher.) When one considers that there are about fifty "hits" of cocaine in a gram, one is startled by the realization that at $20 per gram the cost of a hit will be only forty cents—a figure well within the budget of almost all grade-school children. Nor is the specter of very young children destroyed by the use of cocaine in any way unrealistic; there are ten-year-old cocaine addicts on the streets of Bogota today.

It is true that if the number of those dependent upon cocaine merely doubled, we would arguably be well ahead of the game, considering the large costs imposed by treating those users as criminals. But what if there were a fifty-fold increase in the number of those dependent on cocaine? We simply cannot guarantee that such a situation would not come to pass; since we cannot do so, it is the height of irresponsibility to advocate risking the future of the nation.

If all this is not enough to convince reasonably prudent people that legalizing cocaine is too risky a course, we can also consider the consequences of taking the risk and being wrong. After all, if we had legalized cocaine five years ago, we would not have known how easy it is to make cocaine into "crack," universally considered to be a much more habit-forming and dangerous form of the drug. If we legalize cocaine now, how long should we wait before deciding whether we made a mistake? And if we decided that we had, how would we go about recriminalizing the drug? By then, substantial inventories of legal cocaine would have been built up in private hands, and large numbers of new users would have been introduced to the drug. And once a drug has been made legally available, it is very difficult to prohibit it. This consideration helps to explain why Prohibition failed, and also explains why almost no one advocates the criminalization of tobacco.

Finding a solution

The problem, then, is what we can do about the present situation. Several factors have made our drug policy politically tolerable up to now. First, it has protected most of middle-class America from the kind of continuous exposure to the use of drugs (and encouragement favoring their use) that are most likely to lead to the problems of drug abuse; such exposure and encouragement characterize the underclass areas in which drug use is endemic. Second, although drug enforcement has been expensive, it would have been even more expensive to do more. Third, we have continued to entertain hopes that we could solve our drug problem on the cheap, either by pressuring other nations to prevent the production of illegal drugs or by keeping drugs from being smuggled into the United States.

If we were to choose to take our drug problem more seriously, it is not clear what we could do. According to public-opinion polls, education is currently the most popular method for dealing with our drug problem. A recent Gallup Poll showed that 47 percent of Americans believe it is the best antidrug strategy. (Thirty-six percent favor interdiction, and 6 percent favor drug treatment.)

Our research shows that it is doubtful that education can do much to lower the level of drug abuse, however. Newspaper advertising campaigns to discourage alcohol abuse and drug use have been shown to be ineffective. We have had experience with temperance campaigns, but as far as we can tell, most young people do not appear to pay much attention to them. Nor do school-based programs seem to be able to reduce alcohol and drug abuse.

This is predictable. Young people are notoriously resistant to their elders' efforts to get them to live less risky, more forward-looking lives. Well into adolescence, they tend to retain what psychiatrists refer to as "remnants of infantile omnipotence." Moreover, entirely apart from the question of risk, young people often take pleasure in things that adults tell them are bad. They are constantly told that they should avoid things (like sex or junk food) that they enjoy. At best they tend to disregard such advice—when they do not actually seek out occasions to disobey their elders' counsel. Indeed, the real mystery is how we have managed to convince significant numbers of youths in inner-city school systems— more than 50 percent of whose students drop out of school, despite a massive publicity campaign to the contrary—to avoid taking drugs, since at least in the beginning they would find drug use so enjoyable.

Nevertheless, one kind of drug education does show some promise. Several small-scale experiments have attempted to use peers to teach young students techniques by which they can refuse cigarettes if they want to. They learn, for instance, what to say when others offer them cigarettes or even exert social pressure on them to smoke; this approach has produced significant decreases in the initiation of cigarette use. Such programs are still quite rare, however, and whether we can duplicate them on a large scale with respect to cocaine and heroin, in the neighborhoods that most need them, is by no means clear. At the very least, we need years of research before we can develop programs that can be trusted to do more good than harm.

The charm of education, nonetheless, is seductive. Compared with other means of coping with illegal drugs, it is cheap and seems humane, because it does not require the coercion of our fellow citizens. In this regard, it is similar to bringing pressure upon foreign nations to prevent the production of illegal drugs. Indeed, education may well become the "crop substitution" of the nineties—that is, the supposed panacea for all drug problems.

Conceivably, we will decide simply to continue our present policies. We can spend a great deal on education programs; we can assign the military the task of sealing our borders against drugs; we can seize yachts or fishing boats when passengers or workers have abandoned marijuana cigarettes on them; we can legislate capital punishment for drug-related killings (as when drug dealers murder one another). But by adopting such a course of action, we would only be making an emphatic statement that we were taking the drug problem seriously; we would not really be acting seriously. For to act in this manner would in effect be to choose to keep putting up with our problem.

For most middle-class Americans, the use of heroin and cocaine is not a major threat. Heroin never was a threat; and although cocaine was very popular with some wealthy users—the conventional wisdom held that they were heavily overrepresented in advertising, entertainment, and professional sports—and its use significantly harmed the lives of many middle-class youths, much of the damage has already been done. Today, cocaine—especially in the form of "crack"—is increasingly becoming a drug of the lower classes. It is true that all of us suffer from the intimate connection between these drugs and predatory crime, and in more indirect ways from the enormous dislocation and damage done to lower-class neighborhoods by the sale and use of these drugs. Nonetheless, we learned to live with problems like these many years ago. Indeed, it seems that the public gets really excited about the drug problem only when someone from the middle class is killed in a gang shoot-out.

In an ideal world, the best way to reduce the damage done by illegal drugs would be to convince everyone not to use them. In this world, however, we will probably have to reconcile ourselves to using some coercion. On the other hand, once we give up on finding an inexpensive solution, we may take the problem seriously and apply more careful thought and more resources to the job.

Supply-side enforcement

So long as we are unable to suppress the sale of drugs, we will be remitting large parts of our cities to the terrorization of innocent people, drug-related killings, and the brutalization that comes from constant exposure to the use of drugs. Perhaps equally demoralizing is the sight of the large number of teenage drug lords who own Jaguars or Ferraris before they are old enough to have driver's licenses. Nonetheless, we can accomplish much more than we have in the past.

Apart from our efforts in other countries and at the borders, the major thrust of enforcement within the United States has been the attempt to break up large-scale drug rings, arrest small-scale dealers when they sell drugs outside the areas in which drug use is endemic, and punish users when they commit other crimes. In recent years local police have stepped up their efforts to restrain street-level selling, and private employers have exerted greater efforts to apprehend their workers' "connection," and to weed out illegal drug users from their work force. The result has been a slow but steady loss of ground for law-enforcement agencies.

One cannot say that careful thought and greatly augmented law-enforcement resources will solve our drug problem. There are large numbers of sellers arranged hierarchically within the United States as part of loose but fairly sizable organizations, taking the drug from its importation into the United States through smaller wholesalers down to the small-scale sellers who provide the drug to users. Unfortunately, we cannot expect to achieve much of a reduction in the number of drug suppliers, even if we jail a sizable percentage of them. The high profits at every level of the drug trade guarantee a huge reservoir of individuals prepared to take the places of those who have been imprisoned. At each level in the distribution scheme there are more than enough competitors; and even at the lowest ranks, those who do minor jobs for the sellers (such as acting as lookouts for the police) seem ready to enter the business.

On the other hand, pressure upon the retailing of heroin and cocaine is not necessarily an unattractive option. In fact, it is probably the major governmental means of restraining drug use in the United States today. The number of locations in which an ordinary middle-class individual can buy heroin and cocaine is not very large. In most of the country, cocaine is not widely available to most people. Heroin is less so. A major task of law-enforcement resources is to increase that area of drug unavailability. At the very least, the police should act immediately to suppress the open-air drug markets that spring up whenever the police are distracted by other duties. In most of our urban areas, greater efforts could drive much of the dealing indoors, where a large percentage of potential customers are afraid to go.

At least for the foreseeable future, it is hard to imagine the police being able to do more than gradually drive the dealing back into the public-housing projects and other relatively small areas in which the police are unable to maintain a presence. Nonetheless, increases in law-enforcement efforts at the retail level may lower the availability of heroin and cocaine to large numbers of people without creating a need to involve ourselves in the most hard-core drug-trafficking areas, in which the police would have to maintain a virtual army of occupation.

Apart from the difficulty of policing the hard-core drug areas, the most important constraint upon our ability to suppress the sale of drugs is the cost of incarceration space. Our prisons and jails are full, and despite a massive and continuing effort to provide the infrastructure to imprison more and more lawbreakers, the demand threatens to permanently outrun the supply. Drug sales, moreover, are especially difficult and expensive to restrain through imprisonment. The deterrence we expect from the legal threat is in large part neutralized by the high profits at all levels of the drug trade. And incapacitation, the other major restraint provided by imprisonment, is weakened by the fact that the skills necessary to participate in the drug trade are not at all scarce.

Although we must allocate a large percentage of prison space to the incarceration of drug dealers if we are to make headway, there are other methods that can help. At the higher levels of the drug trade, the forfeiture of assets has proven quite successful. We cannot show that the threat has caused any drug dealers to get out of the business, but at the margin it should have that effect; depriving sellers of working capital makes their reentry into the industry more difficult. At the very least, it assuages our sense of justice, as well as providing additional resources with which to further enforcement. It is likely that we can go a great deal lower in the drug-trade hierarchy before forfeiture is no longer worthwhile. It will require a little more ingenuity by the police and cooperation from the agencies of the criminal-justice system before we can strike at the pocketbook of the small-scale seller, but it can be done—and to good effect.

Demand-side enforcement

While pressure on the small-scale sale of drugs represents an attempt to influence drug supply, it also has an impact on drug demand—perhaps a greater one. The buyer who does not reside in an area of heavy drug sales must not only come up with the money to pay for the drugs; he may also have to search longer to make a purchase and worry more about the danger of being robbed or assaulted. He may also be more conspicuous to the police. To some extent, we can take advantage of this problem faced by drug buyers by using a relatively inexpensive means of lessening the number of those who are willing to obtain their supplies from the areas of heavy drug dealing. On a few occasions police have seized the automobiles of those who drove them to purchase drugs. This is not only inexpensive, but also far less brutal than imprisoning otherwise law-abiding drug users—and it may have more of an impact. This should be a regular feature of all drug enforcement.

Probably the most important aspect of the attack on drugs is the attempt to lower the amount of predatory crime that drug use engenders. We know, for example, that those who use illegal drugs commit a substantial proportion of our urban burglaries, robberies, and thefts. A number of studies have demonstrated that the criminality rate of those using heroin daily—that is, those who were addicted—was about seven times as great as the criminality rate of

the same people when they were using the drug only sporadically or temporarily not using it at all.

Newer studies have shown an even higher correlation between criminality and drug use, and have implicated cocaine as well. Urinalysis of those arrested for crimes in 1986 has revealed that a staggering percentage of those apprehended had recently used cocaine or heroin. In the District of Columbia, 74 percent of non-drug-felony arrestees tested positive for at least one illegal drug other than marijuana. (No one has alleged that marijuana use helps to cause predatory crime, in part because the drug is cheap, in part because it has a tranquilizing effect.) In New York City the figure was 72 percent; in Chicago, 60 percent; and in Los Angeles, 58 percent. It turns out that in large cities about 70 percent of those arrested for robbery, weapons offenses, and larceny tested positive for heroin, cocaine, or (in the few cities where use is common) PCP.

The data on urinalysis suggest an obvious course of action. We must institutionalize routine urinalysis for those arrested for any of the typical crimes arising out of drug use. Then we must act on this information by making maintenance of a urine clean of cocaine, heroin, and PCP a requirement for all those who are released on bail or, after conviction, are placed on probation or released on parole.

A positive urine sample must reliably and immediately mean a return to jail. It is far more important that the enforcement of these rules be consistent than that the jail terms be long. We do not have the jail space that would be needed to provide long terms for this type of offense. And if we try, our efforts will backfire: we will deprive the system of the consistency necessary to get the message through to drug users. But a properly implemented system of imprisonment can make possible a more lasting cure for drug dependency.

This kind of regimen is not without disadvantages. There will inevitably be a dispute over whether we can demand "clean" urine before releasing someone on bail. On the one hand, our jurisprudence tells us that bail is to be used only to guarantee the presence of the accused at judicial proceedings, and there is no firm evidence that drug users are less likely than others to show up in court. On the other hand, more recent precedent seems to allow consideration of the danger to the community if an arrestee is released on bail, and those who use illegal drugs are, on average, much more likely to commit crimes after they have been freed.

Such a system of mandatory urinalysis will also require more money. Parts of the criminal-justice system will simply not give up—even temporarily—the funds they already have and need, even though doing so may help to save money in the long run. The jails are already full, and in many cases under court order not to exceed their present population. Even at two days per failed urinalysis, the increased demand upon those institutions will be substantial. And the maintenance of such a system will require the police to go looking for those who miss urinalysis appointments, a burden that may initially be only partially compensated for by the lower criminality of those now compelled to be drug-free.

Furthermore, the inexpensive urine test, which costs only about $5, but is less than completely accurate, will have to be supplemented by a system in which an arrestee who was confident that he had not used an illegal drug could simply file an affidavit to that effect and be tested by a more expensive but foolproof method (costing about $70). Although there will have to be some sanction for a false affidavit, expensive prosecutions for perjury will not be necessary to deter such conduct (though it is hard to imagine a simpler case to prosecute). The judge, in revoking bail or probation, can simply revoke it for longer.

Then there are the privacy concerns. It should be noted that urinalysis for those who have been arrested involves far fewer restraints on the citizen's right to privacy than the usual attempt to require urinalysis of government employees or members of other large groups, who, as individuals, give us no reason to suspect their drug use. (Nor is it nearly so expensive.) Our statistics on the drug use of those arrested for street crimes already single them out. And apart from the use of urinalysis in the bail decision, there are no real constitutional doubts. If there is a good reason, those arrested for drunken driving, for example, may constitutionally be subjected to blood, urine, or breath analysis, and those released on bail or, after conviction, on probation or parole, forfeit even more of their privacy. They are subject not only to intrusive searches but also to various restrictions on their autonomy. Very few of the restrictions on the privacy and autonomy of defendants in the criminal-justice system make as much practical sense as requiring urinalysis in order to monitor their drug use.

The prognosis

What, then, could we expect from the institutionalization of such a regimen? Many of those using drugs will find themselves constantly in and out of jail. Some would simply decide that enough is enough and clean themselves up. We do know that this can occur when the consequences are immediate and certain enough. Nonetheless, in most cases we will have to rely upon drug treatment to prevent the urinalysis system from becoming a huge, inhumane, and expensive revolving-door operation. While it is true that the most reliable and cost-effective drug treatment—methadone maintenance —is helpful only with heroin addicts, there are other therapies that are more cost-effective than permitting the drug abuser to continue untreated; and it is likely that requiring urinalysis will help persuade drug users to undergo treatment.

Indeed, probably the most foolish aspect of our antidrug posture has been the starvation of drug treatment. In many cities there is a months-long wait for those who want to enter a drug-treatment program; this is a serious problem, considering that the desire to reform is often ephemeral, and disappears if it cannot be acted upon at once. Part of the reluctance to invest in drug treatment stems from the moralistic view that it is wrong to spend resources on making life better for criminals; part stems from the (incorrect) belief that treatment does not work. Treatment is difficult; it is frustrating; and it does not always work. But it is cost-effective—and far more so than its only substitute, imprisonment. A necessary component of any serious effort to lower the social costs of illegal drug use, therefore, is a massive increase in funds for drug treatment.

Another fact about drug treatment is also quite important. Although many believe that compulsory treatment is ineffective, this does not appear to be the case. Virtually everyone undergoing drug treatment is in one way or another forced to do so. Indeed, like many alcoholics, who simply want to become social drinkers again and escape the social, psychological, and physical effects of overindulgence, most drug users do not wish to be abstinent, but rather to return to the early days of their more casual drug use. Nonetheless, one of the effects that those dependent on cocaine and heroin may most wish to escape is the pressure of the criminal-justice system. And a criminal-justice system that makes use of urinalysis will be more effective in driving them into—and keeping them in— treatment.

The approach I am recommending may have another important effect. For years, the drug-producing nations have argued that the United States must share the blame for the drug problem: if they cannot control the production of illegal drugs, neither can we control our consumption. We may now be able to have some success. Those users who are both criminals and drug consumers appear to be not merely a random selection of drug users; they tend, rather, to be the heaviest users. Thus it is likely that these heavy users consume a disproportionate percentage of the illegal drug supply. This should not be surprising: the heaviest-drinking 10 percent of all drinkers drink well over half the total quantity of alcohol—and our evidence, though less conclusive, points in the same direction with regard to illegal drugs. Indeed, the "J curve" seems to be a constant in human behavior: 15 percent of health-insurance users use 90 percent of the resources; 6 percent of Philadelphia's youths commit over 50 percent of its crimes; and 10 percent of Stanford Law School's students file 90 percent of the petitions to be excused from one requirement or another.

As a result, those users we will be focusing on will be those who do the most to support the illegal market. On average, each seller is supported by three heavy users. If we can bring their use under control—in addition to decreasing the number of predatory crimes— we may finally be able to deal a major blow to the illegal retail-distribution networks. We may also create a sizable cohort of former drug users who can help discourage drug use. If the zeal of the convert in this area is as strong as it seems to be in others—think of ex-smokers, for example—we may reap unanticipated and sizable dividends from our efforts. For decades we have attempted to get at the sellers as a way of preventing use; now we may have the means to get at the users as a means of restraining sales.

I do not mean to suggest that we will be able to solve the problem easily. For the foreseeable future we will have a serious drug problem, but we can lessen it considerably if we have the will. Where will the money necessary to accomplish this come from? The additional resources we need for law enforcement and drug treatment will come from the federal government, or they will not come at all. Whether the resources will come is simply a question of whether we have finally begun to take our drug problem seriously. It will be interesting to find out.

CUTTING COSTS OF DRUG ABUSE

Sabin Russell

Chronicle Staff Writer

As the nation launches its latest crackdown on drug abuse, U.S. employers are turning up the heat on the costly private hospitals that treat alcohol and drug abusers.

Declaring that month-long stays in psychiatric hospitals are no more effective in treating addicts than far-less expensive outpatient care, businesses are trimming mental health benefits and challenging the medical decisions at treatment programs.

The economic costs of drug and alcohol abuse in the workplace are staggering. The National Institute on Drug Abuse estimates that alcohol problems cost the U.S. economy $65 billion in lost productivity alone. But there is growing concern among employers that much of the $17 billion spent on alcohol and substance-abuse treatment programs each year is being wasted.

"Psychiatric care is a monster that has gotten out of control," said Walter Afield, a blunt-speaking psychiatrist who is chairman of Tampa-based Mental Health Programs Corp. Employers and insurers increasingly are turning to specialty "utilization review" companies like Afield's. Those companies' own medical staffs can veto payment for mental health services they deem inappropriate.

Afield contends that the psychiatric profession has been corrupted by hospital drives to fill empty beds in order to make up for revenue lost when insurers and regulators capped the cost of other medical services such as surgery. Although Medicare cost-containment guidelines limit payments for most medical conditions, there are no limits on payment for psychiatric hospitalization. For the nation's cash-strapped hospitals, such care has become a big money-maker.

A standard, 28-day program of psychiatric care at a hospital can cost $400 to $700 a day, or as much as $20,000 for a month of treatment—not including $100- to $150-a-day doctor bills.

That kind of revenue, coupled with the drug-abuse epidemic, has been driving mental health costs into the stratosphere.

For many businesses today, mental health benefits consume 20¢ to 30¢ of each health-care dollar.

A study of 1,600 businesses by Princeton employee benefits consultant Foster Higgins found that mental-health and substance-abuse benefits last year rose 27 percent over the previous year to $207 per employee. That pace far outstrips the already high 18.6 percent increase in average health insurance plan costs last year. Mental health and substance abuse benefits accounted for 9.6 of health insurance costs last year, compared with 8.6 percent one year earlier.

"This is the only area of health care where people are actually building new beds, or converting acute-care beds to psychiatric beds," said Eugene Hill, chief executive of U.S. Behavioral Health, an Emeryville utilization-review company.

"There are very fine providers out there, giving very good quality care," said Hill. "We also have providers I think are one step short of fraud."

By moving alcohol and substance-abuse patients quickly to outpatient programs—where they live at home and visit doctors' offices during the day—Hill said costs can be trimmed by as much as 25 percent. Typical outpatient charges are one-half to one-third those of inpatient care, where the patient stays day and night in a hospital.

HOSPITALS IN A PINCH

As a result of pressure from utilization reviewers, Bay Area psychiatric hospitals are suddenly finding it harder to keep their beds full. "It's devastating," said Barbara Stern, director of Merritt Peralta Institute, an Oakland psychiatric-care hospital.

In a survey she conducts of the region's 25 private mental-health clinics, Stern found that only 59 percent of the 445 psychiatric beds were occupied last week. Historically, the hospitals have operated at 80 percent of capacity.

"Many treatment providers just gouged the hell out of insurance companies with outrageous rates," said Stern. "There had to be some cost-containment."

Until a year ago, all 44 of Merritt-Peralta's psychiatric beds were occupied, and there was always a waiting list. Today, the hospital operates at 70 percent of capacity, despite its generally lower rate—about $250 a day. Stern believes her center is suffering the backlash prompted by the lavish ways of her more expensive competitors.

While Stern backs the concept of cost-containment, she feels utilization reviewers are making "capricious and arbitrary" decisions about reimbursement. "To say all patients can be treated in an outpatient setting is not responsible," said Stern. She said she knows of two lawsuits involving addicts who died during withdrawal from drugs, although she declined to identify the cases.

OUTPATIENT ALTERNATIVE TOUTED

Other health-care companies maintain that outpatient care can handle nearly all mental-health cases, and often provides more effective treatment. About 95 percent of the care provided by American Biodyne, a South San Francisco-based mental-health maintenance organization, is conducted on an outpatient basis.

"Inpatient rehabilitation has become a revolving door," said American Biodyne's chairman and chief executive, Nicholas Cummings, a psychologist who spent 25 years running the mental-health program for the Kaiser Permanente Health Plan in the Bay Area. "I've seen people go through it two, three, or four times in a year."

American Biodyne, founded four years ago, covers 1.7 million employees and their dependents in 9 states—but not yet in California. Cummings said the market in the state is so competitive that it is simply easier to build his business elsewhere. The privately held company expects its fiscal year 1989 revenue of $28 million to double within five months.

At a typical cost of $3 per month for each insured employee or dependent, Biodyne provides intensive, 24-hour outpatient care using a staff of 400 doctors and psychologists. Cummings believes the outpatient model allows most alcoholics and addicts to go through detoxification at home. "Most detox is not that painful," he contended. "Rehabilitation should have to take place in the environment where they live."

Cummings boasts that 55 percent of patients who agree to go through with the outpatient program remain "clean" a year later, while in most substance-abuse programs a 10 percent rate is considered "remarkable."

Hospital operators, understandably, take a different view. "If I had my way, I'd keep them for three months," said Merritt Peralta's Stern. "Addicted people need to be in a treatment program for life-style changes, for motivation. There is a high relapse rate, especially for cocaine."

PUBLIC FACILITIES ARE SWAMPED

While private psychiatric hospitals are suddenly scrambling to fill beds, public drug- and alcohol-treatment programs are being overwhelmed by the number of poor people seeking such services. In San Francisco, where a 28-day inpatient program costs only $85 a day to operate, the wait for residential treatment programs is six to nine months.

Most of the addicts and alcoholics treated in the San Francisco program receive outpatient care. This year, the city expects to treat 16,000 people on a budget of $16 million.

Sensitive to the criticism of the profession, the Washington, D.C.-based American Psychiatric Association has established its own utilization-review arm, Advanced PsychSystems, and markets its services to insurers and large corporations. Like many other such firms, the APA group said it achieves an average savings of 25 percent on its clients' mental-health bills.

"Mental-health care is subjective," said Michele Deverich, a spokeswoman for APA. "It is not like taking out an appendix."

Deverich said that the concern over rising mental-health costs is creating some "troubling" trends.

A study by Minneapolis-based Northwestern National Life found that 45 percent of employers plan to exclude or restrict mental-health care benefits to their employees' dependents next year.

Although employers are starting to rebel over the high cost of mental-health programs, experts warn that budget-cutting efforts could be counterproductive if neglect becomes the substitute for treatment. "Employers who cut mental-health benefits in a year or two will encounter the costs again as medical problems, when the lack of treatment brings on physical manifestations," said Deverich.

According to the Mental Health Programs Corp.'s Walter Afield, problem drinkers have 3.6 times more accidents on or off the job than the average worker, require eight times the medical care, and are absent from work 2½ times as often. Recreational drug users use three times the sick leave as the average worker, and are five times as likely to file a workers' compensation claim.

No matter what employers do to get a grip on the nation's thorny drug-abuse problem, it's likely to be expensive, and painful.

CLAIMS AND CAUTIONS
MEGAVITAMIN THERAPY

Because vitamins play such vital roles in the body, many people hope that extra amounts will make them healthier or protect them against disease. So far, however, scientific evidence has not been supportive.

Stephen Barrett

Stephen Barrett, M.D. is the Contributing Editor of PRIORITIES.

Public interest in vitamin C is directly attributable to its promotion by Linus Pauling, Ph.D., winner of the 1954 Nobel Prize in chemistry. His 1970 book *Vitamin C and the Common Cold* suggested that taking 1,000 mg of vitamin C daily would reduce the incidence of colds by 45 percent for most people, but that some people might need larger amounts. The book also recommended that if a cold does strike, you should take 500 or 1,000 mg every hour for several hours (or 4,000 to 10,000 mg daily if symptoms don't disappear with smaller amounts). A second edition, published in 1976 as *Vitamin C, the Common Cold and the Flu*, recommended even higher dosages, and Pauling says he takes 12,000 mg daily, increasing to 40,000 mg daily when symptoms of a cold appear.

Pauling's view of vitamin C is based not on his own experiments but on his evaluation of the research and statistics of others. However, the vast majority of reputable medical and nutritional scientists who have looked at the same evidence believes that supplementation with large doses of vitamin C does not prevent colds and, at best, may slightly reduce the symptoms of a cold.

Scientific "facts" are determined by analyzing the results of all experiments that bear on those particular facts. In the case of vitamin C, at least 16 well-designed studies have been performed to test whether high-dosage vitamin C can prevent colds.

One method of testing is to inoculate the throats of volunteers with cold viruses. Two studies of this type have found that everyone got colds whether they took vitamin C or not. Another way to test vitamin C is to see what happens to matched groups over a period of time. The most comprehensive work of this type was performed during the 1970s by Dr. Terence Anderson and colleagues at the University of Toronto who conducted three studies involving thousands of volunteers. These trials suggest that nothing will be gained by taking vitamin C supplements year-round with the hope of preventing colds. Extra vitamin C may slightly reduce the severity of a cold, but it is not necessary to take the high doses suggested by Pauling to achieve this result. Any possible benefit can be achieved with 250 mg daily (an amount obtainable by drinking fruit juices). Very large amounts of vitamin C are not more effective and can cause diarrhea or other adverse effects.

VITAMIN C AND CANCER

Pauling also believes that massive doses of vitamin C can prolong the lives of cancer patients. This claim is based on a study he reported with Ewan Cameron, a Scottish physician. However, experts who analyzed the report concluded that the experimental and control groups were not comparable. Subsequently, the Mayo Clinic conducted two clinical trials involving 100 or more patients in advanced stages of cancer who were given either vitamin C or a placebo. No differences were found between the vitamin and placebo in survival time, appetite, weight loss, severity of pain, or amount of nausea and vomiting.

MEGAVITAMINS FOR MENTAL ILLNESS

Proponents of "orthomolecular therapy" suggest that abnormal behavior is caused by molecular imbalances that can be corrected by administering the "right" nutrient molecules at the right time. (*Ortho* is Greek for "right.") This approach is also referred to as megavitamin therapy, meganutrient therapy, or nutritional therapy. It began more than 30 years ago when a small number of psychiatrists began using large doses of vitamin B_3 to treat severe mental problems, an approach that they called "megavitamin therapy." Later the treatment regimen was expanded to include other vitamins, minerals, hormones, and diets, which may be combined with conventional psychiatric treatment.

The overwhelming majority of psychiatrists consider the orthomolecular approach ineffective and disreputable. In 1973, a special American Psychiatric Association task force concluded that orthomolecular practitioners use unconventional methods of diagnosis as well as treatment and called the publicity they seek "deplorable." A Research Advisory Committee of the National Institute of Mental Health, reviewed pertinent scientific data through 1979 and agreed that megavitamin therapy is ineffective and may be harmful.

VITAMIN E AND LUMPY BREASTS

Several years ago, preliminary studies by Robert London, M.D., and colleagues at Sinai Hospital of Baltimore suggested that vitamin E supplementation might help women with mammary dysplasia (commonly called benign fibrocystic disease of the breast). But two double-blind studies reported in 1985 found no significant benefit. In one, the Sinai Hospital group treated 128 patients for two months with either a placebo or 150, 300, or 600 International Units of vitamin E. Although slightly more than half the patients improved during the trial period, those receiving vitamin E did no better than those re-

From the American Council on Science and Health's *Priorities*, Spring 1989, pp. 27-29. Reprinted by permission.

ceiving the placebo. The other study by physicians at the University of California in San Francisco involved 62 women who took either 600 International Units of vitamin E or a placebo for 21 months. No differences were observed between the two groups.

NIACIN AND CHOLESTEROL CONTROL

Public attention has been focused on niacin by the recently published book, *The 8-Week Cholesterol Cure*, by Robert E. Kowalski. Although high doses of niacin can lower blood cholesterol levels, they can also cause liver damage and other significant side effects. Thus, megadoses of niacin are not suitable for self-medication and should be taken only under medical supervision as part of a comprehensive treatment program. The first step in a comprehensive program of heart disease prevention is an assessment of risk factors. Cholesterol-lowering drugs (whether niacin or prescription drugs) should not be considered unless cholesterol levels remain dangerously high despite appropriate attention to diet, exercise and weight control. Smoking cessation and normalization of blood pressure are also important.

VITAMIN B₆ FOR PMS

Premenstrual syndrome (PMS), sometimes called premenstrual tension, is a vaguely defined condition said to include headaches, breast swelling or tenderness, bloating, weight gain, backache, irritability, depression, anxiety and other symptoms that resolve during or after each menstrual period. Although high dosages (200 to 800 mg) of vitamin B_6 have been widely advocated for treating this problem, the evidence supporting this practice is slim—based on small studies, some of which showed benefit while others did not. During the past few years, however, doctors have reported more than 100 cases of toxicity from B_6 supplementation. Their symptoms, some of which resembled those of multiple sclerosis, included numbness and tingling of the hands, difficulty in walking, and electric shocks shooting down the spine. Although all the afflicted individuals improved greatly when they stopped taking the vitamin, a few did not recover completely. Some of them had been taking less than 50 mg/day. (The Recommended Dietary Allowance for adult women is 2 mg/day.) In light of these cases, supplementation with high dosages of vitamin B_6 appears inadvisable.

DANGERS OF EXCESS VITAMINS

Although the number of reported cases of vitamin toxicity is small compared to the number of people taking vitamins, amounts higher than the Recommended Dietary Allowances are an invitation to trouble.

Fat-soluble vitamins are not excreted efficiently. They are generally stored until they can be used up, and thus can accumulate to toxic levels. For example, prolonged excessive intake of vitamin A can cause headache, increased pressure on the brain, bone pain, and damage to the liver. Excessive vitamin D can cause kidney damage. And high doses of vitamin E can cause fatigue and other problems.

Water-soluble vitamins are stored in modest amounts, with excesses excreted quickly. But large excesses of the water-soluble vitamins can still cause trouble. High dosages of vitamin C can cause diarrhea, and, if discontinued after months of use, can lead to "rebound" scurvy. Large doses of niacin can cause severe flushes, liver damage and skin disorders. And, as noted above, large doses of vitamin B_6 can damage the nervous system.

ADVERTISING ADDICTION: THE ALCOHOL INDUSTRY'S HARD SELL

Jean Kilbourne, Ed. D.

Jean Kilbourne, Ed.D., is the Chair of the Council on Alcohol Policy and is on the Board of Directors of the National Council on Alcoholism. Two award-winning films, "Still Killing Us Softly: Advertising's Image of Women" and "Calling the Shots: The Advertising of Alcohol," are based on her lectures.

Alcohol is the most commonly used drug in the United States. It is also one of the most heavily advertised products in the United States. The alcohol industry generates more than $65 billion a year in revenue and spends more than $1 billion a year on advertising. The advertising budget for one beer — Budweiser — is more than the entire federal budget for research on alcoholism and alcohol abuse. Unfortunately, young people and heavy drinkers are the primary targets of the advertisers.

What does advertising do?

There is no conclusive proof that advertising increases alcohol consumption. Research does indicate, however, that alcohol advertising contributes to increases in consumption by young people and serves as a significant source of negative socialization for young people. Those who argue that peer pressure is the major influence on young people strangely overlook the role of advertising.

The alcoholic beverage companies claim that they are not trying to create more or heavier drinkers. They say that they only want people who already drink to switch to another brand and to drink it in moderation. But this industry-wide claim does not hold up under scrutiny. An editorial in Advertising Age concluded: "A strange world it is, in which people spending millions on advertising must do their best to prove that advertising doesn't do very much!"

About a third of all Americans choose not to drink at all, a third drink moderately, and about a third drink regularly. Ten percent of the drinking-age population consumes over 60 percent of the alcohol. This figure corresponds closely to the percentage of alcoholics in society. If alcoholics were to recover (i.e. to stop drinking entirely), the alcohol industry's gross revenues would be cut in half. Recognizing this important marketing fact, alcohol companies deliberately devise ads designed to appeal to heavy drinkers. Advertising is usually directed toward promoting loyalty and increasing usage, and heavy users of any product are the best customers but, in the case of alcohol, the heavy user is usually an addict.

Another perspective on the industry's claim that it encourages only moderate drinking is provided by Robert Hammond, director of the Alcohol Research Information Service. He estimates that if all 105 million drinkers of legal age consumed the official maximum "moderate" amount of alcohol — .99 ounces per day, the equivalent of about two drinks — the industry would suffer "a whopping 40 percent decrease in the sale of beer, wine and distilled spirits, based on 1981 sales figures."

Such statistics show the role heavy drinkers play in maintaining the large profit margins of the alcohol industry. Modern research techniques allow the producers of print and electronic media to provide advertisers with detailed information about their readers, listeners and viewers. Target audiences are sold to the alcohol industry on a cost per drinker basis.

One example of how magazines sell target audiences appeared recently in Advertising Age: Good Housekeeping advertised itself to the alcohol industry as a good place to reach women drinkers, proclaiming, "You'll catch more women with wine than with vinegar. She's a tougher customer than ever. You never needed Good Housekeeping more."

The young audience is also worth a great deal to the alcohol industry. Sport magazine promoted itself to the alcohol industry as a conduit to young drinkers with an ad in Advertising Age stating, "What young money spends on drinks is a real eye-opener." Budweiser's Spuds MacKenzie campaign is clearly designed to appeal to young people. Miller has a new television commercial featuring animated clay figures of a monkey, an elephant and a lion with a voice that says "three out of four party animals preferred the taste of Miller Lite." Wine coolers are often marketed as soft drinks with ads featuring puppets, animated characters, Santa Claus and other figures that appeal especially to young people. Even in supposedly commercial-free movies, showing in theaters, viewers are targeted. Many films, especially those appealing to young people, include paid placements of cigarettes and alcohol.

The college market is particularly important to the alcohol industry not only because of the money the students will spend on beer today, but because they will develop drinking habits and brand allegiances that may be

From *Multinational Monitor,* June 1989, pp. 13-16. Reprinted with permission of *Multinational Monitor,* P.O. Box 19405, Washington, D.C. 20036, $22/individual.

with them for life. As one marketing executive said, "Let's not forget that getting a freshman to choose a certain brand of beer may mean that he will maintain his brand loyalty for the next 20 to 35 years. If he turns out to be a big drinker, the beer company has bought itself an annuity." This statement undercuts the industry's claim that it does not target advertising campaigns at underage drinkers since today almost every state prohibits the sale of alcohol to people under 21 years old and the vast majority of college freshman are below that age.

The alcohol industry's efforts to promote responsible drinking must also be evaluated carefully. Much of its advertising promotes irresponsible and dangerous drinking. For example, a poster for Pabst Blue Ribbon features a young woman speeding along on a bicycle with a bottle of beer where the water bottle is supposed to be. Obviously biking and drinking beer are not safely complementary activities.

Even some of the programs designed by the alcohol industry to educate students about responsible drinking subtly promote myths and damaging attitudes. Budweiser has a program called "The Buddy System" designed to encourage young people not to let their friends drive drunk. Although this is a laudable goal, it is interesting to note that none of the alcohol industry programs discourage or even question drunkenness per se. The implicit message is that it is alright to get drunk as long as you don't drive; abuse is acceptable, even encouraged.

Myth making

The industry often targets relatively disempowered groups in society, primarily women and minority groups, and associates alcohol with power. For example, a Cutty Sark Whiskey ad features a retired Black baseball player, Curt Flood, promoting its drink. The ad shows Flood holding forth a glass of whiskey with the text "Some people think you can't beat the system. Here's to those who show the way." This ad associates Flood and his successful athletic performance with his drinking Cutty Sark whiskey.

The link between advertising and alcoholism is unproven. Alcoholism is a complex illness and its etiology is uncertain. But alcohol advertising does create a climate in which abusive attitudes toward alcohol are presented as normal, appropriate and innocuous. One of the chief symptoms of alcoholism is denial that there is a problem. It is often not only the alcoholic who denies the illness but also his or her family, employer, doctor, etc. Alcohol advertising often encourages denial be creating a world in which myths about alcohol are presented as true and in which signs of trouble are erased or transformed into positive attributes.

One of the primary means of creating this distortion is through advertising. Most advertising is essentially mythmaking. Instead of providing information about a product, such as its taste or quality, advertisements create an image of the product, linking the item with a particular lifestyle which may have little or nothing to do with the product itself. According to an article on beer marketing in Advertising Age, "Advertising is as important to selling beer as the bottle opener is to drinking it. . . . Beer advertising is mainly an exercise in building images." Another article a few months later on liquor marketing stated that "product image is probably the most important element in selling liquor. The trick for marketers is to project the right message in their advertisements to motivate those motionless consumers to march down to the liquor store or bar and exchange their money for a sip of image."

The links are generally false and arbitrary but we are so surrounded by them that we come to accept them: the jeans will make you look sexy, the car will give you confidence, the detergent will save your marriage. Advertising spuriously links alcohol with precisely those attributes and qualities — happiness, wealth, prestige, sophistication, success, maturity, athletic ability, virility, creativity, sexual satisfaction and others — that the misuse of alcohol destroys. For example, alcohol is often linked with romance and sexual fulfillment, yet it is common knowledge that alcohol misuse often leads to sexual dysfunction. Less well known is the fact that people with drinking problems are seven times more likely than the general population to be separated or divorced.

Image advertising is especially appealing to young people who are more likely than adults to be insecure about the image they are projecting. Sexual and athletic prowess are two of the themes that dominate advertising aimed at young people. A recent television commercial for Miller beer featured Danny Sullivan, the race car driver, speeding around a track with the Miller logo emblazoned everywhere. The ad implies that Miller beer and fast driving go hand in hand. A study of beer commercials funded by the American Automobile Association found that they often linked beer with images of speed, including speeding cars.

The magic transformation

"It separates the exceptional from the merely ordinary." This advertising slogan for Piper champagne illustrates the major premise of the mythology that alcohol is magic. It is a magic potion that can make you successful, sophisticated and sexy; without it, you are dull, mediocre and ordinary. The people who are not drinking champagne are lifeless replicas of the happy couple who are imbibing. The alcohol has rescued the couple, resurrected them, restored them to life. At the heart of the alcoholic's dilemma and denial is this belief, this certainty, that alcohol is essential for life, that without it he or she will literally die — or at best suffer. This ad and many others like it present the nightmare as true, thus affirming and even glorifying one of the symptoms of the illness.

Glorifying alcoholism

Such glorification of the symptoms is common in alcohol advertising. "Your own special island," proclaims an ad for St. Croix rum. Another ad offers Busch beer as "Your mountain hide-a-way." Almost all alcoholics experience intense feelings of isolation, alienation and loneliness. Most make the tragic mistake of believing that the alcohol alleviates these feelings rather than exacerbating them. The two examples above distort reality in much the same way as the alcoholic does. Instead of being isolated and alienated, the people in the ad are in their own special places.

The rum ad also seems to be encouraging solitary drinking, a sign of trouble with alcohol. There is one drink on the tray and no room for another. Although it is unusual for solitary drinking to be shown (most alcohol ads feature groups or happy couples), it is not unusual for unhealthy attitudes toward alcohol to be presented as normal and acceptable.

The most obvious example is obsession with alcohol.

Alcohol is at the center of the ads just as it is at the center of the alcoholic's life. The ads imply that alcohol is an appropriate adjunct to almost every activity from love-making to white-water canoeing. An ad for Puerto Rican rums says, "You know how to make every day special. You're a white rum drinker." In fact, less than 10 percent of the adult population makes drinking a part of their daily routine.

There is also an emphasis on quantity in the ads. A Johnnie Walker ad features 16 bottles of scotch and the copy, "Bob really knows how to throw a party. He never runs out of Johnnie Walker Red." Light beer has been developed and heavily promoted not for the dieter but for the heavy drinker. The ads imply that because it is less filling, one can drink more of it.

Thus the ads tell the alcoholic and everyone around him that it is all right to consume large quantities of alcohol on a daily basis and to have it be a part of all of one's activities. At the same time, all signs of trouble and any hint of addiction are conspicuously avoided. The daily drinking takes place in glorious and unique settings, such as yachts at sunset, not at the more mundane but realistic kitchen tables in the morning. There is no unpleasant drunkenness, only high spirits. There are never any negative consequences. Of course, one would not expect there to be. The advertisers are selling their product and it is their job to erase any negative aspects as well as to enhance the positive ones. When the product is a drug that is addictive to one out of 10 users, however, there are consequences that go far beyond product sales.

The U.S. culture as a whole, not just the advertising and alcohol industry, tends to glorify alcohol and dismiss the problems associated with it. The "war on drugs," as covered by newspapers and magazines in this country, rarely includes the two major killers, alcohol and nicotine. It is no coincidence that these are two of the most heavily advertised products. In 1987, the use of all illegal drugs combined accounted for about 3,400 deaths. Alcohol is linked with over 100,000 deaths annually. Cigarettes kill a thousand people every day.

A comprehensive effort is needed to prevent alcohol-related problems. Such an effort must include education, media campaigns, increased availability of treatment programs and more effective deterrence policies. It must also include public policy changes that would include raising taxes on alcohol, putting clearly legible warning labels on the bottles and regulating the advertising.

A drug history revealed on a strand of hair

WILLIAM F. BUCKLEY

WILLIAM BENNETT'S drug program calls for random testing for drug abuse of critically situated persons whose physical coordination is a matter of public concern. And of course the Supreme Court has authorized such tests, administered e.g. to pilots, to railroad engineers, to truck drivers. President Reagan, in the last term of his administration, ordered drug testing to be comprehensively administered to federal employees working in sensitive agencies. One remembers mostly about that episode the question directed to Secretary of State George Shultz, namely, "Have you submitted a urine sample for drug testing?" To which the answer was (appropriately) a curt "No."

Dr. Robert DuPont, who was the head of the National Institute on Drug Abuse between 1973 and 1978, has on many occasions pointed out the advantages of hair testing over urine testing. For reasons difficult to understand, it is not widely known that the alternative exists.

That brings us to the various uses of the word "privacy." When the word is used in objection to random testing of urine for drugs, one can't help but think about the aesthetic inconvenience, especially necessary when there is suspicion that the subject may indeed have been taking drugs. In such cases it is absolutely necessary to establish that the urine belongs to the subject, rather than to an obliging friend of the subject being tested at about the same time in private surroundings. Moreover, the usefulness of the urine test can be reduced by adulteration and other means I shan't specify — which really all adds up to urinating under direct observation.

What you then get is an indication whether the subject has been taking drugs during the last two or three days. In fact, if the subject is a very heavy marijuana user, traces of that particular drug will show up in his urine for two or

> (Y)ou can find out the drug history of anybody whose hair you clip. (Y)ou can find out what that person has ingested over the preceding six months.

three weeks. But if he uses cocaine or heroin, for instance, and he knows that he is going to have a urine test in the next few days, he can beat the system by the simple expedient of laying off the stuff for a few days.

But this is not so with human hair. There is something about hair that hangs on to the stuff more or less permanently. Don't ask me what it is, but take the word of DuPont, who is supported by a legion of scientists who verify the reliability of the hair-testing technique, first done in 1979. Here is how the professionals put it: "Sensitive chemical ionization GC/MS confirmation techniques utilizing small samples (5 mg of hair) were developed for cocaine, phencyclidine and heroin. In addition, hair analysis by RIA was extended to amphetamines, methadone and benzodiazepines. An extensive investigation with GC/MS, RIA dilution tests and experimentation with contamination procedures showed no evidence of false-positive problems with hair analysis."

Now what all of this means is that you can find out the drug history of anybody whose hair you clip. And we do mean history. Hair grows about a half-inch per month. On most people it isn't hard to find a strand of hair 3 inches long. Which means that you can find out what that person has ingested over the preceding six months.

If by citing privacy you mean to object to baring your medical history for months, rather than your private parts for a few seconds, then your objection to hair analysis as an invasion of privacy is infinitely more compelling. On the other hand, the examiners would know a great deal more about you than ever they would learn from a urine specimen.

THE COST of the two tests depends to an extent on how many drugs you are looking for. It is, says DuPont, safe to generalize that it's 50 bucks for the hair test and 25 bucks for the urine test. But of course, the hair test is infinitely more valuable.

Why don't we turn uniformly to the hair test, instead of to its alternative? Dr. Werner Baumgartner, the scientific director of the Ianus Foundation, has said that the two tests are in fact complementary, the one (urine) being absolutely reliable for short-term monitoring. But why should we have short-term monitoring when we can have long-term monitoring? The hair test not only tells you what drugs you have imbibed, but also tells you how long ago. So that if you cut out drugs six weeks ago and have been clean ever since, the hair test will reveal this. Moreover, the hair is not confused by such substances as poppy seeds that you find on bagels and other foods, which ring alarm signals unnecessarily. It is correct to predict hair-raising days ahead.

The Dutch Model

Eddy Engelsman

The Netherlands is the only country to have decriminalized drugs such as marijuana and hashish, although its punishment for traffickers is severe. Eddy Engelsman is the Dutch drug czar, in charge of drug policy in the ministry of Welfare, Public Health and Cultural Affairs. We talked to him recently about the Dutch model.

In 1982, the Netherlands amended the 1928 Opium Act and gave the new drug policy the name "normalization." Under this policy, drug use, even heroin and cocaine use, is not prohibited by law. Only possession is prohibited.

Drug normalization should not be misinterpreted as a lenient policy. It is, on the contrary, a well-considered and very practical policy that neither hides the drug problems of our society nor allows them to get out of control.

We never use the words "hard" and "soft" drugs in our legislation. Instead, we refer to Schedule One drugs – cocaine, heroin, amphetamines, LSD – as those with an "unacceptable risk." The other schedule refers only to what we call "traditional cannabis products," including marijuana and hashish.

Possession of these drugs, both Schedule One and the cannabis products, is prohibited, but possession of up to 30 grams of the cannabis products is only a misdemeanor – it is punishable by law, but our pragmatic prosecution policy allows for discretion.

Every country has this kind of prioritized drug policy, though probably not as overt as in the Netherlands. Indeed, if one asks a policeman in any American city what he would do, whether he would choose to catch the dealer of one

> **Normalization is a well-considered and very practical policy that neither hides the drug problems of Dutch society nor allows them to get out of control.**

kilogram of heroin or cocaine, or the dealer of 10 kilograms of marijuana, he would inevitably choose to put his energy into catching the cocaine or heroin dealer. In the Netherlands, this process is just more formalized.

Normalization does not mean everything is legal. If someone traffics in drugs, or if they steal for drugs, they will be punished. In the Netherlands, 30 percent of the prison population is incarcerated for drug-related reasons. In Amsterdam and Rotterdam, the number is 50 percent.

Avoiding A Cure Worse Than Disease | The Dutch drug policy of *de facto* decriminalization of cannabis products has not encouraged more drug use. In fact, the prevalence of cannabis use in the Netherlands is low. In the age bracket between 10 and 18 years, 4.2 percent has ever used cannabis in their lifetime. Among this group, less than two percent are still using occasionally. The number of daily cannabis users appears to be one in 1,000.

The Dutch have been pragmatic and have tried to avoid a situation in which consumers of cannabis products suffer more damage from criminal proceedings than from the use of the drug itself. This same principle accounts for the sale of limited quantities of hashish in youth centers and coffee shops, a policy that aims at separating markets in which hard drugs and soft drugs circulate. According to the Minister of Justice, this policy has succeeded in keeping the sale of hashish out of the realm of hard crime.

Compound Drug-Related Problems | Due to the mind-altering effect of drugs, most governments have tried to discourage their use through law enforcement and health education.

Today, however, we see that in addition to

By Eddy Engelsman. From *New Perspectives Quarterly*, Summer 1989, pp. 44-45. Reprinted by permission.

the mind-altering component of drug use, addicts are also affected by secondary problems – ones that are perhaps more serious than the original medical and social problems caused by addiction.

For the most part, initial medical problems have been compounded by risks of infectious disease, violence and social ostracism – complications that inevitably arise when drugs are pushed into the illegal sphere. On the societal level, additional problems have arisen from an intensified approach toward drug traffickers and the adoption of new, far-reaching legal measures that have led to an increasing corruption of the police, judiciary and government authorities.

These additional consequences – increased criminality and health problems – are the secondary problems, the unintended side-effects of conventional drug policy.

Harm Reduction Policy | The Dutch drug treatment philosophy addresses the socially backward position of most addicts and attempts to focus policy on the primary problems involved in drug abuse. The government encourages forms of treatment that are not intended to end addiction as such, but to improve addicts' physical and social well-being, and to help them function in society.

This kind of assistance may be defined as harm-reduction, or, more traditionally, secondary and tertiary prevention. The effort takes the form of fieldwork in the street, hospitals, jails and open door clinics for prostitutes.

This treatment effort also supplies medically prescribed methadone, material support and social rehabilitation opportunities. In Amsterdam, the conditions for participation in methadone treatment are regular contact with a medical doctor, registration with the methadone clinic, and a prohibition on take-home dosages of methadone.

In spite of the wide availability of medically prescribed methadone, there have never been so many addicts asking for detoxification and drug-free treatment. In Amsterdam, such requests doubled between 1981 and 1986.

The fact that the government has this policy toward addicts who are not able or do not, at least for the time being, want to establish a drug-free lifestyle is indicative of the realistic and pragmatic Dutch approach. It also shows the

The Dutch have been pragmatic and have tried to avoid a situation in which consumers of cannabis products suffer more damage from criminal proceedings than from the use of the drug itself.

determination not to leave drug addicts in the lurch. Failure to provide care of this type would simply increase the risk to the individual and to our society.

The result of Dutch health policy is that it is able to reach a very large segment of the total population of drug addicts. In Amsterdam, about 60-80 percent are being reached by some kind of assistance.

Needle exchange programs have also been instituted, since it is an established fact that many drug users are using intravenously and share needles. The effects of this approach: Only eight percent of the 605 Dutch AIDS patients are intravenous drug users, whereas this figure in Europe generally is 23 percent and is 26 percent in the United States. We have seen no negative side-effects, such as an increasing number of intravenous drug users, nor have we seen reduced interest in drug-free treatment.

Some other data: Reliable estimates on the number of drug addicts in the Netherlands, with a population of 14.5 million, vary between 15,000 and 20,000. Drug use appears to be stabilizing, even decreasing in some cities. Estimates on the number of addicts in Amsterdam, the largest city, vary from 4,000 to 7,000. The prevalence of heroin use in Amsterdam is estimated at 0.4 percent. The use of cocaine has stabilized at 0.6 percent, while crack use is still a virtual rarity. Finally, and perhaps most importantly, between 1981 and 1987 the average age of heroin and cocaine users in Amsterdam rose from 26 to 36 years.

The Dutch drug policy, which is administered by the Minister of Welfare, Health and Cultural Affairs, should not be seen as different from policies toward other areas of our society. Dutch measures for controlling drug abuse can only be understood in the context of history, and, perhaps, geography: The most striking feature of the Netherlands has always been the abundance of water – water that has historically constituted both a threat and a means of livelihood. The Dutch have never conquered the sea, but have succeeded in controlling this enemy. That sort of realistic relationship with the natural world has provided an important stimulus for a realistic and pragmatic approach to life in general for the Dutch, and has now come to typify our national drug policy approach.

Why Not Decriminalize?

Arnold Trebach

Author of The Great Drug War, *Arnold Trebach is a professor of criminal justice at American University in Washington, DC. He is also the director of the privately-funded Drug Policy Center. Because he has taught so many DEA agents in his classes at American University, Trebach has been referred to as "the shadow drug czar." But this czar wants no war. He wants public health and decriminalization.*

Accepting the Presence of Drugs

Approximately one-fourth of the US population uses an illegal drug at least once a year. When our government talks about a war on drugs, it is talking about a war on 25 percent of the American people.

Two of the most reliable sources for this data are federally issued from the National Institute on Drug Abuse. They are the Drug Abuse Warning Network (DAWN), which is a survey of about half to three-quarters of the medical examiners and emergency rooms in the country – and the Household Survey.

These studies show that approximately 50-60 million people use illegal drugs in the US. The most prominent drug is marijuana, with between 18-35 million regular users. There are approximately five million heroin users, five-to-ten million cocaine users and several million users of various other drugs.

Because crack cocaine and PCP are such recent phenomena, there are still no reliable statistics about users. The authorities still do not isolate crack deaths from the general population of cocaine-related deaths, so we have no real data on the toxic effects of that drug.

POWs of the drug war are filling up America's jail cells. With the logic of law enforcement pressed to its limit – the violence still escalating and the drugs still pouring in – questions about the possibility of alternative strategies inevitably arise.

With regard to overall drug use in this country, I am seeing two seemingly contradictory sets of data. One set comes from the Youth Surveys by the Institute of Behavioral Research at the University of Michigan. These studies show a relative decline in youth drug use over recent years, which is the same conclusion I have reached through my own research.

The other set of data comes from the intelligence estimates of the Drug Enforcement Agency (DEA) and other agencies. These reports show enormous amounts of cocaine, *literally tons more*, being imported into the US.

However, what appears to be showing up in both sets of data is a reduction in drug use among some segments of youths, especially among those youths who might show up in a survey, the kids who are staying in school. When we go over all the epidemiological data, we see that despite all the drug use, despite all we hear and despite the pockets of horror that we have, this is the healthiest generation of youth in our history. In 1983, for the first time in our history, the death rate for youths 15-24 went below 100 per 100,000. Though there is a lot of contradictory data concerning the drug situation, one thing is clear: we are not losing our youth to anything, including drugs.

Why A Drug War? | One can legitimately ask, then, why the drug war? Why all the media attention? I think the drug war, like all wars, is built on hysteria.

Throughout history, there have been periodic swings in drug use. We also go through swings in terms of how the society reacts to drug use. Around the turn of the century, we had twin

By Arnold Trebach. From *New Perspectives Quarterly,* Summer 1989, pp. 40-44. Reprinted by permission.

drives against narcotics, particularly opium, and alcohol. During this period, government officials didn't like the fact that the Chinese were using opium, or that by 1910, heroin had become very popular in New York.

Currently, we are caught in a backlash against drug use, a governmental response that began with Reagan and continues with Bush. The conservatives believe their mission is to undo the permissiveness unleashed in America during the sixties.

When Reagan came into office, he proclaimed in a Rose Garden ceremony: "We're taking down the surrender flag that has flown over so many drug efforts. We're running up the battle flag...."

Reagan did, indeed, run up that battle flag. A lot of people say that he didn't conduct a real war, but he did. There is no doubt in my mind, however, that this is the toughest and most vicious campaign we have ever had, the most far-reaching and the most invasive of civil liberties.

For example, historically, the FBI stayed out of drug cases. J. Edgar Hoover viewed drug cases as inherently dirty. He believed that FBI involvement with drugs would corrupt his agency. He didn't want his agents dealing with either the financial temptation or sleazy characters he would have had to use as informants.

In Reagan's first year in office, he began to involve the FBI in drug enforcement, technically putting the DEA under the FBI. Secondly, he got an amendment to the *Posse Comitatus Act* of 1878 that prohibited the use of the military in the enforcement of the criminal law. The amendment stated that, under certain circumstances, the military could lend support to the drug effort. The military has not yet been given the authority to make an arrest on its own, but it can lend support to US law enforcement agencies, as it is now doing along the California-Mexico border, and it can, with the approval of foreign governments, ship troops abroad to destroy coca plantations.

The role of these groups in combatting drugs is roughly akin to sending Marines into Beirut: Their mission is fuzzy *and* extremely difficult.

From Locked Out To Locked Up | Drug Czar William Bennett has proposed that we build prisons, erect chain-link fences around low income housing and require ID cards at the entrance to those facilities in order to fend off the drug crisis. But this amounts to a policy of locking up as many young black males as possible. I am not proposing that Bennett is a racist, but the effects of his policies certainly look that way.

While we may be able to control the drug problem in the general population, the US needs to face up to the fact it cannot deal with the real drug disaster until we address the issue of race. One cannot talk about crime without talking about race, though no one wants to do this. White racial discrimination is still with us. There continues to be huge numbers of blacks who have not been able to make it financially, except through the drug trade. Today, drugs are the nexus between class, race and crime: The recruits in the drug trade come from among people who feel that the only way they can support their families is to grab a piece of the drug action, and they come largely from among young blacks and Hispanics who have been excluded, locked out of the mainstream economy.

Instead of targeting urban, black youth in Washington, DC for prison, Bennett could have announced, along with his prison and fence proposals, that the US Department of Health and Human Services would be asked to provide mobile trailers equipped with treatment specialists in drug-plagued neighborhoods. He could have announced that the people who have drug trouble would be provided with a place to go for help, a place to obtain clean needles and methadone. He could have flooded the streets of Washington, DC with mobile treatment centers, and he could have flooded the area with funds for neighborhood development.

Prohibition Doesn't Work | The record is very clear: We have tried prohibition, many other countries have tried it, and the record around the world, with few exceptions, is dismal. Prohibition is a good idea that doesn't work.

In the US today, all I see are the perverse results of prohibition. Under Reagan, we went from a prison population of 329,821 – people serving a sentence of one year or more for drug-related and other crimes – at the end of 1980 to 627,402 at the end of 1988. The prison population rose 90.2 percent in eight years – the greatest rise in modern history, and this does not include jail populations, juveniles or patients in drug-treatment facilities. The prison numbers

> A lot of people say Reagan didn't conduct a real drug war, but he did – and it has been the toughest and most vicious campaign we have ever had, the most far-reaching and the most invasive of civil liberties.

> Khalkhali had a power that many people here dream of. If he found you with drugs, he put you up against a wall and shot you.

223

only include people serving hard time. Do our government officials want to run the numbers up to a million before they stop and take a look at their policy?

In Iran, there is a story of the roving executioner of the revolution, Ayatollah Khalkhali. Khalkhali had a power that many people here dream of. If he found you with drugs, he put you up against a wall and shot you. According to wire reports, within a seven-week period, he killed 176 people. Khalkhali was photographed standing amidst stacks of opium bags and drug products. Yet, he was criticized because drug use was still rampant. His defensive response was, "If we wanted to kill everybody who had five grams of heroin, we would have to kill five thousand people." And then he added this classic phrase: "And this would be difficult." Despite all his power, drug use was rampant.

I have been radicalized by recent events – traumatized and radicalized. I am scared that if we keep it up we will fill the prisons with young people, especially blacks and Hispanics and we will continue to allow people to die from AIDS, saying, "You use drugs, you deserve to die, because we don't want to give a wrong message to anybody." This lack of civility and safety is going to spread through our society like it did in Rome before its fall.

Beneficial Drug Use | Drugs are a societal problem, but they also offer a societal benefit. People use drugs because it makes them feel better, and something that makes millions of people feel better can't be all bad.

There will always be large numbers of people taking a lot of mind-altering substances, both legal and illegal. This reality becomes a disastrous situation when we say we really mean prohibition and we're really going to enforce it. What we should be worried about is drug abuse, which I define as the use of a chemical substance, a mind-altering substance, legal or illegal, in a manner that adversely affects one's physical health, work performance, or loving relationships. By this standard, simply taking an illegal drug is not drug abuse.

We need to recognize that the line between illegal and legal drugs is a historical accident based primarily upon emotion rather than science. All drugs – including alcohol, tobacco, heroin, cocaine, PCP, marijuana – are danger-

> The line between illegal and legal drugs is a historical accident based primarily upon emotion rather than science.

ous. At the same time, all can be used in relatively nonharmful ways by many people. The difficulty arises when people find they can't get along without these chemical crutches.

I accept the presence of drugs in the society. I know of no way of getting rid of them. What I hope to do is reduce what has become a disaster to a problem. I can live with a problem. I can accept that kind of a problem in the same way that I can accept the presence of people with mental illness because I don't know how to do away with them. I don't want to make them the enemy in yet another war. I don't want to engage in a war on gays, either. I accept the presence of various kinds of different behavior in this society. I don't know how many gay people we have but I accept them. I accept a wide range of religions. I accept a devotion to loud, seemingly barbaric music. And I accept the use of various kinds of mind-altering drugs.

I have come to the conclusion that it is the active enforcement of prohibition that makes the drug problem in the US a disaster. We can continue to make drugs illegal, but we should enforce the drug laws like we enforce our sex laws. We show good sense in the enforcement of sex laws, generally. For example, we have sodomy laws on the books but we don't enforce them. If one looks at the current sex laws they will be appalled. There is absolutely no way to enforce those laws and have anybody out of jail except infants. Basically, the sex laws are on the books for the purposes of moral suasion. We should treat the drug laws the same way.

Square the circle. We cannot do it through prohibition because the financial temptations of drugs are too great. So, we should begin to seriously look at the alternative: decriminalization.

Dutch And British Model | I support a compromise combination of the English and the Dutch systems: For starters, all drugs could remain illegal. We must develop a set of written guidelines on how to uniformly enforce these laws. The Dutch are best on this; they are very proud of their guidelines for arrest and prosecution, worked up by their cops, prosecutors and judges. A perfect example: for possession and small sales, generally speaking, no action is taken.

Under controlled circumstances in Amsterdam, kids can come into what are called youth clubs and can get "soft drugs": marijuana and hashish. And yet, even though kids can get all the pot they want right off the menus of coffee houses, less than one percent of the population uses marijuana daily.

In addition, the Dutch say to people in trouble with drugs: "You are a member of the Dutch family. We want you to work and go to school." I would be much harder. I would say, "If you are going to take drugs, fine, we'll try to get it to you without much hassle, but we don't want you sitting around just getting high and doing nothing. If you are just getting high and nodding off, you're a loser, you should be doing something productive, you should be a good husband, a good wife, a good worker, a good student."

Britain is more aggressive on this point. The British attitude is: "We don't want to give you drugs if you are not functioning well." The test is whether the addict can function in the world.

The most advanced place I know of regarding addicts is Liverpool, England. Liverpool has a wide array of treatment facilities. If addicts need detoxification or drug-free treatment, they can get help in Liverpool. Health officials there make sure that injecting addicts take part in a needle exchange program, receive instructions on injecting, and get general health care.

In addition to providing boxes of clean needles, the addict receives boxes of condoms and instructions on safe sex. The result is that 14 percent of the injecting addicts in the Liverpool area are using condoms, while only 7 percent of the British population is. These statistics show that the injecting addicts of Liverpool are being more conscientious about safe sex than the British population as a whole.

Furthermore, of stunning significance is the fact that AIDS is virtually unknown among addicts who have presented themselves for treat-ment at Liverpool clinics. A study of approximately 2,000 injecting addicts found that not one of them tested positive either for AIDS or the HIV virus, though there have been reports of a few such positive tests recently.

The police in Liverpool are very supportive of these maintenance programs. They admit that much of what the addict does is illegal, but they are comfortable with the compromises that have been made.

If we combine the Dutch and British strategies with neighborhood, family and employment help, we will begin to see a change. Amsterdam has a population of roughly 670,000. In Washington, DC, the population is roughly 622,000. Amsterdam has a lot of drug trade in the street. In 1988, the city had approximately 40 murders, one-third of them connected with the drug trade. Last year Washington, DC had 372 – 60-80 percent connected with the drug trade.

I could see people able to get drugs relatively easily. I could see people smoking in front of a cop and not getting arrested. I could see people in trouble with drugs being able to come in and get clean needles or treatment. I could see 40, 50, 60 murders occurring annually in Washington, DC, one-third connected with the drug trade. Then, the drug trade would be tolerable. It would not be a drug-free situation, but then again, I don't believe it ever will be.

Eventually, we must consider *full* legalization along the line of the alcohol model. This would not be a lawless situation. Indeed, the task of the future is to design new boundaries for the civil and criminal laws controlling drugs. That task is very complicated but it is possible. The mission of creating a drug-free society, on the other hand, is both impossible and destructive.

A Long Time Coming
A skeptic encounters the Twelve Steps

Lily Collett

'Lily Collett' is a pseudonym, in keeping with the pledge of anonymity requested of all participants in Twelve Steps groups. People described in this article have been given new names.

My father was no cartoon drunk. He never passed out on the couch or lost his job or went to jail. He sang me nursery rhymes and taught me to read when I was small, and when people came to dinner, he wore a nice tweed jacket and held the women's coats for them. I loved him so much I thought they ought to make him a movie star.

The year I turned 10, he began getting off the train in the evenings saying, "I need a drink. I deserve a drink." He stared at the TV, bourbon in hand, saying, "This is my anesthetic." One night, at dinner, in the candlelight my mother hoped would teach us better manners, I made a child's pronouncement on a subject now long forgotten.

"No," said my father, and there was a bulge in his thickening jaw. I argued. "Don't contradict me," he shouted. It was the end of friendly dinner-table talks and the beginning of a father who dug his teeth into disagreements like a ferret, shaking and tearing at my words until my dinner ended night after night with slaps and tears and being sent from the table.

My mother sat in the candlelight with a pained expression on her face, but did nothing. It was as though a huge black dog that we all worked hard not to see had moved into the living room. My mother tried to limit my father to tomato juice and caught him secretly adding vodka. The tension spilled over onto us children.

My father shouted at me to improve my schoolwork. "You drive me to drink," he yelled. "You're lazy, and you're sick in the head." My mother said to me,

"You're selfish, you're clumsy, you've got no visual sense, no sense of time." Both of them hit me so frequently that I still flinch at sudden movements. I learned in my bones that alcoholics don't have relationships; they take hostages.

For the first couple of years, no matter how bad the drunken dinner-time scene, I floated up out of sleep each morning with the sense that it was a new day. But when I was 12 I began to wake up feeling as bad as I had the night before. I spent that summer reading in my room, gaining 15 pounds from eating chocolates stolen from supermarkets. I got into fancy schools and got thrown out of them, skipped grades, and then was held back. I blamed myself for my father's pain, for the breakdown of our relationship, for my failure to excel in school, for being an inexplicably bad girl. In high school, I wrote poetry, edited the literary magazine, played the lead in school plays, was a National Merit Scholar, stayed out all night, and nearly slit my wrists.

I escaped from home in the late 1960s like someone who'd done hard prison time and plunged with delight into the world outside. I tried psychedelics, took part in union and student organizing, moved to the mountains, and wrote for an alternative newspaper. When the political community that had sustained me evaporated, I moved, seemingly effortlessly, to a big city paper. In my spare time, I practiced Zen meditation.

My life looked good from the outside, but it didn't feel easy from the inside. By the time I was 35, I had white-knuckled my way to everything I thought stood between me and happiness—a house, a job and a husband—and it had all turned to ashes in my mouth. I didn't think of myself as a "child of an alcoholic," yet I was living on blues power,

depressed and unable to trust. I was a workaholic flake: late everywhere, speeding down the freeways, my car perpetually running on empty. I was in a car crash that knocked me from my psychic moorings. My husband withdrew, and I spent my weekends crying and screaming at him. The world looked flat, and my heart felt enclosed in a Plexiglas box.

Three years ago, when I was 36 and the numbness had become unbearable, I walked into a church basement for a meeting of adult children of alcoholics, clutching a list of meeting places obtained from the local alcoholism council. I thought I was embarking on a last-ditch attempt at personal healing; I later discovered I had joined a cultural movement that incorporates much of the spiritual exploration, group energy, folk wisdom and effective anarchy that I had loved about the '60s. But that came later: On first impression, it seemed corny, passive and pious.

I sat in the back. A volunteer read aloud, "We welcome you to the Monday Night Adult Children Al-Anon Family Group and hope that you may find in it the help and friendship we have been privileged to enjoy." We were asked to introduce ourselves by our first names, and I blushed when the crowd replied, "Hi Lily," the secretary said, "Welcome," and everyone clapped. The crowd wasn't straight-looking—many were gay, some wore leather jackets over their T-shirts and jeans, and only a few wore business suits—but they acted as though they were at a Midwestern summer camp. Or was it a revival meeting?

On a bulletin board, I saw a cloth banner listing The Twelve Steps for spiritual progress adopted from Alcoholics Anonymous: "1. We admitted we were powerless over alcohol—that our lives had become unmanageable. 2. Came to believe that a Power greater than ourselves could restore us to sanity." I stopped there: It didn't apply to me, I'm a Buddhist, a feminist and a big-time reporter, I thought. I'm not powerless, I don't believe in any Power, and my life's not unmanageable. But I stayed: A friend from work who had recently joined Alcoholics Anonymous advised me to forget the religion and go for the group support.

People spoke in monologues—part group therapy and part Quaker meeting—of their own lives and what they called "serenity"—something that had never been a value in my life. Some rambled, full of pain; others spoke in aphorisms. Nobody gave advice, criticism or help.

A volunteer suggested that newcomers find themselves sponsors: "A sponsor is someone with more time in the program than you, who helps you work the steps."

Another volunteer read aloud, "Changing attitudes can aid recovery. . . . You may not like all of us, but in time you will come to love us in a very special way, the same way we already love you." We held hands and recited something that ended with a rah-rah "Keep coming back! It works!" Mystified, I asked someone, "What am I supposed to do now?" She said, "It works by osmosis."

Corny and weird as it was, I went back every week. I was desperate, and there was something intoxicating about listening to a whole roomful of people telling the truth.

But after six months, I still sat in the back and clung to my own sense of personal superiority. Then one night, after a year of meetings, I heard myself tell the group, "I've been depressed for years, and there's no reason for it." After so many years of denying my suffering—and making it so much worse—I had told the truth. I blushed and then cried; I felt sure I would be ostracized for revealing how numb and exhausted I felt. Without knowing it, I had taken the first step: I had admitted my life was unmanageable. It was a radical and empowering moment.

I had become part of a mushrooming national movement. There are an estimated 23 million adult children of alcoholics in the United States, but in 1981, there were only 14 adult children of alcoholics groups registered with the headquarters of Al-Anon, an organization founded in the 1950s by wives of alcoholics. In 1988, there are more than 1,100 such groups, which typically hold meetings once a week.

In a parallel trend among alcoholics, AA members in 1988 reached 750,000, up from 550,000 in 1983. In the last two decades, the movement of Twelve

Steps groups has grown beyond alcoholics and the relatives. Dozens of groups now apply the principles of Alcoholics Anonymous to other human problems—groups like Debtors Anonymous, Overeaters Anonymous, Sex and Love Addicts Anonymous, Cocaine Anonymous, Smokers Anonymous, Incest Survivors Anonymous, Narcotics Anonymous, even Unsafe Drivers Anonymous.

All of the groups use the Twelve Step program for spiritual growth that was originally adapted from a Christian conversion process by a failed New York stockbroker and hopeless drunk named Bill Wilson, who founded AA in 1935. The steps may seem arcane, but in essence they boil down to this: With group help, abstain from your compulsion—alcohol, sex or chronic credit-card debt. Admit you can't do it alone. Straighten out your relationships with your fellow humans by admitting your faults. Accept help from your Higher Power, defining him or her any way you want to. Do these things, help others, and your compulsions will lift as if by magic.

I began consciously working the steps shortly after I confessed my depression to my Al-Anon group. One evening I asked Carl, a bouncy drama student of 24 with streaked blond hair, to be my sponsor. In a coffee shop after a meeting, I told him, "I want to stop being so unhappy," and I started to cry. He put his hand on my arm.

"Buy a spiral notebook," he said. "Write down all the ways that you're powerless over other people's drinking, and over people, places and things. Write how your life is unmanageable. Go to an Alcoholics Anonymous meeting and buy the book called 'Alcoholics Anonymous'—the Big Book. Start reading it."

When things were going badly, I cried my way through two or three meetings in a single week, feeling something like the pain of thawing a frostbite. I realized I had spent my life blaming myself for my father's pain and had called myself crazy for feeling pain of my own. Meanwhile, I systematically filled my spiral notebook with thoughts on how each of the Twelve Steps applied to my own life, talking them over with Carl in our weekly session at the coffee shop. This went well until I hit step three: "Made a decision to turn our will and our lives over to the care of God as we understood Him."

I told Carl I couldn't do it. The AA Big Book said God didn't have to be Christian—it could be anything bigger than my small self, like nature, my Al-Anon group, or a spirit underlying things. Yet

the language of the Big Book was archaic, Christian and patriarchal: God (and the book's assumed reader) was male.

Prayer had repelled me since childhood, and so did Christianity, in both its lukewarm, liberal form and its coercive, fundamentalist form. But because I was so unhappy, I rewrote the Big Book's suggested prayer ("God, I offer myself to Thee to build with me and to do with me as Thou wilt") into a Buddhist form I could live with. Kneeling on my bedroom floor for the first time since childhood, I prayed, "Force of rhythm and meaning moving through all things including me, harmony understood by the Buddha and other enlightened human beings, I offer myself to you. . . . Please relieve me of investment in the illusion of the separate self." It felt foreign; I felt humiliated and embarrassed. I went to sleep.

Surrender, like most religious acts, is a paradox. For years I had felt as though my heart was enclosed in a Plexiglas box. The next day, I went to work with a warmth in my chest, as though someone was home there. Nagging internal voices accusing me of failure—what Twelve Step groups call "the shitty committee"—were temporarily silent. Had I unlocked self-love? Come in tune with The Great Way, or Tao? Been heard by a personal god out there somewhere?

Another night, I read Carl step eight: "Made a list of all persons we harmed, and became willing to make amends to them all." Then I took steps nine and 10: "Made direct amends to such people wherever possible, except when to do so would injure them or others"; and "continued to take personal inventory, and when we were wrong promptly admitted it." I paid off a man whose fender I had dented 10 years ago, apologized to my brother and my husband for treating them as if they weren't smart enough to run their own lives, and wrote a letter to an old friend, admitting I'd betrayed her. My old friend still wouldn't speak to me afterward, but I felt unburdened, because nobody held anything over me anymore.

My life changed in many small ways. I dropped my self-appointed role as chief therapist and manipulator within my marriage. I left the job I had worked at for a decade, a job I had stuck with out of fear—of displeasing my father, or not being famous, of being poor. I whine less about President Reagan and made amends politically by tithing to the Jesse Jackson campaign and to anti-Contra groups, and by writing letters to Congress on issues in which I feel complicit as an American. When it came time to take the 11th step ("Sought through prayer and meditation to improve our conscious contact with God as we understood him . . .") I began taking long, silent walks in the hills.

All this occurred without anybody telling me what to do or what to believe; every meeting closed with, "Take what you like, and leave the rest." But slowly, as I read Al-Anon pamphlets and heard members talk about their lives, serenity became a value of mine—by, you might say, osmosis.

One night after a meeting, when I was feeling particularly happy, a woman—who turned out to be a nurse, six years older than I—nervously asked me to be her sponsor. "Buy a spiral notebook," I told her at the coffee shop. "Go to an AA meeting and get hold of a copy of the Big Book." And so I took the 12th step: "Having had a spiritual awakening as a result of these steps, we tried to carry this message to others and to practice these principles in all our affairs."

I know some people, especially on the left, who think Twelve Step groups encourage conformity and passivity. Perhaps that's inevitable, given our generation's cultural history; rebellion, sex, drugs, and rock and roll splashed over our lives in one big wave that looked like liberation. But I know my friend Walter, a journalist in the alternative press, didn't experience liberation when he smoked so much sinsemilla that he couldn't go to the garage without forgetting what he'd gone for. In true '60s style, he first thought he had a premature case of Alzheimer's contracted from using aluminum cookware. Then a friend in AA suggested he lay off dope for a while, and he found that he couldn't give it up by himself.

And yet—I won't abandon drugs entirely; I know intoxicants can be sacramental. Last New Year's Eve I sat with 11 close friends in silence, by candlelight, drinking champagne and eating a grape for each month of the coming year. It was the peak of an evening in

which one friend had read her translations of Japanese erotic court poetry, and we had all had said things we would not have said sober.

Several years ago, my husband and I once walked the hills and took Ecstasy, speaking to each other in a language deeper than the vulgate of the marketplace and the mortgage payment.

I like being where parts of the self, usually drowned out by conventional life, are heard. I still honor the impulses that once led me to use drugs to get to those parts. But I have to rein in my own romanticism and remember that a little intoxication goes a long way. For some people I know, drinking and drug use have not been gates to a spiritual life, but substitutes for it. Intoxicants have come to symbolize the freedom they crave in their off-work hours. They may not like what they have to do on the job, but within their homes, their families and their bodies—the last unconquered spheres—they express what remains of their freedom: to be left alone, freedom to buy—and freedom to party.

The resulting national epidemic of drug use and alcoholism is the product, I think, of a culture that offers so few sustainable, non-drug opportunities for interconnection, self-expression and spiritual meaning. Religions have traditionally provided such opportunities, and my involvement with adult children of alcoholics give them to me in a non-dogmatic way. I have been able to rethink Buddhism and make it mine, and since I began going to meetings, I don't have to be high to lie alone on a grassy hillside, listening to the sound of a hawk's wings riffling the air.

For years, I had lived my life on the assumption that if I could just figure out how to force other people to behave, I could be happy. Now, my life is not perfect, but Al-Anon helps me give meaning to that part of my suffering that is unavoidable. Talking and listening at meetings helps me accept the given world and helps me see reality. We have a prayer in Al-Anon: "God grant me the

serenity to accept the things I cannot change, the courage to change the things I can, and the wisdom to know the difference."

I keep coming back; it works. After years of trying to stare down my problems, I go at them obliquely, and they melt. After years of locked combat, my relationship with my father eases. I no longer listen on the phone for slurred words like a little detective, I no longer triumph when he stops drinking or get crushed when he begins again. I no longer send him furious letters listing every broken promise, every mean remark, every drunken embarrassment and every blow.

Instead, we talk about writing. I stand up for myself, but with a sense of humor. When he's emotionally absent, I get off the phone instead of trying to suck juice from a stone. I try to face my own life—this mysterious life that I influence, but do not control—instead of trying to live my father's. In the process, I spontaneously recall moments of childhood grace.

The year I turned 10, I spent the day before Christmas with my best friend, Janet. Janet's mother's alcoholism was well advanced—she sometimes passed out on the couch—and Janet was a little adult who ironed her own clothes and made her own meals. In the early afternoon it began to snow, and by nightfall, the highway between Janet's house and my own was closed.

At first, I thought I would spend Christmas Eve with Janet and nobody would much care. But my father called to say he would walk halfway to meet me. It was a long, cold way to go alone, but as I walked through the falling snow, from street lamp to street lamp along the soft, silent highway, I was not afraid. It was a beautiful night, and the snow, caught in the street lamps, sparkled as it whirled and fell. The memory is precious to me, a talisman that reminds me how much my father loved me. He was there to meet me halfway, and sober, and together we walked home.

DRUGS:
The Power of the Placebo

DAVID KLINE

NOT LONG AGO a physician offered a new drug to one of his patients, a man suffering from severe asthma. As the doctor expected, the patient soon felt much better and his breathing capacity improved.

Asthma is a notoriously malleable condition, so the doctor was curious. Was the improvement really due to the drug? Or was it caused by some other factor — a change in diet, perhaps — that the patient had neglected to tell him about? To find out, the doctor substituted a placebo, an inert sugar pill, for the experimental drug, and "treated" the patient with it. As expected, the patient soon complained that the drug no longer worked, and tests confirmed that his condition had worsened.

Confident now in the new drug, the physician called the pharmaceutical company and requested more. The company, after some checking, told the doctor that a mistake had been made. The drug that had worked so well was actually a placebo.

In this incident, reported by Robert Ornstein and David Sobel in *The Healing Brain*, the asthma patient was apparently responding all along to the doctor's varying expectations of the treatment. These were communicated to the patient by subtle cues in the doctor's facial expression, choice of words, or tone of voice. In other words, the doctor's bedside manner—alternately confident and doubtful—was potent enough to produce measurable physical changes. Other research has shown that a placebo can work even when the physician is sure he's dispensing an inactive pill, so long as he expects it to have an effect.

Case studies like this are great fun, if only because they embarrass the medical authorities who still snicker at the notion of "mind over body" healing. These experts would do well to ask themselves why, for thousands of years, physicians were able to dispense chemically useless substances—frog sperm and lizard tongues being just two of the favored elixirs in the antique apothecary—and still see their patients get better.

Part of the answer, of course, is that many diseases go away by themselves. And then, too, every once in a while a sorcerer's potion did contain some active ingredient. But, as Ornstein and Sobel point out, "The long history of medical treatment is, for the overwhelming part, a history of how strong belief heals."

In recent years, studies have consistently demonstrated that when given a sugar pill, 30 to 40 percent of patients suffering from all sorts of disorders — from high blood pressure to arthritis, angina, post-operative pain, and more — will get better. They won't simply feel better; their physical condition will actually improve. And that, when you think about it, is rather amazing.

"What if you discovered a drug that, for a third of all individuals, seemed to effectively treat a variety of conditions?" asks Howard Spiro, professor of medicine at Yale University and the author of *Doctors, Patients, and Placebos*. "You'd think you had invented a wonder drug."

The placebo effect can sometimes even overcome a drug's normal action. In one experiment reported by Ornstein and Sobel, a woman volunteer suffering from intractable nausea and vomiting was given a "new and extremely powerful wonder drug" that would, her doctors promised, cure her nausea. Twenty minutes after she took the drug, her nausea disappeared.

Had she ingested the usual sugar-water solution, the results might not have been so surprising to placebo researchers. But the woman had actually been given syrup of ipecac, a drug used to *induce* vomiting.

"Instead of ignoring the placebo," says Spiro, "we should be studying exactly how it works and trying to discover appropriate ways to use it."

One person doing just that is Jon Levine, a researcher at the University of California Medical Center in San Francisco. He has shown that by apparently raising the patient's expectations of relief, placebos trigger the brain to produce more of the body's natural painkillers, opiatelike substances called endorphins. In a series of carefully controlled experiments, Levine administered naloxone, a drug that blocks the effects of both opiates and endorphins, to patients who had been given placebos and experienced relief from pain. As it turned out, naloxone blocked the painkilling effects of the placebo in the same way it does for morphine. In fact, Levine has calculated that a placebo is as effective as 6 to 8 milligrams of morphine, a common dosage.

"We've always known that placebos can be potent painkillers," says Levine, "but until now it was assumed that their action was psychological. Now we know placebos have direct physical effects on the chemistry of the brain."

Placebos can also influence the functioning of the immune system, as demonstrated by Robert Ader, director of behavioral medicine at the University of Rochester's medical school. He showed that just as a dog can be conditioned to salivate when a bell rings, so could the immune systems of mice be conditioned to suppress their natural reactions to infection. Ader gave mice a saccharin-water solution followed by an injection of a drug that suppressed their ability to make antibodies. Although he later drastically reduced the amount of the immunosuppressive drug in the injection, the mice continued to react as strongly. Their immune systems had "learned" from the taste of sugar water to suppress an antibody reaction.

What mechanism can explain not only how emotions trigger the placebo response, but why its effects are so potent throughout the body?

Neuropeptides, chemical messengers in the brain that include the painkilling endorphins, might provide the answer. Concentrated in the brain's limbic system, which governs human emotional states, neuropeptides flow out from the central nervous system to act upon the immune and endocrine systems. Their role is not only to switch on mood and behavior changes, but also to carry instructions throughout the body for speeding up or slowing down everything from hormone secretions to cell growth to the production of antibodies against infection.

Joanna Hill, a neuroscientist at the National Institute of Mental Health, explains that emotions, such as suppressed rage or euphoria, can change the way neuropeptides in a particular part of the brain

behave. "The altered firing rates and activity patterns of those peptides," she says, "can then change body functions controlled by, for example, the brain stem — things like heart rate, breathing, or the production of infection-fighting lymphocytes by the thymus, which is part of the immune system."

Candace Pert, chief of the brain biochemistry section at the institute, believes

---

The placebo effect can even stop a drug's normal action. One woman's nausea was cured with a "wonder drug"— syrup of ipecac, used to induce vomiting.

---

that research into how mental states influence health is so promising that, as she wrote recently, "I can no longer make a strong distinction between the brain and the body." One can almost hear the wall that western science has built between psychology and biology crumbling.

All manner of "mind over body" therapies, such as biofeedback for hypertension, have gained recognition and acceptance. Now it may be the placebo's turn. In fact, an informal poll conducted

at last year's American College of Physicians convention in New Orleans found that half the doctors in attendance already treat their patients with placebos, at least occasionally.

"Of course, there are a great many medical, ethical, and legal questions raised by the placebo," cautions Spiro. "They should probably not be used to treat an illness where a more specific drug effective against that illness is available." He points to studies showing that a nitroglycerine patch over the heart may actually be no better at preventing or relieving angina than a strip of ordinary tape — a placebo. Yet Spiro would still advocate using the nitroglycerine.

"Placebos should be used only after a careful clinical evaluation," Spiro adds. "And they should never be used to deceive the patient, only to help him." But that said, Spiro says that placebos also present doctors with a wonderful opportunity.

In the 20th century, doctors have come to see themselves as mere conduits of ever-advancing medical technology, as detached purveyors of pills and procedures targeted to deal with specific symptoms. The physician's role as a healer has almost been forgotten.

"Placebos can help physicians regain confidence in the symbolic reality of medicine," Spiro says, "and help restore the bond between themselves and their patients. We need to remember that we are treating patients, not symptoms."

TRANCES THAT HEAL
Rites, Rituals and Brain Chemicals

CAROL LADERMAN

Carol Laderman didn't go to Malaysia in search of shamans; she went to study childbirth practices in an area in which shamanism had died out 75 years earlier—or so it was assumed. Once she got there, she found these healers were still an integral part of the village medical system. And their ceremonies helped her discover "the things the Malays take for granted that everyone knows—that an embryo begins life in the man's brain, for instance."

Laderman, who teaches anthropology at Fordham, has also researched teenage pregnancy and nutrition in New York's Spanish Harlem and South Bronx. Her book is Wives and Midwives *(1983).*

Pak Long Awang is a powerful healer. The Malay villagers he treats believe that he commands spirits and can enter into an altered state at will, becoming a vessel for pronouncements from the invisible world. I first witnessed his power at work while doing anthropological research in a small Malaysian village set between the South China Sea and a tropical rain forest, a village so isolated it lacked electricity. In order to conduct my research, I had to store vials of blood samples in a thermos bottle packed with ice until they could be flown out to the capital, Kuala Lumpur, 180 miles away.

Here, against a backdrop of flickering oil lamps in an atmosphere redolent of a resin used as incense, Pak Long serves as the local version of a country doctor. He treats aches and pains that he diagnoses as "wind sickness" by inducing a deep trance the Malays call "forgetfulness."

Pak Long is a shaman, or spiritual healer, and though his methods seem bizarre, his healing trances may work their apparent magic by actually altering the levels of brain endorphins— the body's natural opiates—in his patients. These endorphins, produced by every human in response to certain extreme situations, may be a link between the trance ceremonies of the East Indies and the most sophisticated neurochemistry laboratories in the West.

For almost two years after my arrival in the village, I refused to undergo one of the shaman's trances. Having become a member of Pak Long's entourage, I attended healing ceremonies with growing regularity; the shaman had even adopted me as his own daughter. Still, as a Westerner and a scientist, I was afraid to enter trance—afraid I might embarrass myself or, worse, never come out at all. My reluctance became a standing joke among the villagers. Although I had learned to love and trust Pak Long, I remained unwilling to place myself under his control. I had asked him and his patients many times to describe their sensations during trance, but no one would. "How could I tell you what red looks like if you had never seen the color?" Pak Long asked.

Still, I had already become a willing subject for some of Pak Long's treatments. I regularly submitted to incantations of release to ward off the dangers the Malays thought accompanied my work on Malay childbirth. I had apprenticed myself to the village midwife, who taught me obstetrics, nursing and the ritual duties of her profession. Malays believe that human birth is too deep a mystery for any but a midwife to witness, and even she runs the risk of failing eyesight unless she is ritually released. Usually, the midwife performed this ritual for both of us, but occasionally Pak Long would squeeze it in at the end of one of his more elaborate healing ceremonies. Unknown to me, the stage was set for my first trance.

One day, instead of beginning the familiar words of release as I sat beside him on the pandanus mat recently vacated by a cured patient, Pak Long signaled the assembled musicians to start the music that accompanies the transition to "forgetfulness." As the drums and gongs set up their steady rhythm, Pak Daud, the shaman's partner, played the introduction to "The Song of the Young Demigod," a story of frustrated love, on his spike fiddle. Pak Daud is the indispensable earthbound member of the shamanistic team; he does not enter into a state of changed reality.

For a moment I hesitated, and then decided to submit to trance. As the vibrations of the drums and gongs entered my body, my eyes seemed to glaze over. As the music became louder my mouth opened, trembling uncontrollably. I began to feel cold winds blowing inside my chest, winds that increased in intensity as the music swelled and accelerated until it felt as if a hurricane was raging within my heart. I put my hands on my chest to try to calm it, but instead I began to move my shoulders and then the whole upper part of my body as if I were about to get up and dance. With the last vestiges of my self-control, I prevented myself; I still feared embarrassment. But as the music swelled to a climax I began to move my head so quickly and violently that, had I not been in trance, my neck would undoubtedly have snapped.

The music stopped abruptly. Instantly, I stopped shaking my head and sank to the floor. Pak Long began reciting spells to bring me out of trance. I came out very quickly, literally as though a spell had been broken. I felt good; the only aftereffect was a slight pain in my stomach. Women crowded around me to wash my face with jasmine water and massage my stomach. The whole thing had taken about 20 minutes.

What was going on?

According to these Malays, the universe and all of its creatures contain four basic elements: earth, air, fire and water. When one of these elements is thrown out of kilter, sickness can result. The talents and desires of individuals are classified as air, or "inner winds." They are powerful when expressed, but when denied or thwarted, they become dangerous, causing "wind sickness." The shaman's cures supposedly release these pent-up winds.

Most Western scientists have a different perspective on the trance experience. Trance is achieved through cultural cues: ritual props, incantations, songs and stories. Percussive music, a steady, musical pulse, is especially important in the transition to altered states in cultures throughout the world. The most effective rhythm is four beats per second, which is exactly the optimum frequency for pain relief through electrically stimulated acupuncture. What's more, it matches the EEG frequency of theta waves, which are produced by the brain during periods of deep meditation but appear only rarely in a normal waking state. English faith healers have been shown to produce continuous theta waves in their patients by the laying-on of hands, and the patient's theta waves exactly match the pattern of the faith healer's.

A more important key may be found in the biochemistry of endorphins. Endorphins (the name is a contraction of "endogenous morphinelike substances") are substances that act on the nervous system, and are generated in the human brain in response to pain, stress or certain kinds of "peak experience." It may be that they are also generated in response to a belief.

The ability of the body to heal in response to belief has long been recognized. Physicians regularly administer placebos, pharmacologically inert substances, in circumstances that don't indicate an active medication. The patient believes he has been given effective medication and, in response to this belief, he recovers. One theory is that his body produces chemicals—perhaps endorphins—that alleviate his ailments. Placebos have been used to control postoperative pain, relieve anxiety, and to cure warts and peptic ulcers.

Endorphins may have evolved in order to protect and preserve our species in its struggle for survival. Pain normally serves as a signal to alert the body that something is amiss. But when pain becomes excessive or too prolonged, it becomes destructive; neurohormones can take over to relieve the pain, sometimes even producing feelings of euphoria. In pregnant women, for instance, endorphin production increases during the last trimester and reaches a peak late in labor. This helps account for the pleasure with which some women remember natural childbirth; endorphins have reduced both the pain and the memory of it.

Nor are endorphins the only chemicals the brain produces. Given the right cues, it will generate tranquilizers as effective as Librium or Valium. A growing number of scientists, from biochemists and pharmacologists to psychiatrists, psychologists

and anthropologists, have speculated that somehow shamans like Pak Long have hit on ingenious methods for turning on production of the brain's natural chemicals. This involves a subtle appreciation of the patient's psychological, as well as his physical, problems.

The shaman carefully tailors his treatment to the patient's needs, and his goal is to choose the appropriate "song of transition" that will move the patient into a trance state. For an asthmatic retired puppeteer, for example, Pak Long chanted his incantations to the accompaniment of musicians playing the overture to the shadow-puppet play.

For the yearly healing of the fattest woman in the neighborhood, known affectionately as "Miss Fatty," Pak Long took another tack. Miss Fatty had an overwhelming desire to dance in the Malay opera, a desire doomed by her enormous girth. She functioned well as wife and businesswoman for most of the year, but as her frustration, or retained wind, built up, she would lose her will and energy and take to her bed. In the healing session, Pak Long and his assistants played the music of the Malay opera to assist Miss Fatty's journey from the normal world to the ideal; there she could realize her ambition. In trance, she would rise from her sleeping mat with the grace of a lithe young girl and dance the role of the beautiful princess before a delighted audience of friends and neighbors. Afterward, her ailments disappeared.

The most striking aspect of the shamans' trances is that they work—sometimes when Western medicine fails. One day, Pak Long was stricken with intense chest pain. I drove him to the hospital, but the resident physician could discover no physical cause for the symptoms and sent us home.

When we got there, Pak Long was placed, pale and trembling, on his sleeping mat. A consulting shaman, summoned for a healing ritual, discovered by divination a cause that would make little sense to Western doctors: Angry, unsatisfied spirits were squeezing the life from Pak Long's heart and lungs. Several weeks earlier, Pak Long had treated a woman for a spirit-induced disease. The spirits, using the shaman's voice, agreed to restore her health in return for a feast. A chicken, eggs, pancakes, custard, rice, cigarettes and a present of white cloth were to be ceremoniously laid out for them near the jungle. But the patient's husband, a rich, urbanized Malay, was skeptical of traditional methods. Instead of fulfilling his promise to the spirits, he took his wife to a clinic in Kuala Trengganu, where she recovered. The couple credited the doctor, and invited neither Pak Long nor the spirits to the feast of thanksgiving. The spirits, insulted and confused, turned on Pak Long.

The consulting shaman announced this to me and to the waiting villagers, and asked that we all join him in calling out to the spirits to leave the shaman alone and attack the real culprits, the unbelieving couple. Immediately Pak Long stopped trembling, color flooded into his face, and he sat up and smiled.

There was clearly no hoax involved here; the consulting shaman believed completely in the results of his divination. But was Pak Long merely responding to the power of suggestion? A Western-trained doctor might have diagnosed his condition as angina pectoris or esophageal spasm; both are often associated with emotional stress. Was his pain brought on by the public denigration of his powers and relieved by a public expression of support?

THE MIND-BODY CONNECTION

The Western interpretation of the shaman's power lies in the growing appreciation of the mind-body connection. Psychosomatic illnesses may have their origins in the mind. But once physical symptoms appear, they are quite real and not "all in the mind." We are discovering that the biochemical changes the mind produces can ravage the body just as a virus or a drug can. In fact, Dr. Raymond Prince of McGill University, a pioneer in the field of transcultural psychiatry, has gone so far as to say that psychiatrists who don't recognize the interaction of mind and body should be known as "former psychiatrists." Malay shamans, it seems, have always inhabited the frontier that Western scientists are just beginning to explore. And they have had company.

There is good evidence to suggest that cultures and cults around the world have long exploited the brain-body link to produce altered states of consciousness without using drugs. The Salish Indians of Canada hold a Winter Spirit Dance designed to help a man achieve the kind of visionary experience that brings power in the form of a tutelary spirit. But the dance is also used to treat "spirit illness," a condition characterized by depression and often connected with drug and alcohol abuse.

The Salish use a number of techniques, from overstimulation to sensory deprivation, to produce the altered state. The patient is alternately immobilized in darkness and silence and forced to run and dance for hours to the beat of drums, rattles and chants. He is underfed and tantalized with food, overheated with heavy blankets and nearly drowned in icy water. The treatment ends only when he becomes a new "baby" and calls out a song that has been revealed to him by the spirits. One can compare the Winter Spirit Dance to experiences brought on by opiates, and the Salish recommend it for tribesmen who have become dependent on drugs. Are the tribesmen substituting natural brain-produced opiates for externally administered drugs?

Dr. Sheila Womack, an anthropologist who has researched Pentecostal Church services in the United States, feels that such a substitution may explain the ability of alcoholics and drug addicts to give up their habits in favor of regular churchgoing as vessels of the Holy Spirit; they speak in tongues and temporarily leave the confines of everyday life. What is even more remarkable is that if they don't go to church at least three times a week, they suffer withdrawal symptoms.

MISSING LINK

Unfortunately, objective proof of a link between ecstatic states and endorphins is difficult to obtain. Lumbar punctures, standard procedure in neurology clinics to obtain spinal fluid for chemical analysis, are too risky in the field. My makeshift blood-refrigeration methods are inadequate for preserving the blood samples until laboratory analysis can detect the unstable chemicals. And even if these problems were solved, we don't really know exactly which chemicals are likely to be the most significant in a shaman's cures. We could block endorphin production with naloxone, a morphine antagonist that also interferes with the action of endorphins. But if the experiment were a success and a patient failed to achieve trance, then the healing ritual would be a failure, and a traumatic one at that.

Such questions may already be academic, at least as far as the Malay shaman is concerned. For years, shamans have practiced in defiance of the ruling Islamic religious authorities. When I returned to my east coast village last summer, Pak Long had retired, Pak Daud, his partner, had suffered a stroke, and Tok Mamat, the consulting shaman, had given up shamanic activities after his pilgrimage to Mecca.

Sadly, we may never discover the exact biochemical components of the shaman's cures, but there is no doubt that by opening the floodgates of emotion he can exorcise the demons of disease.

SHAMANISM IN PRINT

Ecstatic Religion By I.M. Lewis. New York: Penguin, 1971.

Hallucinogens and Shamanism Edited by Michael J. Harner. New York: Oxford University Press, 1979.

Shamanic Voices: A Survey of Visionary Narratives Edited by Joan Halifax. New York: Dutton, 1979.

Shamanism: Archaic Techniques of Ecstasy By Mircea Eliade. Princeton University Press, 1964.

The Way of the Shaman: A Guide to Power and Healing By Michael J. Harner. New York: Harper & Row, 1980.

M.D. VS. HEALER

When Dr. Richard Wedeen first saw the dying child at a city clinic in Enugu, Nigeria, her tiny body bore the signs of kwashiorkor, a severe protein deficiency: retarded growth, puffy limbs, flaking skin. Her face bore other marks: lines of white paint, sketched in during a healing ritual. And by the girl's head lay a portrait of the Madonna. "First they go to the witch doctor, then to the Church and then usually they come to the hospital," Wedeen says.

Western physicians working in the Third World often find themselves competing with unfamiliar health systems and fighting practices that seem to them useless and dangerous. The ritual removal of infant tooth buds in Ethiopia, for example, often leads to infection. And the common practice of spreading mud on the umbilical cord introduces tetanus.

Yet in countries where antibiotics are scarce and sterile gauze unheard of, physicians can't wear scientific blinders. "In western Nigeria it is common to cut the umbilical cord with a red-hot knife," reports Nicholas Cunningham, a pediatrician, "Nurses discouraged it. But it kept everything sterile. You have to look carefully, and not reject practices just because they look primitive."

In Uganda, healers ritually remove the two lower incisors at puberty. Tetanus, or lockjaw, is extremely common, and the spaces are invaluable ports for bamboo feeding straws should a person's jaw freeze. Even the most bizarre remedies may have some scientific rationale. One treatment for malaria is cow's urine. "Maybe the ammonia shrinks the brain and prevents convulsions," Dr. Cunningham suggests.

Steve Robinson, a physician who has worked in Kenya, stresses that Western medicine "can't even begin to touch" some of the indigenous diseases, particularly those of psychiatric or psychosomatic origin. During his time practicing in Haiti, where voodoo is common, Roy Brown recalls seeing "kids coming in temporarily blind" and "epidemics of children dying. We would do examinations and autopsies and find no physical explanation."

Yet even tribal healers recognize that when incantations fail, a shot of penicillin often does the trick. Yaws, a bacterial infection that produces disfiguring eruptions of the skin, clears up quickly after antibiotics. "So people know that for things like yaws, you go to Western doctors," says Cunningham. "But," he adds, "for impotence, you still go to an indigenous healer."
—*Elisabeth Rosenthal*

Chasing Answers to Miracle Cures

SUMMARY: The medical establishment has always been uncomfortable with the idea of spontaneous remission — recovery from a normally incurable disease. As more and more researchers seek the causes of these cures, theories range from mind-body connections to immune functions that are not yet understood to healing powers beyond the immune system. The work could add to the understanding of disease.

The American Academy of Orthopaedic Surgeons describes rheumatoid arthritis as a chronic, long-lasting disease. If the worst cases score a 10 on a scale of 1 to 10, then Gina Covina's was a 9, her doctors told her 15 years ago.

"I had trouble doing simple physical tasks like opening jars," says Covina, 39, who owns Barn Owl Books, a small press in Berkeley, Calif. Doctors wanted to put her on Plaquenil, an antimalarial drug used experimentally for rheumatoid arthritis. "I hit a real bottom at that point, emotionally and spiritually as well as physically."

One night Covina dreamed she was in a doctor's waiting room.

"I was looking at one of those magazines with all the advertisements for drug companies, and I came across a full-page ad for Plaquenil, featuring a photograph of me in a wheelchair as an example of how this drug was keeping someone alive," she says. "I woke up horrified. Something shifted in me at that point, almost beyond my conscious control, to refusing that future."

She began exercising and experimenting with special diets, but says the most important thing she did was change her attitude. Within six weeks, her joint inflammation was gone. Later, blood tests for rheumatoid arthritis were negative.

Recoveries from normally incurable diseases such as this one are called spontaneous remissions or spontaneous regressions. The medical establishment traditionally has dismissed such case histories as misdiagnoses. "Many of the people who write these medical journal reports do so with a great sense of apology, because they seem to be saying to their colleagues, 'Well, we really did diagnose this correctly. We thought that the X rays might have gotten misplaced so we took them again, and we definitely found that this person really had the disease,' " says Brendan O'Regan, research director for the Institute of Noetic Sciences, a tiny nonprofit organization founded by moon-walking astronaut Edgar D. Mitchell that holds conferences and funds research on the limits of human potential. The word "noetic" comes from the Greek *nous*, meaning mind, intelligence or understanding, and the topics the institute studies might best be described as lying somewhere along the continuum from revolutionary to flaky.

Yet such cases are by no means uncommon. Several years ago, O'Regan undertook a massive literature survey of spontaneous remission. "We have about 3,000 papers from about 800 medical journals in 20 different languages, so it's a worldwide phenomenon," he says. "A paper may represent one or 100 cases. And our hunch is that only a very tiny percentage of such cases get written up. It takes a special kind of doctor to do this. He's got to be willing to buck the system a bit."

O'Regan is not the first to survey the field, but he has little company in this endeavor. Warren H. Cole, whose career includes serving as president of several major surgical societies and the American Cancer Society, and colleague Tilden C. Everson published "Spontaneous Regression of Cancer" in 1966. And the International Medical Committee of Lourdes, an international commission of Catholic doctors, investigates reports of cures at the French shrine; since 1858, the doctors have deemed 64 examples of cures to be medically unexplainable.

Spontaneous remissions appear to span the spectrum of normally incurable diseases. Cancers are most heavily represented among the cases O'Regan has compiled, perhaps partly because the disease is so common. In the days before antibiotics, tuberculosis was heavily represented among the remissions at Lourdes, says St. John Dowling, a general practitioner in Hertfordshire, England, and a member of the Lourdes committee. Since the development of antibiotics, the only disease to have seen more than one documented example of cure at Lourdes is multiple sclerosis, although many different types of cancer are represented.

The term "spontaneous" is "a misnomer, because there is obviously a cause of the regression," Cole wrote in 1974. "These causes are a mystery, but there is nothing miraculous about them." O'Regan believes the body can summon resources beyond the immune system to fight disease. He thinks there may be a "healing system that cuts across many systems" and includes the mind's ability to mobilize self-repair mechanisms. He hopes his documentation of remission will prod researchers to study the phenomenon further.

To some extent, hints of where to look for answers have been emerging for years. The power of the placebo effect to influence medical outcomes long has intrigued researchers. "On the average, a placebo is 56 percent as effective as a standard injection of morphine in reducing severe clinical pain of various kinds," Frederick J. Evans of the psychiatry department at the University of Medicine and Dentistry of New Jersey wrote in a recent anthology, "Placebo: Theory, Research and Mechanisms."

In a recent experiment to test a new form of cancer chemotherapy, O'Regan says, some patients received a new drug while others received a placebo, but no one knew who got what. "People expect to lose their hair when given chemotherapy," says research director. In the experiment, 30 percent of those on the placebo lost most of their hair.

One account of remission O'Regan cites involves a cancer patient who got better while taking laetrile. But the cancer returned after the patient discovered that some doctors considered laetrile ineffective. His doctor gave him "new, improved" laetrile and the patient again went into remission, only to become sick again and die after reading in a medical journal that the drug was considered quackery.

Recent experiments with multiple personalities suggest further potential for the mind to influence physiology in ways that might affect the ability to induce remission. At the National Institute of Mental Health, Nicholas R. S. Hall, director of the psychoimmunology division of the University

Herberman believes attitude can play a role, but he is not convinced that "psychological factors can be so potent as to lead to spontaneous regressions."

of South Florida Psychiatry Center, measured the proliferation of T lymphocytes, disease fighting cells of the immune system, as a patient changed personalities. "What was really odd was the enormous variability we would see in the space of 30 seconds, literally the time it would take to take a blood sample at the end of one personality, and again at the beginning of the next," says Hall.

To some researchers, the hypothetical mind-body connection is the most intriguing lead in the study of remissions. But O'Regan believes that, in many instances, regression is a purely biological phenomenon. "One of the common threads that emerges throughout the literature: It doesn't matter whether you are talking about the 1880s or the 1980s, people who have remissions [from cancer] frequently have a bacterial infection of some sort just beforehand," he says.

William Coley observed this in the late 19th century and began treating cancer patients with some success by injecting them with a soup of killed bacteria. Today, it is known that certain components of the bacterial membranes stimulate the body to release Tumor Necrosis Factor, a substance that regulates defenses against cancer and other diseases. But doctors lost interest in "Coley's toxins" in the 1930s, with the coming of radiation and chemotherapy.

Other observations suggest simple involvement of the immune system in regressions. In his 1974 paper, Cole describes 41 examples of regression suggesting that eradication of a cancer patient's primary tumor "may allow the patient's immunologic mechanisms to be effective enough to destroy the metastases."

Some regressions are immunologically mediated, agrees Ronald B. Herberman, director of the Pittsburgh Cancer Institute. Organ transplant patients occasionally develop cancer while undergoing immunosuppression treatment, he says. "What is done in some situations is to either decrease or stop the drugs, and in a number of cases, the tumor may just go away."

It is "interesting to note that in the two types of cancer where regressions have been best documented, renal cell carcinoma [kidney cancer] and malignant melanoma [the deadly form of skin cancer], there are a number of other suggestions that the immune system is playing a role in dealing with the cancer," he adds, noting that the rate of remission in these cancers is "1 to 2 percent at most."

He also believes there is validity in the notion that attitude can play a role in the progression of disease, but he is not convinced "that those psychological factors can be so potent as to lead to these spontaneous regressions."

Studies of regression phenomena may be limited, Herberman adds, because "in order to study the situation you must have a before and after. You are presented with a rare event in which you have only the after. When I was at the National Cancer Institute we saw such a patient. We did a number of immunologic tests and didn't find anything out of the ordinary. The trouble is, negative studies on one or two individuals never get published."

But O'Regan points out that methodologies have improved vastly since then, adding, "The main thing right now is to gather these people into sufficient groups so you can begin to understand what questions to ask.

"Without knowledge about remission," he says, "we are missing an essential piece of the natural history of disease."

— *David Holzman*

Glossary

This glossary of 185 drug terms is included to provide you with a convenient and ready reference as you encounter general terms in your study of drugs and drug and alcohol abuse which are unfamiliar, technical, or require a review. It is not intended to be comprehensive, but, taken together with the many definitions included in the articles themselves, it should prove to be useful.

Absorption The passage of chemical compounds, such as drugs or nutrients, into the bloodstream through the skin, intestinal lining, or other bodily membranes.

Acetylcholine A cholinergic transmitter that forms salts used to lower blood pressure and increase peristalsis, and thought to be involved in the inhibition of behavior.

Addiction Chronic, compulsive, or uncontrollable behavior.

Adrenergic System The group of transmitters, including epinephrine, norepinephrine, and dopamine, that activates the sympathetic nervous system.

Alcohol Abuse *See* Alcoholism.

Alcoholics Anonymous (AA) A voluntary fellowship founded in 1935 and concerned with the recovery and continued sobriety of the alcoholic members who turn to the organization for help. The AA program consists basically of "Twelve Suggested Steps" designed for the personal recovery from alcoholism, and AA is the major proponent of the disease model of alcoholism.

Alcoholism Any use of alcoholic beverages that causes damage to the individual or to society. *See also* Disease Model.

Amphetemines A class of drugs, similar in some ways to the body's own adrenaline (epinephrine), that act as stimulants to the central nervous system.

Analgesics Drugs that relieve pain.

Anesthetics Drugs that abolish the sensation of pain, often used during surgery.

Angel Dust Slang term for phencyclidine.

Anorectic A drug that decreases appetite.

Antagonist Programs Drug treatment programs that use antagonist agents, like naltrexone (antagonist of heroin) or antabuse (used in treating alcoholism), to block the effect of drugs on the body.

Antianxiety Tranquilizers Tranquilizers, like Valium and Librium, used to relieve anxiety and tension, sometimes called minor tranquilizers.

Anticholinergics Drugs that block the transmission of impulses in the parasympathetic nerves.

Antidepressants Drugs that relieve mental depression. *See also* Depression, Mental.

Antihistamines Drugs that relieve allergy or cold symptoms by blocking the effects of histamine production.

Antipsychotic Tranquilizers Drugs used to treat psychosis; include Thorazine (chlorpromazine). Also called major tranquilizers or neuroleptics. *See also* Tranquilizers.

Atropine An alkaloid derivative of the belladonna and related plants that blocks responses to parasympathetic stimulation.

Autonomic Nervous System (ANS) That part of the nervous system that regulates involuntary action, such as heartbeat; consists of the sympathetic and parasympathetic nervous systems.

Axon The core of the nerve fiber that conducts impulses away from the nerve cell to the neurons and other tissue.

Barbiturates Drugs used for sedation and to relieve tension and anxiety.

Binding The attachment of a transmitter to its appropriate receptor site.

Blood Level The concentration of alcohol in the blood, usually expressed in percent by weight.

Caffeine An alkaloid found in coffee, tea, and kola nuts, that acts as a stimulant.

Caffeinism Dependence on caffeine.

Cannabis *See* Marijuana.

Capsule A container, usually of gelatin, that encloses a dose of an oral medicine.

Central Nervous System (CNS) The brain and spinal cord.

Chewing Tobacco A form of tobacco leaves, sometimes mixed with molasses, that is chewed.

Chlorpromazine An antianxiety tranquilizer, manufactured under the name of Thorazine, used for treating severe psychoses. Also used as an antagonist to LSD panic reactions.

Choline A transmitter, part of the cholinergic system.

Cholinergic System Group of transmitters that activate the parasympathetic nervous system.

Cocaine   A white crystaline narcotic alkaloid derived from the coca plant and used as a surface anesthetic and a stimulant.

Codeine   A narcotic alkaloid found in opium, most often used as an analgesic or cough suppressant.

Coke   Slang term for cocaine.

Cold Turkey   Slang expression for abrupt and complete withdrawal from drugs or alcohol without medication.

Compulsive Drug Use   Drug use that is frequent, with intensive levels of long duration, producing physiological or psychological dependence.

Constriction   Narrowing or shrinking.

Contraindication   A condition that makes it inadvisable or hazardous to use a particular drug or medicine.

Controlled Drinking   Moderate drinking by recovered alcoholics, discouraged by AA.

Controlled Drug Use   Use of drugs over a period of time without abusing them.

Controlled Substances   All psychoactive substances covered by laws regulating their sale and possession.

Controlled Substances Act of 1970   Federal act that classifies controlled substances into five categories and regulates their use. Schedule I drugs are those most strictly controlled, and include heroin, marijuana, LSD, and other drugs believed to have high abuse potential. Schedule II drugs are also strictly controlled but have some medicinal uses. These drugs include morphine, methadone, and amphetamines. Schedule III, IV, and V substances include drugs that have increasingly less abuse potential. Over-the-counter medicines not subject to any refill regulations fall into Schedule V.

Craving   Refers to both physical and psychological dependence; a strong desire or need for a substance.

Crisis Intervention   The process of diagnosing a drug crisis situation and acting immediately to arrest the condition.

DMT   Dimethyltryptamine, a psychedelic drug.

DNA   Deoxyribonucleic acid, the carrier of chromosomes in the cell.

DWI   Driving while intoxicated.

Decriminalization   The legal process by which the possession of a certain drug would become a civil penalty instead of a criminal penalty. *See also* Legalization.

Deliriants   Substances, like some inhalants, that produce delirium.

Delirium   State of temporary mental confusion and diminished consciousness, characterized by anxiety, hallucinations, and delusions.

Dendrite   The part of the nerve cell that transmits impulses to the cell body.

Dependence, Drug   A physical or psychological dependence on a particular drug resulting from continued use of that drug.

Dependence, Physical   The physical need of the body for a particular substance such that abstinence from the substance leads to physical withdrawal symptoms. *See also* Addiction; Withdrawal Syndrome.

Dependence, Psychological   A psychological or emotional reliance on a particular substance; a strong and continued craving.

Depression, Mental   The state of mind that ranges from mild sadness to deep despair, often accompanied by a general feeling of hopelessness.

Detoxification   Removal of a poisonous substance, such as a drug or alcohol, from the body.

Dilation   Widening or enlargement.

Disease Model   A theory of alcoholism, endorsed by AA, in which the alcoholism is seen as a disease rather than a psychological or social problem.

Dopamine   An indoleaminergic transmitter necessary for normal nerve activity.

Downers   Slang term for drugs that act to depress the central nervous system.

Drug   Any substance that alters the structure or function of a living organism.

Drug Abuse   Use of a drug to the extent that it is excessive, hazardous, or undesirable to the individual or the community.

Drug Misuse   Use of a drug for any purpose other than that for which it is medically prescribed.

Drug Paraphernalia   Materials, like hypodermic syringes, that are used for the preparation or administration of illicit drugs.

Drunkenness   The state of being under the influence of alcohol such that mental and physical faculties are impaired; severe intoxication.

Dysphoria   Emotional state characterized by anxiety, depression, and restlessness, as opposed to euphoria.

Ecstasy A derivative of nutmeg or sassafras, causing euphoria and sometimes hallucinations; also known as XTC, Adam, or MDMA.

Endorphins Any group of hormones released by the brain that have painkilling and tranquilizing abilities.

Epinephrine An adrenal hormone that acts as a transmitter and stimulates autonomic nerve action.

Ethical Drugs Drugs dispensed by prescription only.

Euphoria Exaggerated sense of happiness or well-being.

Experimental Drug Use According to the US National Commission on Marijuana and Drug Abuse, the short-term, non-patterned trial of one or more drugs, either concurrently or consecutively, with variable intensity but maximum frequency of ten times per drug.

Fetal Alcohol Syndrome (FAS) A pattern of birth defects, cardiac abnormalities, and developmental retardation seen in babies of alcoholic mothers.

Flashback A spontaneous and involuntary recurrence of psychedelic drug effects after the initial drug experience.

Food and Drug Administration (FDA) Agency of the US Department of Health and Human Services that administers federal laws regarding the purity of food, the safety and effectiveness of drugs, and the safety of cosmetics.

Habituation Chronic or continuous use of a drug, with an attachment less severe than addiction.

Hallucination A sensory perception without external stimuli.

Hallucinogen Or, hallucinogenic drugs. Drugs that cause hallucinations. Also known as psychedelic drugs.

Harrison Narcotics Act Federal act passed in 1914 that controlled the sale and possession of prescription drugs, heroin, opium, and cocaine.

Hash Oil An oily extract of the marijuana plant, containing high levels of THC.

Hashish The dried resin of the marijuana plant, often smoked in water pipes.

Herb Commonly, any one of various aromatic plants used for medical or other purposes.

Heroin Diacetylmorphine hydrochloride, an opiate derivative of morphine.

High Intoxicated by a drug or alcohol; the state of being high.

Illicit Drugs Drugs whose use, possession, or sale is illegal.

Illusion A distorted or mistaken perception.

Indole An indoleaminergic transmitter.

Indoleaminergic System A system of neurotransmitters, including indole and serotonin.

Inebriation The state of being drunk or habitually drunk.

Intoxication Medically, the state of being poisoned. Usually refers to the state of being drunk, falling between drunkenness and a mild high.

Involuntary Smoking Involuntary inhalation of the cigarette smoke of others.

Ketamine A general anesthetic, also used as a deliriant.

LSD Lysergic acid diethylamide-25, a hallucinogen.

Legalization The movement to have the sale or possession of certain illicit drugs made legal.

MDMA *See* Ecstasy.

Maintenance Treatment Treatment of drug dependence by a small dosage of the drug or another drug, such as methadone, that will prevent withdrawal symptoms.

Marijuana The dried leaves of the cannabis plant, usually smoked, and resulting in feelings of well-being, relaxation, or euphoria. Also spelled: Marihuana.

Medical Model A theory of drug abuse or addiction in which the addiction is seen as a medical, rather than a social, problem.

Medicine A drug used to treat disease or injury; medication.

Mescaline A hallucinogenic alkaloid drug, either derived from the peyote plant or made synthetically.

Metabolism The set of physical and chemical processes involved in the maintenance of life; or, the functioning of a particular substance in the body.

Methadone A synthetic opiate sometimes used to treat heroin or morphine addiction. *See also* Maintenance Treatment.

Methaqualone A non-barbiturate sedative/hypnotic drug, used to bring on feelings of muscular relaxation, contentment, and passivity. Also known as Quaaludes.

Morphine An organic compound extracted from opium, a light anesthetic or sedative.

Multimodality Programs Programs for the treatment of drug abuse or alcoholism involving several simultaneous treatment methods.

Multiprescribing The situation in which a person is taking more than one prescription or over-the-counter drug simultaneously.

Narcotic Any drug that dulls a person's senses and produces a sense of well-being in smaller doses, and insensibility, sometimes even death, in larger doses.

Nervous System In human beings, the brain, spinal cord, and nerves. *See also* Somatic Nervous System; Autonomic Nervous System.

Neuroleptic Any major, or antipsychotic, tranquilizer.

Neuron The basic element responsible for the reception, transmission, and processing of sensory, motor, and other information of physiological or psychological importance to the individual.

Neurotransmitter *See* Transmitter.

Nicotine The main active ingredient of tobacco, extremely toxic and causing irritation of lung tissues, constriction of blood vessels, increased blood pressure and heart rates, and, in general, central nervous system stimulation.

Norepinephrine Hormone found in the sympathetic nerve endings that acts as an adrenergic transmitter and is a vasoconstrictor.

Opiate Narcotics A major subclass of drugs that act as pain relievers as well as central nervous system depressants; includes opium, morphine, codeine, and methadone.

Opiates The drugs derived from opium—morphine and codeine—as well as those derived from them, such as heroin.

Opium Narcotic derivative of the poppy plant that acts as an analgesic.

Opoids The group of synthetic drugs, including Demerol and Darvon, that resemble the opiates in action and effect.

Overmedication The prescription and use of more medication than necessary to treat a specific illness or condition.

Over-the-Counter Drugs Drugs legally sold without a prescription.

Parasympathetic Nervous System The part of the autonomic nervous system that inhibits or opposes the actions of the sympathetic nerves.

Parasympathomimetics Drugs that produce effects similar to those of the parasympathetic nervous system.

Parkinson's Disease A progressive disease of the nervous system characterized by muscular tremor, slowing of movement, partial facial paralysis, and general weakness.

Patent Medicines Drugs or other medications protected by a patent and sold over the counter.

Peristalsis Wave-like muscular contractions that help move matter through the tubular organs (e.g., intestines).

Phencyclidine (PCP) A synthetic depressant drug used as a veterinary anesthetic and illegally as a hallucinogen. Also known as angel dust.

Placebo An inactive substance used as a control in an experiment.

Placenta The membranous organ that develops in the uterus of a pregnant female mammal to hold the fetus. Though the fetus and mother are thus separated, drugs and alcohol are often still able to reach the developing fetus.

Polyabuse Abuse of various drugs simultaneously.

Pot Slang term for marijuana.

Potency Term used to compare the relative strength of two or more drugs used to produce a given effect.

Prescription Drugs Drugs dispensed only by a physician's prescription.

Primary Prevention Efforts designed to prevent a person from starting to use drugs.

Proprietary Drugs Patent medicines.

Psilocybin A hallucinogenic alkaloid, found in various types of mushrooms, chemically related to LSD.

Psychedelic Drugs Hallucinogens.

Psychoactive Any drug that can cause alterations in the user's mood or behavior.

Psychopharmacology The study of the effects of drugs on mood, sensation, or consciousness, or other psychological or behavioral functions.

Psychosis Severe mental disorder, characterized by withdrawal from reality and deterioration of normal intellectual and social functioning.

Psychotherapeutic Drugs Drugs that are used as medicines to alleviate psychological disorders.

Psychotomimetics Drugs that produce psychosis-like effects.

Receptors The input organs for the nervous system.

Recidivism Return to former behavior.

Recombinant DNA DNA prepared in the laboratory by the transfer or exchange of individual genes from one organism to another.

Recreational Drug Use Drug use that takes place in social settings among friends who want to share a pleasant experience; characterized by less frequency and intensity than addictive drug use. Also called social-recreational drug use.

Rehabilitation Restoration of a person's ability to function normally.

Reinforcement A stimulus that increases the probability that a desired response will occur.

Rush Slang term for an immediate feeling of physical well-being and euphoria after the administration of a drug.

STP Early slang term for phencyclidine.

Schedules Categories of drugs as defined in the Controlled Substances Act of 1970.

Schizophrenia A psychosis characterized by withdrawal from reality accompanied by affective, behavioral, and intellectual disturbances.

Scopolamine Poisonous alkaloid found in the roots of various plants, used as a truth serum or with morphine as a sedative.

Secondary Prevention Early treatment of drug abuse to prevent it from becoming more severe.

Sedative/Hypnotics Class of non-narcotic depressant drugs that calm, sedate, or induce hypnosis or sleep. Sedative/hypnotics are divided into four categories: barbiturates, alcohol, antianxiety tranquilizers (minor tranquilizers), and nonbarbiturate proprietary drugs.

Serotonin An indoleaminergic transmitter found in the blood serum, cells, and central nervous system, that acts as a vasoconstrictor.

Set The combination of physical, mental, and emotional characteristics of an individual at the time a drug is administered.

Setting The external environment of an individual at the time a drug is administered.

Side Effects Secondary effects, usually undesirable, of a drug or therapy.

Snuff A preparation of pulverized tobacco that is inhaled into the nostrils.

Sobriety The quality of being free from alcohol intoxication.

Social-Recreational Drug Use *See* Recreational Drug Use.

Socioeconomic Both social and economic.

Somatic Nervous System That part of the nervous system that deals with the senses and voluntary muscles.

Speed Slang term for methamphetamine, a central nervous system stimulant.

Stereospecificity The matching of both electrical and chemical characteristics of the transmitter and receptor site so that binding can take place.

Stimulants A major class of drugs that stimulate the central nervous system, causing mood elevation, increased mental and physical activity, alertness, and appetite suppression. Primary stimulants include the amphetamines and cocaine. Secondary stimulants include nicotine and caffeine.

Subcutaneous Beneath the skin.

Substance Abuse Refers to overeating, cigarette smoking, alcohol abuse, or drug abuse.

Sympathetic Nervous System That part of the autonomic nervous system that acts to release sugars from the liver, slow digestion, and increase heart and breathing rates.

Sympathomimetic Any drug that produces effects like those resulting from stimulation of the sympathetic nervous system.

Synapse The space, or gap, between two neurons.

THC Tetrahydrocannabinol, a psychoactive derivative of the cannabis plant.

Tars The dark, oily, viscid substances created by burning tobacco, known to contain carcinogenic agents.

Temperance   The practice of moderation, especially with regard to alcohol consumption. The Temperance Movement was a popular movement in the nineteenth and twentieth centuries to restrict or prohibit the use of alcoholic beverages.

Tertiary Prevention   Treatment to prevent the permanent disability or death of a drug abuser.

Therapeutic Community   Setting in which persons with similar problems meet and provide mutual support to help overcome those problems.

Titration   The ability to determine desired drug dosage.

Tolerance   The capacity to absorb a drug continuously or in large doses with no adverse effect.

Trance   Dazed or hypnotic state.

Tranquilizers   Drugs that depress the central nervous system, thus relieving anxiety and tension and sometimes relaxing the muscles, divided into the major tranquilizers, or antipsychotics, and minor tranquilizers, or antianxiety tranquilizers. *See also* Antianxiety tranquilizers; Antipsychotic tranquilizers.

Transmitters   Also known as neurotransmitters. Any substance that aids in transmitting impulses between a nerve and a muscle. Three known categories of transmitters are the cholinergic system, adrenergic system, and indoleaminergic system.

Treatment   Drug treatment programs can be drug-free or maintenance, residential or ambulatory, medical or nonmedical, voluntary or involuntary, or some combination of these.

Uppers   Slang term for amphetamines, and, sometimes, cocaine.

Withdrawal Syndrome   The group of reactions or behavior that follows abrupt cessation of the use of a drug upon which the body has become dependent. May include anxiety, insomnia, perspiration, hot flashes, nausea, dehydration, tremor, weakness, dizziness, convulsions, and psychotic behavior.

Index

abstinence, total, from alcohol use, 109, 148, 160
acetaminophen, side effects of, 140, 144
addictionology, 172–175, 178––182
advertising: of alcohol, 152–154, 216–218; of cigarettes, 120–121, 125–126, 128–138; of cocaine, 21, 22; of smokeless tobacco, 112–113
aggression, and steroid use, 168, 169
AIDS, and intravenous drug use, 28, 38, 59, 86, 88, 199, 200, 201, 221, 224, 225
alcohol(ism): 26, 56, 57, 58, 59, 77, 81, 87, 116, 118, 127, 150, 183, 190, 191, 192, 201, 207, 209; abuse of, by women, 155–157; advertising of, 152–154, 216–218; health effects of, 82, 94, 95, 96, 126, 186, 224; myth of disease model of, 106–109, 148–149, 172–175, 178–182; sports and, 136–137; treatment programs for, 107, 108, 182, 212–213; see also, Prohibition
allergy medicines, side effects of, 139, 140–141
amniotic fluid, norcocaine in, 89, 90
amotivational syndrome, and marijuana use, 95
amphetamines, 37, 79, 98, 99, 100, 117, 150, 155, 178, 181, 186, 194, 208, 217, 220
analogs, drug, see designer drugs
angel dust (PCP), 56, 57, 97, 207, 210, 222, 224
antidepressants, use of, to treat cocaine addiction, 85
Anti-Drug Abuse Act of 1986, 98
anxiety, drug-induced, 32, 35, 87, 93, 94, 95, 140
appetite suppressants, see diet pills
arthritis, rheumatoid, use of thalidomide to treat, 102
aspirin, side effects of, 140, 144
assets, forfeiture of, by drug traffickers, 210
asthma, drug treatment for, 22, 94, 141
athletes: cigarette endorsements by, 128–138; use of performance-enhancing drugs by, 100, 110–111, 155, 167, 168–169, 208
auto racing, tobacco companies' sponsorship of, 130

banks, laundering drug money through legitimate, 66–67
barbiturates, 150, 187, 188
baseball, tobacco companies' sponsorship of, 130
behavioral therapy; for cocaine addiction, 176–177; for smoking, 122
Bennett, William, 32, 65, 73, 87, 122, 173, 185, 219, 223
birth defects: 110; caused by thalidomide, 101, 102, 103
Black Beauties, 98
black tar heroin, 201
blacks: drug use and trafficking by, 28, 41, 45–48, 60–64, 205; false drug arrests of, 52–55
bone-marrow transplants, use of thalidomide for, 101
brain: effect of drugs on, 84–85, 88, 93, 95, 97, 116, 118, 139, 176, 192,

194–195; and healing trances, 231–233; and power of placebos, 229–230
breast, fibrocystic disease of the, and vitamin E, 214–215
Bureau of Alcohol, Tobacco, and Firearms (BATF), 42
Bush, George, anti-drug strategy of, 43–44, 50, 54, 65, 173, 175, 185, 223

caffeine: 23, 77, 98, 150; health effects of, 82, 110–111, 144, 145, 179, 186
cancer: 110, 165, 168, 214; spontaneous remission, 234, 235; tobacco and, 112–113, 134, 136–137, 165–166
cannabis, see marijuana
cartels, Colombian drug, 41, 65, 66, 67
chemotherapy, use of THC with, 94, 99
chewing tobacco, see smokeless tobacco
children: of alcoholics, 148, 155, 158–163, 164, 226–228; side effects of medicine on, 140, 141; see also, teenagers
"China White" heroin, 97
cholesterol, niacin and, 215
cigarettes, see smoking
civil rights abuses, by police, in drug arrests, 52–55, 206, 223
civil rights movement, and victimhood, 26–28
class distinctions, and drug abuse, 78–79
Client Oriented Data Acquisition Process (CODAP), and epidemiology of drug abuse, 200
Coca-Cola, cocaine in, 21–22, 23, 57, 173, 181
cocaine: 77, 115, 117, 150, 151, 166, 169, 173, 175, 178, 187, 188, 194, 206, 209, 210, 220, 221; America's first epidemic of use of, 20–25; health effects of, 35, 82–83, 89–91, 94, 96, 131, 166, 185, 186, 207–209, 224; illegal trade in, 42, 45–49, 50–51, 69, 70, 205; illegal use of, 24, 56, 57, 68, 78, 79, 80, 84–85, 88, 98, 100, 156, 157, 182, 199, 200, 202–203, 211, 217, 222; treatment for addiction to, 176–177; see also, crack
codeine, 140, 150, 176, 187
codependency, in children of alcoholics, 160
cold remedies: drugs in, 99, 150; side effects of, 139, 140, 145
Colombians, drug trafficking by, 40, 41, 45, 46, 48, 49, 65, 66, 68, 205
compulsive activities, as diseases, 172–175, 178–182, 189–193
control, need for, in children of alcoholics, 159, 160
controlled drinking, 109, 149
Controlled Substances Act, 37
crack (cocaine): 34, 100, 175, 178; health risks of, 32, 82–83, 89–91, 185; illegal trade in, 34–38, 43, 45–49, 70, 72, 73, 98; illegal use of, 24, 32, 33, 35, 39–44, 58, 78, 79, 80, 85, 203; see also, cocaine
crib death, in babies exposed to crack, 89, 90
crime, drug-related, 53, 58, 59, 60, 72, 205, 209, 210, 2ll, 223
crystal methamphetamine, see ice
cultural values, and alcohol abuse, 108, 174, 192

culture of refusal, and teenage cocaine traffickers, 45–49

decriminalization, of illegal drugs, 71, 72, 92, 96, 220, 222–225
demand reduction policy, for illegal drug use, 175, 210–211
demon rum, American war against, 15–19, 24, 57–58
denial, in alcoholics, 159, 162, 174, 217
depressants, addictive properties of, 187–188
depression, drug-induced, 32, 85, 87, 95, 110, 141, 159, 163, 164, 167, 177, 179, 208
designer drugs, 37, 97–99
desipramine, use of, to treat cocaine addiction, 85, 176
diet pills: drugs in, 99; side effects of, 139, 140, 145
disease model: and epidemiology of drug abuse, 198–204; myth of alcoholism as, 106–109, 148–149, 172–175, 178–182, 189, 191
doctors: in 1884 America, 7, 8–9; seduction of, by drug company representatives, 29–31
Dominicans, in U.S. drug trade, 40, 41, 43, 46, 49
dopamine, 84, 85, 176, 194, 195
Drug Abuse Warning Network (DAWN), 200, 201, 203, 222
drug company representatives, seduction of doctors by, 29–31
Drug Enforcement Agency (DEA), 22, 40, 41, 43, 50, 65, 69, 79, 80, 86, 97, 98, 99, 222, 223
drug therapy, for cocaine addiction, 176–177

Ecstasy, see MDMA
enabler, role of, in alcoholic's family, 162
endorphins, 144, 191, 229, 230, 231, 232, 233
England, drug policies of, 206, 224–225
entrepreneurs, drug dealers as, 41, 46, 97
environmental factors, in drug and alcohol abuse, 108, 118, 148, 172, 181, 184, 185, 190
ephedrine: 98, 140; use of, to manufacture crank, 35–36, 37
epidemiology, of drug abuse, 198–204, 222
epinephrine, side effects of, 141
ethics, of doctors receiving gifts from drug companies, 29–31
ethnic solidarity, importance of, to blacks, 62–63
ethnic values, and alcohol abuse, 108, 174
euphoria, drug-induced, 20, 32, 33, 37, 79, 85, 86, 88, 93, 94, 141, 169, 176, 187

Fairness Doctrine, and TV cigarette advertising, 131, 132
family hero, role of, in alcoholic's family, 162
fat-soluble vitamins, 215
feminists, and victimhood, 27, 28
fentanyl, 97, 98, 99
freebasing, of cocaine, 40, 47, 88, 176, 203
Freud, Sigmund, observations on cocaine use by, 20–25, 79, 116

gangs, drug: Chinese opium, 87; Hell's Angel's crank, 35, 80; Jamaican posses, 41–42, 43; Korean ice, 32–33; teen cocaine, 40, 43, 45–49

genetics, and alcoholism, 161, 172, 188, 192

glaucoma, use of THC to treat, 94, 99

graft vs. host disease, use of thalidomide to treat, 101

Group Against Smoking Pollution (GASP), 122, 123

gum disease, and smokeless tobacco, 112, 113

habit, vs. addiction, 189–193

hair testing, for drug abuse, 219

hallucinations, drug-induced, 32, 33, 140, 149

hallucinogens, 188

handicapped people, and victimhood, 27, 28

Hansen's disease, use of thalidomide to treat, 102, 103

harm reduction policy, in Dutch drug policy, 221

Harrison Act, 24, 79, 117, 180

hashish, 220, 225

Hawaii, ice epidemic in, 32–33

headaches, drug-induced, 35, 144, 187

heart problems, drug-induced: 32, 35, 95, 110, 115, 126, 128, 166, 167, 202, 203, 208

Hell's Angels, in crank drug trade, 35

heredity, and drinking, 161, 172, 192

heroin: 22, 99, 116, 122, 150, 166, 169, 176, 178, 220; health risks of, 32, 94, 96, 118, 131, 173, 185, 186, 224; illegal trade in, 41, 42, 43, 205; illegal use of, 32, 35, 56, 57, 76, 78, 79, 83, 84, 85–86, 87, 88, 97, 98, 117, 181, 198, 199, 200–201, 207, 208, 211, 217, 222, 223

High School Senior Survey, and epidemiology of drug abuse, 199, 202

homicides, and drug trade, 42, 43, 48, 209, 225

horse racing, tobacco companies' sponsorship of, 130

hydroponics, use of, to grow marijuana, 69, 92

hypersensitivity, in crack babies, 90, 91

ice (methamphetamine), illegal use of, 32–34, 43, 80

immune system: 95, 101; placebos and, 229–230; spontaneous remissions and, 234–235

inhalants, abuse of, 200

intoxication, as basic human drive, 76–77

intravenous drug use, and AIDS, 28, 38, 59, 86, 88, 199, 200, 201, 221, 224, 225

IQ, and addiction, 194–195

Jamaica, drug posses from, 41, 43

kidney damage, drug-induced, 32, 35, 82, 89, 167, 168

kinship networks, importance of, to blacks, 62–63

Korea, illegal trade in ice by, 32–33

laundering, of illegal drug profits, 35, 65–67

laxatives, side effects of, 143–144

learned behavior, alcoholism as, 148–149

learning disabilities, drug-induced, 90–91, 195

legalization, of drugs, 22, 58, 59, 71, 72, 76, 77, 205, 206, 207, 208

leprosy, see Hansen's disease

leukemia, use of thalidomide for, 101

lidocaine, as mixed with illegal drugs, 38, 40, 98

liquor industry, and alcoholism, 107–108, 152–154, 216–218

Lister, Joseph, 10–11

loneliness, as cause of relapse in alcoholics, 149, 155, 217

lost child, role of, in alcoholic's family, 162

loyalty, in children of alcoholics, 158, 159

LSD, 56, 76, 78, 94, 97, 99, 100, 150, 188, 207, 220

lung damage, drug-induced, 32, 95, 125, 128

lupus, use of thalidomide to treat, 102

Madison Avenue sales techniques, of drug company salespersons, to doctors, 29–31

Mafia: drug trade of, 41, 70, 87, 98; see also, organized crime

marijuana: 32, 76, 99, 100, 118, 150, 151, 188, 206, 207, 210, 220; illegal trade in, 68–71; illegal use of, 38, 56, 57, 59, 90–96, 156, 157, 181, 199, 200, 201–202, 217, 222, 224, 225

marketing, of drugs, to doctors, 29–31

mascot, role of, in alcoholic's family, 162

MDMA (Ecstasy), 80, 97–99, 228

medicine, American, in 1884, 6–14

megavitamin therapy, 214–215

mental illness, megavitamins for, 214–215

meperidine, 97, 98, 140

mescaline, 99, 207

methadone, 83, 84, 85, 88, 98, 206, 211, 217, 221, 223

methamphetamine, see ice, crank

Mexicans, drug trafficking by, 67, 68, 205

mind-body connection: and placebos, 229–230; and spontaneous remission, 234–235; and trances, 232–233

misery market, of winos and the liquor industry, 152–154

mood, effect of drugs on, 35, 118, 139, 140, 167, 176

morphine, 21, 22, 23, 57, 100, 114, 115, 116, 118, 150, 176, 180, 194, 208, 229, 234

Musto, David: 79, 80, 81, 181; on America's first cocaine epidemic, 20–25

naloxone, 88, 200, 229, 233

nasal decongestants, side effects of, 144

National Household Survey on Drug Abuse, 200, 202, 222

National Organization for the Reform of Marijuana Laws (NORML), 68, 69, 70

Natural History of Alcoholism, The (Vaillant), 175, 192

needle exchange programs, for addicts, 221, 225

nervous system, central, effect of drugs on, 35, 89, 111, 118, 140, 202

Netherlands, drug policy of, 220–221, 224–225

neurochemistry, of addiction, 194–195

newborns, effect of cocaine on, 82–83, 89–91

niacin, and cholesterol control, 215

nicotine: health effects of, 82, 115–120, 131, 150, 165–166, 173, 183, 186, 189, 218; see also, tobacco

no-name market, for cheap wines, 153

norcocaine, 89, 90

norepinephrine, 37, 176

normalization, Dutch drug policy of, 220–221

nursing schools, growth of American, 13, 14

opium, 7, 10, 11, 21, 23, 77, 86, 87, 114, 116, 117, 176, 180, 223

organized crime: drug trade controlled by, 40–41, 43, 46, 70, 71, 98, 206; see also, Mafia

Oriental flush, 161, 192

orthomolecular therapy, 214

outpatient programs, for substance abusers, 212–213

over-the-counter (OTC) medicines, side effects of, 139–142, 143–145, 150, 186–188

painkillers: placebos as, 229–230; side effects of, 139, 140, 141, 144, 145, 186–188

paranoia, drug-induced, 32, 35, 38, 43, 87, 94

paraquat, 68, 95

passive smoking, dangers of, 121, 122–123

patent medicines, narcotics in, 22, 23, 179

PCP, see angel dust

performance enhancers, drugs as, 100, 110–111, 167, 168–169

Peru, illegal drug production in, 46, 50–51

peyote, 188

phenylpropanolamine (PPA), 98–99, 140, 142, 145

Philip Morris, sponsorship of sports events by, 128–138

phocomelia, and thalidomide, 102

placebo, power of, 229–230, 232, 234

police, false drug arrests by, 52–55

Posse Comitatus Act of 1878, 223

pregnancy, effects of cocaine use during, 82–83

premenstrual syndrome (PMS), vitamin B$_6$ for, 215

prescription medicine: 157; side effects of, 139, 186–188

prescription system, for controlled substances, 206

privacy, right to, and drug testing, 210–211, 217

Prohibition: alcohol, 15–19, 24, 58, 71, 72, 107, 207, 223, 224; drug, 59, 205–206

propaganda, of drug companies, and medical students, 29–31

provoker, role of, in alcoholic's family, 162

psychological damage, drug-induced, 32, 35, 94

psychotherapy, for cocaine addiction, 176–177

Pure Food and Drug Act of 1906, 23

purple hearts, 98

Quaaludes (methaqualone), 97

racism: 28; and drug abuse, 23–24, 57, 58, 223

reaction time, effect of drugs on, 93, 110, 116
rebound effect, of nasal decongestants, 144
Reefer Madness, 81
refusal, culture of, and teenage cocaine traffickers, 45–49
reinforcement, neurobiology of, and addiction, 194–195
relapse prevention, for addictions, 183–184, 191, 192, 213
responsibility, personal, and addiction, 172–175, 182
responsible child, role of, in alcoholic family, 162, 164
reward, neurochemistry of, and addiction, 194–195
R. J. Reynolds, sponsorship of sports events by, 130–138
rock cocaine, *see* crack
Rush, Benjamin, 15–16, 107

Sacramento, CA, as center of illegal methamphetamine (crank) industry, 34–38
saline laxatives, 143, 144
sedation, as effect of marijuana use, 93, 94
self-control, and addiction, 172–175
self-esteem: and addiction, 190, 191; of children of alcoholics, 162–163, 164
Sendero Luminoso, as Maoist rebels controlling Peruvian drug trade, 50–51
sex, effect of drugs on, 35, 141, 148
shamanism, healing trances of, 231–233
Siegel, Ronald, belief of, that intoxication is basic human drive, 76–77
sinsemilla, 69, 99, 199, 228
skiing, tobacco companies' sponsorship of, 130
smack, *see* heroin
small intestine, cocaine-induced damage to, 89, 90
smokeless tobacco, health risks of, 112–113, 135
smoking: 172, 183, 184, 208; health risks of, 114–119, 120–124, 125–126, 151, 189, 190, 191, 192; *see also*, nicotine, tobacco

soccer, tobacco companies' sponsorship of, 130
speed, *see* amphetamines, methamphetamine
speedballing, 200
spontaneous remissions, 234–235
sports: events, tobacco companies' sponsorship of, 128–138; substance abuse in, 155–157
steroids, anabolic, 100, 101, 156, 167, 168–169
stimulant laxatives, 143, 144
stimulants, addictive properties of, 186–187
STP, 188
stress, and drug use, 76, 95, 145, 148, 149, 187, 190
stroke: 126, 145; cocaine-induced, 32, 82, 89, 90, 208
student protest movement, and victimhood, 27

taxes, on legal drugs, 59, 123, 127, 161, 218
team sports, substance abuse in, 156, 157
teenagers: cocaine use and trafficking by, 40, 43, 45–49, 207; and smokeless tobacco, 112–113; and smoking, 125–126, 129, 130, 132, 136; steroid use by, 167, 168–169
temperance movement, history of American, 15–19, 24, 57, 107, 209
tennis, tobacco companies' sponsorship of, 128, 129
testicles, shrinking of, and anabolic steroid use, 167, 168
thalidomide, new medical uses for, 101–103
THC (tetrahydrocannibinol), 68, 69, 70, 92, 93, 94, 99, 199, 206
theophylline, side effects of, 141
THIQ, 88
titration hypothesis, of alcohol abuse, 116, 117
tobacco: as a drug, 56, 58, 59, 77, 94, 95, 96, 206, 207, 224; *see also*, nicotine, smokeless tobacco
tobacco companies, influence of, 120–121, 125–126, 128–138, 189

tooth decay, and smokeless tobacco, 112, 113
trances, healing, 231–233
tranquilizers, side effects of, 142, 186, 187, 188
treatment centers, for substance abuse, 37, 83, 84, 85, 86, 87, 88, 107, 108, 122, 173, 175, 179, 182, 203, 211, 212–213, 223, 225
triprolidine, side effects of, 140
T's and blues, 200
tumor necrosis factor, 235
Twelve Steps, of Alcoholics Anonymous, 226–228

underclass, of drug users, 24, 58, 60–64
United Nations Convention Against Illicit Traffic in Narcotic Drugs and Psychotropic Substances, 65
United States: first cocaine epidemic in, 20–25; medical practice in, in 1884, 6–14; temperance movement in, 15–19; *see also*, Hawaii, Sacramento, CA, Washington Heights
urinalysis, use of, to detect drug use, 92, 93, 210, 211, 219

Vaillant, George, 175, 190, 191, 192
values, and addiction, 108, 172–175, 185
victim, role of, in alcoholic's family, 162
victimhood, joys of, 26–28
violence, drug-related, 32, 47, 48, 54, 60, 72, 87, 100, 178
vitamins, and megavitamin therapy, 214–215

Washington Heights (New York City), as crack capital of America, 39–44, 45–48
water-soluble vitamins, 215
will power, and addiction, 172–175
winos, and the liquor industry, 152–154
wire transfers, use of, in laundering drug money, 65, 66
withdrawal symptoms, from drugs, 82, 88, 117, 118, 122, 142, 149, 179, 180, 185, 190, 193
women, substance abuse among, 155–157, 169, 217

Credits/ Acknowledgments

Cover design by Charles Vitelli

1. Drugs in Perspective
Facing overview—United Nations photo by Y. Nagata.
21, 22—Courtesy of William H. Helfand Collection.

2. Drug Action on the Nervous System
Facing overview—WHO photo.

3. Drugs and Behavior
Facing overview—United Nations photo by John Robaton.

4. Who Uses Psychotropic Drugs?
Facing overview—United Nations photo by John Isaac.
174—United Nations photo by Margot Granitsas.

5. Models of Dependency
Facing overview—WHO photo. 187—WHO photo.

6. Drug Abuse
Facing overview—American Cancer Society.

We Want Your Advice

ANNUAL EDITIONS: DRUGS, SOCIETY AND BEHAVIOR 90/91
Article Rating Form

Here is an opportunity for you to have direct input into the next revision of this volume. We would like you to rate each of the 65 articles listed below, using the following scale:

1. **Excellent: should definitely be retained**
2. **Above average: should probably be retained**
3. **Below average: should probably be deleted**
4. **Poor: should definitely be deleted**

Your ratings will play a vital part in the next revision. So please mail this prepaid form to us just as soon as you complete it.
Thanks for your help!

Annual Editions revisions depend on two major opinion sources: one is our Advisory Board, listed in the front of this volume, which works with us in scanning the thousands of articles published in the public press each year; the other is you—the person actually using the book. Please help us and the users of the next edition by completing the prepaid article rating form on this page and returning it to us. Thank you.

Rating	Article		Rating	Article
	1. What It Was Like to Be Sick in 1884			36. Sneak Addictions to Over-the-Counter Drugs
	2. The War Against Demon Rum			37. Intoxicating Habits
	3. America's First Cocaine Epidemic			38. How to Stay in Right Relationship With Everything From Chocolate to Cocaine
	4. The Joys of Victimhood			39. Wine and Winos: The Misery Market
	5. Madison Avenue Medicine			40. A Male Problem?
	6. The Fire of "Ice"			41. Alcohol and the Family
	7. Crank Capital, U.S.A.			42. Healing Scars of Parental Drinking
	8. Crack's Destructive Sprint Across America			43. Alcohol-Breast Cancer Link / Nicotine: Addictive and Spreads Cancer? / Cocaine Cardiology: Problems, Mysteries
	9. Cocaine Kids: The Underground American Dream			44. Shortcut to the Rambo Look
	10. Why Peru Won't Stop the Cocaine			45. Steroids: The Power Drugs
	11. Caught in the Crossfire			46. Control Yourself
	12. Drug Frenzy: Why the War on Drugs Misses the Real Target			47. Breaking the Cycle of Addiction
	13. Drugs and the Dream Deferred			48. Ain't Misbehavin'
	14. The Drug-Money Hunt			49. A Slip Doesn't Have to Lead to a Fall
	15. Weed It and Reap			50. Drugs Don't Take People; People Take Drugs
	16. The War on Drugs: Let's Surrender Is This Any Way to Fight a War?			51. Nasty Habits
	17. Everybody Must Get Stoned?			52. Out of the Habit Trap
	18. Cycles of Craving			53. Addiction and IQ
	19. Passing a Legacy of Drug Addiction			54. Epidemiology of Drug Abuse: An Overview
	20. New Ways to Crack a Cocaine Addiction			55. Taking Drugs Seriously
	21. The Return of a Deadly Drug Called Horse			56. Cutting Costs of Drug Abuse
	22. The Invisible Line			57. Megavitamin Therapy
	23. Cocaine: Litany of Fetal Risks Grows			58. Advertising Addiction: The Alcohol Industry's Hard Sell
	24. Marijuana			59. A Drug History Revealed on a Strand of Hair
	25. From Crack to Ecstasy			60. The Dutch Model
	26. We've Already Said Yes			61. Why Not Decriminalize?
	27. "Drug of Infamy" Makes a Comeback			62. A Long Time Coming
	28. Alcoholism: The Mythical Disease			63. Drugs: The Power of the Placebo
	29. Caffeine			64. Trances That Heal: Rites, Rituals, and Brain Chemicals
	30. Smokeless Tobacco: The Fatal Pinch			65. Chasing Answers to Miracle Cures
	31. Nicotine Becomes Addictive			
	32. Kick Me: I Smoke			
	33. Achieving a Smoke-Free Society			
	34. Warning: Sports Stars May Be Hazardous to Your Health			
	35. Ordinary Medicines Can Have Extraordinary Side Effects			

(Continued on next page)

ABOUT YOU

Name_____ Date_____

Are you a teacher? ☐ Or student? ☐

Your School Name _____

Department _____

Address _____

City _____ State _____ Zip _____

School Telephone # _____

YOUR COMMENTS ARE IMPORTANT TO US!

Please fill in the following information:

For which course did you use this book? _____

Did you use a text with this Annual Edition? ☐ yes ☐ no

The title of the text? _____

What are your general reactions to the Annual Editions concept?

Have you read any particular articles recently that you think should be included in the next edition?

Are there any articles you feel should be replaced in the next edition? Why?

Are there other areas that you feel would utilize an Annual Edition?

May we contact you for editorial input?

May we quote you from above?